D1584482

Succession
Cases and Materials

Cherry E. Wright LLB
Solicitor,
Lecturer in Law at the
University of Wales Institute
of Science and Technology

London
Butterworths
1986

United Kingdom	Butterworth & Co (Publishers) Ltd, 88 Kingsway, LONDON WC2B 6AB and 61A North Castle Street, EDINBURGH EH2 3LJ
Australia	Butterworths Pty Ltd, SYDNEY, MELBOURNE, BRISBANE, ADELAIDE, PERTH, CANBERRA and HOBART
Canada	Butterworths. A division of Reed Inc., TORONTO and VANCOUVER
New Zealand	Butterworths of New Zealand Ltd, WELLINGTON and AUCKLAND
Singapore	Butterworth & Co (Asia) Pte Ltd, SINGAPORE
South Africa	Butterworth Publishers (Pty) Ltd, DURBAN and PRETORIA
USA	Butterworth Legal Publishers, ST PAUL, Minnesota, SEATTLE, Washington, BOSTON, Massachusetts, AUSTIN, Texas and D & S Publishers, CLEARWATER, Florida

© Butterworth & Co (Publishers) Ltd 1986

Wright, C. E.
  Succession cases and materials
  1. Inheritance and succession—England
  I. Title
  344.2065'2   KD1500

ISBN 0 406 56310 1 (Hardcover)
     0 406 56311 X (Softcover)

Front cover photograph shows a detail from 'A Flaw in the Will' by Philip Richard Morris (1836–1902). Reproduced by kind permission of the Bridgeman Art Library (Wolverhampton Art Gallery).

Typeset by Cotswold Typesetting Ltd., Gloucester
Printed in Great Britain by Billings of Worcester

Preface

It is a truism to say that a student should study law through the source material. Much of this will be readily to hand for the student of the law of succession in his university or polytechnic library; the difficulty for him lies in the amount of it. The aim of this book is to extract for him the key materials which he can then follow up in his own library, and also to direct his attention to the materials of other countries and to committee and commission reports where relevant, in order to develop a critical appreciation of the subject.

In selecting this material I have chosen to follow the growing trend of embracing within the study of the law of succession not only the traditional methods of passing on property on death through a will or the intestacy rules but also some of the other methods alternatively or additionally favoured by large sections of the population such as the lifetime gift, the beneficial joint tenancy and the nomination of pension fund benefits. The second part of the book considers some of the factors that may affect the choice of succession process, predominant of which for the wealthy person is the impact of capital taxation, no prior knowledge of which is assumed for the purpose of the chapters in question. It has been said that a study of tax from its sources is a thankless task for a student as the sources are largely unintelligible; it is hoped that a ruthless pruning of the relevant statutes combined with frequent examples of their application will give the lie to this statement. As few choose to denude themselves of all their property in their lifetime, the passing of property on death will always form a major part of any succession course; the third part of this book is therefore devoted to the winding up of the deceased person's estate. Considerations of space have, sadly, prevented the inclusion of materials relating to the construction of wills and inter vivos documents.

During the final stages of the preparation of the manuscript important changes to the law were introduced, notably in the fields of taxation and insolvency. In the former case, the Budget Speech of March 1986 promised far-reaching changes to capital transfer tax, to be known in future as inheritance tax: these alterations have been included but the relevant extracts are inevitably from the Finance Bill. So far as insolvency is concerned, the new provisions affecting the winding up of the deceased insolvent's estate have been included in so far as they are contained in the Insolvency Act 1985, albeit at the time of writing they have not been brought into force; in so far as they are to be contained in statutory instrument form, those as yet unpublished are perforce omitted.

My thanks are due to my erstwhile mentor, Professor E. C. Ryder, for reading the manuscript: it was his masterly exposition of the subject that first awoke my interest in it. To the extent that some of his thoughts are echoed in this book the plagiarism is unconscious but inevitable from any student of his. I must also thank Mr O. Philip Wylie of our sister College in Cardiff for kindly reading the taxation chapters for me. Any errors that remain are, of course, my responsibility.

Numerous people have had a hand in typing the manuscript in its various stages. I thank them all, in particular Mrs Barbara Lewis, Mrs Margaret Venning and the staff of a well known firm of West Midlands solicitors; a fly on the wall would have derived much entertainment, one suspects, from the comments of the last-mentioned on the vagaries of academics.

Finally, I must express my gratitude for all the encouragement and support I have received from my family and in particular from my long suffering daughter whose arrival coincided with the contract for this book and whose first words (almost) were, 'Haven't you finished the book *yet*?', a sentiment which Butterworths must often have echoed but were too kind to express direct. My thanks to them for their patience and also for the compilation of the index; my colleague, Patrick Parkinson, kindly prepared the table of statutes and list of cases.

The law is as stated at 1 April 1986 but later alterations have been incorporated at proof stage where possible.

C.E.W.
UWIST
Cardiff
April 1986

Contents

Acknowledgements

Extracts from the All England Law Reports have been used wherever available, save where indicated otherwise. Grateful acknowledgement is made to the following authorities and publishers for permission to reprint material from their publications:

The Controller of Her Majesty's Stationery Office

The Incorporated Council of Law Reporting for England and Wales (The Law Reports, Law Times Reports, Law Journal Reports and Weekly Notes)

Professional Books (English Reports as reprinted)

Times Newspapers Ltd (Times Law Reports)

Family Law (Family Law Reports and Family Law)

Sweet & Maxwell Ltd (Jarman on Wills)

Cambridge University Press (Cambridge Law Journal)

Incorporated Council for Law Reporting for Ireland (Irish Reports)

Justice (Report on Home-Made Wills)

Lawyers Co-operative Publishing Company, Rochester, New York (American Law Reports)

The American Law Institute and The National Conference of Commissioners on Uniform State Laws (copies of the United States Uniform Probate Code may be ordered from West Publishing Company, 50 West Kellogg Boulevard, St Paul, Minnesota 55102)

Canada Law Book Inc, 240 Edward Street, Aurora, Ontario, Canada L4G 3S9 (Dominion Law Reports)

Law Society of Upper Canada (Ontario Law Reports)

The Law Book Company Ltd (Commonwealth Law Reports, South Australia State Reports)

New Zealand Council of Law Reporting (New Zealand Law Reports)

Cross-references

The following works have been cross-referenced, and abbreviated as follows:

Cheshire and Burn	*Modern Law of Real Property* 13th edn (1982)
Maudsley and Burn	*Trusts and Trustees, Cases and Materials* 3rd edn (1984)
Mellows	*The Law of Succession* 4th edn (1983)
Pettit	*Equity and the Law of Trusts* 5th edn (1984)
Uniform Probate Code (USA)	'Uniform Probate Code' & Uniform State Laws (1983)
Whitehouse and Stuart-Buttle	*Revenue Law—principles and practice* 3rd edn (1985)
Williams, Mortimer and Sunnucks	*Executors, Administrators and Probate* 16th edn (1982)

Table of statutes

Page references printed in **bold** type indicate where the Act is set out in part or in full

List of cases

Pages on which cases are principally treated are indicated by the use of **bold** figures.

PART ONE
The methods

CHAPTER 1

The lifetime gift—capacity and intention

1 The lifetime gift

The gift inter vivos has been defined as 'the transfer of any property from one person to another gratuitously while the donor is alive and not in expectation of death.'[1] The distinguishing feature of a gift is the gratuitous element, the absence of valuable consideration, a term which includes not just consideration in terms of money or money's worth but marriage consideration. Its scope was illustrated by Lush J in *Currie v Misa*[2] when he said:

> A valuable consideration in the sense of the law, may consist either in some right, interest, profit or benefit coming to one party or some forbearance, detriment, loss or responsibility given, suffered or undertaken by the other.

An inter vivos gift may take the form of an outright transfer of property from A to B, or A may declare himself a trustee of his interest in the property for B, or A may transfer his interest in the property to X and Y to hold in trust for B, but whatever form the gift takes, the donor must have the capacity and intention of making a gift.

2 Capacity

The general rule is that capacity to make a gift is the same as capacity to hold and dispose of any legal or equitable estate or interest in property, so that while any person over 18 may make a gift of any property which is capable of being disposed of (so long as he has the mental capacity to do so), a gift by an infant is voidable by him on attaining 18.[3]

When the donor is suffering from a degree of mental disorder and the management of his affairs has been committed to the Court of Protection,[4] he

---

1. 20 Halsbury's Laws (4th edn) p 2.
2. (1875) LR 10 Ex 153, at 162.
3. See 20 Halsbury's Laws (4th edn) p 9.
4. This is not a court in the usual sense of the word but an office of the Supreme Court for the protection and management of the property of a person who through mental disorder is incapable of managing his own affairs. It is staffed by a master and other officers appointed by the Lord Chancellor, with a right of appeal to a judge. The day to day management of that person's property is put in the hands of a receiver (usually a near relative of the person) appointed by the Court; the receiver acts under the Court's directions. See further Heywood and Massey *Court of Protection Practice* (11th edn, 1985), Macfarlane 'The Court of Protection and its Work' (1984) 128 Sol J 571, 590.

cannot himself make a valid gift inter vivos, even during a lucid interval,[5] although the Court has a statutory power to do so on his behalf. Otherwise, he can still make a valid gift so long as he has a sufficient degree of understanding.

In **Re Walker** [1905] Ch 160, a mentally disordered person whose property had been placed under the control of a committee[6] purported to execute an inter vivos deed declaring that she would henceforth hold certain securities she owned upon trust for herself for her life; after her death the securities were to be held for various other beneficiaries. There was medical evidence indicating that the deed was executed at a time when she was mentally competent and fully understood the terms of the declaration, but the Court of Appeal treated the deed as absolutely null and void. Vaughan-Williams LJ explained their reasoning, at p 172:

It is quite sufficient, as it seems to me, to dispose of the present case to say that the Crown has that control (as distinguished from property) of the real and personal estate of a lunatic, because the moment one sees that the committee, as representing the Crown, has the rights and powers mentioned in s 120 of the Act of 1890, it is perfectly plain that they cannot be effectively exercised by the Crown in the interest and for the benefit of the lunatic, if during the same period someone else is to have the control of the property.

In that event there would be a conflict of control which would be entirely inconsistent with the exercise by the committee of those rights of the Crown which have been delegated to him.

As against this view it is said that if a lunatic is of sufficient mental capacity to do so he can execute a will, and that after his death the will can be proved, if the Court to which the application for probate is made is of opinion that the testator at the time when he executed the will was of testamentary capacity and understood what he was doing. Of that there can be no doubt.

Then it is said, if a lunatic has this capacity to make a will which can be proved after his death, why should he not also have power to execute a deed which on the face of it is only to take effect upon his death, and creates only reversionary interests arising after the death of the lunatic? It does certainly seem at first sight a little inconsistent that the law should recognise the capacity of a lunatic to make a will, and should refuse to recognise his capacity to execute a deed which is intended to take effect only after his death. But the answer to this is, that the beneficiaries under a will have no interest and no locus standi whatever until after the death of the testator. The will is ambulatory and may be revoked by the maker of it at any time before his death, and the result is that the execution of a will gives no immediate interest to the beneficiaries either in possession or in reversion. The will is of no effect until the death of the maker of it, and the consequence is that the making of it does not give rise to any conflict of control. The beneficiaries under such a will cannot, when orders are being made in respect of the lunatic's property, come forward and claim to interfere in any way, whereas those claiming under a deed could successfully insist upon a locus standi to be heard, and immediately thereupon a conflict of jurisdiction would arise.

Mental Health Act 1983

95.   General functions of the judge with respect to property and affairs of patient[7]

(1) The judge may, with respect to the property and affairs of a patient, do or secure the doing of all such things as appear necessary or expedient—

---

5. Cf the testamentary capacity of such a person, p 72 post.
6. A committee appointed by the Judge in Lunacy under the Lunacy Act 1890 (since repealed) to manage the property and affairs of the person concerned. The modern equivalent would be the receiver appointed by the Court of Protection.
7. 'Patient' is defined in MHA 1983, s 94(2) as 'a person incapable by reason of mental disorder of managing and administering his property and affairs.'

(a) for the maintenance or other benefit of the patient,
(b) for the maintenance or other benefit of members of the patient's family,
(c) for making provision for other persons or purposes for whom or which the patient might be expected to provide if he were not mentally disordered, or
(d) otherwise for administering the patient's affairs.

(2) In the exercise of the powers conferred by this section regard shall be had first of all to the requirements of the patient, and the rules of law which restricted the enforcement by a creditor of rights against property under the control of the judge in lunacy shall apply to property under the control of the judge; but, subject to the foregoing provisions of this subsection, the judge shall, in administering a patient's affairs, have regard to the interests of creditors and also to the desirability of making provision for obligations of the patient notwithstanding that they may not be legally enforceable.

96. Powers of the judge as to patient's property and affairs

(1) Without prejudice to the generality of section 95 above, the judge shall have power to make such orders and give such directions and authorities as he thinks fit for the purposes of that section, and in particular may for those purposes make orders or give directions or authorities for—. . .

(d) the settlement of any property of the patient, or the gift of any property of the patient to any such persons or for any such purposes as are mentioned in paragraphs (b) and (c) of section 95(1) above.[8]

Re Beaney [1978] 2 All ER 595, [1978] 1 WLR 770, ChD; Nourse QC (Deputy Judge)

Mrs Beaney, a widow, had three children, Valerie, Peter and Gillian. Valerie returned to the family home to look after her mother who was becoming increasingly senile; no Court of Protection Order was ever sought as to the management of her affairs, however. Some two years after Valerie's return, Mrs Beaney was admitted to a hospital for nervous diseases and whilst there she executed a deed transferring the house to Valerie. A fortnight later she was admitted to a long-term mental hospital where she stayed until her death, intestate, a year or so later. Her assets, without the house, were worth only a few hundred pounds, the house being worth approximately £14,000 and it was only after their mother's death that Peter and Gillian learnt of the transfer of the house to Valerie. They claimed that their mother lacked the necessary mental capacity for the transfer.

Held: Mrs Beaney did not possess sufficient understanding to make a gift of her major asset; the deed of transfer was void and of no effect.

Nourse QC: There appears to be no authority which deals clearly with the degree or extent of understanding required for the validity of a voluntary disposition made by deed. The reason for this, no doubt, is that it is unusual for a person who is, or may be, of unsound mind to make a gift of any substance without his affairs having first been subjected to the jurisdiction of the Court of Protection. . . . Mrs Beaney was not a patient of the Court of Protection. I must therefore consider the position on general principles.

The test in regard to deeds was stated in general terms by the House of Lords in *Ball v Mannin* ((1829) 3 Bli NS 1). From that decision may be extracted the principle that the question in each case is whether the person concerned is capable of understanding what he does by executing the deed in question when its general purport has been fully explained to him. Both counsel for Peter and Gillian and counsel for Valerie accept that this is the correct test. They differ, and the difference could be important, over the

---

8. See further Court of Protection Rules 1984, SI 1984/2035 and Practice Direction [1983] 3 All ER 255, [1983] 1 WLR 1077 as to the procedure.

degree or extent of understanding required before a voluntary disposition of the nature found in the present case is valid. . . .

In the circumstances, it seems to me that the law is this. The degree or extent of understanding required in respect of any instrument is relative to the particular transaction which it is to effect. In the case of a will the degree required is always high. In the case of a contract, a deed made for consideration or gift inter vivos, whether by deed or otherwise the degree required varies with the circumstances of the transaction. Thus, at one extreme, if the subject matter and value of a gift are trivial in relation to the donor's other assets a low degree of understanding will suffice. But, at the other, if its effect is to dispose of the donor's only asset of value and thus for practical purposes to pre-empt the devolution of his estate under his will or on his intestacy then the degree of understanding required is as high as that required for a will, and the donor must understand the claims of all potential donees and the extent of the property to be disposed of. On this view and in the circumstances which I have mentioned, Peter and Gillian must succeed.

3   Intention

(a) In general

There must be a clear intention to make a gift, that is, to transfer the immediate beneficial ownership of the property to another or others.[9] The mere fact of the transfer of the legal title is not usually sufficient, for if A buys property in the name of B or voluntarily transfers pure personalty into the name of B, it is presumed that the intention of the parties was that B should hold that property on resulting trust for A.[10] As Eyre CB said in *Dyer v Dyer* (1788) 2 Cox Eq Cas 92, 30 ER 42, at p 43:

> The clear result of all the cases, without a single exception, is, that the trust of a legal estate, whether freehold, copyhold or leasehold; whether taken in the names of the purchasers and others jointly, or in the name of others without that of the purchaser; whether in one name or several; whether jointly or successive, results to the man who advances the purchase-money.[11]

(b) A presumed intention

If the circumstances are such as to give rise to a presumption of advancement, the intention to make a gift is presumed. This presumption of advancement will arise where the donor is the father of the donee, or *in loco parentis* to the donee; oddly, the presumption does not arise where the donor is the mother of the donee, and although it used to arise where the donor was the husband of the donee, in so far as it still does so, the presumption is regarded as a very weak one. Both the presumption of advancement and the presumption of a resulting trust can be rebutted by evidence of a contrary intention.

9. In *Re Beaney*, p 5 ante, Nourse QC said at p 602 that even if Mrs Beaney had had the capacity to make a gift he would have found against it because he was not satisfied on the evidence that she intended to make a gift. At most, she thought the property was being transferred into her daughter's name in case it was necessary to sell or deal with it for Mrs Beaney's maintenance.
10. See Pettit, Ch 8, Maudsley and Burn, Ch 6. Aliter, it seems, in the case of a voluntary transfer of realty where the effect of LPA 1925 s 60(3) is generally thought to be that there is no presumption of a trust: see Pettit pp 118–119.
11. See eg *Seldon v Davidson* [1968] 2 All ER 755, [1968] 1 WLR 1083.

Bennet v Bennet (1879) 10 Ch D 474; Jessel MR

A widowed mother gave her son £3,000. After his death she claimed it back, alleging that it was a loan; it was argued for the estate that she must be presumed to have intended a gift, on the basis of the presumption of advancement.

Held: No such presumption arose between mother and child; on the evidence, only a loan was intended.

Jessel MR: The doctrine of equity as regards presumption of gifts is this, that where one person stands in such a relation to another that there is an obligation on that person to make a provision for the other, and we find either a purchase or investment in the name of the other, or in the joint names of the person and the other, of an amount which would constitute a provision for the other, the presumption arises of an intention on the part of the person to discharge the obligation to the other; and therefore, in the absence of evidence to the contrary, that purchase or investment is held to be in itself evidence of a gift.

In other words, the presumption of gift arises from the moral obligation to give.

That reconciles all the cases upon the subject but one, because nothing is better established than this, that as regards a child, a person not the father of the child may put himself in the position of one *in loco parentis* to the child, and so incur the obligation to make a provision for the child.

Now what is the meaning of the expression 'a person *in loco parentis*'? . . . (It) means a person taking upon himself the duty of a father of a child to make a provision for that child. It is clear that in that case the presumption can only arise from the obligation, and therefore in that case the doctrine can only have reference to the obligation of a father to provide for his child, and nothing else. But the father is under that obligation from the mere fact of his being the father, and therefore no evidence is necessary to shew the obligation to provide for his child, because that is part of his duty. In the case of a father, you have only to prove the fact that he is the father, and when you have done that the obligation at once arises; but in the case of a person *in loco parentis* you must prove that he took upon himself the obligation. But in our law there is no moral legal obligation—I do not know how to express it more shortly—no obligation according to the rules of equity—on a mother to provide for her child: there is no such obligation as a Court of Equity recognises as such.

From *Holt v Frederick* ((1726) 2 P Wms 356) downwards it has been held that no such obligation exists on the part of a mother; and therefore, when a mother makes an advancement to her child, that is not of itself sufficient to afford the presumption in law that it is a gift because equity does not presume an obligation which does not exist. . . .

We then arrive at this conclusion, that in the case of a mother—this is the case of a widowed mother—it is easier to prove a gift than in the case of a stranger: in the case of a mother very little evidence beyond the relationship is wanted, there being very little additional motive required to induce a mother to make a gift to her child.

In the present case there is strong evidence to shew that this was intended to be a loan and nothing else.[12]

In **Pettitt v Pettitt** [1970] AC 777, [1969] 2 All ER 385, a wife had purchased a cottage in her own name and with her own money but the husband had thereafter spent his own time and money in improving it. His claim of a beneficial interest in the property as a result of his efforts was unsuccessful. One

---

12. Although the report is not clear on this point, it seems that no serious attempt was made to argue that as the son's father was dead at the date of the transfer, the mother stood *in loco parentis* to him; presumably this was because the facts clearly stood in the way of any such argument, the son being married and with a home of his own. On different facts, though, there seems no reason why the argument should not be raised.

of the arguments raised against him by the wife concerned the presumption of advancement. Lord Reid dealt with this succinctly, saying at p 388:

It was argued that the present case could be decided by applying the presumption regarding advancement. It was said that if a husband spends money on improving his wife's property, then, in the absence of evidence to the contrary, this must be regarded as a gift to the wife. I do not know how this presumption first arose, but it would seem that the judges who first gave effect to it must have thought either that husbands so commonly intended to make gifts in the circumstances in which the presumption arises that it was proper to assume this where there was no evidence, or that wives' economic dependence on their husbands made it necessary as a matter of public policy to give them this advantage. I can see no other reasonable basis for the presumption. These considerations have largely lost their force under present conditions, and, unless the law has lost all flexibility so that the courts can no longer adapt it to changing conditions, the strength of the presumption must have been much diminished. I do not think that it would be proper to apply it to the circumstances of the present case.[13]

In **Shephard v Cartwright** [1955] AC 431, [1954] 3 All ER 649, a father purchased shares in the names of his children in 1929. In 1934 he sold the shares, paying the proceeds into the children's bank accounts. Subsequently he withdrew the money from their accounts and when he died, a large part of the amount so withdrawn was unaccounted for. The children had signed all documents placed before them to carry out these transactions without understanding what they were doing, simply acting in adherence to their father's wishes. The father's executors argued that the presumption of advancement had been rebutted by the evidence. The House of Lords disagreed, Viscount Simonds saying at p 652:

I think that the law is clear that, on the one hand where a man purchases shares and they are registered in the name of a stranger, there is a resulting trust in favour of the purchaser; on the other hand, if they are registered in the name of a child or one to whom the purchaser then stood *in loco parentis*, there is no such resulting trust but a presumption of advancement. Equally, it is clear that the presumption may be rebutted, but should not, as Lord Eldon said, give way to slight circumstances.

It must then be asked by what evidence can the presumption be rebutted, and it would, I think, be very unfortunate if any doubt were cast (as I think it has been by certain passages in the judgments under review) on the well settled law on this subject. It is, I think, correctly stated in substantially the same terms in every textbook that I have consulted and supported by authority extending over a long period of time. I will take, as an example, a passage from Snell's *Principles of Equity* (22nd edn), p 122[14] which is as follows:

'The acts and declarations of the parties before or at the time of the purchase, or so immediately after it as to constitute a part of the transaction, are admissible in evidence either for or against the party who did the act or made the declaration; subsequent acts and declarations are only admissible as evidence against the party who did or made them, and not in his favour'. . . .

There must often be room for argument whether subsequent events can be regarded as forming part of the original transaction so as to be admissible evidence of intention, and in this case it has certainly been vigorously argued that they can. But, though I know of no universal criterion by which a link can, for this purpose, be established between one event and another, here I see insuperable difficulty in finding any link at all. The time factor alone of nearly five years is almost decisive, but, apart from that, the events of 1934

---

13. See also Lord Morris' remarks at p 396, Lord Hodson at p 404, Lord Upjohn at pp 406–7, Lord Diplock at p 414.
14. See now 28th edn (1982) p 158. Sed quaere the effect of Civil Evidence Act 1968 as to later declarations: see *Cross on Evidence* (5th edn 1979) p 24.

and 1935, whether taken singly or in their sum, appear to me to be wholly independent of the original transaction.

If, then, these events cannot be admitted in evidence as part of the original transaction, can they be admitted to rebut the presumption on the ground that they are admissions by the appellants (the children) against interest? I conceive it possible, and this view is supported by authority, that there might be such a course of conduct by a child after a presumed advancement as to constitute an admission by him of his parent's original intention, though such evidence should be regarded jealously. But it appears to me to be an indispensable condition of such conduct being admissible that it should be performed with knowledge of the material facts. In the present case, the undisputed fact that the appellants, under their father's guidance, did what they were told without inquiry or knowledge precludes the admission in evidence of their conduct and, if it were admitted, would deprive it of all probative value.[15]

(c) Must the donative intention be mutual?

It seems that while the donor must intend to make a gift, it is not necessary for the donee to intend to receive the property as a gift.

Dewar v Dewar [1975] 2 All ER 728, [1975] 1 WLR 1532, Ch D; Goff J

A mother provided £500 towards the purchase price of a house which her son bought in his own name; she moved in to live there with the son and his family. After her death the question arose whether the £500 was a gift to the son or whether the mother's estate was entitled to a share in the proceeds of sale of the house by way of a resulting trust. The evidence indicated that whereas the mother intended it to be a gift, the son regarded it as a loan and intended to repay it.

Held: The money having been effectively transferred to the son and kept by him without repudiating it, it was an effective gift.

Goff J: The plaintiff (a beneficiary under the mother's will), relying on a passage in Halsbury's Laws of England (3rd edn, vol 18, p 364, para 692) says that it could not be a gift because it was necessary not only that the donor should intend to make a gift, but that the donee should intend to accept it as such. The passage in question is:

> 'It (ie a gift inter vivos) is an act whereby something is voluntarily transferred from the true possessor to another person, with the full intention that the thing shall not return to the donor, and with the full intention on the part of the receiver to retain the thing entirely on his own without restoring it to the giver.'[16]

Only two authorities have been brought to my attention in relation to that proposition, and neither is directly in point. The first was *Cochrane v Moore* ((1890) 25 QBD 57). The headnote reads:

> 'A gift of a chattel capable of delivery, made *per verba de presenti* by a donor to a donee, and assented to by the donee, whose assent is communicated to the donor, does not pass the property in the chattel without delivery.'

---

15. See also *Warren v Gurney* [1944] 2 All ER 472 where a father voluntarily purchased a house in his daughter's name. He retained the title deeds, however, and there was also evidence of declarations he made at the time indicating that he did not intend to make a gift to her, all of which helped to rebut the presumption of advancement.
16. See now 4th edn vol 20 (1978) p 2 para 1 where this proposition stands corrected in the light of *Dewar v Dewar*. See though Roberts 'A Family Matter' (1975) 38 MLR 700, for criticism of *Dewar v Dewar*.

There, of course, the minds were in accord and so the problem with which I am faced did not present itself, but I think I do derive some assistance from a passage in the judgment of Lord Esher MR (at p 76) where he said:

> 'It is a transaction consisting of two contemporaneous acts, which at once complete the transaction, so that there is nothing more to be done by either party. The act done by the one is that he gives; the act done by the other is that he accepts. These contemporaneous acts being done, neither party has anything more to do. The one cannot give, according to the ordinary meaning of the word, without giving; the other cannot accept then and there such a giving without then and there receiving the thing given.'

I must be careful not to attach to those words more meaning than they were intended to have, bearing in mind that this was a case where both parties were in accord, but it is pertinent to observe that the reference there is to 'receiving the thing given'.

The other case was *Standing v Bowring* ((1885) 31 Ch D 282). In that case the donee was, at first, unaware of the gift, and he first learned of it when he was asked to return it. He refused to do so, and it is clear that, at that point in time, which was the first opportunity he had of considering his position, he accepted the gift. So that, again, is not really in point, but once more I do get, I think, some guidance from all the judgments. Lord Halsbury LC said (at p 285):

> 'The facts which I have assumed to be proved seemed upon the argument to have disposed of every question but one, and that one is whether the intended gift was complete, in which case it would not be revocable at the option of the donor, or whether the gift was not complete, but rested only in intention, although the subject matter of the gift did not remain within the control of the donor. If the matter were to be discussed now for the first time, I think it might well be doubted whether the assent of the donee was not a preliminary to the actual passing of the property. You certainly cannot make a man accept as a gift that which he does not desire to possess. It vests only subject to repudiation.'

Cotton LJ said (at p 288):

> 'Now I take the rule of law to be that where there is a transfer of property to a person, even although it carries with it some obligations which may be onerous, it vests in him at once before he knows of the transfer, subject to his right when informed of it to say, if he pleases, "I will not take it". When informed of it he may repudiate it, but it vests in him until he so repudiates.'

Lindley LJ (at p 290):

> 'An incomplete gift can, of course, be revoked by the donor at any time; and I believe that by the civil law and the laws of some, if not all, foreign countries founded upon it, a gift is incomplete until the donee has assented to it, or at least until he has been informed of it and has tacitly assented to it by not objecting to it. But I have not been able to ascertain that this doctrine is ever applied where, as in this case, the donor has put the thing given out of his own power, and has placed it in such a position that he can only get the thing back with the concurrence of the donee.'

The passages to which I have referred lead me to the conclusion that where a person intends to make a gift and the donee receives the thing given, knows that he has got it and takes it, the fact that he says: 'Well, I will only accept it as a loan, and you have it back when you want it' does not prevent it from being an effective gift. Of course, it does not turn it into a loan unless the donor says: 'Very well, let it be a loan.'[17] He could not force the donor to take it back, but the donor, having transferred it to him effectively and completely, intending to make a gift, and he—so far from repudiating it—having kept

---

17. As in *Hill v Wilson* (1873) LR 8 Ch 888.

it, it seems to me that this is an effective gift and, accordingly, I hold that the defendant (the son) has established that the mother's contribution was a gift.

(d) Undue influence

The donor's intention may be vitiated by the existence of undue influence.[18] Where a relationship of confidence and trust exists between the donor and donee and the gift to the donee is a substantial one that cannot reasonably be accounted for, equity raises a presumption of undue influence[19] and the gift[20] will be set aside unless the donee can satisfy the court that the gift really did represent the donor's genuine intention.

Allcard v Skinner (1887) 36 Ch D 145, CA; Cotton, Lindley, Bowen LJJ

Substantial gifts were made to the Lady Superior of a religious foundation by one of the members of the sisterhood. At the time of the gifts, the sister had taken her vows and was accordingly bound to render absolute obedience to the Lady Superior; she had no opportunity of obtaining independent legal advice, indeed this was expressly forbidden by the rules of the sisterhood. The sister subsequently left the foundation and sought the return of her property claiming that she had been unduly influenced by the Lady Superior to make the gifts in question.

Held: Undue influence would be presumed.[1]

Lindley LJ: What then is the principle? Is it that it is right and expedient to save persons from the consequences of their own folly? Or is it that it is right and expedient to save them from being victimised by other people? In my opinion the doctrine of undue influence is founded upon the second of these two principles. Courts of Equity have never set aside gifts on the ground of the folly, imprudence, or want of foresight on the part of donors. The Courts have always repudiated any such jurisdiction. *Huguenin v Baseley* ((1807) 14 Ves 273) is itself a clear authority to this effect. It would obviously be to encourage folly, recklessness, extravagance and vice if persons could get back property which they foolishly made away with, whether by giving it to charitable institutions or by bestowing it on less worthy objects. On the other hand, to protect people from being forced, tricked or misled in any way by others into parting with their property is one of the most legitimate objects of all laws; and the equitable doctrine of undue influence has grown out of and been developed by the necessity of grappling with insidious forms of spiritual tyranny and with the infinite varieties of fraud.

As no Court has ever attempted to define fraud so no Court has ever attempted to define undue influence, which includes one of its many varieties. The undue influence which Courts of Equity endeavour to defeat is the undue influence of one person over

---

18. See *Wingrove v Wingrove* (1885) 11 PD 81 and Winder: 'Undue Influence and Coercion' (1939) 3 MLR 97 for discussion of the meaning of this term.
19. Aliter in relation to gifts by will where undue influence must always be proved by the person alleging it, see p 78 post.
20. The doctrine of undue influence is not limited to transactions by way of gift. As Lord Scarman pointed out in *National Westminster Bank v Morgan* [1985] 1 All ER 821 at 829, [1985] 2 WLR 588 at 600, it can also apply to commercial transactions, where one party assumes a dominating influence over the other and a transaction occurs between them which is manifestly to the disadvantage of that other. See also *Coldunell v Gallon* [1986] 1 All ER 429, [1986] 2 WLR 466.
1. The gift was not in fact set aside, for the court, by a majority, went on to find that the donor's claim was barred by laches (unreasonable delay) and acquiescence, as she allowed more than six years to pass after she left the sisterhood before she made her claim.

another; not the influence of enthusiasm on the enthusiast who is carried away by it, unless indeed such enthusiasm is itself the result of external undue influence. But the influence of one mind over another is very subtle, and of all influences religious influence is the most dangerous and the most powerful, and to counteract it Courts of Equity have gone very far. They have not shrunk from setting aside gifts made to persons in a position to exercise undue influence over the donors, although there has been no proof of the actual exercise of such influence; and the Courts have done this on the avowed ground of the necessity of going this length in order to protect persons from the exercise of such influence under circumstances which render proof of it impossible. The Courts have required proof of its non-exercise, and, failing that proof, have set aside gifts otherwise unimpeachable. In this particular case I cannot find any proof that any gift made by the Plaintiff was the result of any actual exercise of power or influence on the part of the lady superior or of Mr Nihill,[2] apart from the influence necessarily incidental to their position in the sisterhood. . . .

Nevertheless, consider the position in which the Plaintiff had placed herself. She had vowed poverty and obedience, and she was not at liberty to consult externs without the leave of her superior. She was not a person who treated her vows lightly; she was deeply religious and felt bound by her promise, by her vows, and by the rules of the sisterhood. She was absolutely in the power of the lady superior and Mr Nihill. A gift made by her under these circumstances to the lady superior cannot in my opinion be retained by the donee. The equitable title of the donee is imperfect by reason of the influence inevitably resulting from her position, and which influence experience has taught the Courts to regard as undue. Whatever doubt I might have had on this point if there had been no rule against consulting externs, that rule in my judgment turns the scale against the Defendant. In the face of that rule the gifts made to the sisterhood cannot be supported in the absence of proof that the Plaintiff could have obtained independent advice if she wished for it, and that she knew that she would have been allowed to obtain such advice if she had desired to do so. I doubt whether the gifts could have been supported if such proof had been given, unless there was also proof that she was free to act on the advice which might be given to her. But the rule itself is so oppressive and so easily abused that any person subject to it is in my opinion brought within the class of those whom it is the duty of the Court to protect from possible imposition. The gifts cannot be supported without proof of more freedom in fact than the Plaintiff can be supposed to have actually enjoyed. . . .

Where a gift is made to a person standing in a confidential relation to the donor, the Court will not set aside the gift if of a small amount simply on the ground that the donor had no independent advice. In such a case, some proof of the exercise of the influence of the donee must be given. The mere existence of such influence is not enough in such a case; see the observations of Lord Justice Turner in *Rhodes v Bate* ((1866) LR 1 Ch 252 at 258). But if the gift is so large as not to be reasonably accounted for on the ground of friendship, relationship, charity, or other ordinary motives on which ordinary men act, the burden is upon the donee to support the gift.[3]

(e) Mistake

Where the gift has been effected by a written instrument and the donor or his legal advisers have made a mistake in the drafting of that instrument, it may be

---

2. A local vicar who had helped to found the sisterhood; he was described in the case as the plaintiff's spiritual director and confessor. He had introduced the plaintiff to the Lady Superior.
3. See also *Re Craig* [1971] Ch 95, [1970] 2 All ER 390, where a gentle, vulnerable old man of deteriorating health made substantial gifts to his housekeeper, a dominating woman of strong personality and Ungoed-Thomas J held that the presumption of undue influence arose; the donee had failed to rebut it so the gifts would be set aside. Aliter in *Re Brocklehurst* [1978] Ch 14, [1978] 1 All ER 767, where the elderly donor was found to be a strong-willed autocrat whom the donee looked up to as his social superior.

possible for the court to correct the error as a matter of construction, looking only at the other words used in the document and without recourse to extrinsic evidence. Otherwise the court may come to the parties' aid with the equitable remedy of rectification,[4] ordering the instrument to be rectified in such a way as to give effect to the parties' true intention.[5] Although normally a rectification action will only lie if the mistake was mutual to the parties, it seems that where the transaction is a gift it is not necessary for the donor to show that the mistake was shared by the donee or trustees, if they were parties to the instrument.

In **Thomas Bates & Son v Wyndham's Ltd** [1981] 1 All ER 1077, [1981] 1 WLR 505, the Court of Appeal considered the standard of proof required in a rectification action, Brightman LJ saying, at p 1090:

The standard of proof required in an action of rectification to establish the common intention of the parties is, in my view, the civil standard of balance of probability. But as the alleged common intention *ex hypothesi* contradicts the written instrument, convincing proof is required in order to counteract the cogent evidence of the parties' intention displayed by the instrument itself. It is not, I think, the standard of proof which is high, so differing from the normal civil standard, but the evidential requirement needed to counteract the inherent probability that the written instrument truly represents the parties' intention because it is a document signed by the parties.[6]

Re Butlin's Settlement Trusts [1976] Ch 251, [1976] 2 All ER 483, ChD; Brightman J

The settlor executed a voluntary settlement which had been drawn up by counsel, who stated in his accompanying opinion to his instructing solicitors that a particular clause in the draft deed would enable the trustees to act by majority decision in all circumstances. This was what the settlor wanted and he executed the deed on that basis. Goff J subsequently ruled,[7] as a matter of construction, that the deed as drafted only enabled majority decisions to be arrived at in certain circumstances (illness, infirmity or the temporary absence of trustees). The settlor sought rectification of the deed on the basis that as drawn, it did not represent his true intention. The trustees, who were parties to the deed, had executed the deed without realising what his true intention was in relation to the clause and one of the trustees, who had no wish to see decisions taken by majority, opposed his application.

Held: As the settlement was voluntary and not the result of a contractual bargain, the court had power to rectify once it was satisfied that the instrument did not reflect the settlor's intention, even though the mistake was not mutual to all parties to the deed.

Brightman J: There is in my judgment no doubt that the court has power to rectify a settlement notwithstanding that it is a voluntary settlement and not the result of a bargain, such as an anti-nuptial marriage settlement. *Lackersteen v Lackersteen* ((1860) 30 LJ Ch 5) a decision of Page Wood V-C and *Behrens v Heilbut* ((1956) 222 LT Jo 290), a decision of Harman J, are cases in which voluntary settlements were actually rectified. There are also obiter dicta to the like effect in cases where rectification was in fact refused: see *Bonhote v Henderson* ([1895] 1 Ch 742; affd [1895] 2 Ch 202).

---

4. See Pettit, p 570.
5. See *Banks v Ripley* [1940] 1 Ch 719, [1940] 3 All ER 49 as to the unrestricted nature of the evidence admissible for this purpose.
6. Cf *Re Snowden* [1979] Ch 528, [1979] 2 All ER 172.
7. (1974) 118 Sol J 757.

Furthermore, rectification is available not only in a case where particular words have been added, omitted or wrongly written as the result of careless copying or the like. It is also available where the words of the document were purposely used but it was mistakenly considered that they bore a different meaning from their correct meaning as a matter of true construction. In such a case, which is the present case, the court will rectify the wording of the document so that it expresses the true intention: see *Jervis v Howle* ([1937] Ch 67, [1936] 3 All ER 193); *Whiteside v Whiteside* ([1950] Ch 65, [1949] 2 All ER 913) and *Joscelyne v Nissen* ([1970] 2 QB 86, [1970] 1 All ER 1213).

So far, therefore, the plaintiff (the settlor) has surmounted possible problems. The settlement can be rectified though voluntary, and it can be rectified notwithstanding that the mistake arose, not in omitting, or using, words intended, or not intended, to be included, but in ascribing the wrong interpretation to words intended to be used.

There remains, however, one point of some difficulty and that is the relevance or otherwise of the intention of the other parties to the settlement. The plaintiff pleads and proves that both the plaintiff and the solicitor intended the settlement to contain a power for the majority of the trustees to bind the minority. The statement of claim does not allege that that was the intention of the first defendant (the opposing trustee) or of Mr Lakin or of Mrs Lovering or of the second defendant, who were the other trustees at the time the settlement was made. In their defences, both the first defendant and the second defendant plead that they themselves were ignorant that the plaintiff intended the settlement to contain a power for a majority to bind the minority. Nor was any evidence led to the contrary.

I am, therefore, faced with the question, which is not adequately covered by any authority to which I have been referred, to what extent does a settlor, seeking rectification of a voluntary settlement to which trustees are parties, have to establish that the mistake was mutual? Is it enough for the settlor to prove that he alone made a mistake? . . .

I will seek to test the legal position by considering two extremes. First, suppose that on the execution of a voluntary settlement of the family estates a settlor instructs his legal advisers to prepare a settlement which includes annuities of £500 for each of ten retired estate workers. Suppose that, due to a copying error, an extra nought is added to the £500. Suppose that the trustees know nothing of the settlor's intentions and execute the settlement in the form presented to them. I find it difficult to believe that in such a case the court would not have jurisdiction to rectify the settlement by striking out the mistaken nought. Secondly, suppose that a settlement is executed in a usual form. Could the settlor, in defiance of protests by the trustees, rectify the settlement by inserting a power enabling him, for example, to dismiss a trustee at his pleasure, or to dictate sales and purchases of investments, merely upon proof that he had instructed his solicitor to include such powers but they had been omitted by error, and notwithstanding that his intention was wholly unknown to the trustees? Common sense would suggest that the answer is No.

If I have correctly suggested the answers to these two extreme cases, I ask myself, where is the line to be drawn?

It seems to me that the solution to the problem lies in the fact that rectification is a discretionary remedy. In other words, in the absence of an actual bargain between the settlor and the trustees: (i) a settlor may seek rectification by proving that the settlement does not express his true intention, or the true intention of himself and any party with whom he has bargained, such as a spouse in the case of an ante-nuptial settlement; (ii) it is not essential for him to prove that the settlement fails to express the true intention of the trustees if they have not bargained; but (iii) the court may in its discretion decline to rectify a settlement against a protesting trustee who objects to rectification. . . .

In the end, after considerable hesitation, I have reached the conclusion that this is a case in which I ought to exercise my discretion in favour of rectification, despite the opposition of one trustee. I have come to this view because the first defendant has not seen fit to swear an affidavit and disclose her reasons for opposing rectification. It may be that she desires to do no more than put the settlor to proof of his intention. If her opposition is based on more than that, for example, because she felt that her presence was necessary in order that the interests of certain of the discretionary beneficiaries should not be disregarded, then it seems to me that she should have given evidence to that effect. If she merely wished to put the settlor to proof, then it was not necessary for her to give her own evidence. If, however, she wished to persuade the court to reject rectification as a matter of discretion, then I think that she ought to have placed evidence before the court as to her reasons, and if necessary she could have been cross-examined on her evidence. In the absence of any such evidence, I cannot tell if she has any reason for opposing rectification, once the mistake has been proved.

I shall, accordingly, make an order for rectification.

In **Re Slocock's Will Trust** [1979] 1 All ER 358, the mistake was as to the taxation consequences of the words that were deliberately used. A deed of release intended by the donor and donees to release the donor's beneficial interest in certain proceeds of sale with a view to saving taxation on the donor's death, failed to achieve the intended result because of a mistaken understanding of the donor's solicitors as to the nature of the assets concerned, as a result of which all that was released to the donees consisted of shares in a management company of no value. Earlier cases[8] appeared to suggest that rectification would not lie where the only effect of allowing it would be to give some taxation advantage to the parties, but Graham J refuted this suggestion. Granting rectification of the deed of release, he said at p 363:

The true principles governing these matters I conceive to be as follows. (1) The court has a discretion to rectify where it is satisfied that the document does not carry out the intention of the parties. This is the basic principle. (2) Parties are entitled to enter into any transaction which is legal, and, in particular, are entitled to arrange their affairs to avoid payment of tax if they legitimately can. The Finance Acts 1969 and 1975 tell them explicitly how they can do so in the case of estate duty and capital transfer tax. (3) If a mistake is made in a document legitimately designed to avoid the payment of tax, there is no reason why it should not be corrected. The Crown is in no privileged position qua such a document. It would not be a correct exercise of the discretion in such circumstances to refuse rectification merely because the Crown would thereby be deprived of an accidental and unexpected windfall. (4) As Counsel for the trustees submitted, neither *Whiteside v Whiteside* ([1950] Ch 65, [1949] 2 All ER 913) nor any other case contains anything which compels the court to the conclusion that rectification of a document should be refused where the sole purpose of seeking it is to enable the parties to obtain a legitimate fiscal advantage which it was their common intention to obtain at the time of the execution of the document.[9]

QUESTIONS

1. Compare and contrast the capacity and intention required to make a lifetime gift with the capacity and intention required to make a will (see Chapters 6 and 7 post).

2. In *Re Pauling's ST* [1964] Ch 303, [1963] 3 All ER 1 Willmer LJ described the presumption of undue influence as 'in truth a convenient device in aid of decisions on facts often lost in obscurity, whether owing to lapse of time or the death of the parties'. Discuss.

3. Which of the following are effective gifts?

---

8. See eg *Van der Linde v Van der Linde* [1947] Ch 306, *Whiteside v Whiteside* [1950] Ch 65, [1949] 2 All ER 913, *Re Colebrook's Conveyance* [1973] 1 All ER 132, [1972] 1 WLR 1397.
9. For a possible consequence of this ruling, see Sherrin 'Correcting Errors: Rectification of Documents' (1980) 124 Sol J 229.

(a) A buys a house in the name of his daughter B (an 18 year old student). He keeps the title deeds.

(b) A gives his son C (aged 20) a cheque for £3,000 to help towards the purchase of a new car. C says 'Thanks very much Dad, but I'll pay you back when I can.'

(c) A writes to his solicitor instructing him to convey the paddock adjoining his country cottage into the name of D, his wife. By mistake the solicitor prepares a Conveyance of the cottage itself and A executes the Conveyance without noticing this.

CHAPTER 2

The lifetime gift – formalities

1 The requirements

The subject matter of the gift must be duly transferred to the donee (in the case of an outright gift) or to the trustees (if it is a trust gift) using the formalities appropriate for a transfer of property of that nature.

(a) A legal estate in land

A deed is required to create or convey a legal estate or interest in land. Originally this entailed a written document bearing the seal of the parties concerned and duly delivered; the 1925 statute added the requirement of signing. Since then the significance of the seal has declined,[1] and delivery does not mean what it says. As a result it has been suggested that some of these requirements are no longer appropriate and that the formalities for a deed should be brought into line with those for a will.

In **Goddard's Case** (1584) 2 Co Rep 4b, 76 ER 396, at p 398, it was said:

There are but three things of the essence and substance of a deed, that is to say, writing on paper or parchment, sealing and delivery, and if it hath these three, although it wanted *in cujus rei testimonium sigillum suum opposuit*,[2] yet the deed is sufficient, for the delivery is as necessary to the essence of a deed, as the putting of a seal to it, and yet it need not be contained in the deed that is was delivered. And note, the order of making a deed is, first to write it, then to seal it, and after to deliver it; and therefore it is not necessary that the sealing or delivery be mentioned in the writing, forasmuch as they are to be done after. And so, it was said, it was resolved in Henry the Eighth's time.

---

1. It was described by the Law Commission in its Working Paper No 93, p 18 post at para 4.2 as a 'meaningless exercise involving sticking a small circle of red adhesive paper onto the document.' In *First National Securities v Jones* [1978] Ch 109, [1978] 2 All ER 221, the Court of Appeal even accepted as a deed a legal charge impressed with no seal at all but containing expressions such as 'signed, sealed and delivered' which indicated to the Court the mortgagor's intention to execute it as a deed. See further Hoath 'The sealing of documents—fact or fiction' (1980) 43 MLR 415. See also *TCB Ltd v Gray* [1986] 1 All ER 587.
2. The grantor's signature as evidence.

Law of Property Act 1925

52.   Conveyance to be by deed

(1) All conveyances of land or of any interest therein are void for the purpose of creating or conveying a legal estate unless made by deed.[3]

73.   Execution of deeds by an individual

Where an individual executes a deed he shall either sign or place his mark upon the same and sealing alone shall not be deemed sufficient.[4]

Law Commission Working Paper No 93[5]

3.2   The need for formality

What then are the aims of the formalities for making a deed? We would suggest that there are three main aims:

- (a) cautionary: that is, trying to ensure that the maker does not enter into the transaction without realising what he is doing;
- (b) evidential: providing evidence that the maker did enter into a transaction, and evidence of its terms;
- (c) labelling: making it apparent to third parties what kind of a document it is and what its effect is to be.

8.2   Existing formalities

(i) *Writing on paper or parchment*   This is probably the least controversial of the present requirements, and yet recent technological developments mean that it cannot be left unquestioned. Should a deed have to exist on paper? Could it not exist only on a computer disk or in some other electronic form? Alternatively might not a tape or a video of the grantor reciting the terms be sufficient? With the first two queries, there are real problems of verification in the sense of ensuring that the grantor did in fact intend to make an instrument constituting a deed. However, it may be possible to devise satisfactory alternatives to the signature as a method of showing the grantor's intention to authenticate the transaction and we would particularly welcome further information and views upon this possibility. With all of these alternative methods there may be problems of storage and of retrieval of the information if the equipment on which they are recorded becomes obsolete. At present, and without precluding discussion of possible change in the future, we think that the requirement of writing on some permanent substance should be retained, though perhaps extended to cover substances other than paper or parchment.

(ii) *The seal*   We consider that the seal should be abolished as a necessary requirement for a deed. Invalidating a document because of the lack of a small circle of red paper may well seem to laymen, if not to lawyers, to be a clear illustration of the antiquated state of some areas of the English law. The seal is a redundant formality without substantive purpose and easily overlooked.

(iii) *Signature*   We believe this should be retained as a requirement. It helps to fulfil both the cautionary and evidential functions of a deed. Most people, we think, are aware that in signing a document they are committing themselves to some extent, and, while signatures can of course be forged, they are of some help in proving the validity or otherwise of the deed. As we have seen, a signature need not be by handwriting and, for example, can be a rubber stamp. It would be difficult to change this for deeds and not for other documents, and we therefore make no proposals on the point in this paper.

---

3. If the title to the land is registered, any transfer of the land must also be in the form required by the Land Registration Rules 1925, SR & O 1925 No 1093, Rule 98, form 19 (which also requires the signature of the transferor to be attested), and the transfer must be completed by registration: LRA 1925, s 19(1).

4. It will be noted that neither statute nor common law require the attestation of the parties' signatures; in practice deeds are usually attested.

5. (1985) 'Transfer of Land: Formalities for Deeds and Escrows'.

(iv) *Delivery* We consider that the requirement of delivery should be abolished. From being a matter of physical fact, it has become a question of the deliverer's intention to be bound.[6] Although, as a rule, this intention does have to be sufficiently evinced, it need not be communicated to any person in particular (ie not necessarily to the person taking under the deed) and may be difficult to prove. A document may on the face of it be a deed but without the extrinsic element of delivery it will not be one. We consider that the law would be simplified and in general there could be no adverse effects of substance if the requirement of delivery were abolished. Deeds would therefore take effect as such as soon as all the other formalities were completed. If the grantor wished to postpone the actual operation of the deed, for example by preventing the grantee from obtaining the legal estate until the price were paid, he could do so by imposing express conditions to that effect.

8.3 Additional requirements

It would be possible to say that a signature alone should suffice as it does for contracts for the sale of land and declarations of trusts of land. However, this alone could not ensure that deeds are not executed inadvertently and would provide no means of distinguishing between, for example, an unenforceable agreement lacking consideration and an enforceable one made by deed. We therefore provisionally recommend that two additional requirements be introduced:

(i) *Attestation* It is already common practice for the signature on a deed to be attested and in registered conveyancing attestation is already obligatory.[7] We think this should be made a general requirement. This would distinguish deeds from mere signed documents; would emphasise to the person executing the deed the importance of his act; would give rise to an evidential presumption of due execution; and might assist in the prevention or at least the detection of forgery. In our opinion any such requirement should be restricted to one witness but could otherwise follow the recently enacted provision for the attestation of wills.[8]

(b) Stocks and shares

The form of the transfer may be prescribed by the articles of the company concerned. Otherwise the securities may usually be transferred by the simplified form of transfer prescribed by the Stock Transfer Act 1963 which requires the signature of the transferor but no seal or attestation. The transferor will then send the transfer form and share certificate to the transferee who will forward them to the company for registration. Once registered in the company's books the transfer is complete; the company will then issue a new share certificate to the transferee.

Stock Transfer Act 1963

1. Simplified transfer of securities

(1) Registered securities to which this section applies[9] may be transferred by means of an instrument under hand in the form set out in Schedule 1 to this Act (in this Act referred

---

6. See eg *Xenos v Wickham* (1867) LR 2 HL 296.

7. See p 18, n 3 ante.

8. See p 91 post. The second additional requirement suggested by the Law Commission was that it be clear on the face of the document that it was intended to be a deed (para 8.3(ii)). It was pointed out, at paras 6.1, 6.2 that in New Zealand the requirements for sealing and delivery were abolished in 1952, an attested signature being now sufficient whilst the Australian States have generally provided that the deed is not invalid if it is not sealed provided that there is an attested signature and the document is expressed to be a deed.

9. The section applies to, inter alia, fully paid up registered securities issued by a company limited by shares, or (subject to a few exceptions) issued by the Government or by a local authority or to units of a unit trust scheme: s 1(4).

SCHEDULE 1   Section 1

STOCK TRANSFER FORM

	Certificate lodged with the Registrar
Consideration Money[10] £...............	(For completion by the Registrar/ Stock Exchange)

Full name of Undertaking.	
Full description of security.	

	Words	Figures
Number or amount of Shares, Stock or other security and, in figures column only, number and denomination of units, if any.		(units of)

Name(s) of registered holder(s) should be given in full: the address should be given where there is only one holder. If the transfer is not made by the registered holder(s) insert also the name(s) and capacity (e.g., Executor(s), of the person(s) making the transfer.	in the name(s) of

Delete words in italics except for stock exchange transactions. Bodies corporate should execute under their common seal.	I/We hereby transfer the above security out of the name(s) aforesaid to the person(s) named below *or to the several persons named in Parts 2 of Brokers Transfer Forms relating to the above security:* Signature(s) of transferor(s)	Stamp of Selling Broker(s) or, for transactions which are not stock exchange transactions, of Agent(s), if any, acting for the Transferor(s)
	1.. 3..	
	2.. 4..	Date ....

Full name(s), full postal address(es) (including County or, if applicable, Postal District number) of the person(s) to whom the security is transferred. Please state title, if any, or whether Mr., Mrs. or Miss. Please somplete in typewriting or in Block Capitals.	

I/We request that such entries be made in the register as are necessary to give effect to this transfer.

Stamp of Buying Broker(s) (if any).	Stamp or name and address of person lodging this form (if other than the Buying Broker(s))

---

10. 'Nil' for an inter vivos gift.

to as a stock transfer), executed by the transferor only and specifying (in addition to the particulars of the consideration, of the description and number or amount of the securities, and of the person by whom the transfer is made) the full name and address of the transferee.

(2) The execution of a stock transfer need not be attested.

Companies Act 1985

182. Nature, transfer and numbering of shares

(1) The shares or other interest of any member in a company—. . .

    (b) are transferable in manner provided by the company's articles, but subject to the Stock Transfer Act 1963 (which enables securities of certain descriptions to be transferred by a simplified process).

183. Transfer and registration

(1) It is not lawful for a company to register a transfer of shares in or debentures of the company unless a proper instrument of transfer has been delivered to it. . . .

(4) On the application of the transferor of any share or interest in a company, the company shall enter in its register of members the name of the transferee in the same manner and subject to the same conditions as if the application for the entry were made by the transferee.

(5) If a company refuses to register a transfer of shares or debentures,[11] the company shall, within 2 months after the date on which the transfer was lodged with it, send to the transferee notice of the refusal.

185. Duty of company to issue certificates

(1) . . . . every company shall—

    (b) within 2 months after the date on which a transfer of any such shares, debentures or debenture stock is lodged with the company, complete and have ready for delivery the certificates of all shares, the debentures and the certificates of all debenture stock . . . transferred. . . .

186. Certificate to be evidence of title

A certificate under the common seal of the company or the seal kept by the company by virtue of section 40,[12] specifying any shares held by a member, is prima facie evidence of his title to the shares.

(c) Equitable interests

Any transfer of an equitable interest, whether in realty or personalty, must be effected in writing, signed by the transferor.[13]

Law of Property Act 1925

53. Instruments required to be in writing

(1)— . . . (c) a disposition of an equitable interest or trust subsisting at the time of the

---

11. The articles of a private company very often contain an article empowering the directors in their absolute discretion to refuse to register a transfer; so long as they exercise the power in good faith, the courts will not interfere: *Re Smith and Fawcett Ltd* [1942] Ch 304, [1942] 1 All ER 542.
12. This empowers a company to use an official seal when sealing share certificates; it must be a facsimile of the company's common seal with the addition on its face of the word 'Securities'.
13. If a donee disclaims a gift this is regarded as operating as an avoidance of the gift and not by way of a disposition of an equitable interest in the property concerned—see *Re Paradise Motor Co* [1968] 2 All ER 625, [1968] 1 WLR 1125.

disposition, must be in writing signed by the person disposing of the same, or by his agent thereunto lawfully authorised in writing or by will.

In **Vandervell v IRC** [1967] 2 AC 291, [1967] 1 All ER 1, the person seeking to dispose of his equitable interest was a beneficiary under a bare trust,[14] and was therefore in a position to control the legal interest too. In such a case, the House of Lords decided, the equitable owner was in the same position as a person owning the legal and beneficial interest contemporaneously; he could direct a transfer of the legal estate and the equitable interest would follow automatically. Lord Upjohn sought to justify this judicial exception to the statutory requirements by saying at p 7:

> Those words (s 53(1)(c)) were applied in *Grey v Inland Revenue Commissioners* ([1960] AC 1, [1959] 3 All ER 603) and *Oughtred v Inland Revenue Commissioners* ([1960] AC 206, [1959] 3 All ER 623) to cases where the legal estate remained outstanding in a trustee and the beneficial owner was dealing and dealing only with the equitable estate. That is understandable; the object of the section, as was the object of the old Statute of Frauds, is to prevent hidden oral transactions in equitable interests in fraud of those truly entitled, and making it difficult, if not impossible, for the trustees to ascertain who are in truth his beneficiaries. When the beneficial owner, however, owns the whole beneficial estate and is in a position to give directions to his bare trustee with regard to the legal as well as the equitable estate there can be no possible ground for invoking the section where the beneficial owner wants to deal with the legal estate as well as the equitable estate.[15]

(d) Personal chattels

These may be transferred by a deed of gift, or by mere physical delivery; where the chattel concerned is bulky, it seems that a symbolic delivery will suffice.[16] It is particularly difficult to establish delivery where the donor and donee are living together so that the gifted property remains in the apparent possession of the donor. In such circumstances it is usually safer for the donor to use a deed of gift so long as it complies with the requirements of the Bills of Sale Act 1878.[17]

In **Rawlinson v Mort** (1905) 93 LT 555, C had bought an organ and installed it in the local church, it being clearly understood between C and the vicar that the organ was on loan only. Subsequently C visited the organist at the organist's rooms and offered to give him the organ; when the organist accepted, C handed over to him the vicar's letter evidencing the loan and the three receipts C had received for the payments he had made to the organ builder. Not long afterwards, while the organist was playing the organ in church, C said to a former churchwarden, 'I have given this to Walter (the organist)', putting his hand on the organ. Both before and after this event the organist had the control and use of the organ and held the key. Bray J, at p 556, referred to Lord Kenyon's remarks in *Chaplin v Rogers* ((1800) 1 East 192):

> 'When goods are ponderous, and incapable, as here of being handed over from one to another, there need not be an actual delivery; but it may be done by that which is

---

14. Where A holds property on trust for B absolutely, B owning the entire beneficial interest. If B is of age, he can end the trust at any time.
15. See further Pettit, pp 74–78.
16. See Barlow 'Gift inter vivos of a chose in possession by delivery of a key' (1956) 19 MLR 394; he considers whether the use of the symbolic delivery is really confined to bulky chattels.
17. A written instrument for the transfer of personal chattels must be registered as a bill of sale under the Bills of Sale Act 1878 s 8 where the chattels remain in the 'possession or apparent possession' of the transferor, otherwise the transfer will be void as against the transferor's creditors.

tantamount, such as the delivery of the key of a warehouse in which the goods are lodged, or by delivery of other indicia of property.'

I think delivery of a box can be given by handing over the key. Symbolical delivery may be actual delivery. The key was already in the plaintiff's possession, and I think the handing over of the documents evidencing the owner's title, or, as stated in *Chaplin v Rogers* of the indicia of the property, is symbolical delivery and equivalent to actual delivery, at all events where manual delivery is practically impossible. It was not the intention of the donor or the donee that the organ should be removed from the church, and real manual delivery was impossible under those circumstances. In my opinion, there was a valid completed gift at the plaintiff's rooms. I am, however, of the opinion that, if the gift was not completed then, it was completed at the church. I have found that by putting his hand on the organ and using the words (whichever they were) (C) intended to give delivery, and I think that delivery can be made in this way when manual delivery is impossible. In *Cochrane v Moore* ((1890) 25 QBD 57) the learned judges confined their decision to cases where the article was capable of delivery. If the organ was under the circumstances capable of delivery, I think it was delivered. If it was not, I think there was symbolical delivery which was the nearest approach to delivery that could be made.

Re Cole [1964] Ch 175, [1963] 3 All ER 433, CA; Harman and Pearson LJJ, Pennycuick J

Having furnished the new house he had bought, the husband took his wife into their new home, put his hands over her eyes and then uncovered them saying, 'Look! It is all yours.' They thereafter lived together in the house, both regarding the furniture as belonging to the wife. When the husband went bankrupt, the wife claimed the furniture as her property.

Held: There had been no delivery of the furniture to the wife; it would pass to the husband's trustee in bankruptcy.

Pearson LJ: It has been established that oral words of gift, or even written words of gift not embodied in a deed or will, are not sufficient to make an effective gift unless there has been, or is, delivery of possession to the donee. The basic idea is that there must be giving and taking, and, if the donor retains possession, he has not yet given and the donee has not yet taken: *Irons v Smallpeace* ((1819 2 B & Ald 551), *Winter v Winter* ((1861) 4 LT 639) (conflicting opinions), *Cochrane v Moore* ((1890) 25 QBD 57 at pp 72, 73, 76), *Bashall v Bashall* ((1894) 11 TLR 152), *Valier v Wright & Bull Ltd* ((1917) 33 TLR 366). It is also established that the delivery of possession may be prior to or contemporaneous with or subsequent to the words of gift: *Cochrane v Moore* ((1890) 25 QBD 57 at 70), *Re Alderson, Alderson v Peel* ((1891) 64 LT 645), *Re Stoneham, Stoneham v Stoneham* ([1919] 1 Ch 149). In the case of prior delivery, it may not be necessary that the delivery should have been made by the donor; a pre-existing possession of the donee, however it arose, may be sufficient. . . . In the case of husband and wife living together or other persons having a common establishment, the possession, when it would otherwise be doubtful, is attached by law to the title (*Ramsay v Margrett* [1894] 2 QB 18 at pp 25, 27, 28). That was a case of goods bargained and sold, so that the ownership passed from husband to wife without delivery, and when she had become the owner she was considered in law to have the possession. In *French v Gething* ([1922] 1 KB 236 at pp 241, 242, 246, 247), the husband gave furniture in the home to the wife by deed, so that no delivery was required, and when she had become the owner she was considered in law to have the possession. *Youngs v Youngs* ([1940] 1 KB 760 at pp 769, 770), refers to a common establishment.

As to what is necessary to constitute delivery from husband to wife, guidance is afforded by the judgment of Lord Esher MR in *Bashall v Bashall* ((1894) 11 TLR 152) . . . at p 153:

'In an action by the wife it was necessary for her to show that the husband had done that which amounted to a delivery. If the facts proved were equally consistent with the idea that he intended to deliver the thing to the wife so as to be her property, and with the idea that he intended to keep it as his own property, then the wife failed to make out her case. He thought there was not sufficient evidence of delivery here, and the appeal must therefore be allowed.'

As I understand that passage, it is dealing with delivery, and the effect of it is that an act to constitute delivery must be one which in itself shows an intention of the donor to transfer the chattel to the donee. If the act in itself is equivocal—consistent equally with an intention of the husband to transfer the chattels to his wife or with an intention on his part to retain possession but give to her the use and enjoyment of the chattels as his wife—the act does not constitute delivery. In the present case, the intended gift was from husband to wife. Be it assumed that he spoke words of gift—words expressing an intention of transferring the chattels to her, and not merely an intention to give here the use and enjoyment of them as his wife— and that, in the circumstances, the chattels intended to be given were sufficiently identified by the words of gift. There was no pre-existing possession of the donee in this case. The bankrupt was the owner of the chattels and, therefore, considered in law to be in possession of them. No act of delivery has been proved, because the acts relied on are in themselves equivocal—consistent equally with an intention of the bankrupt to transfer the chattels to the applicant or with an intention on his part to retain possession but give to her the use and enjoyment of them as his wife.

(e) Cheques

A cheque must be presented to and passed by the donor's bank.

In **Re Swinburne** [1926] Ch 38, the donor died before the cheque had been met; it had been presented but not honoured, the bank having queried the signature. The Court of Appeal held that the gift was incomplete and therefore ineffective, Pollock MR saying at p 41:

Now a cheque is clearly not an assignment of money in the hands of a banker. A cheque, as explained by Lord Romilly MR in *Hewitt v Kaye* ((1868) LR 6 Eq 198 at 200), is nothing more than an order to obtain a certain sum of money, and it makes no difference whether the money is with the bankers or elsewhere. It is an order to deliver the money; and if the order is not acted upon in the lifetime of the person who gives it, it is worth nothing. Let me assume, therefore, that there was money in the current account ready to meet this cheque as and when it was accepted for payment by the banker, but it is clear law that the fact that this cheque was outstanding did not indicate that there had been any assignment of the money on current account to meet the cheque. It is merely a mandate or authority in the hands of the holder of the cheque to go to the bank and get the money from it.

(f) A declaration of trust

The formalities considered so far apply whether the gift is an outright gift, eg from A to B beneficially, or a trust gift, eg from A to X and Y on trust for B.[18] If the gift is a trust gift and the gifted property is realty, one further formality has to be observed:

---

18. If A decided to declare himself a trustee for B, there would be no need for any of the formalities considered so far as the property would already be vested in A. If the property were realty, however, LPA 1925 s 53(1)(b) post would still apply.

Law of Property Act 1925

53. Instruments required to be in writing

(1) Subject to the provisions hereinafter contained with respect to the creation of interests in land by parol . . .
  (b) A declaration of trust respecting any land or any interest therein must be manifested and proved by some writing signed by some person who is able to declare such trust or by his will;
(2) This section does not affect the creation or operation of resulting, implied or constructive trusts.[19]

2   Effect of want of compliance

(a) In general

Until the appropriate formalities have been used, the gift is said to be imperfect, or incompletely constituted with the result that the donee or beneficiary cannot enforce it.

In **Richards v Delbridge** (1874) LR 18 Eq 11, the would-be donor wrote on his lease of certain business property the following words, not under seal: 'This deed and all thereto belonging I give to Edward Bennetto Richards from this time forth and with all the stock-in-trade.' He signed the memorandum but as it was not under seal it was held to be ineffective to transfer the legal estate to the donee, nor could it operate as a declaration of trust, for this was clearly not the donor's intention; Jessel MR quoted Turner LJ in *Milroy v Lord* ((1862) 4 De G F & J 264) where he said at p 274:

> 'If it (the voluntary settlement) is intended to take effect by transfer, the Court will not hold the intended transfer to operate as a declaration of trust, for then every imperfect instrument would be made effectual by being converted into a perfect trust.'[20]

(b) The *Re Rose* exception

Occasionally the courts have relaxed this strict rule. In *Re Rose* (post) it was established that if the donor has done everything necessary to be done by him to vest the property in the transferee and all that remains is for something to be done by a transferee or by a third party, equity will perfect the gift.

Re Rose [1952] Ch 499, [1952] 1 All ER 1217, CA; Lord Evershed MR, Jenkins and Morris LJJ

The donor, intending to give certain shares to his wife, handed over to her the appropriate share certificates and transfer forms signed by him. She duly

---

19. See eg *Hodgson v Marks* [1971] Ch 892, [1971] 2 All ER 684.
20. See also *Antrobus v Smith* (1805) 12 Ves 39 where the donor endorsed on a share certificate a memorandum to the effect that he assigned his shares in that company to his daughter. He never signed the transfer form required by the company, let alone submitted it for registration, and Grant MR held that the gift was ineffective.

secured the registration of the transfer in the company's books, but it was important to know for estate duty[1] reasons (arising on the donor's subsequent death) whether the gift could be regarded as complete before such registration. **Held:** The gift was complete when the donor had done everything necessary to be done by him to transfer his legal and beneficial interest in the shares; no estate duty would be payable on the gifted property as a result.

Jenkins LJ: If the deceased had in truth transferred the whole of his interest in these shares so far as he could transfer the same, including such right as he could pass to his transferee to be placed on the register in respect of the shares, the question arises, what beneficial interest had he then left? The answer can only be, in my view, that he had no beneficial interest left whatever: his only remaining interest consisted in the fact that his name still stood on the register as holder of the shares, but, having parted in fact with the whole of his beneficial interest, he could not, in my view, assert any beneficial title by virtue of his position as registered holder. In other words, in my view the effect of this transaction, having regard to the form and the operation of the transfers, the nature of the property transferred, and the necessity for registration in order to perfect the legal title, coupled with the discretionary power on the part of the directors to withhold registration, must be that, pending registration, the deceased was in the position of a trustee of the legal title in the shares for the transferees. Thus in the hypothetical case put by the Crown of a dividend being declared and paid (as it would have been paid in accordance with the company's articles) to the deceased as registered holder, he would have been accountable for that dividend to the transferees, on the ground that by virtue of the transfers as between himself and the transferees the owners of the shares were the transferees, to the exclusion of himself.

In my view, to arrive at a right conclusion it is necessary to keep clear and distinct the position as between transferor and transferee and the position as between transferee and the company. It is, no doubt, true that the rights conferred by shares are all rights against the company, and it is, no doubt, true that, in the case of a company with ordinary regulations, no person can exercise his rights as a shareholder vis-à-vis the company, or be recognised by the company as a member unless and until he is placed on the register of members. But, in my view, it is a fallacy from that to adduce the conclusion that there can be no complete gift of shares as between transferor and transferee unless and until the transferee is placed on the register. In my view, a transfer under seal in the form appropriate under the company's regulations, coupled with delivery of the transfer and certificate to the transferee, does suffice, as between transferor and transferee, to constitute the transferee the beneficial owner of the shares, and the circumstance that the transferee must do a further act in the form of applying for and obtaining registration in order to get in and perfect his legal title, having been equipped by the transferor with all that is necessary to enable him to do so, does not prevent the transfer from operating in accordance with its terms as between the transferor and transferee, and making the transferee the beneficial owner.

(c) The rule in *Strong v Bird*

This is a curious rule which depends on the coincidence of the title to the property which is the subject of the incomplete gift, reaching the hands of the donee for some other reason, typically because the donor dies leaving a will appointing the donee as his executor. When this happens the gift is said to be complete.

---

1. Estate duty was a tax chargeable on death and on inter vivos gifts made within a certain period of the donor's death.

Strong v Bird (1874) LR 18 Eq 315, Ch; Jessel MR

The donee borrowed £1,100 from the donor; it was agreed that the loan would be repaid by instalments. After two instalments had been paid, the donor told the donee that she did not want to have any more of the money she had lent returned, but the debt was never formally released.[2] Four years later the donor died; by her will she had appointed the donee as her sole executor.

Held: Title to the debt having vested in the donee as executor, the imperfect gift was perfected.

Jessel MR: The law requires nothing more than this, that in a case where the thing which is the subject of donation is transferable or releasable at law, the legal transfer or release shall take place. The gift is not perfect until what has been generally called a change of the property at law has taken place. Allowing that rule to operate to its full extent, what occurred was this. The donor, or the alleged donor, had made her will, and by that will had appointed Mr Bird, the alleged donee, executor. After her death he proved the will, and the legal effect of that was to release the debt in law, and therefore the condition which is required, namely, that the release shall be perfect at law, was complied with by the testatrix making him executor. It is not necessary that the legal change shall knowingly be made by the donor with a view to carry out the gift. It may be made by the donor with a view to carry out the gift. It may be made for another purpose; but if the gift is clear, and there is to be no recall of the gift, and no intention to recall it, so that the person who executes the legal instrument does not intend to invest the person taking upon himself the legal ownership with any other character, there is no reason why the legal instrument should not have its legal effect. For instance, suppose this occurred, that a person made a memorandum on the title deeds of an estate to this effect: 'I give Blackacre to A.B.,' and afterwards conveyed that estate to A.B. by a general description, not intending in any way to change the previous gift, would there be any equity to make the person who had so obtained the legal estate a trustee for the donor? The answer would be that there is no resulting trust; that is rebutted by showing that the person who conveyed did not intend the person taking the conveyance to be a trustee, and although the person conveying actually thought that that was not one of the estates conveyed, because that person thought that he had well given the estate before, still the estate would pass at law, notwithstanding that idea, and there being no intention to revoke the gift, surely it would get rid of any resulting trust. On the same principle, when a testator makes his debtor executor, and thereby releases the debt at law, he is no longer liable at law. It is said that he would be liable in this Court: and so he would, unless he could show some reason for not being made liable. Then what does he show here? Why he proves to the satisfaction of the Court a continuing intention to give; and it appears to me that there being the continuing intention to give, and there being a legal act which transferred the ownership or released the obligation—for it is the same thing—the transaction is perfected, and he does not want the aid of a Court of Equity to carry it out, or to make it complete, because it is complete already, and there is no equity against him to take the property away from him.

On that ground I shall hold that this gentleman had a perfect title to the £900.[3]

In **Re Freeland** [1952] Ch 110, [1952] 1 All ER 16, the donor told the plaintiff that she intended to give the plaintiff her car. She never actually delivered it to the plaintiff, however; with the plaintiff's agreement she lent it instead to the defendant. When the donor died, she left a will appointing the plaintiff as one of her executrices. The Court of Appeal held that the rule in *Strong v Bird* would not apply to save the gift, Jenkins LJ saying at p 19:

---

2. See *Pinnel's Case* (1602) 5 Co Rep 117a, *Foakes v Beer* (1884) 9 App Cas 605. In the absence of consideration, a seal should have been used.

3. See also *Re Stewart* [1908] 2 Ch 251, *Re Ralli's WT* [1964] Ch 288, [1963] 3 All ER 940.

In my view, the lending of the car to the defendant, albeit with the consent of the plaintiff, is really fatal to the plaintiff's claim that there was a continuing intention to make an immediate gift. In my judgment, the principle of *Strong v Bird* ((1874) LR 18 Eq 315) is directed to perfecting gifts complete in all respects except as regards the legal formalities necessary for the proper transfer of title to the particular property in question. It is confined, in my view, to cases where nothing remains to be done but the mere formality of transfer in order to perfect what was intended by the testator or testatrix to be an immediate gift inter vivos, and surely there can be no room for its application in a case where there is an intention to give, but the gift is not completed because the intending donor desires first to apply the subject matter of the contemplated or promised gift to some other purpose. In that case the intended donee, when appointed as executor, cannot say: 'Nothing remained to complete my title except the transfer,' or, in other words: 'If the testator had been alive today and I had asked him for a transfer, he would have made it at once without question,' for in such circumstances the testator's answer would have been: 'I will not transfer the property to you now. My intention is to give it to you after I have used it for the prior purpose I have in view.' That state of affairs seems to me necessarily to exclude the application of the principle of *Strong v Bird* ((1874) LR 18 Eq 315).[4]

In **Re Gonin** [1979] Ch 16, [1977] 2 All ER 720, Walton J doubted whether the rule in *Strong v Bird* should apply where the donee became the donor's administrator. Miss Gonin had looked after her ageing parents for many years, on the understanding that she would be given the house in which they all lived, which was owned by her mother. No formal gift was ever made. Her father died first; when her mother died intestate some time later, Miss Gonin obtained letters of administration of her estate and claimed perfection of the imperfect gift under the rule in *Strong v Bird*. Walton J found against her on the basis that on the evidence, there was no continuing intention to make an immediate gift to her, and on the subject of donee-administrators, he had this to say at p 734:

It was accepted by both counsel before me, following the decision of Farwell J in *Re James* ([1935] Ch 449) that the doctrine applied to administrators as well as to executors. I shall accordingly proceed on that agreed view of the law but I feel that before I do so I must express my own difficulties in accepting this position, leaving it to a higher court to determine what, if any, validity they have.

I start from the simple proposition that if the defendant in *Strong v Bird* itself had been an administrator instead of an executor the case would have been decided the other way, since it distinctly proceeded on the basis that at law the appointment of the person as an executor effected a release of any debt due from the executor to the testator, a doctrine which was never applied to an administrator; see *Needham's Case* ((1610) 8 Co Rep 1352) *Wankford v Wankford* ((1704) 1 Salk 299), *Seagram v Knight* ([1867] 2 Ch App 628). . . . The appointment of an administrator, on the other hand, is not the act of the deceased but of the law. It is often a matter of pure chance which of many persons equally entitled to a grant of letters of administration finally takes them out. Why, then, should any special tenderness be shown to a person so selected by law and not the will of the testator, and often indifferently selected among many with an equal claim? It would seem an astonishing doctrine of equity that if the person who wishes to take the benefit of the rule in *Strong v Bird* manages to be the person to obtain a grant then he will be able to do so, but if a person equally entitled manages to obtain a prior grant, then he will not be able to do so. This appears to me to treat what ought to be a simple rule of equity, namely that if the legal title to a gift is perfected by the appointment by the intending donor of the intended donee as his executor, and the latter proves his will, then the coincidence of the donor's having intended the gift and having vested the legal estate in the intended donee should coalesce into absolute ownership, as something in the nature of a lottery. I cannot think that equity is so undiscriminating.

---

4. See also *Re Wale* [1956] 3 All ER 280, [1956] 1 WLR 1346, *Re Innes* [1910] 1 Ch 188.

QUESTIONS

1. 'There should be one uniform method for the transfer of property inter vivos, just as there is one uniform method for the transfer of property by will; indeed it would be much simpler for the layman if all inter vivos transfers were brought into line with the current testamentary requirements.'
Discuss.

2. Donald attempts to make a number of gifts to his friends:

(a) He hands over to Susan his share certificate for 1,000 shares in XYZ Ltd, a private company, together with a signed stock transfer form. When Susan applies to the company to register the transfer, the directors refuse her application, acting under their powers in the company's articles of association.

(b) He gives to Percy the key to his strongbox at the bank; the box contains Donald's silver collection.

(c) He says to his mistress Molly, who lives with him: 'The house and all its contents are yours,' indicating them with a sweeping gesture as he stands in the hallway.

(d) He writes a letter to Edwin telling him that he gives Edwin his remainder interest under his late father's will of which his mother is the life tenant.

Which of these items has been effectively transferred? Would it affect your answer if Donald died a month after these events leaving a will appointing Molly his executrix?

CHAPTER 3

The right of survivorship

1 In general

When two or more persons own property jointly, whether realty or personalty, they may do so in one of two ways, namely as joint tenants or as tenants in common.[1] The crucial difference between the two methods of co-ownership is that where the beneficial tenant in common is concerned, his interest on death will pass to his personal representative to devolve under his will or intestacy, whereas the interest of the beneficial joint tenant accrues automatically to the surviving joint tenant(s) by the right of survivorship, the *ius accrescendi*. In its simplicity, the beneficial joint tenancy is a popular method of succession in relation to many kinds of property, such as bank accounts, shareholdings and land, particularly, in the last mentioned case, the matrimonial home.[2]

If this highly convenient method of succession is to be utilised, a number of matters must be carefully considered.

2 Intention to create beneficial co-ownership

If A purchases property in or transfers property into the joint names of himself and B, B having made no contribution to the purchase money and having given no consideration for the transfer, unless A's intention to the contrary has been made plain in the instrument of transfer, the presumption of a resulting trust will arise.[3] As a result, B will acquire no beneficial interest in the property at all, but will be presumed to hold the legal estate in the property as trustee with A, for A as beneficial owner. So if A dies first, B will hold the entire legal estate (as surviving legal joint tenant) on trust for A's estate beneficially. The presumption of a resulting trust can be rebutted by evidence to the contrary;[4] it can also be rebutted where the presumption of advancement lies,[5] and in

---

1. The hallmark of the joint tenancy is the presence of the 'four unities' as between the co-owners, viz unity of time, title, interest and possession; only unity of possession is required for a tenancy in common; see further Cheshire and Burn, pp 208–211.
2. Todd and Jones in their survey on 'Matrimonial Property' (1972) pp 10–11 found that over half of the married couples who took part in the survey were joint owners of the matrimonial home and over 50% of these couples gave as their main reason for the joint ownership the benefit of the automatic transfer of ownership to the survivor on the death of the first to die.
3. See p 6 ante. The presumption will similarly arise if A buys property in his own name but with a contribution to the purchase money from B; A will be presumed to hold the legal estate on trust for himself and B as beneficial co-owners proportionate to the respective contributions. See eg *Bull v Bull* [1955] 1 QB 234, [1955] 1 All ER 253.
4. As in *Standing v Bowring* (1885) 31 Ch D 282. See also *Russell v Scott* (1936) 55 CLR 440, p 38 post.
5. See p 6 ante and *Re Figgis*, post.

relation to joint bank accounts held by a husband and wife, the 'common pool' argument[6] may save the situation for the survivor.[7]

Marshall v Crutwell (1875) LR 20 Eq 328, Ch; Jessel MR

The husband, whose health was deteriorating, transferred his bank account from his own name into the joint names of himself and his wife and directed his bank to honour cheques drawn by either of them. He subsequently paid large sums into the account into which the wife never paid any money of her own. All cheques on the joint account were drawn by the wife at the husband's direction and the proceeds applied in paying household expenses. When the husband died, the wife claimed the balance by survivorship.

Held: She had no such entitlement; the object of the agreement was merely the better management of the husband's affairs, not to provide her with a beneficial interest.

Jessel MR: The mere circumstance that the name of a child or a wife is inserted on the occasion of a purchase of stock is not sufficient to rebut a resulting trust in favour of the purchaser if the surrounding circumstances lead to the conclusion that a trust was intended. Although a purchase in the name of a wife or a child, if altogether unexplained, will be deemed a gift[8] yet you may take surrounding circumstances into consideration, so as to say that it is a trust, not a gift. So in the case of a stranger, you may take surrounding circumstances into consideration, so as to say that a purchase in his name is a gift,[9] not a trust.

Now in the present case the husband, being in failing health, goes to the bank and says 'Change the account from my own name into the name of myself and my wife, and I authorise you to honour the cheques of either of us.'

What afterwards occurred was this: The man's health not improving he never drew a cheque. His wife drew all cheques against the account, and she applied the proceeds to household purposes, and I suppose small sums to her own use. All the sums afterwards paid in by the husband were carried to the credit of the account in the joint names. Of course the theory is, that not only the sum transferred, but all the sums paid in from time to time, would go to the wife. Now, in all the cases in which a gift to the wife has been held to have been intended, the husband has retained the dominion over the fund in this sense, that the wife during the lifetime of the husband has had no power independently of him, and the husband has retained the power of revoking the gift. In transferring a sum of stock there is no obvious motive why a man should put a sum of stock into the name of himself and his wife. She cannot receive the dividends; he can and must, and it is difficult to see any motive of convenience or otherwise which should induce a man to buy a sum of stock, or transfer a sum of stock (if there is any difference between the two) in or into the names of himself and his wife, except the motive of benefiting her in case she survives. But here we have the actual fact, that the man was in such a state of health that he could not draw cheques, and the wife drew them. Looking at the fact that subsequent sums are paid in from time to time, and taking into view all the circumstances (as I understand I am bound to do), as a juryman, I think the circumstances show that this was a mere arrangement for convenience, and that it was not intended to be a provision for the wife in the event which might happen, that at the husband's death there might be a fund standing to the credit of the banking account. I take into account the circumstance that the wife could draw upon the fund in the husband's lifetime, so that it would not necessarily be a provision for her after his death; and also the circumstance that the

---

6. See p 33 post.
7. See Cretney *Principles of Family Law* (4th edn 1984) pp 635–660 with particular reference to the application of these principles to married couples.
8. By virtue of the presumption of advancement, see p 6 ante.
9. As in *Fowkes v Pascoe* (1875) LR 10 Ch 343.

amount of the fund at his death must be altogether uncertain; and, having regard to the rule which is now binding on me, that I must infer from the surrounding circumstances what the nature of the transaction was, I come to the conclusion that it was not intended to be a provision for the wife, but simply a mode of conveniently managing the testator's affairs, and that it leaves the money therefore still his property.[10]

Re Figgis [1969] 1 Ch 123, [1968] 1 All ER 999, Ch D; Megarry J

Whilst serving in the Army during the 1914–18 War, the husband opened a joint current bank account in the name of himself and his wife; shortly thereafter he opened a joint bank deposit account in their names also. The bank was authorised to accept cheques drawn by either of them but there was no mention in the letter of authority as to ownership of the balances should either of them die. The accounts were fed and operated entirely by the husband save for a few cheques drawn on the current account by the wife shortly before the husband died, when he was too ill to sign them himself. The husband had no separate bank account of his own, whereas the wife had a separate current account in her own name into which she paid her own money and money transferred from the deposit account by the husband. Some fifty years after opening the joint accounts, the husband died, both accounts being at that time substantially in credit.

Held: The presumption of advancement would apply; the wife was entitled to the balances by survivorship.

Megarry J: The applicability of the presumption of advancement to a joint bank account seems undoubted; and so the question here is whether that presumption has been rebutted. Counsel for the second defendant relied on the facts of the case as establishing that the joint current account was opened merely for convenience within the doctrine of *Marshall v Crutwell*[11] ((1875) LR 20 Eq 328) and that throughout it was treated by both husband and wife as belonging to the husband alone. The husband opened the account so that the wife could draw on it while he was abroad during the first world war, and this, he said, characterised the account throughout its life. The joint deposit account, which was opened by a transfer from the joint current account, had the same origin in convenience, he added. He also put some emphasis on the wife's acquiescence over a long period in the husband treating the joint account as his own.

I am not persuaded by these contentions. The difficulties in ascertaining a man's intentions are great enough when there is a plenitude of evidence. Here there is a paucity. Convenience may well have been one reason why the husband opened the joint current account in 1917; but after his return from France some fifty years ago until he lay on his deathbed I cannot see any evidence of convenience. The case is very different from *Marshall v Crutwell*.[11] There the joint account was opened by the husband less than six months before his death, when he had for some time been in failing health; every cheque on that joint account was drawn by the wife, and not by the husband. Here it cannot be said what was in the husband's mind when he opened the joint current account. If convenience was one consideration, as I think that it was, that does not mean that the husband had no thought of the account forming a provision for his wife if he were to be killed. At a time when a bloody war had lasted for over three years, he was leaving a bride of less than two years standing and facing the risks of that war; and although one is in the sphere of inference and speculation, I should be slow to hold that an account

---

10. See also *Hoddinott v Hoddinott* [1949] 2 KB 406 where the Court of Appeal found that the joint bank account was created solely for convenience to enable the wife to draw money from the account (of which the husband was the sole provider), the bank being open only three days a week and the husband finding it difficult to get there because of his work.
11. See p 31 ante.

opened in such circumstances was opened merely for convenience. If the husband had intended to make arrangements for mere convenience, there was indeed no need for him to open a joint account. He could simply have given instructions to the bank to honour cheques drawn on the current account that he had in his sole name. Furthermore, I bear in mind the husband's carefulness in money matters. Once the war was over he might have been expected to terminate the joint current account and to resume a current account in his own name, if all that he had intended was to make convenient arrangements. The more careful the man, the more significant the long subsistence of the joint account seems to be.

I regard the joint deposit account as being a fortiori. In any case, the mere fact that it was opened with moneys taken from the joint current account could not, I think, suffice to stamp it with the quality of the joint current account, even if that had been opened merely for convenience. Furthermore, in the nature of things a deposit account is far less appropriate than a current account as a provision made for convenience.[12]

In **Jones v Maynard** [1951] Ch 572, [1951] 1 All ER 802, the joint bank account differed from those referred to above in so far as both husband and wife paid money into the account from their own resources and drew on it for their own purposes. Vaisey J said at p 803:

In my judgment, where there is a joint purse between husband and wife—a common pool into which they put all their resources—it is not consistent with that conception that the joint account should thereafter (in this case in the event of a divorce) be divided up with reference to the respective contributions of husband and wife, crediting the husband with the whole of his earnings and the wife with the whole of her dividends. I do not believe that when once the joint pool has been formed it ought to be, and can be, dissected in any such manner. I take the view that when spouses have a common purse and a pool of their resources, the husband's remuneration is earned on behalf of them both, and the idea that years afterwards one can dissect the contents of the pool by taking an elaborate account as to how much was paid in by the husband and how much was paid in by the wife is not consistent with the original fundamental idea of a joint purse or a common pool. When the money goes into the pool it is there as a joint property.

The question of survivorship was not in issue on the facts of this case. The husband and wife were still alive but divorced, and the dispute concerned their respective entitlement to investments which the husband had made in his own name by his withdrawals from the joint account. Vaisey J was satisfied from the parties' evidence that they regarded the joint account and investments made therefrom as 'our savings' such that the wife was intended to have a beneficial interest therein and he concluded at p 804:

That being the position, I take the view that investments made out of the joint account, although in the name of the husband, were made by him in his own name as a trustee as to a moiety for his wife. If the investments out of the joint account had been made in the name of the wife alone, there is no doubt that the ordinary presumption of law would have applied and she would have been entitled to the investments, but, as they were made in the name of the husband, it seems to me that the assumption of half and half is the one which I ought to apply. Plato said that equality was a sort of justice, that is to say, if in such a matter as this one cannot find any other basis, equality is the proper basis. I think that is a principle which applies here. When moneys were taken out of the joint

---

12. See also *Re Pattinson* (1885) 1 TLR 216, *Re Harrison* (1920) 90 LJ Ch 186: both cases relate to joint bank accounts held by married couples and in each case the court on the facts upheld the presumption of advancement enabling the surviving wife to claim the balance. It should be noted however that *Re Figgis* was decided in 1968; some twelve months later in *Pettitt v Pettitt* [1970] AC 777, [1969] 2 All ER 385, the House of Lords was to describe the strength of the presumption of advancement in favour of the wife as much diminished in modern times, see p 8 ante.

account for the purpose of making an investment the intention which I attribute to the parties is equality and not some proportion to be ascertained by an inquiry as to the amounts which were respectively contributed by the husband and the wife to the common purse.

Re Bishop [1965] Ch 450, [1965] 1 All ER 249, Ch D; Stamp J

The husband and wife opened a joint bank account to which each contributed from time to time (in unequal amounts) out of their respective resources. The account was not opened for any particular purpose. Both drew on it for their own purposes and for house-keeping and investment purposes. Some of these investments were made in the wife's name and some in the name of the husband. When the husband died, the question was raised as to the extent of the wife's beneficial interest in the investments and in the balance in the joint bank account.

Held: The balance in the bank account would pass to the wife by survivorship but the investments made from the bank account would belong to the person in whose name they were made.

Stamp J: Now, where a husband and wife open a joint account at a bank on terms that cheques may be drawn on the account by either of them, then in my judgment, in the absence of facts or circumstances which indicate that the account was intended, or was kept, for some specific or limited purpose, each spouse can draw upon it not only for the benefit of both spouses but for his or her own benefit. Each spouse, in drawing money out of the account, is to be treated as doing so with the authority of the other, and in my judgment, if one of the spouses purchases a chattel for his own benefit or an investment in his or her own name, that chattel or investment belongs to the person in whose name it is purchased or invested; for in such a case there is in my judgment, no equity in the other spouse to displace the legal ownership of the one in whose name the investment is purchased. What is purchased is not to be regarded as purchased out of a fund belonging to the spouses in the proportions in which they contribute to the account or in equal proportions, but out of a pool or fund of which they were, at law and in equity, joint tenants. It also follows that if one of the spouses draws on the account to make a purchase in the joint names of the spouses, the property purchased, since it is purchased in joint names, is, prima facie, joint property and there is no equity to displace the joint legal ownership. There is, in my judgment, no room for any presumption which would constitute the joint holders as trustees for the parties in equal or some other shares. . . . Now I am asked by Counsel appearing for Mrs Bishop and other members of the family who support her contention, and relying on the decision of Vaisey J in *Jones v Maynard*[13] ([1951] Ch 572, [1951] 1 All ER 802) to hold that as regards investments purchased in the sole name of Mr Bishop, he is a trustee of those investments holding them on trust for himself and Mrs Bishop in equal shares and that as regards investments which were made in the sole name of Mrs Bishop, she is, if I understood the argument correctly, entitled to one half by virtue of the doctrine of equality and to the other half by the effect of the presumption of advancement. The way the argument goes is that the money standing to the credit of the joint account is to be regarded as belonging to the spouses in equal shares and that when an investment is purchased in the name of the husband, that investment is accordingly held on trust for the husband and the wife in equal shares, but that when an investment is purchased in the name of the wife, the share which the husband would be entitled to by the effect of the doctrine of equality is to be deemed to be given by him to his wife by the effect of the doctrine of advancement. I pause to observe that if the circumstances were such that the parties intended that moneys standing to the joint account should belong to them in equal shares and that investments

---

13. See p 33 ante.

purchased out of those moneys should be held on trust for the husband and wife in equal shares, it seems to me quite impossible, in the case of an investment in the name of the wife, to presume that the husband intended a gift to his wife of his share. I cannot, it seems to me, presume that a trust was intended when moneys in the joint account are invested in the name of the husband but no trust when they are made in the name of his wife.

In my judgment, however, not only the facts of *Jones v Maynard* but the question of law which was there considered, are wholly different from the questions of fact and the questions of law which I have to consider in this case. . . .

(He recited the facts of *Jones v Maynard* and continued:)

Now the only question which fell for determination in the case was whether the investments which the husband had purchased in his own name by drawing on the joint account were held by him on trust for the wife and himself in equal shares, or whether they were held by him for himself and his wife in the shares in which they had contributed the moneys in the joint account. That was the only question which fell for determination, and manifestly, the argument which has been put in the present case, that Mr Bishop was entitled to the investments purchased in his own name for his own use and benefit, was not open in that case. Both husband and wife agreed that investments were to be 'our savings'. It was quite impossible to contend, in those circumstances, that the wife had no interest in the investments made in the name of the husband. I have to read that case in the light of those facts, and I have to bear in mind that that was the only issue between the parties. . . .

I do not conclude that Vaisey J was there laying down any general principle that wherever one finds money standing to a joint account and there are investments in the name of the husband that those investments are held by the husband on trust for the husband and the wife in equal shares. It must, in my judgment, depend on the facts of the case and I do not think that Vaisey J was coming to any other conclusion. Vaisey J went on to say that if the investments were made in the name of the wife alone, the ordinary presumption of law would apply and she would be entitled to the investments. That question had not been argued before Vaisey J and, again, in my judgment, he was not attempting to lay down any general principle of law, but was merely stating his conclusion on the facts of that particular case.[14]

3 Intention to create a beneficial joint tenancy

It must next be plain that the intended form of co-ownership is that of a beneficial joint tenancy as opposed to a beneficial tenancy in common, if the *ius accrescendi* is to apply. This should be done by indicating as clearly as possible the parties' intentions in this respect at the time when the property concerned is put or transferred into joint names.[15]

If there is no clear indication of the beneficial interests in the instrument giving rise to the joint ownership or otherwise, in relation to both realty and

---

14. The Law Commission in its Working Paper No 90 'Family Law' (1985) has stated its intention of securing the reversal of *Re Bishop* as between spouses. It is proposing that unless otherwise agreed, (i) money made available by one spouse to the other for joint purposes and property acquired with that money shall be owned by them both, and (ii) where both spouses make money available for joint purposes in such a way as to create a 'notional pool' of their resources, then that money and any property acquired with it should be owned by them both.

15. Ideally this should be done in the instrument of transfer, see eg *Goodman v Gallant* [1986] 1 All ER 311, [1986] 2 WLR 236 but this is not possible in the case of pure personalty transferred by delivery; in the case of stocks and shares, companies are not concerned with the equitable status of their shareholders and will treat the survivor of joint shareholders as absolute owner of the shareholding, see Companies Act 1985 s 360.

personalty there is a long established presumption in favour of a beneficial joint tenancy, a presumption created by the common law courts attracted by the convenience of the doctrine of survivorship. This presumption is much disliked by equity[16] which has always been prepared to look for evidence to rebut the presumption either in the instrument itself by finding 'words of severance' indicating the parties' intention to take separate shares, or by reference to the surrounding circumstances. In addition there are three situations where equity presumes the existence of a tenancy in common, namely (i) where purchasers of property contribute the purchase money in unequal shares,[17] (ii) where property is bought by partners, (iii) where money is advanced on mortgage by two or more persons,[18] so that in these three situations it is particularly important to make it plain that the form of ownership intended by the parties is a beneficial joint tenancy, if this is in fact the parties' intention.

Morley v Bird (1798) 3 Ves Jun 628, 30 ER 1192, Rolls Court; Arden MR

The testator had left a legacy to 'the four daughters of my brother John Collins', three of whom died in the testator's lifetime. The surviving daughter claimed the entire legacy.

Held: The presumption of a joint tenancy would apply; as the surviving joint tenant she was entitled to the whole.

Arden MR: Great doubts have been entertained by Judges both at Law and in Equity as to words creating a joint tenancy or a tenancy in common; and it is clear, the ancient law was in favour of a joint tenancy; and that law still prevails: unless there are some words to sever the interest taken, it is at this moment a joint tenancy notwithstanding the leaning of the Courts lately in favour of a tenancy in common. A legacy of a specific chattel, a grant of an estate, is a joint tenancy. It is true, the Courts seeing the inconvenience of that have been desirous, wherever they could find any intention of severance, to avail themselves of it; and their successive determinations have laid hold of any words for that purpose. 'Equally to be divided' (*Rigden v Vallier* 2 Ves Sen 252), 'equally, among, between,' even in Law I believe, certainly in Equity, create a tenancy in common: but without those words it is a joint tenancy. But many distinctions have been raised in Equity (see 1 Ves Jun 434, 435; 2 Ves Sen 258; *Jackson v Jackson* 7 Ves 535; 9 Ves 591; and the note, 597. *Aveling v Knipe* 19 Ves 441); as where persons are in trade, and have joint debts due to them; the Courts say, it could not be intended to the prejudice of the family of the deceased partner; therefore not doubting that it would be a joint tenancy at Law, in Equity they say, it could not be the agreement. So if two people join in lending money upon a mortgage, Equity says, it could not be the intention, that the interest in that should survive. Though they take a joint security, each means to lend his own and take back his own. But that was never extended to grants. A voluntary bond

---

16. Courts of equity regarded the doctrine of survivorship as grossly unfair: *R v Williams* (1735) Bunb 342 at 343: 'survivorship is looked upon as odious in equity'; *Gould v Kemp* (1834) 2 My & K 304 at 309: 'That joint tenancy is not favoured in equity is certain'. In Canada most jurisdictions have statutorily reversed the common law rule so far as realty is concerned and provide that a conveyance or devise to two or more persons will create a tenancy in common unless the instrument indicates that a joint tenancy is intended: McLean 'Severance of Joint Tenancies' (1979) 57 Can BR 761.

17. See eg *Lake v Gibson* (1729) 1 Eq Cas Abr 290, *Lake v Craddock* (1732) 3 P Wms 158.

18. See eg *Steeds v Steeds* (1889) 22 QBD 537. In *Malayan Credit v Jack Chia-MPH Ltd* [1986] 1 All ER 71 the Privy Council added a fourth situation: where two or more persons hold premises as legal joint tenants for their several business purposes.

would survive, if no intention of the party to make a severance appears. Therefore legacies, gifts, grants, etc, are both at Law and in Equity joint; except from the nature of the contract or from the words some intention of severance appears.

This is a legacy to four persons; and there are no words of severance; therefore it is a joint legacy; and the whole interest survives to the survivor, three being dead; and though I agree with those, who think it the least evil, that it should be a tenancy in common, this is one of those cases, in which it is more convenient, that it should remain joint.

In **Robinson v Preston** (1858) 4 K & J 505, 70 ER 211, Page Wood V-C emphasised the rebuttable nature of these presumptions. Some stock had been purchased in the joint names of two sisters, A and B, who also held a joint bank account; in each case the money had been provided by equal contributions. A died before B and A's executors claimed one half of the stock and bank balance for A's estate, on the basis that A and B were tenants in common. Holding in their favour, Page Wood V-C said at p 213:

The law is settled as to the investment of moneys in the names of two or more persons in the purchase of property. If invested in unequal shares, the purchasers remain tenants in common of the purchased property; if in equal shares, and the matter on the face of it purports to be a joint tenancy, then it is considered by this Court to be a joint tenancy, and no equity is supposed to intervene by which it can be reduced to a tenancy in common.

Therefore, if this had been a simple case of so much money advanced by each sister, and laid out in stock, then, inasmuch as the sisters were residing together, and nearly of the same age, and the chances were nearly even as to which would be the survivor, the case would have been a strong one in favour of the presumption that there might be a desire on the part of both ladies to avoid probate and legacy duty, and to that end there should be an actual joint tenancy.

But the circumstances of the case are peculiar.

In the first place, the property has all arisen in this way: The ladies were tenants in common of certain freehold lands; and the money which was at the banker's and the money which had been invested in these several securities appear to have been the rents of those lands, which had been paid into the banker's to their joint account.

On one occasion when the investment was made in the form of a mortgage there was an express declaration by the ladies that they were to be tenants in common of the mortgage security—a declaration which, as it was observed, in the argument was unnecessary, inasmuch as in the case of *Petty v Styward* (1 Ch Rep 57), one of the earliest authorities, it was held that a mortgage taken by two, although in equal shares, is a tenancy in common. Perhaps the ground of the distinction in this respect between a mortgage and a purchase is not particularly clear; but it has been settled, and therefore it was unnecessary that any such declaration should be made. Still the fact of making it indicated, no doubt, the intention, and showed what was their desire, at all events with reference to that portion of their savings. . . .

Then I find further the third point—perhaps the strongest of all, viz., that the sister who proved to be the survivor, and against whom of course her own declaration may be read, by her will, executed in the lifetime of her sister not only speaks of 'her share' of the property in question, but affects to dispose of it in favour of her sister; and, further, on the assumption that her sister will survive her, she directs that, after her sister's decease, a legacy of £350 stock should be paid out of a part of the stock in question, that part standing exactly in the same position as the rest.

These three circumstances concurring, and the whole being a question of intention to be ascertained from the circumstances of the case, it is not illogical to say that the three combined have a force and carry a conviction which, perhaps, any one of them taken alone would not produce.

4   Testamentary in nature?

If the doctrine of survivorship is to operate, the deceased must create the beneficial joint tenancy in his lifetime, so in making the transfer into or purchase in joint names, he must satisfy the appropriate formalities for an inter vivos transfer. [19]

Sometimes, however, the deceased's intention at the time of such transfer is that he alone shall have the beneficial enjoyment and control of the property during his lifetime, the gift to be limited to such of the property as may be remaining at his death, should he be the first to die. It has been argued that in such a case the disposition is really testamentary in nature[20] and must fail unless it complies with the formal requirements for a will.

In the Canadian case of **Hill v Hill** (1904) 8 Ont LR 710, a father had placed 400 dollars in a bank account in the joint names of himself and his son with the intention that the money should remain subject to the father's control and disposition whilst alive, only the balance on his death to belong to his son. When the father died it was argued that the son was entitled to the balance, the transaction being equivalent to a voluntary inter vivos settlement which reserved to the father a life interest with a power of revocation, but Anglin J refused to accept this saying at p 711:

Upon the plaintiff's own evidence I find myself driven to the conclusion that the purpose of William Hill, deceased, was by this means to make a gift to his son, the plaintiff, in its nature testamentary. As such it could only be made effectually by an instrument duly executed as a will. The father retaining exclusive control and disposing power over the 400 dollars during his lifetime, the rights of the son were intended to arise only upon and after his father's death. This is, in substance and in fact, a testamentary disposition of the money, and as such ineffectual.[1]

Russell v Scott (1936) 55 CLR 440, High Court of Australia; Starke, Dixon, Evatt and McTiernan JJ

An elderly woman and her nephew opened a joint bank account which was fed entirely by the aunt and was solely to meet the aunt's needs, withdrawal slips being signed by both of them. It was found as a fact that the aunt's intention was that any balance remaining in the account at her death was to belong to the nephew beneficially. When she died, the nephew claimed the balance but it was argued that he held the funds on resulting trust for the aunt's estate.
Held: He was entitled both legally and beneficially to the balance.

Dixon and Evatt JJ: It is said that the deceased's intention that her nephew on surviving her should take the amount of the bank account is a testamentary wish to which effect could be given only by a duly executed will.

This must mean that, while retaining full beneficial property in a corpus, she intended that on her death some other person should succeed to her property in that corpus or to some interest therein to which he was not before entitled either absolutely or contingently, and to which the law gave him no title to succeed. It is only in this sense that an intention to benefit can be said to be testamentary. Law and equity supply many

---

19. See Ch 2 ante.
20. See Ch 5 post.
1. See also *Shortill v Grannen* (1920) 55 DLR 416, *McKnight v Titus* (1933) 6 Mar Prov R 282, *Larondeau v Laurendeau* (1954) 4 DLR 293 (all Canadian authorities), and *Owens v Greene* [1932] IR 225 (Irish Supreme Court) where similar decisions were reached.

means by which the enjoyment of property may be made to pass on death. Succession *post mortem* is not the same as testamentary succession. But what can be accomplished only by a will is the voluntary transmission on death of an interest which up to the moment of death belongs absolutely and indefeasibly to the deceased. This was not true of the chose in action created by opening and maintaining the joint bank account. At law, of course, it was joint property which would accrue to the survivor. In equity, the deceased was entitled in her lifetime so to deal with the contractual rights conferred by the chose in action as to destroy all its value, namely, by withdrawing all the money at credit. But the elastic or flexible conceptions of equitable proprietary rights or interests do not require that, because this is so, the joint owner of the chose in action should in respect of the legal right vested in him be treated as a trustee to the entire extent of every possible kind of beneficial interest or enjoyment. Doubtless a trustee he was during her lifetime, but the resulting trust upon which he held did not extend further than the donor intended; it did not exhaust the entire legal interest in every contingency. In the contingency of his surviving the donor and of the account then containing money, his legal interest was allowed to take effect unfettered by a trust. In respect of his *ius accrescendi* his conscience could not be bound. For the resulting trust would be inconsistent with the true intention of that person upon whose presumed purpose it must depend.

In **Young v Sealey** [1949] Ch 278, [1949] 1 All ER 92, the point was for the first time considered by an English court, in a case that involved similar facts to those in *Russell v Scott* (ante). Romer J found in favour of the surviving joint tenant but admitted to sympathy with decisions such as *Hill v Hill*,[2] *Owens v Green*,[3] saying at p 108:

I confess that the reasoning of those cases appeals to me, and if there had been no English authority relevant to the question I should have felt inclined to apply that reasoning notwithstanding that, by so doing, I should have defeated Miss Jarman's (the deceased joint tenant's) expressed intentions. I find it difficult to regard Miss Jarman's deposit account transactions as voluntary settlements by her in the defendant's favour coupled with a power of revocation. I find it equally difficult to regard them as operating as immediately effective gifts of anything, seeing that, as between Miss Jarman and the defendant, the defendant was to have no power of withdrawal so long as Miss Jarman was living, whilst she retained the entire beneficial title to the funds. Further, it is impossible to regard the transactions as *donationes mortis causa*. There only remains the view, therefore, that the gifts were intended to be postponed until Miss Jarman's death and to operate then so as to pass for the first time to the defendant a beneficial right to assets of Miss Jarman as then ascertained. In my judgment, however, it would not be right for me to defeat the defendant by applying this course of reasoning. In the first place, the cases which have come before the courts of this country in which a depositor has put funds in the joint names of himself and another, intending to retain control over the funds and to withdraw from them if he thought proper, but with the further intention that the other party (if surviving) should take beneficially whatever might be left of the funds at the death of the depositor, have all, so far as I am aware, resulted in the surviving beneficiary taking free from any trust. . . . Secondly, there is the fact that a court whose decisions are entitled to very great respect, namely, the Appellate Division of the Supreme Court of Ontario, had the very point before them but did not accept it.[4] In these circumstances, and having regard to the disturbing effect which an acceptance of the argument might well have on titles already acquired, I think it is better that the change in the current of authority which I am invited to make should be made rather by the appellate court than by a court of first instance, assuming that it is to be made at all.

---

2. P 38 ante.
3. P 38 n 1 ante.
4. *Re Reid* (1921) 64 DLR 598 (Hodgin JA dissenting). See now also *Edwards v Bradley* (1956) 2 DLR (2d) 382.

QUESTIONS

1. See Bandali 'Injustice and Problems of Beneficial Joint Tenancies' (1977) 41 Conv 243. He advocates the abolition of the concept of joint tenancy on the ground that it has the effect of producing the fortuitous and unintended enrichment of the surviving joint tenant. Do you agree?

2. Alfred opens a bank account in the joint names of himself and his mistress Betty, instructing the bank to honour cheques drawn by either of them. Thereafter he pays £400 a month into the account whilst Betty pays into it her Bingo winnings, which average about £40 a month. Betty draws on the account for all their household expenses, for her personal expenses and also to finance the purchase of investments which she buys from time to time in her own name. Who will own the balance in the account and the investments if (i) Alfred dies first, (ii) Betty dies first? Would it make any difference to your answer if (a) Alfred and Betty were married, or (b) Alfred's health was deteriorating when he opened the joint bank account?

3. It is an attempt to make an ambulatory and postponed gift of such (if any) moneys as shall remain undrawn from the account at the depositor's death which, in my opinion, is contrary to the established principles, in as much as it is really testamentary in character and intention

(per Kennedy CJ, *Owens v Green* [1932] IR 225 at 238).

The gift of the joint interest was, I think, intended to be effective from the moment of the deposit so as to carry with it the legal right to title by survivorship; the promise and agreement in reference to drawing were not intended to and did not prevent the vesting of the title to the joint interest, as to which there was, I think, a complete and perfect gift inter vivos

(per Ferguson JA, *Re Reid* (1921) 64 DLR 598 at 608).

Discuss these conflicting statements, both of which were made with reference to a joint bank account which was to be drawn on only by the depositor in his lifetime. In the United States the Uniform Probate Code solves the problem by a simple provision that the balance shall pass to the survivor by virtue of the contract with the bank and the provisions of the Code (s 6–101 to 105) and any transfers relating thereto 'are not to be considered as testamentary' (s 6–106). For a general discussion on this topic see Cullity 'Joint Bank Accounts with Volunteers' (1969) 85 LQR 530.

CHAPTER 4

Nominations

1 In general

The nomination is a method of succession made available by various statutes in relation to certain assets,[1] usually up to a specified limit,[2] and by private pension schemes, usually with no limit. Originally conceived as a form of poor man's will, the availability of the nomination nowadays in passing on benefits payable on the death of an employee under many company pension and superannuation schemes often makes the nomination responsible for the transfer of a substantial proportion of the property realisable on the death of the nominator.[3]

In **Eccles Provident Industrial Co-operative Society Ltd v Griffiths** [1912] AC 483 at 490, Lord Mersey described the object of the nomination process (in relation to the power of nomination given by the Industrial and Provident Societies Act 1893 s 25[4]) in the following terms:

The object of s 25 is, in my view, to give to the poorer members of a society, that is to say to those who have not more than £100[5] to their credit, the power to make provision for the disposal, at their death, of this small sum without the expense being incurred of the making of a will or administering this part of their estate . . . . Once made the nomination takes effect, not by creating any charge or trust in favour of the nominee as against the nominator, as was suggested during the argument (for the nominator can at any moment revoke the nomination), but by giving to the nominee a right as against the society, in the event of the death of the member without having revoked the nomination, to require the society to transfer the property in accordance with the nomination. Until death the property is the property of the member, and all benefits accruing in respect of it during his lifetime are his also.

---

1. Eg property in a registered industrial and provident society, Industrial and Provident Societies Act 1965, ss 23–24; sums due from a registered friendly society, Friendly Societies Act 1974, ss 66–69; sums due to members of a trade union, Trade Union and Labour Relations Act 1974, Sch 1 para 31, as amended by Employment Protection Act 1975, Sch 16 Pt III paras 31–32, Trade Union (Nominations) Regulations 1977, SI 1977/789.
2. Currently £5,000: Administration of Estates (Small Payments) (Increase of Limit) Order 1984, SI 1984/539.
3. See Samuels, 'Nominations in favour of a Nominee to take effect on Death,' (1967) 31 Conv 85. The nomination process is very popular in relation to death benefits payable under superannuation schemes because the benefits generally escape inheritance tax on the death of the nominator (see Ch 16 post); they also avoid family provision claims (see Ch 17 post).
4. Now Industrial and Provident Societies Act 1965, s 23.
5. Now £5,000, see n 2 ante.

2   Formal requirements

Each statute or set of regulations made thereunder lays down the formal requirements to be satisfied by the nominator, as does the individual pension scheme trust deed or rules made thereunder; the appropriate trade union nomination regulations are extracted as a typical example of the former. Non-compliance with the designated requirements will normally render the nomination ineffective although in one instance relating to a company pension scheme,[6] substantial compliance was accepted as sufficient and there are other instances where the courts have been prepared to accept that although the nomination as such fails, since it is testamentary in character it can operate as a valid will, if it happens to satisfy the formal requirements of the Wills Act 1837, s 9.[7]

The Trade Union (Nominations) Regulations 1977[8]

2.   Power to make nominations
(1) Subject to the provisions of these Regulations a member of a trade union being a person who has attained the age of 16 years may nominate any person to receive the whole or part of any moneys not exceeding [£5,000[9]] payable on his death out of any funds of the trade union of which he is a member.
(2) Every nomination shall be made in writing in a form approved by the trade union, and shall be signed by the nominator.
(3) A nomination shall be of no effect unless it is delivered at or sent to the principal office of the trade union during the lifetime of the nominator.
(4) The trade union shall register every nomination and notify the registration to the nominator.
(5) A nomination may be in favour of one person or of several persons (who shall be clearly designated in the nomination) and, where there is more than one nominee, may direct that specific sums be paid to one or more of the nominees or that the nominees shall take the money nominated in specified shares, or may give directions to both effects.
(6) A nomination shall not be valid in respect of any nominee who at the date of the nomination is an officer or employee of the trade union unless that person is the husband, wife, father, mother, child, brother, sister, nephew or niece of the nominator.

In **Pearman v Charlton** (1928) 44 TLR 517, the deceased had nominated the balance in his Post Office Savings Bank Account[10] in favour of X. Under the then regulations[11] the nominator was required to make his nomination in writing, sign it in the presence of a witness and deposit it with the Post Office Savings Bank Controller. The deceased had signed the form, the name of a witness did appear on it and he had lodged the form with the Controller, but it transpired after his death that he had not signed the form in the presence of the witness. Wright J held that the nomination was invalid saying at p 517 that

---

6. *Re Danish Bacon Co Ltd Staff Pension Fund Trusts* [1971] 1 All ER 486, [1971] 1 WLR 248. As this aspect of the case was in fact concerned with the formalities for revocation of the nomination, it is considered in Ch 11 post.
7. Ch 8 post.
8. SI 1977/789.
9. See p 41 n 2 ante.
10. Until 1st May 1981 National Savings Bank (formerly Post Office Savings Bank) balances could be nominated without limit. The practice was formally discontinued as from that date but nominations made before that date will be honoured: National Savings Bank Regulations 1972 SI 1972/764, as amended by SI 1981/484.
11. Post Office Savings Bank Regulations 1921.

it was a testamentary document and he thought it was as necessary that it should be signed by the nominator in the presence of a witness as that the provisions for the due execution of a will should be observed.

X, to whom the Post Office had paid out in accordance with the nomination, had to hand over the money to the deceased's administrators for those entitled on his intestacy.

In **In the Goods of Baxter** [1903] P 12, the deceased had signed a nomination of his property with an industrial and provident society which turned out to be invalid because the deceased's property exceeded the then permitted limit of £100.[12] The Industrial and Provident Societies Act 1893, s 25 only required the nomination to be signed by the nominator, but the deceased's signature had in fact been witnessed by two persons who swore affidavits to the effect that the requirements of Wills Act 1837, s 9 had in fact been satisfied. This enabled Gorrell Barnes J to hold that it took effect as a will saying at p 15:

If the document had been operative as a nomination, sub-s 2 of s 25 of the Act of 1893 would have taken effect, and the document would only have been revocable in the manner therein indicated, and it would not have been revocable by any will or codicil. But, as the document is not operative as a nomination, the sub-section has no effect in this case; and, that being so, I do not see why I should not accept it as a will.

3 Testamentary in nature?

Although it is not a will and does not depend on compliance with the requirements of Wills Act 1837, s 9[13] for its validity, the nomination clearly has testamentary characteristics, which has enabled the courts to apply the wills doctrine of lapse[14] when the nominee dies in the nominator's lifetime. These same characteristics however have led courts in other jurisdictions to invalidate nominations for non-compliance with the formal requirements for a will. The United States Uniform Probate Code[15] has sought to overcome the problem by labelling the nomination as non-testamentary, so freeing it from testamentary formalities.

Re Barnes [1940] 1 Ch 267, Ch D; Farwell J

The deceased had nominated his property in a registered industrial and provident society in favour of X, but X died in the nominator's lifetime.
Held: The nomination was ineffective; the deceased's personal representative was entitled to the property, not the nominee's estate.

Farwell J: (Having quoted Lord Mersey in *Eccles Provident Industrial Cooperative Society Ltd v Griffiths* [1912] AC 483 at 490.[16])

---

12. Now £5,000, see p 41 n 1. Under the Industrial and Provident Societies Act 1965, s 23(3) the nomination would have been valid up to the permitted limit and only invalid as to the excess.
13. See Ch 8 post.
14. See Ch 22 post.
15. Approved by the National Conference of Commissioners on Uniform State Laws in 1969 and recommended for adoption in all States. The references to it hereafter incorporate amendments up to August 1983.
16. See p 41 ante.

The same view was expressed quite shortly by Farwell LJ in the same case in the Court of Appeal. He delivered a dissenting judgment which was not approved by the House of Lords, but a sentence in it to which I wish to refer is wholly consistent with what I have read from Lord Mersey's speech, and I think may be taken to be quite accurate. Farwell LJ said this ([1911] 2 KB 275, 284):

> 'Section 25 of the Act of 1893, like several other sections of the same character in similar Acts, is in my opinion intended to confer a benefit on members of societies of this kind by giving them a limited power of disposition in its nature testamentary without the formality and expense of making a will or obtaining probate. The nomination in pursuance of such a power is, like any other testamentary disposition, revocable, as, under the Wills Act, a will is revocable, and, like a will, does not, prior to the nominator's death, affect his property, but leaves him free to deal with it as he pleases, either by withdrawing it in accordance with the rules of the society, or receiving payment of his loans to the society, without any power of interference by the nominee. The nominator is in the position of a testator, and the nominee of a legatee.'

From that I think it is quite clear that this section has the effect of giving the depositor a power, in its nature testamentary, to deal up to £100, with his interest in the society. I say 'in its nature testamentary', because it has all the characteristics of a testamentary document, that is to say, it is a nomination which has no effect at all until the death of the nominator who is left completely free during his lifetime to deal with his share irrespective of it. The nominee would have no right to complain of, nor could he take any steps to prevent, the nominator dealing with his interest during his lifetime. The nomination has no operation and is not intended to have any operation until the death of the nominator. Whether or not it then operates depends upon whether or not the nominator has during his lifetime either revoked it or used the money which he purported to nominate for his own purposes, by withdrawing it from the society or in some other way. The result, as I said, is that the nature of the nomination in a case of this sort is clearly testamentary. . . . Now as this nomination is in its nature ambulatory and operates only on and at death of the nominator, one would have thought that if the nominee died in the lifetime of the nominator, the consequence would be that his title would lapse, and that, accordingly, his legal personal representative would not be entitled to the money, which would remain part of the property of the nominator. Speaking for myself, I should have had no difficulty in coming to that conclusion, because, as I said, it appears to me that this nomination has all the elements of a testamentary disposition and is, therefore, governed, so far as the question of lapse is concerned, by the ordinary rule in regard to a testamentary disposition.[17] It has been suggested that such a decision might give rise to all sorts of difficulties—questions as to whether s 33 of the Wills Act 1837,[18] applied, and problems of that kind. But those are matters which can be dealt with if and when they arise. So far as I am concerned, I should have no doubt, provided the matter were open to me and free from authority, in coming to the conclusion that the death of the nominee in the lifetime of the nominator operated to cause lapse.

In **Re Danish Bacon Co Ltd Staff Pension Fund Trusts** [1971] 1 All ER 486, [1971] 1 WLR 248, it was argued (inter alia) that a nomination made under the terms of a company pension scheme was invalid because it was either an inter vivos disposition of a subsisting equitable interest in which case it failed to comply with the requirements of the Law of Property Act 1925, s 53(1)(c)[19] or it was a testamentary disposition in which event it failed for want of compliance with Wills Act 1837, s 9,[20] the nominator's signature not having

---

17. See p 353, post.
18. See p 357, post.
19. See p 20 ante.
20. See Ch 8 post.

been witnessed. Holding that on the facts the requirements of s 53(1)(c) had been met, whether or not this was necessary, Megarry J continued at p 493:

Nominations made under a statute, of course, do not face this problem; they take effect by force of the statute, and have nothing to fear from the Wills Act 1837 or s 53(1)(c). But where there is no statutory authority, then, said counsel for the first and second defendants, if the nomination is of a testamentary nature it must be executed like a will.

It was on this issue that counsel for the plaintiffs joined in the argument; for the trustees were understandably concerned for the fate of other nominations as well as this. His argument, when conjoined to that of counsel for the third defendant on this point was twofold. First, although a nomination had certain testamentary characteristics, and not least that of being ambulatory, it took effect as a contractual arrangement and not as a disposition by the deceased. The contributions and interest did not come to the deceased and then pass on from him by force of his will or the nomination; they went directly from the fund to the nominee, and formed no part of the estate of the deceased. I may say that I think that *Bennett v Slater* ([1899] 1 QB 45) and *Eccles Provident Industrial Co-operative Society Ltd v Griffiths* ([1912] AC 483 at 490) provide some support for this view. Despite certain testamentary characteristics, the nomination takes effect under the trust deed and rules, and the nominee in no way claims through the deceased. Secondly, there is a vast difference, it was said, between a testamentary paper and a disposition of a testamentary nature. A testamentary paper must satisfy the Wills Act 1837; but a disposition might have certain testamentary characteristics without the paper containing it being a testamentary paper. Indeed, counsel for the plaintiffs urged that a nomination was *sui generis*, with some of the characteristics of an appointment under a power, some of the characteristics of a will, and some of the characteristics of a *donatio mortis causa*. As Alice said, curiouser and curiouser.

I appreciate the force of these arguments. Non-statutory nominations are odd creatures, and the cases provide little help on their nature. I do not, however, think that a nomination under the trust deed and rules in the present case requires execution as a will. It seems to me that such a nomination operates by force of the provisions of those rules, and not as a testamentary disposition by the deceased. Further, although the nomination has certain testamentary characteristics, I do not think that these suffice to make the paper on which it is written a testamentary paper. Accordingly, in my judgment the requirements of the Wills Act 1837 have no application.[1]

In **Re MacInnes** [1935] 1 DLR 401 (Supreme Court of Canada) by contrast, the deceased had nominated his wife as a beneficiary under his company's pension fund scheme. His signature to the nomination was witnessed by only one person, as was sufficient under the rules of the scheme. Hughes J, citing with approval the remarks of Lord Mersey in *Eccles Provident Society Ltd v Griffiths*,[2] Farwell LJ in *Griffiths v Eccles Provident Society Ltd*[3] and Gorrell Barnes J *in the Goods of Baxter*,[4] held that the nomination was void as a testamentary document that failed to comply with the formal requirements for a will,[5] saying at p 409:

An employee . . . could withdraw for himself approximately the balance at his credit. Any participating employee could revoke the benefits or change the beneficiaries or divert the money to his estate by instrument in writing or by will. The 'Employee's Acceptance' (the nomination) did not, in the words of Lord Mersey, supra, create any

---

1. See also *Gill v Gill* [1938] SC 65 at 71.
2. AC 483 at 490, p 41 ante.
3. [1911] 2 KB at 284, p 44 ante.
4. [1903] P 12 at 14, p 43 ante.
5. Wills Act RSO 1927, c 149, requiring two witnesses to the testator's signature. The decision was followed by the Saskatchewan Queen's Bench in *Re Shirley* (1965) 49 DLR (2d) 474. For an Australian viewpoint which supports the Canadian decisions see, Nunan 'The Application of the Wills Acts to Nominations of Beneficiaries under Superannuation or Pension Schemes and Insurance Policies' (1966) 40 ALJ 13.

charge or trust in favour of the nominee against the nominator. Until death the beneficial interest in the amount which the participating employee could withdraw was in the employee. If he died while a participating employee, his beneficiary had a right to his share of the Fund. The right of the beneficiary was dependent upon the death of the participating employee for its vigour and effect.

Uniform Probate Code (USA)

6–201   Provisions for payment or transfer at death

(a) Any of the following provisions in an insurance policy, contract of employment, bond, mortgage, promissory note, deposit agreement, pension plan, trust agreement, conveyance or any other written instrument effective as a contract, gift, conveyance or trust is deemed to be nontestamentary, and this Code does not invalidate the instrument or any provision:

(1) that money or other benefits therefore due to, controlled or owned by a decedent shall be paid after his death to a person designated by the decedent in either the instrument or a separate writing, including a will, executed at the same time as the instrument or subsequently;

(2) that any money due or to become due under the instrument shall cease to be payable in the event of the death of the promisee or the promisor before payment or demand; or

(3) that any property which is the subject of the instrument shall pass to a person designated by the decedent in either the instrument or a separate writing, including a will, executed at the same time as the instrument or subsequently.

FURTHER READING

Read Langbein 'The Nonprobate Revolution and the Future of the law of Succession' (1984) 9.7 Harv LR 1108 in which he argues that the true testamentary nature of nominations, joint bank accounts (see p 38 ante) and other commonly used 'will-substitutes' should be recognised and that they should be legitimated as 'non-probate wills', ie wills not requiring compliance with Wills Act formalities and not requiring a grant of probate for successors to obtain title.

CHAPTER 5

Nature and contents of a will

1 Nature of a will

The statutory definition of a will provides little information as to its nature. A more frequently quoted definition is that supplied by Halsbury which suggests that a will has certain essential characteristics, considered below.

Wills Act 1837

1. Meaning of certain words in this Act . . . the words and expressions hereinafter mentioned, which in their ordinary signification have a more confined or a different meaning, shall in this Act, except where the nature of the provisions or the context of the Act shall exclude such construction, be interpreted as follows; (that is to say) the word 'will' shall extend to a testament, and to a codicil, and to an appointment by will or by writing in the nature of a will in exercise of a power, and also to a disposition by will and testament or devise of the custody and tuition of any child, . . . and to any other testamentary disposition.

Halsbury's Laws of England[1]

'A will or testament is the declaration in a prescribed manner of the intention of the person making it with regard to matters which he wishes to take effect upon or after his death.'

(a) Made in a prescribed manner[2]

The formal requirements for a will are described in Chapter 8 post and are contained in Wills Act 1837, s 9; briefly, it must be in writing, signed by the testator in the presence of two witnesses who must themselves then sign.

(b) Ambulatory

A will only takes effect on the testator's death. As a result, no interest passes to a beneficiary until then, so that if a beneficiary dies before the testator his estate

---

1. 4th edn (1984) Vol 50, 91.

2. The reference in the definition to a prescribed manner has been criticized by Miller 'The Machinery of Succession' p 113 on the basis that it is only when the declaration in question *has* been classified as testamentary in intention, that compliance with the prescribed formalities has to be considered. See eg *The Foundling Hospital (Governors and Guardians) v Crane* [1911] 2 KB 367.

usually derives no benefit from the will,[3] whilst the testator is free in his lifetime to give away or otherwise dispose of any property he has given by will.[4]

Jarman on Wills (8th edn, 1951)[5]

It is this ambulatory quality which forms the characteristic of wills; for although a disposition by deed may postpone the possession or enjoyment, or even the vesting, until the death of the disposing party, yet the postponement is in such case produced by the express terms and does not result from the nature of the instrument.

(c) Revocable

The will is only a declaration of intention by the testator. He can always change his mind and replace it with another will or simply revoke it and die intestate. This principle, that a will can always be revoked, applies to the following, notwithstanding initial appearances to the contrary.

(i) *A contract to make a will*[6]

A contract to make a will in a particular form or not to revoke a will already made appears to breach the principle, but in fact any will subjected to such a contract is still revocable, although the testator and his estate may be liable for breach of contract.[7]

Synge v Synge [1894] 1 QB 466, CA; Lord Esher MR, Lopes and Kay LJJ

The defendant, who was anxious to marry the plaintiff, wrote the following letter to her:

> You my love thoroughly understand the terms (and I daresay have told Mr Woodruff (the plaintiff's trustee)) on which we are to put a stop to all this bother by becoming one another which are that I leave house and land to you for your lifetime. . . .

She accepted these terms and the marriage took place but the defendant subsequently conveyed the property in his lifetime to other persons. The plaintiff sued for damages for breach of contract.

Held: The defendant having made performance of his part of the contract impossible, the plaintiff had an immediate right of action to recover damages[8]

---

3. See the doctrine of lapse, Ch 22 post.
4. See the doctrine of ademption, Ch 22 post.
5. P 26.
6. See p 268 post for the court's powers to modify or annul such a contract when awarding provision out of the estate under the Inheritance (Provision for Family and Dependants) Act 1975.
7. For such an action to lie, the contract must satisfy the usual contractual requirements of offer, acceptance, intention to create legal relations and consideration or a seal. In addition, in so far as it concerns realty, it must be evidenced in writing to comply with LPA 1925, s 40 or supported by acts of part performance—see eg *Re Gonin* [1979] Ch 16, [1977] 2 All ER 720 and generally, Cheshire and Burn 112–122. Cf New Zealand: by the Law Reform (Testamentary Promises) Act 1949 an express or implied promise by the deceased in his lifetime to reward another by way of testamentary provision, for services or work performed, can be enforced by way of a claim for reasonable remuneration from the estate, if no such provision is made, irrespective of whether the work or services were performed before or after the making of the promise, whether legal relations were intended and whether evidenced in writing or not.
8. An anticipatory breach—see Cheshire and Fifoot *Law of Contract* 10th edn (1981) pp 484–485.

being the value of the life interest in the property to which she would have been entitled had she survived him.

Kay LJ: We are of opinion that the proposal of terms in this case was made as an inducement to the lady to marry, that she consented to the terms, and married the defendant on the faith that he would keep his word, and that accordingly there was a binding contract on the defendant's part to leave to his wife the house and land at Ardfield for her life.

Then, secondly, what is the remedy? Marriage is a valuable consideration for such a contract of the highest order, and where, as here, the contract is in writing, so that there is no question upon the Statute of Frauds,[9] in the language already quoted, a Court of Equity will take care that the party who marries on the faith of such a proposal 'is not disappointed, and will give effect to the proposal'. . . .[10]

Then what is the remedy where the proposal relates to a defined piece of real property? We have no doubt of the power of the Court to decree a conveyance of that property after the death of the person making the proposal against all who claim under him as volunteers.

It is argued that Courts of Equity cannot compel a man to make a will. But neither can they compel him to execute a deed. They, however, can decree the heir or devisee in such a case to convey the land to the widow for life, and under the Trustee Acts can make a vesting order, or direct that someone shall convey for him if he refuses. And under the like circumstances, the Court has power to make a declaration of the lady's right.

But counsel do not press for such relief, or ask for a declaration to bind the house and land. The relief they ask is damages for breach of contract. It seems to be proved that the grantees of the property under the deeds executed by Sir R Synge (the defendant) took without notice of the letter; they acquired, as we understand, the legal estate by the grant. If there was any valuable consideration moving from them, no relief in the nature of specific performance could be given against them; and it is suggested that the property, being partly leasehold, according to the decision in *Price v Jenkins* ((1877) 5 Ch D 619), there was such valuable consideration. It is not necessary to examine this argument, as counsel elect to ask for damages only.

Sir R Synge had all his lifetime to perform this contract; but, in order to perform it, he must in his lifetime make a disposition in favour of Lady Synge (the plaintiff). If he died without having done so, he would have broken his contract. The breach would be omitting in his lifetime to make such a disposition. True, it would only take effect at his death; but the breach must take place in his lifetime, and as by the conveyance to his daughters he put it absolutely out of his power to perform this contract, Lady Synge, according to well-known decisions (*Hochster v De la Tour* ((1853) 2 E & B 678); *Frost v Knight* ((1872) LR 7 Ex 111), had a right to treat that conveyance as an absolute breach of contract, and to sue at once for damages; and as this Court has both legal and equitable jurisdiction, we are of opinion that such relief should be granted.

We have not before us the materials for assessing such damages. The amount must depend on the value of the possible life estate which Lady Synge would be entitled to if she survived her husband. Their comparative ages would, of course, be a chief factor in such a calculation. There must be an inquiry as to the proper amount of damages.

In **Re Marsland** [1939] Ch 820, [1939] 3 All ER 148, the Court of Appeal had to consider the revocatory effect of marriage[11] on a will which the testator was under contract not to revoke. He had entered into a separation deed with his wife in which he covenanted that he would not revoke the will he had made in favour of the wife and their children. The wife subsequently died and he remarried, thereby automatically revoking the will.[11] Holding that this did not amount to a breach of the contract, Lord Greene MR said at p 153:

---

9. See now LPA 1925, s 40.
10. *Hammersley v De Biel* (1845) 12 Cl & Fin 45 at 78, per Lord Lyndhurst LC.
11. See Ch 12 post.

The covenant must be construed with reference to the sections of the Wills Act 1837, which describe the ways in which a will may be revoked. Section 20 states exhaustively the ways by which the testator by his own act can revoke a will—that is to say, by another will or codicil or by destruction *animo revocandi*. In these cases, the action of the testator is directed to revocation of his will, and to that alone, and revocation takes place as the intended consequence of his action. Section 18 provides that a will shall be revoked by marriage. Here revocation takes place, not by virtue of some action of the testator directed to the revocation of the will, but as a collateral consequence, imposed by law, of an action performed *alio intuitu*.[12] In our opinion, when the testator here covenanted not to 'revoke' his will, his words are to be confined to acts of revocation performed as such and for that purpose namely, to revocation under s 20—and do not extend to the case under s 18, where revocation follows as a matter of law, whether or not the testator wishes it.

(ii) *Mutual wills*

These are wills made by two or more persons, usually in substantially the same terms and conferring reciprocal benefits, pursuant to an agreement to that effect which is intended to bind the survivor of them. If one of them dies performing his part of the bargain, the survivor holds the property subject to the agreement on trust to perform its terms. If he fails to do so, for example because he revokes his will and replaces it with another on different terms, his first will is validly revoked but on his death his personal representatives will stand in his shoes to perform his trust. The essential characteristic of a will is thus preserved but the obligation undertaken is protected through the medium of the trust.

In **Dufour v Pereira** (1769) Dick 419, 21 ER 332, Lord Camden considered the consequences of mutual wills saying at p 333:

It might have been revoked by both jointly; it might have been revoked separately, providing the party intending it had given notice to the other of such revocation. But I cannot be of opinion that either of them could, during their joint lives, do it secretly; or that after the death of either, it could be done by the survivor by another will. It is a contract between the parties which cannot be rescinded, but by the consent of both. The first that dies carries his part of the contract into execution. Will the court afterwards permit the other to break the contract? Certainly not!

Birmingham v Renfrew (1937) 57 CLR 666, High Court of Australia; Latham CJ, Dixon and Evatt JJ

A husband and wife made wills on the same occasion and in similar terms: she left all her property to him but if he died first then her property was to go to four named relatives of hers; he left all his property to her, but if she died first then all his property was to go to those same four relatives. The wife predeceased the husband who took his entitlement under her will and subsequently made a new will revoking his prior will and benefitting his own relatives. On his death his second will was admitted to probate.

Held: The wills were made pursuant to an agreement which created a trust which the wife's relatives could enforce in equity against the husband's executors.

Dixon J: The four persons who would have taken a fourth part each in residue had he died leaving unaltered the will he made on that occasion set up an agreement between

---

12. 'For another motive'.

husband and wife by which, in consideration of her making her will, he agreed to make his corresponding will and, if he should be the survivor, to leave it unrevoked. Such an agreement can be established only by clear and satisfactory evidence.[13] . . . Gavan Duffy J[14] found that an agreement had been made and I do not think that his finding can be set aside. He found, too, that the arrangement was not of a character leaving legal relations unaffected. So far as this is a question of fact, I think he was fully justified in taking the view that the wife meant to obtain from her husband a promise and meant that it should be communicated to the intended beneficiaries in order the better to ensure its fulfilment. I think the legal result was a contract between husband and wife. The contract bound him, I think, during her lifetime not to revoke his will without notice to her. If she died without altering her will, then he was bound after her death not to revoke his will at all. She on her part afforded the consideration for his promise by making her will. His obligation not to revoke his will during her life without notice to her is to be implied. For I think the express promise should be understood as meaning that if she died leaving her will unrevoked then he would not revoke his. But the agreement really assumes that neither party will alter his or her will without the knowledge of the other. It has been long established that a contract between persons to make corresponding wills gives rise to equitable obligations when one acts on the faith of such agreement and dies leaving his will unrevoked so that the other takes property under its dispositions. It operates so as to impose on the survivor an obligation which is regarded as specifically enforceable. It is true that he cannot be compelled to make and leave unrevoked a testamentary document and if he dies leaving a last will containing provisions inconsistent with his agreement it is nevertheless valid as a testamentary act. But the doctrines of equity attach the obligation to the property. The effect is, I think, that the survivor becomes a constructive trustee[15] and the terms of the trust are those of the will which he undertook would be his last will . . .

The purpose of an arrangement for corresponding wills must often be, as in this case, to enable the survivor during his life to deal as absolute owner with the property passing under the will of the party first dying. That is to say, the object of the transaction is to put the survivor in a position to enjoy for his own benefit the full ownership so that, for instance, he may convert it and expend the proceeds if he choose. It is only by the special doctrines of equity that such a floating obligation, suspended, so to speak, during the lifetime of the survivor can descend upon the assets at his death and crystallize into a trust. No doubt gifts and settlements, inter vivos, if calculated to defeat the intention of the compact, could not be made by the survivor and his right of disposition, inter vivos, is, therefore, not unqualified. But, substantially, the purpose of the arrangement will often be to allow full enjoyment for the survivor's own benefit and advantage upon condition that at his death the residue shall pass as arranged.[16]

---

13. In *Re Cleaver* [1981] 2 All ER 1018, [1981] 1 WLR 939, Nourse J described this as amounting to no more than the ordinary civil standard of proof, viz balance of probabilities. In that case he was satisfied, primarily from statements by the deceased in his lifetime and by his widow thereafter, that there was such evidence. Cf *Re Oldham* [1925] Ch 75, *Gray v Perpetual Trustee Co Ltd* [1928] AC 391 where there was not. The evidential problem can be avoided by an express reference in the wills to the existence of the agreement—see eg *Re Green* [1951] Ch 148, [1950] 2 All ER 913. In the United States Uniform Probate Code, at s 2—701, there must be either such a reference or separate writing signed by the deceased evidencing the agreement for the mutual wills to be upheld; evidence of oral testimony alone is not sufficient.

14. At first instance, *Renfrew v Birmingham* [1937] VLR 180.

15. In *Re Cleaver* [1981] 2 All ER 1018, [1981] 1 WLR 939 Nourse J described this constructive trust as an example of that wider category of cases such as secret trusts in which the court of equity intervened to prevent a person to whom property was transferred by way of a gift but on the faith of an agreement that it be dealt with in a particular way for the benefit of a third person, from dealing with that property inconsistently with that agreement. Any attempt by him to do so after receiving the benefit of the gift would be forestalled by equity imposing a constructive trust on the property the subject of the agreement. See also *Ottaway v Norman* [1972] Ch 698, [1971] 3 All ER 1325 at 1330–2.

16. In *Re Cleaver* [1981] 2 All ER 1018, [1981] 1 WLR 939, this judgment was adopted and applied in extenso by Nourse J, who described it at p 1023 as 'a correct analysis of the principles on which a case of enforceable mutual wills depends'.

Law Reform Committee: Twenty-Second Report[17]

3.51   Mutual wills   It is not altogether clear whether the surviving testator's remarriage will revoke a mutual will. In *Re Marsland* [1939] Ch 820,[18] Greene MR said:

> 'In our opinion when the testator here covenanted not to 'revoke' his will, his words are to be confined to acts of revocation performed as such and for that purpose . . . and do not extend to the case under section 18 where revocation follows as a matter of law'.

This case suggests that whether or not a mutual will will be 'revoked' by the surviving testator's remarriage will depend on exactly what the parties must be taken to have agreed. If the obligation on the survivor was not to revoke his will, that obligation would not extend to revocation by operation of the law. If, on the other hand, his obligation was to ensure that the property passed on the terms of the mutual wills in any event, that obligation would probably stand and survive a remarriage. A further problem which arises in cases of mutual wills is the difficulty of establishing what property the parties intended should be subject to the terms of the wills and what property should be held on the constructive trust which arises when a mutual will is revoked by the survivor. It is unclear whether the constructive trust will bind only the property of the mutual testators held at the death of the first to die or whether in addition any property subsequently acquired by the survivor is included. In trying to find the answer to such questions, the court has to construe the agreement as best it can in order to determine what it was that the parties actually covenanted to do.

3.52   One criticism of mutual wills is that they can create injustice because they are based on the often fallacious assumption that the needs of the beneficiaries will remain constant over a period of time. We have considered the suggestion that the law should be amended to enable the surviving testator (at least in husband and wife cases) to amend his will in order to take account of changed family circumstances. This could be done by conferring on the court a power to vary mutual wills, upon the application of the survivor. . . . Whilst we have some sympathy with this proposal, in principle we think it right that people should remain bound by their agreements. That circumstances may change is known to the parties when they make their wills and the fact that it is rarely, if ever sensible to enter into mutual wills does not of itself justify the creation of the power proposed. Other witnesses suggested that the law applying to mutual wills is so shrouded in uncertainty that mutual wills should be abolished altogether. We do not think it would be right to prevent people from entering into mutual wills should they choose to do so and we think that the difficulties they create would be better clarified by judicial development than by legislation.

2   Classification of ambiguous documents

It will usually be apparent from the document itself if it is intended to take effect as a will.[19] Sometimes, however, the application of the above characteristics, considered in the light of extrinsic evidence, will give testamentary effect to a document that on the face of it does not purport to be testamentary at all.

In **Milnes v Foden** (1890) 15 PD 105, the testatrix had a power of appointment over certain property, exercisable by revocable deed or will. She executed a will in 1884 which did not expressly include this property. Subsequently she executed two revocable deeds-poll which were duly attested by two witnesses; by these she appointed the property concerned on certain trusts to take effect from her death. In holding that the instruments were

---

17. 'The Making and Revocation of Wills' (1980) Cmnd 7902.
18. P 49 ante.
19. See eg the example of a professionally drawn will at p 62 post.

testamentary and should be admitted to probate together with the will, Hannen P said at p 107:

The true principle to be deduced from the authorities, as stated in Williams on Executors, appears to be that if there is proof, either in the paper itself or from clear evidence dehors, first, that it was the intention of the writer of the paper to convey the benefits by the instrument which would be conveyed by it if considered as a will; secondly, that death was the event that was to give effect to it, then whatever may be its form it may be admitted to probate as testamentary. It is not necessary that the testator should intend to perform or be aware that he has performed a testamentary act. In my opinion both the deeds-poll fulfil the essential conditions just mentioned, and are, together with the will of 1884, entitled to probate.

In **Re Brennan** [1932] IR 633, the document in question appeared to be only the deceased's instructions for a will. The would-be testatrix had appeared at her solicitor's office one day without an appointment, announcing that she wanted to make a new will straightaway, to replace an earlier will which the solicitor had prepared for her. The solicitor told her that he was too busy to arrange this on the spot but that he would take down her instructions and she should return the next day to execute the new will. He took a piece of paper, headed it 'Mrs Catherine Brennan. Instructions for new will', and beneath the heading wrote down her requirements as she stated them. As she was leaving his office she suggested that as a precaution, in case she had an accident, she sign the instructions and this she duly did in the presence of the solicitor and a typist who both signed the paper. The solicitor drew up the new will for her to sign the next day, but she never came back. Two years later she died. Hanna J held that the document 'Instructions for new will' should be admitted to probate as a valid will saying at p 636:

Having regard to . . . the circumstances of the drawing of the instructions, the lady's statements and actions, and the use of the word 'new' in the document signed by her. I am satisfied that she intended, when she signed the instructions, to revoke her previous will and substitute these instructions until a more formal document was drawn up. And the mere fact that she executed the instructions indicates that she had in her mind that a more formal document might never be drawn up. The informality of the document or its brevity is no bar to its being admitted to probate once I find that she intended it to be her last will, but the surplusage in the form of notes, added by the solicitor for his own information, will be omitted from the grant.[20]

3 Nature of a codicil

(a) In general

A codicil is a testamentary document having all the characteristics required of a will[1] but written as a supplement to an earlier will. The expression 'will' is defined in the Wills Act 1837, s 1 as including a codicil, however,[2] and strictly speaking all a person's testamentary instruments which are unrevoked at his death together constitute his will. Any codicil the testator may have made has to

---

20. See also *Jones v Nicolay* (1850) 2 Rob 288 (banker's order), *In the Goods of Baxter* [1903] P 12 (nomination) p 43 ante, *Hill v Hill* (1904) 8 Ont LR 710 (joint bank account) p 38 ante.
1. See p 47 ante.
2. Ibid.

be construed with the will and with any other codicils there may be; a codicil only revokes a will or a later codicil an earlier codicil to the extent of any express or implied inconsistency. As Lord Robertson said in *Dougal-Menzies v Umphelby* [1908] AC 224, at 233:

Whether a man leaves one testamentary writing or several testamentary writings, it is the aggregate or the net result that constitutes his will or, in other words, the expression of his testamentary wishes. The law on a man's death, finds out what are the instruments which express his last will. If some extant writing be revoked, or is inconsistent with a later testamentary writing, it is discarded. But all that survives this scrutiny form part of the ultimate will or expression of his wishes about his estate. In this sense it is inaccurate to speak of a man leaving two wills; he does leave and can leave but one will.

(b) Republication

One important effect of a codicil is that so long as it confirms the earlier will (save in so far as it alters it) the earlier will is said to be republished as at the date of the codicil[3] so that it operates as if executed at the date of its republication, although not where to do so would be to defeat the testator's intention. Express words of confirmation, although usual,[4] are not essential; a mere reference to an earlier will is regarded as sufficient to republish it.

Wills Act 1837

34. Act not to extend to wills made before 1838

. . . This Act shall not extend to any will made before the first day of January One thousand eight hundred and thirty-eight, and every will re-executed or republished or revived[5] by any codicil shall for the purpose of this Act be deemed to have been made at the time at which the same shall be so re-executed republished or revived . . .[6]

In **Re Smith** (1890) 45 ChD 632, the testatrix, a married woman, made a will in 1878 at a time when married women had only limited powers of disposition by will.[7] After her husband's death, she executed an instrument in the following terms:

> Dunmow, July 30, 1885.
> This is a present to Oswald Newman Roper from his aunt, Maria Smith, by the express wish of his late uncle, Joseph Smith, a few weeks before his death, 10 shares of £10 each in the Dunmow Gas Company.
>
> (signed) Maria Smith.
> Witness:
> (signed) Henry C. Smith
> Eliza Clark.

---

3. The doctrine of republication also applies if the will is simply re-executed: WA 1837, s 34 post.
4. See the specimen codicil at p 64 post.
5. As to the doctrine of revival, see p 184 post.
6. Before the passing of the Act it was possible to republish a will of personalty by a mere parol declaration, an obvious inducement to fraud or imprecise recollection, so the Real Property Commissioners in their Fourth Report (1833) p 34 recommended this change.
7. The will was made before the passing of the Married Women's Property Act 1882 which gave married women complete freedom of testamentary disposition.

Both the will and the instrument were admitted to probate and it was argued for the residuary legatee under the will that the will was republished by the instrument and that as this occurred after the husband's death at a time when the testatrix had complete power of testamentary disposition, it would be effectual to pass all her property of whatever nature, other than the shares referred to in the instrument. Stirling J held otherwise, saying at p 639:

It seems to me, then, that in order that republication may be implied, something must be found in the second testamentary instrument from which the inference can be drawn that, when making and executing it, the testator 'considered the will as his will'. If I apply that test to the present case, I find nothing from which I can draw any such inference, and I accordingly think that this testamentary instrument does not amount to a republication of the will.

Re Hardyman [1925] Ch 287, Ch D; Romer J

The testatrix made a will in 1898 bequeathing a legacy of £5,000 on trust for her cousin and then for 'his wife' for life with remainders over. At the date of the will the cousin was married to his first wife; she died in January 1901. In November 1901, the testatrix, knowing of the first wife's death, made a codicil to the will which began as follows:

'This is the codicil of one Charlotte Jeanette Hardyman . . . to the said will bearing date of February the 25th, 1898'

and proceeded to make dispositions which in no way affected the settled legacy. Two years after the testatrix's death, the cousin married again.
Held: The second wife would benefit under the settled legacy.

Romer J: It appears to me, in the circumstances, and having regard to the authorities, that I must construe the present will in light of the fact that by republication the testatrix has said to me: 'This will expresses my intentions at this date' (ie, the date at which this codicil was made), and that I must not disregard that fact. But Mr Swords, on behalf of those interested in contesting the claim of Colonel McClintock's (the cousin's) second wife, has asked me to pursue the following line of reasoning: he says that I must take the will first of all and substitute for the word 'wife' the name of Colonel McClintock's first wife and then, he says, having done that, the testatrix has by her codicil only republished a will in which she has given a benefit to his first wife by name, and that, as his first wife predeceased the testatrix, the second wife cannot possibly take under that devise. It appears to me that to adopt such a course would not be to apply the rules as to republication with good sense and with discrimination, but to construe the will as though it had not been republished. I cannot substitute the Christian name of the first wife for the word 'wife', unless I disregard the fact of the republication of the will and construe the will as though there had been no republication. What I have to construe is a will which the testatrix tells me expressed her wishes as they were at the date of her codicil. Approaching the document in that light, I find that the testatrix, knowing full well that Colonel McClintock's first wife was dead, has directed that this legacy of £5,000 shall be held for the benefit of Colonel McClintock, his wife and children. Now, he had no wife at that time; therefore, if those were the testatrix's wishes at the date of the codicil, the only person who could take under that provision would be, and is, the lady whom Colonel McClintock married after the testatrix's death in 1903. It appears to me, therefore, that I ought to answer the questions that have been asked by the summons by declaring that according to the true construction of the will and codicil, and in the events which have happened, the second wife of Colonel McClintock has an interest for her life or until she shall re-marry in the sum of £5,000.[8]

---

8. See also *In the Goods of Truro*, p 120 post, *Re Reeves* [1928] Ch 351, *Re Harvey* [1947] Ch 285, [1947] 1 All ER 349.

In the Irish case of **Re Moore** [1907] 1 IR 315, Barton J was at pains to point out that republication would not lie in the face of the testator's intention. The Charitable Donations Act 1844, s 16 stated that no devise for charitable purposes in Ireland should be valid to create any estate in land 'unless the will or other instrument containing the same shall be duly executed three calendar months at least before the death.' Holding that a charitable devise by will dated more than three months before the death was valid notwithstanding that a codicil confirming it was made within three months of the death, he said at p 318:

> It is well settled that for many purposes republication brings the will down to the date of the codicil, and makes it speak as a new will of that date, and take effect as if it had been re-inserted in the codicil and re-executed at the date of the codicil. But it is equally well settled that there are limits to the doctrine. 'The rule is subject to the limitation that the intention of the testator is not to be defeated thereby': per Patteson J in *Doe d Biddulph v Hole* ((1850) 15 QB 848). It does not necessarily operate as if the will had been originally made at the date of the codicil: per Lord Campbell LC in *Hopwood v Hopwood* ((1859) 7 HLC 728). The effect of the decision of the Court of Appeal in *Mountcashell v Smyth* ([1895] 1 IR 346) is that republication republishes the will with all its contents, including its original date. It is as if the old document, with its old date, were translated into the codicil. Republication gives to the will a fresh starting point, but it does not erase the old date. Nor does it, in my opinion, falsify the fact that the will contained a particular devise and was executed at a particular time. The authorities which have been cited lead me to the conclusion that the courts have always treated the principle that republication makes the will speak as if it had been re-executed at the date of the codicil not as a rigid formula or technical rule, but as a useful and flexible instrument for effectuating a testator's intentions, by ascertaining them down to the latest date at which they have been expressed.[9]

4 Contents of a will

(a) In general

No particular form is required for a will nor does a will have to be professionally drawn. Many people draw their own wills without legal advice ('home-made' wills), sometimes on printed will forms available from many stationers,[10] sometimes even more informally, although few have gone so far as the would-be testator who wrote out his will on an egg-shell.[11] Professionally drawn wills appear to be more common, however. When the Justice Committee reported on home-made wills in 1971 it observed from Probate Registry statistics compiled from probate grants issued during a thirteen week period, that 77% of

---

9. See also *Re Park* [1910] 2 Ch 322, *Re Heath's WT* [1949] Ch 170, [1949] 1 All ER 199 and generally Mitchell 'The Present State of Testamentary Republication' (1954) 70 LQR 353.
10. The 'printed' part of these forms usually consists of the introductory words of a will: 'This is the last will of . . .' followed by an express revocation clause. After a gap for the testator to enter his appointment of executors and his dispositions (often with 'lead in' words to assist him) the form usually ends with a printed testimonium and attestation clause. There is at least one local law society reputed to raise an annual toast to the manufacturers of printed will forms in gratitude for the legal costs engendered by the litigation resulting from their use. But in fairness it should be said that unlike other makers of home-made wills, the testator who uses a printed will form at least has some sort of guidance as to what is expected of him; often helpful advice is printed thereon.
11. See *Hodson v Barnes* (1926) 43 TLR 71: the 'will' was refused probate for a number of reasons but not because of the substance on which it was written.

the wills admitted to probate during that period appeared to have been drafted by solicitors.

(b) Classification of gifts by will

Gifts by will are either legacies (gifts of personalty) or devises (gifts of realty); the former may be specific, general, demonstrative or residuary, the latter may be specific or residuary.[12]

(i) *Specific gifts* [13]

A specific gift was defined by Jessel MR in *Bothamley v Sherson* (1875) LR 20 Eq 304 at p 308 in the following terms:

In the first place it is a part of the testator's property. A general bequest may or may not be a part of the testator's property. A man who gives £100 money or £100 stock may not have either the money or the stock, in which case the testator's executors must raise the money or buy the stock; or he may have money or stock sufficient to discharge the legacy, in which case the executors would probably discharge it out of the actual money or stock. But in the case of a general legacy it has no reference to the actual state of the testator's property, it being only supposed that the testator has sufficient property which on being realised will procure for the legatee that which is given to him, while in the case of a specific bequest it must be of a part of the testator's property itself. That is the first thing.

In the next place, it must be a part emphatically, as distinguished from the whole. It must be what has been sometimes called a severed or distinguished part. It must not be the whole, in the meaning of being the totality of the testator's property, or the totality of the general residue of his property after having given legacies out of it. But if it satisfy both conditions, that it is a part of the testator's property itself, and is a part as distinguished, as I said before, from the whole, or from the whole of the residue, then it appears to me to satisfy everything that is required to treat it as a specific legacy.

The particular gift he had to classify was one of 'all my stock in the Midland Railway Company' and it was argued that as the stock had been described in generic terms[14] such that the subject matter of the gift would not be identifiable until the testator died, it could not be specific, but Jessel MR disagreed, saying at p 309:

Now there can be no question, as I understand the authorities, that the part may be defined in any way which distinguishes it. If a testator gives 'the black horses which I now have', or 'the black horses of which I shall be possessed at the time of my death', or at any other specified time, the gift satisfies the definition of a specific legacy. . . . Therefore the mere fact of death being referred to as the period for ascertainment does not make the gift less specific.

(ii) *General legacies*

A general legacy is a gift of personalty of a particular kind or description which is not identified as a particular part of the testator's estate, for example a gift of '1,000 shares in Marks & Spencer PLC' (general) as opposed to a gift of 'my

---

12. See the specimen will p 62 post for examples of each kind of gift.
13. Legacies and devises.
14. The subject matter being so described as to be capable of fluctuating between the date of the will and the date of death ('all my stock in the Midland Railway Company' as opposed to 'my £1,000 Midland Railway Company stock').

1,000 shares in Marks & Spencer PLC' (specific). The most common form of general legacy is a pecuniary legacy: 'I give £500 to X'. A specific legacy is at risk of ademption; if the subject matter of the gift no longer exists among the testator's assets at his death, the gift is said to be adeemed and the legacy fails.[15] A general legacy will be valid even if there is no property in the estate at the date of the testator's death of the description mentioned in the gift; at the option of the legatee the executors must acquire such property and give it to the legatee, or the legatee can have the value of the object in question given to him without the executors having to purchase it.[16] If the value of the object is not ascertainable at the testator's death, however, the general legacy will fail for uncertainty.

Re O'Connor [1948] Ch 628, [1948] 2 All ER 270, Ch D; Roxburgh J

By Clause 5 of his will, the testator had left his son 'ten thousand preference shares of one pound each fully paid' in X Ltd, a private company in which the testator had only 9,000 such shares at the date of his death. If the legacy was specific, the gift would fail as to the outstanding 1,000 shares. If it was general, the legatee would be entitled to have the additional 1,000 shares purchased for him.

Held: The gift was general.

Roxburgh J: The question which I have to determine is whether this legacy of 10,000 preference shares of £1 each is a general legacy or a specific legacy, and there are two points in favour of either view. In favour of it being a general legacy is the fact that there is nothing in the language of cl 5 of the will to indicate that the testator is describing specific property of his. For example, the testator does not use the word 'my' or any possessive word at all. The second point, a very strong one, in favour of the legacy being general, is that the testator never had 10,000 preference shares either at the date of his will or at the date of his death, but only 9,000 and, accordingly, if he did intend by this clause to make a specific disposition of his own property, he must have been misinformed as to the extent of that property.

The two points in favour of the legacy being specific are, first, the circumstance that the bequest deals with a private company of which the testator was the manager and governing director and in which the shares were subject to the restrictions usual in the case of a private company, and secondly—and this is very important—the testator clearly did not include the disposition in cl 5 of the preference shares among the dispositions which his executors and trustees were to satisfy out of residue. It will be remembered that the direction to the trustees in cl 8 was that out of the moneys arising from the sale, calling in and conversion they were to pay the pecuniary legacies therein before bequeathed. The property devised and bequeathed in the trust for sale was the property 'not hereby otherwise disposed of.' Seeing that the testator introduces cl 6 with the words 'I bequeath the following pecuniary legacies', I cannot, as a matter of construction of the will, hold that the testator was treating this bequest of the preference shares as included in the phrase 'pecuniary legacy' and as one which was to be satisfied out of residue. I should reach that conclusion notwithstanding that 'pecuniary legacy' is so defined in the Administration of Estates Act, 1925,[17] as to include a general legacy. Though it is so defined for the purposes of that Act, as a matter of construction I do not think that the phrase 'pecuniary legacy' was intended to include a general legacy in this will.

In the circumstances, what ought I to hold? There is no doubt that the court leans

---

15. See p 349 post.
16. See eg *Re Gage* [1934] Ch 536.
17. S 55(i)(ix).

strongly in favour of a general legacy. How strongly is apparent from *Re Willcocks* ([1921] 2 Ch 327).[18] Yet if the testator, instead of referring to 10,000 preference shares had referred to 9,000 or less preference shares in cl 5, I should have held that there was sufficient context here to carry me to the other side of the line, notwithstanding the leaning of the court to which I have referred, but it is impossible to construe this will without doing some violence to some of its language. If the argument of counsel for the second defendant that this is a specific legacy is right, I must treat the figure 10,000 as a *falsa demonstratio*.[19] If the argument advanced by counsel for the first defendant is right, I must treat the testator as having forgotten to include the bequest in cl 5 within the description of 'pecuniary legacy', another *falsa demonstratio*. Having regard to the leaning of the court in these matters, between those two *falsae demonstrationes* I decide in favour of the first defendant that this is a general legacy, and that the *falsa demonstratio* lies in the use of the word 'pecuniary' and not in the use of the word 'ten'.[20]

In **Re Gray** (1887) 36 Ch D 205, the testator made a gift of 'fifty shares' in Y Ltd. He owned 70 shares in the company in question at the date of the will, but by the date of his death it was no longer in existence. If this was a specific legacy it was clearly adeemed, but even if it was a general legacy, as he thought it was, Kay J held that it must fail, saying at p 211:

A general legacy of this kind amounts in effect to a direction to the testator's executors to buy the shares or other property designated, that is, in the present case, fifty shares in the unincorporated company. Of course the Court will do its utmost to maintain the legacy, and if for any reason the shares could not be bought, or if the legatee had a choice in the matter and said that he would rather not have shares, he would then take the amount of money which would have had to be expended in buying them. But when this testator died, suppose the legatees had come to the executors and said 'now hand over to us the legacy'. The difficulty would have arisen at once, and the answer would have been 'it is impossible to buy shares in the company to which the testator referred. That company has been extinct for a long time. How is it possible to tell what amount you are entitled to?' If this be a general legacy it is impossible to take as a criterion the value of the shares at the date of the will, still less can you take as a criterion their value when the unincorporated company ceased to exist. It seems to me that the legacy fails, not because of any ademption, but because it has become, by circumstances of which the testator was aware, utterly impossible to determine what amount of money should be set apart for the persons entitled under the gift.

(iii) *Demonstrative legacies*

The demonstrative legacy is a general legacy, usually of a specified sum of money, but where the testator has pointed out particular property, separate from the rest of his estate, as available to satisfy the gift.[1] If the designated fund is not available at the testator's death or is insufficient, the legatee is still entitled to be paid any shortfall out of the rest of the estate as if the legacy were general,

---

18. The testatrix in that case bequeathed £948.3s.11d. Queensland $3\frac{1}{2}\%$ Inscribed Stock to X, having exactly that amount of stock at the date of her will, but the court held that it was a general legacy; as such it was not adeemed by the subsequent sale of the stock.

19. *Falsa demonstratio non nocet cum de corpore constat*: an incorrect description of a person or thing will not vitiate the gift so long as the meaning is otherwise clear.

20. He added at p 273 that if it was not possible to purchase the shares before the end of twelve calendar months after the testator's death (being the end of the executor's year, see p 389 post) the legatee would be entitled to such sum as at that date would have been required to buy the shares in question, with interest at 4% pa from that date (see p 383 post). Cf *Re Rose* [1949] Ch 78, [1948] 2 All ER 971.

1. See specimen will at p 62 post for an example.

but in so far as the particular fund is available, the legacy ranks as specific and the beneficiary is entitled to be satisfied out of the fund as a specific legatee.

Re Webster [1937] 1 All ER 602, CA; Lord Wright MR, Romer and Greene LJJ

The testator had left his son £3,000 'to be paid to him out of the share of my capital and loans' in a particular partnership. The testator's share at his death was worth substantially less than £3,000. If the gift was specific, the shortfall could not be made up from any other part of the estate.

Held: The gift was demonstrative; any deficiency would be met out of the testator's residuary estate.

Lord Wright MR: The question has been raised whether the bequest is a demonstrative or a specific gift. Whether that is so is to be determined on a construction of the clause, with such help as any other part of the will may afford, and, in this case, that appears to me to be non-existent, but the clause has to be read as a whole. It may be convenient here to refer to the judgment of Sir William Page Wood V-C, in the case of *Paget v Huish* ((1863) 1 H & M 663) at p 671:

> 'These are, therefore, the three classes of gifts: first, a general gift, in which no special fund is pointed at for payment; secondly, a specific gift out of a particular fund alone; and, thirdly, a gift where a particular fund is pointed out as primarily applicable, but where the gift is not to fail by the failure of the particular fund. In this case I think there is a clear intention that the gift should take effect in any event, because, after bequeathing several legacies, the testator proceeds thus: 'I give and devise the following annuities', specifying them, and then adds a declaration that these annuities shall be paid by the trustees out of the rents of the real estate thereby devised. Subsequently, there is a gift to the trustees of all the real estate and the residuary personal estate, upon trust, out of the rents of the realty to pay the annuities, and subject thereto to apply the real and residuary personal estate upon certain specified trusts. All this appears to me only to show that the testator, after making a positive gift, points out the particular fund which he desires to have first applied, and which he supposes to be adequate for the purpose. It is clear that he preferred that the gift should be satisfied out of the realty rather than the personalty; but the question now is, whether he preferred that it should fail altogether rather than be thrown upon the personalty. I think the case is very similar to *Mann v Copland* ((1817) 2 Madd 223) and that there is no indication of an intention that the gift was to fail on failure of real estate.'

Applying that here, I ask myself whether there is an indication of an intention that the gift was to fail on failure or insufficiency of the partnership interest. Now, the first words 'I bequeath to the said Frank Eric Webster the sum of £3,000' are, in themselves, obviously only appropriate to a specific gift. Then come the words 'to be paid to him out of the share of my capital and loans in the business of Webster and Bullock, City Meat Market, Birmingham'. These words ought, I think, to be construed as meaning 'to be paid to him primarily out of the share', and not as meaning 'to be paid to him only out of the share of the capital and loans'. That is very much on the same lines as the view expressed by Page Wood, V-C in the case to which I have just referred.

In **Re Tetsall** [1961] 2 All ER 801, [1961] 1 WLR 938, the testatrix left 'my seven hundred and fifty ordinary shares' in a named company, to X. In fact she held 7,500 such shares both at the date of the will and at the date of death, for although she had originally inherited 750 shares under her late husband's will, there had subsequently been a bonus issue of nine fully paid up shares for each ordinary share. On the face of it this was a specific gift which would fail for uncertainty (which 750 shares?) but Cross J held otherwise, saying at p 804:

Do 750 shares pass, or does the whole gift fail for uncertainty? In that connection I should refer to the decision of the Court of Appeal in *Re Cheadle* ([1900] 2 Ch 620). There a testatrix made a gift of 'my 140 shares in the Crown Brewery Company' to trustees on certain trusts. The position at the date of her will and at the date of her death was that she held 280 shares in the Crown Brewery Company of which 40 were fully paid up—they were £5 shares—and the other 240 were only paid-up to the extent of £2. 10s per share. It was not argued in that case by the legatees of the shares (indeed, on the facts I do not think that it could have been argued) that the whole 280 shares passed under the gift of 'my 140 shares'. What was argued was that the legatees had a right of selection, and, therefore, they could take the forty fully paid-shares and one hundred of the partly paid-up shares. On the other side, the residuary legatees . . . argued that the fact that the gift was a specific gift, ie, that the testatrix was referring to some particular 140 shares, was inconsistent with a right of selection in the legatees. On that point, the Court of Appeal, reversing the judgment of Kekewich J, held that the residuary legatees were right and that the legatees of the shares had no right of selection. It does not appear to have been argued by the residuary legatees that, on that footing, the gift failed for uncertainty because one could not say which of the shares were referred to by the gift of 'my 140 shares'; but the Court of Appeal took the view that, as there were more than 140 partly paid shares out of which the gift could be satisfied, it should be treated as equivalent to a gift of 140 of the partly paid shares. That conclusion may perhaps be open to some criticism from the point of view of logic, because, having emphasised when dealing with the suggested right of selection, that the gift was a specific gift the court then appears to have treated it as equivalent to a general or demonstrative gift in order to prevent it failing altogether. But where one is dealing with a number of identical objects the conclusion makes a considerable appeal to one's common sense.

He accordingly declared that the gift should pass to X 750 of the shares in the company held by the testatrix at her death, so that the remaining 6,750 of the shares fell into residue.

(iv) *The residuary gift*

This is a gift of the general mass of the testator's property (be it realty or personalty or, most commonly, both together) after any specific, general and demonstrative gifts have been granted.

In **Re Wilson** [1967] Ch 53, [1966] 2 All ER 867, the testatrix left various pecuniary legacies and then concluded: 'I devise and bequeathe all my real estate and the residue of my personal estate to my daughter absolutely'. It was argued that the gift of realty could only be residuary if there had been a previous devise, but Pennycuick J disagreed, saying at p 871:

The natural view, so it seems to me, is that where a testator makes a general or universal gift of his real estate, that is 'all my property', the subject matter of that gift falls under the second head,[2] that is as being property not specifically devised but included in a residuary gift. A gift in this form does not indicate any particular item of property but covers all items of real property to which the testator may be entitled at his death. In ordinary language today lawyers would, I think, not inaptly describe such a gift as a residuary devise. They would certainly not describe it as a specific devise.[3]

---

2. For the purpose of the statutory order of application of assets for the payment of debts, see p 340 post. As a residuary devise it would be liable for the payment of debts at a much earlier stage (the second head of the statutory order) than if it had been classified as a specific devise (the sixth head).
3. Cf *Re Ridley* [1950] Ch 415, [1950] 2 All ER 1, but there the context indicated otherwise; after making the gift of 'all my real estate' the testatrix went on to give 'the residue of my property' to X absolutely which enabled Harman J to describe the latter (at p 3) as the 'true residuary clause which would sweep up realty as well as personalty if any were undisposed of'.

Specimen will[4]

THIS IS THE LAST WILL of me DAI TUP of 21 Sunny Street, Splott, South Glamorgan, which I make this   28th   day of September One thousand nine hundred and eighty - three

Revocation Clause[5]

1. I REVOKE all former testamentary dispositions.

Funeral Instructions[6]

2. I WISH my funeral to be carried out as simply as possible. I wish to be cremated.

Appointment of Executors and Trustees[7]

3. I APPOINT as my Executors and Trustees (hereinafter together referred to as 'my Trustees') my father CYRIL OWEN TUP of 19 Rhubarb Row, Radyr, South Glamorgan, and my brother GWYN TUP of 6 Lampire Lane, Llandaff, South Glamorgan, Solicitor.

Legacies

4. I GIVE:

Specific

(a) All my personal chattels as defined by Administration of Estates Act 1925 s 55(1) (x) to my friend SALLIE SIREN of 21 Sunny Street aforesaid;

General

(b) A copy of the current edition of Cheshire & Burn's 'Real Property' to my said brother beneficially;

General (Pecuniary)

(c) The sum of £50 to my mother MAIR TUP of 19 Rhubarb Row aforesaid;

Demonstrative

(d) The sum of £100 payable out of my Barclays Bank Current Account to my said father beneficially.

Devise: *Specific* *Substitutional gift*[8]

5. I GIVE my freehold property known as 21 Sunny Street aforesaid to the said SALLIE SIREN but if she dies before me I give the said property to my said mother in her stead.

Residuary gift

6. MY TRUSTEES shall hold the residue of my estate on trust for sale and:

(a) to pay debts executorship expenses and any general legacies[9] given by this will or any codicil hereto;

Life interest

(b) to pay the income from the residue to the said SALLIE SIREN during her lifetime and after her death;

Ultimate residuary gift

(c) to divide the capital equally between such of them my said brother and my sister RHIAN TUP of 19 Rhubarb Row aforesaid as survive both me and the said SALLIE SIREN.

4. A typical professionally drawn will save that the side-headings would not usually be included.
5. A revocation clause is not essential but is sensible even where no previous wills have been made, in order to inhibit fraudulent claims after the testator's death as to the existence of such wills. See Chapter 14 post.
6. There is in fact no property in a dead body: *Williams v Williams* (1881) 20 Ch D 659; the deceased cannot therefore demand that his instructions be carried out. It is for his executors to bury the deceased in a manner suitable to the estate he leaves behind him, but they will obviously pay attention to his expressed wish.
7. The executors are also appointed trustees because of the trust contained in the residuary gift. The same persons do not have to be appointed as executors and trustees but it is a convenient and common practice.
8. To avoid the doctrine of lapse, see Ch 22 post.
9. Drafting oneself out of the problem concerning the incidence of general legacies considered in Ch 23 post.

Investment clause[10]	7. MY TRUSTEES shall have power to invest and change investments freely as if they were beneficially entitled thereto.
Charging clause[11]	8. ANY of Trustees who is engaged in a profession or business shall be entitled to be paid fees for work done by him or by his firm on the same basis as if he were not one of my Trustees but employed to act on behalf of my Trustees.
Testimonium	IN WITNESS whereof I have hereunto set my hand the day and year first before written
Attestation clause[12]	SIGNED by the said DAI TUP) in our joint presence) *Dai Tup* and by us in his presence:)

Albert Smith
19 Sunny St, Splott
Investment analyst

Doreen Smith
19 Sunny St. Splott
Secretary

10. To widen the trustees' investment powers for the duration of the trust, otherwise they would be restricted to those authorised by the Trustee Investments Act 1961, see Pettit, pp 277–279, Maudsley and Burn pp 479–489.

11. Included because one of the executors and trustees is a solicitor. Without such authority he would be unable to charge for his services for acting, see eg *Robinson v Pett* (1734) 3 P Wms 249 at 251: 'It is an established rule that a trustee, executor or administrator shall have no allowance for his care and trouble' (per Talbot LC).

12. See Ch 8 on formalities.

Specimen codicil

THIS IS A FIRST CODICIL to the Will of me DAI TUP of 21 Sunny Street Splott South Glamorgan which I made on the 28th day of September One thousand nine hundred and eighty-three _____

1. IN place of the gift of £50 to my mother MAIR TUP in Clause 4(c) of my said Will I GIVE my said mother the sum of £250 _____

2. IN all other respects I confirm my said Will[13] _____

IN WITNESS whereof I have hereunto set my hand this   *10th*

day of   *June*   One thousand nine hundred and eighty-five __

SIGNED by the said DAI TUP)
)
in our joint presence and   )   *Dai Tup*
)
by us in his presence:)

John Rees
23 Sunny St, Splott
University Lecturer

Mary Rees
23 Sunny St, Splott
Company Director

13. See p 54 ante on republication.

QUESTIONS

1. For a wide-ranging discussion of the problem of classification of ambiguous documents, see Gulliver and Tilson 'Classification of Gratuitous Transfers' (1941) 51 Yale LJ 1.
2. X and Y make mutual wills in each other's favour, the survivor leaving everything to Z. X dies first. What is Z's position in the following alternative situations:
   (a) Y disclaims his entitlement under X's will;
   (b) As (a) but all X's property passes to Y anyway by virtue of the intestacy rules;

(c) **Y** marries;

(d) **Y** gives away a substantial amount of property in his lifetime?

For a discussion of these and other problems affecting mutual wills, see Mitchell 'Some Aspects of Mutual Wills' (1951) 14 MLR 136, Burgess 'A Fresh Look at Mutual Wills' (1970) 34 Conv 230.

3. Four years ago Poppy made a will containing a gift of 'my three Siamese cats' to George. She did originally have three Siamese cats, but by the date of the will she had acquired two more and she still owned all five when she died. Advise George. Would your answer be different if (a) the gift had been of '3 Siamese cats' or (b) Poppy had made a codicil shortly before her death appointing another executor and otherwise confirming her will?

CHAPTER 6

Wills – capacity

1 Age

The old common law rule was that a male of 14 years or more and a female of 12 years or more could make a valid will of personalty (but not realty[1]); this was altered by the Wills Act 1837 which denied testamentary capacity of any property, realty or personalty, to persons under the age of twenty-one. It was not until 1967 that the Latey Committee, reporting generally on the age of majority,[2] recommended that full testamentary capacity be granted at 18 and this recommendation was put into effect by the Family Law Reform Act 1969. The sole exception to this statutory age limit relates to infant 'soldiers in actual military service and seamen at sea'[3] but other common law jurisdictions often extend testamentary capacity to married infants[4] whilst New Zealand also permits unmarried infants over the age of sixteen to make a will on obtaining the requisite approval.

Report of the Committee on the Age of Majority[2]

414 Wills The case for allowing young people of, say, 18 to make wills is indeed a strong one. With many more people of that age marrying, it seems only fair that they should be able to make provision for their families in the event of death. With their greater earning power they have more to dispose of and should they be enabled to make contracts and own houses as a result of the recommendations of this Committee there would be an even stronger case for giving them the power to dispose of the property thus acquired. While the intestacy provisions would, of course, look after the young wife and her children for the most part, there may be people with equally good claims on a dying youngster about whom he could do nothing—a fiancée, for example, or a foster-mother. It also seems unjust, as was pointed out to us by some witnesses, that those under 21 awaiting a divorce have no way of stopping their property going to the estranged spouse if they die—a thought particularly galling, presumably, to those who are busy divorcing a fortune-hunter.

---

1. Statute of Wills 1542 s 14 '. . . Wills or Testaments made of any Manors, Lands, Tenements or other Heriditaments, by any Woman covert or Person under the Age of twenty-one years, Idiot or any person de non sane Memory shall not be taken to be good or effectual in the Law.'
2. (1967) Cmnd 3342.
3. See Ch 9 post.
4. Eg New South Wales, Queensland and Tasmania, also most Canadian States, see eg Succession Law Reform Act 1977 (Ontario) s 8(1) which also provides that a minor who is contemplating marriage may make a will which will be valid upon marriage provided the will states that it is made in contemplation of marriage to a particular person.

Wills Act 1837

7. No will of a minor valid
No will made by any person under the age of eighteen years[5] shall be valid.

Wills Amendment Act 1969 (New Zealand)

2. Wills of Minors
(1) Every minor after his or her marriage or on or after attaining the age of 18 years shall be competent to make a valid will or revoke a will in all respects as if he or she were of full age.

(2) Every minor who is of or over the age of 16 years, but has never been married and has not attained the age of 18 years may, with the approval of the Public Trustee or of a Magistrate's Court, make a will or revoke a will, and every will so made and every revocation so effected shall be valid and effective as if he or she were of full age.

(3) The approval required by subsection (2) of this section shall be given if the Public Trustee or the Court is satisfied that the minor understands the effect of the will or the revocation, as the case may be.

2 Soundness of mind

As Knight Bruce V-C said in *Bird v Luckie* (1850) 8 Hare 301, 68 ER 375 at 378:

> 'No man is bound to make a will in such a manner as to deserve approbation from the prudent, the wise or the good. A testator is permitted to be capricious and improvident, and is moreover at liberty to conceal the circumstances and the motives by which he has been activated in his dispositions. Many a testamentary provision may seem to the world to be arbitrary, capricious and eccentric, for which the testator, if he could be heard, might be able to answer most satisfactorily'.[6]

(a) The test

The dividing line between eccentricity and such mental impairment as affects a person's testamentary abilities can be very hard to draw. As Lord Cranworth said in *Boyse v Rossborough*:[7]

> ... the difficulty to be grappled with arises from the circumstances that the question (of mental incapacity) is almost always one of degree. There is no difficulty in the case of a raving madman or a drivelling idiot in saying that he is not a person capable of disposing of property; but between such an extreme case and that of a man of perfectly sound and vigorous understanding there is every shade of intellect, every degree of mental capacity. There is no possibility of mistaking midnight for noon, but at what precise moment twilight becomes darkness is hard to determine.

For centuries it was thought that any degree of mental unsoundness, however slight and however unconnected with the testamentary disposition in question would be fatal to capacity,[8] but in the nineteenth century with the advance of

---

5. As substituted by Family Law Reform Act 1969, s 3(1)(a).
6. For a light-hearted look at some illustrations of seemingly eccentric provisions, see Turing 'Testators—Vicious and Capricious' (1982) 79 LSG 1361.
7. (1857) 6 HL Cas 1, at p 45.
8. See eg *Waring v Waring* (1848) 6 Moo PC 341, *Smith v Tebbitt* (1867) LR1 P & D 398.

medical knowledge, judicial attitudes began to change and the classic statement of the test of mental capacity now applied was formulated in the case of *Banks v Goodfellow*.[9]

Banks v Goodfellow (1870) LR 5 QB 549, QB; Cockburn CJ, Blackburn, Mellor, Hannen JJ

The testator was convinced that he was being pursued by evil spirits, in particular by one Featherstone Alexander, a man long dead and quite unconnected with him in his lifetime. He was quite capable of looking after his own financial affairs, however, and gave clear instructions to his solicitor about his will which was perfectly sensible. He left the greater part of his estate to his niece who had looked after him.

Held: The delusion had in no way influenced his testamentary dispositions; the will was valid.

Cockburn CJ: The Roman law, and that of the Continental nations which have followed it, have secured to the relations of a deceased person in the ascending and descending line a fixed portion of the inheritance. The English law leaves everything to the unfettered discretion of the testator, on the assumption that, though in some instances, caprice, or passion, or the power of new ties, or artful contrivance, or sinister influence, may lead to the neglect of claims that ought to be attended to, yet, the instincts, affections, and common sentiments of mankind may be safely trusted to secure, on the whole, a better disposition of the property of the dead, and one more accurately adjusted to the requirements of each particular case, than could be obtained through a distribution prescribed by the stereotyped and inflexible rules of a general law.

It is unnecessary to consider whether the principle of the foreign law or that of our own is the wiser. It is obvious, in either case, that to the due exercise of a power thus involving moral responsibility, the possession of the intellectual and moral faculties common to our nature should be insisted on as an indispensable condition. It is essential to the exercise of such a power that a testator shall understand the extent of the property of which he is disposing; shall be able to comprehend and appreciate the claims to which he ought to give effect; and, with a view to the latter object, that no disorder of the mind shall poison his affections, pervert his sense of right, or prevent the exercise of his natural faculties—that no insane delusion shall influence his will in disposing of his property and bring about a disposal of it, which if the mind had been sound, would not have been made.

Here, then, we have the measure of the degree of mental power which should be insisted on. If the human instincts and affections or the moral sense, become perverted by mental disease; if insane suspicion, or aversion, take the place of natural affection; if reason and judgment are lost, and the mind becomes a prey to insane delusions calculated to interfere with and disturb its functions, and to lead to a testamentary disposition, due only to their baneful influence—in such a case it is obvious that the condition of the testamentary power fails, and that a will made under such circumstances ought not to stand. But what if the mind, though possessing sufficient power, undisturbed by frenzy or delusion, to take into account all the considerations necessary to the proper making of a will, should be subject to some delusion, but such delusion neither exercises nor is calculated to exercise any influence on the particular disposition, and a rational and proper will is the result; ought we, in such case, to deny to the testator the capacity to dispose of his property by will?

It must be borne in mind that the absolute and uncontrolled power of testamentary disposition conceded by the law is founded on the assumption that a rational will is a better disposition than any that can be made by the law itself. If therefore, though mental disease may exist, it presents itself in such a degree and form as not to interfere

---

9. Post.

with the capacity to make a rational disposal of property, why, it may be asked, should it be held to take away the right? It cannot be the object of the legislator to aggravate an affliction in itself so great by the deprivation of a right the value of which is universally felt and acknowledged. If it be conceded, as we think it must be, that the only legitimate or rational ground for denying testamentary capacity to persons of unsound mind is the inability to take into account and give due effect to the considerations which ought to be present to the mind of a testator in making his will, and to influence his decision as to the disposal of his property, it follows that a degree or form of unsoundness which neither disturbs the exercise of the faculties necessary for such an act, nor is capable of influencing the result, ought not to take away the power of making a will, or place a person so circumstanced in a less advantageous position than others with regard to this right. . . .

In the case before us two delusions disturbed the mind of the testator, the one that he was pursued by spirits, the other that a man long since dead came personally to molest him. Neither of these delusions—the dead man not having been in any way connected with him—had, or could have had any influence upon him in disposing of his property. The will, though in one sense an idle one, inasmuch as the object of his bounty was his heir at law, and therefore would have taken the property without its being devised to her, was yet rational in this, that it was made in favour of a niece, who lived with him, and who was the object of his affection and regard. And we must take it on the finding of the jury that irrespectively of the question of these dormant delusions, the testator was in possession of his faculties when the will was executed.

In a leading Canadian case, **Leger v Poirier** [1944] 3 DLR 1, the Supreme Court of Canada was faced with the difficult decision of finding the point at which the elderly testatrix's state of senility had declined to the extent that she lost her testamentary capacity. When she executed the disputed will, the old lady was childish in her ways, unable to carry on any but the most simple of conversations and had lost her memory of certain persons and events. Finding against the will, Rand J said at p 11:

A 'disposing mind and memory' is one able to comprehend, of its own initiative and volition, the essential elements of will-making, property objects, just claims to consideration, revocation of existing dispositions and the like . . . . Merely to be able to make rational responses is not enough, nor to repeat a tutored formula of simple terms. There must be a power to hold the essential field of the mind in some degree of apreciation as a whole, and this I am satisfied was not present here.

In **Dew v Clark** (1826) 3 Add 79, 162 ER 410, Nicholl J pronounced against the will of a testator who had developed an extreme aversion for his only child. The testator beat her often and reviled her as 'a fiend, a monster, Satan's special property' notwithstanding evidence on all sides that she was a charming girl of strictly moral and religious habits. He had left the bulk of his property—a considerable fortune—to two nephews and made only small provision for her. Nicholl J held that the testator's conception of his daughter was the result of an insane delusion that had obviously affected the dispositions in his will. Describing such a delusion as 'the pertinacious adhesion of the patient to some delusive idea in opposition to plain evidence of its falsity',[10] he said at p 454:

Now, the daughter being in this case a sole next of kin, the deceased's only child, it is quite impossible, I think, to disconnect the daughter from the subject matter of his will; from the disposal by will, that is, of his property—they are subjects, in effect, identified. Hence, the deceased's insanity on the subject of his daughter, generally speaking, being proved at all times in my judgment; it follows that his insanity, at the time of making his

---

10. At p 91.

will, is also proved in my judgment—unless the contrary is to be inferred from the will itself. But the inference furnished by the will itself (and it is for this only that I refer to the dispositive part—to the contents—of the will at all) is quite the other way. For the prominent feature of the deceased's insanity, in respect of the daughter, was aversion or antipathy to the daughter—so pleaded and so proved: and the will is a will plainly inofficious, so far as regards the daughter; being a will by which she, in effect, is disinherited—disinherited, too, in favour of parties nearly utter strangers to the deceased (for so it appears); though not remotely connected with him by blood, as being his sister's children. Therefore, it follows that, in my judgment, the deceased is proved upon the whole matter to have been insane at the time of his making this will; which was the daughter's case.[11]

(b) Burden of proof

As Parke B said in *Barry v Butlin*:[12]

> 'The *onus probandi* lies in every case upon the party propounding a will and he must satisfy the conscience of the court that the instrument so propounded is the last will of a free and capable testator.'

Where the will is rational on the face of it, however, the evidential burden of proof will shift to the party seeking to upset the will.[13] Once that party has established the existence of mental impairment, the evidential burden shifts back to the party propounding the will to establish that the mental unsoundness had no effect on the testator's dispositions. As Cockburn CJ said in *Banks v Goodfellow*:[14]

No doubt, where the fact that the testator has been subject to any insane delusion is established, a will should be regarded with great distrust, and every presumption should in the first instance be made against it. . . . And the presumption against a will made under such circumstances becomes additionally strong where the will is, to use the term of the civilians, an inofficious one, that is to say, one in which natural affection and the claims of near relationship have been disregarded.[15]

In **Cartwright v Cartwright** (1793) 1 Phill 90, 161 ER 923 the testatrix made a will that was perfectly rational on the face of it, legibly written by her and with no mistakes or corrections. The dispositions it contained were natural ones for her to make. It was proved, however, that six months before she made her will she was declared medically insane and that she remained in this condition thereafter. Sir William Wynne nevertheless held that the will was valid, saying at p 926:

Now what is the legal effect of such a proof as this? Certainly not wholly to incapacitate such a person, and to say a person who is proved to be in such a way was totally and necessarily incapacitated from making a legal will. . . . If you can establish that the party afflicted habitually by a malady of the mind has intermissions, and if there was an intermission of the disorder at the time of the act, that being proved is sufficient, and the general habitual insanity will not affect it; but the effect of it is this, it inverts the order of

---

11. See also *Boughton v Knight* (1873) LR 3 P & D 64 (father, conceiving an insane dislike of his son, gave the bulk of his estate to strangers); *Smee v Smee* (1879) 5 P & D 84 (testator under an insane delusion that he was a son of George IV and that a large sum of money held in trust for him in that regard had been wrongly diverted to his brother and sister, gave the bulk of his estate to the town of Brighton, making no provision for them).
12. (1838) 2 Moo PC 480 at 482.
13. *Symes v Green* (1839) 1 Sw & Tr 401. See also *Sutton v Sadler* (1857) 3 CB(NS) 87.
14. (1870) LR 5 QB 549 at p 570.
15. See also *Boughton v Knight* (1873) LR 3 P & D 64 at 76.

proof and of presumption, for, until proof of habitual insanity is made, the presumption is that the party agent like all human creatures was rational; but where an habitual insanity in the mind of the person who does the act is established, there the party who would take advantage of the fact of an interval of reason must prove it; that is the law; so that in all these cases the question is whether, admitting habitual insanity, there was a lucid interval or not to do the act. Now I think the strongest and best proof that can arise as to a lucid interval is that which arises from the act itself; that I look upon as the thing to be first examined, and if it can be proved and established that it is a rational act rationally done the whole case is proved.

(c) Time for testing capacity

As a general rule, capacity is tested at the time of the execution of the will but one inroad has been made on this principle.

Parker v Felgate (1883) 8 PD 171, PDA; Hannen P

The testatrix was fully competent when she gave instructions to her solicitor (Mr Parker) for the drawing up of a will but by the time she came to execute it her condition had deteriorated. For much of the time she was in a coma but she could still be roused and could answer general questions and she was aware that it was her will that was being executed.
Held: The will was valid.

Hannen P: If a person has given instructions to a solicitor to make a will, and the solicitor prepares it in accordance with those instructions, all that is necessary to make it a good will, if executed by the testator, is that he should be able to think thus far, 'I gave my solicitor instructions to prepare a will making a certain disposition of my property. I have no doubt that he has given effect to my intention, and I accept the document which is put before me as carrying it out.' Now, I have only put into language that which flashes across the mind without being expressed in words. Do you believe that she was so far capable of understanding what was going on? Did she at that time know and recollect all that she had done with Mr Parker? That would be one state of mind. But if you should come to the conclusion that she did not at that time recollect in every detail all that had passed between them, do you think that she was in a condition, if each clause of this will had been put to her, and she had been asked, 'Do you wish to leave So-and-So so much?' or 'Do you wish to do this?' (as the case might be), she would have been able to answer intelligently 'Yes' to each question? That would be another condition of mind. It would not be so strong as the first, viz., that in which she recollected all that she had done, but it would be sufficient. There is also a third state of mind which, in my judgment, would be sufficient. A person might no longer have capacity to go over the whole transaction, and take up the thread of business from the beginning to the end, and think it all over again, but if he is able to say to himself, 'I have settled that business with my solicitor. I rely upon his having embodied it in proper words, and I accept the paper which is put before me as embodying it'; it is not, of course, necessary that he should use those words, but if he is capable of that train of thought in my judgment that is sufficient. It is for you to say whether, having regard to the circumstances under which this will was prepared and executed, you accept the view of those who were present at the time, and who have given their evidence, and who say that in their judgment she was conscious.[16]

---

16. See also *Perera v Perera* [1901] AC 354 (PC). Cf *Battan Singh v Amirchand* [1948] AC 161, [1948] 1 All ER 152 where the House of Lords refused to apply the *Parker v Felgate* exception because the testator had not given his instructions to the solicitor direct but through a lay intermediary. ('The opportunities for error in transmission and of misunderstanding and of deception in such a situation are obvious,' per Lord Normand at p 155.)

(d) Effect of mental incapacity

The effect of lack of capacity is usually the invalidity of the whole will, but in one instance the court was satisfied that the incapacity only affected a part of the instrument and allowed probate to issue of the remainder.

In **Re Bohrmann** [1938] 1 All ER 271, the testator was making a codicil to his will. At the time of doing so, he was suffering from an insane delusion that he was being persecuted by his local authority, the then London County Council. By clause 2 of the codicil he revoked a clause in his will leaving money to English charities and declared that the money be held for American charities instead. Holding that the codicil should be admitted to probate except for clause 2 which should be deleted, Langton J said at p 282:

Having regard to the fact that he was in the end suffering from this delusional insanity, and to the fact that it is very difficult to put any reasonable interpretation upon this particular declaration in his codicil, I think that it is right and proper that I should consider that clause apart from the rest of the codicil, which is in reasonable and quite natural terms, and must have been quite unaffected by this particular delusional insanity. I have paused a good deal in taking this view, because, again, I am impressed by the danger of departing from well-known rules. I know of no case, and counsel have not been able to give me a case, in which any judge of this court has divided a testamentary instrument, such as a will or a codicil, and has said, as to one part: 'I see no reason to disturb it, because in any event it cannot have been affected by the delusion from which the testator suffered, but, as regards another part of it, I think this must have been dictated by some form of delusion,' or 'I think it is fairly proved to have been so dictated.' As a matter of law, I feel that this is, perhaps, going a step beyond what has yet been decided, but I cannot see that it is in conflict with the well-known decisions. I do not think that I am here taking it upon myself to transgress upon what is really the field of the legislature. It has been the practice in this court for many years to delete from instruments of testamentary disposition anything which the court is satisfied is not brought to the knowledge and approval of the testator. I conceive that I am doing no more now in declaring for this codicil without cl 2 than I should be doing in deleting from the codicil something which I believe was never brought to his knowledge and approval as a sane, balanced man. I think that he was at that time, so far as I can judge of the matter, with all the material at my disposal, suffering from a delusion at the moment when he inserted cl 2 into his fourth codicil.

(e) Execution of a statutory will

When a person is no longer mentally capable of managing his affairs for himself, the property of that person (the patient) may be placed under the control of the Court of Protection[17] and a receiver appointed to manage the patient's affairs for him. In such a situation the Court of Protection has very wide powers for dealing with the patient's property for the benefit of the patient, including the power to direct the execution of a will on behalf of the patient.[18]

Mental Health Act 1983[19]

96. Powers of the judge as to patient's property and affairs
. . . (1) Without prejudice to the generality of section 95,[20] the judge shall have power to

---

17. See p 3 n 4 ante.
18. The patient may still make a will for himself but unless he does so in a lucid interval as in *Cartwright v Cartwright*, p 70 ante, such a will will fail for lack of capacity. See *Re Davey* [1980] 3 All ER 342, [1981] 1 WLR 164 for a dramatic example of the usefulness of the statutory power.
19. This Act consolidated the law relating to mentally disordered persons.
20. See p 4 ante.

make such orders and give such directions and authorities as he thinks fit for the purposes of that section, and in particular may for those purposes make orders or give directions or authorities for . . .

(e) the execution for the patient of a will making any provision (whether by way of disposing of property or exercising a power or otherwise) which could be made by a will executed by the patient if he were not mentally disordered;

(4) The power of the judge to make or give an order, direction or authority for the execution of a will for a patient—

(a) shall not be exercisable at any time when the patient is a minor, and
(b) shall not be exercised unless the judge has reason to believe that the patient is incapable of making a valid will for himself.[1]

Re D(J) [1982] Ch 237, [1982] 2 All ER 37, Ch D; Megarry V-C

The patient, a widower, had made a will in 1962 leaving her property equally among her five children. By 1972 she was becoming senile; she went to live with one of the children, A, and A's husband, who looked after her thereafter. In 1978 the patient's affairs were placed under the control of the Court of Protection. A subsequently applied to the Court for the exercise of its powers under Mental Health Act 1959 s 103(1)(dd)[2] to increase the testamentary provision for her out of the patient's property, which was then worth £50,000. The deputy master ordered the execution of a will giving A a legacy of £10,000 and the residue of the estate to the five children equally (including A), with gifts over to their children and a gift over of A's share of the residue to her husband if she died childless before the patient's death. A appealed, seeking increased provision.

Held: The will as directed by the master should be executed, subject to an increase in A's legacy to £15,000; in addition, the substitutional clause in favour of A's husband should apply to the legacy as well as to the share of residue.

Megarry V-C: The first of the principles or factors which I think it is possible to discern is that it is to be assumed that the patient is having a brief lucid interval at the time when the will is made. The second is that during the lucid interval the patient has a full knowledge of the past, and a full realisation that as soon as the will is executed he or she will relapse into the actual mental state that previously existed, with the prognosis as it actually is. These propositions emerge, I think, from the judgment of Cross J in *Re WJGL* [1965] 3 All ER 865 at 871–872, [1966] Ch 135 at 144–145. In that case the judge was dealing with the making of a settlement for the patient,[3] not a will: but I cannot see that the distinction matters. Paragraph (dd), dealing with wills, has been inserted immediately after para (d), dealing with settlements and gifts,[3] and both are governed by the same general statutory provisions.

The third proposition is that it is the actual patient who has to be considered and not a hypothetical patient. One is not concerned with the patient on the Clapham omnibus. . . . Before losing testamentary capacity the patient may have been a person with strong antipathies or deep affections for particular persons or causes, or with vigorous religious or political views; and of course the patient was then able to give effect to those views when making a will. I think that the court must take the patient as he or she was before losing testamentary capacity. No doubt allowance may be made for the

---

1. S 97 contains supplementary provisions as to the method of execution and declares that subject thereto, the will should have effect in every way as if executed by the patient being capable. See further the Court of Protection Rules 1984, SI 1984/2035 and Practice Note [1983] 3 All ER 255, [1983] 1 WLR 1077. For a general examination of the topic, see Thurston 'Wills for Mentally Disordered Persons' (1985) 82 LSG 1617.
2. Now Mental Health Act 1983 s 96(1)(e).
3. See p 5 ante.

passage of years since the patient was last of full capacity, for sometimes strong feelings mellow into indifference, and even family feuds evaporate. Furthermore, I do not think that the court should give effect to antipathies or affections of the patient which are beyond reason. But subject to all due allowances, I think that the court must seek to make the will which the actual patient, acting reasonably, would have made if notionally restored to full mental capacity, memory and foresight. If I may adapt Dr Johnson's words, used for another purpose, the court is to do for the patient what the patient would fairly do for himself, if he could.

Fourth, I think that during the hypothetical lucid interval the patient is to be envisaged as being advised by competent solicitors. The court will in fact be making the will, of course, and the court should not make a will on the assumption that the terms of the will are to be framed by someone who, for instance, knows nothing about lapse and ademption. Furthermore, as the court will be surveying the past and the future, the hypothetically lucid patient should be assumed to have a skilled solicitor to draw his or her attention to matters which a testator should bear in mind. In *Re DML* [1965] 2 All ER 129 at 133, [1965] Ch 1133 at 1139, a case on a proposed purchase of an annuity in order to save estate duty, Cross J put a lucid explanation of the proposal into the mouth of a hypothetical legal adviser to the hypothetically lucid patient. In any case, I cannot imagine that Parliament intended the court to match the sort of home-made will that some testators make. I do not, of course, say that one must treat the patient as being bound to accept the imaginary legal advice that is given to him: but the patient is to be treated as doing what he does either because of the advice or in spite of it, and not without having had it.

Fifth, in all normal cases the patient is to be envisaged as taking a broad brush to the claims on his bounty, rather than an accountant's pen. There will be nothing like a balance sheet or profit and loss account. There may be many to whom the patient feels morally indebted; and some of that moral indebtedness may be readily expressible in terms of money, and some of it may not. But when giving legacies or shares of residue few testators are likely to reckon up in terms of cash the value of the hospitality and gifts that he has received from his friends and relations, and then seek to make some form of testamentary repayment, even if his estate is large enough for this. Instead, there is likely to be some general recognition of outstanding kindnesses by some gift which in quantum may bear very little relation to the cost or value of those kindnesses. . . .

I can now at last return to the facts of the case. What disposition of the patient's estate should now be made according to the principles or factors which I have stated and the general requirements of fairness and appropriateness for all concerned? The main claim of Mrs A to the larger share of the estate which it is conceded that she should have rests on the burden that she and her husband have discharged over the past nine years or so; for throughout that period the patient has lived with them nearly continuously. . . . The advantage of having a settled home with a daughter, instead of living on her own, or being moved every few weeks or months from the house of one of her children to the house of another, or living in some old persons' home is one which must stand very high, not only in its own right but also as showing the strength of filial affection and duty. I do not doubt that Mrs A has acted with devotion and kindliness, and not reluctantly or grudgingly. She has supplied what so many old people need and crave. I am, of course, making a number of assumptions about the patient, for I have very little evidence about her nature: but I do not think that in those circumstances it is wrong to assume that she follows the usual pattern. She is plainly not one of those sturdy individualists who demand independence and seclusion.

It also seems to me that the future would loom large in the patient's thoughts, and that until mental or physical infirmity made it impossible for her to continue living with Mrs A, she would want to continue there. Her recognition for the past would therefore include an element of expectation for the future. She would realise (I am assuming, of course, that she has the advice of a skilled solicitor) that whereas at present her income is more than sufficient to pay the £40 a week that Mrs A is receiving from her estate, there is a very real risk of having to resort to capital if she has to go to a home or hospital and live there for some while . . . .

In the end my conclusion is that Mrs A should be given a legacy of £15,000 . . . it strikes me as being about right for Mrs A to receive a little over £20,000 in all[4] and for each of the others to receive a little over £5,000 in all, with the figures varying upwards or downwards with the size of the estate. This represents giving about half the estate to Mrs A and the other half to her sister and brother. This seems to me to give substantial recognition to the claims of all the children, as such, and at the same time to reflect Mrs A's special claims.[5]

QUESTIONS

1. 'If an infant is able to marry, he ought to be able to make a will too.' Discuss.
2. A died recently, aged 89, leaving a will made two months before his death by which he gave all his estate to charities for the benefit of animals. He was a generous supporter of such charities during his lifetime and often stated his belief that the souls of all human beings passed on death into animals. During the last two years of his life, A had become increasingly senile although there were periods when he was able to hold rational conversations and discuss his financial affairs sensibly. Advise B, his brother, and only near relative.
3. Do you think the rule in *Parker v Felgate*[6] is justified? What if the testator had changed his mind since giving instructions for the will?
4. In *Kenward v Adams* (1975) The Times 25th November 1975, Templeman J advised solicitors acting for elderly and infirm testators (a) to consult with the testator's nearest relatives before drawing up his will and (b) to ensure that at least one of the witnesses was medically qualified and prepared to record at the time of execution his satisfaction with the testator's capacity and understanding. Do you envisage any practical problems in compliance with this rule which Templeman J himself described as 'golden but tactless'? See also Law Reform Committee: Twenty-Second Report 'The Making and Revocation of Wills' (1980) Cmnd 7902, paras 2.17–2.19.

4. Including her share of the residue and allowing for the costs of the hearing and of the administration.
5. He added at p 49, that the substituted clause in favour of A's husband should apply to A's legacy as well as to her share of the residue, in recognition of his involvement in the patient's care.
6. P 71 ante.

CHAPTER 7

Wills–intention

1 Animus testandi

The testator does not necessarily have to realise that he is making his will; to have *animus testandi* he need only intend that his wishes, as expressed in the document in question, should take effect only on death.

In **Re Chalcraft** [1948] P 222, the deceased on her deathbed had signed a document which simply read:

> '96 Osborne Road Acton. I wish my house to be sold and £500 made over to Mr C F West for purchase of Stilecroft Gardens.'[1]

It was duly attested. Nothing was stated either in the document or at the time as to it constituting a will or codicil. Holding that the document should be admitted to probate as a codicil, Willmer J said at p 230 (Probate report):

The document itself being equivocal, what is the effect of the evidence which I have heard? As was pointed out by counsel for the defendants, Miss Helen Chalcraft's own evidence was really silent as to any intention, express or implicit, to execute a testamentary document; but it is an undoubted fact that the deceased became conscious of the seriousness of her condition, and was apprehensive lest she should die before her arrangements were all carried out. It was with that object in view that, at her request, Mr West was sent to fetch the solicitor as soon as possible. That was followed by the conversation in which the deceased asked Mrs Giles[2] to see that in the event of anything happening to her—that means in the event of her death—her arrangements were carried out; that is to say, the deceased was apprehensive as to her wishes being carried out after her death.

In those circumstances, the conclusion to which I come, by way of inference from facts proved in evidence before me, is that when the deceased was invited to sign this document, and when, as I have said, she signified her knowledge and approval of its contents, she was regarding it as a document of the nature she wanted, namely a document which would govern the disposition of her property in the event of her death before she was able to execute the deed. Putting that into other words, I feel satisfied that the correct inference to draw is that the deceased did intend this to be a testamentary document'.[3]

---

1. A new house which the gentleman concerned was in the process of buying at the time.
2. A daughter of the deceased and also one of the defendants to the action.
3. See also *Re Brennan*, Ch 5 ante. Cf *Nicholls v Nicholls* (1814) 2 Phill Ecc 180 where the deceased's children propounded a paper in these terms as a will: 'I leave my property between my children; I hope they will be virtuous and independent; that they will worship God and not black coats.' It was held that the deceased never intended this to operate as a will; the court was satisfied on the evidence that it was written as a post prandial joke, in the context of a conversation ridiculing the verbosity of lawyers and their documents. See also *Lister v Smith* (1863) 3 Sw & Tr 282.

2 Vitiating factors

Sometimes however, even where the intention appears obvious on the face of the document, it may be vitiated by other factors.

(a) An unfulfilled precondition

The testator's intention may be only conditional in which case the will will only be valid if the condition is satisfied.

In **In the Goods of Robinson** (1870) LR 2 P & D 171, the deceased was a master mariner in command of a merchant ship in the course of a return voyage from London to Sicily. Having reached the port of Cette in France, on the way out, he called in at the British Consular Office there and wrote out a will which commenced as follows:

> 'Cette, May 16th 1868. This is the last will and testament of me, George Twizall Robinson, that in case anything should happen to me during the remainder of the voyage from hence to Sicily and back to London that I give and bequeath . . .' (various dispositive provisions followed).

He returned safely from that voyage and died some two years later, leaving in addition to the will of 1868, an earlier will made in 1864 which contained no such conditional phrase. Pronouncing against the 1868 will, Lord Penzance said at p 172:

> The deceased in this case commences his will with the following words:— 'This is the last will and testament of me'. What is? '*That* in case anything should happen to me during the voyage from hence to Sicily and back to London, that I give and bequeath, etc.' He therefore makes the dispositions of his will dependent on a certain event, namely something happening on the voyage. . . . I am against this paper. I think it is conditional. By it the deceased distributes his property only in case he died on his voyage from Cette to London, whereas he survived it by two years. Administration with the will of June, 1864, alone will be granted.[4]

In the Goods of Spratt [1897] P 28, PD; Jeune P

An Army officer serving in New Zealand during the Maori War wrote to his sister as follows.

> If we remain here taking pahs[5] for some time to come the chances are in favour of more of us being killed, and as I may not have another opportunity of saying what I wish to be done with any little money I may possess in case of an accident, I wish to make everything I possess over to you. . . . Keep this until I ask you for it. Your affectionate brother C. Spratt.

It appeared to satisfy the requirements of Wills Act 1837, s 11 and to constitute a valid privileged will,[6] but was the testator's intention conditional on his death during the Maori War? If it was, the will would fail for he survived the War and died over 30 years later.

---

4. See also *Re Hugo* (1877) 2 P D 73, *Re Thomas* [1939] Ch 513, [1939] 2 All ER 567.
5. Native forts in New Zealand.
6. See Ch 9 post.

Held: The disposition of his property was not conditional on his death in active service; it was a valid privileged will.

Jeune P: In cases of the character of the present, the difficulty which arises in determining the intention of the testator as expressed in his will is that an ambiguity is caused by the use of language which renders it doubtful whether the testator meant to refer to a possible event as his reason for making a will, or as limiting the operation of the will made. If the will is clearly expressed to take effect only on the happening, or not happening, of any event, *cadit quaestio*, it is conditional. If the testator says, in effect—that he is led to make his will by reason of the uncertainty of life in general, or for some special reason, *cadit quaestio*, it is not conditional, but if it be not clear whether the words used import a reason for making a will or impress a conditional character on it, the whole language of the document, and also the surrounding circumstances, must be considered. In such cases there are two criteria which are especially useful for determining the problem: first, whether the nature of disposition made appears to have relation to the time or circumstances of the contingency; and, secondly, where the contingency is connected with a period of danger to the testator, whether it is coincident with that period, because, if it is, there is ground to suppose that the danger was regarded by the testator only as a reason for making a will, but, if it is not, it is difficult to see the object of referring to a particular period unless it be to limit the operation of the will. . . .

Applying the tests which I have above indicated to the present case, I think that the words 'in case of an accident' point only to the reason why the testator desired to make a will. There is no expression of any period to be found in the document within which alone it was to be operative; on the contrary, the request that the will should be kept by his sister till he asked for it appears to me to shew that the testator had not in his mind any defined period of time at the expiration of which he intended that his will should cease to be effective. Nor is there anything in the disposition of the property which indicates that it was temporary, or that it did not apply to whatever property of which the testator might at any time be possessed. I am of the opinion, therefore, that probate should be granted of the document in question.[7]

(b) Undue influence

Gifts by will, like inter vivos gifts, will be invalidated by the presence of undue influence, but unlike inter vivos gifts,[8] no presumption of undue influence arises in relation to a gift by will, however close the relationship between the testator and the beneficiary may be.

Parfitt v Lawless (1872) LR 2 P & D 462, Court of Probate; Lord Penzance, Brett J, Pigott B

The testatrix left all her property to a Roman Catholic priest who had been a member of her household for many years, acting as a domestic chaplain and father confessor. It was argued that the equitable rules in relation to inter vivos gifts[9] should be adopted to raise a presumption of undue influence which the priest would have to disprove.

---

7. See also *In the Goods of William Cawthron* (1863) 3 Sw & Tr 417 where the testator's intention on the face of the will appeared to be conditional on his death during a long journey that he was about to undertake, but extrinsic evidence established that he did not complete his execution of the will until his return home.

8. See p 11 ante.

9. Ibid.

Held: No such presumption would arise and on the facts there was no evidence of undue influence either.

Lord Penzance: But in truth the cases in equity apply to a wholly different state of things. In the first place, in those cases of gifts or contracts inter vivos there is a transaction in which the person benefited at least takes part, whether he unduly urges his influence or not; and in calling upon him to explain the part he took, and the circumstances that brought about the gift or obligation, the Court is plainly requiring of him an explanation within his knowledge. But in the case of a legacy under a will, the legatee may have, and in point of fact generally has, no part in or even knowledge of the act; and to cast upon him, on the bare proof of the legacy and his relation to the testator, the burthen of shewing how the thing came about, and under what influence or with what motives the legacy was made, or what advice the testator had, professional or otherwise, would be to cast a duty on him which in many, if not most cases, he could not possibly discharge. A more material distinction is this: the influence which is undue in the case of gifts inter vivos is very different from that which is required to set aside a will. In the case of gifts or other transactions inter vivos it is considered by the Courts of equity that the natural influence which such relations as those in question involve, exerted by those who possess it to obtain a benefit for themselves, is an undue influence. Gifts or contracts brought about by it are, therefore, set aside unless the party benefited by it can shew affirmatively that the other party to the transaction was placed 'in such a position as would enable him to form an absolutely free and unfettered judgment': *Archer v Hudson* ((1844) 7 Beav 551).

The law regarding wills is very different from this. The natural influence of the parent or guardian over the child, or the husband over the wife, or the attorney over the client, may lawfully be exerted to obtain a will or legacy, so long as the testator thoroughly understands what he is doing and is a free agent. There is nothing illegal in the parent or husband pressing his claims on a child or wife, and obtaining a recognition of those claims in a legacy, provided that that persuasion stop short of coercion, and that the volition of the testator, though biased and impressed by the relation in which he stands to the legatee, is not overborne and subject to the domination of another. . . .

This difference, then, between the influence which is held to be undue in the case of transactions inter vivos, and that which is called undue in relation to a will or legacy is all-important when a question arises of making presumptions or adjusting the burden of proof. For it may be reasonable enough to presume that a person who had obtained a gift or contract to his own advantage and the detriment of another by way of personal advice or persuasion has availed himself of the natural influence which his position gave him. And in casting upon him the burden of exculpation, the law is only assuming that he has done so. But it is a very different thing to presume, without a particle of proof, that a person so situated has abused his position by the exercise of dominion or the assertion of adverse control.

For these reasons it seems to me that it would be improper and unjust to throw upon a man in the position of the plaintiff, without any proof that he had any hand whatever in the making of this will, the onus of proving negatively that he did not coerce the testatrix into devising the residue of her land to him. . . .

No amount of persuasion or advice, whether founded on feelings of regard or religious sentiment, would avail, according to the existing law, to set aside this will, so long as the free volition of the testatrix to accept or reject that advice was not invaded. And what, it must therefore be asked, is the proof that any attempt ever was made to control her free will? There was not a fact, a word, or an event proved which shewed that on any occasion the testatrix had subordinated her own will to that of the plaintiff. It was stated, indeed, that he managed her affairs for her; but even this was confined to the last three years of her life, many years after the date of the will, and at a time when her health had failed. But of evidence to shew that, in the common affairs of life, or in business, or in anything else, she was under the plaintiff's dominion, there was an absolute and total dearth.

In **Craig v Lamoreux** [1920] AC 349, Viscount Haldane added a further reason for withholding the inter vivos presumption of undue influence from gifts by will. Considering a will that was wholly in favour of the testatrix's husband who had been instrumental in its preparation and execution, he said at p 356:

A will which merely regulates succession after death, is very different from a gift inter vivos, which strips the donor of his property during his lifetime.

In the absence of any evidence of undue influence, the Privy Council upheld the will. [10]

Justice Committee: Report on Home-Made Wills[11]

14. We believe that there is a certain number of cases in which undue influence is brought to bear on elderly testators, acting without legal advice, by proprietors of old people's homes or other persons on whom the testators are physically dependent. We think that the presumption of undue influence might well be extended to include persons (or employees of such persons) who at the date of the will were providing residential care for a testator over the age of (say) 60 under a contract—again excluding small gifts.

(c) Want of knowledge and approval

The testator must know and approve the contents of his will; failure to do so will vitiate an apparent testamentary intention and render the will, or the part of it affected, invalid. Proof of the testator's testamentary capacity and of due execution normally raises a rebuttable presumption of knowledge and approval of the contents, throwing the evidential burden on the person opposing the will to rebut the presumption. [12] No such presumption arises, however, where the circumstances attending the execution of the will are suspicious; as Parke B stated in *Barry v Butlin* (1838) 2 Moo PC 480, 12 ER 1089, at p 1090:

If a party writes or prepares a Will under which he[13] takes a benefit, that is a circumstance that ought generally to excite the suspicion of the Court, and calls upon it to be vigilant and jealous in examining the evidence in support of the instrument, in favour of which it ought not to pronounce unless the suspicion is removed, and it is judicially satisfied that the paper propounded does express the true Will of the deceased.

Wintle v Nye[14] [1959] 1 All ER 552, [1959] 1 WLR 284, HL; Viscount Simonds, Lords Reid, Tucker, Keith of Avonholm and Birkett

An elderly woman had a large estate of over £100,000. Unversed in business affairs (her doctor described her as a 'very unintelligent woman'), she was

---

10. It seems unfortunate on these facts that those challenging the will did not rely instead on the rule in *Barry v Butlin* (1838) 2 Moo PC 480, post, as this would have shifted the burden of proof on to the husband to establish positively the testatrix's knowledge and approval of the contents of her will.

11. Published 1971. This recommendation has not received legislative support as yet.

12. Except where the testator is blind or illiterate: see NCPR 1954 r 11, p 311 post. In such a case the registrar will normally require evidence that the will was read over to the testator before execution. This evidence will usually take the form of a special attestation clause in the will, otherwise the registrar will probably call for affidavit evidence from witnesses.

13. Or a relative of his—see eg *Tyrrell v Painton* [1894] P 151 where the will was prepared and witnessed by the beneficiary's son.

14. A case that attracted considerable notoriety at the time, not least because the plaintiff who took on the solicitor defendant, conducted his own case (with the help of his local library), lost at first instance, lost in the Court of Appeal and succeeded in the House of Lords.

housebound and her solicitor, Nye, was the only person who visited her. He made a will for her, a very complicated document which left the residue of her estate to himself, and subsequently a codicil, the effect of which was to swell the residuary gift even further. She had no independent legal advice and he made little effort to persuade her to get it. Once the documents were executed Nye kept them at his office and did not even give her copies. After her death the will and codicil were challenged, not on the ground of undue influence but on the basis that she did not know and approve of their contents.

Held: In these suspicious circumstances it was for the solicitor to prove affirmatively that she knew and approved the contents of both documents: the jury had not been sufficiently directed on this point by the trial judge and their verdict in favour of the will and codicil could not stand. The codicil was declared invalid, also the will, in so far as concerned the gifts to the solicitor.

Viscount Simonds: It is not the law that in no circumstances can a solicitor or other person who has prepared a will for a testator take a benefit under it. But that fact creates a suspicion that must be removed by the person propounding the will. In all cases the court must be vigilant and jealous. The degree of suspicion will vary with the circumstances of the case. It may be slight and easily dispelled.[15] It may, on the other hand, be so grave that it can hardly be removed. In the present case the circumstances were such as to impose on the respondent as heavy a burden as can well be imagined. Here was an elderly lady who might be called old, unversed in business, having no one upon whom to rely except the solicitor who had acted for her and her family; a will made by him under which he takes the bulk of her large estate; a will made, it is true, after a number of interviews extending over a considerable time, during which details of her property and of her proposed legacies and annuities were said to have been put before her, but in the end of a complexity which demanded for its comprehension no common understanding: on her part, a wish disclosed in January, 1937, to leave her residuary estate to charity which was by April superseded by a devise of it to him, and, on his part, an explanation of the change which was calculated as much to aggravate as to allay suspicion: the will retained by him and no copy of it given to her: no independent advice received by her, and, even according to his own account, little pressure exercised by him to persuade her to get it: a codicil cutting out reversionary legacies to charities allegedly for the benefit of annuitants but in fact, as was reasonably foreseeable, for the benefit of the residuary beneficiary. All these facts and others that I do not pause to enumerate demanded a vigilant and jealous scrutiny by the judge in his summing-up and by the jury in the consideration of their verdict.[16]

In **In the Estate of Fuld (No 3)** [1968] P 675, [1965] 3 All ER 776, Harman J, commenting on the reemergence of the rule in *Barry v Butlin*[17] said at p 722 (Probate report):

It may well be that positive charges of fraud and undue influence will not feature as largely in the pleadings of probate cases, now that *Wintle v Nye* has been decided, as they have done in the past; clearly it would be preferable if they did not.[18]

---

15. Parke B in *Barry v Butlin* (1838) 2 Moo PC 480 at 485, gave as an example of such a case the instance of a man of acknowledged business competence with an estate of £100,000, leaving all his property to his family except £50 to his solicitor who prepared the will.

16. A further danger for a solicitor-beneficiary who falls foul of the rule in *Barry v Butlin* is that he stands to lose not just his benefit under the will but also his livelihood. See *Re A Solicitor* [1975] QB 475, [1974] 3 All ER 853, where the Court of Appeal upheld the decision of the Disciplinary Committee of the Law Society in striking off the roll two solicitor-beneficiaries who had failed to advise their clients to obtain independent advice before making wills in the solicitors' favour.

17. (1838) 2 Moo PC 480, p 80 ante.

18. He went on to warn, at p 722, that a party with strong grounds for pleading the rule in *Barry v Butlin* who added unnecessarily to the costs by pleading fraud or undue influence (with all the evidential problems associated therewith) on the same facts, might well find that the costs he thereby incurred were disallowed.

(d) Mistake

The deceased's apparent testamentary intention may have its foundation in a mistake; that mistake may take a number of possible forms with varying effects on the validity of the disposition concerned.

(i) *Mistake as to the document*

Sometimes two parties make wills in each other's favour, often in precisely the same terms, but inadvertently, each signs the will of the other. In such a case neither document can be admitted to probate for want of the requisite *animus testandi* in relation to the will concerned. In other jurisdictions the problem has been overcome by allowing both wills to be admitted to probate with the omission from each of any mistaken reference to the testator.

In **Re Meyer** [1908] P 353, two sisters executed codicils in similar terms but, by mistake, each sister had executed the document intended for the other. When one of them died, the other applied for probate of the codicil executed by the deceased sister. Holding that probate could not be granted, Gorell Barnes P said, at p 354:

It is quite clear that this lady, though her signature is on the document, never meant to sign this particular codicil at all. She meant to sign a totally different document. It may be that this document contains provisions corresponding with what she wished to sign, because the two documents were cross-codicils by two sisters. But, as a matter of fact, the deceased in signing her name to this codicil never intended to do that at all, but intended to put her signature to another document; and, unless some authority can be produced to me to shew that in such a case the document she did not intend to sign is to be treated as the one she did intend to sign, I do not mean to support it. In my opinion this codicil cannot stand. The will, of course, can be proved in the ordinary way.

Guardian Trust & Executors Company of New Zealand Ltd v Inwood [1946] NZLR 614, New Zealand CA; Johnston, Fair and Cornish JJ

Two sisters, Maude Lucy Remington and Jane Remington, decided to make identical wills, apart from a life interest in each other's favour. They attended together to execute their respective wills and by mistake each of them was given and executed the will that should have been signed by the other. As a result, when Jane Remington died she left a will signed by her but expressed in its opening words to be the last will of Maude Lucy, who was also identified as the testatrix in the attestation clause, and leaving 'my sister Jane Remington' a life interest in the residuary estate.

Held: The will should be admitted to probate omitting the word 'Jane'; the references to Maude Lucy in the opening words and attestation clause could be ignored, neither of those parts being a necessary or essential part of a will.

Fair J: Clearly, on the face of it, the document propounded as the will of Jane Remington appears to be irregular. There would, however, be no difficulty in clearing up the irregularity as to the attestation if evidence were available for that purpose, for an attestation clause is neither necessary nor is it an essential part of the will: *Mortimer on Probate Law and Practice* 2nd Ed 1, 25, and R 519 of the Code of Civil Procedure. Obviously, too, the opening words are no essential part of the will, but, if inappropriate, would call for consideration and, if necessary, explanation: *Whyte v Pollok*, per Lord Watson ((1882) 7 AC 400, 424). . . .

Then, too, it may be shown that clauses or expressions have been inadvertently introduced into the will, contrary to the testator's intentions and instructions, or, in other words, that a part of the executed instrument is not his will: *Jarman on Wills*, 7th Ed 469. At the foot of that page it is said:

> Under the modern practice, the question whether the words have been introduced into a will by mistake is often considered by the Court of Probate and if it is found that they do not form part of the will, the Court directs them to be omitted from the probate. . . .

See also *Mortimer on Probate Law and Practice* 2nd Ed 86. When a will has been proved, evidence is not admissible in a court of construction to show that certain words contained in a probate copy were inserted in the original will by mistake: *Re Bywater, Bywater v Clarke* ((1881) 18 Ch D 17, 22).

It is admitted by all counsel that there was no other sister named 'Jane Remington' or passing by that name, and in the circumstances of the case it appears clear that the words 'Jane Remington' in the disposing part of the will are there owing to a mistake and do not represent the intentions of the late Jane Remington.

It is to be noted from this recital of the facts that the operative parts of the document propounded, in spite of its striking inaptness of recital and attestation clause, do express literally and exactly the testamentary wishes and intentions of the signatory except by the inclusion of the word 'Jane'. If the document is admissible to probate as a testamentary instrument, the Court has, according to the authorities to which we have referred, ample power to strike out the words inserted by mistake, and that is now the usual practice in the Probate Court.

But it is submitted on behalf of the defendants, who are entitled under the intestacy, that it is not admissible to probate on the ground that it was not executed *animo testandi*— that is, that the testatrix did not intend to sign this document and that this document was never intended by her or by any one to be her will. This would appear, upon careful examination, to be a very technical basis for its rejection, and, upon an exact appreciation of the true facts, to lack substance. True, the physical document was not the paper that the testatrix intended to sign, but it was a paper that contained everything that she wished included in the paper she intended to sign except the Christian names of her sister. She adopted it believing that it expressed her intentions in every respect. It does in most, and can be read as carrying out her intentions. It appoints the executor she intended to appoint in the exact terms she intended to appoint it. That in itself if it stood alone would be enough, apart from this formal objection, to entitle it to probate: *Mortimer on Probate Law and Practice* 2nd Ed 205, 246. It also disposes of the residue after the life interest in the exact terms which the other will contains. The life interest is in correct terms except for the Christian name. There is no doubt that she intended the document to which she put her signature to operate as her will.

If she had intended to sign the document in the original typewriting, and she had, by mistake, been given a carbon copy, she would have been executing a paper physically different from that which she intended to sign, but if it had contained a duplicate carbon copy it appears unarguable that document in carbon would be invalid on that ground. The present will seems to us to differ from such copy only in degree and not in substance. No doubt the circumstances of the recital with the wrong Christian name would call for explanation as the preliminary headings of the will in *Whyte v Pollok* ((1882) 7 AC 400). But the fact that the paper put before the testatrix was different from that which she thought she was signing should not, we think, prevent that part of the document which she wished and believed, and which was, in fact, included, being her testamentary act. The testatrix did really know and approve of the effective provisions contained in it: *Parker v Felgate* ((1883) 8 PD 171)[19] and *Perera v Perera* [1901] AC 354, 361.[20]

---

19. P 71 ante.
20. See also *Re Brander* [1952] 4 DLR 688 (British Columbia Supreme Court), *Re Bonachewski* (1967) 60 WWR 635 (Saskatchewan Surrogate Court), *Re Snide* (1981) 52 NY 2d 193 (New York Court of Appeals), all decided similarly.

(ii) *Mistake as to the relevant facts*

Where the facts are of a kind likely to influence the testator in making his will, such a mistake will invalidate the gift concerned if induced by fraud, but not otherwise.

In **Re Posner** [1953] P 277, [1953] 1 All ER 1123, the testator left a gift to a woman described in his will as 'my wife'. In fact they were not validly married, but neither party knew that. Holding that in the absence of fraud, the gift would stand, Karminski J said at p 1125:

> Two things (suffice) to defeat the gift. One is a legacy given to a person of a character which the legatee does not fill, but that by itself is not enough. In order to defeat the legacy there must also be a fraudulent assumption of that character, and furthermore, the testator must have been deceived by that fraud.

On the pleadings before him there was no allegation of fraud against the woman concerned and no justification therefore for upsetting the gift.[1]

(iii) *Mistake as to the legal effect*

Where words were deliberately chosen by the testator or his draftsman but under a mistaken belief as to their legal effect, the testator is bound by those words;[2] the only recourse for a beneficiary who suffers loss thereby is to sue the draftsman of the will (if any) in negligence.[3]

Collins v Elstone [1893] P1, PD; Jeune P

The testatrix made a will disposing of the whole of her estate. She then decided to make a different disposition in relation to her insurance policy and asked a friend, who was not a professional draftsman to draft another will to dispose of the policy only. Instead of preparing a codicil, the friend obtained a printed will form for the purpose and this contained a printed clause revoking all previous wills. The testatrix read the will form through and queried the printed clause but the friend assured her (wrongly) that its effect was to revoke the earlier will in respect of the policy only. She executed the will.

Held: The revocation clause could not be struck out; the testatrix knew the clause was there and had approved it even though she did not understand its legal effect.

Jeune P: I cannot help regretting—as I suppose everybody would regret—that I am compelled to come to a conclusion the effect of which I am conscious will be that the real intentions of the testatrix will not be carried out. But on the facts of the case the conclusion is quite clear. The last will contains words which in law revoke all previous wills. Those words were inserted, as I have no doubt, because the testatrix

---

1. Cf *Wilkinson v Joughin* (1866) LR 2 Eq 319 where the testator thought he was married to the woman he described in his will as 'my wife' but she was already married at the time when she went through the marriage ceremony with him and the judge found that she had deliberately misled him. See also *Kennell v Abbott* (1799) 4 Ves Jun 802.
2. Cf such mistakes occurring in an inter vivos disposition—see p 15 ante.
3. *Ross v Caunters* [1980] Ch 297, [1979] 3 All ER 580, where Megarry V-C decided that a solicitor owes a duty of care to an identified beneficiary under a will that he makes for a client; a beneficiary who incurs loss by a want of care on the solicitor's part may thus at least sue the solicitor in negligence. See further, Mithani 'The Rights of Disappointed Beneficiaries—Part II' (1982) 79 LSG 1425.

misunderstood their meaning, and I have no doubt how she came to misunderstand their meaning. It is clear on the evidence that the person who drew the will was ignorant—there is no fraud—as to the effect of putting that clause in, and doubly ignorant; for he told her it would be inoperative, and he told her further, if it was struck out the rest of the will would be vitiated. Misinformed by this statement, she allowed the clause to remain. The question is, under these circumstances, can I strike it out consistently with the authorities? I am afraid I cannot. . . .

(Counsel) refers me to the case of *Morrell v Morrell* ((1882) 7 PD 68), and it seems to me that the language used in that case expresses the law which is applicable to this case, and expresses what is some reason for it, because the view of Lord Hannen in that case is this, that if a testator employs another to convey his meaning in technical language, and that other person makes a mistake in doing it, the mistake is the same as if the testator had employed that technical language himself. Now, that view appears to me exactly to meet the present case. This lady thought it right to employ this gentleman to make her will for her; she thought it right to trust to him. No doubt he was mistaken; but, according to the view of Lord Hannen, his mistake was her mistake.[4]

(iv) *Clerical errors*

Words inserted by the clerical error of the testator or his draftsman are not binding on the testator unless they are brought to his notice before execution and he deliberately adopts them.[5] Where a mistake by way of clerical error is proved, the court has power to delete the offending words from probate but until 1982, it had no power to rectify such mistakes by ordering the insertion of what the testator really intended the will to contain.[6] The Administration of Justice Act 1982 introduced the equitable remedy of rectification for wills, to correct not only the clerical error but also mistakes due to the draftsman's failure to understand the testator's instructions.

Re Morris [1971] P 62, [1970] 1 All ER 1057, PD; Latey J

By Clause 7 of her will the testatrix made no fewer than 20 pecuniary legacies (numbered 7(i) to xx)). She subsequently decided to alter the provisions contained in Clauses 3 and 7(iv). Her solicitor prepared a codicil which she duly executed, having cast her eye over it without taking in its effect. It contained the words: 'I revoke clauses 3 & 7 of my said Will'. To give effect to the testatrix's intention it should have read: 'I revoke clauses 3 and 7(iv) of my said Will'.

Held: The introduction of the words 'clause 7' instead of 'clause 7(iv)' was a mere clerical error by the solicitor which had not been adopted by the testatrix. Probate would be granted with the reference to '7' deleted from the codicil, the court having no power simply to insert '(iv)'.

---

4. Aliter, he conceded (p 5) had there been any fraud on the draftsman's part, but there was no evidence of any fraud on the facts before him. See also *Re Horrocks* [1939] P 198, [1939] 1 All ER 579.
5. *Fulton v Andrew* (1875) LR 7 HL 448, *Re Morris* [1971] P 62, [1970] 1 All ER 1057; cf *Guardhouse v Blackburn* (1866) LR 1 P & D 109, *Atter v Atkinson* (1869) LR 1 P & D 665.
6. See *Re Morris*, post. See also *Re Reynette-James* [1975] 3 All ER 1037, [1976] 1 WLR 161; Lee 'Correcting Testator's Mistakes: The Probate Jurisdiction' (1969) 33 Conv 322; Sherrin 'Correcting Errors: Rectification of Documents' (1980) 124 Sol J 229; Langbein and Waggoner 'Reformation of Wills on the Ground of Mistake: Change of Direction in American Law' (1982) 130 U Pa L Rev 521.

Latey J: The introduction of the words 'Clause 7' instead of 'Clause 7(iv)' was *per incuriam*. The solicitor's mind was never applied to it, and never adverted to the significance and effect. It was a mere clerical error on his part, a slip. He knew what the testatrix's instructions and intentions were, and what he did was outside the scope of his authority. And he did it, of course, without knowing and approving what he himself was doing. How can one impute to the principal the agent's knowledge and approval which the agent himself has not got? Accordingly, I hold that the testatrix was not bound by this mistake of the draftsman which was never brought to her notice. The discrepancy between her instructions and what was in the codicil was to all intents and purposes total and was never within her cognisance.

Accordingly, the case is one in which the court has power to rectify, using that word in a broad sense, so far as it can. Which is the proper course? To pronounce against the instrument in its entirety? Or to exclude part and admit the rest?

Certainly to reject the whole instrument would come much nearer to giving effect to the testatrix's dispositive intentions (both in the number of beneficiaries and in the amounts involved) than would the admission of the whole instrument. But is the instrument severable, and can one get nearer still by excluding part? In my judgment, I can. I cannot add the numeral '(iv)' after '7' but if '7' is excluded, cl 1 of the codicil would read as follows: '1. I revoke Clauses 3 and (   ) of my said Will.'

I agree with counsel for the plaintiff bank's submission that this would have one of the following effects. The Chancery Court as the court of construction might deduce from the two documents (the will and the codicil so altered) read together that the testatrix's intention was that the other clause after the words 'Clauses 3 and (   )' should be 7(iv). Or the court might decide from a reading of the documents alone that there was not enough intrinsic evidence to fill in the blank but that the revocation of cl 3 of the will, coupled with the reinstatement of the same gift in cl 2(a) of the codicil, rebutted the presumption that the gifts in cl 3 of the will and cl 2 of the codicil were cumulative, and thus lead to the construction that those in cl 2 of the codicil were intended to be substitutional. Either of those decisions would give full effect to what in fact the testatrix intended. Or the court might decide that the presumption prevailed and the gifts were cumulative.

Counsel for the plaintiff bank submitted that the court would probably come to one or other of the first two conclusions, but that is not a matter on which I can express any opinion other than to take it into account. Of course, the ambiguity being a patent one, the court of construction will not be able to admit the external evidence which makes the testatrix's intentions as clear as crystal, or to have regard to the findings of fact in that regard in this action. One can only say that that is a situation which W S Gilbert would have found ripe, but is otherwise unattractive; and perhaps the Lord Chancellor's committee may find an acceptable improvement.

Law Reform Committee: Nineteenth Report[7]

17   Rectification   The evidence received by the Committee has been predominantly in favour of conferring on the court of construction some power to rectify a will so as to make it accord with what the testator intended. With this we agree: the facts in *Re Morris*[8] speak for themselves. But it is one thing to say that the court should have some such power; it is something very different to prescribe what limits, if any, there should be on the circumstances in which it should be exercisable, or the nature of the evidence which should be adduced before the court is satisfied that rectification is called for. Those who have submitted evidence to us are divided on these questions, and we ourselves have not found them easy to resolve. . . .

19   Clerical errors   Where there is a demonstrable clerical error, the case for rectification seems to us to be unanswerable. If (and it may be a big 'if') it can be proved

---

7. 'Interpretation of Wills', (1973) Cmnd 5301.
8. P 85 ante.

that '£100' in the will is a clerical error and that '£1,000' was meant, there can in our view be no grounds on which the court ought to be debarred from giving effect to what the testator meant. How his true intention should be provable is another question, which we consider below. At this stage, it is sufficient to say that we see no difference in principle between a slip made by the testator himself, his solicitor, or the typist of either.

20 Misunderstanding of the testator's instructions[9] This is a more difficult case. One may suppose, for example, that the testator has instructed his solicitor to draw his will in such a way as to leave certain property to X. The solicitor, failing to understand what is wanted, draws the will in such a way as to leave the property to Y, and the testator, not appreciating the mistake, executes the will. To some extent, this situation overlaps the next one, where the testator (and possibly his solicitor as well) fails to understand the legal effect of the words actually used, and thus produces the wrong result, though using the intended expression. But there does appear to us to be a real distinction between the two kinds of error, even though they may often co-exist. In the first case, the testator's intention is apparently frustrated solely because his solicitor has failed to ascertain what it is; in the second, all concerned may know what the testator wants, but fail to use the right technique to achieve it.

21 In our view, where it can be established, first, that the will fails to embody the testator's instructions, and secondly what those instructions were, it ought to be open to the court to rectify the will so as to make it embody them. Those instructions, if faithfully carried out, may not achieve what the testator really wanted. That is another question. But if the testator said to his solicitor: 'I want my wife to have my house for her life and then it is to go to my son John', and if the solicitor draws a will which, on its literal construction, leaves the house to the wife absolutely, then we see no reason why the court should not be able to rectify the will. Once again, how the testator's instructions are to be proved, and whether he may have changed his mind between giving them and executing the will, are questions which do not affect the principle.

22 Failure to appreciate the effect of the words used The typical case here is the unintended life interest, created by a holograph will leaving 'all my property to my wife and, after her death, to my son John'. It may be demonstrable that what the testator really meant was that his widow should take all absolutely, and that John should take anything left when she died. In principle, this differs from the last case only to the extent that there is no interposition of a professional adviser; in a more complicated case, even if both testator and solicitor are fully agreed on the words to be used and their likely effect in law, both may be wrong.

23 This seems to us to be more a matter of construction than of rectification. . . . But we do not consider that rectification is an appropriate remedy where it cannot be shown that the words of the will are not those which the testator meant to use, or intended to be used on his behalf. To go beyond that is to pass into the wider realm of the testator's purpose.

28 Restrictions on evidence We are very conscious of the argument that if the doctrine of rectification is applied to wills in the way that we recommend, there may be a temptation for those whom a will disappoints to 'have a go' on insufficient material. Even if no court would look seriously at the claim, nervous or impatient executors and beneficiaries might feel the pressure to compromise the claim, even if only at its nuisance value. We think that this argument may be exaggerated; but it raises the further question whether there ought to be any specific rules confining the admissible evidence to particular categories. Three such possible categories which have been suggested are—
   (i) evidence related to the instructions for the will;

---

9. In *Re Morris* [1971] P 62 at p 80, [1970] 1 All ER 1057 at p 1066, Latey J considered this form of mistake, but as it was not germane to the facts in issue, he left the point open although clearly favouring the view that such mistakes should be treated in the same way as clerical errors.

(ii) evidence arising before the execution of the will; and

(iii) written evidence.

29   While we find it attractive to restrict the admissible evidence to that which is connected in some way with the instructions for the will, we do not think this would be practicable. In the first place, much cogent evidence would not fall into this category: for example, the testator may have written to his stockbroker or accountant in terms which demonstrate conclusively what he thinks he has told his solicitor to put into his will. Equally, where the testator has drawn his own will, there will have been no instructions; yet the evidence of contemporary correspondence as to his purpose and intention may be overwhelming.

30   Any kind of time-barrier also seems to us unrealistic. A letter to the testator's accountant written the day after the execution of the will may be just as cogent as one written the day before. Either both should be admitted or both excluded. The same argument applies to oral statements: many testators give no written instructions and speak, rather than write, to their stockbrokers and accountants. Obviously, written communications are much more reliable than oral, and contemporaneous statements will be more reliable than subsequent ones; but we see no difference in principle between oral and written communications, or between those which are previous, contemporaneous or subsequent. All these factors go to their weight, but should not affect their admissibility.

Administration of Justice Act 1982

20. Rectification[10]

(1) If a court is satisfied that a will is so expressed that it fails to carry out the testator's intentions, in consequence—

(a) of a clerical error; or

(b) of a failure to understand his instructions,

it may order that the will shall be rectified so as to carry out his intentions.[11]

(2) An application for an order under this section shall not, except with the permission of the court, be made after the end of the period of six months from the date on which representation with respect to the estate of the deceased is first taken out.

(3) The provisions of this section shall not render the personal representatives of a deceased person liable for having distributed any part of the estate of the deceased, after the end of the period of six months from the date on which representation with respect to the estate of the deceased is first taken out, on the ground that they ought to have taken into account the possibility that the court might permit the making of an application for an order under this section after the end of that period; but this subsection shall not prejudice any power to recover, by reason of the making of an order under this section, any part of the estate so distributed.[12]

QUESTIONS

1. The day before departing on a round the world sailing trip, Archie wrote on a scrap of paper: 'In case I don't come back, I want my girlfriend Jane to have

10. The section came into force on 1 January 1983 for testators dying on or after that date: AJA 1982 s 73(6) and 76(11).

11. Rectification is therefore still impossible for the beneficiary who suffers loss through his own or his draftsman's failure to appreciate the legal effect of the words he has used.

12. Applications for rectification are to be made to the registrar (unless a probate action has commenced) and must be supported by an affidavit setting out the grounds of the application together with such evidence as can be obtained as to the testator's intention and the nature of the mistake: Non-Contentious Probate (Amendment) Rules 1983, SI 1983/623.

everything I possess'. He signed the paper and two sailing friends also signed as witnesses. Two days after departure, Archie was drowned in a storm. Will the paper have any testamentary effect? Would your answer be different if Archie had died in a car accident the day after his return?

2. Trevor, bedridden for the last few years of his life, died recently aged 90, leaving a will wholly in favour of his housekeeper Harriet, a dominating woman of whom he had seemed to be afraid. John, Trevor's nephew and only near relative discovers that it was Harriet who had written to Trevor's solicitor with his instructions for the will and she had also been present when the solicitor called with the will for Trevor to execute it. Has John any grounds for contesting the will?

3. Compare *Re Meyer* with *Guardian Trust & Executors Company of New Zealand v Inwood* (p 82 ante). Which decision do you prefer? Would the latter case have been decided differently if Jane Remington had accidently signed a stranger's will which happened to be substantially the same as hers? Or if instead of a will she had signed a mortgage document thinking it was her will?

4. For a general discussion of the provisions of Administration of Justice Act 1982 s 20 see Mithani 'Rectification of Wills' (1983) 80 LSG 2589. He argues that the section is too restricted in its application and should also apply to instances of fraud and undue influence. Do you agree?

CHAPTER 8

Wills – formal requirements

1 Introduction

Before 1838 there was a bewildering assortment of formal requirements governing the making of wills, the appropriate formality depending on the nature or value of the property in some cases, the circumstances of the testator in others, and sometimes even on the nature of the testator's directions. The Real Property Commissioners considered this problem in their Fourth Report[1] and recommended one common set of formalities to govern all situations;[2] their recommendations were embodied in Wills Act 1837, s 9 which remained largely untouched until 1983. By then growing concern had been expressed about the number of wills that were failing to obtain probate through want of compliance with these statutory requirements; a Law Reform Committee had been set up to look into the matter, and the result was a revised version of s 9 incorporating a relaxation of the requirements in two fairly minor respects. The modest nature of the reform surprised many critics, some of whom had been advocating a substantial relaxation of the requirements, as in many other common law countries, whilst others had been urging the other extreme of compulsory notarial certification of wills, a feature of many civil law jurisdictions.

Real Property Commissioners: Fourth Report[3]

There are ten different laws for regulating the execution of Wills under different circumstances. . . .

The unnecessary multiplication of rules has the effect of diminishing the respect which ought to be entertained for the Laws, because it tends to create litigation when there is no substantial question in dispute. It also occasions mistakes which defeat lawful and proper intentions. A person who has seen copyhold and leasehold estates, and personal property of great value, pass by an unattested Will, is induced to believe that freehold land may be devised in the same manner, and if he considers it right, as a measure of prudence, to procure the attestation of witnesses, he will not think it necessary to have three witnesses, when he has never seen a deed attested by more than two.

Perhaps the most serious evil produced by such mistakes is the rendering a Will void as to some property intended to be comprised in it, while it is valid as to other property. A

---

1. Of 1833.
2. Except the wills of soldiers in actual military service and seamen at sea; their wills remained exempt from any formal requirements, see Ch 9 post.
3. 1833, p 12.

Will is commonly of the whole property of the Testator for the benefit of all his family; and his intentions may be defeated to a greater extent by giving a partial effect to the Will, than by totally setting it aside. . . .

There appears to be no good reason for making any distinction between the forms required for the execution of Wills, with respect to different descriptions of property. All Wills are open to the same danger of forgery and fraud, and their genuineness depends on the same circumstances.

We think it of great importance that, as a general rule, Wills of every description should be required to be executed according to one simple form which may be easily and generally understood.

[Wills Act 1837

9. Every will to be in writing and signed or acknowledged by the testator in the presence of two witnesses
No will shall be valid unless it shall be in writing and executed in manner hereinafter mentioned; (that is to say) it shall be signed at the foot or end thereof by the testator, or by some other person in his presence and by his direction; and such signature shall be made or acknowledged by the testator in the presence of two or more witnesses present at the same time, and such witnesses shall attest and shall subscribe the will in the presence of the testator, but no form of attestation shall be necessary.][4]

Law Reform Committee: Twenty-Second Report[5]

2.2 Present law In considering whether these formalities should be retained or relaxed, and if so to what extent, we took as our starting point the principle that the purposes of the law are, first, to ensure that documents genuinely representing the testator's intentions should be valid and secondly, to prevent the admission to probate of wills which, because they are forged or for any other reason, do not represent the true wishes of the testator . . . most of our witnesses thought that the present rules achieved the right balance between these two aims. It is of course important that the law should be clear and certain, and on the whole we do not think that it places unnecessary restraints on testators. The existing requirements import an element of formality or ceremony into the making of a will which we think is appropriate for so important an act as the disposition of an estate. Moreover the evidence we received supported the view that the present rules provide a safeguard not only against forgery and undue influence, but against hasty or ill-considered dispositions which can lead to family dissension and consequent litigation.

2.3 Although we therefore consider that some degree of formality is appropriate to the execution of a will, we recognise that there are cases where a will which in fact represents the testator's true intention fails for technical reasons, and that to this extent the law does not achieve its object.

Wills Act 1837

9.[6] Signing and attestation of wills
No will shall be valid unless—

4. Replaced for testators dying after 1982 by a revised version (see post) substituted by AJA 1982 s 17.
5. 'The Making and Revocation of Wills' (1980) Cmnd 7902.
6. As substituted by AJA 1982 s 17. The amendments thereby introduced were those recommended by the Law Reform Committee and are considered at p 94 and p 101 post; they take effect in relation to the wills of testators dying after 1982.

   (a) it is in writing, and signed by the testator, or by some other person in his presence and by his direction; and

   (b) it appears that the testator intended by his signature to give effect to the will; and

   (c) the signature is made or acknowledged by the testator in the presence of two or more witnesses present at the same time; and

   (d) each witness either

      (i) attests and signs the will; or

      (ii) acknowledges his signature, in the presence of the testator (but not necessarily in the presence of any other witness),

but no form of attestation shall be necessary.

2   Writing

The Real Property Commissioners had recommended that all wills be made in writing, finding that even where it was possible to do so 'the power of making a nuncupative[7] Will is very rarely exercised and in the present general state of education can scarcely ever be required.'[8] The requirement for writing does not demand the testator's own handwriting;[9] the word is given a wide statutory interpretation in the Interpretation Act 1978.

Interpretation Act 1978

5. Definitions
In any Act, unless the contrary intention appears, words and expressions listed in Schedule 1 to this Act are to be construed according to that Schedule.

Schedule I

'Writing' includes typing, printing, lithography, photography and other modes of representing or reproducing words in a visible form, and expressions referring to writing are construed accordingly.

3   Signed by the testator

The will must be signed by the testator or by some other person in his presence and by his direction.

(a) What constitutes a signature?

This requirement has been interpreted flexibly by the courts; it does not mean that the deceased actually has to write his name, but whatever mark he does put on the document must be intended by him to represent his signature.

---

7. le oral.
8. Fourth Report (1833), p 16.
9. Where the testator does write the will out in his own hand it is technically known as a holograph will.

In the Estate of Cook [1960] 1 All ER 689, [1960] 1 WLR 353, PD; Collingwood J

The testatrix signed her will simply 'Your loving Mother'; it was duly attested. **Held:** It should be admitted to probate; she intended these words to represent her signature.

Collingwood J: Counsel for the plaintiff has referred me to several authorities, the most important of which is *In the Goods of Sperling* ((1863) 3 Sw & Tr 272). That was a case where the deceased having signed his will in the presence of a servant, the servant described himself as 'Servant to Mr. Sperling', not writing his name or giving any further identification. That was held to be a sufficient attestation and subscription and Wilde J, giving the short judgment said (at p 273):

'I think that there is a sufficient attestation and subscription. I am satisfied that Saunders [ie the servant] wrote the words which appear on the will, intending thereby an identification of himself as the person attesting.'

I think that the same test would be applicable to the case of a testator. In *Baker v Denning* ((1838) 8 Ad & E 94) the headnote read as follows:

'Under the Statute of Frauds [1677] the making of a mark by a devisor, to a will of real estate, is a sufficient signing; and it is not necessary to prove that he could not write his name at the time'.

In his judgment Coleridge J said (at p 98):

'I should be sorry if our decision were to lead to the practice of substituting a mark for a name, for this might give much opportunity for fraud. But here we are on the question of law, whether, if a party make his mark, that be a signature, although he could have written his name. How can we say that it is not, when we look at the statute [ie, the Statute of Frauds, 1677] and find what is admitted in argument? The statute has only the word 'signed'; and it is admitted that, in some cases, this is satisfied by a mark. When I consider the inconvenience which would result from inquiring, in all cases, whether the party who has made a mark could write at all, or could write at a particular time, I think it would be wrong to raise a doubt by granting a rule.'

Then, in *In the Goods of Redding (otherwise Higgins)* ((1850) 2 Rob Eccl 339) the headnote reads:

'A testatrix, having duly executed her will under an assumed name, subsequently altered the will by erasing that name, and signing her true name; but the witnesses did not subscribe the will as altered. Probate was granted of the will as it originally stood, as the court considered the assumed name might be regarded as the mark of the testatrix'.

Finally, there is the decision in *Hindmarsh v Charlton* ((1861) 8 HL Cas 160) where Lord Campbell LC, in the course of his opinion said (at p 167):

'I will lay down this as my notion of the law: that to make a valid subscription of a witness, there must either be the name or some mark which is intended to represent the name.'

Applying those principles to the present case, I am quite satisfied here that the words 'Your loving mother' were meant to represent the name of Emma Edith Cook, the testatrix, and, accordingly, I pronounce for the will.

In **Re Chalcraft** [1948] P 222, [1948] 1 All ER 700, the testatrix was on her deathbed and had just been given a large dose of morphia. A codicil to her will was handed to her for signing; she wrote part of her name but was too weak to finish it, so that it read 'E. Chal' instead of 'E. Chalcraft'. The attesting witnesses quickly signed in her presence and shortly afterwards she became unconscious. Upholding the document as a validly executed codicil, Willmer J said, at p 702:

> In my opinion, I must have regard to all the facts of this case—the fact that this lady was in an extremely weak condition and was lying, if not quite on her back, very nearly on her back, in a position in which it must have been very difficult to write at all. I must ask myself the question whether on all the facts I can draw the inference that what she wrote was intended by her to be the best she could do by way of writing her name. If I come to that conclusion, then I think I ought to accept this writing of 'E. Chal' as being in law the signature of the deceased. Bearing in mind all the circumstances of the case—the weakness of the deceased, the difficulty of writing in that position—I come to the conclusion that this mark 'E. Chal' on this document does amount, in all the circumstances, to a signature on the part of the deceased.[10]

(b) Place of signature

As originally drawn,[11] s 9 required the testator to 'sign at the foot or end' of the will, a requirement that was relaxed by the Wills Act Amendment Act 1852 which, with one important exception, validated any signature provided it was 'apparent on the face of the will that the testator intended to give effect by such his signature to the writing signed as his will.'[12] The exception related to a signature at the top of the will which was not to be accepted as effective, and over the years this exception caused a number of wills to fail.[13] When the Law Reform Committee was considering the formalities for making a will, it was an obvious candidate for their attention and in fact formed one of their two recommendations for reform, now embodied in the revised version of s 9. In the case of testators dying after 1982,[14] all that is necessary is that 'it appear that the testator intended by his signature to give effect to the will';[15] the Wills Act Amendment Act 1852 has been repealed.[16]

Law Reform Committee: Twenty-Second Report[17]

2.8   The position of the testator's signature   Whilst we accept that the end of the narrative is the normal place for putting the signature on any document, we see no compelling reason why a will should be invalid where the signature is at the top. The original reason for providing that the signature should be at the end of the will may have been to ensure that testators did not leave space in which to add further dispositions after execution. However those who use printed will forms[18] often leave a large space between

---

10. Cf *Re Colling* [1972] 3 All ER 729, [1972] 1 WLR 1440, p 102 post where the testator's partial signing of his name was not intended to represent his name as was evidenced by the fact that he subsequently went on to complete the signature.
11. See p 91 ante.
12. S 1.
13. Eg *Re Stalman* (1931) 145 LT 339, *Re Harris* [1952] P 319, [1952] 2 All ER 409, *Re Beadle* [1974] 1 All ER 493, [1974] 1 WLR 417.
14. AJA 1982 s 73(6), s 76(11).
15. See p 91 ante. As a result the courts should no longer have to indulge in the mental gymnastics they sometimes performed to prevent a signature from invalidating the will by virtue only of its position: see eg *Re Hornby* [1946] P 171, [1946] 2 All ER 150, *Re Roberts* [1934] P 102.
16. AJA 1982, s 75 Sch 9, Pt I.
17. 'The Making and Revocation of Wills' (1980) Cmnd 7902.
18. See p 56 n 10 ante.

the end of the narrative and the signature, so that the present rule does not necessarily avoid this danger. Moreover, section 1 of the 1852 Act makes it clear that the validity of a will cannot be challenged merely by the existence of such a space, which reinforces our conclusion that whatever the original reasons for the rule were, it is no longer necessary. The survey to which we have referred[19] showed that of the 93 wills that were rejected for failure to comply with the strict formalities, 8 failed because the testator's signature was incorrectly placed. In our view, the test should simply be whether the testator intended his signature to give effect to his will, regardless of where that signature was placed. We therefore conclude and recommend that a will should be admitted to probate if it is apparent on the face of the will that the testator intended his signature to validate it. It is our view that, if this conclusion is accepted, the cumbersome provision contained in the 1852 Act can be repealed.

In **In the Estate of Bean** [1944] P 83, [1944] 2 All ER 348,[20] the testator made his will on a printed will form.[1] There was a place indicated on the form for the testator's signature, but he did not sign there. He wrote his name, address and the date on the back of the form and also on an envelope which was lying near the form at the time. The witnesses then signed their names at the place indicated on the will form for that purpose. Holding that neither the writing of his name on the back of the form nor on the envelope constituted the testator's signature to the will, Hodson J said at p 349:

The executrix has sworn that she did not know that the deceased had not signed the will form, and it appears to me to be plain that this omission on the part of the deceased was purely accidental in that he failed to sign his name in the space provided for the purpose. The writing on the envelope was equally clearly, I think, put there for the purpose of identifying the contents of the envelope and not as a signature at all. The deceased never indicated that the testamentary document and the envelope together constituted his will. He had written his name not only on the envelope, but also on the indorsement which appears on the back sheet. It is true that the indorsement was not visible to the attesting witness whereas the writing on the envelope was seen. Nevertheless, in my opinion, it is impossible to be satisfied that the deceased intended to give effect to the will by writing on the envelope since in all probability, he, like the executrix, was under the impression that he had already signed the will on the form itself.

(c) The rule of connection

Where the will is written on more than one piece of paper the courts have developed a rule that requires the various pieces to be connected in some way at the moment of execution if all are to be validated by the signature in question. Only one exception to the rule, the so-called 'envelope' exception, has been generally accepted although there is some authority to suggest that it may be sufficient if all the pieces, albeit unconnected, are in the same room at the time of execution.

---

19. This was a three month survey of all wills submitted to probate in England and Wales, carried out for the Law Reform Committee by the Senior Registrar of the Family Division. The results are set out in Annex 2 of the Report and indicate that of the 40,664 wills submitted to probate during the period, 97 were rejected, 93 of which were for failure to comply with the formalities. Of the 97 failures, 69 were made on printed will forms, 22 were other home-made wills and 6 were professionally drawn.
20. Decided before the passing of the AJA 1982 but the same decision would have been reached under the redrawn version of WA 1837 s 9, see p 91 ante.
1. See p 56 n 10 ante.

In **Re Little** [1960] 1 All ER 387, [1960] 1 WLR 495, the will was written on five sheets of paper which were not fastened together as such at the moment of execution but the other four sheets were beneath the fifth sheet on which the testator made his signature. Sachs J held that all five sheets should be admitted to probate, saying at p 391:

There was clear evidence, wholly undisputed, that, during the period of signing, the five sheets were pressed together on the table by the deceased. In my view, even though there was no mechanical attachment between those sheets, such a pressing provides a sufficient nexus between all five of them for the purpose of establishing that there was a single testamentary document. In that behalf I follow the lead given in *Lewis v Lewis* ([1908] P 1) where it was stated that two pieces of paper being held together for the moment by the testator's finger and thumb was a sufficient nexus.

In the Goods of Mann [1942] P 146, [1942] 2 All ER 193, PD; Langton J

In the presence of two witnesses, the testatrix wrote out her will in her own handwriting on a piece of paper, but she did not sign the paper. She then wrote on an envelope: 'The last will and testament of Jane Catherine Mann', her name. She then pointed out to the two witnesses that the documents she had written were her will and asked them to sign their names as witnesses to it. They then signed the paper under the attestation clause it contained; there was no testimonium clause. She then put the paper in the envelope.

Held: She clearly intended the signature on the envelope to constitute the signature to her will despite the fact that the paper was not connected to the envelope at the time when she signed the latter document.

Langton J: The courts have laid down and held fast to the rule that no document can be allowed to form part of a will which was not physically or otherwise connected to the signed portion of the will at the moment of signature . . . .

The rule as to attachment, physically or otherwise, of the documents is clearly designed to obviate the possibility of fraud. In this case it has been urged upon me, without undue insistence, by counsel opposing the grant that any relaxations of the just and salutary rule of long-standing might open an undesirable door. Speaking generally, I am not much impressed by forensic forebodings of indeterminate future disaster. I have a comforting conviction that the judges who succeed me will prove able to safeguard the law, but in this instance I own to a certain feeling of uneasiness lest the relaxation of a good rule in a most exceptional case should amount to good news for bad people by making it appear that this court was now less jealous than of yore to secure the door against fraud.

Therefore, although I am prepared to order that this will be admitted to probate by accepting the signature on the envelope as the signature to the will, I desire to draw attention pointedly to the very exceptional circumstances which have impelled me to this course. To begin with, the rule as to attachment of documents is . . . a rule intended as security against fraud. Where the circumstances are so plain and so well-ascertained as to preclude all possibility of fraud, the reasons supporting the strict application of the rule are greatly diminished. I do not say that they altogether disappear, for there is always a certain safeguard against subsequent possibilities of fraud in the preservation of an unvarying rule. Secondly, if an unattached paper is to be admitted at all, there is much to be said in favour of an envelope which may reasonably be held to have a far closer relationship to a document which it encloses than a second and wholly disconnected piece of paper. Envelopes are, by their nature, designed to have what may be described as a dependent and secondary existence rather than an independent and primary life of their own. This consideration clearly distinguishes the present case from

In the Goods of Hatton[2] ((1881) 6 PD 204). Thirdly, the will in the present case is a holograph document,[3] and was written with the same pen and on the same occasion as the envelope. Fourthly, both paper and envelope were written in the presence of the attesting witnesses, the first witness being present during the whole of the writing of both documents, and the second during the writing of the envelope and the latter part of the dispositive paper. Finally, the history of the documents between the time of their making and the date of death of the testatrix has been clearly ascertained and provides strong confirmatory evidence of the completely genuine nature of the transaction. It is always imprudent to attempt anything in the nature of prophecy in matters of this description, but it is difficult to imagine that circumstances of this kind will easily or frequently repeat themselves, and in this reflection I find a certain measure of consolation in departing reluctantly from a rule which I believe to be both salutary and wise.[4]

In **In the Goods of Tiernan** [1942] IR 572, the will consisted of three separate sheets of paper, only one of which had been signed by the testator and the witnesses, and this one sheet contained only the attestation clause and the signatures. There was no evidence to suggest that the three sheets had been connected in any way at the time when those signatures were made, indeed the witnesses could not recall seeing the other two sheets at all. Hanna J nevertheless admitted all three sheets to probate as the testator's will on the presumption that the whole will was in the room and under the testator's control at the time of execution, saying at p 578:

The earliest case that I can find that is relevant to the point is in 1765—the case of *Bond v Seawell* ((1765) 3 Burr 1773). In that case the witnesses never saw the first sheet of the will, nor was the same or any other paper on the table, but they were shown the codicil and the last sheet of the will which they attested. The headnote of the case, inserted in the English Reports, Vol 97, p 1092, is as follows:

'It may be presumed when the witnesses only saw the last sheet of the will that the whole will was in the room.'

Lord Mansfield, who gave the judgment in the case, stated he had a conference with all the Judges (except one) upon this subject, and, after indicating that it was not necessary that each page or sheet should be particularly shown to the witnesses, he said:

"But the fact 'whether the first sheet of his will was or was not in the room at the time of executing and attesting the latter' may be material to be known. If it was, the jury ought to find for the will generally; and they ought to find all things favourable to the will. If it be doubtful 'whether the first sheet was then in the room or not'; we all think the circumstances sufficient to presume 'that it was in the room' and 'that the jury ought to be so directed.'"

This is an important decision, for the sheets were not attached, and only the sheet which was attested by the witnesses was signed. It differs in the facts from the case under

---

2. In that case the will was written in duplicate; one copy was signed by the testator and the other copy by the attesting witnesses. Hannen P held that whilst a will might be made up of numerous papers which together comprised one instrument, 'these are separate and independent documents' (p 204) and probate was refused.

3. Ie written in the testator's handwriting.

4. In both *Re Bean* [1944] P 83, [1944] 2 All ER 348, p 95 ante, and *Re Beadle* [1974] 1 All ER 493, [1974] 1 WLR 417 this 'envelope' exception to the rule of connection was accepted by the respective first instance judges but the wills in question failed to obtain probate because in neither case was the court satisfied that the signature on the envelope was intended to be a signature to the will as a whole.

consideration where the witnesses only saw a blank attestation sheet, but the established principle should, I think, apply.[5]

4   Witnessed

The testator's signature must be made or acknowledged in the joint presence of two or more witnesses who must then sign or acknowledge their signatures in the testator's presence.[6]

Real Property Commissioners: Fourth Report[7]

There is no written Instrument which stands so much in need of the protection afforded by the attestation of witnesses, as a Will. If it is considered expedient for Deeds, it must be allowed to be much more necessary for Wills. Deeds are usually made between several parties, and are acted upon immediately or while the parties are alive; they must have been executed at a time generally known, are often protected by valuable considerations and antecedent treaties, and usually affect only a part and sometimes only a small part of the persons by whom they are made. On the contrary, a Will does not appear until after the death of the only person who is necessarily aware of its existence; it may by possibility have been executed at any time during the life of the testator that a fabricator may think it most safe to fix upon, and it usually disposes of the whole property of the testator. Forgery is not the only, nor by much the most usual, question affecting the validity of a Will. The incapacity of the Testator, or the circumstances of fraud or coercion under which a false Will may have been obtained, and which may be attempted to be disproved by perjury, render the validity of a Will one of the most complicated and perplexing subjects of litigation, and make it particularly necessary to require the protection of attesting witnesses . . . These considerations induce us to recommend that every Will shall be attested, and we think it expedient and sufficient to require two witnesses.

Where more than one witness is required, there is the greater probability that a witness will be living at the death of the testator, and a greater difficulty is opposed to the fabrication of a Will. If a Will be forged, the same person may write the false Will, and affix his own signature as a witness. The protection against forgery is greatly increased by requiring a second witness, on account of the difficulty of engaging an accomplice, the necessity of rewarding him, and the danger to be apprehended from his giving information, or not being able to elude a discovery of the fraud by a searching cross-examination.[8]

---

5. Neither *Bond v Seawell* nor *Re Tiernan* itself was mentioned in *Re Mann* p 96 ante. In *Re Little* p 96 ante Sachs J referred at p 391 to Hanna J's careful judgment in *Re Tiernan*, but on the facts before him there was no need for the plaintiff to rely on Hanna J's presumption, so he did not consider it further.

6. This requirement was in the original form of WA 1837, s 9 as well as the version substituted by AJA 1982, s 17 p 91 ante, save that it was only by virtue of the latter Act that witnesses were able to acknowledge their signatures.

7. 1833, p 17.

8. The Law Reform Committee in their 22nd Report, 'The Making and Revocation of Wills' Cmnd 7902 evidently agreed with this, stating at para 2.9: 'We think that a rule requiring two witnesses provides a greater safeguard against forgery and undue influence than would a rule requiring only one. The present law is generally well known and we see no reason to recommend that it should be altered.'

(a) Who can be a witness?

It seems that anyone except a blind person can be a witness. A beneficiary under the will or a spouse of a beneficiary is an effective witness but by Wills Act 1837, s 15 the gift to the beneficiary is void.[9]

Wills Act 1837

14. Will not void on account of incompetency of witness
If any person who shall attest the execution of a will shall at the time of the execution thereof or at any time afterwards be incompetent to be admitted a witness to prove the execution thereof, such will shall not on that account be invalid.[10]

16. Creditor attesting to be admitted a witness
In case by any will any real or personal estate shall be charged with any debt or debts, and any creditor, or the wife or husband of any creditor, whose debt is so charged, shall attest the execution of such will, such creditor notwithstanding such charge shall be admitted a witness to prove the execution of such will, or to prove the validity or invalidity thereof.

17. Executor shall be admitted a witness

. . . No person shall, on account of his being an executor of a will, be incompetent to be admitted a witness to prove the execution of such will, or a witness to prove the validity or invalidity thereof.

In **In the Estate of Gibson** [1949] P 434, [1949] 2 All ER 90, the question before Pearce J was whether a blind man could be a witness: He said at p 91:

There is no direct authority on the capacity of a blind man to witness a will. The normal meaning of 'attesting' is testifying or bearing witness to something, and the normal meaning of 'witness' is one who is a spectator of an incident or one who is present at an incident. Is mere presence, without the faculty of sight, enough to constitute a person as 'witness' for the purposes of s 9? And is an act which he cannot see done 'in his presence'? The object of the Act is clear. One witness is not enough. The presence of two witnesses is made necessary to give certainty and avoid fraud. In the light of commonsense and without any authority I should be inclined to hold that for the purposes of the Act a 'witness' means one who, in regard to things audible, has the faculty of hearing, and in regard to things visible, has the faculty of seeing. The signing of a will is a visible matter, and, therefore, I think a will is not signed 'in the presence of' a blind person, nor is he a 'witness' for the purposes of the section.

(b) What constitutes an acknowledgement by the testator?

If the testator has not signed in the simultaneous presence of both witnesses, he must have acknowledged his signature in their joint presence. He may do so expressly or the acknowledgement may be implied from the circumstances.

In **Keigwin v Keigwin** (1843) 3 Curt 607, 163 ER 841, Fust J outlined the circumstances in issue in that case, at p 842:

---

9. See p 359 post.
10. The meaning of this section is regarded as doubtful, see Mellows pp 84–85. It has been suggested that it adverts not to mental competence but to those persons who were by law in 1837 incompetent to give evidence in court, such as persons of no religious belief: see Williams, Mortimer and Sunnucks, p 134.

They were at work in a room in the deceased's house; she brought this paper into that room, and addressing them both, said, 'I want you to sign this paper,' and pointed out the place where they were to sign; they both observed her name signed thereto; they have no doubt whatever that the paper produced to them by the deceased had been signed by her; but they do not recollect that she pointed out the signature to them as being her name; they are sure she did not say anything in particular about her handwriting. The question comes to this, whether this will has been duly executed according to the requisites of the statute; the deceased did produce this paper, having her signature affixed to it at the time, to two witnesses present at the same time; and the two witnesses did attest it in her presence; was this a sufficient acknowledgement? I am clearly of opinion that it was; it is not necessary that the party should say in express terms 'that is my signature'; it is sufficient if it clearly appears that the signature was existent when they did, at her request, subscribe the will. On these circumstances, I hold that this paper has been sufficiently executed.

(c) The simultaneous presence of the witnesses

The need for the witnesses to be present at the same time when the testator signs or acknowledges his signature was emphasised by the Real Property Commissioners in 1833; their presence on separate occasions will not suffice. In 1966 the Law Commission drew attention to the hardship that strict compliance with this requirement was causing, but to no avail; the Law Reform Committee had no recommendation to make on this score.

Real Property Commissioners: Fourth Report[11]

It is important that the competency of the Testator at the time of execution of his Will should be satisfactorily established; and if the transaction must be witnessed by both witnesses at one time, they must then agree in the same story, and perjury will be more easily detected by cross-examination.

We therefore propose that every Will should be signed by the Testator in the presence of, or the signature acknowledged to, two witnesses present at one time.[12]

Law Commission Working Paper: Should English Wills be Registrable?[13]

43. During the year beginning 28th September 1961 approximately 9,600 wills were submitted to the Personal Application Department of the Principal Probate Registry at Somerset House. Probate was refused in only 52 cases, in 31 of which the only defect in the execution was that the will had been produced by the testator to each attesting witness separately. In five other cases the witnesses were not 'present at the same time' but the will was invalid for other reasons as well.

44. In view of the fact that a number of home-made wills are invalidated each year for non-compliance with this requirement and the probability that many more would be if the true situation were known, it seems right to consider whether the requirements of s 9 about attesting witnesses could safely be relaxed by amending legislation.

---

11. 1833, p 18.
12. The Real Property Commissioners further recommended that the witnesses should subscribe in each other's presence for the same reason, although not necessarily in the testator's presence; as will be seen (p 102 post) the recommendation was not followed.
13. (1966) PW P 4.

Re Groffman [1969] 2 All ER 108, [1969] 1 WLR 733, a few years later provided a further example of the situation to which the Law Commission had drawn attention. The testator had signed his will when by himself and had put it in his pocket. He then asked his friends, A and B, to witness it. They had not seen him sign it, but he pointed to his pocket where the document was. He went into another room with A, but not with B, took the will from his pocket and asked A to sign it. A could see the testator's signature; he signed the will and went out of the room. B then came in; he also saw the testator's signature and signed the document. Simon P reluctantly held that the will was invalid. The testator's signature had not been acknowledged in the presence of both witnesses when they were together and the testator's earlier indication of his pocket could not constitute an acknowledgement of his signature because A and B had not seen the document or the testator's signature at that stage. As Simon P sadly remarked at p 111:

As must appear from the fact that I have been satisfied that the document does represent the testamentary intentions of the deceased, I would very gladly find in its favour; but I am bound to apply the Act, which has been enacted by Parliament for good reason.

Law Reform Committee: Twenty-Second Report[14]

2.10   The attestation requirements   A number of those who submitted evidence to us thought that this rule was unnecessary and that the law should merely require the testator to write or to acknowledge his signature in the presence of each witness, but not necessarily the two together. However, we do not consider that this requirement causes any great injustice and on the whole we think it is right that the three necessary participants in the 'ritual' of execution of a will should be present together during the essential part of it, namely the signature or acknowledgement of his signature by the testator.[15]

(d) The witnesses must sign or acknowledge their signatures

This step must be carried out after the testator has signed or acknowledged his signature to them jointly. Before 1983 a witness could not acknowledge his signature[16] with the result that if he signed before the testator had signed (or acknowledged his signature) in their joint presence, the will would fail[17] unless that witness signed again afterwards. A number of wills failed for this reason and so on the recommendation of the Law Reform Committee, s 9 was altered to enable witnesses to acknowledge.[18]

---

14. 'The Making and Revocation of Wills' (1980) Cmnd 7902.
15. Cf the Uniform Probate Code (USA) s 2–502 whereby the testator is not obliged to sign (or acknowledge his signature) in the joint presence of the witnesses, nor do they have to sign in his presence. Section 2–502 simply states 'Except as provided for holograph wills . . . every will shall be in writing signed by the testator or in the testator's name by some other person in the testator's presence and by his direction, and shall be signed by at least 2 persons each of whom witnessed either the signing or the testator's acknowledgement of the signature or of the will'.
16. See the original version of WA 1837 s 9 at p 91 ante.
17. As in *Hindmarsh v Charlton* (1861) 8 HL Cas 160, *Re Colling* [1972] 3 All ER 729, [1972] 1 WLR 1440, see post.
18. The alteration takes effect in relation to the wills of testators dying after 1982: AJA 1982 ss 73(6), 76(11).

Law Reform Committee: Twenty-Second Report[19]

2.11   The attestation requirements   We would like to prevent the recurrence of a case such as *re Colling* [1972] 1 WLR 1440. In that case the testator, who was a patient in hospital, asked a nurse and another patient to witness his signature but, while he was signing and before he had completed his signature, the nurse was called away to attend to another patient. The testator nevertheless continued signing and the other witness then signed. When the nurse returned, the testator and the other witness both acknowledged their signatures and the nurse then added her own signature. The will was held to be invalid and some have thought that the invalidity resulted from the failure on the part of the testator to sign in the simultaneous presence of the two witnesses. However, in our view, it was not the requirement of simultaneity which invalidated the will in *re Colling* because in that case the testator did acknowledge his signature in the presence of both witnesses. What invalidated the will was the requirement that both the attesting witnesses must subscribe after the operative signature or acknowledgement of the testator. In *Colling*, when the testator acknowledged his signature one of the witnesses had already subscribed and did not actually subscribe again although he acknowledged his earlier signature. We do not think that testators' intentions should be defeated by such a technicality. We therefore recommend that the effect of *re Colling* should be reversed by providing that an acknowledgement by a witness of his signature should have the same effect as his signature, just as under the present law a testator's acknowledgement of his signature is as operative as his actual signature. The method of making a will would then consist of two successive steps whereby the testator would sign or acknowledge his signature in the simultaneous presence of the two witnesses and the witnesses would then sign or acknowledge their respective signatures.

(e) In the presence of the testator

The witnesses must sign or acknowledge their signatures in the presence of the testator (although not necessarily in each other's presence), a requirement that is said to provide 'some safeguard against the substitution of a spurious will by one of the witnesses'[20] but it has to be said that it is in any case applied very benevolently by the courts.

In **Casson v Dade** (1781) 1 Bro CC 99, 28 ER 1010, the testatrix went to her solicitor's office to execute her will. The report continues (at p 1010):

Being asthmatical, and the office very hot, she retired to her carriage to execute the will, the witnesses attending her: after having seen the execution, they returned into the office to attest it, and the carriage was accidentally put back to the window of the office, through which, it was sworn by a person in the carriage, the testatrix might see what passed; immediately after the attestation, the witnesses took the will to her, and one of them delivered it to her, telling her they had attested it; upon which she folded it up and put it into her pocket.—The Lord Chancellor inclined very strongly to think the will well executed, and the case of *Shires v Glasscock,* 2 Salk 688 [1 Lord Raym 507], 1 Eq Abr 403, was relied upon to that purpose. Mr Arden pressed much for an issue: but, finding Lord Chancellor's opinion very decisive against him declined it.[1]

---

19. 'The Making and Revocation of Wills' (1980) Cmnd 7902.
20. Law Reform Committee: Twenty-Second Report, 'The Making and Revocation of Wills' (1980) Cmnd 7902 para 2.13.
1. One has some sympathy for Mr Arden. See also the notorious four-poster bed cases: *Newton & Thomas v Clarke* (1839) 2 Curt 320, cf *Tribe v Tribe* (1849) 1 Rob Ecc 775.

5 Attestation clause

A will does not have to contain an attestation clause[2] but it is advisable that it should do so as it is then regarded as prima facie evidence that the formal requirements have been observed.[3] Without such a clause, the probate registrar will require further evidence of due execution.[4] There is a useful presumption which may come to the rescue in the absence of such evidence viz: *omnia praesumuntur rite esse acta.*[5]

In **Harris v Knight** (1890) 15 PD 170, the testator's will contained no attestation clause. Three signatures appeared at the end, one of which appeared to be the testator's; the other two were the names of friends of the testator who had both died by the time the proceedings were brought. The Court of Appeal was prepared to presume the will duly executed, Lindley LJ saying at p 179:

> The maxim, *Omnia praesumuntur rite esse acta*, is an expression, in a short form, of a reasonable probability, and of the propriety in point of law of acting on such probability. The maxim expresses an inference which may reasonably be drawn when an intention to do some formal act is established; when the evidence is consistent with that intention having been carried into effect in a proper way; but when the actual observance of all due formalities can only be inferred as a matter of probability. The maxim is not wanted where such observance is proved, nor has it any place where such observance is disproved. The maxim only comes into operation where there is no proof one way or the other, but where it is more probable that what was intended to be done was done as it ought to have been done to render it valid; rather than that it was done in some other manner which would defeat the intention proved to exist, and would rend what is proved to have been done of no effect.[6]

In **Re Bercovitz** [1962] 1 All ER 552, [1962] 1 WLR 321, the testator had signed at the top of the will (an invalid signature before the substitutional version of s 9 was enacted[7]). He had signed again, however, at the end of the will, but the witnesses gave evidence to the effect that they only saw the signature at the top of the will and it was to attest this invalid signature that they signed. It was argued, inter alia, that the court should apply the maxim *omnia praesumuntur* to save the will, but Danckwerts LJ refused to do so, saying at p 559:

> Now in the present case, the evidence accepted by the judge is not consistent with the intention to execute the will in the proper way, and that is not established. The appearance of the will is against it, and the observance of the legal formalities required is disproved by the evidence which was accepted by the judge. So, as Lindley LJ said,[8] the presumption has no place; and I can see no reason for reversing the conclusions of the judge, who had the opportunity of seeing the witnesses.

---

2. As WA 1837, s 9 itself makes plain, see p 92 ante.
3. For an example of an attestation clause, see the specimen will at p 63 ante.
4. See NCPR 1954 r 10, p 311 post.
5. Roughly translated: 'In the absence of anything to indicate to the contrary, it is presumed that all the formalities were duly carried out.'
6. See also *In the Estate of Denning* [1958] 2 All ER 1, [1958] 1 WLR 462, *Re Webb* [1964] 2 All ER 91, [1964] 1 WLR 509, p 189 post.
7. By AJA 1982, s 17, see p 91 ante.
8. In *Harris v Knight, ante.*

6   The case for further reform

It will have been seen[9] that the reforms as to the making of wills suggested by the Law Reform Committee in their Twenty-Second Report[10] and subsequently embodied in the Administration of Justice Act 1982 were of a relatively minor nature, but the limited nature of the recommendations resulted from an extensive consultative process combined with statistical returns indicating that the size of the problem was not perhaps so great as recent notorious cases[11] had suggested that it might be.[12] The Committee did consider the following suggestions for more radical reform but as will be seen, each one was rejected.

(a) A general dispensing power

Law Reform Committee: Twenty-Second Report[13]

2.4   A dispensing power   The results of the survey[14] and indeed the evidence we received indicate that most wills which fail do so because of formal defects. One possibility, canvassed in our consultative document, would be to confer upon the courts a general dispensing power to admit a will to probate if satisfied that it was genuine, notwithstanding its failure to comply with the requirements of section 9. The evidence on this question was fairly evenly divided, the support for the proposal resting on the argument that it would provide the courts with a valuable long-stop and enable them to prevent the sort of injustice which can occur when a will which is in fact genuine is rejected.

2.5   While the idea of a dispensing power has attractions, most of us were more impressed by the argument against it, namely that by making it less certain whether or not an informally executed will is capable of being admitted to probate, it could lead to litigation, expense and delay, often in cases where it could least be afforded, for it is the home-made wills which most often go wrong. Recent legislation in South Australia[15] allows the courts just such a discretion and we have read with interest the first case in which that legislation was successfully invoked.[16]

The judgment contains an interesting discussion of the relationship between the formalities and the new discretion which in our view indicates that the courts will not find the application of their dispensing power an easy matter. We think that to attempt to cure the tiny minority of cases where things go wrong in this way might create more problems than it would solve and we have therefore concluded that a general dispensing power should not be introduced into our law of succession.[17]

Wills Act 1936–1975 (South Australia)

12.(2)   A document purporting to embody the testamentary intentions of a deceased

---

9. See pp 94–5, 102.
10. 'The Making and Revocation of Wills', (1980) Cmnd 7902.
11. Eg *Re Groffman*, p 101 ante, *Re Colling*, p 102 ante, *Re Bercovitz*, p 103 ante.
12. See p 95 n 19 ante.
13. 'The Making and Revocation of Wills', (1980) Cmnd 7902.
14. See p 95 n 19.
15. See post. For an interesting commentary on the legislation in question see Palk 'Informal Wills: From Soldiers to Citizens' (1976) 5 Adel LR 382.
16. *In Re Graham* post.
17. See also Ormiston 'Formalities and Wills: A Plea for Caution' (1980) 54 ALJ 451, advocating a very limited dispensing power. Cf the 'substantial compliance' doctrine put forward by Langbein 'Substantial Compliance with the Wills Act' (1975) 88 Harv LR p 489, advocating that even an unsigned will might be admitted to probate, depending on the circumstances.

person shall, notwithstanding that it has not been executed with the formalities required by this Act,[18] be deemed to be a will of the deceased person if the Supreme Court, upon application for admission of the document to probate as the last will of the deceased, is satisfied that there can be no reasonable doubt that the deceased intended the document to constitute his will.[19]

In Re Graham (1979) 20 SASR 198, South Australia Supreme Court; Jacobs J

The testatrix signed her will; she then handed it to her nephew and asked him 'to get it witnessed'. He took the will to two neighbours who knew the testatrix, and they both signed the document, as witnesses, in the place provided in the attestation clause. On the face of it the document appeared to be validly executed but in fact the testatrix had not signed in the witnesses' presence nor they in hers.

Held: Pursuant to Wills Act 1936–1975, s 12(2) the document should be admitted to probate.

Jacobs J: Has (Parliament), by the language it has used, opened the flood-gates to admit proof of informal testamentary documents much as they might have been proved prior to 1837, and notwithstanding s 8 of the Wills Act? I do not think it has, but neither am I persuaded that it is necessary to read down the plain and natural meaning of the words which Parliament has used in order to reach that conclusion.

In the first place, s 12(2) speaks of a document that 'has not been executed with the formalities required by this Act'. I cannot think that Parliament had in mind a document that had not been executed by the testator at all. If one reads s 12(2) with the opening words of s 8, which says that 'no will shall be valid unless it is in writing and executed in the following manner . . . ,' it is to the absence of the formalities prescribed by paragraphs (a), (b) and (c) of s 8 that Parliament is directing its attention in s 12(2), not to the execution of the will by the testator. Thus, unsigned documents which might have been admitted to probate prior to 1837 (*Huntington v Huntington* (1814) 2 Phill Ecc 213, and *Allen v Manning* (1825) 2 Add 490) would not come within the ambit of s 12(2).[20]

It was nevertheless suggested that there must be some further implied limitation, if sub-paragraphs (a), (b) and (c) of s 8 are themselves not to be swept away; and that since those provisions have been retained Parliament must have intended that there should be at least some attempted compliance with them, before s 12(2) can be successfully invoked. I can find no warrant for such a limitation in the language that Parliament has used, and indeed if it were adopted, it would defeat the present will, notwithstanding that I am clearly satisfied, in the plain terms of s 12(2), that the deceased intended the document to constitute her will. It cannot really be said that she ever *attempted* to comply with s 8 at all. She herself signed the document in the absence of witnesses, and made no 'attempt' to have them present when she signed; and far from attempting to have them both sign in her presence, she arranged for them to sign in her absence. On the face of the document, there is certainly a purported compliance with s 8, but equally clearly on the evidence there was no attempted compliance.

---

18. Contained in s 8, these formalities are in identical terms to those contained in WA 1837, s 9 before its alteration by AJA 1982, s 17 (see p 91 ante).

19. Similarly, in Queensland the Succession Act 1981 s 9 permits the court to admit to probate 'a testamentary instrument executed in substantial compliance with the formalities prescribed by this section if the Court is satisfied that the instrument expressed the testamentary intention of the testator.'

20. This dictum was subsequently followed by Mitchell J in *Baumanis v Praulin* (1980) 25 SASR 423 (South Australia Supreme Court) when he refused to apply Wills Act 1936–1975 s 12(2) in the case of a document that had not been signed by the testator at all.

But although I am not prepared to read into the section any such limitation, or any other limitation that would thereby alter the plain and natural meaning of the words, I think that the section itself contains a significant restraint, and some control against abuse of the relief which it offers, in the requirement that the Court should be 'satisfied that there can be no *reasonable doubt* that the deceased intended the document to constitute his will'. It seems to me that in most cases, the greater the departure from the requirements of formal validity dictated by s 8, that is to say, to the extent that those requirements have not been, or do not appear to have been, observed, the harder will it be for the Court to reach the required state of satisfaction. For example, I do not think I could have reached that state of satisfaction in the present case if the deceased had done no more than sign the will herself, without evidence of any other act of the kind envisaged by s 8, or that might amount at least to publication of the will. I say in most cases, because different considerations may well apply to a will which has been executed *in extremis,* eg by a person dying of thirst in the desert, or stranded in the ice-fields of Antarctica. It will be sufficient to consider such cases when they arise, but I am, for the present at least, not prepared to take any narrower view of the section than I have indicated. Upon that view I have no hesitation in making the order sought by the motion.[1]

(b) Holograph wills

Law Reform Committee: Twenty-Second Report[2]

2.22   The law of several countries, including Scotland, allows special consideration for holograph wills, ie wills written as to all essential parts by the testator in his own handwriting.[3] In Scotland such a will, provided that it is signed by the testator himself, is valid without any witnesses at all although by section 21 of the Succession (Scotland) Act 1964 it is now necessary that two persons should give evidence that the writing and the signature are in the handwriting of the testator before a holograph will can be confirmed.[4] In our consultative document we invited views as to whether the holograph form of will should be admitted to probate in England. Despite the fact that there is no evidence that holograph wills do not operate successfully elsewhere, the majority of our witnesses thought that they would be likely to be confused with draft wills. In the light of this evidence we do not see any further case for change.[5]

In **Re Kimmel's Estate** (1924) 31 ALR 678, 123 A 405, the Pennsylvania Supreme Court had to consider whether a letter written in the following terms could be said to amount to a holograph will:

'Johnstown, Dec. 12.

The Kimmel Bro. and Famly We are all well as you can espec fore the time of the Year. I received you kind & welcome letter from Geo & Irvin all OK glad you poot your Pork down in Pickle it is the true way to keep meet every piece gets the same, now always poot it down that way & you will not miss it & you will have good pork fore smoking you can keep it from butchern to butchern the hole year round. Boys, I wont agree with you

---

1. See also *In the Estate of Radziszewski* (1982) 29 SASR 256 (South Australia Supreme Court).
2. 'The Making and Revocation of Wills' (1980) Cmnd 7902.
3. See also the Uniform Probate Code (USA) s 2–503 which permits as an alternative to the witnessed will referred to at p 101, n 15 ante, a holograph will where the signature and 'material' provisions are in the handwriting of the testator. Most Canadian states provide similarly.
4. Ie admitted to probate.
5. The Real Property Commissioners in their Fourth Report (1883) at p 21 had similarly rejected the holograph will; whilst they thought it would reduce the danger of forgery, the handwriting of an entire will being more difficult to imitate than a mere signature, they decided that 'the mischiefs of making this exception from the general rule would preponderate over the benefits.'

about the open winter I think we are gone to have one of the hardest. Plenty of snow & Verry cold verry cold! I dont want to see it this way but it will will come see to the old sow & take her away when the time comes well I cant say if I will come over yet I will wright in my next letter it may be to ruff we will see in the next letter if I come I have some very valuable papers I want you to keep fore me so if enny thing hapens all the scock money in the 3 Bank liberty lones Post office stamps and my home on Horner St goes to George Darl & Irvin Kepp this letter lock it up it may help you out. Earl sent after his Christmas Tree & Trimmings I sent them he is in the Post Office in Phila. working.

Will clost your Truly,
Father.'

Admitting the letter to probate as a valid will, Simpson J said at p 680:

As is often the case in holographic wills of an informal character, much of that which is written is not dispositive; and the difficulty, in ascertaining the writer's intent, arises largely from the fact that he had little, if any, knowledge of either law, punctuation, or grammar. In the present case this is apparent from the paper itself; and in this light the language now quoted must be construed: (Quoting from the letter, he continued:) When resolved into plainer English, it is clear to us that all of the quotation, preceding the words 'I have some very valuable papers,' relate to the predicted bad weather, a doubt as to whether the decedent will be able to go to Glencoe because of it, and a possible resolution of it in his next letter; the present one stating, 'We will see in the next letter if I come.' This being so, the clause relating to the valuable papers begins a new subject of thought, and since the clearly dispositive gifts which follow are made dependent on no other contingency than 'if enny thing hapens,' and death did happen suddenly on the same day, the paper, so far as respects those gifts, must be treated as testamentary.

It is difficult to understand how the decedent, probably expecting an early demise,—as appears by the letter itself, and the fact of his sickness and inability to work during the last three days of the first or second week preceding,—could have possibly meant anything else than a testamentary gift when he said, 'so if enny thing hapens [the property specified] goes to George Darl & Irvin;' and why, if this was not intended to be effective in and of itself, he should have sent it to two of the distributees named in it, telling them to 'Kepp this letter lock it up it may help you out'.[6]

(c) Notarial wills[7]

Law Reform Committee: Twenty-Second Report[8]

2.23 Finally, we considered whether there was a case for introducing a form of notarial will into our law. By this we mean a will made under a system which allows the testator

---

6. See also *Bennett v Gray* [1958] 14 DLR (2d) 1 where the Supreme Court of Canada faced similar difficulties in deciding whether the deceased's letter to his solicitor amounted to a valid holograph will.

7. A compulsory notarial system had been strongly advocated by the Justice Committee reporting in 1971 on home-made wills. The Committee felt that the relative lack of formality for making a will was a serious disadvantage because it 'conceals from the ordinary testator the difficulties inherent in disposing of his estate,' (para 5). The Committee recommended that the existing system be replaced by a rule requiring all wills to be witnessed by the English equivalent of a notary; in addition to thereby eliminating the problem of formal validity, it was thought that such a system would encourage testators to take proper legal advice before executing their wills and would form a 'more effective barrier against the more blatant forms of undue influence' (para 6). Civil Law countries generally have such a system although a holograph will is often also recognised as an alternative. See Amos and Walton 'Introduction to French Law' (3rd edn, 1966) Ch XIV and Cohn 'Manual of German Law' (2nd edn, 1968) Vol 1 Ch 6.

8. 'The Making and Revocation of Wills' (1980) Cmnd 7902.

either to dictate his testamentary wishes to a notary or to hand the notary an instrument which he declares contains them. The notary then sees to the attestation requirements and records the transaction. Nearly all of those who gave evidence on this point were opposed to this suggestion, although there was some support for the proposal that recourse to a solicitor should be compulsory. We believe that to impose compulsory recourse to a solicitor would be unacceptable and that it would deter some people from making a will at all. Further, we are not persuaded that there is a sufficient case for the introduction of an optional notarial system because we doubt whether it would be used; it would certainly not be used by those testators who prefer to make their wills without assistance. A more compelling reason for not introducing a notarial system into our law is that there are a number of differences between continental notaries and solicitors in this country and a notarial system would not be workable here without conferring upon solicitors powers which they do not at present have.[9]

QUESTIONS

1. *Re Groffman, Re Colling* and *Re Bercovitz* (ante) were all decided before the passing of the Administration of Justice Act 1982. Would the same decision have been reached in each case: (a) if the testator had died after 1982 or (b) if the court had had the benefit of a general dispensing power as in South Australia?

2. What advantages and disadvantages would you envisage for the introduction of (i) holograph wills as an alternative to satisfying the s 9 formalities; (ii) a scheme for the compulsory notarial certification of wills?

3. What do you understand by the 'rule of connection'? Can you justify its existence especially in the light of the exceptions that have been made to it?

---

9. See now AJA 1982, ss 27–28, not yet in force, providing for the International Will as prescribed by the 1973 Washington Convention on International Wills; it will establish a formal procedure for the execution of a will in the presence of a solicitor or notary public, compliance with which will guarantee the will recognition of formal validity by all states ratifying the Convention.

CHAPTER 9

Will formalities – exceptions

There are three instances where testamentary effect is given to declarations that do not comply with the requirements contained in the Wills Act 1837 s 9.

1 The secret trust

This arises where the testator makes a gift by will to A, apparently beneficially, but at some time before his death he asks A to hold it on certain trusts and A agrees to do so. Despite the fact that the terms of the trusts are not set out in the will and may even have been communicated orally, equity requires A to carry out his trusteeship.[1] Similarly, where A is named as trustee on the face of the will (the half secret trust as opposed to a fully secret trust as previously described) but no mention is made of the terms of his trusteeship, these having been communicated to and accepted by A at or before the execution of the will, equity will enforce the trust.[2] Varying arguments have been put forward to justify this exception to s 9. The modern trend is to argue that it is not a testamentary trust at all but an inter vivos trust, expressly created by the testator in his lifetime, but incompletely constituted until he dies leaving a will which leaves the property concerned to the secret trustee.[3] Others have argued that as it takes effect only on death and is de facto freely revocable until then by the testator simply altering his will so that nothing will pass to A on his death, it is a testamentary trust; it is then an example, they say, of equity stepping in to prevent statutory requirements being used as an 'engine of fraud',[4] the secret trustee's conscience being bound by the trust he has accepted.[5]

2 The privileged will

(a) In general

The Statute of Frauds 1677, s 23 enabled any 'soldier in actual military service or mariner or seaman at sea' to make a will disposing of his personalty

---

1. See eg *Ottaway v Norman* [1972] Ch 698, [1971] 3 All ER 1325.
2. See eg *Blackwell v Blackwell* [1929] AC 318.
3. See eg Hanbury and Maudsley 'Modern Equity', (12th edn, 1985), pp 160–165.
4. See eg Hodge 'Secret Trusts: The Fraud Theory Revisited', (1980) Conv 341.
5. See further, Pettit pp 106–113, Maudsley and Burn pp 131–151.

informally, even verbally. The privilege was continued in the Wills Act 1837 and extended to realty in 1918.

Wills Act 1837

11.   Savings as to wills of soldiers and mariners

Provided always, that any soldier being in actual military service, or any mariner or seaman being at sea, may dispose of his personal estate as he might have done before the making of this Act.

Wills (Soldiers and Sailors) Act 1918

1.   Explanation of s 11 of 7 Will 4 & 1 Vict c 26

In order to remove doubts as to the construction of the Wills Act 1837, it is hereby declared and enacted that section eleven of that Act authorises and always has authorised any soldier being in actual military service, or any mariner or seaman being at sea, to dispose of his personal estate as he might have done before the passing of that Act, though under the age of [eighteen years[6]]

2.   Extension of s 11 of Wills Act 1837

Section eleven of the Wills Act 1837 shall extend to any member of His Majesty's naval or marine forces not only when he is at sea but also when he is so circumstanced that if he were a soldier he would be in actual military service within the meaning of that section.

3.   Validity of testamentary dispositions of real property made by soldiers and sailors

(1) A testamentary disposition of any real estate in England or Ireland made by a person to whom section eleven of the Wills Act 1837 applies, and who dies after the passing of this Act, shall, notwithstanding that the person making the disposition was at the time of making it under [eighteen years[7]] of age or that the disposition has not been made in such manner or form as was at the passing of this Act required by law, be valid in any case where the person making the disposition was of such age and the disposition has been made in such manner and form that if the disposition had been a disposition of personal estate made by such a person domiciled in England or Ireland it would have been valid.[8]

5.   ... Interpretation

(2) For the purposes of section eleven of the Wills Act 1837 and this Act the expression 'soldier' includes a member of the Air Force, and references in this Act to the said section eleven include a reference to that section as explained and extended by this Act.

(b) Soldier in actual military service

Any member of the armed forces, including one whose role is non-combatant, can qualify for the privilege, so long as he or she was in actual military service at

---

6. As substituted by Family Law Reform Act 1969, s 3(1)(b).

7. Ibid.

8. The extension of the privilege to realty was subsequently nullified for unmarried infants by AEA 1925, s 51(3) which provides that if an infant dies entitled to an equitable interest in fee simple (the most an infant can hold as he cannot hold a legal fee simple, LPA 1925, s 1(6)) and has never married, he is deemed to have died entitled to an entailed interest which will devolve as such and not under any will he may leave. LPA 1925, s 176 which enables a tenant in tail in possession to bar the entail by will only applies to a tenant of full age. To escape s 51(3) the infant privileged testator must therefore marry; his equitable fee simple will then pass under his will.

the time. Most of the cases involving this limb of the privilege arose out of wartime wills but a state of war is not a prerequisite; service in connection with internal security operations will suffice.

Re Wingham [1949] P 187, [1948] 2 All ER 908, CA; Bucknill, Cohen and Denning LJJ

The testator was a member of the Royal Air Force; he made an informal will in 1943 whilst completing his training as a pilot in Canada. It was argued that he could hardly be said to be in actual military service at that time as Canada was not a theatre of war and the military operations then afoot were taking place in Europe and the Far East.

Held: When the testator executed the document he was in actual military service; the informal will should be admitted to probate.

Denning LJ: This court has to decide what is the proper test (of actual military service). It must be both simple and certain—simple, because it is to be understood by all ranks and certain, because every soldier must be able to apply it without difficulty in the situation in which he finds himself. It is quite beside the mark to inquire what are the reasons for the privilege. The privilege is one thing. The reasons for it are another. The reasons are, no doubt, that a soldier 'in actual military service' is likely to be in danger and to be bereft of legal advice. It would be a great mistake, however, to argue therefrom that a soldier who is not in danger or who has legal advice at his elbow cannot make a soldier's will. That would be to confound the reasons for the rule with the rule itself. The rule is that a soldier 'in actual military service' is privileged to make a will without any formalities. The plain meaning of the statutes is that any soldier, sailor or airman is entitled to the privilege if he is actually serving with the armed forces in connection with military operations which are, or have been, taking place, or are believed to be imminent. It does not, of course, include officers on half pay or men on the reserve, or the Territorials, when not called up for service. They are not actually serving. Nor does it include members of the forces serving in this country, or on routine garrison duty overseas, in time of peace, when military operations are not imminent. They are actually serving, but are not in actual 'military' service, because no military operations are afoot. It does, however, include all our men serving—or called up for service—in the wars, and women too, for that matter. It includes not only those actively engaged with the enemy, but all who are training to fight them. It also includes those members of the forces who, under stress of war, both work at their jobs and man the defences, such as the Home Guard. It includes not only the fighting men but also those who serve in the Forces, doctors, nurses, chaplains, Women's Royal Naval Service, Auxiliary Transport Service, and so forth. It includes them all, whether they are in the field or in barracks, in billets or sleeping at home.[9] It includes them although they may be captured by the enemy or interned by neutrals. It includes them, not only in time of war but also when war is imminent.[10] After hostilities are ended, it may still include them, as, eg, when they garrison the countries which we occupy,[11] or when they are engaged in military operations overseas. In all these cases they are plainly 'in actual military service'. Doubtful cases may arise in peace-time when a soldier is in, or is about to be sent to, a

---

9. Cf *Re Gibson* p 112 post.

10. As was held in *Re Rippon* [1943] P 61, [1943] 1 All ER 676, where a territorial army officer made an informal will in August 1939 when under orders to join his unit in England. No declaration of war had been formally made at the time but it was obvious that war was imminent and the territorial army had been mobilised.

11. As was subsequently held in *Re Colman* [1958] 2 All ER 35, [1958] 1 WLR 457, where a soldier on leave in England in 1954 from the British Army of the Rhine made an informal will while under orders to rejoin his unit at the end of his leave. Karminski J held that this was service connected with operations that had already taken place, namely the 1939–45 war and so s 11 applied.

disturbed area or an isolated post, where he may be involved in military operations. As to these cases, all I say is that, in case of doubt, the serving soldier should be given the benefit of the privilege.

In **Re Gibson** [1941] P 118, [1941] 2 All ER 91, the testator made an informal will at a time when he was a dental officer in the Royal Army Dental Corps attached to the District Command Headquarters in England. He lived at home but attended daily at his camp nearby. Henn Collins J, holding that he was not in actual military service, said at p 92:

> When all the civilian amenities which were available to the deceased are considered, it would be going against the principle laid down in the authorities to grant this motion. I can understand the privilege being extended to a man mobilised for service abroad or told to go to a certain place for embarkation, but a soldier who is carrying out peace-time duties, although he is under military authority, is no more a fighting soldier because he is in the Army than an ordinary civilian, who, in the circumstances of the present war, may be said to be in the front rank of the fighting. The foundation of the rule is that a man is parted from civil surroundings and the deceased never was.[12]

In **Re Jones** [1981] Fam 7, [1981] 1 All ER 1, a soldier serving in Northern Ireland was shot whilst on patrol in Londonderry, and made an informal will while he was dying. It was argued that for the privilege to apply, the military service had to take place in the context of a war rather than internal security operations but Arnold P disagreed, saying at p 5:

> When the deceased in the present case was ordered to go out on his patrol, the fatal patrol, he was obliged, by the conditions of his service in accordance with the discipline which prevailed in his military unit, so to do. That the service was military, that the service was active, seems to me to be beyond contest. The fact that the enemy was not a uniformed force engaged in regular warfare, or even an insurgent force organised on conventional military lines, but rather a conjuration of clandestine assassins and arsonists, cannot in my judgment affect any of those questions and I have no hesitation in pronouncing for this will as a valid nuncupative will. It is not the state of the opponent, or the character of the opponent's operations, in my judgment, which affect the answers to the questions which arise. They must be answered by reference to the activities of the deceased and those with whom he is associated; and it is *nihil ad rem* in relation to the answers to the questions whether there is service, whether it is active and whether it is military that the context in which it occurs is that of foreign expedition, foreign invasion or local insurrection.[13]

(c) Seaman at sea

To qualify under this limb of the privilege there is no need for any military involvement. The expression 'seaman' includes women as well as men, and members of the merchant navy[14] as well as members of the Royal Navy. The

---

12. This decision which was doubted by all three members of the Court of Appeal in *Re Wingham* ante, has been supported by Potter 'Soldiers' Wills' (1949) 12 MLR 183 where he suggests that the remarks of Denning LJ in *Re Wingham* were far too wide and would have the effect of extending the privilege to anyone who happened to be in uniform. He argues persuasively that the intention of the legislature in stating 'actual military service' as opposed to 'every soldier' must have been to restrict the privilege to soldiers so circumstanced as to be 'inops consilii' ie out of their usual peace-time routine and so unable to take advantage of the normal facilities for making a formal will.
13. See also *In the Will of Anderson* (1958) 75 WN (NSW) 334.
14. See eg *In the Goods of Sarah Hale* [1915] 2 IR 362 (a typist employed by a steamship company on a transatlantic liner); *Re Knibbs* p 114 post (barman in the merchant navy).

words 'at sea' are liberally construed by the Courts so as to include shore leave in certain circumstances.

Re Rapley's Estate [1983] 3 All ER 248, [1983] 1 WLR 1069, Ch D; Finlay J, QC[15]

A seaman, apprenticed to a shipping company, was on leave at home in Sussex when he made an informal will. He had been discharged from one ship at the time but not yet posted to another. It was argued that as he was at the time contemplating another voyage he could be said to be 'at sea' for the purpose of the privilege.

Held: The will was invalid. A seaman on shore leave between postings must be under instructions to join his next ship for the privilege to apply.

Finlay J: In those cases, where it has been held that the maker of the testamentary document of a nuncupative type (and for convenience I will refer to the maker in each case as 'the testator') was a seaman being at sea in circumstances where that was not in any obvious and ordinary sense the case, there appear to be the following features. In the first place, one finds that there is material that justified a finding that the testator was serving either in the Royal Navy or the Merchant Navy. It matters not whether he be a man or a woman, nor in what capacity he or she served or was employed, provided that the nature of the service is sea service. Second, the evidence, it appears to me, must also justify a finding that the testator either (a) is already (that is at the time of signing the document in question or making the nuncupative will) in post as a ship's officer (see, for example, *Re M'Murdo's Goods* (1868) LR 1 P & D 540, where the testator was the mate in HMS Excellent, and *Re Lay's Goods* (1840) 2 Curt 375, 163 ER 444, where the testator was the mate of HMS Calliope and made a will when on shore leave from that vessel), or (b) is already a member of a particular ship's company serving in that ship (and an instance of that is *Re Patterson's Goods* (1898) 79 LT 123), or on shore leave (an example of that is *Re Lay's Goods*) or on long leave ashore (of which *Re Newland's Estate* itself is an instance), or (c) being employed by owners of a fleet of ships and having been discharged from one such is already under orders to join another ship in that fleet (and examples of that are *Re Hale's Goods* [1915] 2 IR 362 and *Re Wilson's Estate* [1952] 1 All ER 852 [1952] P 92). . . .

Now in the present case the deceased was, in my judgment, clearly a mariner or seaman by calling. He was an apprentice indentured for training as a sea officer. It is further clear that he made and signed the questioned document when he was ashore. Is he then to be treated as a mariner or seaman being at sea within the meaning of the section bearing in mind that he had not, at the time when he signed the document, been posted to a seagoing ship? . . .

Counsel for the plaintiff submits that in *Re Newland's Estate* [1952] 1 All ER 841, [1952] P 71 is authority that it is enough if the testator makes a will in contemplation of sailing on a fresh voyage. The facts in *Re Newland's Estate* were that the deceased was an apprentice in the Merchant Navy and he executed a testamentary document shortly before rejoining his ship, which sailed a day or two later. The document was executed in compliance with the formalities of the 1837 Act in that it was attested by two witnesses but, as he was then a minor, it was only a valid will if it was validated by virtue of s 11 on the basis that he was a mariner or seaman being at sea at the time when he executed it. He was an apprentice serving in the SS Strathmore. He had joined that ship in April 1944 and continued to serve in her until 24 October 1944. In July of that year, while the Strathmore was docked in Liverpool, the deceased went on shore leave, and at Walton-on-Thames in Surrey he executed the will in the presence of two witnesses. It appears from the facts as stated in the judgment that Havers J inferred that he had received

---

15. Sitting as a judge of the High Court.

instructions to rejoin the Strathmore before he wrote and executed the document in question. . . .

In my judgment *Re Newland* is a case distinguishable from the present. There the testator was on leave from the Strathmore, he had been discharged from one ship and gone on leave awaiting a posting to another. He was at all times, when on leave, one of the complement of the Strathmore. Here the deceased had been discharged from the City of Ely on 7 October 1960 and at some time after 22 October 1960 he was posted to or received orders to join the City of Melbourne. . . .

I find that none of the authorities which have been cited to me goes so far as to decide that when one who is a mariner or seaman by calling and employment makes a will when on shore on leave and is not at that time a member of the complement of a particular ship and has not at that time been posted to a ship, he is yet to be treated as being at sea. To extend the meaning of s 11 to such a case would appear to me to result in according no significance to the words 'at sea' in the section, because it would make the section applicable to anyone who at the relevant time was a mariner or seaman, since any mariner or seaman must always be in contemplation of another voyage until in fact he gives up the sea, retires from the marine service and so ceases from that point to be a mariner or seaman.

The cases have gone very far to extend the meaning of 'at sea' to include those who are in a state of preparation for going to sea, being under orders to do so, but to go beyond that and to extend the ambit of the section to cover the case where a mariner or seaman is on furlough or leave, knows well that he may at any time be instructed to join another ship but has not at the moment received such instructions is, I think, to extend the operation of the section beyond the circumstances which were no doubt in the contemplation of the legislature when this provision was originally enacted and when it was re-enacted in 1837. The ground and justification for the privilege is no doubt the circumstance that those who are at sea are both without the advantage of legal assistance and also the justification for the privilege is no doubt the danger of the calling and the fact that to those who follow the sea, death is an always present likelihood and not the remote certainty which it is for others.

I do not think that, considering the basis for this privilege, I can find any ground in that for extending the operation of the section to the extent that counsel invites me now to do.

(d) A testamentary intention

No formalities whatever apply to the making of the will once a person is in a privileged situation,[16] but there must be an intention on his part to indicate how his property is to be disposed of on his death.

In the Estate of Knibbs [1962] 2 All ER 829, [1962] 1 WLR 852, PDA; Wrangham J

The testator was employed as a barman on a liner. One day, in the course of a voyage, he and the head barman (Mr Wills) were chatting casually about their respective families. The testator, emphasizing how good his sister, Iris, had always been to him, said, 'If anything ever happens to me, Iris is to get all I've got'.

---

16. Cf Canada where most states permit the privileged will but require it to be made in writing, relaxing only the need for attestation: see eg the Ontario Succession Law Reform Act 1977 s 5. Similarly, the Russian Civil Code 1964 Art 451, which relaxes only the requirement for notarial registration.

Held: These words were not uttered with any testamentary intention and so did not constitute a valid privileged will.

Wrangham J: Although a testamentary act may be one not recognised by the testator to be an actual will, it must I think, be an act which is intended to operate so far as possible as a disposition of his goods after his death. As Salter J said in *Beech's case*:[17]

> 'I think that, in order to constitute a will, the words used by a testator must be intended by him, at or after the time he uses them, to be preserved or remembered so as to form the guide to those who survive in carrying out his wishes.'

In other words, in order to be a testamentary act there must be a statement of the deceased's wishes for the disposition of his property which is not merely imparted to his audience as a matter of information or interest, but is intended by him to convey to that audience a request explicit or implicit to see that his wishes are acted on.

I take two extreme cases to illustrate my meaning. A man who telephoned to his solicitor (under the conditions under which the privilege would be applicable) telling him what dispositions of property he intended to operate after his death, and asking him to do that which was required, would clearly be performing a testamentary act because he would not only be stating what his intentions were, but stating them in circumstances which showed that he wished his intentions to be carried out as a result of what he was then saying. On the other hand, if one can imagine a man who said to a friend of his, 'Well, my intention is to cut out my wife and family altogether from my will and leave everything to my mistress but don't you ever say a word to anybody about what I have told you', such a conversation could not possibly be a testamentary act because although it revealed clearly what the intentions of the deceased were, the person hearing the words could not be expected, and was, indeed, forbidden, to take any step to see that they were put into effect. So also where a testator has indicated what his intentions for the dispositions of his property were, but only by way of summarising an existing will as in *Beech's case* ([1923] P 46) or by way of explanation why he was not making a will at all as in *Re the Estate of Donner* ((1917) 34 TLR 138), it has been held that the expression of his intentions did not constitute a testamentary act.

In other cases, such as *Stable's* case ([1919] P 7) . . . or *In the Goods of Spicer, Spicer v Richardson* ([1949] P 441) where a soldier on the last day of his leave before going abroad on active service in 1944 told his mistress and her friend that he wished everything to belong to the mistress if anything happened to him, in such cases as those, the court has been able to draw the inference that the testator intended his words to be acted on, that is to say, intended that those who heard his words both should remember them as the record of his intentions and should help to see that those intentions were carried out.

That being, as I think, the law applicable to this matter, I have to determine whether or not the deceased, when he spoke to Mr Wills in 1960, was performing a testamentary act, that is to say, was recording his wishes as to the disposition of his property with the intention that his words should be remembered and should be acted on by the person to whom they were uttered, namely, Mr Wills.

I am quite satisfied that the deceased did form a clear and definite intention that his sister, Iris, should have all his property. If I were able to give effect to that intention I should be very glad to do so. I think that would, indeed, be just by perhaps what I might call natural law; but I have to administer the law as it exists, and I cannot think that the deceased when he was having this casual conversation in the bar with Mr Wills was in any sense of the phrase performing a testamentary act. I think that he was merely exchanging with Mr Wills a discussion of family affairs. . . . If, for example, he had even said to Mr Wills, 'I want my sister, Iris, to be certain to have everything that I possess after my death. Will you please see to it, and tell the captain. Please make sure that that is all right', I think the situation might well have been different. As it is, I think that what was said was the mere exchange of family gossip, of opinions and information about family matters, which cannot be regarded as a testamentary act.

---

17. *In the Estate of Beech* [1923] P 46 at 57.

(e) Reform

The Latey Committee on the Age of Majority, reporting in 1967,[18] felt that the distinction between what is and is not 'actual military service' had become 'blurred to the point of extinction by long-range weapons and informal hostilities'. They recommended that to avoid the confusion, the privilege should simply apply to any member of the armed forces, of any age, whether or not in actual military service, but this recommendation has not been implemented. The privilege was recently reconsidered by the Law Reform Committee.

Law Reform Committee: Twenty-Second Report[19]

2.21 Privileged wills On the general question whether soldiers' and sailors' privilege to make wills which do not comply with section 9 of the 1837 Act should be abolished, the evidence we received was divided. The privilege was first introduced in the 17th century when servicemen were more likely to be engaged in long campaigns abroad and thus cut off from the facilities for making a will than they are today. Certainly there has been a decline in the number of such wills in recent years and a number of our witnesses thought that the privilege was no longer necessary or justified. Servicemen and sailors are now more literate than formerly and there is usually ample opportunity for them to make a will before going to sea or embarking upon active service. As against this, however, it was suggested that even if not many privileged wills are submitted for probate at present, circumstances can be envisaged when the privilege may again be needed. The Ministry of Defence, for example, was strongly in favour of its retention unaltered for this reason. They also pointed out that, even in peace-time, there were occasional cases of servicemen making privileged wills in the course of certain military operations, giving as an example a case where a soldier in Northern Ireland was fatally injured by terrorists and gave oral instructions as to the disposal of his property.[20] On balance, therefore, we think that there is a case for retaining the privilege in its present form and do not recommend either its abolition or modification.

3   The document incorporated by reference

This is a judicially created exception, the effect of which is that if certain conditions are satisfied, a document that has not been executed in accordance with the Wills Act 1837 will nevertheless be regarded as incorporated into a duly executed will and its provisions applied just as if it had been written originally into the will.

(a) Conditions to be satisfied

For incorporation to apply, the document must be in existence at the date of the will, it must be referred to in the will as being already in existence and it must be

---

18. Report of the Committee on the Age of Majority (1967) Cmnd 3342, para 417.
19. 'The Making and Revocation of Wills' (1980) Cmnd 7902.
20. Presumably a reference to *Re Jones*, p 112 ante, decided a few months after the date of the Law Reform Committee's Report. The 1982 Falklands Islands campaign adds further point to the MOD's views.

possible to identify it from the words used in the will.[1] The United States Uniform Probate Code provides a similar exception albeit excluding the second condition, and there is another exception which goes much further in that it permits the testator to refer in his will to a separate document disposing of certain tangible property, which may be prepared after the execution of the will and may even be altered from time to time.

In **University College of North Wales v Taylor** [1908] P 140, the testator executed his will in June 1905 leaving a legacy of £10,000 to the University of Wales to be held on such terms 'as are contained and specified in any memorandum among my papers written or signed by me relating thereto'. After his death a written memorandum was found among his papers, setting out the terms and dated March 1905. Farwell LJ held that the memorandum could not be incorporated into the will saying at p 147:

> It is well settled that in order to incorporate a document of this nature the will must necessarily refer to a particular specified paper then in existence . . . reading the words fairly I find it impossible to doubt that the words 'as are contained and specified in any memorandum amongst my papers written or signed by me relating thereto' do not refer to any particular document, but refer to any number of documents which may or may not answer the description of being written, or in the alternative signed, and which may or may not be in existence. So far as regards the word 'are' is concerned, it is well settled that in wills it may well point to futurity, and I cannot doubt that the testator in using those words has intended to reserve to himself the right to declare from time to time the rules and regulations and the trusts which he desires to apply to his gift. If this is decided to be the true construction of the words, it is obvious that parol evidence cannot be admitted in order to contradict that which has already been held to be the meaning of the words.

In **Re Jones** [1942] Ch 328, the will included a gift to trustees under a special declaration of trust for the benefit of Tettenhall College 'executed by me bearing even date with this my last will and testament or any substitution thereof or addition thereto which I may hereafter execute'. The testator had executed a declaration of trust in favour of Tettenhall College on the same date as he executed his will. Simonds J held that the declaration could not be incorporated into the will. As in *University College of North Wales v Taylor*[2] the terms used in the will were such as to include a future document and parol evidence was not admissible to show that no substitutional document had in fact been executed after the date of the will. Simonds J stated at p 334:

> The testator's intention was that subsequent declarations should have testamentary validity, though they might not satisfy the formal requirements of the Wills Act. That intention must, however, fail.

Uniform Probate Code (USA)

2–510 Incorporation by Reference Any writing in existence when a will is executed may be incorporated by reference if the language of the will manifests this intent and describes the writing sufficiently to permit its identification.

---

1. For an example of a document that satisfied all three conditions see *Allen v Maddock* (1858) 11 Moo PC 427 where an unattested 'will' was duly incorporated by a subsequently executed codicil which commenced 'This is a Codicil to my Last Will and Testament' but otherwise contained no reference to the earlier 'will'.
2. Ante.

2–513   Separate Writing Identifying Bequest of Tangible Property   Whether or not the provisions relating to holographic wills apply,[3] a will may refer to a written statement or list to dispose of items of tangible personal property not otherwise specifically disposed of by the will, other than money, evidences of indebtedness, documents of title, and securities, and property used in trade or business. To be admissible under this section as evidence of the intended disposition, the writing must either be in the handwriting of the testator or be signed by him and must describe the items and the devises with reasonable certainty. The writing may be referred to as one to be in existence at the time of the testator's death; it may be prepared before or after the execution of the will; it may be altered by the testator after its preparation; and it may be a writing which has no significance apart from its effect upon the dispositions made by the will.

(b) Incorporation of an existing settlement[4]

Often the document sought to be incorporated is an existing inter vivos settlement. Where the settlement on its terms contemplates its own variation or replacement, the possible inclusion of future documents is avoided by incorporating the settlement as it stands at the execution of the will, to the exclusion of later amendments, although this could be said to interfere with the testator's intention. In the United States the problem is overcome in many states by treating the testamentary gift as an addition to the inter vivos settlement to be disposed of in accordance with the terms of the settlement including any amendments made to it before the testator's death.

Re Edwards' Will Trust [1948] Ch 440, [1948] 1 All ER 821, CA; Lord Greene MR, Somervell and Cohen LJJ

The testator left his residuary estate to trustees to be held on the trusts of a settlement which was already in existence and which he fully identified in his will. There was nothing in the will referring to its replacement by any subsequent document, but cl 2 of the settlement contained a power to substitute new trusts by memorandum and one such memorandum was made by the testator after the date of the will. It was argued that the existence of the power prevented incorporation of the settlement.

Held: The settlement as it stood at the date of the will was duly incorporated, but not the subsequent memorandum

Lord Greene MR: The testator makes quite clear what his testamentary wishes are. He directs that those concerned with the administration of his estate shall turn to the settlement to find what those wishes are. The identification of that document is a simple matter. There is no question what the document is, and there is no rule of law which makes it impossible to lead evidence to identify it. I say that at the outset, because reliance has been placed on a decision of Simonds J in *Re Jones*.[5] That was a case in which the testator directed payment of a legacy to trustees. (His Lordship quoted the words of the will and continued:) In the very gift itself the testator was endeavouring to reserve power to himself to modify or alter the gift at some later date by a subsequent instrument not executed in accordance with the Wills Act, 1837. Simonds J pointed out that,

---

3. See p 106 n 3 ante.
4. Described in Canada as a 'pour-over will' because its provisions 'pour-over' additional property to the inter vivos trust from the will, see eg *Re Johnson* (1962) 30 DLR (2d) 474 (British Columbia Supreme Court).
5. P 117 ante.

whereas in the case of a document in existence it is always possible to lead evidence to identify the document, in the case before him it never would be possible to lead evidence to identify any subsequent document. On that ground he held that, if effect were given to the direction, it would be equivalent to giving a power to change a testamentary disposition by an unexecuted codicil in violation of the Wills Act, 1837 and, therefore, that the gift failed for uncertainty. That seems to me to be a different case from that which we have here. This settlement was a document which can be identified and there is no rule of law to the contrary. It can, accordingly, be incorporated as a piece of writing into the testamentary disposition. Indeed, if the settlement, instead of being a thing having value and force in itself, had been merely a memorandum previously executed to which, in his will, the testator referred, it could have been admitted to probate as a testamentary instrument. The question then would have arisen: what provisions in this instrument are valid and what are invalid?

In other words, I start with the proposition that the incorporation of this document into the will is a permissible and easy matter. When I say incorporation, I am referring to what I may call the mechanical act of incorporation by reading the language of the document into the will itself. The effect is that we have now got to a stage where there is a document, part of the directions in which cannot operate any more than they could operate if they had been contained, as in the case of *Re Jones*, in the will itself. The presence of that invalid provision in *Re Jones* did not involve that it was to be struck out of the probate and treated as not being part of the will at all, nor do I see any reason why the invalidity of a provision contained in this settlement should be any reason for excluding it from the testamentary directions of the deceased. The result of his having in that identifiable document included something which the law does not allow to have effect, is a matter to be considered after probate when the question of the validity of his testamentary dispositions arises. The result, therefore, is that there is here, so to speak, a composite will consisting of a combination of provisions of the actual will itself plus those of the settlement. . . .

The trial judge took the view that the directions for incorporation must be read as meaning the whole settlement and nothing but the settlement, and that, in so far as the law prevented the effective incorporation of any part of the settlement, all the directions for incorporation fell to the ground. I do not take that view. It seems to me that the directions for incorporation are directions to read into the will the entirety of a document which the testator, no doubt, thought would be effective, but if, on writing them into the will, it turns out that part of them is invalid from some rule of law, as in the present case, I cannot read the testator's directions as meaning that, therefore, the whole process of incorporation must be abandoned. I think that the effect of it is that so much of the settlement as can validly have operation as part of a testamentary disposition is left to have its proper operation according to its true construction.[6]

Uniform Probate Code (USA)

2–511 Testamentary Additions to Trusts A devise or bequest, the validity of which is determinable by the law of this state, may be made by a will to the trustee of a trust established or to be established by the testator or by the testator and some other person or by some other person (including a funded or unfunded life insurance trust, although the trustor has reserved any or all rights of ownership of the insurance contracts) if the trust is identified in the testator's will and its terms are set forth in a written instrument (other than a will) executed before or concurrently with the execution of the testator's will or in the valid last will of a person who has predeceased the testator (regardless of the existence, size, or character of the corpus of the trust). The

---

6. See also *Re Schintz WT* [1951] Ch 870, [1951] 1 All ER 1095 where the will itself mentioned the power in the settlement to vary its provisions but the settlement as it stood at the date of the will was nevertheless incorporated. Wynn Parry J decided, at p 1100, that the words were 'merely descriptive of the powers contained in the settlement'.

devise is not invalid because the trust is amendable or revocable, or because the trust was amended after the execution of the will or after the death of the testator. Unless the testator's will provides otherwise, the property so devised (1) is not deemed to be held under a testamentary trust of the testator but becomes a part of the trust to which it is given and (2) shall be administered and disposed of in accordance with the provisions of the instrument or will setting forth the terms of the trust, including any amendments thereto made before the death of the testator (regardless of whether made before or after the execution of the testator's will) and, if the testator's will so provides, including any amendments to the trust made after the death of the testator. A revocation or termination of the trust before the death of the testator causes the devise to lapse.

(c) Effect of a codicil

Sometimes a subsequent codicil will save a document that otherwise fails to satisfy all the conditions for incorporation.

In **In the Goods of Truro** (1866) LR 1 P & D 201, the will referred to 'such articles of silver plate and plated articles as are contained in the inventory signed by me and deposited herewith'. No such inventory was in existence at the date of the will but one was drawn up later and subsequently the testator executed a codicil which republished[7] the will as at the date of the codicil. Holding that the articles in question would pass under the will, Sir JP Wilde said at p 205:

> Now construing these words by the light of the events which had then happened, they appear with sufficient distinctness to refer to a document then existing. For the inventory referred to had then been signed by the testatrix and deposited at the bankers. The operation of the codicil as a re-execution of the will, therefore gets rid of all difficulty, and I admit the will and the codicil to probate, together with the inventory signed by the testatrix.[8]

QUESTIONS

1. The privileged will for soldiers has been described as an 'outdated anachronism'—Cole 'How Active is Actual Military Service?' [1982] Conv 185. Do you agree? Would your answer be different in relation to the 'seaman's will'?

2. Could you justify an extension of the privilege? The Russian Civil Code 1964, for example, relaxes testamentary formalities not only for soldiers and sailors but for citizens under treatment in medical institutions and citizens on prospecting, arctic or other similar expeditions (Art 451).

3. Compare the judicial attitude to the incorporation of future documents in this country with the provisions of the United States Uniform Probate Code. Do you think the requirements in this country should be similarly relaxed?

4. In 1982 Albert made a will leaving all his residuary estate to Bill and Clarice 'to be held by them on the trusts of the settlement I have executed in favour of

---

7. P 54 ante.

8. Aliter where the reference in the will itself lets in the possibility of a future document. See, eg *In the Goods of Smart* [1902] P 238 where the testator left a gift to 'such of my friends as I may designate in a book or memorandum that will be found with this my will'. By the time a codicil was executed there were various memoranda in existence but it was held that these could not be incorporated; the will, as republished at the date of the codicil, was still referring to possible future documents.

my grandchildren'. It was not until a week after execution of the will that Albert executed the settlement which included a power for Albert to vary the trusts thereof in certain respects. In 1983 Albert executed a deed making alterations to the trusts in the settlement. In 1984 he made a codicil to his will and in 1985 he died. Is the residuary gift effective? Would your answer have been different if no codicil had been executed but shortly before execution of the will Albert had shown the drafts of the intended settlement and the will to Bill and Clarice?

CHAPTER 10

Intestacy

1 Introduction

Previous chapters[1] have examined the position of those who die testate, that is, leaving a valid will which effectively disposes of the whole of their property. This chapter is concerned with succession to property on intestacy, whether the deceased dies wholly intestate, that is, without leaving a valid will at all, or partially intestate, that is, leaving a will which does not dispose of the whole of his property.

The Administration of Estates Act 1925 introduced the present system of intestate succession which is applicable to realty and personalty alike.[2] All the deceased's undisposed of property is put on trust for sale and after payment of the deceased's debts and liabilities the balance, known as the 'residuary estate' of the intestate, is applied in accordance with the statutory order of entitlement contained in s 46 of the Act.[3]

2 The statutory trust for sale

Administration of Estates Act 1925

33. Trust for sale

(1) On the death of a person intestate as to any real or personal estate, such estate shall be held by his personal representatives—

    (a) as to the real estate upon trust to sell the same; and

    (b) as to the personal estate upon trust to call in sell and convert into money such part thereof as may not consist of money,

with power to postpone such sale and conversion for such a period as the personal representatives, without being liable to account, may think proper, and so that any reversionary interest be not sold until it falls into possession, unless the personal representatives see special reason for sale, and so also that, unless required for purposes of

---

1. Chs 5–9 ante.
2. Previously realty went to the heir at law, applying the Inheritance Act 1833 whilst personalty devolved in accordance with the Statutes of Distribution 1670 and 1685.
3. This order was based on a survey of the dispositive provisions in wills filed at the Probate Registry over a period of time and it was aimed at thereby reflecting the probable wishes of the deceased had he died testate. A similar exercise was carried out between 1950 and 1952 for the Committee on the Law of Intestate Succession set up, inter alia, to consider the position of the surviving spouse; most of its recommendations (Cmd 8310) were implemented by the Intestates' Estates Act 1952.

administration owing to want of other assets, personal chattels be not sold except for special reason.

(2) Out of the net money to arise from the sale and conversion of such real and personal estate (after payment of costs), and out of the ready money of the deceased (so far as not disposed of by his will, if any), the personal representative shall pay all such funeral, testamentary and administration expenses, debts and other liabilities as are properly payable thereout having regard to the rules of administration contained in this Part of this Act, and out of the residue of the said money the personal representative shall set aside a fund sufficient to provide for any pecuniary legacies bequeathed by the will (if any) of the deceased.

(3) During the minority of any beneficiary or the subsistence of any life interest and pending the distribution of the whole or any part of the estate of the deceased, the personal representatives may invest the residue of the said money, or so much thereof as may not have been distributed, in any investments for the time being authorised by statute for the investment of trust money, with power, at the discretion of the personal representatives, to change such investments for others of a like nature.

(4) The residue of the said money and any investments for the time being representing the same, including (but without prejudice to the trust for sale) any part of the estate of the deceased which may be retained unsold and is not required for the administration purposes aforesaid, is in this Act referred to as 'the residuary estate of the intestate.'

(7) Where the deceased leaves a will, this section has effect subject to the provisions contained in the will.[4]

3 Order of entitlement to the residuary estate[5]

Administration of Estates Act 1925

46. Succession to real and personal estate on intestacy

(1) The residuary estate of an intestate shall be distributed in the manner or be held on the trusts mentioned in this section, namely:

  (i) If the intestate leaves a husband or wife, then in accordance with the following table:

TABLE

If the intestate—

(1) leaves— 　(a) no issue and 　(b) no parent, or brother or sister of the whole blood, or issue of a brother or sister of the whole blood	the residuary estate shall be held in trust for the surviving husband or wife absolutely.
(2) leaves issue (whether or not persons mentioned in subparagraph (b) above also survive)	the surviving husband or wife shall take the personal chattels[6] absolutely and, in addition, the residuary estate of the intestate (other than the personal chattels) shall stand charged with the payment of

---

4. See p 142 post as to a partial intestacy.
5. The order can be varied by agreement between the beneficiaries or by a simple disclaimer (see Ch 22 post). It may also be affected by public policy considerations (see Ch 22 post).
6. As defined in AEA 1925, s 55(1)(x) p 126 post.

a fixed net sum[7] free of death duties and costs, to the surviving husband or wife with interest thereon from the date of the death at such rate as the Lord Chancellor may specify by order[8] until paid or appropriated, and, subject to providing for that sum and the interest thereon, the residuary estate (other than the personal chattels) shall be held—

(a) as to one half upon trust for the surviving husband or wife during his or her life, and, subject to such life interest, on the statutory trusts[9] for the issue of the intestate, and

(b) as to the other half, on the statutory trusts[9] for the issue of the intestate.[10]

(3) leaves one or more of the following, that is to say, a parent, a brother or sister of the whole blood, or issue of a brother or sister of the whole blood, but leaves no issue

the surviving husband or wife shall take the personal chattels[6] absolutely and, in addition, the residuary estate of the intestate (other than the personal chattels) shall stand charged with the payment of a fixed net sum,[11] free of death duties and costs, to the surviving husband or wife with interest thereon from the date of the death at such rate as the Lord Chancellor may specify by order[8] until paid, or appropriated, and, subject to providing for that sum and the interest thereon, the residuary estate (other than the personal chattels) shall be held—

(a) as to one half in trust for the surviving husband or wife absolutely, and

(b) as to the other half—

(i) where the intestate leaves one parent or both parents (whether or not brothers or sisters of the intestate or their issue also survive) in trust for the parent absolutely or, as the case may be, for the two parents in equal shares absolutely,

(ii) where the intestate leaves no parent on the statutory trusts[9] for the brothers and sisters of the whole blood of the intestate.

(ii) If the intestate leaves issue but no husband or wife the residuary estate of the intestate shall be held on the statutory trusts[9] for the issue of the intestate;

(iii) If the intestate leaves no husband or wife and no issue but both parents, then the

---

7. The Family Provision Act 1966, s 1(1) empowered the Lord Chancellor to make orders by statutory instrument as to the amount of this sum (the statutory legacy). The current figure, for those dying after February 1981, is £40,000: Family Provision (Intestate Succession) Order 1981, SI 1981/255.

8. Currently 6% for those dying intestate after September 1983: Intestate Succession (Interest and Capitalisation) Order 1977 (Amendment) Order 1983, SI 1983/1374.

9. As defined in AEA 1925, s 47(1)(i) p 137 post.

10. In some jurisdictions the surviving spouse's entitlement where the intestate leaves children, depends on the number of children, eg in most Canadian states after receiving the statutory legacy the surviving spouse takes half the remainder outright if the intestate left only one child (or issue of one child), as opposed to one-third the remainder where the intestate left more than one child.

11. See n 7 ante. The current figure, for those dying after February 1981 is £85,000: Family Provision (Intestate Succession) Order 1981, SI 1981/255.

residuary estate of the intestate shall be held in trust for the father and mother in equal shares absolutely;

(iv) If the intestate leaves no husband or wife and no issue but one parent, then the residuary estate of the intestate shall be held in trust for the surviving father or mother absolutely;

(v) If the intestate leaves no husband or wife and no issue and no parent, then the residuary estate of the intestate shall be held in trust for the following persons living at the death of the intestate, and in the following order and manner, namely:—

First, on the statutory trusts[9] for the brothers and sisters of the whole blood of the intestate; but if no person takes an absolutely vested interest under such trusts; then

Secondly, on the statutory trusts[9] for the brothers and sisters of the half blood[12] of the intestate;[9] but if no person takes an absolutely vested interest under such trusts; then

Thirdly, for the grandparents of the intestate and, if more than one survive the intestate, in equal shares; but if there is no member of this class; then

Fourthly, on the statutory trusts[9] for the uncles and aunts of the intestate (being brothers or sisters of the whole blood of a parent of the intestate); but if no person takes an absolutely vested interest under such trusts; then

Fifthly, on the statutory trusts for the uncles and aunts of the intestate (being brothers or sisters of the half blood[12] of a parent of the intestate);

(vi) In default of any person taking an absolute interest under the foregoing provisions, the residuary estate of the intestate shall belong to the Crown or to the Duchy of Lancaster or to the Duke of Cornwall for the time being, as the case may be, as *bona vacantia*, and in lieu of any right to escheat.[13]

The Crown or the said Duchy or the said Duke may (without prejudice to the powers reserved by section nine of the Civil List Act 1910, or any other powers), out of the whole or any part of the property devolving on them respectively, provide, in accordance with the existing practice, for dependants, whether kindred or not, of the intestate, and other persons for whom the intestate might reasonably have been expected to make provision.[14]

4 The spouse's entitlement

(a) Who is a 'spouse'?

The intestate's spouse must survive the intestate, however briefly,[15] to claim on the intestacy; the presumption that where the order of death is uncertain the elder predeceased the younger[16] does not apply in favour of the younger spouse

---

12. In many other jurisdictions these distinctions between collaterals of the whole blood and collaterals of the half blood have been abolished as inappropriate given the frequency nowadays of divorce and remarriage, with children of each union being brought up as one family: see eg the United States Uniform Probate Code, s 2–107, the Ontario Succession Law Reform Act 1977, s 48(8), the New Zealand Administration Act 1969, s 77.

13. The right of escheat to land on the death of a person intestate and without heirs was abolished by AEA 1925, s 45(1)(d).

14. For comparison with the intestacy order of entitlement in a civil law jurisdiction, see MacDonald Allen 'Dying Intestate in France' (1983) 127 Sol J 850.

15. Cf the Uniform Probate Code (USA) which requires a person to survive the intestate for a minimum of 120 hours to benefit under his intestacy: s 2–104.

16. LPA 1925, s 184, see p 353 post.

of an intestate. A former spouse has no entitlement, nor will any claim lie for the judicially separated spouse.[17]

Administration of Estates Act 1925

46.   Succession to real and personal estate on intestacy

(3) Where the intestate and the intestate's husband or wife have died in circumstances rendering it uncertain which of them survived the other and the intestate's husband or wife is by virtue of section one hundred and eighty-four of the Law of Property Act 1925, deemed to have survived the intestate, this section shall, nevertheless, have effect as respects the intestate as if the husband or wife had not survived the intestate.[18]

Matrimonial Causes Act 1973

18.   Effects of judicial separation

(2) If while a decree of judicial separation is in force and the separation is continuing either of the parties to the marriage dies intestate as respects all or any of his or her real or personal property, the property as respects which he or she died intestate shall devolve as if the other party to the marriage had then been dead.[19]

(b) The personal chattels

The surviving spouse is always entitled to the 'personal chattels'. This expression, as defined in the Administration of Estates Act 1925, is frequently adopted by testators when making gifts of their personal chattels by will.

Administration of Estates Act 1925

55.   Definitions

(1) In this Act, unless the context otherwise requires, the following expressions have the meanings hereby assigned to them respectively, that is to say:

(x) 'Personal chattels' mean carriages, horses, stable furniture and effects (not used for business purposes), motor cars and accessories (not used for business purposes), garden effects, domestic animals, plate, plated articles, linen, china, glass, books, pictures, prints, furniture, jewellery, articles of household or personal use or ornament, musical and scientific instruments and apparatus, wines, liquors and consumable stores, but do not include any chattels used at the death of the intestate for business purposes nor money or securities for money.

In **Re Ogilby** [1942] Ch 288, [1942] 1 All ER 524, the intestate's herd of shorthorn cattle was held to be outside the definition on account of business user, Simonds J saying, at p 525:

It is said that it was her hobby and that, at least, it was not the business of her life. It is

---

17. Many Canadian states go further than this and disentitle a spouse from benefit if the spouse had been guilty of adultery at the intestate's death.
18. The subsection was added by the Intestates' Estates Act 1952, s 1. See eg *Re Dellow's WT* [1964] 1 All ER 771, [1964] 1 WLR 451.
19. Aliter where a magistrates' court order contains an order excluding a spouse from the matrimonial home (Domestic Proceedings and Magistrates' Courts Act 1978, s 16(3)) or where the spouses have separated by agreement rather than by court order; in either case the surviving spouse will be entitled to benefit on the intestacy of the first to die.

said that she consistently made a loss, and for that reason, as I understand the argument, it is said that she did not carry on the business of farming and that she did not keep these cows and the other live and dead stock, the accompaniment of her farm, as a business.

I am wholly unable to follow that argument. . . . It may be that there are cases where an intestate keeps a cow or two for her own use, or it may be a pig or it may be humbler domestic animals, and in such case it may be right to say of those animals that they are not kept for business purposes. It may in fact be difficult to draw the line; but where you find farming on this scale—a home farm with a substantial acreage and live and dead stock which may be valued for the purpose of probate at between £1,400 and £1,500, including 31 head of cattle and 35 head of sheep—in such a case as that there is no doubt upon which side of the line the case falls. There is a farming business being carried on, and the live and the dead stock are being used for the purpose of that business.

Re Crispin's Will Trusts [1975] Ch 245, [1974] 3 All ER 772, CA; Russell, Stamp and James LJJ

By his will the testator left 'all my personal chattels as defined in the Administration of Estates Act 1925,' to his sister. When he died, his estate included a valuable collection of clocks and watches (the Todhunter collection) which had been bequeathed to the testator a few years before his death. He had not made the collection himself nor did he add to it; he simply kept it together. This led Burgess V-C[20] to decide that it was not an article of personal use and so would not pass under the definition. The sister appealed.

Held: The collection was within the definition and would pass to her.

Russell LJ: The scope of the bequest must be decided in exactly the same way in which it would have been decided on an intestacy, what articles were within the widow's statutory right to personal chattels as defined. [His Lordship referred to the definition in the Administration of Estates Act 1925, s 55[1] and continued:] It is to be observed of this definition that there are express exceptions of articles used for business purposes, money, and securities for money. Apart from the question of use for business purposes, and 'articles of household or personal use or ornament,' we apprehend that the only question is whether an article comes within the ordinary meaning of the word used: for example, jewellery, *Re Whitby* ([1944] 1 All ER 299, [1944] Ch 210): horses, *Re Hutchinson* ([1955] 1 All ER 689) and, we apprehend, furniture. When considering whether an article is an article of household use or ornament, or of personal use or ornament, an examination of the circumstances of the particular article may be required in addition to its actual physical character. . . .

So far as the clocks are concerned, in our opinion a clock, whether long case or bracket, is an article of furniture in the ordinary sense of the word, and it matters not whether it is keeping good or bad time or no time at all, whether it is standing in the room in the testator's house which is in everyday use or stored in a locked room therein, or stored at a repository, or on loan to a museum. The fact that it is one of a collection of clocks bought by the testator or inherited by the testator from another seems to us nothing to the point. Nor, to our minds, is the fact that it is one of a collection which could be said to be a hobby of the testator; if anything, that fact would incline us to think that it was not only an article of furniture but also an article of personal use, as was the stamp collection in *Re Reynolds* ([1965] 3 All ER 686, [1966] 1 WLR 19): though we would venture to doubt the soundness of the reference to a bought collection, ([1965] 3 All ER at 688, [1966] 1 WLR at 22),[2] as to which see a note in the Law Quarterly

---

20. [1973] 2 All ER 141.
1. P 126 ante.
2. In *Re Reynolds* Stamp J had held that a stamp collection kept up by the deceased as his main hobby was an article of personal use even though its value was such that it might also be regarded as an investment, but he suggested obiter, that he might have decided otherwise had the deceased simply bought the collection from a stamp dealer and installed it in his flat. This suggestion was criticised by Megarry: (1966) 82 LQR 18.

Review ((1966) 82 LQR 18). There was some discussion, as to some of the clocks, whether they were or were not in cases; but the evidence was obscure, nobody suggested that the answer was other than 100 per cent one way or the other, and in those circumstances we conclude that all the clocks passed by the bequest.

We turn to the watches. . . . The evidence showed that they were or substantially were kept in a chest with suitable compartments in which Todhunter had kept them; that the testator constructed a special window in the wall of the house to throw light on the area of the chest so that the testator, when opening the chest, could the more readily see them; that he treasured them and from time to time worked on them; and that it was his custom to wear them, or some of them, one at a time, changing them. Burgess V-C dismissed the contention that these watches were within the bequest on the short ground that they were in substance derived from or part of the Todhunter collection, and therefore followed the clocks into residue. We cannot agree. A watch is in its nature an article of personal use, and in the present case we regard the cherishing by eye and hand of the collection as well as the wearing of selected items from time to time as bringing them within the definition of articles of personal use.[3]

(c) The life interest

When the deceased leaves issue, the surviving spouse is entitled to a life interest in half the residue, after deduction of the personal chattels, statutory legacy and interest thereon. The Committee on the Law of Intestate Succession whose recommendations led to the passing of the Intestates' Estates Act 1952 recommended that the surviving spouse be given the right to capitalise this life interest and as a result of this recommendation, s 47A was added to the Administration of Estates Act 1925.

Report of the Committee on the Law of Intestate Succession[4]

32. If our recommendations are adopted, a life interest will arise only when the intestate is survived by the spouse and issue and then in a greatly reduced number of instances because of the increase in the statutory legacy to be given to the spouse.[5] Still, in cases where the net estate is not much in excess of £5,000, the existence of such life interests will be attended by difficulties in administration and may not be of much benefit to the spouse compared with a capital sum. Section 48(1) of the Act of 1925[6] provides that the intestate's personal representative, with the consent of the surviving spouse, or, if the latter is the sole personal representative, then with the consent of the Court, may purchase or redeem the life interest of the spouse by paying to the latter a capital sum out of the estate. This capital sum is reckoned in accordance with tables which are to be selected by the personal representative. There is already in existence, therefore, one means whereby a spouse may receive a capital sum in lieu of the life interest and whereby the personal representative may avoid being saddled with the burden of administration of a small estate during the spouse's lifetime. We understand that this procedure is not made use of to any great extent, perhaps because the existence of this particular Section of the Act is not widely known to personal representatives. In our opinion the scope of this remedy against the continuance of life interests can be usefully widened. Under the existing law the initiative for taking action must come from the personal representative, who may not be the surviving spouse. As the right to

---

3. See also *Re Chaplin* [1950] Ch 507, [1950] 2 All ER 155 where the deceased's 60 foot motor yacht was held to be an article of personal use.
4. (1950) Cmd 8310.
5. The Committee had recommended, at para 13, that the statutory legacy be increased from £1,000 to £5,000.
6. Subsequently repealed by Intestates' Estates Act 1952, s 2(a).

surrender the life interest for a capital sum affects the spouse more than anyone else, we recommend that the spouse alone, irrespective of whether he or she is the sole personal representative or one of the personal representatives, should have the right to elect that a payment be made to him or her of a capital sum out of the estate representing the value of the life interest. We are not in favour of the children having a similar power, owing to the difficulties which are likely to arise where some of the children are infants or where adult children are living in widely separated parts of the world or are unable to agree as to whether the power should be exercised or not.

Administration of Estates Act 1925

47A.[7] **Succession to real and personal estate on intestacy**

(1) Where a surviving husband or wife is entitled to a life interest in part of the residuary estate, and so elects, the personal representative shall purchase or redeem the life interest by paying the capital value[8] thereof to the tenant for life, or the persons deriving title under the tenant for life, and the costs of the transaction; and thereupon the residuary estate of the intestate may be dealt with and distributed free from the life interest.

(5) An election under this section shall be exercisable only within the period of twelve months from the date on which representation with respect to the estate of the intestate is first taken out:

Provided that if the surviving husband or wife satisfies the court that the limitation to the said period of twelve months will operate unfairly—

(a) in consequence of the representation first taken out being probate of a will subsequently revoked on the ground that the will was invalid or,

(b) in consequence of a question whether a person had an interest in the estate, or as to the nature of an interest in the estate, not having been determined at the time when representation was first taken out, or

(c) in consequence of some other circumstances affecting the administration or distribution of the estate,

the court may extend the said period.[9]

(6) An election under this section shall be exercisable, except where the tenant for life is the sole personal representative, by notifying the personal representative (or, where there are two or more personal representatives of whom one is the tenant for life all of them except the tenant for life) in writing; and a notification in writing under this subsection shall not be revocable except with the consent of the personal representative.

(7) Where the tenant for life is the sole personal representative an election under this section shall not be effective unless written notice thereof is given to the Senior Registrar of the Family Division of the High Court within the period within which it must be made; and provision may be made by probate rules for keeping a record of such notices and making that record available to the public.[10]

(9) In considering for the purposes of the foregoing provisions of this section the question when representation was first taken out, a grant limited to settled land or to trust property shall be left out of account and a grant limited to real estate or to personal estate shall be left out of account unless a grant limited to the remainder of the estate has previously been made or is made at the same time.

---

7. Added by Intestates' Estates Act 1952, s 2.

8. The rules for calculating the capital sum are now contained in the Intestate Succession (Interest and Capitalisation) Order 1977, SI 1977/1491 to which is annexed separate tables for husbands and wives owing to their differing expectations of life, with a multiplier in each table which varies according to the age of the surviving spouse and the prevailing rate of interest on medium-term government stocks.

9. See eg *Re Phelps* [1978] 3 All ER 395, [1978] 1 WLR 1501 where Foster J refers at p 396 to an earlier hearing (unreported) where the spouse having made an ineffective election under s 47A (she sent it before letters of administration had been granted and not to the eventual administrators), applied for leave to make an election out of time but 'the judge was not satisfied on the facts that it came within paragraph (c) and refused to extend the time' (p 397). See further p 133 post.

10. This is provided for by NCPR 1954, r 56.

(d) The right to appropriate the matrimonial home

The Committee on the Law of Intestate Succession reporting in 1950 was most concerned to secure the position of the surviving spouse in relation to the matrimonial home. Under the Administration of Estates Act 1925, s 41[11] the personal representatives already had power to appropriate the matrimonial home in satisfaction of the surviving spouse's statutory legacy, but they could not be compelled to do so, and with the statutory legacy standing at only £1,000[12] the legacy was normally insufficient for this purpose. The Committee's recommendations were subsequently embodied in the Intestates' Estates Act 1952.

Report of the Committee on the Law of Intestate Succession[13]

23 . . . Therefore, unless the intestate's children are able to agree to allow the spouse to remain in the house, it must often be sold, where the estate is over £1,000, in order to provide the children's immediate share of the estate. Those who have submitted evidence to us have made varying suggestions as to the provision which should be made for the spouse in respect of the matrimonial home and the proposals fall naturally into three groups:

    (a) merely to increase the statutory legacy;
    (b) to give the matrimonial home to the spouse;[14]
    (c) to give the spouse an option to purchase the matrimonial home at a fixed value.

If the statutory legacy is increased to £5,000 as we are recommending, the spouse will usually be able to set off the value of the house against this larger sum and the hardship which occurs under the present law should disappear. However, in view of the emphasis which has been placed on the position of the spouse with regard to the matrimonial home in the evidence before us, we feel that it would be unjust merely to increase the statutory legacy and not to give the spouse some right in respect of the home. It is to be remembered that because of our recommendations for a further capital sum to be given to the spouse when there are no children, it is only necessary to consider the position as between the spouse and the children. In our view it would seem unjust to the children to allow the spouse to take the matrimonial home, as well as the statutory legacy of £5,000. Supposing, however, that the amount of the statutory legacy were to be decreased to £3,000 and that the spouse were to receive the matrimonial home in addition, then an unfair distinction would be drawn between those circumstances where the intestate had chosen to own his house and those where he had merely rented a house. To provide that the latter suggestion should rank as an alternative wherever the intestate had owned the house would lead to uncertainty and might be to the prejudice of the children's interests. It appears to us, therefore, that the balance of interest is maintained if the right to be given to the surviving spouse is an option to purchase from the estate the intestate's interest in the matrimonial home. This right will give the spouse an advantage which he or she does not possess under the existing law because, provided a limit is set on the

---

11. P 391 post.
12. For those dying intestate between 1926–1952.
13. (1950) Cmd 8310.
14. This is the solution that has been adopted in Scotland, where the surviving spouse is entitled to the deceased's interest in any dwellinghouse in which the surviving spouse was ordinarily resident at the deceased's death up to the value of £50,000 (if the interest is worth more than £50,000 the surviving spouse is entitled to a cash sum of £50,000 in lieu). The surviving spouse is also entitled to the furniture and furnishings of the house up to the value of £10,000. These rights are in addition to the surviving spouse's statutory legacy (currently £15,000 where the deceased leaves issue, otherwise £25,000): Succession (Scotland) Act 1964, ss 8, 9; the Prior Rights of Surviving Spouse (Scotland) Order 1981, SI 1981/806.

period during which the option can be exercised, the personal representatives will not be able to sell the house against the wishes of the spouse until the option expires.[15]

Intestates' Estates Act 1952

5. Rights of surviving spouse as regards the matrimonial home
The Second Schedule to this Act shall have effect for enabling the surviving husband or wife of a person dying intestate after the commencement of this Act to acquire the matrimonial home.

SCHEDULE 2—RIGHTS OF SURVIVING SPOUSE AS RESPECTS THE MATRIMONIAL HOME

1.—(1) Subject to the provisions of this Schedule, where the residuary estate of the intestate comprises an interest in a dwelling-house in which the surviving husband or wife was resident at the time of the intestate's death, the surviving husband or wife may require the personal representative, in exercise of the power conferred by section forty-one of the principal Act[16] (and with due regard to the requirements of that section as to valuation[17]) to appropriate the said interest in the dwelling-house in or towards satisfaction of any absolute interest of the surviving husband or wife in the real and personal estate of the intestate.

(2) The right conferred by this paragraph shall not be exercisable where the interest is—

  (a) a tenancy which at the date of the death of the intestate was a tenancy which would determine within the period of two years from that date; or

  (b) a tenancy which the landlord by notice given after that date could determine within the remainder of that period.[18]

(3) Nothing in subsection (5) of section forty-one of the principal Act (which requires the personal representative, making an appropriation to any person under that section, to have regard to the rights of others)[19] shall prevent the personal representative from giving effect to the right conferred by this paragraph.

(4) The reference in this paragraph to an absolute interest in the real and personal estate of the intestate includes a reference to the capital value of a life interest which the surviving husband or wife has under this Act elected to have redeemed.[20]

(5) Where part of a building was, at the date of the death of the intestate, occupied as a separate dwelling, that dwelling shall for the purposes of this Schedule be treated as a dwelling-house.

3.—(1) The right conferred by paragraph 1 of this Schedule—

  (a) shall not be exercisable after the expiration of twelve months from the first taking out of representation with respect to the intestate's estate;

---

15. The Committee also considered, at para 27 an alternative suggestion that the surviving spouse be given merely the right to reside in the house, but rejected it because of the difficulties it would introduce in relation to the spouse's liability for repairs, rates and taxes, and responsibility for providing a home for the children, 'besides adding a complication in the case of leasehold premises to the relationship between landlord and tenant.'
16. AEA 1925. See p 391 post.
17. Open market value at the date of the appropriation, see *Re Collins* p 392 post.
18. But see now Leasehold Reform Act 1967, s 7(8) which excludes para 1(2) of the Schedule (a) where the surviving spouse would as a result of the appropriation under the Schedule become entitled by s 7 to acquire the freehold or an extended lease under the Leasehold Reform Act 1967 either immediately on the appropriation or before the tenancy can determine or be determined under the Schedule, (b) when the deceased spouse, having been entitled to acquire the freehold or an extended lease under the Act had given notice of his desire to have it before his death and the benefit of that notice had been appropriated with the tenancy.
19. See p 392 post.
20. See p 128 ante. In *Re Phelps* p 133 post, the surviving spouse would have been able to secure her appropriation of the matrimonial home without using any of her own funds for this purpose had she complied with the time limit for electing to capitalise her life interest (see p 129 ante).

(b) shall not be exercisable after the death of the surviving husband or wife;

(c) shall be exercisable, except where the surviving husband or wife is the sole personal representative,[1] by notifying the personal representative (or, where there are two or more personal representatives of whom one is the surviving husband or wife, all of them except the surviving husband or wife) in writing.

(2) A notification in writing under paragraph (c) of the foregoing sub-paragraph shall not be revocable with the consent of the personal representative; but the surviving husband or wife may require the personal representative to have the said interest in the dwelling-house valued in accordance with section forty-one of the principal Act[2] and to inform him or her of the result of that valuation before he or she decides whether to exercise the right.

(3) Subsection (9) of the section forty-seven A[3] added to the principal Act by section two of this Act shall apply for the purposes of the construction of the reference in this paragraph to the first taking out of representation, and the proviso to subsection (5) of that section[4] shall apply for the purpose of enabling the surviving husband or wife to apply for an extension of the period of twelve months mentioned in this paragraph.

4.—(1) During the period of twelve months mentioned in paragraph 3 of this Schedule the personal representative shall not without the written consent of the surviving husband or wife sell or otherwise dispose of the said interest in the dwelling-house except in the course of administration owing to want of other assets.

(3) Where the court under sub-paragraph (3) of paragraph 3 of this Schedule extends the said period of twelve months, the court may direct that this paragraph shall apply in relation to the extended period as it applied in relation to the original period of twelve months.

(4) This paragraph shall not apply where the surviving husband or wife is the sole personal representative or one of two or more personal representatives.

(5) Nothing in this paragraph shall confer any right on the surviving husband or wife as against a purchaser from the personal representative.

5.—(1) Where the surviving husband or wife is one of two or more personal representatives, the rule that a trustee may not be a purchaser of trust property shall not prevent the surviving husband or wife from purchasing out of the estate of the intestate an interest in a dwelling-house in which the surviving husband or wife was resident at the time of the intestate's death.

(2) The power of appropriation under section forty-one of the principal Act[5] shall include power to appropriate an interest in a dwelling-house in which the surviving husband or wife was resident at the time of the intestate's death partly in satisfaction of an interest of the surviving husband or wife in the real and personal estate of the intestate and partly in return for a payment of money by the surviving husband or wife to the personal representative.

6.—(1) Where the surviving husband or wife is a person of unsound mind or a defective, a requirement or consent under this Schedule may be made or given on his or her behalf by the committee or receiver, if any, or, where there is no committee or receiver, by the court.

(2) A requirement or consent made or given under this Schedule by a surviving husband or wife who is an infant shall be as valid and binding as it would be if he or she were of age; and, as respects an appropriation in pursuance of paragraph 1 of this

---

1. If the surviving spouse is the sole personal representative therefore, the right of appropriation under the Schedule will not apply; such a spouse must apply to the court for permission or obtain the consent of all the other beneficiaries if all are sui iuris.

2. See p 391 post.

3. P 129 ante.

4. Ibid.

5. AEA 1925.

Schedule, the provisions of section forty-one of the principal Act[6] as to obtaining the consent of the infant's parent or guardian, or of the court on behalf of the infant, shall not apply.

7.—(1) Except where the context otherwise requires, references in this Schedule to a dwelling-house include references to any garden or portion of ground attached to and usually occupied with the dwelling-house or otherwise required for the amenity or convenience of the dwelling-house.

In **Re Phelps** [1980] 1 Ch 275, [1979] 3 All ER 373, the surviving spouse's statutory legacy, at the then rate of £8,750, was less than the value of the matrimonial home.[7] She sought to exercise the right to demand appropriation of the home under the Intestates' Estates Act 1952 on paying the difference out of her own pocket. At first instance, Foster J held[8] that in view of the words 'in or towards satisfaction' in para 1(1) of the Second Schedule, the Act would only apply where the value of the surviving spouse's absolute interest in the intestate's estate was greater than the value of the home. The Court of Appeal disagreed, Templeman LJ saying, at p 374:

The effect of para 5(2) is that for the purposes of Sch 2 a transaction which in essence is partly appropriation and partly sale becomes an appropriation and Sch 2 must be read as if s 41 of the 1925 Act included this new hybrid power of appropriation. When a widow, pursuant to para 1(1) of Sch 2, requires the personal representatives to appropriate, in exercise of the power conferred by s 41, she is requiring them to exercise that power as enlarged by para 5(2). Where the dwelling-house and the widow's interests are equal in value, the personal representatives are required to appropriate in satisfaction of the widow's interest; where the dwelling-house is worth less than the widow's interest they are required to appropriate towards satisfaction of the widow's interest; and where the dwelling-house is worth more than the widow's interest, they are required to appropriate, in the words of para 5(2) 'partly in satisfaction' of the interest 'and partly in return for a payment of money.'

5 The issue's entitlement

(a) Meaning of 'issue'

Does it include the intestate's adopted children, legitimated children, illegitimate children, children en ventre sa mère? The answer nowadays is that it includes them all.[9]

---

6. AEA 1925, see p 391 post.
7. Having failed to obtain leave to capitalise her life interest out of time (see p 129 n 9 ante), she was unable to use this to supplement the statutory legacy as permitted by para 1(4) of the Schedule.
8. [1978] 3 All ER 395, [1978] 1 WLR 1501.
9. Personal representatives who would be at risk as a result are given protection from liability to such beneficiaries (other than children en ventre sa mère) if they distribute without knowledge of their entitlement: Children Act 1975, s 8(9) Sch 1, Part IV, para 15; Legitimacy Act 1976 s 7; Family Law Reform Act 1969, s 17.

(i) *Adopted children*

Children Act 1975

Section 8
SCHEDULE I
PART II ADOPTION ORDERS

3. Status conferred by adoption
(1) An adopted child shall be treated in law—
  (a) where the adopters are a married couple, as if he had been born as a child of the marriage (whether or not he was in fact born after the marriage was solemnized);
  (b) in any other case, as if he had been born to the adopter in wedlock (but not as a child of any actual marriage of the adopter).
(2) An adopted child shall be treated in law as if he were not the child of any person other than the adopters or adopter.
(3) It is hereby declared that this paragraph prevents an adopted child from being illegitimate.[10]

(ii) *Legitimated children*

Legitimacy Act 1976

5. Rights of legitimated persons and others to take interests in property
(3) A legitimated person[11] and any other person shall be entitled to take any interest as if the legitimated person had been born legitimate.[12]

(iii) *Illegitimate children*

Before 1970 an illegitimate child could claim only on his mother's intestacy and then only if the mother had no legitimate issue.[13] The illegitimate child had no rights whatever on his father's intestacy, nor on the intestacy of remoter relations such as grandparents and brothers. If the illegitimate child himself died intestate, leaving no spouse or issue, the mother would take the whole,[14] the father (and remoter relatives) having no rights at all. For deaths after 1969, the succession rights of illegitimate children were substantially improved by the Family Law Reform Act 1969[15] but an element of discrimination remained[16] and the Law Commission has recommended further reform with a view to equating the succession rights of 'marital and non-marital' children.[17]

---

10. This paragraph applies to entitlement on the intestacy of those dying after 1975 (paras 5(1)(3) and 1(5)). For those dying before 1976 but after 1949, similar provisions were contained in the Adoption Act 1958, ss 16, 17.

11. Ie a child born illegitimate but legitimated by his natural parents' subsequent marriage: s 10(1).

12. The section applies to entitlement on the intestacy of those dying after 1975 (ss 5(2), 10(1)). For those dying before 1976 but after 1925, similar provisions were contained in the Legitimacy Act 1926, s 3.

13. Legitimacy Act 1926, s 9(1).

14. Legitimacy Act 1926, s 9(2).

15. Embodying the recommendations of the Russell Committee on the Law of Succession in relation to Illegitimate Persons, (1966) Cmnd 3051.

16. See Ryder 'Property Law Aspects of the Family Law Reform Act 1969' (1971) 24 CLP 157 at pp 161–63.

17. As is already the case, for example, in Ontario, see Succession Law Reform Act 1977, s 1(2).

Family Law Reform Act 1969

14. Right of illegitimate child to succeed on intestacy of parents, and of parents to succeed on intestacy of illegitimate child

(1) Where either parent of an illegitimate child dies intestate as respects all or any of his or her real or personal property, the illegitimate child or, if he is dead, his issue, shall be entitled to take any interest therein to which he or such issue would have been entitled if he had been born legitimate.[18]

(2) Where an illegitimate child dies intestate in respect of all or any of his real or personal property, each of his parents, if surviving, shall be entitled to take any interest therein to which that parent would have been entitled if the child had been born legitimate.

(3) In accordance with the foregoing provisions of this section, Part IV of the Administration of Estates Act 1925 (which deals with the distribution of the estate of an intestate) shall have effect as if—

   (a) any reference to the issue of the intestate included a reference to any illegitimate child of his and to the issue of any such child;

   (b) any reference to the child or children of the intestate included a reference to any illegitimate child or children of his; and

   (c) in relation to an intestate who is an illegitimate child, any reference to the parent, parents, father or mother of the intestate were a reference to his natural parent, parents, father or mother.

(4) For the purposes of subsection (2) of this section and of the provisions amended by subsection (3)(c) thereof, an illegitimate child shall be presumed not to have been survived by his father unless the contrary is shown.[19]

Report of the Law Commission on Illegitimacy[20]

8.6 .... there remain a number of differences between marital and non-marital children in matters of inheritance. The most significant difference is that the child cannot inherit on the intestacy of his grandparents, brothers, sisters, uncles or aunts, whether or not any of these relations were themselves born in marriage. Conversely, these relations cannot inherit on the intestacy of the child born outside marriage. Moreover, on an intestacy it is only the legitimate descendants of a deceased non-marital child who are entitled to succeed to the share which he would have taken had he survived the intestate.[1]

8.8 The argument of principle against extending the rights of the non-marital child to inherit on intestacy may be stated thus: it is right that the non-marital child should be able to inherit on the intestacy of either of his parents, who have moral and may have legal responsibilities for him, and who can be presumed to have wished to benefit him. However, this does not apply to remoter relations, since the deceased may not know of the illegitimate beneficiary, let alone wish to benefit him. It could even be said that a relation of this kind, such as a grandparent, might choose to die intestate on the assumption that his or her estate would go to the grandchildren of marital birth and that it would be wrong in such circumstances partially to frustrate the grandparent's positive intentions by allowing other grandchildren to share.

8.9 There are four reasons why we do not consider that this argument should prevail. First, we think that the point of principle was really decided in the Family Law Reform

---

18. See eg *Re Trott* [1980] CLY 1259 where the intestate's illegitimate daughter successfully claimed the whole of her father's estate which would otherwise have passed to his brothers and sisters. Such a claim would have been impossible had the intestate died before 1970.

19. The Russell Committee on the Law of Succession in relation to Illegitimate Persons (1966) Cmnd 3051, at para 47, had recommended this presumption as a rule of convenience, taking the view that in many cases the identity of the father would be unknown.

20. (1982) Law Com 118.

1. On the statutory trusts, see p 137 post.

Act 1969, which gave to illegitimate children extended, but still incomplete, succession rights. The result is now somewhat illogical. A child and his father have mutual rights of succession, even if they have had no real contact; but there are no such rights in respect of the mother's relatives, or of the child's siblings, with any or all of whom the child may have had close personal links.

8.10   Secondly, a right on the part of a non-marital child to inherit on the intestacy of his remoter relations in the same way as a marital child would make for consistency between intestate and testamentary succession. At present, if a man leaves property by will to 'my grandchildren' an illegitimate grandchild will, because of the changed rule of construction,[2] have a right to share in the bequest in the absence of any contrary intention in the will, whether the testator knows of that grandchild or not. If the man dies intestate, that grandchild will not benefit under the law as it stands.

8.11   Thirdly, the argument assumes that the grandparent in question would have wished to exclude any grandchildren of non-marital birth if he or she had known of their existence. This seems to us to be speculation. If the grandparent feels particularly strongly about the possibility of illegitimate descendants benefiting, he will be able to exclude the possibility by making a will in appropriate terms. Fourthly, it seems to us that the argument should be treated as of significant weight only if it is true that a substantial number of those who choose not to leave wills do so because they wish their property to devolve on those entitled under an intestacy and thus exclude those born outside marriage. Such evidence as there is suggests that this is not the case.

8.12   Finally we should stress that the United Kingdom's signature and ratification of the European Convention on Human Rights and the European Convention on the Legal Status of Children Born Out of Wedlock strengthens the arguments for removing, wherever possible, legal discrimination against children born outside marriage. The United Kingdom has placed a reservation against Article 9 of the Legal Status Convention. This Article reads as follows—

> 'A child born out of wedlock shall have the same right of succession in the estate of its father and its mother and of a member of its father's or mother's family, as if it had been born in wedlock.'

Under English law, at present, the non-marital child manifestly does not have the same right of succession in the estate of 'a member of its father's or mother's family' as if it had been of marital birth. Extension of rights on intestacy such as we have discussed would, in our opinion, allow the United Kingdom to remove, so far as the law of England and Wales is concerned, the reservation against Article 9. The removal of discrimination against non-marital children in matters of succession would also bring English law into line with the provisions of the European Convention on Human Rights as laid down by the judgment of the European Court of Human Rights in the *Marckx* case.[3]

8.13   Accordingly we conclude that there is no significant argument of principle to justify retention of the existing rules discriminating against illegitimate persons in relation to intestate succession.[4]

---

2. See FLRA 1969, s 15(1)(b). Before 1970, words in a will describing a blood relationship meant only those coming within the description by way of legitimate links, unless the testator had shown a contrary intention.

3. *Marckx v Belgium* (1979–80) 2 EHRR 330.

4. The Law Commission recommended that the protection afforded to personal representatives under FLRA 1969, s 17 (p 133 n 9 ante) should be extended to claims by persons becoming entitled as a result of their recommendation (para 8.29) and that the presumption against the father's survival contained in FLRA 1969, s 14(4), p 135 ante, should be extended to include any persons related to the father (para 8.33).

(iv) *Children en ventre sa mère*

Administration of Estates Act 1925

55. Definitions
(2) References to a child or issue living at the death of any person include a child or issue en ventre sa mère at the date of death.

(b) The statutory trusts

The deceased's issue hold their entitlement on the 'statutory trusts'.[5]

Administration of Estates Act 1925

47. Statutory trusts in favour of issue and other classes of relatives of intestate[6]
(1) Where under this Part of this Act the residuary estate of an intestate, or any part thereof, is directed to be held on the statutory trusts for the issue of the intestate, the same shall be held upon the following trusts, namely:
  (i) In trust, in equal shares if more than one, for all or any of the children or child of the intestate, living at the death of the intestate, who attain the age of eighteen[7] years or marry under that age, and for all or any of the issue living at the death of the intestate who attain the age of eighteen years or marry under that age of any child of the intestate who predeceases the intestate, such issue to take through all degrees, according to their stocks, in equal shares if more than one, the share which their parent would have taken if living at the death of the intestate, and so that no issue shall take whose parent is living at the death of the intestate and so capable of taking;
  (ii) The statutory power of advancement,[8] and the statutory provisions which relate to maintenance and accumulation of surplus income,[9] shall apply, but when an infant marries such infant shall be entitled to give valid receipts for the income of the infant's share or interest;
  (iii) (see p 139 post).
  (iv) The personal representatives may permit any infant contingently interested to have the use and enjoyment of any personal chattels[10] in such manner and subject to such conditions (if any) as the personal representatives may consider reasonable, and without being liable to account for any consequential loss.
(2) If the trusts in favour of the issue of the intestate fail by reason of no child or other issue attaining an absolutely vested interest—
(a) the residuary estate of the intestate and the income thereof and all statutory accumulations, if any, of the income thereof, or so much thereof as may not have been paid or applied under any power affecting the same, shall go, devolve and be held under the provisions of this Part of this Act as if the intestate had died without leaving issue living at the death of the intestate;
(b) references in this Part of this Act to the intestate 'leaving no issue' shall be construed as 'leaving no issue who attain an absolutely vested interest';

---

5. AEA 1925, s 46, p 124 ante.
6. By s 47(3) (not extracted) the provisions of subs (1) and (2) (other than the hotchpot provision of subs (1)(iii)) are applied to the entitlement of other classes of relatives, eg the intestate's brothers and sisters.
7. Eighteen substituted for twenty-one by FLRA 1969, s 3(2).
8. Trustee Act 1925, s 32.
9. Trustee Act 1925, s 31.
10. As defined in AEA 1925, s 55, p 126 ante.

(c)   references in this Part of this Act to the intestate 'leaving issue' or 'leaving a child or other issue' shall be construed as 'leaving issue who attain an absolutely vested interest'.

EXAMPLE

A dies intestate, a widower. He had two children: a son, B, who is alive when A dies and aged 20, and a daughter, C, who died before A leaving a daughter D, aged 16 at A's death. A's residuary estate will go as to one half to B at once; the other half will be held on trust for D until she attains 18 or marries under that age.

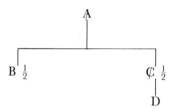

D being under 18, the income of her share will be used for her maintenance, education and benefit[11] (the surplus being accumulated and handed over to her along with the capital at 18 or earlier marriage) and the trustees can also apply for her benefit up to one half of the capital due to her.[12] If C had died without leaving a child, B would have taken the whole of A's estate; if B had been under 18 at A's death in such circumstances, and had subsequently died under 18, unmarried and without leaving issue, the statutory trusts would have failed and A would be treated as having died without issue surviving him.

(c) Hotchpot[13] for advancements

The basis of the statutory trusts is to achieve equality between the stirpes.[14] It may be that one of the intestate's children has already received a substantial gift from his parent by way of an advancement during the intestate's lifetime. In fairness to the other children and on the assumption that this must be what the intestate would have intended, the advancee is required to bring that gift into account at its value at the intestate's death, in order to achieve an overall equality between the stirpes, unless he can establish that this is not what the intestate intended.

---

11. Trustee Act 1925, s 31.
12. Trustee Act 1925, s 32.
13. Derived from the French 'hochepot', a dish shaken up, a pudding; 'hache en poche', 'a confusing mingling of diverse things'—Jowitt *Dictionary of English Law* (2nd edn, 1977). 'A tiresome irritating subject, hotchpot' per Danckwerts J, *Re Morton* [1956] Ch 644, 647, [1956] 3 All ER 259, 260.
14. The branches of the family, derived from stirps (Lat).

Administration of Estates Act 1925

47. Statutory trusts in favour of issue and other classes of relatives of intestate

(1) . . .

(iii) Where the property held on the statutory trusts for issue[15] is divisible into shares, then any money or property which, by way of advancement or on the marriage of a child of the intestate, has been paid to such child[16] by the intestate or settled by the intestate for the benefit of such child (including any life or less interest and including property covenanted to be paid or settled) shall, subject to any contrary intention expressed or appearing from the circumstances of the case, be taken as being so paid or settled in or towards satisfaction of the share of such child or the share which such child would have taken if living at the death of the intestate, and shall be brought into account, at a valuation (the value to be reckoned as at the death of the intestate), in accordance with the requirements of the personal representatives.

EXAMPLE

If in the previous example[17] A's net residuary estate had been worth £30,000, but in his lifetime A had made an advancement of £10,000 to B, in order to achieve equality between the stirpes, each branch of the family would have to receive (£30,000 + £10,000) ÷ 2 = £20,000. B has already received £10,000 by way of the advancement and so will only receive a further £10,000 from A's residuary estate. C received no advancements from A, so his branch of the family will receive £20,000 from A's residuary estate, to be held in trust for D until she reaches 18 or marries under that age. Any advancements made to D will not have to be brought into account by C's branch of the family, as s 47(1)(iii) only relates to advancements to the deceased's children.

Taylor v Taylor (1875) LR 20 Eq 155, Ch; Jessel MR

During his lifetime the intestate paid his son's admission fees for the Inns of Court when the son was intending to become a barrister; when the son abandoned the law and entered the army the intestate paid for his commission, outfitting and part of his passage money to India; he also paid the debts his son incurred as an army officer, in the sum of £650. The son gave up the army, whereupon his father bought him a mining plant worth about £850 to enable him to set up in a mining business. When that failed, the son entered the Church and his father thereafter paid him considerable sums from time to time to assist him with his living expenses. Which of these sums had to be brought into account as advancements?

Held: Only those sums paid by the father to establish the son in life or to make a permanent provision for him would have to be accounted for.

Jessel MR: I shall not be[18] the first Judge to hold that sums of money given by a father, without covenant, without agreement, not at any definite time, of various amounts,

---

15. See AEA 1925, s 47(1)(i), p 137 ante.
16. Note that s 47(1)(iii) only applies to gifts to the intestate's children. Advancements to grandchildren or remoter issue are not brought into account under this provision.
17. P 138 ante.
18. Ie: 'I am not prepared to be' . . . .

sometimes amounting to £200, sometimes more or sometimes less, given to a curate to aid him in his maintenance, are advancements by way of portion or provision within the statute.[19] I have always understood that an advancement by way of portion is something given by the parent to establish the child in life, or to make what is called a provision for him—not a mere casual payment of this kind. You may make the provision by way of a marriage portion on the marriage of the child. You may make it on putting him into a profession or business in a variety of ways: you may pay for a commission, you may buy him the goodwill of a business and give him stock-in-trade; all these things I understand to be portions or provisions. Again, if in the absence of evidence you find a father giving a large sum to a child in one payment, there is a presumption that that is intended to start him in life or make a provision for him; but if a small sum is so given you may require evidence to shew the purpose. But I do not think that these words 'by portion' are to be disregarded, nor is the word 'advancement' to be disregarded. It is not every payment made to a child which is to be regarded as an advancement by way of portion. In every case to which I have been referred, there has either been a settlement itself, or the purpose for which the payment was made has been shewn to be that which every one would recognise as being for establishing the child or making a provision for the child. . . .

Prima facie, an advancement must be made in early life; but any sum given by way of making a permanent provision for the child would come within the term establishing in life. The entry money at the *Middle Temple* was clearly for the establishment of the child, and must be accounted for; but the payment to the special pleader appeared to be rather in the nature of a payment for preliminary education, and need not be accounted for. The price of the commission and the outfit was an advancement on entering the army, and must be accounted for, but not the price of the outfit for *India* or the passage money, neither of which were payments for the Plaintiff's establishment in life. Again, the sums paid for debts in *India* appeared to be in the nature of temporary assistance; thus, if a child were in business and required further capital, a sum given for that purpose would be an advancement; but a sum given merely to assist him temporarily would not. The sum given to pay the debts in *India* therefore need not be accounted for. On the other hand, the payments in respect of the mining operations in *Wales* appeared to have been made for starting the Plaintiff in business, and ought to be accounted for.

In **Re Hayward** [1957] Ch 528, [1957] 2 All ER 474, the intestate had nominated the balance in his Post Office Savings Bank Account and his National Savings Certificates totalling about £500 to his elder son X, who was 43 when the intestate died, married and in regular employment. The total estate, including the nominated property, amounted to only £1,500. The deceased's other son, Y, claimed that X should bring the £500 into account as an advancement. The Court of Appeal disagreed, Jenkins LJ saying at p 482:

I think that in order to raise a prima facie case for accounting, it must be shown that the fund in question was sufficiently substantial in itself to be in the nature of a permanent provision without pressing too far the question of proportion. If that were not so an intestate who only had £50 in the world, £25 in cash and £25 in National Savings Certificates, could properly be held to be making a permanent provision for one of his sons by giving him a nomination in respect of the certificates, because they represented no less than half his estate, although the sum given would in itself be trifling.

In **Re Reeve** [1935] Ch 110, the intestate during his life appointed the capital of a settled fund to a child of his under a special power of appointment conferred on him by a settlement under which he himself had a life interest. He then released his life interest in favour of that child, who took the settled fund

---

19. Statute of Distributions 1670 which was repealed by AEA 1925. Section 5 of the 1670 Statute contained a similar provision to that now contained in AEA 1925, s 47(1)(iii).

absolutely as a result. Clauson J held that the capital value of the fund was not liable to be brought into account under Administration of Estates Act 1925, s 47(1)(iii) since it was not property paid or settled by the intestate, merely a decision by the intestate as to where someone else's property should go. He went on to consider whether the intestate's life interest should be brought into account as that was the intestate's own property which he had given to the child, saying at p 117:

I think it may well be argued that . . . the life interest which he so surrendered is 'money or property which by way of advancement . . . has been paid to such child'. The language is not apt, but I can conceive that the words might cover the life interest so surrendered. I think it is recognised that, if it be that only (namely, the surrendered life interest) upon which the clause operates, the result is nil, because that which is paid is to be brought into account at a valuation to be reckoned at the time of the death of the intestate, and it is quite obvious that at the death of the intestate the life interest surrendered by him five years before, which of course comes to an end on his death, if it is reckoned as at the death of the intestate, is of the value of nil, and accordingly nothing is to be brought into account.

In **Hardy v Shaw** [1976] Ch 82, [1975] 2 All ER 1052, the father of three children, H, V and M, carried on a small printing business by way of a family company. He held 1,000 shares in the company whilst the children, all of whom had worked in the business since leaving school, held 600 shares each. Following her marriage, M left the business, which so annoyed her father that he decided that she should have no more shares in the company. By his will, he left his 1,000 shares in the company entirely to his wife, the children's mother. She subsequently gave H and V 499 of her shares each, keeping only two for herself, and died 14 years later. M demanded that H and V bring the two blocks of 499 shares into account on a hotchpot on their mother's intestacy. They argued that their mother had shown that she intended to prefer them so that the hotchpot provisions would not apply. Having decided that the share transfers were advancements by the mother, Goff J said at p 1057:

I therefore turn to the second question: does a contrary intention appear from the circumstances of the case? I would first observe that in my judgment the test is not objective: that is if the intestate had thought of everything what would her intention be likely to have been? but subjective: looking at all the circumstances, do they require an inference that her intention was that the gift should not be brought into hotchpot? I have no doubt that is right, not only on the language of the section itself but because that was clearly the approach of the whole court in *Re Lacon* ([1891] 2 Ch 482 at 496, 500, 504).

That, however, does not, in my judgment, mean that it must be shown that the mother's attention was specifically drawn to the section or its effect, or that she formed an intention expressly in relation thereto. The question, in my view, is whether the facts as a whole indicate an intention on her part not simply to anticipate as to the defendants the provision her children would get on her death, but an intention and desire to prefer them to the plaintiff (M) not only in point of time but in point of the amount and nature of that provision. . . .

(Having reviewed the evidence, he concluded:) I have therefore come to the conclusion that there is not sufficient evidence that she ever directed her mind to the question what should happen on her death, and so could not have had a contrary intention, or, at any rate, that the circumstances are not so clearly inconsistent with the statutory presumption that I must infer the contrary intention.[20]

---

20. Cf the United States Uniform Probate Code, s 2–110 which requires any beneficiary, not just a child of the deceased, to bring the deceased's lifetime gifts into account against his entitlement on the deceased's total (not partial) intestacy, but only where there is written evidence that the deceased intended the gift to constitute an advancement.

6   Partial intestacy

(a) Effect first given to the will

A partial intestacy arises where the deceased leaves a will but it fails to dispose of the whole of his property.[1] When this happens, full effect is first given to the will and only then are the intestacy rules applied to the extent that the will has not disposed of the property concerned.

Administration of Estates Act 1925

49. Application to cases of partial intestacy
(1) Where any person dies leaving a will disposing of his property, this Part of the Act shall have effect as respects the part of his property not so disposed of subject to the provisions contained in the will and subject to the following modifications. . . .[2]

Re McKee [1931] 2 Ch 145, Ch D; Maugham J[3]

The testator had declared an express trust for sale of his residuary estate, giving a life interest therein to his widow, followed by a remainder to such of his brothers and sisters as survived her. The last of his brothers and sisters having died in the widow's lifetime, the remainder interest was undisposed of property. Was it subject to the administration trusts of the Administration of Estates Act 1925, s 33,[4] and could the widow claim her statutory legacy under the intestacy rules straightaway or would it be payable only on her death?
Held: The statutory trust for sale was superseded by the express trust for sale in the will. The widow was not entitled to any immediate payment in respect of the undisposed of property; she would receive the benefit of her life interest under the will and on her death her personal representative would be entitled to receive her statutory legacy, with interest thereon as from the testator's death.

Maugham J: I approach the construction of the (Administration of Estates Act 1925) with the remark that in a case of only partial intestacy, whether it be immediate (ie, evident at the date of the death) or contingent (ie, dependent on events subsequent to the death), the will is the controlling instrument, and I think the statutory provisions of ss 33, 46, 47 and 48 of the Act ought to be applied so far as they can be applied consistently in all respects with the terms of the will.

Taking the present case as an example of what will frequently occur, a question that presents itself *in limine* is whether the statutory trust for sale with the necessary corollary as to the application of the proceeds of sale (sub-s 2) can subsist in a case where the testator has by his will given his real and personal property upon trust for conversion. There cannot, I think, be two subsisting trusts for conversion of the testator's estate and for application of the proceeds with, it may be, different incidents. For example, there may be in the will a requirement as to the consent to the sale of the tenant for life, or a special provision as to the legacies which are to be discharged out of the proceeds or a number of other matters not provided for in s 33. I hold that the words in sub-s 7[4] are intended to have the effect in such a case as the present of preventing sub-ss 1 and 2

---

1. Eg because the testator failed to make a residuary gift or the residuary beneficiary died before him.
2. See p 143 post.
3. Affirmed by the Court of Appeal, [1931] 2 Ch 153.
4. P 123 ante.

having any application, at any rate at the death of the testator. I may observe parenthetically that, if the will is so drawn as to give property in specie to any beneficiary for life or for some other period, the sub-sections pro tanto must obviously be superseded. . . .

There is in the present case an effective trust for conversion and an effective life interest created by the will, and for the reasons given it follows that the statutory trust for sale mentioned in sub-s 1 of s 33 is not applicable, and that sub-s 2 is not applicable, because the testator has stated how the funeral and testamentary expenses and debts and the legacies bequeathed by his will are to be paid. . . .

A question will however arise on the death of the widow whether, when the testator's residue falls into possession, her personal representatives will be entitled under the provisions of the Fourth Part of the Act to receive the sum of £1,000 and any other interests given to the widow of an intestate by that part of the Act[5]. . . .

The words 'subject to the provisions contained in the will' must be borne in mind. The will it is true has given the widow a life interest in the testator's residue; but it seems to me that it is consistent with that provision, though it may be a surprising result, that on the death of the widow the residue then undisposed of shall stand charged with the payment of a net sum of £1,000 to her, or rather to her personal representatives, with interest thereon from the date of the death at the rate of 5 per cent per annum until paid. Support is gained for this view by the fact, above alluded to, that the issue of the deceased have to bring into account any beneficial interests acquired under the will of the deceased, while the widow, or widower, has not,[6] It does not, in my opinion, follow that the widow has any interest under the subsequent provisions of s 46, sub-s 1. According to the opinion I have expressed there is nothing in the Act requiring a sale of the reversionary interest in question before the death of the widow;[7] and, since under s 49 the interest is to be held 'subject to the provisions contained in the will,' my view is that on a fair construction of those words the widow is not entitled to any life interest in the property which will fall in on her death nor on its estimated value as at the death of the testator. There is no provision for any notional conversion as from the death of the testator, nor, I think, any reason for thinking that any such provision, elaborate as it would need to be, should be implied. She is therefore, I think, precluded from claiming any further interest beyond the £1,000 and interest thereon in the property falling into possession upon her own death.[8]

(b) Hotchpot[9]

On a partial intestacy there are three situations where something may have to be brought into account against a beneficiary's entitlement.

(i) *By the surviving spouse*

Administration of Estates Act 1925

49(1) . . . (aa)[10] where the deceased leaves a husband or wife who acquires any

---

5. Under the then intestacy rules (AEA 1925, s 46 unamended by the Intestates' Estates Act 1952) the entitlement of the surviving spouse (in default of issue) was to the personal chattels absolutely, a statutory legacy of £1,000 charged on the intestate's residuary estate with interest at 5% pa from the intestate's death and subject thereto, a life interest in the whole.

6. The hotchpot provision for the surviving spouse (AEA 1925, s 49(aa) post) was introduced into the AEA many years after this decision, by Intestates' Estates Act 1952, s 3(2).

7. It had been argued that the undisposed of remainder was a reversionary interest that should be sold in view of the express trust for sale to provide the widow with her entitlement under the intestacy rules straightaway.

8. The personal chattels had been left to her in the will so this part of her entitlement under the intestacy rules was not in issue.

9. See p 138 n 13 ante.

10. The paragraph was added by the Intestates' Estates Act 1952.

beneficial interests under the will of the deceased (other than personal chattels specifically bequeathed) the references in this Part of this Act to the fixed net sum,[11] payable to a surviving husband or wife, and to interest on that sum, shall be taken as references to the said sum diminished by the value at the date of death of the said beneficial interests, and to interest on that sum as so diminished and, accordingly, where the said value exceeds the said sum, this Part of this Act shall have effect as if references to the said sum, and interest thereon, were omitted.

EXAMPLE

The testator leaves a surviving spouse and issue; his undisposed of property is worth £80,000. On the face of it the surviving spouse will take £40,000 of this absolutely as her statutory legacy and a life interest in half the remainder. In the will, however, she receives a legacy of £10,000 which must be brought into account and so will reduce her statutory legacy to £30,000. The 6% interest to which the spouse is entitled is calculated on the reduced amount of the legacy, she still gets intact any undisposed of personal chattels and she still gets her life interest in one half of the remaining undisposed of property—in this instance, assuming no undisposed of personal chattels, a life interest in $\frac{1}{2} \times £50,000 = £25,000$. The issue take the other half and the half subject to her life interest, on the statutory trusts.[12]

Re Bowen-Buscarlet's Will Trusts [1972] Ch 463, [1971] 3 All ER 636, [1971] Ch D; Goff J

The deceased left his surviving spouse by will a life interest in his estate, but failed to dispose of the capital thereafter so that there was a partial intestacy. The value of her life interest had to be brought into account against the statutory legacy, but on the authority of *Re McKee*[13] it was argued she would have no right in her lifetime to the balance of the statutory legacy which would simply fall into her estate on her death.

Held: She was entitled to claim forthwith the statutory legacy, reduced by the value of the life interest.

Goff J: The matter was apparently decided . . . by Maugham J and unanimously by the Court of Appeal in the case of *Re McKee* ([1931] 2 Ch 145), but while I must, of course, pay great respect to the views there expressed, it is not, in my judgment, an authority binding on me because the point canvassed before me was never raised or argued. The question originally raised in that case was whether the will having, as in the present case, given the widow a life interest and, having regard to the events which had happened, failed to dispose of the residue, she was entitled under general equitable principles to have the undisposed of reversionary interest sold for the dual purpose of giving her a further life interest and paying her the statutory legacy. The court held that she was not entitled to have the reversion sold because it was not an asset of the estate but a beneficial interest arising in the estate and coming into effect under the will and the statutory provisions applicable to an intestacy.

The question seems to have arisen in the court of first instance whether, if that were to

---

11. Ie the statutory legacy.
12. If the value of the gift by will had been, say £45,000, ie it had exceeded the amount of the statutory legacy, she would get no statutory legacy at all, but she would still get her life interest in half the undisposed of property, ie $\frac{1}{2} \times £80,000 = £40,000$.
13. See p 142 ante.

be the answer, she or her estate would have any right at all in respect of the statutory £1,000 and the court caused this question to be added by amendment to the originating summons to ask—

> 'whether on the death of the widow: (i) the net sum of £1,000 with interest thereon at the rate of £5 per cent per annum from the date of the testator's death, and (ii) any other and what sum ought to be paid out of the residuary estate of the testator to the personal representatives of the widow.'

It will be observed that it was assumed that apart from the sale of the reversion point, the widow could not claim payment during her lifetime, and the contrary was never argued, but it has been argued before me. . . .

In these circumstances I am free and I think bound to make up my own mind. . . .

It is simply a case in which the widow is entitled to say:

> 'I am the only person having any interest under this charge. There is a charge in my favour postponed to a life interest it is true, but that life interest is mine and therefore I merge it and claim payment.'

Why cannot she do that? It seems that the answer must be that she can. . . .

It is also interesting to observe that Maugham J felt himself fortified by the fact that whereas under the law as it stood then certain persons had to bring into account interests which they took under the will, a widow was not so accountable. That has now been changed by s 49(1)(aa), inserted by the Intestates' Estates Act 1952.

If, of course, the decision in *Re McKee* ([1931] 2 Ch 145) were authority, settling the law and binding on me, I do not think I could regard that provision as amending the law by a side-wind, but it is, I think, a consideration which one is entitled to have in mind when the point comes to be argued that the provision which Maugham J thought helped him to his conclusion is not, now, open. There is moreover an indication in support of the conclusion I have reached in that the new section directs the widow to bring into account an actuarial valuation of her life interest.[14] If Parliament regarded the law as being such that the widow had no beneficial interest and there was merely a charge in favour of her estate, one would have thought that the direction would have been to bring in the actual value of the life interest as ascertained on the date of her death and the legislature would not have speculated where there could be certainty.

In the end it comes back to this. In my judgment, the effect of the will and the statutory charge is to give the widow a right to the benefit of the charge and the right to the income, and therefore, to give her an interest which is, I think, immediate. In my judgment, therefore, subject to the adjustments which have to be made, the widow is entitled, forthwith, to be paid the statutory legacy, and I so declare.

(ii) *By the children*

The deceased's children have to bring into account against their entitlement on a partial intestacy any lifetime advancements by the deceased.[15]

Administration of Estates Act 1925

47. Statutory trusts in favour of issue and other classes of relatives of intestate

(1)(iii) (p 139 ante).

---

14. AEA 1925, s 49(1)(aa) p 143 ante does not require this in so many words, but an actuarial valuation will be inevitable in practice for valuing at the date of death a life interest given by the deceased's will.

15. Grandchildren and remoter issue who benefit under the statutory trusts on the deceased's partial intestacy do not have to bring into account any benefits they received from the deceased in his lifetime nor do the deceased's children themselves have to bring such lifetime benefits to their issue into account. Cf the position under s 49(1)(a) post.

(iii) *By the children and remoter issue*

Both the deceased's children and more remote issue are required to bring into account any benefits they receive under the will. It seems that a stirpital construction is given to this requirement so that a child of the deceased entitled under the partial intestacy, has to bring into account against that entitlement not only any benefits he receives under the will but also any benefits left by the will to his issue.

Administration of Estates Act 1925

49. Application to cases of partial intestacy
(1)(a) The requirements of section forty-seven of this Act as to bringing property into account shall apply to any beneficial interests acquired by any issue of the deceased under the will of the deceased, but not to beneficial interests so acquired by any other persons.[16]

Re Young [1951] Ch 185, [1950] 2 All ER 1040, Ch D; Harman J

The testator settled a one-seventh share of his residuary estate on a discretionary trust of income and capital for the benefit of his son Charles and Charles' children during Charles' lifetime; the balance was then to pass to Charles' children equally. A partial intestacy arose as to another part of the estate and Charles was entitled to share in it but what did he have to bring into account on a hotchpot under the Administration of Estates Act 1925, s 49(1)(a)?
Held: He must bring into account not just the value of his interest under the discretionary trust but also the beneficial interest of his children, and as he and his children were between them entitled to the whole of the settled share, this meant the capital value of the entire one-seventh share.

Harman J: It is contended by counsel for Charles' personal representative that only a person who has acquired a beneficial interest under the will has to bring anything into account under s 49(a), and, therefore, Charles, who, as one of the testator's children, is entitled to a share of the part of the residue which was not disposed of after the widow's death, has nothing to bring into account because, in the events which happened, not he, but his children, took the one-seventh share which was settled on him and his children, and he himself never had more than a very limited interest in the income of that share at the discretion of the trustees—or, at the most, all that needs to be brought into hotchpot by Charles' estate is the interest which he took, viz, his life interest, which must be valued, and would, I suppose, be of very little value. The result would be that the whole fund would go to Charles's estate. The contrary view is that s 49(a) of the Act of 1925 is meant to produce, as it were, a stirpital division which is as equal as possible, and that is why the word 'issue' is used here, although the word 'children' is used in s 47(1)(iii). Any member of the family belonging to a certain branch must bring in everything that has been taken or acquired under the will by that branch. Therefore, in taking his share under the intestacy, Charles should bring into account the one-seventh share in which his children have taken an absolute interest under the will.

On the whole, I prefer the view last stated. It seems to me that 'issue' in the words, 'any beneficial interests acquired by any issue of the deceased,' must mean children or

---

16. This paragraph was described by Danckwerts J in *Re Morton* [1956] Ch 644 at 647, [1956] 3 All ER 259 at 260 as 'as bad a piece of draftsmanship as one could conceive'; cf (1956) 72 LQR 483 for a defence of the draftsman by Megarry.

remoter issue, and, therefore, that what is to be brought into account is the beneficial interest which the issue acquired. Who are the issue in question? The father and the children, the two generations between them, are the issue, and it seems to me therefore, that anything that the father and children together acquired under the will is a beneficial interest acquired by the issue. I would add that although there was a trust, in the event of the whole or part of the income of Charles' share not being applied during Charles' lifetime for the benefit of him or his children, to apply it to other members of the family, that trust never arose and I think it should be ignored. I think that, in effect, Charles and his children between them had the one-seventh share which was settled on them by the testator, and that is what, in my judgment, ought to be brought into account.[17]

QUESTIONS

1. The statutory provisions for the distribution of an intestate's estate are intended to reflect the probable wishes of the deceased had he died testate. Do you think that they succeed?

2. Ian recently died intestate. He leaves the following assets:
  (a) the matrimonial home, worth £70,000;
  (b) furniture and household equipment, worth £7,000;
  (c) a collection of stamps worth £8,000; he built up the collection himself but deposited it with his bank 6 years ago when he lost interest in it;
  (d) a car worth £6,000 which he used partly for the purpose of his practice as a solicitor and partly as a family car;
  (e) investments and cash amounting to £50,000.

He is survived by his mother, Martha, his wife, Wanda, a son Stuart (aged 40) and the two daughters, Daisy (aged 16) and Frances (aged 21) of his deceased son, William.

Advise as to the distribution of Ian's estate.

3. There is no sufficient argument of principle to justify retention of the existing rules discriminating against illegitimate persons in relation to intestate succession.
(Law Com 118 para 8.13).
Discuss.

4. In 1982 Isabel gave her husband, Harry, a painting worth £6,000 on their golden wedding anniversary, in the same year she gave their son, Sam, £10,000 to help in his purchase of a grocery business. In 1986 she died. By her will she left £2,000 to her grandson, Graham (Sam's son), and the rest of her estate worth £150,000, to Harry for life and then to their three children, Sam, Jane and Dora in equal shares. Dora died, childless, a week before Isabel's death. Harry's life interest under Isabel's will has been valued at £20,000 as at her death.

Who is entitled to Isabel's estate?

---

17. See also *Re Grover's WT* [1971] Ch 168, [1970] 1 All ER 1185. Cf *Re Morton*, p 146 n 16 ante, where the interests taken under the will by the child and the child's issue did not together amount to the whole beneficial interest in the fund in question and Danckwerts J held that their several beneficial interests in the fund should be separately valued in order to find the value of the interests actually taken by the child and his issue, so that the child had to bring into account something less than the capital value of the fund. See further Ryder 'Hotchpot on Partial Intestacy' (1973) 26 CLP 208. For an example of the application of all three hotchpot situations in one hypothetical estate, see Mellows pp 169–170.

PART TWO

Choice factors

CHAPTER 11

Revocation of the arrangements

Can the donor who has put into effect his chosen method(s) for passing on his property thereafter change his mind and restore the status quo in relation to that property? This topic will be examined in this chapter in relation to the various succession methods considered so far, except for intestate succession which is inevitably irrevocable and testate succession which is considered in the following chapters.

1 The lifetime gift

The essence of an inter vivos gift is that it takes effect immediately, once the appropriate formalities have been satisfied.[1] There is a presumption that every gift is irrevocable and so unless the donor expressly or by necessary implication reserves a right to revoke the gift or settlement, or unless the gift is subject to a condition which is not fulfilled,[2] once completely constituted the gifted property cannot be recalled in the absence of some invalidating cause. As was said in *Villers v Beaumont* (1682) 1 Vern 100, 23 ER 342 at 342 by Lord Nottingham LC:

> If a man will improvidently bind himself up by a voluntary deed and not reserve a liberty to himself by a power of revocation, this court will not loose the fetters he hath put upon himself, but he must lie down under his own folly: for if you would relieve in such a case, you must consequently establish this proposition, viz. that a man can make no voluntary disposition of his estate, but by his will only, which would be absurd.

In this case the donor had settled his beneficial interests in a certain leasehold estate in favour of his cousins 'by a little scrap of paper at an ale-house, but under hand and seal', intending to pay his debts to them thereby and make them a gift of the surplus. He subsequently changed his mind and made a will in which he left his beneficial interest in the lease to his half-brother. The Lord Chancellor held that the deed of gift would prevail.

In **Ogilvie v Littleboy** (1897) 13 TLR 399,[3] the donor's late husband had left her his entire fortune worth about one million pounds. They had both been

---

1. If the gift is incompletely constituted, the donor can of course disregard it with impunity and treat the property as his own, no one being in a position to enforce the gift against him; see *Fortescue v Barnett* (1834) 3 My & K 36, and p 25 ante.
2. Eg *Jacobs v Davis* [1917] 2 KB 532 (gift of an engagement ring which the defendant had to return when she broke the engagement).
3. Affd HL sub nom *Ogilvie v Allen* (1899) 15 TLR 294.

associated with charitable works, and with the object of fulfilling what she believed he would have wished, she executed deeds giving the greater part of that fortune to various charities. She subsequently changed her mind and tried to have the deeds set aside in their entirety on the basis that they did not carry out her intention. The Court of Appeal refused to accept this, finding that the donor's advisers had taken her carefully through the deeds several times, clause by clause, and that she thoroughly knew and approved their provisions. Lindley LJ said at p 400:

> Gifts cannot be revoked, nor can deeds of gift be set aside, simply because the donors wish they had not made them and would like to have back the property given. Where there is no fraud, no undue influence, no fiduciary relationship between donor and donee, no mistake induced by those who derive any benefit by it, a gift, whether by mere delivery or by deed, is binding on the donor.[4]

2   The nomination

A nomination is revocable at any time before the nominator's death; the nominator should comply with the formal requirements of the statute or pension scheme concerned although it seems that 'substantial compliance' will suffice in the latter case.

Industrial and Provident Societies Act 1965[5]

23.   Nominations to property in society

(4) A nomination by a member of a society under subsection (1) of this section may be varied or revoked by a subsequent nomination by him thereunder or by any similar document in the nature of a revocation or variation signed by the nominator and delivered at or sent to the society's registered office during his lifetime, but shall not be revocable or variable by the will of the nominator or by any codicil thereto.

(5) Every registered society shall keep a book in which the names of all persons nominated under subsection (1) of this section and any revocation or variation of any nomination under that subsection shall be recorded.

(6) The marriage of a member of a society shall operate as a revocation of any nomination made by him before the marriage and after 31st December 1913; but if any property of that member has been transferred by an officer of the society in pursuance of that nomination in ignorance of a marriage contracted by the nominator subsequent to the date of the nomination, the receipt of the nominee shall be a valid discharge to the society and the society shall be under no liability to any other person claiming the property.

In **Bennett v Slater** [1899] 1 QB 45, the nominator had nominated in favour of the plaintiff the sums due to him from a policy with a friendly society in accordance with the requirements of the Friendly Societies Act 1875, s 15(3).[6] He subsequently made a will disposing of his entire estate elsewhere and after

---

4. See also *Coleby v Coleby* (1866) LR 2 Eq 803.
5. Extracted as a typical example of statutory requirements. See also Friendly Societies Act 1974 s 66(6)(8) and s 69; the Trustee Savings Bank Regulations 1972, SI 1972/583, Reg 12, as amended by SI 1979/259; the National Savings Bank Regulations 1972, SI 1972/764, Reg 35, as amended by SI 1981/484; the Savings Certificate Regulations 1972, SI 1972/641, Reg 16 as amended by SI 1981/486.
6. See now Friendly Societies Act 1974, s 66.

his death, his executors claimed the policy moneys as part of his estate. The Court of Appeal found in favour of the nominee, AL Smith LJ saying at p 49:

(Can) a nomination under the sub-section be revoked otherwise than in the manner therein prescribed? In my judgment it cannot. The sub-section prescribes a special manner in which the nomination may be made, and a special manner in which it may be revoked; and it appears to me that, upon the true construction of the enactment, as a nomination can only be made in the prescribed manner, so it can only be revoked in the prescribed manner. It is provided, in the absence of a revocation, that, on receiving satisfactory proof of the death of the nominator, the society 'shall' pay to the nominee the amount due to the deceased member not exceeding the sum aforesaid. All that the society have to do under the Act is to see that there has been a proper nomination, and that the nominator is dead, and then, if there has been no revocation as provided for by the section, the enactment is imperative that they shall pay the amount to the nominee. They are not bound to inquire whether there is a will or not. In my opinion, assuming that the will is to be construed as revoking the nomination, which I think it is not, that revocation is ineffective. For these reasons I think the appeal must be allowed, and judgment entered for the plaintiff.

Re Danish Bacon Staff Pension Fund [1971] 1 All ER 486, [1971] 1 WLR 248, Ch D; Megarry J

The rules of a company pension scheme permitted each member to appoint, in a form set out in an appendix to the rules, a nominee to receive any moneys payable on his death to his personal representatives. The rule in question (16(b)) went on to provide that any member of the fund could at any time 'cancel any such appointment made by him and simultaneously appoint a new nominee in a similar form': any monies due on the nominator's death would then be paid to the nominee 'in respect of whom a form of appointment is then in force'. The deceased had signed a valid nomination in favour of A. Many years later he wrote to the secretary of the fund (who was also one of its trustees) asking him to strike out the name of A and insert the name of B instead, and the secretary accordingly did so, writing beside the amendment 'see letter attached 12/6/59'. The appendix to the rules required the deceased to sign his nomination and for the signature to be witnessed; the only signature the deceased had made to the amended nomination was that contained in his letter and that signature was unwitnessed.

Held: The alteration was effective and the nomination in favour of B would stand.

Megarry J: The worst, I think, that can be said against the nomination as read with the letter of 12th June is that the form in Appendix II provides for a witness, and that although the signature of the deceased to the nomination as it originally stood was duly witnessed, there was no witness to his signature of the letter. In the case of wills, of course, there are express statutory requirements for alterations. In the present case, the rules impose no such requirement.

I am here concerned with an equitable interest in a case where the intention of the deceased to benefit the third defendant was perfectly clear; and, of course, equity traditionally looks to the substance rather than the form. In my judgment there is here, in the nomination and the letter, a sufficiently substantial compliance with the requirements of rule 16(b) to constitute a new nomination in favour of the third defendant to replace the former nomination in favour of the first defendant. The original nomination was altered under the authority of the only person with power to make a nomination; and on the footing that the alterations were duly authorised, the altered nomination is in the requisite form. I do not think that equity, which has long been ready to grant certain classes of persons relief against formal defects in the execution of powers, will be astute to seize on such a debatable matter as the absence of a witness's signature in this case in order to invalidate the nomination, whether or not in favour of a member of the favoured classes of person. Indeed, counsel for the first and second defendants ultimately stated that he could not rely on the absence of any signature of a witness. In my judgment, the lack of a witness to the unquestioned signature of the deceased to the letter of 12th June ought not to invalidate the whole transaction, and does not do so. The trustees have a document which originally was in full compliance with the rules, and they have clear and explicit alterations to that document made by one of their number in obedience to signed directions of the deceased lodged with them which can leave them in no doubt who is intended to be the nominee. In my judgment, there is a valid nomination in favour of B.[7]

3 The beneficial joint tenancy

(a) In general

If a beneficial joint tenant decides that he does not want the doctrine of survivorship to apply, he can sever the joint tenancy in his lifetime and so turn it into a beneficial tenancy in common so that his share as tenant in common will devolve instead under his will or intestacy (unless he gives it away or sells it in the meantime). There are four generally accepted methods of severing a beneficial joint tenancy, three of which were established by common law before 1925; whilst the fourth is contained in the Law of Property Act 1925, s 36(2), namely a unilateral notice in writing by one joint tenant to the other(s) indicating the desire to sever. On its terms the last method relates only to a beneficial joint tenancy in land, but it has been argued that a unilateral declaration of an intent to sever, whether in written or verbal form, will in any case suffice to sever a beneficial joint tenancy, whether the property is realty or personalty.

(b) The three common law methods

In **Williams v Hensman** (1861) 1 John & H 546, 70 ER 862, at p 867, Page Wood V-C described the three methods available (before 1926) for severing a joint tenancy of personalty as follows:

A joint tenancy may be severed in three ways: in the first place, an act of any one of the persons interested operating upon his own share may create a severance as to that share. The right of each joint tenant is a right by survivorship only in the event of no severance having taken place of the share which is claimed under the *jus accrescendi*. Each one is at liberty to dispose of his own interest in such manner as to sever it from the joint fund— losing, of course, at the same time, his own right of survivorship. Secondly, a joint tenancy may be severed by mutual agreement. And, in the third place, there may be a severance by any course of dealing sufficient to intimate that the interests of all were mutually treated as constituting a tenancy in common. When the severance depends on an inference of this kind without any express act of severance, it will not suffice to rely on

---

7. Megarry J made it plain (at p 494) that he was reaching his decision in relation to a non-statutory nomination; it does not necessarily follow that his 'substantial compliance' doctrine would apply to the revocation of a statutory nomination, see eg *Pearman v Charlton* (1928) 44 TLR 517, p 42 ante.

an intention, with respect to the particular share, declared only behind the backs of the other persons interested. You must find in this class of case a course of dealing by which the shares of all the parties to the contest have been affected.

(c) The statutory method

Law of Property Act 1925

36. Joint tenancies

(2) No severance of a joint tenancy of a legal estate, so as to create a tenancy in common in land, shall be permissible, whether by operation of law or otherwise, but this subsection does not affect the right of a joint tenant to release his interest to the other joint tenants, or the right to sever a joint tenancy in an equitable interest whether or not the legal estate is vested in the joint tenants:

Provided that, where a legal estate (not being settled land) is vested in joint tenants beneficially, and any tenant desires to sever the joint tenancy in equity, he shall give to the other joint tenants a notice in writing of such desire[8] or do such other acts or things as would, in the case of personal estate, have been effectual to sever the tenancy in equity, and thereupon under the trust for sale affecting the land the net proceeds of sale, and the net rents and profits until sale, shall be held upon the trusts which would have been requisite for giving effect to the beneficial interests if there had been an actual severance.

In **Neilson-Jones v Fedden** [1974] 3 All ER 38, [1974] 3 WLR 583,[9] Walton J described the subsection at p 43, as:

a rather elliptic method of legislation, but since it is, I think, not in dispute that the methods of severance of a joint tenancy in personal estate before 1926 were precisely the same as the methods of severance of a joint tenancy in real estate (see *Williams on Personal Property* 18th ed (1926), p 524) the final effect of this subsection is merely to add another method to the ways in which the severance of a joint tenancy in real estate may be effected. Why this highly convenient method of severance was not also extended to personal estate, I am at a loss to understand.

Harris v Goddard [1983] 3 All ER 242, [1983] 1 WLR 203, CA; Lawton, Kerr and Dillon LJJ

A husband and wife were beneficial joint tenants of the matrimonial home. When the marriage broke down, the wife served on the husband a divorce petition which included a prayer for the court to exercise its jurisdiction under the Matrimonial Causes Act 1973, s 24 'by way of transfer of property and/or settlement of property and/or variation of settlement in respect of the former matrimonial home . . . and otherwise as may be just'. Before the court could consider the matter the husband was killed in a car accident. The house was subsequently sold by the wife and the husband's executors claimed half the net proceeds on the basis that the wife's prayer in her petition amounted to a notice of severance under the Law of Property Act 1925, s 36(2).

Held: The prayer was not an effective notice of severance as it did not indicate a desire to sever forthwith; the wife was entitled to the whole of the proceeds of sale.

---

8. See *Re 88 Berkeley Road NW9* [1971] Ch 648, [1971] 1 All ER 254 from which it seems that service of such notice by registered post on the other joint tenant(s) under LPA 1925, s 196(4) satisfies the requirements of s 36(2) even if the notice is never in fact received by the other tenant(s).
9. See further at p 157 post.

Lawton LJ: In *Williams v Hensman* (1861) John & H 546, 70 ER 862 Page Wood V-C said that a joint tenancy could be severed in three ways, that is by disposal of one of the interests, by mutual agreement and 'by any course of dealing sufficient to intimate that the interests of all were mutually treated as constituting a tenancy in common'. The words in s 36(2) 'do such other acts or things as would . . . have been effectual to sever the tenancy' put into statutory language the other ways of effecting severance to which Page Wood V-C referred in *Williams v Hensman*. The words 'and any tenant desires to sever the joint tenancy in equity, he shall give to the other joint tenants a notice in writing of such desire' operate to extend the mutual agreement concept of severance referred to in *Williams v Hensman*. Unilateral action to sever a joint tenancy is now possible. Before 1925 severance by unilateral action was only possible when one joint tenant disposed of his interest to a third party. When a notice in writing of a desire to sever is served pursuant to s 36(2) it takes effect forthwith. It follows that a desire to sever must evince an intention to bring about the wanted result immediately. A notice in writing which expresses a desire to bring about the wanted result at some time in the future is not, in my judgment, a notice in writing within s 36(2). Further the notice must be one which shows an intent to bring about the consequences set out in s 36(2), namely that the net proceeds of the statutory trust for sale 'shall be held upon the trust which would have been requisite for giving effect to the beneficial interests if there had been an actual severance'. I am unable to accept the submission of counsel for the plaintiffs that a notice in writing which shows no more than a desire to bring the existing interest to an end is a good notice. It must be a desire to sever which is intended to have the statutory consequences. Paragraph 3 of the prayer of the petition does no more than invite the court to consider at some future time whether to exercise its jurisdiction under s 24 of the 1973 Act and, if it does, to do so in one or more of three different ways. Orders under s 24(1)(a) and (b) could bring co-ownership to an end by ways other than by severance. [10] It follows, in my judgment, that para 3 of the prayer of the petition did not operate as a notice in writing to sever the joint tenancy in equity. This tenancy had not been severed when Mr Harris died, with the consequence that Mrs Harris is entitled to the whole of the fund held by the first and second defendants as trustees. [11]

(d) Any unilateral declaration of an intent to sever?

In **Hawksley v May** [1956] 1 QB 304, [1955] 3 All ER 353, a settled fund was held by trustees on trusts by which on attaining 21 the plaintiff and his younger sister would become absolutely entitled as joint tenants. When the plaintiff became 21 the trustees took no steps to transfer to him his share of the capital and pay him the income from it but retained the whole fund and accumulated the income waiting for the sister to reach 21 also. When she did, she wrote to them instructing them to pay the dividends from her share into her bank account; a few months later her share of the capital of the fund was also transferred to her. Havers J held that the joint tenancy of the fund had been severed by the sister's letter. Referring to Page Wood V-C's three methods of severance as set out in *Williams v Hensman* [12] he continued at p 356:

The first method indicated there, an act of any one of the persons interested operating on his own share, obviously includes a declaration of intention to sever by one party. The position therefore, of the plaintiff and his sister as joint tenants under the Musgrave settlement, was this. The right of each of them in a joint tenancy is a right to take by

---

10. Eg the court might have made an order extinguishing the husband's interest in the property and directing that the property be vested in the wife as sole beneficial owner or an order directing the resettlement of the property on the husband and the wife successively and not concurrently.
11. Cf *Re Draper's Conveyance* p 157 post and see in particular n 13 post.
12. See p 154 ante.

survivorship only in the event of the severance not having taken place. As to capital, the plaintiff on attaining twenty-one was entitled to sever by one of the methods which I have indicated and to be paid his share. If the plaintiff did not exercise this right before his sister attained twenty-one, then on his sister attaining twenty-one each had a right to sever. If then, there had been no severance, on the sister attaining twenty-one the plaintiff and his sister were entitled to have the trust funds transferred to them jointly. . . . As regards the severance, I hold that when the sister wrote the letter in which she said: 'Thank you for your letter of 17th instant with the particulars of the investments. I should like the dividends to be paid into my account at Martin's Bank, 208 Kensington High Street' (which was a letter in reply to the first defendant), that was a sufficient act on her part to constitute a severance of the joint tenancy. If I am wrong about that, there clearly was a severance when her share of the trust funds was transferred to her in September, 1942.

In **Re Draper's Conveyance** [1969] 1 Ch 486, [1967] 3 All ER 853, the husband and wife were joint tenants of a house. The wife obtained her decree nisi of divorce and took out a summons under the Married Women's Property Act 1882 with supporting affidavit, seeking an order for the sale of the property and an equal division of the proceeds. Shortly thereafter the husband died. Holding that she had effectively severed the beneficial joint tenancy and so failed to take the husband's share by survivorship, Plowman J referred to the above passage in *Hawksley v May* and said at p 857:

So from that case I derive this, that a declaration by one of a number of joint tenants of his intention to sever, operates as a severance.

Counsel for the defendants also relied on the notice in writing which under s 36(2) of the Law of Property Act 1925, is allowed in the case of a joint tenancy in land, although not in personalty, and he submits that the summons to which I have already referred, although not signed, amounted to a notice in writing on the part of the plaintiff that she desired to sever the joint tenancy in equity. I say 'although not signed by the plaintiff or by anybody on her behalf' because there is no requirement of signature in the subsection. . . .

Now, dealing with the matter up to this point, it seems to me that counsel for the defendant's submissions are right, whether they are based on s 36(2) of the Law of Property Act 1925, or on the old law which applied to severing a joint tenancy in the case of a personal estate. The summons, coupled with the affidavit in support of it, clearly evinced an intention on the part of the plaintiff that she wished the property to be sold and the proceeds distributed, a half to her and a half to the deceased. It seems to me that that is wholly inconsistent with the notion that a beneficial joint tenancy in that property is to continue.[13]

Neilson-Jones v Fedden [1974] 3 All ER 38, [1974] 3 WLR 583, Ch D; Walton J

Mr and Mrs Todd were joint tenants of the former matrimonial home; they had separated and were contemplating a divorce. They drew up a memorandum which both of them signed, authorising Mr Todd to use his discretion to sell the matrimonial home and to use the proceeds to provide a new home for himself. They then put their affairs into the hands of their respective solicitors who

---

13. In *Harris v Goddard*, p 155 ante, the CA distinguished *Re Draper's Conveyance* in its application of LPA 1925, s 36(2) on the basis that the relief claimed in the wife's summons in *Re Draper's Conveyance* plainly called for a severance of the beneficial joint tenancy whereas the relief sought in *Harris v Goddard* was in 'the most general and unparticularised terms under s 24 of the Matrimonial Causes Act 1973', per Dillon LJ at p 247.

began negotiations for a financial settlement between them but before the negotiations came to fruition, Mr Todd died. The house was subsequently sold. Was Mrs Todd entitled to the entire proceeds by survivorship or had the beneficial joint tenancy been severed before her husband's death?

Held: The beneficial joint tenancy had not been severed; she was entitled to the entire proceeds of sale.

Walton J: (Having found that there was no express or implied agreement between the parties such as would sever the joint tenancy under the second and third heads described by Page Wood V-C in *Williams v Hensman* [14], he continued:) I shall assume in favour of counsel for the executors that the correspondence does indeed disclose an unequivocal declaration by Mr Todd to the effect that he wishes to sever the joint tenancy so as to make himself master of a one half share of the net proceeds of sale of the property. The question then is, can such a declaration—a unilateral declaration—ever be effective to sever a beneficial joint tenancy? It appears to me that in principle there is no conceivable ground for saying that it can. So far as I can see, such a mere unilateral declaration does not in any way shatter any one of the essential unities. [15] Moreover, if it did, it would appear that a wholly unconscionable amount of time and trouble has been wasted by conveyancers of old in framing elaborate assignments for the purpose of effecting a severance, when all that was required was a simple declaration.

The question, moreover, is not untouched by authority. One may start with *Moyse v Gyles* ((1700) Prec Ch 124). In this case one joint tenant made a deed of gift of his moiety to his wife, with the expressed intention of severing the joint tenancy, in order to make provision for her. As the deed was made in favour of the wife, it was void at law; and, the deed being made without consideration, it was held that equity could not relieve.

Again, in *Partriche v Powlet* ((1740) 2 Atk 54), a decision of Lord Hardwicke LC, the sidenote is as follows: 'An actual alienation only can sever a joint tenancy; a declaration of one of the parties that it shall be severed, is not sufficient.' It is quite clear from that case that Lord Hardwicke LC regarded severance as only effected (if one leaves out of account the acquisition of a mergeable interest) by either (i) an agreement to that effect or (ii) actual alienation. He would, I think, have regarded the third head, which is often referred to in the cases, namely, a course of conduct, as merely being material from which an agreement is to be inferred. For a modern instance of the adoption of this analysis, see per Hanna J in *Flynn v Flynn* ([1930] IR 337, 343). The final authority in this line is *Re Wilks*, ([1891] 3 Ch 59), a decision of Stirling J. . . . [16] Accordingly, down to that case I think it is fair to say that the whole current of authority was against severance by means of such a declaration as is now envisaged.

(He then referred to the judgment of Havers J in *Hawksley v May* [17] and continued:) With very great respect to that learned judge, I think he had, in deciding as he did that the letter written by the sister was a sufficient act on her part to constitute a severance of the joint tenancy, entirely misapprehended the judgment of Lord Hatherley (then Sir Page Wood V-C) in *Williams v Hensman*, ((1861) 1 John & H 546). The first method of severance of which Lord Hatherley was talking was actual alienation, or something equivalent thereto. The learned judge (Havers J) appears to have been very poorly assisted by counsel on this point, for they did not cite any of the relevant authorities to him, so far as the report shows. . . .

(He then turned to *Re Draper's Conveyance*:) [18] Since I have already concluded above that Havers J's dictum was wholly unwarranted, I regret that I can place no greater reliance upon it when blandly repeated in *Re Draper's Conveyance*. I am also troubled

---

14. See p 154 ante.
15. See p 30 n 1 ante.
16. Stirling J held in that case that the issue of proceedings by one plaintiff seeking the payment of his share of funds held by the court to the credit of the three plaintiffs as joint tenants, did not sever that joint tenancy.
17. See p 156 ante.
18. P 157 ante.

about the suggestion that the mere issue of the originating summons, coupled with the affidavit in support, could amount to a notice in writing under section 36(2). It appears to me that the reasons so cogently stated by Stirling J in *Re Wilks* ([1891] 3 Ch 59) apply with equal force: until any order had been made, the wife was *domina litis*,[19] and entitled to withdraw the proceedings entirely. In other words, it appears to me that section 36(2) contemplates an irrevocable notice, and that the issue of proceedings is the very reverse of an irrevocable act. If the proceedings are, indeed, to constitute a severance, it must, I think, follow as a consequence that they themselves become irrevocable, and this I find difficult to appreciate.

Of course, there can be no doubt but that an order for sale and payment out of the proceeds of sale in defined proportions made with jurisdiction to make it would sever the joint tenancy; but if the only order that the court can make under section 17 of the Married Women's Property Act 1882, as assumed by Plowman J, is to declare the rights of the parties, then it appears to be even more surprising that he should have held that an application thereunder could change the rights of the parties. It would appear to me that on the judge's own hypothesis (which I do not pause to examine) the only result of the application at the end of the day must have been a declaration that the parties were entitled to the property as joint tenants.

Counsel for the executors very naturally and properly, relied upon these two last cases very heavily; but, in my opinion, they did not represent the law, being, at any rate, so far as the instant relevant parts of *Hawksley v May* ([1956] 1 QB 304, [1955] 3 All ER 353) and of *Re Draper's Conveyance* ([1969] 1 Ch 486, [1967] 3 All ER 853) are concerned, clearly contrary to the existing, well-established law, to which the attention of the respective learned judges who decided them was in neither case directed. Accordingly, I regard the relevant parts of these two decisions as having been given per incuriam, and I do not propose to follow them.

I would finally add on this branch of the case that my misgivings as to the two cases referred to are clearly shared by the learned writer of a note appearing in the Law Quarterly Review ((1968) 84 LQR 462) and also that, if they were correct, so far as I can see, section 36(2) of the Law of Property Act 1925 would be wholly otiose, since there was already in existence an even simpler method of severing a joint tenancy. Indeed on one view, it might even have been restrictive! I find either conclusion impossible to reach.

The result is that on the third question posed in this matter, I hold that the joint tenancy between Mr Todd and his wife could not, as a matter of law, be severed by any such declaration as is now under consideration, and was accordingly not severed.

The final result is that I hold that Mrs Todd, now Mrs Nielson-Jones, has become, by survivorship, beneficially entitled to the whole of the net proceeds of sale of the former matrimonial home.

Burgess v Rawnsley [1975] Ch 429, [1975] 3 All ER 142, CA; Lord Denning MR, Browne LJ, Sir John Pennycuick

A house was transferred into the names of Mr Honick and Mrs Rawnsley, an unmarried couple, as beneficial joint tenants. Mr Honick had intended the house to be their matrimonial home, but Mrs Rawnsley had never intended to marry him. When this became clear, he attempted to buy her share from her and she orally agreed to sell it to him for £750, but she subsequently changed her mind. Mr Honick left matters as they were and three years later he died. The house was sold. Was Mrs Rawnsley entitled to the whole of the proceeds by survivorship or had the beneficial joint tenancy been severed before Mr Honick's death?

---

19. Lit mistress of the suit, ie the party with the carriage and control of the action.

Held: Although the oral agreement as such was unenforceable,[20] it still indicated a mutual agreement to sever and that was sufficient to sever the joint tenancy.

Sir John Pennycuick: In the present case the judge found as a fact that Mr Honick and Mrs Rawnsley at the beginning of July 1968 agreed upon the sale by her to him of her share at the price of £750. . . . Once that finding of fact is accepted, the case falls squarely within rule 2 of Page Wood V-C. It is not contended that it is material that the parties by mutual consent did not proceed to carry out the agreement. Rule 2 applies equally, I think, whether the agreement between the two joint tenants is expressly to sever it or to deal with the property in a manner which involves severance. Counsel for Mrs Rawnsley contended that in order that rule 2 should apply, the agreement must be specifically enforceable. I do not see any sufficient reason for importing this qualification. The significance of an agreement is not that it binds the parties; but that it serves as an indication of a common intention to sever, something which it was indisputably within their power to do. It will be observed that Page Wood V-C in his rule 2 makes no mention of specific enforceability. Contrast this position where severance is claimed under his rule 1 by reason of alienation by one joint tenant in favour of a third party. We were referred to a sentence in Megarry and Wade's *Law of Real Property* 3rd ed, (1966) p 418 where, under the heading of 'Alienation in equity' it is said:

'In equity . . . a specifically enforceable contract to alienate creates an equitable interest in the property even though the legal act of alienation has not taken place.'

That statement has, I think, no application to an agreement between the two joint tenants themselves. The only other authority relied on by counsel for Mrs Rawnsley on this point is a sentence in the old Irish case of *Wilson v Bell* ((1843) 5 Ir Eq Rep 501 at 507) where it is said:

'. . . it is settled, that an agreement to sever will in equity amount to a severance: and as this is personal property, there is no doubt that even a parol agreement would be sufficient for that purpose.'

I think that sentence is altogether inadequate to support counsel for Mrs Rawnsley's contention.

Counsel for Mrs Burgess[1] advanced an alternative argument to the effect that even if there were no agreement by Mr Honick to purchase Mrs Rawnsley's share, nevertheless the mere proposal by Mr Honick to purchase her share would operate as a severance under rule 3 in *Williams v Hensman*, ((1861) 1 John & H 546, 558). That rule is stated by Page Wood V-C in the following terms: (having set out Page Wood V-C's third ground, he continued:)

I do not doubt myself that where one tenant negotiates with another for some rearrangement of interest, it may be possible to infer from the particular facts a common intention to sever even though the negotiations break down. Whether such an inference can be drawn must I think depend upon the particular facts. In the present case the negotiations between Mr Honick and Mrs Rawnsley, if they can be properly described as negotiations at all, fall, it seems to me, far short of warranting an inference. One could not ascribe to joint tenants an intention to sever merely because one offers to buy out the other for £X and the other makes a counter-offer of £Y.

We were referred to a long series of authorities going back to *Partriche v Powlet* ((1740) 2 Atk 54) and culminating in the conflicting decisions of Plowman J in *Re Draper's Conveyance* ([1969] 1 Ch 486, [1967] 3 All ER 853); and Walton J in *Nielson-Jones v Fedden* ([1974] 3 All ER 38, [1974] 3 WLR 583). Once it has been determined that an

---

20. For want of compliance with LPA 1925, s 40: 'No action may be brought upon any contract for the sale or other disposition of land or any interest in land, unless the agreement upon which such action is brought, or some memorandum or note thereof, is in writing, and signed by the party to be charged or by some other person thereunto by him lawfully authorised.'
1. Mr Honick's administratrix.

agreement was made, as in the present case, anything more one may say on this line of authorities must necessarily be obiter; but I think it may be helpful to state very shortly certain views which I have formed in the light of the authorities.

(1) I do not think rule 3 in Page Wood V-C's statement ((1861) 1 John & H 546, 557), is a mere sub heading of rule 2. It covers only acts of the parties, including, it seems to me, negotiations which, although not otherwise resulting in any agreement, indicate a common intention that the joint tenancy should be regarded as severed.

I do not overlook the words which I have read from Page Wood V-C's statement, namely, that you must find a course of dealing by which the shares of all the parties to the contract have been affected. But I do not think those words are sufficient to import a binding agreement.

(2) Section 36(2) of the Law of Property Act 1925 has radically altered the law in respect of severance by introducing an entirely new method of severance as regards land, namely, notice in writing given by one joint tenant to the other.

(3) Pre-1925 judicial statements, in particular that of Stirling J in *Re Wilks* ([1891] 3 Ch 59), must be read in the light of this alteration in the law; and, in particular, I do not see why the commencement of legal proceedings by writ or originating summons or the swearing of an affidavit in those proceedings, should not in appropriate circumstances constitute notice in writing within the meaning of s 36(2). The fact that the plaintiff is not obliged to prosecute the proceedings is I think irrelevant in regard to notice.

(4) Perhaps in parenthesis because the point does not arise, the language of s 36(2) appears to contemplate that even under the existing law notice in writing would be effective to sever a joint tenancy in personalty: see the words 'such other acts or things'. The authorities to the contrary are rather meagre and I am not sure how far this point was ever really considered in relation to personalty before 1925. If this anomaly does exist, and I am afraid I am not prepared to say positively, that it does not exist, the anomaly is quite indefensible and should be put right as soon as possible.

(6) An uncommunicated declaration by one party to the other or indeed a mere verbal notice by one party to another clearly cannot operate as a severance.

(7) The policy of the law as it stands today, having regard particularly to s 36(2) of the 1925 Act, is to facilitate severance at the instance of either party, and I do not think the court should be over zealous in drawing a fine distinction from the pre-1925 authorities.

(8) The foregoing statement of principles involves criticism of certain passages in the judgments of Plowman J and Walton J in the two cases cited. These cases, like all the other cases, depend on their own particular facts, and I do not myself wish to go on to apply these obiter statements of principle to the actual decisions in these cases.

QUESTIONS

1. Should Megarry J's 'substantial compliance' doctrine (*Re Danish Bacon Staff Pension Fund*, p 153 ante) apply to the formalities governing statutory nominations as well as non-statutory? What difficulties might lie in the way of this?

2. A, B, C and D were beneficial joint tenants of Blackacre. If A, B and C were all killed in a car crash and D died a week later, how would this affect the beneficial ownership? Would your answer be different if (a) A, B, C and D were tenants in common or (b) the day before the car crash A had posted letters to B, C and D telling them that he intended selling his interest in Blackacre to E?

3. When will a unilateral declaration of intent to effectively sever a joint tenancy? See further on this: Bandali 'Injustice and Problems of Beneficial Joint Tenancy' (1977) 41 Conv 243; Garner 'Severance of a Joint Tenancy' (1976) 40 Conv 77; Hayton 'Joint Tenancies—Severance' (1976) 35 CLJ 20; McClean 'Severance of Joint Tenancies' (1979) 57 Can BR 1.

CHAPTER 12

Revocation of a will by marriage/divorce

A will can be revoked in any one of five ways. Three of these methods depend on the testator's intention and are considered in the next chapter. The other two operate automatically, not necessarily in accordance with the testator's intention, because of a change in the testator's circumstances and are considered in this chapter.

1 Revocation by marriage

(a) In general

Before 1837 the will of a woman was automatically revoked by her marriage whereas there was only a rebuttable presumption to that effect in the case of a man and even then, only if the marriage was followed by the birth of a child. The Wills Act 1837, s 18 simplified the position by providing for the automatic revocation of every will on marriage. The Law Reform Committee reporting in 1980 recommended the retention of this rule, contenting itself with titivating the two established exceptions to it[1] so that when s 18 was redrawn by the Administration of Justice Act 1982, the rule remained.[2] Other jurisdictions vary in their adoption of the rule.[3]

Law Reform Committee: Twenty-Second Report[4]

Revocation by marriage
3.2 ... The reasons to justify the retention of the present rule may be summarised as follows:—

---

1. Pp 164–7 post.
2. Solicitors should therefore continue to heed the warning dicta of the CA in *Hall v Meyrick* [1957] 2 QB 455 at 482, [1957] 2 All ER 722 at 730 to the effect that a solicitor has a duty to advise his client-testator of the automatic rule if the solicitor has definite information of the testator's intention to marry.
3. Eg in Scotland wills are not revoked by marriage, the spouse being regarded as provided for by the doctrine of legal rights, p 241 post, see Walker *Principles of Scottish Private Law* (3rd edn 1983) Vol IV p 159. In Canada the basic rule applies in all provinces except Quebec, but in Ontario the spouse can nevertheless elect to take under the will by filing a written and signed instrument to that effect within a year of the testator's death: Succession Law Reform Act 1977 s 16. See p 164 post for the solution adopted by the Uniform Probate Code (USA).
4. 'The Making and Revocation of Wills' (1980) Cmnd 7902.

(a) Marriage represents a fundamental change in a person's life and with it he or she acquires new personal and financial responsibilities. It is, therefore, a time for starting with a clean slate.

(b) A spouse and children should not inadvertently be deprived of the rights which they would have upon the intestacy of the other spouse and parent. In so far as people fail to make fresh wills after marriage, or at least fail to revoke a pre-marriage will, this is normally the result of inadvertence and most persons marrying would wish their spouse and children to benefit from their estate: the deceased's intentions are, therefore, more likely to be achieved by the statutory imposition of an intestacy than by preservation of his earlier will. This may, indeed, prevent hardship to the family.

(c) The present rule is well known and accords with the intentions and expectations of the great majority of those who marry.

3.3 The case against section 18 of the Wills Act 1837 can be stated as follows:

(a) *The wife* The rule is no longer necessary to protect the wife. A woman's personal property no longer automatically becomes that of her husband upon marriage, so there is no need to ensure that her property does not go to strangers under the terms of a will made by the husband before the marriage. Secondly, the retention by the wife of her own property means that she is less likely to be in need under the husband's will. Further, the development since 1938 of the legislation on family provision[5] means that any injustice done to the wife by the old will can be remedied by an application to the court under the Inheritance (Provision for Family and Dependants) Act 1975.

(b) *Children* The revocation of the will on marriage could be unfair, at least in the case of a second marriage, in relation to children of an earlier marriage, who might find that the provision made for them by the deceased during that marriage was cut down by the intrusion of the second wife's rights on intestacy. Further, the rights of children under the family provision legislation differ from those of a wife, in that children are only entitled to apply for reasonable financial provision for maintenance.

(c) *Cohabitation* The rule operates only on marriage and does not therefore apply in the case of unmarried persons living together as husband and wife not least because there would be obvious practical difficulties in determining at what time a cohabitation arrangement should revoke a prior will by either party. Abolition of the rule would put such persons on the same footing as spouses.

(d) *Other purposes of wills* The present rule can have effects well outside the primary purpose of protection of the wife and children. Thus small legacies to friends or remoter relations, bequests of a charitable or quasi-charitable nature and expressions of the deceased's wishes (such as the gift of his eyes or internal organs for medical or medical research purposes or a desire to be cremated) are cancelled by the revocation of the will. Further, the loss of appointed executors can be inconvenient.

3.7 In our view, the case for repealing section 18 is by no means made out. The rule is well known to lawyers and laymen, it has operated satisfactorily since 1837 and the social and legislative changes which have taken place since then have not created a need to amend it.

Wills Act 1837

18.[6] Wills to be revoked by marriage, except in certain cases
(1) Subject to subsections (2) to (4) below,[7] a will shall be revoked by the testator's marriage.

---

5. See Ch 17 post.
6. As substituted by AJA 1982, s 18.
7. See pp 164–7 post.

Uniform Probate Code (USA)

2-301 Omitted Spouse

(a) If a testator fails to provide by will for his surviving spouse who married the testator after the execution of the will, the omitted spouse shall receive the same share of the estate he would have received if the decedent left no will unless it appears from the will that the omission was intentional or the testator provided for the spouse by transfer outside the will and the intent that the transfer be in lieu of a testamentary provision is shown by statements of the testator or from the amount of the transfer or other evidence . . .[8]

(b) The exception for powers of appointment

The Wills Act 1837, s 18 as originally drawn contained an exception to the rule in so far as the will exercised a power of appointment. The justification for this exception was considered by the Law Reform Committee which recommended its continuance subject to modernisation of its terminology and their recommendation was embodied in the Administration of Justice Act 1982 in the redrawn version of s 18.

Law Reform Committee: Twenty-Second Report[9]

3.9 (i) Wills made in the exercise of a power of appointment
Section 18 of the Wills Act 1837 reads as follows:

'Every will made by a man or woman shall be revoked by his or her marriage (except a will made in exercise of a power of appointment, when the real or personal estate thereby appointed would not in default of such appointment pass to his or her heir, customary heir, executor, or administrator, or the person entitled as his or her next of kin under the Statute of Distributions).'

The reason for this exception is that the testator's new family can derive no benefit from the revocation of a will of the kind described in the exception. If the purpose of the basic rule that marriage revokes a will is to protect and benefit the testator's widow, the purpose of the exception is to disapply that rule where revocation could not confer any advantage on the widow or next of kin, because the gift over in default in favour of others would take effect. The exception was discussed in *Re Gilligan* [1950] P 32, where its principal purpose was neatly summarised in the following passage from Pilcher J's judgment:

'I think the intention of the section was that a will exercising a power of appointment should only be wholly revoked by the subsequent marriage of the testator in those cases in which the instrument creating the power provides that in default of appointment the fund shall devolve as on an intestacy, in which event the widow of the deceased will take her portion of the fund.'

3.10 Although we have received some evidence recommending that the exception should be repealed, we think that it is consistent with the principle underlying the basic rule in section 18 and that it should be retained. However, the language of the exception has never been modified to take account of the abolition of heirship and of the repeal of

---

8. There is a similar provision at s 2-302 for children born or adopted by the testator after execution of his will. So in states adopting this provision, whilst the will is valid notwithstanding the marriage, the spouse and/or children as the case may be nevertheless receive the share(s) they would have been respectively entitled to on an intestacy.

9. 'The Making and Revocation of Wills' (1980) Cmnd 7902.

the Statutes of Distribution and it may not fit those persons now entitled on intestacy under sections 46 and 47 of the Administration of Estates Act 1925.[10] Accordingly, we recommend that in any legislation following our report the wording of this exception should be updated.

3.11 The question then arises how best to modernise the exception. We have considered how it ought to operate in cases where in default of appointment the property would not have passed exactly as on an intestacy, but very nearly so. For example, the default gift might be to all or some of those who would have taken on an intestacy or even to the testator's widow and children or other relatives in proportions different to those set out in the statutory intestacy trusts. Although we appreciate that our conclusion could cause some illogicalities, we think that the best course would be to provide that the exception to section 18 should operate in all cases except where, in default of appointment, the subject property of the power would pass exactly as on an intestacy, or to the deceased's personal representatives as part of his estate.

Wills Act 1837

18.[11] **Wills to be revoked by marriage, except in certain cases**
(2) A disposition in a will in exercise of a power of appointment shall take effect notwithstanding the testator's subsequent marriage unless the property so appointed would in default of appointment pass to his personal representatives.[12]

(c) The exception for wills made in contemplation of marriage

This exception was originally contained in the Law of Property Act 1925, s 177. It was considered by the Law Reform Committee in 1980 and its retention recommended subject to amendments rendered necessary by the decision in *Re Coleman*.[13] These recommendations were implemented by the Administration of Justice Act 1982 by way of two new sub-sections to the Wills Act 1837, s 18 and the repeal of the Law of Property Act 1925, s 177 for wills made after 1982.

Law Reform Committee: Twenty-Second Report[14]

3.13 (ii) **Wills expressed to be made in contemplation of marriage**
Section 177 of the Law of Property Act 1925 provides:—

> 'A will expressed to be made in contemplation of marriage shall, notwithstanding anything in section 18 of the Wills Act 1837, or any other statutory provision or rule

---

10. AEA 1925, s 50 converts references to the Statutes of Distribution to references to Part IV of the AEA 1925, but it relates only to references to the Statutes in instruments inter vivos made or wills coming into operation after 1925, not to references to the Statutes of Distribution in other statutes, such as the Wills Act 1837: see Mitchell 'The Revocation of Testamentary Appointments on Marriage' (1951) 67 LQR 351; cf Russell (1952) 68 LQR 455.
11. As substituted by AJA 1982, s 18; WA 1837, s 18(2) takes effect for wills executed after 1982: AJA 1982, s 73(7), s 76(11).
12. It will be noted that the subsection does not follow the Law Reform Committee's recommendation at para 3.11 precisely. It remains to be seen whether the new provision will be interpreted literally so that the gift over in default of appointment must in so many words be one to the testator's personal representatives before the appointment will be revoked, or whether it will be sufficient that to reach the persons entitled under the gift over, the property must first pass through the hands of the testator's personal representatives.
13. [1976] Ch 1, [1975] 1 All ER 675, p 166 post.
14. 'The Making and Revocation of Wills', (1980) Cmnd 7902.

of law to the contrary, not be revoked by the solemnisation of the marriage contemplated'.

None of the evidence submitted to us suggested that there should not be an exception on these general lines. We agree that a will made with the evident intention that it should survive the testator's forthcoming marriage should not be revoked by that marriage and we are therefore agreed that the principle underlying section 177 of the Law of Property Act 1925 is sound. We did, however, receive a certain amount of evidence to suggest that the formulation of that principle may be in need of amendment.

3.14   Criticism of the present law centres on the recent case of *Re Coleman* [15] where a will leaving to a named fiancée the testator's personal chattels, stamp collection, £5,000 and a freehold house was revoked by the testator's marriage two months after the will was made. It was held firstly that no extrinsic evidence was admissible to ascertain the testator's intentions. Secondly, in order to comply with section 177, the fact that the will had been made in contemplation of the marriage had to be sufficiently expressed in the will itself. This could normally be deduced from the use of the word 'fiancée' which not only described an existing state of affairs but also contemplated a change in them. [16] Thirdly, however, it was the will and not merely some gift in it, which had to be expressed to be made in contemplation of marriage, and so a will containing some beneficial dispositions, which could not be described as trivial and which lacked any expression of such contemplation, could not be described as a 'will' made in contemplation of marriage. [17]

3.15   The first point that has been made is that the law ought no longer to insist on the will being 'expressed to be' in contemplation of marriage and that evidence which shows that the will was in fact made in contemplation of marriage should be admissible. The admissibility of evidence in the construction of wills has already been fully considered in our 19th Report on the Interpretation of Wills. . . . [18]

3.16   In our view, the admission of extrinsic evidence of the testator's dispositive intentions would, in this context, result in undesirable uncertainty and be a virtual invitation to litigation, particularly in the case of small estates, the bulk of which might then be dissipated in costs. Recent legislation in Victoria [19] provides that a will shall not be revoked on marriage if either it is expressed to be made in contemplation of that marriage or it appears from its terms or from those terms taken in conjunction with the circumstances existing at the time of the making of the will, that the testator had in contemplation that he would or might marry and intended the disposition made by the will to take effect in that event. Extrinsic evidence will therefore be admissible to explain the testator's intention as indicated by the terms of the will but not to supply an intention not so indicated. We think that this is the right approach. Accordingly we think that it should continue to be the requirement of the law that the language of the will should show that it was made in contemplation of marriage, that is that it was intended to survive the marriage, and that the rules recommended in our 19th Report as to the admission of extrinsic evidence, short of direct evidence of dispositive intention, should be applied to determine whether the will in fact expressed such an intention.

3.17   The second criticism of section 177 is that the 'contemplation of marriage' test is inappropriate and that the question which should be asked is whether it was the

---

15. [1976] Ch 1, [1975] 1 All ER 675. See Edwards and Langstaff 'The will to survive marriage' (1975) 39 Conv 121.

16. Cf the use of the word 'my wife' to describe the woman the testator subsequently marries. In *Pilot v Gainfort* [1931] P 103 this expression was enough to invoke the exception but this decision was not followed in *Re Gray* (1963) 107 Sol J 156 and was criticised by Megarry J in *Re Coleman*, ante at p 678, the description being an 'expression of the present rather than a contemplation of the future'.

17. The rock on which the *Coleman* will foundered, the deceased having left his not insubstantial residuary estate to his brother and sister.

18. (1973) Cmnd 5301.

19. The Wills (Interested Witnesses) Act 1977, s 4.

testator's intention that the will should survive the marriage. We see force in this objection, although we think that the application of the 'contemplation of marriage' test rarely defeats the testator's intentions and that in practice the courts usually construe wills so as to give effect to those intentions by treating the words 'contemplation of marriage' as equivalent to 'with the intention that the will should survive the impending marriage'.

3.18 Thirdly, we have received considerable criticism of that part of the decision in *Coleman* where it was held that a will is revoked on marriage unless the *whole* will is expressed to be in contemplation of the marriage. We agree with these criticisms. Once it is accepted that a bequest in a will is made in 'contemplation of marriage' ie with the intention that it should survive the marriage, it seems illogical to suppose that the testator did not intend that will to survive the marriage; for the bequest cannot survive unless the will survives. The construction of the section upheld by the court in *Re Coleman* seems to us an unduly narrow one and we would ourselves have expected a decision that the will did survive the marriage. We appreciate that it may sometimes be difficult to determine whether a bequest to a fiancée is sufficient for the inference to be drawn that it was made in contemplation of marriage. For example we do not think that a will can be said to have been made in contemplation of marriage where it contains, say, one trivial gift to a fiancée. Certainly the use of the word 'fiancée' should not be conclusive. We should like to see an amendment to section 177 in which the 'contemplation of marriage' test is replaced by a provision that, if a will or any part of a will is shown by its language to be intended to survive a particular marriage, the presumption should be that the whole will survives. Such a presumption should in our view be capable of being rebutted to the extent that the will shows affirmatively that any particular provisions were not intended to survive the contemplated marriage. So for example, where a will which contains provisions intended to survive a contemplated marriage also contains a bequest so worded as to indicate that the testator did not intend it to survive the marriage, that bequest, but that bequest only, should be treated as having been revoked.

Wills Act 1837

18.[20] **Wills to be revoked by marriage, except in certain cases**
(3) Where it appears from a will that at the time it was made the testator was expecting to be married to a particular person and that he intended that the will should not be revoked by the marriage, the will shall not be revoked by his marriage to that person.
(4) Where it appears from a will that at the time it was made the testator was expecting to be married to a particular person and that he intended that a disposition in the will should not be revoked by his marriage to that person,
  (a) that disposition shall take effect notwithstanding the marriage; and
  (b) any other disposition in the will shall take effect also, unless it appears from the will that the testator intended the disposition to be revoked by the marriage.

(d) Voidable marriages

Marriage means a valid marriage; s 18 will not apply to a marriage which is void *ab initio*. If the marriage is only voidable, however, it will revoke any existing will, whether the marriage is subsequently avoided or not, because the marriage is treated as valid up to the time of avoidance.

---

20. As substituted by AJA 1982, s 18, the new subsections take effect for wills executed after 1982: AJA 1982, s 73(7), s 76(11).

Matrimonial Causes Act 1973

16. Effect of decree of nullity in case of voidable marriage

A decree of nullity granted after July 31st, 1971,[1] in respect of a voidable marriage shall operate to annul the marriage only as respects any time after the decree has been made absolute, and the marriage shall, notwithstanding the decree, be treated as if it had existed up to that time.

In **Re Roberts** [1978] 3 All ER 225, [1978] 1 WLR 653, the testator had made a will in 1973 in favour of his brother. Subsequently, when suffering from mental disorder he went through a marriage ceremony.[2] He died 18 months later without the marriage being annulled. The Court of Appeal held that the voidable marriage had nevertheless operated to revoke the will so that the estate would pass to his wife on his intestacy, Buckley LJ concluding at p 232:

A marriage which is voidable, but not void, under the Act[3] must in every case operate to revoke an earlier will of a party to such marriage, whether the marriage is subsequently annulled or not. Whether this effect was appreciated by Parliament may, I think, be doubtful, but it is, in my judgment, the inescapable effect of the legislation.[4]

2 Effect of divorce or annulment

Until 1983 a decree of divorce or annulment of marriage did not affect wills already made by the parties involved although they were of course free to expressly revoke them if they so wished, and any subsequent remarriage would bring about an automatic revocation by virtue of Wills Act 1837, s 18.[5] When the Law Reform Committee come to consider the matter in 1980, it found itself to be divided.[6] The majority view was that the divorced spouse should be treated as predeceasing the testator and this recommendation was substantially implemented by the Administration of Justice Act 1982 by way of a new section, s 18 A of the Wills Act 1837. Difficulties have since arisen in applying this section due to the draftsman's use of the word 'lapse' in the new section, which has been interpreted as not meaning the same as 'predecease' with the result that substitutional provisions very commonly included in wills to cover the possibility of the testator's spouse predeceasing the testator cannot take effect

---

1. Before 1st August 1971 (when the Nullity of Marriages Act 1971 came into force) it seems that when a decree of annulment of a voidable marriage was obtained, the marriage was treated as if it had never existed, not even prior to the decree, with the result that any will entered into before the 'marriage' was unaffected by the marriage.

2. Lack of consent to a marriage renders the marriage voidable: Matrimonial Causes Act 1973, s 12.

3. Matrimonial Causes Act 1973.

4. As a testator whose marriage is voidable through unsoundness of mind will seldom have the mental capacity to make a new will, he will usually die intestate as in this case. The possible unfairness of this result was considered by the Law Reform Committee in its 22nd Report (1980) Cmnd 7902 and it recommended, at para 3.25 that any person or charity which would have benefited under the will revoked by such a marriage should be able to apply for provision from the estate (see Ch 17 post). This recommendation has not yet been adopted.

5. See p 162 ante.

6. The Committee was agreed, however, that if the law was changed, (a) any solution adopted for divorce should also apply to nullity, but not judicial separation; (b) a will expressed to be made with the intention that it should survive the divorce should not be affected; (c) if the divorce was to have a revocatory effect regarding benefits to the divorced spouse, the appointment of that spouse as executor should also be treated as revoked (para 3.31).

when the original provisions fail because of the operation of s 18A. In other jurisdictions with similar statutory provisions this problem has been successfully avoided.

Law Reform Committee: Twenty-Second Report[7]

The majority view: treat the divorced spouse as pre-deceasing the testator

3.32 Because the courts now have wide powers of settling property disputes on divorce, we believe that one of the most common results of divorce is a permanent division of property between the ex-spouses which is intended by both parties to be a once and for all settlement. The finality of such settlements has recently been recognised by the House of Lords in *Minton v Minton* [1979] AC 593 as being in accordance both with statute law and with public policy. The majority of us take the view that in almost all cases a will made during the subsistence of the marriage providing for quite a different division of the property will no longer be appropriate in the changed circumstances produced by the divorce. While no solution can be guaranteed to avoid unfortunate results in occasional cases, it would be most unusual for a divorced spouse to wish to make greater provision for the former wife or husband than that made on the divorce and equally unusual for him or her to want a will made while they were married to subsist unaltered.

3.33 Secondly, because the incidence of divorce is increasing and its procedure has been greatly simplified, we suspect that significant numbers of people are divorced without the benefit of legal advice. This means that failure to think about making a new will or to reconsider the benefits conferred on the other spouse by a will made during the marriage is probably common. Statutory revocation or lapse of those benefits would be more likely to accord with the wishes of unadvised or inadvertent testators than would the maintenance of the provisions in the old will. If the proposal that a divorced spouse should be treated as pre-deceasing the testator is adopted, the Inheritance (Provision for Family and Dependants) Act 1975[8] would be available to mitigate any injustice caused to the divorced spouse in individual cases, since he or she would be a dependant for the purposes of that Act.

The minority view: no change

3.35 Those of us who are not persuaded that a case has been made out in favour of any change in the present law believe that because marriage revokes a will it does not follow that divorce should have any effect, even though it also involves a change of status. The two situations are factually quite different. In the case of marriage, a common intention of the parties to provide for each other and for any future children can safely be assumed. It is therefore reasonable to have a rule of law revoking a previous will that might frustrate that intention, the more so since the need for a formal act of revocation might well be overlooked in the euphoria of impending marriage.

3.36 No parallel assumptions can be made in the case of divorce. It cannot even be assumed that both parties want the divorce, since one party frequently does not. The circumstances leading to the breakdown of a marriage are of course infinitely variable, but during the period leading up to the divorce questions of money and property tend to loom large and have to be dealt with, often with legal assistance. At a time when the minds of both husband and wife are likely to be turned to questions of financial provision, it seems highly improbable that they will overlook their wills; indeed, they may well deliberately alter them in the light of the financial arrangements of the divorce. A minority of us therefore think it unlikely that if a will is left unaltered after a divorce it will be as a result of its having been overlooked entirely.

3.37 Divorce does not, like marriage, place new responsibilities on the parties, even if it

7. 'The Making and Revocation of Wills', (1980) Cmnd 7902.
8. See Ch 17 post.

indirectly qualifies existing responsibilities. If a will including bequests to a former spouse is consciously left unaltered on divorce, the law should not intervene to revoke those bequests and so deprive the former spouse of provision that he or she was intended, or at any rate may have been intended, to receive. Frequently, no doubt, divorce leaves a party so bitter that he wishes his former spouse to have nothing and then he is of course free to revoke or alter his will if he wishes. But there must be many other cases in which a party wishes to continue to make provision for a person with whom he may have spent much of his life and in such cases it should not be the policy of the law to frustrate this welcome lack of bitterness by providing that bequests to a former spouse should be revoked, thus putting such a person to the trouble and expense of making a new will in order to give effect to his wishes. If he does take on new responsibilities by marrying again, then that marriage will of course revoke a will surviving from the earlier marriage.

Wills Act 1837

18A.[9]   Effect of dissolution or annulment of marriage on wills
(1) Where, after a testator has made a will, a decree of a court dissolves or annuls his marriage or declares it void,
    (a) the will shall take effect as if any appointment of the former spouse as an executor were omitted; and
    (b) any devise or bequest to the former spouse shall lapse,
except in so far as a contrary intention appears by the will.[10]
(2) Subsection (1)(b) above is without prejudice to any right of the former spouse to apply for financial provision under the Inheritance (Provision for Family and Dependants) Act 1975.
(3) Where—
    (a) by the terms of a will an interest in remainder is subject to a life interest; and
    (b) the life interest lapses by virtue of subsection (1)(b) above,
the interest in remainder shall be treated as if it had not been subject to the life interest and, if it was contingent upon the termination of the life interest, as if it had not been so contingent.[11]

In **Re Cherrington** [1984] 2 All ER 285, [1984] 1 WLR 772, the testator made a will by which he appointed his wife to be his sole executrix and gave her all his estate with a proviso (cl 3) that if she predeceased him his estate should instead pass to his two sons who would then also be his executors, together with his solicitor (cl 4 and 5). The testator's marriage was subsequently dissolved and in 1983 he died. The division of the small estate was agreed by the parties concerned and the only question before the court was whether the substitutional appointment of the sons and the solicitor as executors could take effect

---

9. As substituted by AJA 1982, s 18(1). The new section takes effect for testators dying after 1982 regardless of when the will was made: ss 73(6), 76(11). By the Matrimonial Causes (Amendment) Rules 1984, SI 1984/1511, the recipient of a certificate of making a decree nisi of divorce or nullity absolute has the effect of s 18A on any existing will drawn specifically to his attention.
10. As the Law Reform Committee mentions at para 3.27, this is the position adopted by New Zealand (Wills Amendment Act 1977), by a number of Canadian states (adopting a similar provision in the Uniform Wills Act of Canada), and by many states of the USA following a similar provision in the Uniform Probate Code, s 2-508, p 172 post. Cf Scotland where there is no equivalent provision, see Walker *Principles of Scottish Private Law* (3rd edn 1983) vol IV p 159.
11. An odd form of wording, as pointed out by Clark 'Darning the Law of Succession', (1984) 37 CLP 115 at 121, as the termination of a life interest can hardly be regarded as a contingency, something that may or may not happen, rather it is an inevitability. He suggests that the draftsman must have intended the 'termination of the life interest' to refer simply to the time at which a particular contingency was required by the will to be satisfied.

when the testator's wife had not literally predeceased him. Holding that it could, Butler-Sloss J said at p 287:

The devise to the wife must lapse under s 18A(1)(b), but does the effect of the lapse bring into effect the proviso under cl 3 of the will, since she is still alive? Counsel for the applicant, in his admirable submission, urged me to equate lapse with predecease. In order for cll 4 and 5 of the will to take effect, the word 'lapse' in s 18A(1)(b) requires to be considered as if intended to refer to predeceasing the testator.

The section in Jarman on Wills 8th ed (1951), vol 1, p 438 dealing with the doctrine of lapse shows that the general principle assumes lapse to refer to predecease.

In the new s 33 of the Wills Act 1837, substituted by s 19 of the Administration of Justice Act 1982, which deals with gifts to children who predecease the testator, the section is referred to in the note at the side as, 'Gifts to children or other issue who leave issue living at the testator's death shall not lapse', and the word is used as meaning death before the testator.

Section 18A(3) is somewhat difficult to follow if lapse is intended to refer to predecease, since the second part of the subsection will be unnecessary, but it is probable that it is set out for avoidance of doubt.

The alternative possibility is that lapse means 'shall be of no effect'. The effect of that interpretation, in the present will, would cause a residual intestacy and defeat the purpose of the testator, and is likely to do so in many other wills. . . .

For the purposes of simplicity, certainty, and to give effect to the intentions of the testator, I propose to interpret s 18A(1)(b) of the 1982 Act as referring to the former spouse predeceasing the testator and hold, therefore, that the proviso to cl 3 of the will takes effect. In those circumstances, the appointment of the executors under cl 4 takes effect.

Re Sinclair [1985] 1 All ER 1066, [1985] 2 WLR 795, CA; O'Connor and Slade LJJ, Bristow J

The testator left all his estate by will to his wife, directing that if she predeceased him or failed to survive him by one month, the estate was to pass to a named research fund. Subsequently the testator and his wife were divorced and in 1983 the testator died. The gift to her was clearly invalidated by Wills Act 1837, s 18A(1)(b) but the question was whether the gift over to the research fund could take effect as neither of the contingencies to which it was subject had actually taken place.

Held: The word 'lapse' in s 18A(1)(b) meant 'fail'. The terms of the gift over not having been met, the testator's estate would devolve as on his intestacy.

Slade LJ: The construction of the relevant wording favoured by (Butler-Sloss J in *Re Cherrington*)[12] in truth involves reading (s 18A(1)(b)) as meaning 'any devise or bequest to the former spouse shall fail with the same consequences as if the former spouse had died in the testator's lifetime'. It involves reading it as a deeming provision. For my part, I find it impossible to read the opening words of s 18A(1)(b) in this manner. First, as I have said, it must be and is accepted that the word 'lapse' is, in an appropriate context, perfectly apt to cover the happening of any event in a testator's lifetime which prevents the intended legatee from being entitled to the legacy, and thus to mean nothing more than 'fail'. In my opinion, the natural meaning of the word 'lapse' in the context of s 18A(1)(b) is to refer to the happening of an event, namely divorce, in the testator's lifetime which is to prevent the intended legatee, the former spouse, from becoming entitled to the legacy. The natural meaning of the word 'lapse' in this particular context is that, in the relevant contingency, the devise or bequest to the former spouse shall fail, no more and no less.

---

12. P 170 ante.

Second, if the legislature had intended that s 18A(1)(b) should have the effect, not only of preventing the former spouse from receiving the gift in cases such as this, but also of designating the consequences which would ensue in relation to the other provisions of the will, it would in my opinion inevitably have said so. To spell out a deeming provision from this one word 'lapse' would in my opinion be impermissible according to any proper principles of statutory construction.

Third, the conclusion that the legislature did not regard s 18A(1)(b) as designating the consequences that would ensue from the failure of the gift to the former spouse, in relation to the other provisions of the will, is in my opinion clearly supported by the presence of sub-s(3). For this subsection does designate such consequences in those cases where the will has given the former spouse a life interest. The provisions of sub-s(3) would have been wholly unnecessary if s 18A(1)(b) had itself been intended to provide that the effects of the failure of the gift on all the other provisions of the will was to be the same as if the former spouse had died in the testator's lifetime. I am not at all convinced by the submission of counsel for the fund that sub-s(3) was inserted by the legislature merely for the avoidance of doubt. If the legislature had intended 'lapse' in s 18A(1)(b) to bear the deeming sense suggested by him, no possible doubt, as I see the position, could have arisen.

As to the other sections of the 1837 Act to which reference has been made, ss 32 and 33 deal with situations which have arisen by reason of the death of a testamentary beneficiary during the testator's lifetime.[13] If one reads the word 'lapse' in these sections as meaning 'fail', no more and no less, it makes perfect sense in its context. Likewise, if one reads the word 'lapsed' in the sidenote to s 25 as meaning 'failed', no more and no less, it makes perfect sense in its context.[14] Furthermore, there is no question of the word 'lapse' or 'lapsed' in any of these other statutory provisions bearing a deeming sense. I do not therefore think that these provisions give any support to the construction of s 18A(1)(b) which is submitted on behalf of the fund.[15]

Uniform Probate Code (USA)

2-508   Revocation by divorce; no revocation by other changes of circumstances

If after executing a will the testator is divorced or his marriage annulled, the divorce or annulment revokes any disposition or appointment of property made by the will to the former spouse, any provision conferring a general or special power of appointment on the former spouse, and any nomination of the former spouse as executor, trustee, conservator, or guardian, unless the will expressly provides otherwise. Property prevented from passing to a former spouse because of revocation by divorce or annulment passes as if the former spouse failed to survive the decedent, and other provisions conferring some power or office on the former spouse are interpreted as if the spouse failed to survive the decedent.[16] If provisions are revoked solely by this section, they are revived by testator's remarriage to the former spouse.[17] For purposes of this section, divorce or annulment means any divorce or annulment which would exclude

---

13. See p 357 post.
14. See p 348 post.
15. The decision of the first instance judge was thus upheld (*Re Sinclair* [1984] 3 All ER 362, [1984] 1 WLR 1240). That decision had provoked considerable concern among practitioners in view of the extremely common wording of the substitutional gift which failed; see Mithani 'The Effect of Dissolution or Annulment of Marriage on Wills', (1984) 81 LSG 3323, SM 'The Effect of a Testator's Divorce on His Will', (1984) 128 Sol J 651 and see the correspondence that followed at (1984) 128 Sol J pp 706, 719, 754.
16. See also Wills Amendment Act 1977 (New Zealand), s 2 and Succession Law Reform Act 1977 (Ontario), s 17(2), where the provision is similarly worded and thus in each case avoids the problem for substitutional provisions that has resulted from the drafting of Wills Act 1837, s 18A.
17. A provision not generally to be found in other jurisdictions; perhaps the phenomenon of remarriage to the former partner is more common in the United States than elsewhere.

the spouse as surviving spouse within the meaning of section 2-802(b). A decree of separation which does not terminate the status of husband and wife is not a divorce for purposes of this section. No change of circumstances other than as described in this section revokes a will.[18]

QUESTIONS

1. Given the reasons that have been expressed for the general rule that marriage automatically revokes a will, could you justify (a) a similar rule for the birth of children or (b) a distinction between a first and subsequent marriage for the purpose of the rule?

2. Adam is married and has two children, John and Mary, but lives with a mistress, Eve. Certain settled property is held in trust for Adam for life with remainder to such of his issue as he shall appoint by will and in default of appointment, in trust for his children in equal shares. In 1984 Adam makes a will by which he leaves a legacy of £5,000 to 'my fiancée' Eve', the remainder of his property to John and Mary in equal shares and appoints his settled property to John absolutely. Later that year Adam's wife dies and he marries Eve. In 1986 Adam dies, leaving an estate worth £30,000. Who is entitled to (a) Adam's estate (b) the settled property?

3. Consider the two opposing views on the effect that divorce should have on a will, as expressed in the Law Reform Committee Report. Which view do you find more compelling?

4. Under the United States Uniform Probate Code, divorce operates to revoke a will but not marriage. Can you justify this distinction?

---

18. It will be noted therefore that under the Uniform Probate Code, marriage as such does not operate to revoke a will.

CHAPTER 13

Revocation of a will by instrument or destruction

1 Introduction

There are three methods of revoking a will which depend on the intention of the testator namely, revocation by a formal testamentary instrument, revocation by destruction and revocation by informal declaration where the testator has privileged status. Each of these methods was available before the passing of the Wills Act 1837 but there were at that time many distinctions between realty and personalty, as well as alternative methods such as revocation by parol declaration of wills of copyholds and of appointments of testamentary guardians, which attracted the concern of the Real Property Commissioners.

Real Property Commissioners: Fourth Report[1]

As to the Revocation of Wills . . .
The variety of rules relating to the revocation of Wills with respect to different properties and purposes, is attended with inconveniences similar to those which arise from the rules requiring different modes of execution.[2] It frequently happens that a Will is revoked as to personal and copyhold property, while the revocation does not extend to estates in fee simple; and thereby the Will becomes partially void, and the general arrangement intended by the Testator is frustrated.

The reasons which were given for proposing that the rules relating to Wills, with respect to different descriptions of property, should be rendered uniform in other respects, induce us to recommend that all Wills should be revocable in the same manner.

Wills Act 1837

20. In what cases wills may be revoked
No will or codicil, or any part thereof, shall be revoked otherwise than as aforesaid,[3] or by another will or codicil, executed in manner hereinbefore required, or by some writing declaring an intention to revoke the same, and executed in the manner in which a will is hereinbefore required to be executed, or by the burning, tearing, or otherwise destroying the same by the testator, or by some person in his presence and by his direction, with the intention of revoking the same.

---

1. 1833, p 31.
2. See p 90 ante.
3. See WA 1837, ss 18 and 18A (as substituted by Administration of Justice Act 1982, s 18), Ch 12 ante.

2 Methods of revocation

(a) By formal testamentary instrument

There are two requirements under this head; a document executed in accordance with the requirements of Wills Act 1837, s 9,[4] which will usually be in the form of a will or codicil but may take some other form such as a duly executed letter, and an intention to revoke shown by that document.[5]

In **In the Goods of Durance** (1872) LR 2 P & D 406, the testator had made a will which he deposited with his solicitor; he later wrote the following letter to his brother:

'My dear Joe,—Enclosed, I hand you an order to get my will from Mr Denman, which please burn as soon as you receive it without reading it. I will leave you my share as a deed of gift, leaving it to your honour to pay out of it £100 each to each of my two sisters, and £100 to Thomas Plant. I am very ill, so good bye. God bless you.
Your affectionate brother,
Thos. J. Durance.'

Witnesses,
 John Greenshields,
 Frank Booth.

Holding that the letter was effective to revoke the will, Lord Penzance said at p 407:

If a man writes to another 'Go and get my will and burn it', he shews a strong intention to revoke his will. In the language of the 20th section of the Wills Act the letter is a writing declaring an intention to revoke the will, and it is duly executed. It is also of a testamentary character, and therefore I shall grant administration with it annexed to Joseph Durance the brother and one of the next of kin.[6]

Re Hawksley's Settlement [1934] Ch 384, Ch D; Luxmoore J

The testatrix made a will in 1922 and a codicil thereto in 1925. In 1927 she made another will which commenced 'Last will and testament of Florence Hawksley Musgrove'; it contained no express revocation clause but it did purport to dispose of the whole of her estate and also property over which she had powers of appointment. It also referred to the 'cancelled will' and after the testatrix's death a copy of the 1922 will was found on which the testator had written 'cancelled'.
Held: The 1922 will and codicil to it had been revoked by the 1927 will.

Luxmoore J: (Counsel) argue that—apart from the inconsistent gifts contained in the 1927 will—there is in fact an expression of intention to revoke which as a matter of construction is to be found in the description of the document as the testatrix's last will and testament, and the reference contained in it to a document called a 'cancelled will'. It is admitted that the testatrix only made one will before she made the 1927 will—that is the 1922 will—and that she wrote on a copy of that will the word 'cancelled' and the document referred to in the 1927 will as the 'cancelled will' is the 1922 will. I do not think these words by themselves are sufficient to effect a complete revocation of the 1922 will

---

4. See Ch 8 ante.
5. In a professionally drawn will the intention will usually be shown by an express revocation clause; see the specimen will at p 62 ante.
6. See also *Re Gosling* (1886) 11 PD 79.

and codicil; and that if revocation of these two documents is to be found, it must be by reason of the fact that the testatrix has disposed of the whole of her own property and the property over which she had a testamentary power of disposition in a manner wholly inconsistent with the provisions of the two earlier documents. Of course, in considering the 1927 will from this point of view the fact it is described as 'Last will and testament', and the fact that there is a reference to the 1922 will as a 'cancelled will' must be taken into consideration. If the 1927 will is read alone, it is fairly plain that it would operate as a complete disposition of the whole of the testatrix's own estate and also of all property over which she had a general power of appointment. It is I think also fairly plain that it would operate as an exercise of the special power conferred on the testatrix by the 1893 settlement, to take effect immediately on the testatrix's death, in favour of the defendants Harold Stephen Ronald Hawksley and Cicely Winifred Hawksley. On this basis the provisions of the 1927 will are either entirely inconsistent with the provisions of the 1922 will and codicil, or repeat the provisions therein contained. I am consequently of opinion that, as a matter of construction, the 1927 will in fact renders the whole of the provisions of the 1922 will and codicil ineffective, because so far as any of them are repeated in the 1927 will, those provisions take effect under that will and not under the 1922 will and codicil.[7]

In **Re Howard** [1944] P 39, the testator had executed a will in 1933 leaving all his estate to his son. In 1940 he executed two more wills both on the same day, one leaving all his estate to his wife and the other leaving all his estate to his son again. There was no indication as to the order of execution but each of the 1940 wills contained a clause expressly revoking all former wills.[8] Holding that the testator died intestate, Henn Collins J said at p 41:

To be an effective revocation, a document need not be susceptible to probate (so much is clear on the authorities), though it must comply in form with s 20 of the Wills Act, 1837. It is contended on the part of the Crown that the true reason why inconsistent wills cannot be admitted to probate is that they are void for uncertainty, and that, being void, they are of no effect, either as wills or as revocations, but to substitute the word 'uncertainty' for 'inconsistency' seems to me to carry the matter no further. On the face of the documents it is apparent that the testator did not intend both to operate, but did intend one or other to do so, though one cannot say which. That is why neither can be admitted to probate, but since the testator contemplated that one or other would be operative and both revoked all earlier dispositions one is on safe ground in supposing that he intended that no earlier dispositions should have effect.

(b) By destruction

A mere direction by the testator to destroy his will is not enough unless the destruction follows and is in the testator's presence.[9] There must be both a substantial degree of destruction, coupled with a contemporaneous intention of thereby revoking the will. A partial mutilation of the document may constitute

---

7. For another example of an intention to revoke shown by implication, see the 'shortest will ever known', *Thorn v Dickens* [1906] WN 54 per Gorrell Barnes P at 54, where the later will simply said 'All to mother'.
8. There was method in his madness; heavy air raids were taking place at the time and the testator thought he was covering all contingencies by making the separate wills; unfortunately he failed to provide for the third possibility that duly materialised—a bomb which demolished the house in which he and his wife and son were all sleeping, killing all of them on the same day.
9. In *In the Goods of Dadds* (1857) Dea & Sw 290, the testatrix, who was bedridden, requested a neighbour and her executor to burn her codicil in the kitchen, there being no fire in her bedroom. They duly did so, but probate of the codicil was still granted; it had not been destroyed in her presence.

a partial revocation of the will if the court is satisfied that that is what the testator intended.[10]

In **Gill v Gill** [1909] P 157, the testator had come home drunk and made some irritating remark to his wife who lost her temper and retaliated by tearing up the nearest thing to hand which happened to be his will in her favour. Holding in favour of the validity of the will, Bargrave Deane J said at p 161:

In this particular case the will was torn up in the presence of the testator by his wife. Was it done by his authority? There is not a particle of evidence to suggest that he authorized it. The wife says that he did not, and on that I accept her evidence that she did it in a fit of temper. It was about as silly a thing to do as could possibly be imagined; but she was at the time beside herself with anger, just as he was beside himself with drink. I doubt whether he had capacity at the time to give any authority, and I do not think that she was sufficiently self-possessed to appreciate what she was doing. Under these circumstances it is impossible to hold that the act of destruction was performed with the authority of the testator. If it was not done with his authority at that time, the dictum of Butt J in *Mills v Millward* ((1889) 15 PD 20) indicates what in my opinion is good law, namely, that no amount of authority afterwards can be brought into play so as to ratify an act done without authority at the time. If a testator under such circumstances desired that the act of destruction, performed without his authority at the time, should prevail, he had it in his power effectually to revoke his will in accordance with the provisions of the Wills Act. He could either execute a document expressly revoking his will, or he could make a fresh will dealing with his property in any way he chose. In the present instance, so far from doing anything of the sort, the testator always treated the act of destruction by his wife rather as a joke and as of no effect in law—and he was right. He told people what she had done in her temper, and he laughed at it; he spoke, within a few months of his death, of having left everything to his wife if she survived him. I am satisfied that this will was never revoked, and accordingly I admit it to probate.

In **Cheese v Lovejoy** (1877) 2 PD 251, the testator wrote across the back of his will 'All these are revoked', and put a pen stroke through the text, although this left the text still legible. He then kicked it into the corner of the room among a pile of waste paper which was subsequently collected by the housemaid. She kept the will lying around in the kitchen, where it was found some eight years later when he died. Holding in favour of the will, James LJ said at p 253:

It is quite clear that a symbolical burning will not do, a symbolical tearing will not do, nor will a symbolical destruction. There must be the act as well as the intention. As it was put by Dr Deane in the Court below, 'All the destroying in the world without intention will not revoke a will, nor all the intention in the world without destroying; there must be the two.'[11]

Hobbs v Knight (1838) 1 Curt 768, 163 ER 267, Prerogative Court; Fust J

The testator had cut off his signature at the foot of the will which was otherwise left intact.

Held: The will was wholly revoked.

---

10. There is a presumption of destruction where the last known custodian of the will was the testator and the will cannot be found after his death; see Ch 14 post.
11. See also *Andrew v Motley* (1862) 12 CB (NS) 514. It was suggested to the Law Reform Committee that in the light of *Cheese v Lovejoy*, the court should have a discretion to give effect to any act which manifested an intention on the testator's part to revoke his will but the Committee, in its Twenty-Second Report (1980) Cmnd 7902, at para 3.41, declined to recommend legislation on the point taking the view that the *Cheese v Lovejoy* situation of a manifest intention to revoke but an insufficient act of destruction, was 'extremely rare, amounting to 2 or 3 out of the 29,000 wills admitted to probate in the Principal Registry each year.'

Fust J: Assuming, then, that this act was done by the deceased, it must be taken to have been deliberately done; the effect of that act is now to be considered. The signature of the testator being an essential part of a will, it is difficult to comprehend when that which is essential to the existence of a thing is destroyed, how the thing itself can exist. There can be no doubt that if the name of the testator had been burnt or torn out, the revocation would have been as complete as if the will had been torn into twenty pieces. If this were not the case, it would lead to many absurd consequences. But it has been argued that, as the present act of Parliament has pointed out certain modes with regard to the revocation of wills, the Court cannot go beyond the express terms of the act; that the words being confined to burning, tearing, or otherwise destroying, omitting the terms 'obliterating' and 'cancelling' used in the statute of frauds; there must be an actual burning or tearing, or as to 'otherwise destroying', that the whole instrument must be destroyed; that the cutting in the present case, is not tearing (burning is out of the question), and, the instrument not being destroyed, that there is no revocation. . . .

Suppose a will to be written in pencil, and the words removed by means of Indian rubber, could there be any doubt that that would be a sufficient revocation? Cutting is a mode of destroying as effectual as tearing, and it appears to me that if tearing a will to this extent be a sufficient destruction of it, the same effect must be attributed to the act of cutting it; what would be the consequences of a different construction? Suppose a will were torn into two or more pieces, the will, no doubt, would be revoked; but if it were cut into twenty pieces with a knife, that would be no revocation, and if the pieces could be collected and pasted together, the will must be pronounced for by the Court. I cannot conceive it possible that it was the intention of the legislature to leave the law in that state. The question then comes to this: whether this be or be not a destruction of the will. I consider the name of the testator to be essential to the existence of a will and that, if that name be removed, the essential part of the will is removed and the will is destroyed.[12]

Law Reform Committee: Twenty-Second Report[13]

3.43 Destruction   Destruction is the only method of revocation which can be effected by the unwitnessed act of the testator and, on the basis that revocation of a will may have effects which are just as far reaching as the making of one from the point of view of beneficiaries and those who would inherit under the laws of intestate succession, we asked for views on the question whether destruction ought to be witnessed in order to be an effective revocation. The replies to this question were almost unanimously against such a requirement on the basis that it would frequently frustrate the testator's intentions and would create complications in practice. For example, it would be necessary to record the witnessed destruction of the will and to prove the contents of a will which has been destroyed without witnesses would often be difficult, if not impossible.

(c) By informal declaration

A person who is entitled to make a privileged will[14] can revoke his will, whether a duly executed will or an informal privileged will, informally whilst the privilege continues.[15] Once privileged status ends, the will whether formal or informal, can only be revoked in one of the formal ways; unless and until so

---

12. Cf *Re Everest* [1975] Fam 44, [1975] 1 All ER 672, where the testator had cut out only the trusts of the residuary estate leaving the remainder intact, including his signature and the attestation clause; probate was granted of the remainder.
13. 'The Making and Revocation of Wills' (1980) Cmnd 7902.
14. See Ch 9 ante.
15. Marriage of the privileged testator will also revoke his will as it will for any other testator (see Ch 12 ante) *Re Wardrop* [1917] P 54.

revoked, it will remain in force.[16] Section 3(3) Family Law Reform Act 1969 was passed to rescue the infant who makes a privileged will but, on losing his privileged status while still an infant, lacks the capacity to make a formal revoking instrument.

In the Estate of Gossage [1921] P 194, CA; Lord Sterndale MR, Warrington and Younger LJJ

A soldier whilst enjoying privileged status made a formal will. Whilst still within his privileged status, he wrote an (unwitnessed) letter from South Africa to his sister in England asking her to burn the will 'for I have already cancelled it'. She did burn it but when he died a few years later, a copy of the will was found among his possessions and the main beneficiary thereunder sought to propound it.

Held: The will had been validly revoked by the letter to his sister.

Lord Sterndale MR: The will in this case could not have been burnt in the presence of the testator, because it was in England whilst he was in Africa. It was said however that there was here no valid revocation of the will because by s 20 a soldier's will could not be revoked although it could be made without the formalities required, that is, by another will or codicil or by a document executed with the same formalities as are required in the case of a will which is not a soldier's will. This appears to me to be an absurd result, but however absurd it may appear, effect must be given to it if that result arises from the Act.

I do not think, however, that it requires any straining of the language of the Wills Act to arrive at an opposite conclusion. It is quite clear, apart from the Act, that a soldier could at common law make or revoke a will without any formalities. Is this letter of January 9, 1918 a 'writing declaring an intention to revoke the [will] and executed in the manner in which a will is hereinbefore required to be executed' or is it 'another will or codicil' within the meaning of s 20? The word 'revocation' postulates the existence of a previous will, and I think the words of the section must mean 'executed in the manner hereinbefore required for the execution of the will which it is intended to revoke'. If you read ss 9 and 11 together no formalities are prescribed for the execution of a soldier's will, but soldiers are allowed to dispose of their personal estate as they might have done before the Act, that is to say, as they might have done before the Statute of Frauds.

If that is the correct view then it seems to me that the letter of January 9 1918, is a sufficient writing declaring an intention to revoke the will and executed in the manner required by the Act with regard to that particular will. In the case of a civilian's will certain formalities are required, in that of soldier's will no formalities at all are necessary, and therefore upon the interpretation of the Act no formalities are required to revoke a soldier's will. That being my view I think there was here a valid revocation of the will and the appeal must be dismissed.[17]

Family Law Reform Act 1969

3. Provisions relating to wills and intestacies
(3) Any will which
   (a) has been made, whether before or after the coming into force of this section by a person under the age of eighteen; and

---

16. See *Re Booth* [1926] P 118; Bagwell Purefoy 'Have you revoked your privileged will?' (1982) 79 LSG 570.

17. Warrington and Younger LJJ reached the same conclusion, but whereas Warrington LJ agreed with Lord Sterndale MR's reasoning, Younger LJ arrived at his decision independently of WA 1837, s 20. He relied instead on the wording of WA 1837, s 11 (as extended by Wills (Soldiers and Sailors) Act 1918, s 1), p 110 ante, declaring that the power of revocation was merely another aspect of the privileged power of disposition conferred by that section.

(b) is valid by virtue of the provisions of section 11 of the said Act of 1837 and the said
    Act of 1918,

may be revoked by that person notwithstanding that he is still under that age whether or
not the circumstances are such that he would be entitled to make a valid will under those
provisions.[18]

3   Dependent relative (conditional[19]) revocation

This doctrine arises where the testator appears to revoke his will in one of the
three ways described in this chapter, but his intention to revoke is found to be
conditional; if the condition is not fulfilled, the intention to revoke is vitiated
and the will remains valid. It has been the subject of some criticism as sometimes
the courts have employed it where its application would seem to fly in the face of
the testator's intention.

In **Re Southerden** [1925] P 177, the testator burnt his will, undoubtedly
with the intention of revoking it, but the reason for the revocation was that he
wanted the whole of his estate to go to his wife and he thought that this would be
achieved under the intestacy rules. His belief was wrong and the Court of
Appeal held that as a result, the will had never been validly revoked, Atkin LJ
saying at p 185:

There has been brought into existence in recent years[20] a doctrine which has been
described as 'dependent relative revocation'. The question in each case is, had the
testator the intention of revoking his will? The intention may be conditional, and if the
revocation is subject to a condition which is not fulfilled, the revocation does not take
effect. Cases of dependent relative revocation are mostly cases where the testator has
supposed that if he destroyed his will his property would pass under some other
document. But the condition is not necessarily limited to the existence of some other
document. The revocation may be conditional on the existence or future existence of
some fact. If that is proved full effect can be given to the Wills Act 1837. You must prove
that there was in fact a condition. It is a question of fact in each case. . . .

I think the true inference of fact in the present case, is that when the testator destroyed
his will in the presence of his wife he did it on the condition that she would take the whole
of the property. The condition was not fulfilled, and therefore the revocation was not
operative.

In **In the Goods of Middleton** (1864) 3 Sw & Tr 583, 164 ER 1402, the
testatrix's first will left legacies to a niece. A second will was made primarily in
order to exclude the niece from benefit but was invalid for lack of due

---

18. It is not clear from the section whether the infant who loses his privileged status during infancy
can nevertheless revoke his privileged will informally or whether he is intended to adopt one of the
formal methods notwithstanding his infancy. Probably the safest course for the infant testator with
revocatory intentions is to destroy the will.

19. The Law Reform Committee has expressed the hope that the doctrine may in future be
described simply as 'conditional revocation' rather than as 'dependent relative revocation'
(Twenty-Second Report (1980) Cmnd 7902 para 3.46), a suggestion with which Langton J would
agree: 'This doctrine seems to me somewhat overloaded with unnecessary polysyllables', *Re Hope
Brown* [1942] P 136 at 138, [1942] 2 All ER 176 at 178.

20. Its origins are more respectable than this; as Roskill LJ pointed out in *Re Jones* [1976] Ch 200 at
212, [1976] 1 All ER 593 at 601, it seems to have been invoked for the first time in *Onions v Tyrer*
(1716) 1 P Wms 343 where a testator revoked his will by destroying it, because he was making a new
will on similar terms which would replace it. The new will was invalid for want of due attestation
and Lord Cowper held that as the intention to revoke the first will was conditional on its effective
replacement, the first will remained valid.

attestation. Subsequently the attestation clause in the first will was torn off and burned. Sir JP Wilde upheld the first will saying at p 1402, that he was satisfied that the testratrix 'only intended to revoke it on the assumption that the later will had been duly executed'.[1]

Re Jones [1976] Ch 200, [1976] 1 All ER 593, CA; Buckley, Roskill and Goff LJJ

The testatrix made a will in 1965 in which she left her smallholding to two nieces. In a conversation with her bank manager in 1970 she complained about the attitude of these nieces and said that she intended to leave the smallholding to a nephew's children instead. A few days later, in conversation with another nephew, she said that she had not made a will. She made arrangements to see a solicitor with a view to making a new will, but before she could so so, she was taken ill and died. After her death, the 1965 will was discovered, mutilated in such a way as could constitute its revocation. The nieces contended that her intention to revoke it must have been conditional on the making of the new will she had in mind, and since she never had made that new will, dependent relative revocation would apply, the condition was unsatisfied and the 1965 will would stand.

Held: Her intention to revoke the will was unconditional; she died intestate.

Buckley LJ: Where a testator mutilates or destroys a will, the questions which arise, I think, are these: (1) Did he do so with the intention of revoking it? . . . If there is no intention of revoking it, the act of destruction or mutilation will not effect a revocation.

If, however, the answer to that question is that the testator did have a revocatory intention, the second question arises, which is this: (2) If he had an intention of revoking the will, was his intention absolute or qualified, so as to be contingent or conditional? If it was absolute, that is the end of the investigation, for the act takes effect as a revocation.

If, however, it was qualified, the further question which arises is: (3) What was the nature of the qualification? The testator's intention may have been dependent upon an intent to revive an earlier testamentary document, founded on an erroneous belief that the cancellation of the later will would have that effect, as in *Powell v Powell* ((1866) LR 1 P & D 209); or it may have been wholly and solely dependent upon an intention to displace it by some new testamentary disposition. An example of this may be taken to be *Dixon v Treasury Solicitor* ([1905] P 42) where there was evidence that the testator thought that the cancellation of an earlier will was a necessary pre-condition of making a new one.

If the testator's intention is found to have been a qualified one, subject to some condition or contingency, the final question arises, which is this: (4) Has that condition or contingency been satisfied or occurred? If the condition or contingency to which the intention to revoke was subject has not been satisfied or occurred, the revocation is ineffective; if it has been satisfied or occurred, the revocation is effective.

The fact that at the time of the mutilation or destruction the testator intended or contemplated making a new will, is not, in my judgment, conclusive of the question whether his intention to revoke was dependent upon his subsequently making a new will. A testator who has made a will in favour of A may become disenchanted with A and decide not to benefit him. He may well at the same time decide that in these circumstances he will benefit B instead of A. It does not by any means follow that his intention to disinherit A will be dependent on his benefiting B, or making a will under which B could take. . . .

---

1. Yet the final wish of the testatrix was clearly that the niece should not benefit. For other examples of the application of the doctrine see *Re Itter*, p 183 post, *Re Carey* (1977) 121 Sol J 173, *Re Crannis* (1978) 122 Sol J 489.

With deference to the learned judge, it seems to me that the inference which most convincingly fits these facts is that the testatrix was not content that the revocation of her existing will should depend upon her making a new one, but that she wished and intended to achieve what she could, namely, the revocation of her existing will, there and then, and that this was her reason for mutilating it. This is not necessarily inconsistent with her having at the same time an intention to make a new will at the earliest opportunity devising 'Dryslwyn' to the children of her nephew.

Law Reform Committee: Twenty-Second Report[2]

3.47   The doctrine of dependent relative or conditional revocation

This rule can operate to preserve an earlier will where its revocation was conditional upon the effectiveness of a later will. The chief criticism of the rule is that the preservation of a prior will may be directly contrary to the testator's wishes.[3] The testator might have intended the revocation of his earlier will to survive in any event and preferred his property to pass as on an intestacy on failure of the later will. It was suggested that the rule should be abolished in favour of a discretion enabling the Court to validate a later will in such a case. However, most witnesses welcomed the approach in *Re Jones* [1976] Ch 200[4] which makes it clear that a revocation will not be held to be conditional unless there is evidence that such was the testator's intention. We think that the rule, which is a flexible and useful compromise between a complete discretionary power and rigid rules, should be retained. In our view *Re Jones* not only limits its scope but also provides clear guidance as to its application.

4   Alterations

If an alteration is made before execution of the will, the will takes effect as altered. If made after execution of the will the alteration will be admitted to probate if duly executed; otherwise it will be of no effect unless the original wording is no longer 'apparent' on the face of the will, in which event to that extent the will is partially revoked.

Wills Act 1837

21   No alteration in a will after execution shall have any effect unless executed as a will

No obliteration, interlineation, or other alteration made in any will after the execution thereof shall be valid or have any effect, except so far as the words or effect of the will before such alteration shall not be apparent, unless such alteration shall be executed in like manner as herein-before is required for the execution of the will; but the will, with such alteration as part thereof, shall be deemed to be duly executed if the signature of the testator and the subscription of the witnesses be made in the margin or on some other part of the will opposite or near to such alteration, or at the foot or end of or opposite to a

---

2. 'The Making and Revocation of Wills' (1980) Cmnd 7902.
3. See eg FH Newark's criticisms in (1955) 71 LQR 374 'Dependent Relative Revocation', with particular reference to the application of the doctrine in *In the Goods of Middleton* (1864) 3 Sw & Tr 583 (p 180 ante) and *Powell v Powell* (1866) LR 1 P & D 209.
4. P 181 ante.

memorandum referring to such alteration and written at the end or some other part of the will.[5]

In **Townley v Watson** (1844) 3 Curt 761, 163 ER 893, the testatrix, some time after executing her will, had so obliterated with a pen and ink certain legacies as to make them wholly illegible. The obliterations were not executed in accordance with Wills Act 1837, s 9. A draft copy of the will was available to establish the contents of the obliterated passages but Fust J held that this evidence was not admissible, the missing passages having been revoked in accordance with Wills Act 1837, s 21, saying at p 895:

What, then is the interpretation to be put on this section, when either words in a will, or the effect of words, are so completely effaced or obliterated as not to be apparent? Now, I think the prima facie construction must be apparent on the face of the instrument itself, and not that suggested in argument, namely, capable of being made apparent by extrinsic evidence. What is an obliteration? Is it not by some means covering over words originally written, so as to render them no longer legible? I cannot understand, if the Legislature really intended that extrinsic evidence should be admitted, why a few more words were not added, which would have freed the section from all doubt; for instance, why was it not thus penned, 'unless the words shall be capable of being made apparent'.

There may be inconsistencies and there may be inconveniences—I do not say there are—in the construction I am putting on the section; but I think it is impossible to read the words and not say it was the intention of the Legislature that if a testator shall take such pains to obliterate certain passages in his will, and shall so effectually accomplish his purpose that those passages cannot be made out on the face of the instrument itself, it shall be a revocation as good and valid as if done according to the stricter forms mentioned in the Act of Parliament.[6]

In **Re Itter** [1950] P 130, [1950] 1 All ER 68, the doctrine of dependent relative revocation[7] came to the rescue of some post execution alterations. Some time after executing a codicil the testatrix had pasted strips of paper over the amount of the legacies it contained and on top of these strips she had written different amounts. These substituted figures were not signed and attested and so were clearly not valid as alterations to the codicil. The original amounts could not be deciphered from the face of the codicil, although they could when infra-red photography was used. It was argued that the original legacies had been revoked so that the legatees would get nothing but Ormrod J held that the original legacies should stand, saying at p 70:

From the fact that the amounts of the legacies only were obliterated in this way and not the whole of the bequests, I think that the inference should be drawn that it was the intention of the testatrix to revoke the part of the bequests covered by the slips only if new bequests were effectually substituted. This seems to me to be the only reason that the testatrix could have for dealing with the codicil in the way in which she did. If this be so,

---

5. It is therefore a sensible precaution for the testator and witnesses to initial even pre-execution alterations as there will then be no need to establish that the alterations had been made before the will was executed.

6. Cf *Ffinch v Combe* [1894] P 191 where slips of paper had been pasted over certain words but the words could still be read by placing a piece of brown paper around them and holding the document up to the light; it was held that the words were still 'apparent' on the face of the instrument. The Law Reform Committee in its Twenty-Second Report: 'The Making and Revocation of Wills' (1980) Cmnd 7902, considered this construction of the word 'apparent' at para 3.44. It found it logically a little difficult to justify but was satisfied that if the testator had so obliterated part of his will that it could not be read even with a magnifying glass, then he must have intended to take that part out of his will and it was right that it be treated as revoked.

7. See p 180 ante.

it follows that the slips may be taken off the document, if necessary, or any other means used to ascertain the writing which was on the document before the slips were pasted on, and accordingly there must be judgment for the plaintiffs (the original legatees).[8]

5   Revival of a revoked will

Revival is the act of restoring validity to a will which has been revoked. Once revived the will is republished as at the date of the revival.[9] Before 1837 it was comparatively easy to revive a revoked will or codicil. A revoked will of personalty, for example, could be revived merely by parol evidence that the testator had treated it as unrevoked, whilst revocation of the revoking instrument automatically revived the will it had revoked whether the will concerned realty, personality or both. This laxity led the Real Property Commissioners in their Fourth Report[10] to make the recommendation subsequently embodied in the 1837 Act.

Wills Act 1837

22.   No revoked will shall be revived otherwise than by re-execution or a codicil

No will or codicil, or any part thereof, which shall be in any manner revoked, shall be revived otherwise than by the re-execution thereof, or by a codicil executed in manner hereinbefore required and showing an intention to revive the same; and when any will or codicil which shall be partly revoked, and afterwards wholly revoked shall be revived, such revival shall not extend to so much thereof as shall have been revoked before the revocation of the whole thereof, unless an intention to the contrary shall be shown.

In the Goods of Davis [1952] P 279, [1952] 2 All ER 509, PD; Willmer J

The testator made a will leaving all his property to one Ethel Phoebe Horsley, whom he later married. The will was not expressed to be made in contemplation of marriage[11] and so was revoked by that marriage. Some 10 years later he wrote on the envelope in which the will was kept: 'The herein named Ethel Phoebe Horsley is now my lawful wedded wife', then followed his signature and that of two attesting witnesses.

Held: The writing on the envelope was in effect a codicil showing an intention to revive the will which should therefore be admitted to probate.

Willmer J: I have been referred to the case of *In the Goods of Steele, In the Goods of May, In the Goods of Wilson* ((1868) LR 1 P & D 575). In that case the meaning of section 22 of the Wills Act was fully considered, and the effect of the decision, as I understand it, is summarized in one sentence of the headnote, the words of which are reproduced from those used in the judgment. I can therefore read them as amounting to the decision of this court. It was held 'In order to satisfy those words [ie the words of section 22 of the

---

8. This was not a novel solution to the problem; see Real Property Commissioners' Fourth Report (1833) p 26.
9. As to republication, see p 54 ante.
10. 1833, p 34.
11. See p 165 ante.

Act] the intention must appear on the face of the codicil, either by express words referring to a will as revoked and importing an intention to revive the same, or by a disposition of the testator's property inconsistent with any other intention, or by some other expression conveying to the mind of the court with reasonable certainty the existence of the intention.'

It would seem that three possibilities are there expressed. The first two do not arise in the present case, for there are no express words here referring to the will as revoked, nor is there any disposition of property contained in the purported codicil. The question remains whether it can be said that there is some expression conveying to the mind of the court with reasonable certainty the existence of an intention to revive the will. I was very much impressed with the argument of counsel for the applicant when he pointed out that one must assume that the testator intended to execute some sort of effective document when he executed the document of 1943; he cannot be credited with an intention to execute a wholly ineffective codicil to a wholly ineffective will. The words which he wrote refer specifically to what is written within, that is to say, within the envelope, and within the envelope was the will itself. It is pointed out, and I think with force, that the testator could only make this an effective codicil by making the will an effective will. If I am not to infer that in preparing this document, and having it executed in the form of a codicil, the testator intended to revive this will, what other intention can possibly be imputed to him? . . . It appears to me that the words ought to be construed, if they legitimately and fairly can be construed, so as to have some effect. The only effect I can give them is the effect of making the will effective.

In **Rogers & Andrews v Goodenough** (1862) 2 Sw & Tr 342, 164 ER 1028, Cresswell J held that there could be no revival of a will that had been destroyed. The testator had made a will in 1858 and then another will in 1859 which contained a general revocation clause. The 1858 will was then burnt with his consent. Subsequently he made a codicil, expressed to be a codicil 'to my last will, made 1858'. Cresswell J said at p 1031:

The first question is, whether the codicil could revive that will, assuming that the reference to it by date was correct, and that it was the intention of the testator that it should be so revived. That is a question to be determined by the Stat 1 Vict c 26 (Wills Act 1837). When the instrument had been destroyed, it no longer existed either in law or fact; it did not exist as a will from the time when the second will was executed; it no longer existed as a written instrument, as a paper writing, from the time when it was burnt. Not being either a will or a writing, how could it again become a will? That question seems to be decided by the statute; the 9th section says, 'that no will shall be valid unless it be in writing and executed in the manner hereinafter mentioned.' It has been said that it could again become a will, because it was revived by the codicil; but it could only be revived in its original condition of a written instrument, and thus the very first thing required by the statute in order to make a will, cannot be satisfied. It appears to me that the expression 'no will shall be valid' applies equally to an original will and a revived will. . . .

I say nothing as to what would be the effect if the instrument had been destroyed without his knowledge. The question may arise on another day whether a person can revive an instrument, or rather the contents of an instrument, which no longer exists,— whether in that case the terms of the 9th section of the statute would be satisfied. My judgment is limited to the facts before the Court in the present case'.[12]

QUESTIONS

1. A testator tears his will, but not quite in two; he then throws it on the fire

---

12. As the codicil showed no intention to revoke the 1859 will, however, he was able to hold that that will, together with the codicil, should be admitted to probate.

where it is singed but not completely destroyed. Has he done enough to revoke the will? See *Bibb v Thomas* (1775) 2 Black W 1043.

2. The justification for the doctrine of dependent relative revocation is said to be that it gives effect to the testator's intention, yet the results of its application sometimes seem to fly in the face of that intention.

Discuss.

3. Terry executes his will which includes a legacy of £300 to Lucy. He subsequently crosses out the reference to '£300' and puts '£500' immediately above the crossing out, but the alteration is not attested. The original figure of '£300' is still apparent. What amount, if any, would Lucy receive on Terry's death? Would your answer be different in any of the following alternative circumstances:

(a) instead of crossing out '£300', Terry so scribbles over it that the amount is not apparent on the face of the will;

(b) Terry and two witnesses sign and initial the figure '£500';

(c) the alterations are made (though not as such signed and attested) before Terry executes his will?

4. 'Revival always involves republication, but republication does not always involve revival'.

Is this correct?

CHAPTER 14

The problem of the lost will

When a will that is known to have been in existence cannot be found at or after the testator's death, a number of problems are posed.

1 Has the will been revoked?

Where the last known custodian of the will was the testator himself and the will cannot be produced after his death, the testator is presumed to have destroyed the will with the intention of revoking it. The presumption is rebuttable by evidence to the contrary.

In **Welch v Phillips** (1836) 1 Moo PC 299, 12 ER 828, the testatrix made a new will some months before her death; she kept it in her own custody and after her death it could not be found. Holding that the presumption of revocation would apply and that there was insufficient evidence to rebut it, Parke B said at p 829:

> Now the rule of the law of evidence on this subject, as established by a course of decisions in the Ecclesiastical Court, is this: that if a Will, traced to the possession of the deceased, and last seen there, is not forthcoming on his death, it is presumed to have been destroyed by himself; and that presumption must have effect, unless there is sufficient evidence to repel it. It is a presumption founded on good sense; for it is highly reasonable to suppose that an instrument of so much importance would be carefully preserved, by a person of ordinary caution, in some place of safety, and would not be either lost or stolen; and if, on the death of the maker, it is not found in his usual repositories, or else where he resides, it is in a high degree probable, that the deceased himself has purposely destroyed it. But this presumption, like all others of fact, may be rebutted by others which raise a higher degree of probability to the contrary.

The onus of proof of such circumstances, is undoubtedly on the party propounding the will.[1]

Sugden v Lord St Leonards (1876) 1 PD 154, CA; Cockburn CJ, Jessel MR, James and Mellish LJJ, Baggallay JA

Lord St Leonards, a former Lord Chancellor, made no less than eight codicils to his will in the last few years of his life. The will and codicils were all kept in a

---

1. Aliter if the testator becomes mentally unsound after executing his will. As a mentally unsound person is not usually capable of forming an *animus revocandi*, the presumption will not apply in such a case; the burden of proof will be on those asserting the revocation to establish that the will was destroyed whilst he was still of sound mind: *Re Broome* (1961) 29 DLR (2d) 631 (Manitoba Court of Appeal), *Sprigge v Sprigge* (1868) LR 1 P & D 608.

small black box in a locked writing-desk in his home. After his death the box was opened; the codicils were inside but the will could not be found.

Held: The will was not revoked. The presumption of revocation was rebutted by satisfactory evidence to the contrary.

Cockburn CJ: Now, where a will is shewn to have been in the custody of a testator, and is not found at his death, the well-known presumption arises that the will has been destroyed by the testator for the purpose of revoking it, but of course that presumption may be rebutted by the facts. Although *presumptio juris*, it is not *presumptio de jure*, and of course the presumption will be more or less strong according to the character of the custody which the testator had over the will.

Now here we have to observe that the custody was anything but a close custody. The box was kept in a room on the ground floor, common not only to the inmates of the house, but to any one who had obtained access to it. It was kept in a common box, easily opened, and the key was kept in an escritoire not always under lock and key. It is in evidence, that of the different keys in the house there were no less than five by which the escritoire might be opened, and the will was, no doubt, known to the inmates of the house or to those who had been its inmates, as being kept in this box, for, as a matter of fact, Lord St Leonards was constantly, or, at all events, frequently, engaged in making wills or codicils, testamentary dispositions of one sort or another, and upon all these occasions some of the servants of the house were called in to witness the execution of the testamentary document, and, therefore, would well know that the box was the place for the deposit of the testamentary papers of Lord St Leonards.

Next comes the question whether it is or is not probable that the will should have been destroyed by the testator, and here we must look at the position and character of the man. It would be difficult to find a more methodical man of business than the late Lord St Leonards; it would be difficult to find any one who had a deeper sense of the importance of testamentary dispositions. We find that between 1867 and 1873 he made no fewer than two wills and eight codicils. He always exhibited the greatest possible anxiety to make a proper provision for the members of his family, and more especially for his daughter, Miss Sugden, for whom it is quite clear that he entertained the warmest and fondest affection, and who would be left wholly unprovided for in the absence of testamentary provision made in her favour. He upon all occasions expressed a deep sense of the duty, which every man ought to act upon, of making testamentary provision for those who were dependent upon him. We know, also, although, of course, we might have presumed it independently of any specific knowledge of the fact, that he was quite alive to the danger of destroying one will with the view of making another, and of the necessity of making a will, as it were, *uno flatu*,[2] to prevent the possibility of any question arising as to his intention. It must be remembered that it is in evidence that upon two occasions when he was making his will, in 1867 and 1870, there was the greatest difficulty in prevailing upon him to take refreshment, because he would not be interrupted in the work, and he gave as a reason that, if anything should happen to him while the will was, as it were, in suspense, questions might afterwards arise upon it.

Now besides that, we have the fact that, from the time of making his will in 1870 down to the time of his death, he was in the constant habit of talking to every one with whom he came into contact, most certainly to all the inmates of the house with whom he was brought into daily contact, of the testamentary provisions he had made, expressing his satisfaction at what he had been able to do for the different members of his family, more especially for Miss Sugden, and at his having acquired, by his own professional powers and exertions, so large an amount of property. The possession of that property, the disposition of that property, and the satisfaction he felt in having made provision for the peerage which he had founded, and for the various members of his family who were dependent upon his bounty, seem to have been constant subjects of his thoughts, upon which his mind delighted to dwell, and also constant topics of his daily discourse with almost all the persons with whom he was brought into contact. It seems to me utterly

---

2. In the same breath, ie straightaway.

impossible to suppose that, under these circumstances, such a man as Lord St Leonards would voluntarily have destroyed this will, whether for the purpose of revoking it, or making another, or for any other purpose that could be conceived. My mind revolts from arriving at any such conclusion, and I feel bound to reject it.[3]

In **Homerton v Hewett** (1872) 25 LT 854, it was argued that the doctrine of dependent relative revocation[4] should operate to save a missing will otherwise revoked by the application of the presumption, for during his lifetime the testator had declared his intention of making another will disposing of his property in a different way, an intention that he never put into effect. Pronouncing nevertheless against the missing will, Lord Penzance said at p 855:

But then it is said that if this will has been destroyed it was for the purpose of setting up the codicil,[5] and the case therefore comes within the principle of dependent relative revocation. But the force of that is destroyed by this remark, that the court has never been in the habit of applying that doctrine to any case in which there was not proof of the destruction of the document. Here there is no proof of the fact of destruction. It is merely a surmise of law, and we do not know when the testator destroyed it, or what he said or did when he destroyed it. It would be a dangerous thing to surmise a transaction, and build upon it some theory by which the effect of revocation could practically be destroyed. In both the cases cited[6] there was evidence of destruction, and in all cases before it applies the principle of dependent relative revocation the court must have some such evidence.[7]

2 Was the will duly executed?

Assuming the missing will has not been revoked, its due execution now has to be established.[8] In the first instance the court will look to the evidence of the attesting witnesses, but if they are dead, or of unsound mind, or cannot be traced, the court will look to the evidence of anyone else who saw the will executed or any other evidence from which an inference of due execution can be drawn. If there is evidence as to the existence of an attestation clause, this may enable the court to apply the maxim *omnia praesumuntur rite esse acta*[9] to save the will.

Re Webb [1964] 2 All ER 91, [1964] 1 WLR 509, PD; Faulks J

The testatrix's original will had been seen in the custody of her solicitor when it was destroyed during an air raid in 1940 which extensively damaged the

---

3. The Law Reform Committee in its 22nd Report 'The Making and Revocation of Wills' (1980) Cmnd 7902 found that the presumption was often rebutted in practice; they accepted that it served a useful purpose in determining where the burden of proof should lie and recommended no change in this respect.
4. See p 180 ante.
5. An earlier revoked instrument which contained the different provision which the testator had declared he had in mind.
6. *Powell v Powell* (1866) LR 1 P &D 209, *In the Goods of Weston* (1869) LR 1 P & D 633.
7. See *In the Estate of Botting* [1951] 2 All ER 997, *In the Estate of Bridgewater* [1965] 1 All ER 717, [1965] 1 WLR 416. In each of these cases dependent relative revocation saved the missing will, but there was positive evidence of the destruction of the will concerned.
8. As to the procedure, see NCPR 1954 r 53 p 312 post.
9. See p 103 ante.

solicitor's office. The solicitor had since died. After the death of the testatrix, a draft of the will was found; it contained an attestation clause and the names of the witnesses were entered beneath it. One of the witnesses was called to give evidence of due execution but could not remember signing the document at all. She did remember being called into the testatrix's shop on one occasion and noticing a little man in a Homburg hat.[10]

Held: There was sufficient evidence of due execution; the draft will could be admitted to probate.

Faulks J: I think it is right in this case for the court to have regard to the completed draft. That is in application of the principle laid down in *Sugden v Lord St Leonards* ((1876) 1 PD 154)[11] and in a case, to which counsel for the defendants referred me, called *In the Estate of Phibbs* ([1917] P 93).[12] In the former case, however, the execution of the will that was lost was duly proved by the evidence of persons who were in attendance at the time and saw it executed in accordance with the provisions of the Wills Act 1837. The question here is whether the court is entitled to say that although there is no such affirmative evidence, the completed draft being used as secondary evidence to prove the contents of the last will,[13] the maxim *omnia praesumuntur rite esse acta*[14] allows the court to say that there being an attestation clause in the completed draft, which speaks to the regularity of the execution of the document, that in the absence of cogent negative evidence is enough. In my view that is enough.

In the case of *In the Estate of Phibbs* ([1917] P 93), where the original will had been lost, what was proved was not the actual contents of the will, but an epitome thereof, just as in *Lord St Leonards' case* (1876) 1 PD 154), the daughter having memorised the contents, it was admitted to probate in its entirety. Here there is no doubt as to the contents of the document. The document, which is validly in evidence, and is the best evidence in the absence of the original, states on its face that it was 'Signed by the above named Mabel Beatrice Webb as her last will in the joint presence of herself and us who at her request and in such joint presence have hereunto subscribed our names as witnesses.' In those circumstances, I think that it is right to apply the authorities succinctly set out in *Mortimer on Probate Law and Practice* (2nd edn 1927), pp 123–129.[15] In particular I rely on the passage at p 126, where the text reads: 'The court will not allow a defective memory alone to overturn a will which is upon the face of it duly executed; if the witnesses are utterly forgetful of the facts, the presumption *omnia rite esse acta* will prevail.' So the plaintiff is in no way handicapped by the honesty of (the attesting witness) and there will be an admission of the completed draft to probate as prayed.

3   Proving the contents of a missing will

Secondary evidence is admissible for this purpose, the best possible evidence being a photocopy of the executed will or a draft copy of the will that has been completed with particulars of the execution,[16] particularly if someone such as a solicitor is in a position to swear that the actual will was executed in the form of

---

10. The assumption drawn from this by the court was that he must have been the solicitor who drew the will and who was attending on the testatrix for its execution.
11. See p 191 post in relation to the problem of proving the contents of a missing will.
12. In this case there was evidence from people who had actually seen the will to the effect that it contained a proper attestation clause even though they could not remember the names of the attesting witnesses.
13. See post.
14. See p 103 ante.
15. See now Williams, Mortimer and Sunnucks, pp 135–137.
16. As in *Re Webb*, ante. See also NCPR 1954 r 53 p 312 post.

the draft without alterations. Otherwise the oral evidence of someone familiar with the terms of the will, even an interested beneficiary, has been accepted by the court.

In **Sugden v Lord St Leonards** (1876) 1 PD 154, having decided that the missing will had not been revoked,[17] the Court of Appeal then had to reconstruct its contents. There was no direct documentary evidence available, but the testator's daughter, Miss Sugden, was able to recall almost verbatim the terms of his long and very complicated will, a will by which, on her recollections, she was a major beneficiary. The Court of Appeal accepted her evidence, which was supported both by the contents of the codicils which fitted in with her recollections of the will and by her evidence of the declarations of the testator himself. Cockburn CJ said at p 222:

Now we have to ask ourselves how far, Miss Sugden's veracity and honesty of purpose not being for a single moment questioned, we can place implicit reliance upon that lady's recollection of the various testamentary dispositions contained in the will upon which she has spoken. No doubt the observation naturally presents itself that in a matter of this kind, with details more or less of a technical character, it is not likely that these things should have impressed themselves upon a lady's mind, or that she should be able to produce them with anything like satisfactory accuracy. But then we must look at the peculiar position of Miss Sugden, and the peculiar training which she had undergone. She lived with, and devoted her life to a great lawyer, who may be said, literally, to have lived in the law, who seems to have devoted his whole life, even to the last, to the study of the law and to the production of those works which are so highly valued by the profession. Then he was in the habit of employing Miss Sugden as his amanuensis, and when he was preparing the various editions of his works, he employed her to correct the proofs; he was fond of explaining to her the various points of law, as they from time to time presented themselves, in going through his works, and explaining to her things which, otherwise, no doubt, she would not have been able to understand. Now, besides that, she had on various occasions, an opportunity of reading these two wills of 1867 and 1870; upon each occasion when Lord St Leonards had completed his will he read it over to her, and she had other opportunities of seeing the will, and she tells us that she read it over three times; besides being called upon him, on different occasions, when he was making a codicil, to refer to the will for the particulars which he wanted. That, of course, places her in a very different position from what would have been the case with a lady otherwise circumstanced; her story, therefore, I am prepared to believe, that, with all these advantages, she had become familiar with the testamentary dispositions made in these wills by her father. It is true, when we look at the will as propounded, at the paper purporting to contain the provisions of the will as propounded, the language may be found to assume a technical character, of which it would be little likely that, even with all her opportunities and advantages, Miss Sugden should have acquired the command. But then, the answer to that is given, I think, by Sir James Hannen,[18] namely, that her statement is not clothed in that technical and professional form, but is the simple statement of a layman, of what the provisions in the will were.[19]

---

17. P 187 ante.
18. At first instance.
19. Jessel MR, agreeing with Cockburn CJ's acceptance of the daughter's reconstruction of the will, thought the circumstances of the case were likely to be unique in this respect, but see now *Re Yelland* (1975) 119 Sol J 562 where probate was granted of a lost will, the contents of which were reconstructed by the main beneficiary with no corroborative evidence, although one of the alleged witnesses did recall attesting the will.

4   Establishing the effect of the lost will on earlier wills

If the contents of the lost will have been fully established, it will be known whether it expressly or by implication revoked earlier wills.[20] If the contents are not sufficiently established, the mere fact that a later will has been made will not necessarily mean that it revoked the earlier will, and probate of the earlier will will issue.[1]

Re Wyatt [1952] 1 All ER 1030, [1952] 1 TLR 1294, PDA; Collingwood J

The testatrix made a will in 1935 and a codicil in 1937. Later on in 1937 she instructed a solicitor to prepare another will, which she duly executed and took away with her. On her death it could not be found.[2] The solicitor who drew it up had not kept a copy of it and could not swear positively that it contained the usual express revocation clause; he could only say that it was his usual practice to include such a clause in all wills drawn up by him.

Held: This was not sufficient evidence to establish the revocation of the first will and codicil; nothing short of stringent and conclusive evidence would suffice. Probate of the first will and codicil would therefore be granted.

Collingwood J: The mere fact of making a subsequent testamentary paper does not effect a total revocation of a prior one unless the later document expressly or impliedly revokes the former one. On the other hand, the executor of a second will which expressly revokes—or is entirely inconsistent with a former one—revokes the first even though the second will is not forthcoming at the death of the testator, and its contents are proved by oral evidence: *Brown v Brown* ((1858) 8 E & B 876); *Wood v Wood* ((1867) LR 1 P & D 309). But in such a case the authorities show that there must be clear proof of the provisions of the missing will. . . . In his affidavit of Feb 12 1952, the solicitor states that it was his practice to include a revocation clause in any draft will prepared by him on the instructions of a client, and he went on to describe the various stages of preparation which were customary, including the sending of the draft for perusal and approval, and the making of any amendments or deletions necessitated thereby, and final engrossment. He had, however, no recollection of any of these matters in relation to the will in question. From this I was invited on behalf of the Treasury Solicitor to draw the conclusion that the lost will contained a revocation clause. I was referred to the report of *In the Estate of Hampshire* ([1951] WN 174). The report is a short one, but I think it is clear from the judgment that the learned judge had evidence before him which he felt (to quote his own word) 'compelled' him to find that the missing will contained both a revocation clause and an effective disposition of the whole estate of the testator.[3]

In this case, on the evidence before me, I think that so to find involves the assumption that the solicitor's usual procedure was in fact followed in the present instance, and the further assumption that the testatrix accepted the draft as correctly expressing her intentions in the matter. In my opinion, I ought not to make these assumptions in respect of a will the contents of which are wholly unknown. To do so would, I think, be to

---

20. See p 175 ante.
1. Whether or not the lost will is presumed revoked.
2. The presumption that it had been destroyed by the testator with the intention of revoking it accordingly applied, see p 187 ante.
3. The solicitor who drew up the missing will in that case could not say for certain that it contained a revocation clause, but Karminski J said at p 174: 'I find it very hard to believe that a solicitor would be likely to draw a will without a revocation clause. If possible, he would be even less likely to draw a will which did not, so far as he could, dispose of the whole estate of the testator'.

substitute surmise for the 'stringent and conclusive' oral evidence required by Dr Lushington in *Cutto v Gilbert* ((1854) 9 Moo PC 131) and thereby, to use his words, 'to pursue a course of proceedings not unattended with danger.'[4]

5 Deposit/registration of wills

In addition to the above problems, there is always a risk that a will will be suppressed by an interested party or simply not found after the testator's death. This problem was considered by the Law Commission in a Working Paper in 1966 and a system of compulsory registration of wills suggested, but the suggestion has not been implemented.[5] There is presently a system for the voluntary deposit of wills in the Principal Registry[6] but this is little used[7] and will ultimately be replaced by the provisions for the voluntary deposit and registration of wills contained in ss 23–26 Administration of Justice Act 1982 which are aimed at implementing the voluntary system provided for by the Convention on the Establishment of a Scheme of Registration of Wills concluded in Basle on 16th May 1972. The United Kingdom is a signatory to the Convention but has not yet ratified it so that these provisions of the 1982 Act have not yet been brought into force.

Law Commission Working Paper: Should English Wills be Registrable?[8]

19. In the Netherlands registration of wills has been compulsory since 1918. Under Dutch law no will is valid unless it has been deposited with a notary in the presence of witnesses. The notary holds a semi-official position and is subject to very stringent disciplinary rules. The will remains in the notary's custody, whether or not he knows its contents, but he is under a duty to inform the custodian of the central registry of wills that the will has been deposited with him, together with the name and address of the testator and the date of deposit. This information is entered in the register which is open to inspection 'by any interested party'. We understand that in practice no dispute ever arises about the authenticity or date of Dutch wills and the system has won general approval.

Possible remedies

20. While one cannot pretend that the present position in England is so unsatisfactory as to cry out for a remedy as a matter of urgency, we think that public dissatisfaction is unlikely to die away and public opinion may come sooner or later to accept the need for

---

4. Cf *Barkwell v Barkwell* [1928] P 91 where the testator's missing will had been made on a printed will form supplied by a firm of law stationers which always included a printed revocation clause; the court was satisfied that it therefore revoked all previous wills.
5. The Law Reform Committee in its Twenty-Second Report 'The Making and Revocation of Wills' (1980) Cmnd 7902 also briefly considered the problem at para 2.24, but concluded that it was not so significant as to justify the introduction of compulsory registration: 'a suspicion that there may be a missing will arises in less than one in a thousand cases'.
6. As originally provided for by the Supreme Court of Judicature (Consolidation) Act 1925, s 172, now replaced by Supreme Court Act 1981, s 126. See also the Wills (Deposit for Safe Custody) Regulations 1978, SI 1978/1724.
7. See Gillis 'Missing Wills, a Solution to the Problem' (1975) 72 LSG no 4 p 4; he states that only 21 wills on average had been deposited in each of the previous five years.
8. Law Com PWP no 4 (1966).

the setting up of some machinery to ensure that wills are not overlooked, to diminish the chances of their being suppressed and to do away with the time consuming and expensive searches and advertisements which solicitors now have to put in train. This machinery might be of either of two kinds:

(a) there could be a depository in which all original wills would be stored or (b) there could be a registry of wills in which certain facts about each will must be recorded within a certain time after it is made. Under the latter scheme it would not be compulsory to deposit the original will in the registry, but the voluntary system, so little used at present, would continue in being, so that a testator could deposit his will there if he wished.

21. There is no reason to think that any voluntary system of deposit or registration would fare better than the existing facilities for deposit, which are almost a dead letter. Moreover, if the system is to be voluntary, there can be no assurance that the latest will registered or deposited would be the last made by the testator and the searches and advertising by solicitors would have to continue. It is, therefore, for consideration whether one of these two schemes should be made compulsory so that all wills and codicils made after an appointed day would depend for their validity on deposit or, as the case may be, registration within a certain time—say, two months—after the date of execution.[9]

22. The obvious objection to any compulsory requirement that a will should be dependent for its validity on compliance with some such formality as we have just mentioned is that a number of home-made wills might be invalidated. We understand, however, that home-made wills are nearly always made on will forms[10] and steps could be taken to ensure that all will forms on sale should bear appropriate warning about the need for deposit or registration, as the case might be. There remains the danger that stocks of out-of-date will forms would still be in circulation and might be held in stationers' shops for a number of years. It is not, however, unrealistic to hope that, if the change in the law were given suitable publicity, the risk that home-made wills would continue to be made in an invalid form could be reduced to an acceptable level and that after a very short time the number would be smaller than the number overlooked under the present state of the law.

23. Wills made before the appointed day would, of course, continue to be valid and would not be affected by the change in the law. For this reason the usefulness of the new machinery would be small at the start; with the passage of time more wills would be readily discovered from the registry and the work of solicitors and others in finding wills after the testator's death would be simplified.[11]

Law Commission: Third Annual Report 1967–68[12]

71(c) **Registration of wills**. . . . Comments we received on our tentative proposals show that they are regarded as more controversial than we had supposed. We were also informed that they would raise difficulties in Scotland where home-made holograph wills are frequently resorted to. In the circumstances we have decided to take no further action for the time being.

---

9. To allow for 'deathbed' wills, the Commissioners suggested (at para 29) that for wills made within two months of death, the period should be extended to two months after the date of death.
10. See p 56 n 10 ante.
11. At para 24–26, the Commissioners considered the respective merits of deposit or registration and found themselves favouring the latter; registration would require fewer staff and less storage space than deposit, most testators would prefer to keep their wills somewhere where they could readily refer to them, and compulsory deposit would make it impossible for testators to revoke their wills by destruction.
12. Law Com 15.

Administration of Justice Act 1982

23. Deposit and registration of wills of living persons[13]
(1) The following, namely—
   (a) the Principal Registry of the Family Division of the High Court of Justice;
   (b) the Keeper of the Registers of Scotland; and
   (c) the Probate and Matrimonial Office of the Supreme Court of Northern Ireland,
shall be registering authorities for the purposes of this section.
(2) Each registering authority shall provide and maintain safe and convenient depositories for the custody of the wills of living persons.
(3) Any person may[14] deposit his will in such a depository in accordance with regulations under section 25 below and on payment of the prescribed fee.
(4) It shall be the duty of a registering authority to register in accordance with regulations under section 25 below any will deposited in a depository maintained by the authority.
(5) A will deposited in a depository provided—
   (a) under section 172 of the Supreme Court of Judicature (Consolidation) Act 1925 or section 126 of the Supreme Court Act 1981; or
   (b) under Article 27 of the Administration of Estates (Northern Ireland) Order 1979,[15]
shall be treated for the purposes of this section as if it had been deposited under this section.

QUESTIONS

1. On A's death, a will made by him in 1983 is found, by which he leaves all his property to B. C says that three months before he died, A made another will, wholly in her favour, but that will cannot be found. What arguments will B raise in support of the first will? What arguments will C raise in support of the second will? To what extent would their respective positions be altered by the discovery of a draft copy of the missing will?

2. Do you consider that the voluntary deposit and registration scheme embodied in the Administration of Justice Act 1982 is likely to receive any more support from the public than the existing scheme (described by the Law Commissioners, p 194 ante, as 'almost a dead letter'? What difficulties would you envisage for the implementation of a compulsory scheme such as the Netherlands system described at p 193 ante?

---

13. See p 193 ante. These provisions are not yet in force.
14. Ie the scheme is to be voluntary, as required by the Basle Convention (see p 193 ante), not compulsory as suggested by the Law Commission, p 194 ante. The Uniform Probate Code (USA) at s 2–901 also provides for the voluntary deposit of wills during the testator's lifetime, the will to be kept confidential and released only to the testator or someone authorised by him in writing.
15. Ie wills already deposited under the present systems for voluntary deposit.

CHAPTER 15

Capital gains tax

The impact of taxation on capital is often the predominant influence on the choice of succession process for those with substantial assets, for the transfer of property, inter vivos or on death, has long been regarded by governments as an ideal opportunity for levying tax. Income tax considerations should not be disregarded[1] but it is usually capital taxation that is uppermost in a taxpayer's mind when he considers the succession process and two taxes in particular: capital gains tax (CGT) and inheritance tax[1a] (IHT). CGT will be considered in this chapter; IHT in the next chapter.[2]

1   In general

Introduced by the Finance Act 1965, the relevant provisions, as subsequently amended, were reproduced in consolidated form in the Capital Gains Tax Act 1979 which has itself been amended by subsequent Finance Acts. It is a tax levied on the capital gains accruing to a person on the disposal of chargeable assets[3] in a year of assessment[4] after deducting any capital losses for that year. Each person has the benefit of an annual exempt amount of gains;[5] any gains for the year in excess of that amount are then taxed at 30%. If offsetting the losses produces an overall capital loss for the year, that loss can be carried forward and set off against the following year's chargeable gains and so on without time limit.

House of Commons debates: Rt Hon James Callaghan[6]

Budget Statement 1965
The failure to tax capital gains is widely regarded, outside as well as inside the Labour

---

1. Eg higher rates of income tax start to bite on incomes over £17,200 for 1986–87 (Fin. Bill 1986. s 15). So A, a higher rate taxpayer, might be prompted by the amount of income tax he was paying to gift, say, £10,000 worth of shares to B, a basic rate (presently 29%) taxpayer who would thus derive more actual benefit from the income from the shares than A.
1a. Formerly known as capital transfer tax.
2. These taxes are examined below in outline only and with emphasis on those provisions that affect the succession process. For more detailed consideration see Whitehouse and Stuart-Buttle, Pinson *Revenue Law* (16th edn 1985).
3. Many assets are exempt—see p 206 post.
4. April 6–April 5 of the following year.
5. £6,300 for 1986–87.
6. Chancellor of the Exchequer. HC Deb. 1965–65 Vol 710 Col 245.

Party, as the greatest blot on our existing system of direct taxation. There is little dispute nowadays that capital gains confer much the same kind of benefit on the recipient as taxed earnings more hardly won. Yet earnings pay tax in full while capital gains go free. This is unfair to the wage and salary earner . . . this new tax will provide a background of equity and fair play.

Capital Gains Tax Act 1979

1. Taxation of capital gains
(1) Tax shall be charged in accordance with this Act in respect of capital gains, that is to say, chargeable gains computed in accordance with this Act and accruing to a person on the disposal of assets.

2. Persons chargeable
(1) Subject to any exceptions provided by this Act, a person shall be chargeable to capital gains tax in respect of chargeable gains accruing to him in a year of assessment during any part of which he is resident in the United Kingdom, or during which he is ordinarily resident in the United Kingdom.[7]

3. Rate of tax
The rate of capital gains tax shall be 30 per cent.

4. Gains chargeable to tax
(1) Capital gains tax shall be charged on the total amount of chargeable gains accruing to the person chargeable in the year of assessment, after deducting—
  (a) any allowable losses accruing to that person in that year of assessment, and
  (b) so far as they have not been allowed as a deduction from chargeable gains accruing in any previous year of assessment any allowable losses accruing to that person in any previous year of assessment (not earlier than the year 1965–66).

19. Disposal of assets
(1) All forms of property shall be assets for the purposes of this Act, whether situated in the United Kingdom or not, including—
  (a) options, debts and incorporeal property generally, and
  (b) any currency other than sterling, and
  (c) any form of property created by the person disposing of it, or otherwise coming to be owned without being acquired.
(2) For the purposes of this Act—
  (a) references to a disposal of an asset include, except where the context otherwise requires, references to a part disposal of an asset . . . .

2   Calculating the gain

The gain on disposal of a chargeable asset is computed by deducting from the consideration on disposal any allowable expenditure and an indexation allowance.

---

7. Husband and wife living together are usually treated as one person for CGT purposes; thus they have only one annual exempt amount between them and are assessed on their joint capital gains less losses, except in the year of the marriage itself. See further p 208 post.

(a) Allowable expenditure

Capital Gains Tax Act 1979

32. Expenditure: general

(1) Except as otherwise expressly provided, the sums allowable as a deduction from the consideration in the computation under this Chapter of the gain accruing to a person on the disposal of an asset shall be restricted to—

    (a) the amount or value of the consideration, in money or money's worth, given by him or on his behalf wholly and exclusively for the acquisition of the asset, together with the incidental costs to him of the acquisition or, if the asset was not acquired by him, any expenditure wholly and exclusively incurred by him in providing the asset,

    (b) the amount of any expenditure wholly and exclusively incurred on the asset by him or on his behalf for the purpose of enhancing the value of the asset, being the expenditure reflected in the state or nature of the asset at the time of the disposal, and any expenditure wholly and exclusively incurred by him in establishing, preserving or defending his title to, or a right over, the asset,[8]

    (c) the incidental costs to him of making the disposal.

EXAMPLE

In 1980 A bought a house as a holiday home[9] for £15,000; in the same year he spent £3,000 on putting in a new kitchen. He sells it in June 1987 for £50,000. His chargeable gains (ignoring for the moment indexation allowance)[10] will be:

	£	£
Sale proceeds		50,000
LESS Acquisition cost	15,000	
Legal costs on purchase	500	
Cost of improvement	3,000	
Legal costs and estate agents' commission on sale	1,100	19,600
		£30,400

(b) Indexation allowance

Before 1982 CGT was often criticized as a tax on 'paper gains', that is, gains due merely to the effects of inflation and not gains in real terms. The Finance Act 1982[11] therefore introduced an indexation allowance for an asset disposed of on or after 6 April 1982 by which its allowable expenditure is increased by the rise in the Retail Prices Index (RPI). The allowance, which is calculated separately for each item of allowable expenditure, is arrived at by applying the formula:

$$\frac{RD - RI}{RI}$$

---

8. See *Passant v Jackson* (1986) Times, 20 February; see also *IRC v Richard's Executors* [1971] 1 All ER 785, [1971] 46 TC 626, p 202 post.

9. It is assumed for the purpose of the example that he never occupied the house as his 'only or main residence' so the private residence exemption (p 208 post) was not available.

10. See post.

11. Ss 86, 87, not reproduced here; they were substantially amended by FA 1985, s 68 and Sch 19.

RD is the Retail Prices Index for the month of disposal and RI is the Retail Prices Index for the month in which the expenditure in question was incurred. It only applies to a rise in the index since March 1982; there is no backdating, so that inflationary gains on assets held before that date will still be fully taxable on disposal, but the taxpayer is allowed to choose in such a case to have the allowance calculated by reference to market value of the asset at 31 March 1982 and he will obviously do so when this is greater than the acquisition cost.[12]

EXAMPLE

A buys a painting in April 1983 for £10,000 and disposes of it in March 1987 for £25,000. Assuming that RPI for April 1983 is 300 and RPI for March 1987 is 450, the indexation allowance will be:

$$£10,000 \times \frac{(450-300)}{300} = £5,000.$$

The net gain will therefore be £25,000 − (10,000 + 5,000) = £10,000.

3 Disposal

CGT is only levied on the 'disposal' of a chargeable asset.[13] The word is not comprehensively defined in the Act but is generally interpreted to include any occasion (except death) when the beneficial ownership of the asset is transferred, whether in whole or in part, from one person to another, for example by sale, exchange, or gift. When the transfer is by way of gift (outright or settled), market value of the asset at the date of the gift is deemed to be the consideration on the disposal and the chargeable gain is reckoned accordingly. Similarly, the market value at the date of the gift becomes the donee's acquisition cost for calculating his chargeable gain when he comes to sell or give away the asset. An obvious method of reducing CGT liability would be to sell an asset at an undervalue rather than give it away, but the Revenue is entitled to substitute market value for the consideration in such a case and is particularly watchful in this respect where the vendor and purchaser are 'connected persons' (as defined in the Act)[14] in which event the burden is on the vendor to prove that the sale price represents market value.

Capital Gains Tax Act 1979

29A.[15] **Disposals and acquisitions treated as made at market value**
(1) Subject to the provisions of this Act, a person's acquisition or disposal of an asset shall for the purposes of this Act be deemed to be for a consideration equal to the market value of the asset—

---

12. Eg in the example on p 198 ante, assuming that the market value of the house at 31 March 1982 was £25,000, that RPI for March 1982 was 250 and for June 1987 was 450, the indexation allowance would be £25,000 × (450 − 250) ÷ 250 = £20,000. A's chargeable gain would therefore be £10,400 and not £30,400 as there stated.
13. CGTA 1979 s 1(1), p 197 ante.
14. See n 16 p 200 post.
15. Inserted by FA 1981 s 90(1).

   (a) where he acquires or, as the case may be, disposes of the asset otherwise than by way of a bargain made at arm's length, and in particular where he acquires or disposes of it by way of gift or on a transfer into settlement by a settlor . . . .

62. Transactions between connected persons

(1) This section shall apply where a person acquires an asset and the person making the disposal is connected with him.[16]

(2) Without prejudice to the generality of section 29A(1) above the person acquiring the asset and the person making the disposal shall be treated as parties to a transaction otherwise than by way of a bargain made at arm's length.

EXAMPLE

March 1979: A buys a painting for £15,000.

February 1981: A gives the painting to B. Market value at the date of the gift is £20,000. There is a chargeable gain of £5,000 (less any allowable expenditure) for A to include in his tax return for 1980–81.[17]

May 1986: B sells the picture to C for £30,000. There is a chargeable gain of £10,000 for B to include in his tax return for 1986–87 (less any allowable expenditure and the indexation allowance).[18]

In **Turner v Follett** [1973] STC 148, (1973) 48 TC 614, the taxpayer claimed that Parliament had attempted to introduce a gifts tax in the guise of a tax on capital gains. He argued before the General Commissioners that:

In giving shares to my children I have in fact made a capital loss to the extent of the full value of the shares, and any attempt by the Finance Act to describe that as a capital gain is gross misrepresentation which I view with the utmost contempt, creating as it does a contradiction in the true meaning of the English language and consequently an incomprehensible law.

His appeal reached the Court of Appeal where he received a sympathetic but unsuccessful hearing, Russell LJ concluding, at p 154:

We have listened to the taxpayer's criticisms of this method of legislation, particularly this method of fiscal legislation. To say that his criticisms fall on deaf ears would be impolite; but, speaking judicially, our ears can but be deaf to such an approach. We can do nothing but construe the Act to the best of our ability, stifling any distaste which out of court we might find ourselves sharing with the taxpayer.

4   Death

There is no charge to CGT on death;[19] the deceased's assets are simply deemed to be acquired by the personal representatives for a consideration equal to market value at the date of death. Any gain up to that point thus escapes CGT

---

16. CGTA 1979, s 63 defines 'connected persons' very widely; it includes spouses, their relatives (defined as meaning brothers, sisters, ancestors or lineal descendants), and partners.

17. A & B could elect for hold-over relief: see p 211 post.

18. See p 198 ante.

19. This has not always been the case. Death was regarded as a disposal of assets by the deceased giving rise to a charge to CGT until FA 1971, s 59 Sch 12 provided otherwise in order to avoid occasioning a double charge to tax with estate duty, now IHT.

completely. If the personal representatives transfer those assets or any part of them to a beneficiary under the deceased's will or intestacy, again there is no deemed disposal but the beneficiary is deemed to acquire the assets at their market value at the deceased's death and that will be the beneficiary's acquisition cost for reckoning the chargeable gains on any subsequent disposal.

If the personal representatives instead sell assets in the course of administration[20] they will be liable to CGT only on the difference between the sale consideration and market value at the deceased's death with the normal deduction for any allowable expenditure[1] and for the indexation allowance[2] including an appropriate proportion of the cost of obtaining the grant of representation. They can offset any capital losses against their chargeable gains in the year of assessment, carrying forward any excess losses to the next year.[3] They have the benefit of the individual's yearly exempt amount[4] for the year of assessment in which the deceased died and for the two following years, after which their chargeable gains are taxed at 30%.

Capital Gains Tax Act 1979

49. Death: general provisions
(1) For the purposes of this Act the assets of which a deceased person was competent to dispose—
-   (a) shall be deemed to be acquired on his death by the personal representatives or other person on whom they devolve for a consideration equal to their market value at the date of the death, but
-   (b) shall not be deemed to be disposed of by him on his death (whether or not they were the subject of a testamentary disposition).

(4) On a person acquiring any asset as legatee (as defined in section 47[5] above)—
-   (a) no chargeable gain shall accrue to the personal representatives, and
-   (b) the legatee shall be treated as if the personal representatives' acquisition of the asset had been his acquisition of it.

(5) Notwithstanding section 29A(1) above (gifts) no chargeable gain shall accrue to any person on his making a disposal by way of donatio mortis causa.

(10) In this section references to assets of which a deceased person was competent to dispose are references to assets of the deceased which (otherwise than in right of a power of appointment or of the testamentary power conferred by statute to dispose of entailed interests) he could, if of full age and capacity, have disposed of by his will, assuming that all the assets were situated in England and, if he was not domiciled in the United Kingdom, that he was domiciled in England, and include references to his severable share in any assets to which, immediately before his death, he was beneficially entitled as a joint tenant.

---

20. See p 280 post.
1. See p 198 ante.
2. See p 198 ante.
3. Any losses unrelieved at the end of the administration of the estate cannot be transferred to the beneficiaries, so personal representatives should avoid this by instead transferring a loss-making asset to a legatee who can then sell it himself and get the benefit of the capital loss to set off against his own chargeable gains. On this and other aspects of a personal representative's CGT liability see Alexander: 'Tips and Traps for Practical Post-mortem Capital Gains Tax Planning' (1978) 75 LSG 782.
4. Currently £6,300 see p 206 post.
5. 'Legatee' is defined in s 47(2) as including 'any person taking under a testamentary disposition or on an intestacy or partial intestacy, whether he takes beneficially or as trustee, and a person taking under a donatio mortis causa shall be treated . . . as a legatee and his acquisition as made at the time of the donor's death.'

EXAMPLE

1974: A buys shares for £20,000.
1982: A dies. Shares now worth £50,000. No charge to CGT.
1983: Personal representatives transfer shares now worth £55,000 to B in accordance with A's will. No charge to CGT.
1986: B sells the shares to C for £70,000. B's chargeable gain (less any allowable expenditure and indexation allowance) is £70,000 − 50,000 = £20,000.[6]

In **IRC v Richards' Executors** [1971] 1 All ER 785, [1971] 46 TC 626, the deceased's executors sold some of the deceased's shares, realising a capital gain of £1,183 on which they were assessed to CGT. They sought to deduct from the gain the sum of £242 as representing a proportion of their solicitors' costs for valuing the deceased's stocks and shares, preparing the Inland Revenue Affidavit[7] and procuring confirmation.[8] The Revenue argued that this expenditure was also incurred in order to pay the estate duty[9] and was not therefore incurred 'wholly and exclusively' for the purpose of establishing title under the Finance Act 1965, Sch 6, para 4.[10] The House of Lords (Lords Morris of Borth-yr-Gest and Upjohn dissenting) upheld the executors' claim, Lord Reid saying at p 790:

If then one is entitled to construe 'wholly and exclusively' not strictly but so as to give a reasonable result I am of opinion that the fact that the work necessary to obtain confirmation also serves the ancillary purpose of determining the amount of stamp duty does not prevent the cost of that work from being held to have been wholly and exclusively incurred in establishing the executors' title. Payment of estate duty is another matter. The respondents do not claim that as a deduction. No doubt they had to pay the duty before they could get confirmation, but I could not regard payment of duty as merely ancillary. This may be a matter of degree. When stamp duty[11] is very small it might be possible so to regard it. But in 1965 estate duty could be very large and no one could reasonably say that paying it was merely an incidental step towards getting a title to what remained after it had been paid.[12]

5 Settlements

The effect of CGT on settled property is relatively mild in comparison with IHT.[13]

---

6. Note that the £30,000 gain that accrued before A's death has thus escaped CGT completely.
7. Now Inland Revenue Account—see p 309 post.
8. The Scottish equivalent of an English grant of probate.
9. A forerunner of IHT, the estate duty on personalty had to be paid before the grant would issue (FA 1894, s 6).
10. Now CGTA 1979, s 32(1), p 198 ante.
11. Ie estate duty, this being technically a form of stamp duty.
12. The Inland Revenue has since published a scale of allowable expenditure for the personal representative's expenses in establishing title, ranging from 1.5% of the probate value of the assets sold to 0.75%, see SP7/81 ((1981) 78 LSG 1112). In practice the Revenue will accept computations based either on this scale or on the actual expenditure.
13. See p 221 post.

(a) Meaning of 'settled property'

The term is defined in the Capital Gains Tax Act 1979, s 51 as 'any property held in trust other than property to which section 46 above (nominees and trustees) applies'. Where there is property within a s 46 trust, it is treated for CGT purposes as belonging to the beneficiary.

Capital Gains Tax Act 1979

46. Nominees and bare trustees

(1) In relation to assets held by a person as nominee for another person, or as trustee for another person absolutely entitled as against the trustee, or for any person who would be so entitled but for being an infant or other person under disability (or for two or more persons who are or would be jointly so entitled)[14] this Act shall apply as if the property were vested in, and the acts of the nominee or trustee in relation to the assets were the acts of, the person or persons for whom he is the nominee or trustee (acquisitions from or disposals to him by that person or persons being disregarded accordingly).[15]

(2) It is hereby declared that references in this Act to any asset held by a person as trustee for another person absolutely entitled as against the trustee are references to a case where that other person has the exclusive right, subject only to satisfying any outstanding charge, lien or other right of the trustees to resort to the asset for payment of duty, taxes, costs or other outgoings, to direct how that asset shall be dealt with.

Tomlinson v Glyn's Executor & Trustee Co [1970] Ch 112, [1970] 1 All ER 381, CA; Lord Denning MR, Sachs and Phillimore LJJ

The settlor gave property in trust for such of his son's children as should attain 21 years[16] or marry under that age, provided that once one child reached the age of 21, no afterborn children could come into the class of beneficiaries. (At the time of the hearing the eldest child was still only 11 so the class was still open). The trustees subsequently sold investments, realising a gain of £374 and claimed the alternative rate of CGT then available for individuals as opposed to trustees.[17] They claimed that by the Finance Act 1965, s 22(5)[18] the property was not settled.

Held: The property was settled. The minority of the beneficiaries was not the only bar to their absolute entitlement; their interests were contingent on their survival to their majority.

Lord Denning MR: (having read s 22(5))[18] That is all very complicated, but I will try and explain it simply. It means that if property is held by a person as a *nominee* for an ordinary individual, then the beneficiary can obtain the benefit of the alternative rate. Similarly, if property is held by a *bare trustee* for an ordinary individual who is of full age and entitled as of right to call for that property, then the beneficiary can obtain the

---

14. As beneficial joint tenants or as beneficial tenants in common, see *Kidson v MacDonald* [1974] Ch 339, [1974] 1 All ER 849.

15. So eg the beneficiary would have the benefit of the individual's annual exempt amount, whilst if the property was settled, only the trustees' lower exempt amount would be available, see p 206 post.

16. The then age of majority, the trust being created before the Family Law Reform Act 1969 came into force.

17. The alternative rate has since been replaced by the differential in the annual exempt amount for the individual and trustees, see p 206 post.

18. Now CGTA 1979, s 46(1).

benefit of the alternative rate. Then the section goes on to deal with trusts for children or persons of unsound mind. If property is held by trustees 'for any person who would be (absolutely) entitled but for being an infant or other person under disability' then the infant or other person can obtain the benefit of the alternative rate. In my opinion, those words are directed to a case where property is held by a trustee for a person who would be absolutely entitled to call for the property but for the fact that he is an infant or is of unsound mind. If his infancy or other disability is the *only* impediment which prevents his being absolutely entitled, then he can be regarded as an ordinary individual and he is entitled to the benefit of the alternative rate.

I am afraid that I cannot accept this argument. It assumes not only that each is over 21. It also assumes that the closing date has been reached. That assumption is not permissible. I think that the right way of looking at the section is to *take the time* when the capital gain was made and to ask the question: if he was not an infant at that time, would he be absolutely entitled to call for his money so as himself to be able to give directions to the trustees and to give a good receipt to them? In short: is the infancy the *only* bar? In the present case none of these four children, if they were not infants, would be absolutely entitled at that time to call for the money or to give the trustees a proper receipt. Their interests were contingent on their living to the age of 21. They were defeasible pro tanto if other children were born. The section only applies where a child has, in the Chancery phrase to which second counsel for the Crown referred, a vested and indefeasible interest in possession. None of these four children came within that category; none of them was absolutely entitled to the money. Each of their interests was defeasible and contingent. It might never vest at all.

(b) Creation of the settlement

If the settlement is created inter vivos there is a deemed disposal to the trustees giving rise to a chargeable gain on its creation,[19] but if created on death by will or intestacy there is no charge to CGT on the 'death principle'[20] whereby the trustees are simply deemed to acquire the settled assets at market value at the date of death.

Capital Gains Tax Act 1979

53. Gifts in settlement
A gift in settlement, whether revocable or irrevocable, is a disposal of the entire property thereby becoming settled property notwithstanding that the donor has some interest as a beneficiary under the settlement and notwithstanding that he is a trustee or the sole trustee of the settlement.

(c) Subsequent events

If the trustees sell any of the settled assets they will be liable to CGT in the usual way[1] on the difference between the consideration on sale and market value at the date of creation of the settlement[2] or acquisition cost if subsequently purchased. As trustees they will have their annual exempt amount;[3] chargeable gains in excess of this will be liable at the usual 30% rate. On termination of a life interest in the settled property there will be no charge to CGT (on the death

---

19. As with any other gift, see p 199 ante. Hold-over relief is available at the option of the settlor, see FA 1980, s 79, p 211 post.
20. See CGTA, s 49, p 200 ante.
1. See p 197 ante.
2. This will be the date of death if created by will or intestacy.
3. £3,150 for 1986–87, see p 207 post.

principle)[4] but there will be a charge to CGT when a beneficiary becomes absolutely entitled to settled property as against the trustees[5] unless he owes that entitlement to the termination of a life interest in which event no charge will lie.

Capital Gains Tax Act 1979

54. Person becoming absolutely entitled to settled property

(1) On the occasion when a person becomes absolutely entitled to any settled property as against the trustee all the assets forming part of the settled property to which he becomes so entitled shall be deemed to have been disposed of by the trustee, and immediately re-acquired by him in his capacity as a trustee within section 46(1) above, for a consideration equal to their market value.

(2) On the occasion when a person becomes absolutely entitled to any settled property as against the trustee, any allowable loss which has accrued to the trustee in respect of property which is, or is represented by, the property to which that person so becomes entitled (including any allowable loss carried forward to the year of assessment in which that occasion falls), being a loss which cannot be deducted from chargeable gains accruing to the trustee in that year, but before that occasion, shall be treated as if it were an allowable loss accruing at that time to the person becoming so entitled, instead of to the trustee.[6]

55. Termination of life interest etc

(1)[7] On the termination on death of the person entitled to it of a life interest[8] in possession in all or any part of the settled property—

    (a) the whole or a corresponding part of each of the assets forming part of the settled property and not ceasing at that time to be settled property shall be deemed for the purposes of this Act at that time to be disposed of and immediately re-acquired by the trustee for a consideration equal to the whole or a corresponding part of the market value of the asset; but

    (b) no chargeable gain shall accrue on that disposal.

56. Death of life tenant: exclusion of chargeable gain

(1) Where, by virtue of section 54(1) above, the assets forming part of any settled property are deemed to be disposed of and re-acquired by the trustee on the occasion when a person becomes absolutely entitled thereto as against the trustee, then, if that occasion is the termination of a life interest (within the meaning of section 55 above) by the death of the person entitled to that interest—

    (a) no chargeable gain shall accrue on the disposal . . . .[9]

EXAMPLE

By inter vivos deed S settles shares worth £50,000 on A for life, B for life, then for C absolutely. S will be liable to CGT on the disposal to the trustees on the

---

4. See CGTA 1979, s 49, p 200 ante.
5. Eg when a beneficiary whose interest is contingent ('To A if he attains 25') satisfies the contingency. Hold-over relief is available if the trustees and beneficiary jointly so elect, see FA 1980, s 79, FA 1982, s 82, p 211 post.
6. Cf personal representatives' unrelieved losses, see p 201 ante.
7. Substituted by FA 1982, s 84(1).
8. 'Life interest' does not include any right which is contingent on the exercise of a discretion by the trustee or some other person—CGTA 1979, s 55(4)(6), so eg, the death of a beneficiary under a discretionary trust will not give rise to any uplift in the base value.
9. So there is an uplift in the base value or acquisition cost of the assets concerned but no charge to CGT.

creation of the settlement, market value at that date being the consideration for the disposal and the trustees' acquisition cost.[10] When A dies there will be no charge to CGT but the trustees' acquisition cost will be raised to the market value of the shares at A's death. When B dies, C becomes absolutely entitled to the shares but by virtue of B's death; there will accordingly be no charge to CGT then either[11] and C will have the market value of the shares at B's death as his acquisition cost.

6   The main exemptions and reliefs

National Savings Certificates,[12] Premium Savings Bonds[12] and money in the form of sterling[13] are not chargeable assets for CGT purposes. Gains not exceeding the annual exempt amount escape CGT[14] as do gains on the disposal of certain chattels,[15] most gilt-edged securities[16] and authorised unit and investment trusts.[17] Gains are also exempt if made by a charity.[18] There is no charge to CGT on a disposal to a charity[19] nor an inter-spouse disposal[20] but no uplift of the acquisition cost either; the donee simply takes over the acquisition cost of the donor. Gains on the disposal of a dwelling house which has been the only or main residence of the taxpayer are exempt.[1] There are also two important reliefs, namely business relief for an individual over the age of 60 who disposes of the whole or part of his business[2] and a hold-over relief enabling the payment of CGT to be postponed.[3] Some of these exemptions and reliefs are now examined in more detail.

(a) The annual exempt amount

Capital Gains Tax Act 1979

5. Exemption for first [£6,300][4] of gains
(1) An individual shall not be chargeable to capital gains tax in respect of so much of his taxable amount for any year of assessment as does not exceed the exempt amount for the year.

---

10. Applying normal gift principles, see p 199 ante. Note that S may elect for hold-over relief, see p 211 post. Had S created the settlement by his will there would have been no such charge—see CGTA 1979, s 49, p 201 ante.
11. Aliter if the ultimate remainder had been 'to C if he attains 35' and C was less than 35 when B died.
12. CGTA 1979, s 71.
13. CGTA 1979, s 19(1), p 197 ante.
14. See post.
15. See p 207 post.
16. CGTA 1979, s 67 as amended by FA 1985, s 67.
17. FA 1980, s 81(1).
18. CGTA 1979, s 145.
19. CGTA 1979, s 146.
20. See p 208 post.
1. See p 208 post.
2. See p 210 post.
3. See p 211 post.
4. Subs (1B) and (1C) (not extracted) link the exempt amount to the yearly rise (if any) in the retail prices index. £6,300 is the exempt amount for 1986–87: Capital Gains Tax (Annual Exempt Amount) Order 1986, SI 1986/528.

(1A)[5] Subject to subsection (1B) below, the exempt amount for any year of assessment shall be £6,300.[4]

(4) For the purposes of this section an individual's taxable amount for a year of assessment is the amount on which he is chargeable under section 4(1)[6] above for that year but—

    (a) Where the amount of chargeable gains less allowable losses accruing to an individual in any year of assessment does not exceed the exempt amount for the year, no deduction from that amount shall be made for that year in respect of allowable losses carried forward from a previous year or carried back from a subsequent year in which the individual dies, and

    (b) where the amount of chargeable gains less allowable losses accruing to an individual in any year of assessment exceeds the exempt amount for the year, the deduction from that amount for that year in respect of allowable losses carried forward from a previous year or carried back from a subsequent year in which the individual dies shall not be greater than the excess.[7]

(6) Schedule 1 to this Act shall have effect as respects the application of this section to . . . personal representatives and trustees.

SCHEDULE 1   APPLICATION OF EXEMPT AMOUNT IN PARTICULAR CASES

1. In this Schedule references to any subsections not otherwise identified are references to subsections of section 5 of this Act.

Personal representatives
4. For the year of assessment in which an individual dies and for the two next following years of assessment subsections (1)(4) and (5)[8] shall apply to his personal representatives as they apply to an individual.

Trustees[9]
6. (1) For any year of assessment during the whole or part of which any property is settled property . . . subsections (1)(4) and (5)[8] shall apply to the trustees of a settlement as they apply to an individual but with the following modifications:
(2) In subsections (1) and (4) there shall be substituted one half of the exempt amount for the year.[10]

(b) Chattels

Capital Gains Tax Act 1979

127. Wasting assets
(1) . . . No chargeable gain shall accrue on the disposal of, or of an interest in, an asset which is tangible movable property and which is a wasting asset.[11]

---

5. Subs (1A), (1B) and (1C) were inserted by FA 1982, s 80(2).
6. See p 197 ante.
7. Ie the annual exempt amount is to be utilised in full first to relieve chargeable gains of the current year before losses carried forward from previous year(s) so that such losses still unused may be carried forward to the next year.
8. This subsection simply provides that if the chargeable gains for the year do not exceed the annual exempt amount and the disposal consideration does not exceed twice the annual exempt amount, the taxpayer is only required to note that fact on his tax returns, without supplying a full computation.
9. Other than trustees of a trust for the benefit of a mentally or physically disabled person; in this case the whole of the annual exempt amount is available (provided the requirements of CGTA 1979, para 5 Schedule 1 as amended by FA 1981, s 89 are satisfied).
10. As amended by FA 1982, s 80(3). The exempt amount for 1986–87 for trustees is therefore £3,150, see Capital Gains Tax (Annual Exempt Amount) Order 1986, SI 1986/527.
11. 'Wasting asset' is defined by CGTA 1979, s 36(1) as 'an asset with a predictable life not exceeding fifty years'.

128. Chattel exemption

(1) ... A gain accruing on a disposal of an asset which is tangible movable property shall not be a chargeable gain if the amount or value of the consideration for the disposal does not exceed £3,000.[12]

130. Passenger vehicles

A mechanically propelled road vehicle constructed or adapted for the carriage of passengers except for a vehicle of a type not commonly used as a private vehicle and unsuitable to be so used, shall not be a chargeable asset; and accordingly no chargeable gain or allowable loss shall accrue on its disposal.

(c) Spouses

Capital Gains Tax Act 1979

44. Husband and wife

(1) If, in any year of assessment, and in the case of a woman who in that year of assessment is a married woman living with her husband, the man disposes of an asset to the wife, or the wife disposes of an asset to the man, both shall be treated as if the asset was acquired from the one making the disposal for a consideration of such an amount as would secure that on the disposal neither a gain nor a loss would accrue to the one making the disposal.[13]

(d) Private residence[14]

This important exemption was introduced from the inception of the tax 'to encourage home ownership, to avoid any feeling of resentment there might be—and I think it would be widespread if this was subject to tax—and also from a social point of view to assist greater mobility.'[15] Not only the individual has the benefit of the exemption from the gain made on the disposal of a dwelling-house which has been his only or main residence,[16] trustees also have the benefit of it when disposing of a house which has been the only or main residence of a beneficiary entitled to occupy it by the terms of the settlement.

Capital Gains Tax Act 1979

101. Relief on disposal of private residence

(1) This section applies to a gain accruing to an individual so far as attributable to the disposal of, or of an interest in—

---

12. As amended by FA 1982, s 81. Marginal relief is available, see s 128(2).

13. The donee spouse is thus treated as acquiring the asset at the acquisition cost of the donor spouse. Where the donor spouse is entitled to an indexation allowance (see p 198 ante) the acquisition cost is uplifted by this amount. If the donee spouse acquires the asset on the death of the donor spouse there is an uplift of the acquisition cost to the value of the asset at the date of death under the death principle, see p 200 ante.

14. See Ratcliffe 'Tax Considerations for the House Owner-Occupier' (1981) 78 LSG 114; Williams 'Private Residences: Tax Incidence and Exemptions' (1977) 41 Conv 389.

15. Financial Secretary to the Treasury, Vol 713 HC Deb cols 990–1006 at col 997.

16. An individual can also claim the benefit of the exemption in respect of no more than one other property owned by him but occupied rent free as a residence by a dependent relative: see CGTA 1979, s 105.

(a) a dwelling-house[17] or part of a dwelling-house[18] which is, or has at any time in his period of ownership been, his only or main[19] residence, or

(b) land which he has for his own occupation and enjoyment with that residence[20] as its garden or grounds up to the permitted area.

(2) In this section 'the permitted area' means, subject to subsections (3) and (4) below, an area (inclusive of the site of the dwelling-house) of one acre.

(3) In any particular case the permitted area shall be such area, larger than one acre, as the Commissioners concerned may determine if satisfied that, regard being had to the size and character of the dwelling-house, that larger area is required for the reasonable enjoyment of it (or of the part in question) as a residence.

(4) Where part of the land occupied with a residence is and part is not within subsection (1) above, then (up to the permitted area) that part shall be taken to be within subsection (1) above which, if the remainder were separately occupied, would be the most suitable for occupation and enjoyment with the residence.

102. Amount of relief

(1) No part of a gain to which section 101 above applies shall be a chargeable gain if the dwelling-house or part of a dwelling-house has been the individual's only or main residence throughout the period of ownership, or throughout the period of ownership except for all or any part of the last twenty-four months[1] of that period.

(2) Where subsection (1) above does not apply, a fraction of the gain shall not be a chargeable gain, and that fraction shall be—

(a) the length of the part or parts of the period of ownership during which the dwelling-house or the part of the dwelling-house was the individual's only or main residence, but inclusive of the last twenty-four months of the period of ownership in any event, divided by

(b) the length of the period of ownership.[2]

104. Private residence occupied under terms of a settlement

Sections 101 to 103[3] above shall also apply in relation to a gain accruing to a trustee on a disposal of settled property being an asset within section 101(1) above where during the period of ownership of the trustee the dwelling-house or part of the dwelling-house mentioned in that subsection has been the only or main residence of a person entitled to occupy it under the terms of the settlement, and in those sections as so applied—

(a) references to the individual shall be taken as references to the trustee except in relation to the occupation of the dwelling-house or part of the dwelling-house and

(b) the notice which may be given to the inspector under section 101(5)(a)[4] above

---

17. In *Makins v Elson* [1977] 1 All ER 572, [1977] STC 46, a caravan jacked up on supports and with water, electricity and telephone connections was held to be a dwelling-house within the exemption. Cf *Moore v Thompson* (1986) Times, 18 March (caravan on wheels with no mains connections).

18. In *Batey v Wakefield* [1982] 1 All ER 61, [1981] STC 521, a caretaker's bungalow built in the garden of the taxpayer's main residence was held to be a part of the taxpayer's residence.

19. Where an individual has two or more residences he can nominate either as his residence for the purpose of this exemption by notice in writing to his tax inspector: s 101(5). A husband and wife living together may have only one main residence for the purpose of the section: s 101(6).

20. If the taxpayer has in mind separate disposals of his house and garden he should ensure that he disposes of the garden first to have the benefit of the exemption for both disposals: *Varty v Lynes* [1976] 3 All ER 447, [1976] STC 508.

1. Substituted by FA 1980, s 80(2).

2. For the purpose of subs (1) and (2) periods of absence not exceeding three years in toto can be ignored and also certain periods of absence for work reasons: CGTA 1979, s 102(3). In so far as any part of the property has been let out, the exemption is still available for that part up to the lesser of £20,000 and the exempt gain attributable to the part occupied by the owner: FA 1980, s 80 as amended by FA 1984 s 63.

3. S 103 provides a partial exemption in so far as any part of the residence has at any time been used exclusively for trade or professional purposes.

4. See n 19 ante.

shall be a joint notice by the trustee and the person entitled to occupy the dwelling-house or part of the dwelling-house.

In **Sansom v Peay** [1976] 3 All ER 375, [1976] STC 494, the taxpayers were trustees of a discretionary trust by which they were expressly empowered to permit one or more of the beneficiaries to reside in any dwelling-house subject to the trust 'upon such conditions as to payment of rent rates . . . and for such period and generally upon such terms as the Trustees in their absolute discretion shall think fit.' The trustees bought a house and permitted the beneficiaries, who were all members of one family, to occupy it as their main residence for five years, at which point the trustees sold it. The gains on sale of the house would only be within the exemption if the beneficiaries were 'entitled to occupy it under the terms of the settlement.' It was argued that their entitlement was derived not from the terms of the settlement but merely from the licence of the trustees which was revocable at any time at the trustees' will and that such an arrangement was outside the terms of the exemption. Brightman J disagreed however, saying at p 379:

In this case the beneficiaries were in occupation of Wickwoods throughout the relevant period as their only or main residence. They were in occupation pursuant to the exercise by the trustees of a power expressly conferred by the settlement to permit those beneficiaries to go into occupation and remain in occupation. The trustees exercised that power, and the beneficiaries thereupon became entitled to go into occupation and to continue in occupation until the permission was withdrawn. The trustees never did withdraw permission until they required vacant possession in order to complete the exchange. Therefore, looking at the matter at the date of disposal, the beneficiaries were the persons who, in the events which happened, were entitled to occupy the house and did occupy it under the terms of the settlement. That, in my view, is the correct approach to the subsection in dealing with the type of case which is before me, and in those circumstances I reach the view that the terms of s 29(9)[5] have been satisfied and that the gain is exempt from capital gains tax.[6]

(e) Business 'retirement' relief

This is an important relief for a person with business assets, whether he is a sole trader, a trader in partnership or someone who trades through the medium of a family company.[7] Despite the side-heading in the Act, he does not necessarily have to retire to benefit from it; the relief applies to any individual who has attained 60[8] or who has retired because of ill-health below 60, and disposes by way of sale or gift of business assets which he has owned for at least a year before their disposal. Gains on the disposal are then exempt up to a maximum of £100,000, which is available where he owned the asset for at least 10 years before disposal; for any lesser period the relief is reduced by a proportionate percentage of £100,000 down to 10%, ie £10,000, where the asset has been held for the minimum of 1 year.[9]

---

5. FA 1965, now CGTA 1979, s 104.
6. This decision has been criticised, see eg Vollans: 'CGT residence relief—a trustee's bonanza?' (1980) 77 LSG 114.
7. Defined as one in which the transferor owns a minimum of 25% of the voting shares, or at least 5% but he and his family together own more than 50%: FA 1985, Sch 20 para 1.
8. Whether or not he retires.
9. The relief is also available for settlements in so far as there is a beneficiary entitled to an interest in possession, such as a life tenant, who satisfies the appropriate conditions: FA 1985, s 70(3).

Finance Act 1985

69.[10] **Relief for disposals by individuals on retirement from family business**
(1) Relief from capital gains tax shall be given, subject to and in accordance with
Schedule 20 to this Act, in any case where a material disposal of business assets is made
by an individual who, at the time of the disposal—
  (a) has attained the age of 60, or
  (b) has retired on ill-health grounds below the age of 60, ...
(2) For the purposes of this section and Schedule 20 to this Act, a disposal of business
assets is—
  (a) a disposal of the whole or part of a business, or
  (b) a disposal of one or more assets which, at the time at which a business ceased to be
    carried on, were in use for the purposes of that business, or
  (c) a disposal of shares or securities of a company (including a disposal of an interest
    in shares which a person is treated as making by virtue of section 72 of the Capital
    Gains Tax Act 1979—capital distributions),[11]
and the question whether such a disposal is a material disposal shall be determined in
accordance with the following provisions of this section.[12]

SCHEDULE 20

13. The amount available for relief: the basic rule
(1) Subject to the following provisions of this Part of this Schedule, on a qualifying
disposal by an individual the amount available for relief by virtue of sections 69 and 70 of
this Act is a percentage of £100,000 determined according to the length of the qualifying
period which is appropriate to the disposal on a scale rising arithmetically from 10 per
cent, where that period is precisely one year to 100 per cent, where it is ten years.
(2) The amount available for relief by virtue of section 70 of this Act on a trustees'
disposal shall be determined, subject to sub-paragraph (3) below, in accordance with
sub-paragraph (1) above on the assumption that the trustees' disposal is a qualifying
disposal by the qualifying beneficiary.
(3) If, on the same day, there is both a trustees' disposal and a material disposal of
business assets by the qualifying beneficiary, the amount available for relief shall be
applied to the beneficiary's disposal in priority to the trustees' disposal.

EXAMPLE

A has owned a grocery business for 8 years. He gives it to his son on A's 63rd
birthday. This will give him relief of £80,000, ie 10% of £100,000 for each year
of ownership, to be set off against his chargeable gains on that disposal. Had he
waited another two years he would have qualified for the maximum £100,000
exemption. Had he made the gift when he was 59 the exemption would not have
been available at all, unless he was retiring through ill-health.

(f) Hold-over relief

This is an important relief which is available for disposals by way of gift only. It
enables the donor and donee on their joint election to have the gain held-over,

---

10. Previously CGTA 1979, s 124; the FA 1985 recast its provisions and relaxed some of its
qualifying conditions. See further (1985) 82 LSG 3231.
11. To qualify for the relief in (c) the transferor must be a full-time working director of the
company concerned or of another company in the same group.
12. The detailed provisions are contained in subs (3)–(5) and in Sch 20, not extracted here except
for para 13 of the Schedule post.

so that no CGT is payable at the time of the gift but the donee is deemed to acquire the asset at the donor's base value or acquisition cost.

Finance Act 1980

79. General relief for gifts
(1) If after 5 April 1980 an individual (in this section referred to as 'the transferor') makes a disposal otherwise than under a bargain at arm's length, to an individual[13] resident or ordinarily resident in the United Kingdom (in this section referred to as 'the transferee') and the transferor and transferee make a claim for relief under this section—
- (a) the amount of any chargeable gain, which apart from this section, would accrue to the transferor on the disposal,[14] and
- (b) the amount of the consideration for which, apart from this section, the transferee would be regarded for the purposes of capital gains tax as having acquired the asset in question,

shall be reduced by an amount equal to the held-over gain on the disposal.

EXAMPLE

A buys shares for £20,000.
A gives shares to B; market value of shares now £30,000.
Chargeable gain is £10,000[15] for which A is liable.
However, if A and B so elect, instead of CGT being paid now on the £10,000, that gain can be held over; B is deemed to have acquired the shares for £20,000,[15] so that if he subsequently sells them for £50,000 he will be liable to CGT on a chargeable gain of £30,000, not £20,000.[16] If B dies without having sold the shares the capital gain will escape CGT altogether by the death principle.[17]

QUESTIONS

1. What advice about capital gains tax would you give to the following:
   - (a) A, who has a large portfolio of shares which he wants to give to his son now. A is terminally ill with cancer.
   - (b) B, who owns a plot of land presently worth £2,000 but likely to be worth £20,000 if planning permission can be obtained. He plans at that stage to give the land to his daughter.

---

13. FA 1981, s 78 extended this relief to a gift by an individual to trustees of a settlement but in such a case it is for the donor-individual to choose whether to claim the relief, whereas for transfers between individuals under FA 1979, s 79(1) a joint election by donor and donee is required. FA 1982, s 82 extended the relief to disposals by trustees to an individual and this time a joint election by the transferring trustees and the individual is required.
14. After applying the indexation allowance to the donor's allowable expenditure in the normal way, see p 198 ante. The donee also has the benefit of the indexation allowance for his period of ownership: FA 1982, Sch 13 paras 2, 3.
15. Ignoring the indexation allowance for the sake of simplicity.
16. FA 1980, s 79(5) provides that where an election for hold-over relief is made, the donee when he comes to dispose of the property, can deduct from the proceeds of sale in computing his CGT liability, not only the donor's acquisition cost, but also any IHT paid on the gift to the donee (including IHT which proves to be payable in the case of a potentially exempt transfer), whether the IHT is paid by the donor or donee. See further, Ch 16.
17. See p 200 ante.

(c) C, who want to make a lifetime gift of about £10,000 to her granddaughter, using either £10,000 she has on bank deposit, or government stocks to that value or £10,000 worth of shares she owns in the ABC Company Limited.

(d) D, a newsagent aged 58 who wants to transfer the business to his son.

(e) E, who is planning to make a lifetime gift to his wife of the matrimonial home and a gift of his holiday bungalow to his son.

(f) F, who wants to create a settlement of £20,000 worth of shares on X for life, then for X's son Y if he attains the age of 30.

2. 'Capital gains tax has become in effect a voluntary tax so far as gifts are concerned.'

Explain and discuss.

CHAPTER 16

Inheritance tax

1 In general

If capital gains tax (CGT) was the only taxation factor to consider, as will have been seen[1] there would be little to discourage the would-be donor who could simply leave his property to pass on death and avoid the tax completely. However, CGT was preceded by many years by another fiscal levy in the form of estate duty[2] which provided the main system for taxing property passing on death and by way of lifetime gift within a certain period[3] before the death until 1975. By that time many critics were describing it as a voluntary tax because it was so easy to avoid by a lifetime gift followed by survival for the required number of years. It was therefore replaced in the Finance Act 1975 by capital transfer tax which charged to tax not only property passing on death, but also lifetime transfers, no matter how long afterwards the donor survived.

The 1975 Act provisions as amended were consolidated in the Capital Transfer Tax Act 1984 and the tax appeared to have settled down to an established form, only for the Chancellor of the Exchequer to propose a major amendment in his Budget Speech of March 18 1986, namely the removal from the charge of gifts between individuals made more than seven years before the donor's death;[4] he also proposed that thenceforward the tax be known as inheritance tax (IHT) and the 1984 Act as the Inheritance Tax Act 1984 (IHTA 1984).[5] These proposals and other amendments are presently found in the Finance Bill 1986;[6] when enacted they will provide a major impetus to lifetime giving, for the charge on death, at a top rate of 60% of the value of the property concerned, is still an onerous one.

---

1. See Ch 15 ante.
2. Introduced by FA 1894.
3. Seven years (by the time estate duty was abolished): FA 1968, s 35(1).
4. Described in The Times, 19 March 1986 as 'a move which took the legal and accountancy professions completely by surprise' and as 'a shift back to the days of the old estate duty tax'.
5. Other EEC countries have an inheritance tax, usually combined with a lifetime gifts tax but in their case the tax is charged at differing rates depending on each beneficiary's relationship to the deceased and running total of receipts from the deceased. See eg MacDonald Allen 'Property Taxes in France' (1983) 127 Sol J 131, 'Winding up an Estate in Spain' (1977) 121 Sol J 433.
6. The amendments introduced by the Finance Bill have been incorporated into the text where relevant and the tax and the 1984 Act are referred to under their new nomenclature for ease of identification; it will be appreciated, however, that it is always possible that the Bill may be amended before it reaches the statute book.

2 The charge to tax

Inheritance tax is charged at progressive rates on the cumulative total of an individual's lifetime gifts (transfers of value) in excess of the nil rate band,[7] with a final charge to tax in respect of the assets he possesses when he dies (the final transfer of value). A lifetime gift drops out of the cumulation process seven years after it has been made.[8] The rate of tax on a lifetime gift is one half the death rate unless the donor dies within seven years of the gift in which event the full death rate will apply,[9] subject to tapering relief for gifts made more than three years before the donor's death.

Inheritance Tax Act 1984

1. Charge on transfers
Inheritance tax shall be charged on the value transferred by a chargeable transfer.

2. Chargeable transfers and exempt transfers
A chargeable transfer is a transfer of value which is made by an individual but is not (by virtue of Part II of this Act or any other enactment) an exempt transfer.[10]

7. Rates
(1) Subject to subsections (2), (4) and (5) below[11] the tax charged on the value transferred by a chargeable transfer made by any transferor shall be charged at the following rate or rates, that is to say—
   (a) if the transfer is the first chargeable transfer made by that transferor in the period of seven[12] years ending with the date of the transfer, at the rate or rates applicable to that value under the appropriate Table in Schedule 1 to this Act;
   (b) in any other case, at the rate or rates applicable under that Table to such part of the aggregate of—
      (i) that value, and
      (ii) the values transferred by previous chargeable transfers made by him in that period,
   as is the highest part of that aggregate and is equal to that value.
(2) Except as provided by subsection (4) below, the tax charged on the value transferred by a chargeable transfer made before the death of the transferor shall be charged at one half the rate or rates referred to in subsection (1) above.
(3) In the Table in Schedule 1 to this Act any rate shown in the third column is that applicable to such portion of the value concerned as exceeds the lower limit shown in the first column but does not exceed the upper limit (if any) shown in the second column.
(4) Subject to subsection (5) below, subsection (2) above does not apply in the case of a chargeable transfer made at any time within the period of seven years ending with the death of the transferor but, in the case of a chargeable transfer made within that period but more than three years before the death, the tax charged on the value transferred shall be charged at the following percentage of the rate or rates referred to in subsection (1) above—
   (a) where the transfer is made more than three but not more than four years before the death, 80 per cent;

---

7. £0–71,000, see Table at p 216 post.
8. Many lifetime gifts will now escape the cumulation process completely as potentially exempt transfers, see p 217 post.
9. With a credit for any IHT paid at the lifetime rate when the gift was made.
10. See p 228 post.
11. Subs (2)(4) and (5) were introduced by Finance Bill 1986, s 80, Sch 18 Pt I, para 2.
12. The cumulation period is reduced from 10 years to 7 years by Finance Bill 1986, s 80, Sch 18 Pt I, para 2.

(b) where the transfer is made more than four but not more than five years before the death, 60 per cent;

(c) where the transfer is made more than five but not more than six years before the death, 40 per cent; and

(d) where the transfer is made more than six but not more than seven years before the death, 20 per cent.

(5) If, in the case of a chargeable transfer made before the death of the transferor, the tax which would fall to be charged in accordance with subsection (4) above is less than the tax which would have been chargeable (in accordance with subsection (2) above) if the transferor had not died within the period of seven years beginning with the date of the transfer, subsection (4) above shall not apply in the case of that transfer.[13]

SCHEDULE 1[14] RATES OF TAX[15]

Portion of value		Rate of tax
Lower limit	*Upper limit*	*Per cent*
£	£	
0	71,000	Nil
71,000	95,000	30
95,000	129,000	35
129,000	164,000	40
164,000	206,000	45
206,000	257,000	50
257,000	317,000	55
317,000	—	60

EXAMPLE

(The example assumes for simplicity that none of the exemptions and reliefs considered post[16] are available, that IHT on the lifetime gifts is paid by the donee[17] and that the rates and rate bands remain constant.[18])

June 1986: A, having made no previous transfers of value, settles £80,000 on a discretionary trust for his brothers and sisters. Applying the rates set out in the Table (one half thereof for a lifetime gift):

$$£71,000 = \text{nil}$$
$$£9,000 \times 15\% = 1,350$$

IHT for trustees to pay = £1,350

---

13. Ie if the effect of tapering relief would be to bring the tax payable on a gift made within 7 years of death below the amount of tax that would be payable on the normal half death rate rule for lifetime gifts, the half death rate rule is to apply instead to that gift.

14. As amended by Finance Bill 1986, s 80, Sch 18 Pt I, para 29.

15. The rate bands, including the nil rate band, are linked to the yearly rise (if any) in the Retail Prices Index: IHTA 1984, s 8. The rate bands shown in the Table are those provided for 1986–87 by the Capital Transfer Tax (Indexation) Order 1986 SI 1986/528.

16. See p 228 post. It should also be noted that none of the transfers in the example are potentially exempt transfers, see p 217 post.

17. To avoid grossing up, see p 219 n 13 most.

18. The rate bands will inevitably vary from year to year because of the index-linking provisions; see n 15 ante.

March 1991: A gives £50,000 to Company X. A's cumulative total before this transfer was £80,000, so applying the rates as from that point (one half thereof for a lifetime gift):

$$£15,000 \times 15\% = \quad 2,250$$
$$£34,000 \times 17\tfrac{1}{2}\% = \quad 5,950$$
$$£1,000 \times 20\% = \quad\quad 200$$

IHT for X to pay = £8,400 [19]

July 1993: A dies,[20] leaving an estate valued at £90,000. The transfer in June 1986 can be ignored,[1] so A's cumulative total before the transfer on death will be £50,000. Applying these rates as from that point:

$$£21,000 \qquad\quad = \qquad\quad \text{nil}$$
$$£24,000 \times 30\% = \quad 7,200$$
$$£34,000 \times 35\% = \quad 11,900$$
$$£11,000 \times 40\% = \quad 4,400$$

IHT for A's personal representatives to pay = £23,500

3 Transfers of value

Cumulation and the charge to IHT (once over the current nil rate band) only apply to transfers of value, ie lifetime gifts and property passing on death. The value of the lifetime gift is the amount by which it has reduced the value of the donor's estate; a sale at market value is therefore not regarded as a transfer of value,[2] although a sale at an undervalue would be. A lifetime gift on or after March 18th 1986[3] made by an individual to another individual, or into an accumulation and maintenance trust,[4] or into a disabled person's trust[5] will escape IHT altogether as a potentially exempt transfer(PET), so long as the donor survives for seven years after making the gift.[6] If he dies within the seven year period, the PET will become chargeable on its value at the date of the gift:[7] it will be cumulated with other transfers made within seven years of it and charged to IHT at the death rate, albeit with tapering relief if the donor survived the PET by at least three years.[8]

Inheritance Tax Act 1984

3. Transfers of value
(1) Subject to the following provisions of this Part of the Act, a transfer of value is a

---

19. Cf the IHT payable on the earlier transfer. X will wish that A had reversed the order of the gifts.
20. As A has died within 7 years of the gift to X, that gift will now be charged to IHT at the full death rate, credit being given for the £8,400 IHT paid.
1. As it is outside the 7 year cumulation period, see p 215 ante.
2. As the sale proceeds fall into the transferor's estate, there is no actual loss in value of his estate.
3. Budget Day.
4. See p 225 post.
5. See p 225 post.
6. Provided the gift is not caught by the reservation of benefit rules, see p 219 post.
7. The usual lifetime exemptions will be available, see p 228 post.
8. See p 215 ante.

disposition[9] made by a person (the transferor) as a result of which the value of his estate[10] immediately after the disposition is less than it would be but for the disposition; and the amount by which it is less is the value transferred by the transfer.

[EXAMPLE

A has a complete set of Chippendale chairs; he gives one chair to B. The gift will be a transfer of value. Whilst the value of the chair to B may be quite small, the reduction in value of A's estate may be considerable as he no longer has a complete set of chairs, and it is the latter figure which provides the value of the transfer for the charge to IHT. This is a point to watch in particular when the donor has a controlling interest, say 51%, in a private company and gives away eg 2% of those shares to B, so losing control.]

3A.[11]   Potentially exempt transfers

(1) Any reference in this Act to a potentially exempt transfer is a reference to a transfer of value—

    (a) which is made by an individual on or after 18th March 1986; and

    (b) which, apart from this section, would be a chargeable transfer (or to the extent to which, apart from this section, it would be such a transfer); and

    (c) to the extent that it constitutes either a gift to another individual or a gift into an accumulation and maintenance trust or a disabled trust;

but this subsection has effect subject to any provision of this Act which provides that a disposition (or transfer of value) of a particular description is not a potentially exempt transfer.

(2) A potentially exempt transfer which is made seven years or more before the death of the transferor is an exempt transfer and any other potentially exempt transfer is a chargeable transfer.

(3) During the period beginning on the date of a potentially exempt transfer and ending immediately before—

    (a) the seventh anniversary of that date, or

    (b) if it is earlier, the death of the transferor,

it shall be assumed for the purposes of this Act that the transfer will prove to be an exempt transfer.

[EXAMPLE

If the gifts made in June 1986 and March 1991 in the example on page 216 had instead been made to A's son S and daughter D, respectively, both gifts would have been PETs. The gift to S would have become fully exempt seven years after it was made, whilst the gift to D would have become chargeable on A's death in July 1993; the earlier exempt gift would not have been cumulated, however, so there would have been no IHT for D to pay. A's cumulative total before the transfer on death would still have been £50,000, however.]

4. Transfers on death

On the death of any person tax shall be charged as if, immediately before his death, he had made a transfer of value and the value transferred by it had been equal to the value of his estate immediately before his death.

---

9. 'Disposition' includes a disposition effected by associated operations: IHTA 1984, s 27, see p 326 post.

10. 'Estate' is explained in s 5(1) post.

11. The section was introduced by the Finance Bill 1986, s 80, Sch 18 Pt I, para 1.

5. Meaning of estate

(1) For the purposes of this Act a person's estate is the aggregate of all the property to which he is beneficially entitled, except that the estate of a person immediately before his death does not include excluded property.[12]

(3) In determining the value of a person's estate at any time his liabilities at that time shall be taken into account, except as otherwise provided by this Act.

(4) The liabilities to be taken into account in determining the value of a transferor's estate immediately after a transfer of value include his liability for inheritance tax on the value transferred[13] but not his liability (if any) for any other tax or duty resulting from the transfer.[14]

10. Dispositions not intended to confer gratuitous benefit

(1) A disposition is not a transfer of value if it is shown that it was not intended, and was not made in a transaction intended, to confer any gratuitous benefit on any person and either—

(a) that it was made in a transaction at arm's length between persons not connected with each other,[15] or

(b) that it was such as might be expected to be made in a transaction at arm's length between persons not connected with each other.

4 Gifts with reservation of benefit

The Finance Bill 1986 reintroduced an old estate duty concept in order to protect the charge to IHT on death, namely the lifetime gift with reservation of benefit to the donor, as for example, where the donor gives his house to his son but continues to live in it, or where the settlor creates a discretionary trust but includes himself as a beneficiary.[16] Such a gift will be treated in the same way as any other transfer of value at the time it is made[17] but unless the benefit has been released by the donor at least seven years before his death, it will be liable on the donor's death to the death rate charge, subject to tapering relief[18] and with credit for any IHT paid at the date of the gift.

Finance Bill 1986

81. Gifts with reservation

(1) Subject to subsection (5) below, this section applies where, on or after 18th March

---

12. Ie property situate outside the UK and beneficially owned by someone domiciled outside the UK: IHTA 1984, s 6.

13. So unless the donor and donee agree that the donee shall pay the IHT (a gross transfer), a chargeable lifetime gift will have to be grossed up to find the total reduction in the donor's estate by virtue of the gift and IHT will then be charged on the grossed up amount. There is no grossing up when the transfer of value occurs on death, see IHTA 1984, s 4, p 218 ante.

14. So eg if CGT is payable by the transferor on a lifetime gift (because hold-over relief has not been claimed, see p 211 ante) that payment of CGT by the transferor is ignored in calculating the loss in value of his estate for IHT, so ensuring that IHT is not paid on the amount of the CGT.

15. S 210 adopts the CGT definition of 'connected persons' (see p 200 n 16 ante) and extends the meaning of 'relatives' to include uncles, aunts, nephews and nieces.

16. The new provision has also brought to an abrupt halt the burgeoning market in insurance based schemes such as the 'inheritance trust', specially designed by certain life companies to reduce the individual's IHT liability on death by enabling him to give away a capital sum through the medium of an insurance contract or a trust, or both, whilst still receiving benefits from the scheme in his lifetime.

17. Ie if potentially exempt (see p 217 ante) it will not be taxed at that time; otherwise it will be taxable, at the lifetime rate, at the time it is made.

18. See p 217 ante.

1986, an individual disposes of any property by way of gift and either—

(a) possession and enjoyment of the property is not bona fide assumed by the donee at or before the beginning of the relevant period; or

(b) at any time in the relevant period the property is not enjoyed to the entire exclusion, or virtually to the entire exclusion, of the donor and of any benefit to him by contract or otherwise;

and in this section 'the relevant period' means a period ending on the date of the donor's death and beginning seven years before that date or, if it is later, on the date of the gift.

(2) If and so long as—

(a) possession and enjoyment of any property is not bona fide assumed as mentioned in subsection (1)(a) above; or

(b) any property is not enjoyed as mentioned in subsection (1)(b) above;

the property is referred to (in relation to the gift and the donor) as property subject to a reservation.

(3) If, immediately before the death of the donor, there is any property which, in relation to him, is property subject to a reservation then, to the extent that the property would not, apart from this section, form part of the donor's estate immediately before his death, that property shall be treated for the purposes of the 1984 Act as property to which he was beneficially entitled immediately before his death.

(4) If, at a time before the end of the relevant period, any property ceases to be property subject to a reservation, the donor shall be treated for the purposes of the 1984 Act as having at that time made a disposition of the property by a disposition which is a potentially exempt transfer.

(5) This section does not apply if or, as the case may be, to the extent that the disposal of property by way of gift is an exempt transfer by virtue of any of the following provisions[19] of Part II of the 1984 Act—

(a) section 18 (transfers between spouses);

(b) section 20 (small gifts);

(c) section 22 (gifts in consideration of marriage);

(d) section 23 (gifts to charities);

(e) section 24 (gifts to political parties);

(f) section 25 (gifts for national purposes, etc.);

(g) section 26 (gifts for public benefit);

(h) section 27 (maintenance funds for historic buildings); and

(i) section 28 (employee trusts).

(6) Schedule 19 to this Act has effect for supplementing this section.

Schedule 19—Gifts with reservation

Exclusion of benefit

6. (1) In determining whether any property which is disposed of by way of gift is enjoyed to the entire exclusion, or virtually to the entire exclusion, of the donor and of any benefit to him by contract or otherwise—

(a) in the case of property which is an interest in land or a chattel, retention or assumption by the donor of actual occupation of the land or actual enjoyment of an incorporeal right over the land, or actual possession of the chattel shall be disregarded if it is for full consideration in money or money's worth;[20]

(b) in the case of property which is an interest in land, any occupation by the donor of the whole or any part of the land shall be disregarded if—

(i) it results from a change in the circumstances of the donor since the time of the gift, being a change which was unforeseen at that time and was not brought about by the donor to receive the benefit of this provision; and

(ii) it occurs at a time when the donor has become unable to maintain himself through old age, infirmity or otherwise; and

---

19. See pp 228–231 post.
20. So a gift of a house followed by a lease back to the donor at full market rent would not be treated as a gift with reservation of benefit.

> (iii) it represents a reasonable provision by the donee for the care and maintenance of the donor; and
>
> (iv) the donee is a relative of the donor or his spouse;
>
> (c) a benefit which the donor obtained by virtue of any associated operations (as defined in section 268 of the 1984 Act)[1] of which the disposal by way of gift is one shall be treated as a benefit to him by contract or otherwise.
>
> (2) Any question whether any property comprised in a gift was at any time enjoyed to the entire exclusion of the donor and of any benefit to him shall (so far as that question depends upon the identity of the property) be determined by reference to the property which, under the principal section, is at that time treated as property comprised in the gift.

In **Chick v Commissioner of Stamp Duties** [1958] AC 435, [1958] 2 All ER 623, the Privy Council was concerned with the interpretation of the New South Wales Stamp Duties Act 1920–56, s 102:

> For the purposes of the assessment and payment of death duty . . . the estate of a deceased person shall be deemed to include and consist of the following classes of property: . . .
>
> (2)(d) Any property comprised in any gift made by the deceased at any time . . . of which bona fide possession and enjoyment has not been assumed by the donee immediately upon the gift and thenceforth retained to the entire exclusion of the deceased . . .

The donor had transferred grazing land to one of his sons by way of a gift which he made without any reservation or qualification at the time. Some 17 months after the date of the gift, father, the donee son and another son entered into partnership to carry on the business of graziers and stockdealers; father was to manage the business and the partnership was to have the use of each partner's respective landholdings although those holdings would remain the separate property of the partner concerned. Holding that the value of the gifted land must as a result be included in computing the value of father's estate for death duty purposes, Viscount Simonds said at p 625:

> The respondent took his stand on the plain words of the section. How, he asked, could it be said that the deceased was entirely excluded from the property, the subject of the gift, or from the possession and enjoyment thereof, when for some seventeen years before his death he had been a member of a partnership, whose right it was to agist their stock on it, and himself moreover was the manager of the partnership business with the power to make final and conclusive decisions upon all matters relating to it? The 'objective and outward facts' (to use an expression of Isaacs J in *New South Wales Stamp Duties Comrs v Thompson* [1928] 4 CLR 394) were, he urged, wholly inconsistent with such exclusion. To this simple presentation of the case no adequate answer, as it appeared to their Lordships, was given by the appellants.[2]

5 Settlements

(a) Classification

Special considerations apply to a settlement, which is widely defined by the IHTA 1984 but excludes property held by a nominee or bare trustee where the

---

1. See p 236 post.

2. Cf *Munro v Stamp Duty Commissioners* [1934] AC 61 where the benefit or interest was carved out by the donor *before* he made the gift and the gifted property was held not dutiable on the donor's death.

beneficial owner is treated for all purposes as the absolute owner.[3] On creation of the settlement there will be the usual charge to IHT.[4] Thereafter the IHT treatment of the settlement will depend on whether it is a settlement with an 'interest in possession' or not. The expression 'interest in possession' is not defined in the Act. A settlement limited 'To A for life then to B absolutely' or 'To A until he is 25 and then to B absolutely' would clearly give A a beneficial interest in possession. The typical discretionary trust: '£10,000 to my trustees to apply the income to such of them, A, B and C as my trustees in their absolute discretion shall think fit' would clearly fall into the other category.[5] Not all settlements fall neatly into one category or the other, however.

Inheritance Tax Act 1984

43. Settlement and related expressions

(1) The following provisions of this section apply for determining what is to be taken for the purposes of this Act to be a settlement, and what property is, accordingly, referred to as property comprised in a settlement or as settled property.

(2) 'Settlement' means any disposition or dispositions of property, whether effected by instrument, by parol or by operation of law, or partly in one way and partly in another, whereby the property is for the time being—

   (a) held in trust for persons in succession or for any person subject to a contingency; or

   (b) held by trustees on trust to accumulate the whole or part of any income of the property or with power to make payments out of that income at the discretion of the trustees or some other person, with or without power to accumulate surplus income; or

   (c) charged or burdened (otherwise than for full consideration in money or money's worth paid for his own use or benefit to the person making the disposition) with the payment of any annuity or other periodical payment payable for a life or any other limited or terminable period;

or would be so held or charged or burdened if the disposition or dispositions were regulated by the law of any part of the United Kingdom; or whereby, under the law of any other country, the administration of the property is for the time being governed by provisions equivalent in effect to those which would apply if the property were so held, charged or burdened.

In **Pearson v Inland Revenue Commissioners** [1981] AC 753, [1980] 2 All ER 479, trustees had power to appoint the capital and income of a settled fund to any of the settlor's children and their issue. Pending such an appointment the trustees were to accumulate[6] such of the income as they thought fit, and to the extent that they did not so accumulate it, it was to be divisible equally between those of the settlor's children who had attained 21. Did this mean that his three daughters, who had all attained 21, had interests in possession? The House of Lords[7] held that it did not. An interest in possession meant a present right of present enjoyment, and the daughters had no such

---

3. CGTA 1979, s 46, p 203 ante, provides similarly for CGT.
4. See p 215 ante. If an inter vivos settlement, there will be a transfer of value from the donor to the trustees; if the settlement is created by will the personal representatives will vest the property in the trustees but there will be no charge to IHT at that point, the property concerned having already been subjected to IHT on the transfer of value occurring on the testator's death.
5. As would the grant of a contingent interest, eg 'To A contingent on him attaining 21'; until he does, there will be no interest in possession.
6. Ie capitalise.
7. By a three to two majority.

right, not because of the overriding power of appointment but because of the trustees' power to deny them the income by exercising their power to accumulate. Viscount Dilhorne said at p 485:

In *Gartside v Inland Revenue Comrs* [1968] 1 All ER 121 at 128, [1968] AC 553 at 607, an estate duty case, Lord Reid said:

> 'In possession' must mean that your interest enables you to claim now whatever may be the subject of the interest. For instance, if it is the current income from a certain fund your claim may yield nothing if there is no income, but your claim is a valid claim, and if there is any income you are entitled to get it; but a right to require trustees to consider whether they will pay you something does not enable you to claim anything. If the trustees do decide to pay you something, you do not get it by reason of having the right to have your case considered; you get it only because the trustees have decided to give it to you.'

That case concerned a discretionary trust where payment was made to the beneficiaries at the discretion of the trustees. Here the three sisters' entitlement to income was subject to the trustees' power to accumulate. On reaching 21 they had no valid claim to anything. If there was any income from the settled property, they were not entitled to it. Their right to anything depended on what the trustees did or did not do and the receipt of income by them appears to me to have been just as much at the discretion of the trustees as was the receipt of income by the beneficiaries in the *Gartside* case.

It was recognised by the trustees that, if cl 3 had created a trust to accumulate subject to which the trust fund was to be held in trust for the three sisters absolutely on their attaining 21, they would not have secured an interest in possession on reaching that age. It makes all the difference, so it was said, that the trustees were not under a duty to accumulate but only had power to do so if they thought fit. I am not able to accept this for in neither case can it in my opinion be said that the sisters on attaining that age secured the right to the present enjoyment of anything.[8]

In **Moore v Inland Revenue Commissioners** [1984] 1 All ER 1108, [1984] STC 236, the settlor had created a discretionary trust for his life, the discretionary beneficiaries being himself, any future wife he might marry and any child of such marriage, as the trustees should think fit. He never did marry. On his death the Inland Revenue claimed that as the sole object of the discretionary trust, he was beneficially entitled to an interest in possession immediately before his death.[9] Peter Gibson J disagreed. Pointing out that immediately before the settlor's death the class of discretionary objects was not closed for it was always possible that the settlor might marry and might have children, he said at p 1115:

So long as that possibility exists, the sole object's entitlement is subject to the possibility that the income will be properly diverted by the trustees to the future object once he comes into existence or is ascertained. Indeed, in strictness the entitlement of the sole object is only an entitlement that the trustees should consider whether to pay income to him. In respect of income received it may be possible to say that such an entitlement has arisen, but for present purposes I must consider the position immediately before the death of the settlor not in relation to income previously received by the trustees but in relation to the settlor's rights to income then or thereafter accruing. Such income as it

---

8. For criticism of this decision, see Thomas *Taxation and Trusts* (1981) pp 192–194, Chapman *Capital Transfer Tax* (5th edn 1982) pp 162–167, Venables, Thornhill and Jepson *Tax Planning through Wills* (1981) pp 20–27. Extracts from all three sources are to be found in Maudsley and Burn, pp 503–508. See also Shipwright 'Interest in Possession: the Pearson case' (1980) 124 Sol J 535.

9. So that the settled funds would be treated as forming part of his estate on his death, see p 224 post.

accrued was subject to the possibility that it could properly be withheld by the trustees from the settlor and diverted to a future beneficiary, unlikely though the possibility of such beneficiary coming into existence or being ascertained undoubtedly was in the present case. On that footing the settlor did not immediately before his death have an interest in possession.

(b) Interest in possession settlements

A typical example of a settlement where there is a beneficiary entitled to an interest in possession arises where property is settled on 'A for life then to B absolutely'. The general rule is that the person so entitled (A) is treated as if he were entitled to the capital of the fund (or that part of the fund) in which he has an interest in possession. So if A dies, or his interest otherwise terminates, or he disposes of it by inter vivos gift, he is regarded as having made a transfer of value and IHT is charged not on the actual value of his life interest but on the underlying assets in which his life interest subsisted,[10] the IHT being payable primarily by the trustees out of the trust property. The IHT rates are those applicable to A personally, so that if A has a high cumulative total of his own, the capital of the settled fund will be severely caught for IHT, especially if A's interest terminated on death or within seven years of death.[11]

EXAMPLE

In January 1987 X settles £100,000 on A for life, B for life, then for C absolutely (a gross transfer[12]). X having made no chargeable transfers but having exhausted his annual exemptions, the charge to IHT, payable by the trustees (at half the death rate) will be £4,475. A dies in 1992 leaving assets of his own worth £90,000; the capital of the settled fund is now worth £110,000. If A has not used up any part of his £71,000 nil rate band[13] in making lifetime gifts, the total IHT payable on the basis of transfers of value of £200,000 (£90,000 + 110,000) will be £49,300. This sum will be apportioned proportionately between A's own estate (payable by A's personal representatives) and the settled property (payable by the trustees out of the settled property) as follows:

A's estate: $\dfrac{90,000}{200,000} \times 49,300 = £22,185$

Settled property: $\dfrac{110,000}{200,000} \times 49,300 = £27,115$

If A had in fact used up his £71,000 nil rate band by making chargeable transfers within seven years of his death, the total transfers of value on his death would still amount to £200,000, but they would be taxable at the rate bands starting at £71,000, so that even more IHT would be payable. The same

10. IHTA 1984, s 49–52. No attempt is made to reproduce these lengthy and complex provisions here; their effect is summarised in this paragraph.
11. Subject to tapering relief, see p 215 ante.
12. To avoid grossing up, see p 219 n 13 ante.
13. The example assumes for simplicity that the rates and rate bands will remain at the 1986–87 levels which, being index-linked, will not be the case.

process will then apply on the death of B (termination of his interest in possession) and so it can be seen that to create a series of interests in possession can be very expensive from the IHT point of view, particularly where the life tenant has a substantial estate of his own.

(c) Settlements with no interest in possession

A typical example of a settlement where no person is beneficially entitled to an interest in possession arises in the case of a discretionary trust, for example: '£100,000 to my trustees to apply the income to such of them A, B and C as my trustees in their absolute discretion shall think fit.' Originally these were treated very harshly by the IHT legislation and a mass tax-planning exodus from the discretionary trust followed, so a much fairer system was introduced in 1982 as a result of which it may be that discretionary trusts with their useful flexibility will figure more widely in future.

Under the new provisions,[14] IHT is payable in the usual way on the transfer of value to the trustees on the creation of the settlement.[15] Thereafter the cornerstone of the IHT regime for non interest in possession settlements is a 10 yearly charge to IHT whereby the settled fund is charged to IHT every 10 years[16] at 30% of the appropriate lifetime rates, taking as the starting point for cumulation purposes (in order to ascertain the appropriate rates) the settlor's own cumulative total immediately before making the settlement.[17] If property leaves the settlement during any 10 year period, eg because the trustees make a capital payment to a beneficiary or because a beneficiary becomes entitled to an interest in possession, there is a proportionate charge to IHT based on the principle that if the property concerned had stayed in the settlement for the full 10 year period, it would attract the full periodic charge, so if it comes out after, say, 3 years it should attract 3/10 of the full charge.[18]

(d) The accumulation and maintenance settlement

Certain settlements which would otherwise be caught by the discretionary trust rules[19] are given privileged treatment under the IHT regime. These favoured settlements include trusts for the mentally disabled,[20] discretionary trusts for the benefit of employees in a particular trade, profession or employment or for

---

14. Now contained in IHTA 1984, ss 58–69; only a summary is provided here. The provisions have been extracted in Maudsley and Burn, pp 516–524; see in particular pp 524–525 for a useful worked out example illustrating their application. See also Ivison 'Capital Transfer Tax: Settlements without an Interest in Possession' (1983) 80 LSG 2732.
15. See p 222 n 4 ante.
16. IHTA 1984, s 64.
17. Ibid, s 66.
18. Ibid, s 65. So if the settlor's cumulative total before making the settlement was nil, and the amount settled was within the nil rate band, ie for a settlement created in 1986–87, no more than £71,000, so long as the value of the fund increased by no more than the index-linked increase in the IHT threshold, the amount of IHT payable every 10 years and on distributions during the 10 year period would be nil. A small discretionary trust of this sort therefore has nothing to fear from IHT.
19. Ie the rules for settlements without an interest in possession, ante.
20. IHTA 1984, s 89: a transfer into such a trust is potentially exempt (see p 217 ante); thereafter the mentally disabled person is treated as if he had an interest in possession.

their relatives and dependants[1] and protective trusts[2] where the protected life interest has been forfeited and replaced by a discretionary trust.[3]

By far the most important of the privileged settlements from a general tax-planning point of view is the 'accumulation and maintenance' settlement which is particularly relevant where property is to be held in trust for young beneficiaries. When he wishes to provide for a young beneficiary, a donor will usually prefer to create a trust in the beneficiary's favour (until the child reaches a sensible age) rather than an outright gift which the child might squander, and he will usually prefer the gift to be contingent rather than vested, in case the child fails to survive to that age. In the meantime he will usually want the income to be available at the trustees' discretion, to help maintain the child, any income not so required being accumulated and added to the capital. Without saving provisions, such a trust would suffer heavily under the IHT discretionary trust regime, so there are special statutory provisions to ensure that so long as certain qualifying requirements (set out below) are satisfied, the initial transfer to the trustees (if made by lifetime gift) is potentially exempt[4] and thereafter IHT is avoided completely. There will be no periodic charge;[5] a capital payment made to a beneficiary under a statutory or express power of advancement[6] will not be chargeable to IHT;[7] when a beneficiary becomes entitled to the settled property or an interest in possession therein, there will be no charge to IHT.[8]

Inheritance Tax Act 1984

71. Accumulation and maintenance trusts

(1) Subject to subsection (2) below, this section applies to settled property if—
  (a) one or more persons (in this section referred to as beneficiaries) will, on or before attaining a specified age not exceeding twenty-five, become beneficially entitled to it or to an interest in possession in it,[9] and
  (b) no interest in possession subsists in it and the income from it is to be accumulated so far as not applied for the maintenance, education or benefit of a beneficiary.
(2) This section does not apply to settled property unless either—
  (a) not more than twenty-five years have elapsed since the commencement of the

---

1. IHTA 1984 s 86: their creation will not usually involve a transfer of value and once created the fund generally escapes the discretionary trust regime, in particular the periodic charge.
2. See Trustee Act 1925, s 33.
3. IHTA 1984, s 88: the termination of the protected beneficiary's life interest is ignored for IHT purposes; he is treated as if he were still entitled to a beneficial interest in possession, see eg *Thomas v IRC* [1981] STC 382.
4. See p 217 ante.
5. IHTA 1984, s 58(1)(b).
6. See Trustee Act 1925, s 32 empowering trustees at their discretion to advance up to one half of a beneficiary's presumptive capital entitlement; an express power in the settlement may vary this, eg by extending it to the whole of the beneficiary's presumptive entitlement.
7. See *Inglewood v IRC* p 227 post.
8. IHTA 1984, s 71(4). If any of the qualifying requirements is broken, (eg on the expiration of the 25 year period when the beneficiaries do not have a common grandparent, see post), there will be a charge to IHT, see IHTA 1984, s 71(5).
9. 'To X's children contingent on attaining the age of 30' would satisfy this requirement because Trustee Act 1925, s 31 provides that a person with a contingent interest in capital becomes automatically entitled to the income on reaching 18 (unless the settlor has directed otherwise eg by a direction to accumulate) even though his interest in capital is still contingent. See eg *Swales v IRC* [1984] 3 All ER 16, [1984] STC 413. Of course the settlement will cease to be a qualifying settlement at that point as he will then have an interest in possession. See further McCutcheon: 'Interests in Possession Again—s 31 of the Trustee Act 1925', (1980) 77 LSG 951.

settlement or, if it was later, since the time (or latest time) when the conditions stated in paragraphs (a) and (b) of subsection (1) above became satisfied with respect to the property, or

(b) all the persons who are or have been beneficiaries are or were either—
    (i) grandchildren of a common grandparent, or
    (ii) children, widows or widowers of such grandchildren who were themselves beneficiaries but died before the time when, had they survived, they would have become entitled as mentioned in subsection (1)(a) above.

EXAMPLE

F transfers £100,000 to trustees for the benefit of his 3 sons, then aged 6, 5 and 4 contingent on them attaining 21, directing that the income in the meantime be accumulated.[10] No IHT will be paid on the creation of the settlement.[11] On the three sons becoming entitled on the vesting of their interests when they respectively attain 21, no IHT liability will arise.[12] If the trustees advance capital to any of them in the meantime, or if one of them dies, there will be no IHT to pay and there will be no periodic charge.

In **Inglewood (Lord) v Inland Revenue Commissioners** [1983] 1 WLR 366, [1983] STC 133, settled property was held on trust for the children of X contingent on them attaining 21. The settlement deeds specifically empowered the trustees to revoke all or any of these trusts and appoint the property to a wide class which would include persons over 25 years of age. The Inland Revenue argued that the conditions for an 'accumulation and maintenance' settlement were not satisfied because it could not be said in the light of the power of revocation and reappointment that one or more of the beneficiaries would become entitled to an interest in possession on or before attaining 25.[13] The trustees argued that if this were correct, then a settlement which incorporated the usual statutory power of advancement[14] would also fail to qualify for privileged status, enabling as it did trustees to resettle up to half a beneficiary's presumptive capital entitlement on new trusts under which the beneficiary's interest might be postponed to an age greater than 25.[15] The Court of Appeal upheld the Revenue's argument distinguishing a power of revocation and reappointment from a power of advancement, Fox LJ saying at p 373:

The word 'will' in paragraph 15[16] does import a degree of certainty which is not satisfied if the trust can be revoked and the fund re-appointed to some other person at an age exceeding 25. But a power of advancement has been for so long such a normal provision in a settlement for a person contingently on attaining a specified age, and since its sole purpose is to enable the trust property to be applied for that person's benefit before he attains the specified age, it would be impossible to see any rational ground why a trust for A if he attains 25 and with a power of advancement should not satisfy it also—more particularly since the exclusion of a power of advancement in such a case must be rare indeed . . . .

---

10. The direction to accumulate prevents the settlement from ceasing to qualify under IHTA 1984, s 71 once the son reaches 18, see n 9 ante.
11. So long as F survives for 7 years thereafter, see p 217 ante.
12. Although CGT may be payable (subject to hold-over relief), see p 205 ante.
13. As required by IHTA 1984, s 71(1)(a), see p 226 ante.
14. See p 226 n 6 ante.
15. As occurred in *Re Hampden Settlement Trusts* [1977] TR 177.

Looking at the whole matter more widely it appears to us unlikely that Parliament can have intended that a trust should have the benefit of paragraph 15[16] if it was subject to a power of revocation which could be exercised for the benefit of other persons at ages exceeding 25. The Finance Act 1975 plainly continued and extended the policy of the Finance Act 1969 of reducing the fiscal advantages enjoyed by discretionary trusts. It did that by imposing the discretionary trust régime. That régime was burdensome on trusts for persons contingently upon attaining a specified age—which are necessarily very common because it is undesirable to give capital to persons absolutely at too early an age. Paragraph 15[16] was enacted accordingly. Existing trusts could be converted into paragraph 15[16] trusts at low rates of tax under the provisions of paragraph 14. Parliament, having decided on assistance for contingent trusts, would, it seems to us, in the context of this legislation, be likely to confine it within fairly strict boundaries. In particular, it seems to us, highly unlikely that the benefit of paragraph 15[15] was intended to be available to what were, in effect, discretionary trusts, by reason of the existence of wide powers of revocation and reappointment, merely by the device of a primary trust for a person at 25 which could be revoked at any time.

6　The main exemptions and reliefs

Some of the exemptions and reliefs are available for lifetime transfers only, some for transfers on death only, and some for lifetime or death transfers.

(a)　Lifetime transfers only[17]

Inheritance Tax Act 1984

11.　Dispositions for maintenance of family
(1) A disposition is not a transfer of value if it is made by one party to a marriage in favour of the other party or of a child of either party and is—
    (a) for the maintenance of the other party, or
    (b) for the maintenance, education or training of the child for a period ending not later than the year in which he attains the age of eighteen or, after attaining that age, ceases to undergo full-time education or training.[18]

19.　Annual exemption
(1) Transfers of value made by a transferor in any one year are exempt to the extent that the values transferred by them (calculated as values on which no tax is chargeable) do not exceed £3,000.
(2) Where those values fall short of £3,000, the amount by which they fall short shall, in relation to the next following year, be added to the £3,000 mentioned in subsection (1) above.
(3) Where those values exceed £3,000, the excess—
    (a) shall, as between transfers made on different days, be attributed so far as possible to a later rather than an earlier transfer, and

---

16. FA 1975, Sch 5, para 15 originally set out the requirements for an accumulation and maintenance settlement. See now IHTA 1984, s 71 p 226 ante.
17. Including PETs (see p 217 ante) which become chargeable on the donor's death within 7 years.
18. Subss (3) and (4) extend the benefit of the exemption to dispositions for the maintenance of dependent relatives (as defined in subs (6)) and for the maintenance, education or training of the illegitimate child of the disposer. The importance of the exemption is that it is not limited to dispositions out of income, which would usually be covered by the 'normal expenditure out of income' exemption post, but applies to capital payments too.

(b) shall, as between transfers made on the same day, be attributed to them in proportion to the values transferred by them.

(3A)[19] A transfer of value which is a potentially exempt transfer[20]—

(a) shall in the first instance be left out of the account for the purposes of subsections (1) to (3) above; and

(b) if it proves to be a chargeable transfer, shall for the purposes of those subsections be taken into account as if, in the year in which it was made, it was made later than any transfer of value which was not a potentially exempt transfer.

(4) In this section 'year' means period of twelve months ending with 5th April.

EXAMPLE

Year 1: A makes no transfer of value.

Year 2: A gives away £4,000 to Company X and £4,000 to D.

Year 3: A dies. The gift to X (which will have the benefit of the exemption first before the chargeable PET to D) will be wholly exempt using the Year 2 exemption and £1,000 of the unused exemption from Year 1.[1] The remainder of the Year 1 exemption will be available for D whose gift will only be chargeable as to £2,000.

Inheritance Tax Act 1984

20.   Small gifts

(1) Transfers of value made by a transferor in any one year by outright gifts to any one person are exempt if the values transferred by them (calculated as values on which no tax is chargeable) do not exceed £250.[2]

(2) In this section 'year' means period of twelve months ending with 5th April.

21.   Normal expenditure out of income

(1) A transfer of value is an exempt transfer if, or to the extent that, it is shown—

(a) that it was made as part of the normal expenditure of the transferor, and

(b) that (taking one year with another) it was made out of his income, and

(c) that, after allowing for all transfers of value forming part of his normal expenditure, the transferor was left with sufficient income to maintain his usual standard of living.[3]

22.   Gifts in consideration of marriage

(1) Transfers of value made by gifts in consideration of marriage are exempt to the extent that the values transferred by such transfers made by any one transferor in respect of any one marriage (calculated as values on which no tax is chargeable) do not exceed—

(a) in the case of gifts within subsection (2) below by a parent of a party to the marriage, £5,000,

---

19. Introduced by Finance Bill 1986, s 80, Sch 18 Pt I, para 5.

20. See p 217 ante.

1. The current year's exemption must be used up first before recourse can be had to any unused part of the previous year's exemption.

2. A donor can give away £250 to as many people as he wishes in the course of the year and still be within the exemption. There is no provision for any carry forward to the next year.

3. A particularly useful exemption encouraging, for example, regular allowances to one's children. It is also useful in the funding of life policies containing trust provisions for the benefit of the children of the life assured; so long as the premiums are paid out of income, the premium payments will be within the exemption and the policy proceeds will pass free of IHT to the children on the death of the life assured.

(b) in the case of other gifts within subsection (2) below, £2,500, and
(c) in any other case £1,000;

any excess being attributed to the transfers in proportion to the values transferred.

(2) A gift is within this subsection if—

(a) it is an outright gift to a child or remoter descendant of the transferor, or
(b) the transferor is a parent or remoter ancestor of either party to the marriage, and either the gift is an outright gift to the other party to the marriage or the property comprised in the gift is settled by the gift, or
(c) the transferor is a party to the marriage, and either the gift is an outright gift to the other party to the marriage or the property comprised in the gift is settled by the gift;

and in this section 'child' includes an illegitimate child, an adopted child and a stepchild and 'parent', 'descendant' and 'ancestor' shall be construed accordingly.

EXAMPLE

On the marriage of X and Y, their respective parents can give them up to £20,000 within the exemption (4 × £5,000), their respective grandparents can give them up to £20,000 within the exemption (8 × £2,500) and anyone else can give them up to £1,000 and be within the exemption.[4]

(b) Lifetime or death transfers

Inheritance Tax Act 1984

18. Transfers between spouses

(1) A transfer of value is an exempt transfer to the extent that the value transferred is attributable to property which becomes comprised in the estate of the transferor's spouse or, so far as the value transferred is not so attributable, to the extent that that estate is increased.

(3) Subsection (1) above shall not apply in relation to property if the testamentary or other disposition by which it is given—

(a) takes effect on the termination after the transfer of value of any interest or period, or
(b) depends on a condition which is not satisfied within twelve months after the transfer;

but paragraph (a) above shall not have effect by reason only that the property is given to a spouse only if he survives the other spouse for a specified period.

(4) For the purposes of this section, property is given to a person if it becomes his property or is held on trust for him.[5]

EXAMPLE

A gives £100,000 in his lifetime to his wife B: no IHT will be payable (s 18(1)).

---

4. The donors could each increase their gifts by the amount of the annual exempt amount (see p 228 ante) together with the previous year's exempt amount if unused. Marriage is therefore a splendid opportunity for enriching a couple without adverse IHT consequences for the benefactor no matter how soon afterwards they may die.

5. There are detailed provisions in IHTA 1984, ss 36–42 to ensure that when one or more of ss 18, 23–26 applies but the transfer is not wholly exempt (eg because the deceased left his residuary estate to be divided equally between his spouse and their children—a partially exempt transfer) any IHT payable is born wholly by the non-exempt part of the estate. See further Whitehouse and Stuart-Buttle, pp 323–330.

On his death, A leaves a will giving all his remaining property to B for life and on her death to their child C absolutely: no IHT will be payable on A's death (s 18(4)).[6] If by his will A had left his property to X for life and then for B, s 18 would not have exempted the later transfer to B (s 18(3)(a)).

Inheritance Tax Act 1984

23. Gifts to charities

(1) Transfers of value are exempt to the extent that the values transferred by them are attributable to property which is given to charities.[5,7]

24. Gifts to political parties

(1) Transfers of value are exempt to the extent that the values transferred by them—
   (a) are attributable to property which becomes the property of a political party qualifying for exemption under this section, and
   (b) so far as made on or within one year of the death of the transferor, do not exceed £100,000.

(2) A political party qualifies for exemption under this section if, at the last general election preceding the transfer of value—
   (a) two members of that party were elected to the House of Commons, or
   (b) one member of that party was elected to the House of Commons and not less than 150,000 votes were given to candidates who were members of that party.[5]

BUSINESS PROPERTY[8]

104. The relief

(1) Where the whole or part of the value transferred by a transfer of value is attributable to the value of any relevant business property, the whole or that part of the value transferred shall be treated as reduced—
   (a) in the case of property falling within section 105(1)(a) or (b) below, by 50 per cent;
   (b) in the case of other relevant business property, by 30 per cent;
but subject to the following provisions of this Chapter.

105. Relevant business property

(1) . . . 'relevant business property' means, in relation to any transfer of value—
   (a) property consisting of a business or interest in a business;
   (b) shares in or securities of a company which (either by themselves or together with other such shares or securities owned by the transferor) gave the transferor control of the company immediately before the transfer;
   (c) shares in a company which do not fall within paragraph (b) above and are not quoted on a recognised stock exchange;
   (d) any land or building, machinery or plant which, immediately before the transfer, was used wholly or mainly for the purposes of a business carried on by a company of which the transferor then had control or by a partnership of which he then was a partner; and

---

6. There will be IHT to pay, however, when B's interest in possession terminates (see p 224 ante).
7. A similar exemption applies to gifts for national purposes such as the National Gallery, the British Museum, any local authority and any UK University: IHTA 1984, s 25 and Sch 3, and for gifts to a non-profit making body of property of outstanding scenic, historic or scientific interest, subject to undertakings as to maintenance and public access: IHTA 1984, s 26.
8. Ss 103–14. Only the main provisions governing the relief are extracted. The Finance Bill 1986, s 80, Sch 18 Pt I, para 14, adds a new section, s 113A, whereby the relief will apply to a PET (see p 217 ante) on the donor's death within 7 years provided the donee still owns the property in its original form.

(e) any land or building, machinery or plant which, immediately before the transfer, was used wholly or mainly for the purposes of a business carried on by the transferor and was settled property in which he was then beneficially entitled to an interest in possession.[9]

106. Minimum period of ownership

Property is not relevant business property in relation to a transfer of value unless it was owned by the transferor throughout the two years immediately preceding the transfer.

EXAMPLE

A, a solicitor, has been in sole practice for the last 40 years. On his retirement he transfers his business by way of gift to his son B; the business is worth £110,000. A dies the following year; B is still carrying on the business. A's estate includes a 60% shareholding in Company X, worth £140,000, which A had owned for the previous 20 years and a 25% shareholding in Company Y worth £12,000, which A had owned for the previous 3 years. The gift of the business is a PET[10] rendered chargeable by A's death within 7 years; its value for IHT will be £55,000 (s 105(1)(a) ante).[11] The value of the X shares will be £70,000 (s 105(1)(b) ante); the value of the Y shares will be £8,400 (s 105(1)(c) ante).

Inheritance Tax Act 1984

AGRICULTURAL PROPERTY[12]

116. The relief

(1) Where the whole or part of the value transferred by a transfer of value is attributable to the agricultural value of agricultural property[13] the whole or that part of the value transferred shall[14] be treated as reduced by the appropriate percentage, but subject to the following provisions of this Chapter.

(2) The appropriate percentage is 50 per cent if either—

(a) the interest of the transferor in the property immediately before the transfer carries the right to vacant possession or the right to obtain it within the next twelve months, or

(b) the transferor has been beneficially entitled to that interest since before 10th March 1981 and the conditions set out in subsection (3) below[15] are satisfied:

and, subject to subsection (4)[15] below, it is 30 per cent in any other case.

---

9. For the purpose of business relief, where a settlement with an interest in possession includes business property, that property is treated as if owned by the life tenant and it is the life tenant who is required to fulfil the conditions for the relief to apply, see *Featherstonaugh v IRC* [1984] STC 261. Where a settlement has no interest in possession, the condition for the relief must be met by the trustees: IHTA 1984, s 103.

10. See p 217 ante.

11. The relief is given before deducting other exemptions, eg the annual exempt amount and any part of the annual exempt amount unused from the previous year.

12. Ss 115–124. Only the main provisions are extracted. The Finance Bill 1986, s 80, Sch 18 Pt 1, para 15, adds a new section, s 124A whereby the relief will apply to a PET (see p 217 ante) on the donor's death within 7 years, provided the donee still owns the property in its original form.

13. Defined in s 115(2) as agricultural land or pasture including such cottages, farm-buildings and farmhouses as are appropriate to the property concerned.

14. The relief is mandatory, ie, if the transferor is entitled to agricultural relief he must take it rather than business relief. The relief is given before deducting other exemptions, eg the annual exempt amount etc.

15. Not extracted; subs (3) and (4) provide transitional relief for transferors who became entitled to their interest in agricultural property before 10 March 1981 and would have been entitled to 50% relief under the previous rules.

117. Minimum period of occupation or ownership
Subject to the following provisions of this Chapter, section 116 above does not apply to any agricultural property unless—
  (a) it was occupied by the transferor for the purposes of agriculture throughout the period of two years ending with the date of the transfer, or
  (b) it was owned by him throughout the period of seven years ending with that date and was throughout that period occupied (by him or another) for the purposes of agriculture.[16]

EXAMPLE

A dies owning a farm which he occupied and farmed himself for the previous 10 years; it is worth £100,000 at his death. He also owned two fields adjoining his farm for the same period but throughout his ownership they were let out to a neighbouring farmer; the two fields are worth £10,000 at A's death. The value of the farm (for IHT purposes) will be reduced to £50,000 (s 116(2)(a)): the value of the two fields to £7,000 (s 116(2)).

(c) Death transfers only

Inheritance Tax Act 1984

141. Two or more transfers within five years
(1) Where the value of a person's estate was increased by a chargeable transfer ('the first transfer') made not more than five years before
  (a) his death, or
  (b) a chargeable transfer which is made by him otherwise than on his death and as to which the conditions specified in subsection (2)[17] below are satisfied,
the tax chargeable on the value transferred by the transfer made on his death or, as the case may be, referred to in paragraph (b) above ('the later transfer') shall be reduced by an amount calculated in accordance with subsection (3) below.
(3) The amount referred to in subsection (1) above is a percentage of the tax charged on so much of the value transferred by the first transfer as is attributable to the increase mentioned in that subsection; and the percentage is—
  (a) 100 per cent if the period beginning with the date of the first transfer and ending with the date of the later does not exceed one year;
  (b) 80 per cent if it exceeds one year but does not exceed two years;
  (c) 60 per cent if it exceeds two years but does not exceed three years;
  (d) 40 per cent if it exceeds three years but does not exceed four years; and
  (e) 20 per cent if it exceeds four years.

EXAMPLE[18]

A gives £90,000 to B.[19] A dies the following year[20] so B pays IHT of £5,700 on

---

16. The relief applies to settlements on the same basis as business relief, see p 232 n 19, and IHTA 1984, s 115(1). See also Mellows 'Agricultural Tenancies of Settled Property' (1983) 80 LSG 2109.
17. Not extracted: it applies to settled property in which an interest in possession subsisted and which is the subject of two chargeable transfers made within 5 years of each other, eg where property is settled by A on B for life, remainder to C and B dies three years after A created the settlement.
18. Applying 1986–87 rates and rate bands throughout.
19. A gross gift so that if IHT becomes payable on the PET (see p 217 ante) there will be no grossing up.
20. Within 7 years of the gift so the PET becomes chargeable.

the gift. B's estate has therefore been increased as a result of the gift by £84,300. $3\frac{1}{2}$ years later B dies. Section 141 relief will be calculated as follows:

(i) $\dfrac{84,300 \text{ (gift less IHT borne by B)}}{90,000 \text{ (value transferred)}} \times 5,700 = £5,339$[1]

(ii) Relief: $40\% \times 5,339$ $= £2,135.60$

So IHT chargeable on B's death will be reduced by £2,135.60.

7   Effect of IHT on the succession process

This leaves the person considering the most tax effective method of passing on his property in a quandary. If he decides to make inter vivos gifts, IHT and CGT may be payable.[2] If he leaves the transfer of his property until death, there will be no CGT but his estate will be liable to IHT at the full death rate. There is no obvious solution to his dilemma, only certain advice:

(a) If he can afford to part with capital in his lifetime, he should take full advantage of the potentially exempt transfer[3] in making lifetime gifts. In so far as the gifted property falls within the IHT lifetime exemptions there will be no charge to IHT even if the donor dies within seven years of the gift.[4] The donor should ensure that he is entirely excluded from any benefit from the gifted property. He should select the gifted assets from those CGT exempt if possible; otherwise hold-over relief can be used if necessary to postpone the CGT reckoning day.[5]

(b) He should ensure that he uses up any unused part of his £71,000 nil rate band at his death by gifting assets or legacies by will to other members of the family up to that amount and only the balance to the spouse. If he simply leaves all his estate by will to his spouse, there will be no IHT to pay on his death[6] but when she subsequently dies, her estate being swollen by the property she received on the earlier death (the 'bunching' effect), there will be a heavy IHT bill to pay.

(c) As he cannot assume that he will die before his spouse, he must make sure that she is in a position to make use of any unused portion of her own £71,000 nil rate band by transferring to her, inter vivos, assets up to this amount (in so far as her own assets do not amount to this figure). If she dies first, she will then be in a position to leave £71,000 by will direct eg to the children.

(d) In so far as it is not practicable to avoid substantial 'bunching' on the second death,[7] the couple should consider taking out a 'joint life survivor' policy to produce a fund to meet the IHT liability on the second death. Taken out on

---

1. Only the proportion of the IHT on the first transfer which corresponds to the increase in B's estate as a result of the first transfer qualifies for the relief (see s 141(3)) so this proportion of the figure must first be ascertained.
2. Although he may be able to set off the IHT bill against his CGT liability (see p 212 n 16 ante).
3. See p 217 ante.
4. Otherwise, the donee can insure against the risk by taking out, eg a reducing term assurance policy on the life of the donor.
5. See p 211 ante.
6. Because of the transfer between spouses exemption.
7. Eg because the main asset is the matrimonial home and the spouses want the survivor to have sole control of this, or because it is felt that to allow for inflation the surviving spouse will need a fair amount of capital to maintain a reasonable standard of living.

the lives of both spouses and stated to be for the benefit of the children, it will mature on the death of the survivor and will provide an IHT free fund[8] to help to meet the IHT payable on the survivor's estate.

(e) The creation of an interest in possession settlement is generally to be avoided unless the immediate life tenant is to be the spouse[9] and even then it is not very tax effective as with the capital tied up, the beneficiary is not in a position to make PETs and otherwise use the full range of the inter vivos exemptions.[10] The discretionary trust is now a much more attractive vehicle for the person wishing to postpone the final distribution of his property,[11] but it suffers from the same disadvantage, whilst it is also expensive to administer as professional help is needed at regular intervals, indeed professional trustees may be desirable. A person wishing to provide for young beneficiaries should ensure that he takes full advantage of the privileged position of the accumulation and maintenance trust.[12]

EXAMPLE

Assume that husband (H) and wife (W) have made no inter vivos chargeable transfers, that they have one child (C), that H has assets of £150,000 and W has none, at the beginning of each alternative sequence of events and that the 1986–87 rates and rate bands apply throughout.

1. H and W make wills in each other's favour, the survivor leaving all to C.
   H dies first: all to W—no IHT because of spouse exemption, but his IHT nil rate band has been wasted.
   W then dies: all to C—estate worth £150,000 (inherited from H).

$$IHT = \underline{£27,500}$$

Had W died first, the result would have been the same. Having no assets to pass under her will, her nil rate band would have been wasted and on H's subsequent death, IHT of £27,500 would have been payable on his £150,000 estate.

2. H transfers inter vivos £71,000 to W, leaving H with £79,000.
   H dies first: by will he leaves £71,000 to C and the rest (£8,000) to W. No IHT payable.[13]
   W then dies: by will she leaves all to C. Estate worth £79,000 (her own £71,000 and the £8,000 inherited from H).

$$IHT = \underline{£2,400}$$

---

8. So long as the premiums are paid out of income, there should be no charge to IHT on the gift element as the normal expenditure exemption will apply, see p 229 ante. See Gaselee 'Life and Pension Policies and Capital Transfer Tax' (1981) 125 Sol J 421.
9. In which event the 'transfer to spouse' exemption will apply. See IHTA 1984, s 18(4), p 230 ante.
10. The life tenant's own annual £3,000 exemption and the exemption for gifts in consideration of marriage can both be used by the life tenant on the inter vivos termination of his interest in possession, wholly or in part, (IHTA 1984, s 57(1)(2)); business property relief and agricultural property relief may also be available, on a lifetime or death transfer, see p 232 n 9, p 233 n 16 ante.
11. Even though IHT is likely to be paid at more frequent intervals than in the case of an interest in possession settlement, the sums involved will be relatively small and the date of each charge will be known well in advance and can be planned for.
12. See p 225 ante.
13. Because of nil rate band (gift to C), and spouse exemption (gift to W).

Had W died first, the result would have been the same. By her will she would have left everything to C; no IHT would have been payable because of her nil rate band. On H's subsequent death, IHT of £2,400 would have been payable on his £79,000 estate.[14]

8   Associated operations

Any tax planner seeking to avoid or reduce IHT has to bear in mind the statutory anti-avoidance provision known as the associated operations rule. Broadly defined as two or more operations affecting one piece of property or one paving the way for the other, their consequences are complex and depend on the nature of the operations concerned.

Inheritance Tax Act 1984

268.   Associated operations

(1) In this Act 'associated operations' means, subject to subsection (2) below, any two or more operations of any kind, being—
   (a) operations which affect the same property, or one of which affects some property and the other or others of which affect property which represents, whether directly or indirectly, that property, or income arising from that property, or any property representing accumulations of any such income, or
   (b) any two operations of which one is effected with reference to the other, or with a view to enabling the other to be effected or facilitating its being effected, and any further operation having a like relation to any of those two, and so on,
whether those operations are effected by the same person or different persons, and whether or not they are simultaneous: and 'operation' includes an omission.
(2) The granting of a lease for full consideration in money or money's worth shall not be taken to be associated with any operation effected more than three years after the grant, and no operation effected on or after 27th March 1974 shall be taken to be associated with an operation effected before that date.
(3) Where a transfer of value is made by associated operations carried out at different times it shall be treated as made at the time of the last of them; but where any one or more of the earlier operations also constitute a transfer of value made by the same transferor, the value transferred by the earlier operations shall be treated as reducing the value transferred by all the operations taken together, except to the extent that the transfer constituted by the earlier operations but not that made by all the operations taken together is exempt under section 18 above.[15]

House of Commons Debates: Mr Joel Barnet[16]

Finance Bill Debate

It is reasonable for a husband to share capital with his wife when she has no means of her own. If she chooses to make gifts out of the money she has received from her husband, there will be no question of using the associated operations provisions to treat them as gifts made by the husband and taxable as such. In a blatant case, where the transfer by a

---

14. It will be appreciated that the surviving H or W in the second sequence should have little difficulty in fact in bringing the estate down below the nil rate band by lifetime gifts when capital can be spared for this purpose.
15. The 'transfer between spouses' exemption, see p 230 ante.
16. Chief Secretary to the Treasury, H C Deb 1974–75, Vol 888 Col 56.

husband to a wife was made on condition that the wife should at once use the money to make gifts to others, a charge on a gift by the husband might arise under (s 268).[17]

9 Post-mortem tax planning

(a) In general

When effective tax planning steps are not taken by the deceased in his lifetime, post-mortem tax planning may be the answer. It has always been possible for beneficiaries to rewrite their testator's will or their entitlement under the intestacy rules under the principle of *Saunders v Vautier*[18] with the court consenting on behalf of infant or unborn beneficiaries.[19] Without statutory intervention, there could be adverse taxation consequences arising from any such variation however; the deceased's IHT position would remain the same whilst a beneficiary giving up something to which he was entitled under the will or intestacy would be making a transfer of value for his own IHT purposes and a disposal for CGT purposes giving rise to a charge to CGT on any increase in value from the date of death to the date of the disposal.

(b) Arrangements IHT and CGT effective

Statute has intervened, however, currently by the Inheritance Tax Act 1984, s 142 (for IHT) and the Capital Gains Tax Act 1979, s 49 (for CGT), with the result that any variation or disclaimer, so long as it is made in writing, within two years of the death and (in the case of variation) notified to the Inland Revenue within 6 months of the date of the instrument, is for IHT and CGT purposes written back as if made by the deceased himself.[20]

Inheritance Tax Act 1984[1]

142. Alteration of dispositions taking effect on death
(1) Where within the period of two years after a person's death—
  (a) any of the dispositions (whether effected by will, under the law relating to

---

17. So it seems that the tax planning suggestions at p 235 ante would escape attack under s 268. Sed quaere the effect of *Furniss v Dawson* [1984] 1 All ER 530, [1984] STC 153 where the House of Lords established (in the context of a charge to CGT liability) that whenever taxpayers entered into transactions that amounted to a scheme whose purpose was the avoidance or deferrment of tax, the various steps in the scheme could be viewed as a whole and taxed accordingly, a decision described by Whitehouse and Stuart-Buttle in (1984) 81 LSG 565 as a 'judicial associated operations rule.'
18. (1841) 4 Beav 115; affirmed Cr & Ph 240, 10 LJ Ch 354.
19. Nowadays under its powers under the Variation of Trusts Act 1958; the court will only give its consent if satisfied the variation is for the benefit of the infant or unborn beneficiary concerned.
20. Unfortunately there is no corresponding provision for income tax relief; any income receivable between the date of death and date of the variation or disclaimer is taxable as that of the original beneficiary. The gift element of a post-mortem variation used to attract ad valorem stamp duty too, but FA 1985, s 84 removed this charge; variations are now subject only to a 50p fixed duty.
1. The corresponding provisions as to CGT in CGTA 1979, s 49(6)–(10) are virtually word for word identical with those for IHT and are therefore not extracted.

intestacy or otherwise)[2] of the property comprised in his estate immediately before his death are varied, or

(b) the benefit conferred by any of those dispositions is disclaimed,[3]

by an instrument in writing made by the persons or any of the persons who benefit or would benefit under the dispositions,[4] this Act shall apply as if the variation had been effected by the deceased or, as the case may be, the disclaimed benefit had never been conferred.

(2) Subsection (1) above shall not apply to a variation unless an election to that effect is made by written notice given to the Board within six months after the date of the instrument, or such longer time as the Board may allow, by—

(a) the person or persons making the instrument, and

(b) where the variation results in additional tax being payable, the personal representatives;

but personal representatives may decline to join in an election only if no, or no sufficient, assets are held by them in that capacity for discharging the additional tax.

(3) Subsection (1) above shall not apply to a variation or disclaimer made for any consideration in money or money's worth other than consideration consisting of the making, in respect of another of the dispositions, of a variation or disclaimer to which that subsection applies.

(4) Where a variation to which subsection (1) above applies results in property being held in trust for a person for a period which ends not more than two years after the death, this Act shall apply as if the disposition of the property that takes effect at the end of the period had had effect from the beginning of the period; but this subsection shall not affect the application of this Act in relation to any distribution or application of property occurring before that disposition takes effect.

(5) For the purposes of subsection (1) above the property comprised in a person's estate includes any excluded property[5] but not any property to which he is treated as entitled by virtue of section 49(1) above[6] (or section 81 of the Finance Act 1986).[6a]

(6) Subsection (1) above applies whether or not the administration of the estate is complete or the property concerned has been distributed in accordance with the original dispositions.[7]

EXAMPLE

Hywel Jones dies, leaving his entire estate of £250,000 to his wife, Wendi. As he has therefore failed to utilise his nil rate band[8] Wendi enters into the following deed of variation.

THIS DEED OF VARIATION is made the 12th day of July 1986 BETWEEN *Wendi Jones* of 1 Bryn Road, Cardiff (hereinafter called 'Mrs Jones') of the first part, *Carys*

---

2. 'Or otherwise' will include the deceased's severable share in any assets to which immediately before his death he was beneficially entitled as joint tenant, ie which passes by survivorship to the other joint tenant(s), as CGTA 1979, s 4(10) specifically makes plain for CGT purposes.

3. As to disclaimer generally, see p 369 post.

4. Ie the consent of the person giving up the whole or part of his entitlement is a prerequisite for a variation or disclaimer, so that if he refuses to comply, no advantage can be taken of the sections; if he is an infant or unborn beneficiary the court will have to be asked to consent on his behalf.

5. See p 219 n 12 ante.

6. Ie settled property in which the deceased had an interest in possession at his death. So if property is settled on X for life, remainder to Y, it is not open to Y on X's death to vary his reversionary interest under these provisions although he could effectively disclaim it under IHTA 1984, s 93.

6a. Words in brackets added by Finance Bill 1986, s 80, Sch 18 Pt I, para 17 (a gift with reservation of benefit, see p 219 ante).

7. See 'Instruments of Variation: The Latest Position', (1985) 82 LSG 1454 for a note on the Inland Revenue's interpretation of these requirements.

8. Having made no inter vivos chargeable transfers, it is assumed.

Jones of 45 Castell Road, Cardiff (hereinafter called 'Carys') of the second part[9] and *Edwin Evans* of 25 Higher Street, Cardiff (hereinafter called 'the Executor') of the third part.

WHEREAS:

(1) Hywel Jones late of 1 Bryn Road aforesaid (hereinafter called 'the Testator') made his will dated 3rd July 1977 by which he appointed the Executor to be the executor thereof and gave the whole of his estate to Mrs Jones.

(2) The Testator died on the 4th April 1986 and his said will was proved by the Executor in the Llandaff District Registry of the Family Division of the High Court on the 2nd day of June 1986.

(3) Mrs Jones being absolutely entitled to the Testator's estate desires to vary the terms of the said will to make some provision for Carys (being the only child of the Testator and Mrs Jones).

NOW THIS DEED WITNESSETH that the said will shall thenceforth be read as if the Testator himself had included the following clause in it:

'I GIVE to my daughter *Carys Jones* the sum of £71,000 subject to all liability in respect of any Inheritance Tax payable by reason of my death on this gift.'[10] IN WITNESS whereof the parties hereto have hereunto set their hands and seals the day and year first before written.

SIGNED SEALED and DELIVERED etc.

Written Notice to Inland Revenue[11]

WE, *Wendi Jones* of 1 Bryn Road Cardiff, *Carys Jones* of 45 Castell Road Cardiff and *Edwin Evans* of 25 Higher Street Cardiff being parties to an instrument dated the 12th day of July 1986 varying the dispositions of the estate of Hywel Jones deceased (a copy of which is enclosed for your attention) hereby give notice of election that the provisions of section 142(1) of the Inheritance Tax Act 1984 and of section 49(6) of the Capital Gains Tax Act 1979 shall apply thereto.

Dated the 14th day of July 1986
Signed . . . . etc.

(c) Arrangements IHT effective only

The IHT legislation provides three further opportunities for post-mortem arrangements free of adverse IHT consequences but with no corresponding CGT relief.

---

9. It is not strictly necessary for Carys to be a party to this deed or to the following notice of election, but in practice this is usually done when the recipient is of full age.

10. The legacy is made to bear its own IHT (which should be nil by virtue of the nil rate band) to avoid grossing up, see Whitehouse and Stuart-Buttle, pp 323–330.

11. Although the election could be included in the deed of variation, the deed will have to be submitted for adjudication for stamp duty purposes first, so that it is considered better practice, in order to ensure compliance with the 6 months time limit, to submit it to the Inland Revenue (Capital Taxes Office) by way of a separate document.

Inheritance Tax Act 1984

143. Compliance with testator's request

Where a testator expresses a wish that property bequeathed by his will should be transferred by the legatee to other persons, and the legatee transfers any of the property in accordance with that wish within the period of two years after the death of the testator, this Act shall have effect as if the property transferred had been bequeathed by the will to the transferee.

144. Distribution etc from property settled by will

(1) This section applies where property comprised in a person's estate immediately before his death is settled by his will and, within the period of two years after his death and before any interest in possession has subsisted in the property, there occurs—

- (a) an event on which tax would (apart from this section) be chargeable under any provision, other than section 64 or 79, of Chapter III[12] of Part III of this Act, or
- (b) an event on which tax would be so chargeable but for section 75 or 76 above or paragraph 16(1) of Schedule 4 to this Act.

(2) Where this section applies by virtue of an event within paragraph (a) of subsection (1) above, tax shall not be charged under the provision in question on that event; and in every case in which this section applies in relation to an event, this Act shall have effect as if the will had provided that on the testator's death the property should be held as it is held after the event.[13]

145. Redemption of surviving spouse's life interest

Where an election is made by a surviving spouse under section 47A of the Administration of Estates Act 1925[14] this Act shall have effect as if the surviving spouse, instead of being entitled to the life interest, had been entitled to a sum equal to the capital value mentioned in that section.

QUESTIONS

1. Consider again question 1, p 212 ante. How would your answers be affected by IHT considerations?

2. You are called to the bedside of Midas who is likely to die in the next few days. He is a widower with 4 adult children, his assets amount to £750,000 and he has never made a will. What measures, if any, can you suggest to reduce the IHT payable on his death? Would it make any difference to your answer if he were married? Read Cox 'Death-Bed Estate Planning' (1985) 82 LSG 422.

3. 'When one considers the effect of capital taxation on the timing of the succession process, one is faced with a dilemma: what suits one tax will not suit another.'
Discuss.

---

12. The Chapter containing the provisions relating to settlements without an interest in possession.
13. So if the deceased's will creates a discretionary trust which is ended within two years of death, the dispositions of the trustees are read back into the will for IHT purposes. Without a corresponding rule for CGT there is a potential charge under CGTA 1979, s 54(1) (p 205 ante) on any absolute appointment to a beneficiary before the two year trust is ended, but hold-over relief would be available in such a case (see p 211 ante). The one substantial tax planning advantage that this has over the post-mortem variation or disclaimer (p 237 ante) is that the consent of the beneficiaries is not required. However desirable a variation or disclaimer may be from a tax planning viewpoint, the beneficiary whose consent is requisite cannot always be expected to view the matter objectively.
14. See p 129 ante.

CHAPTER 17

Family provision claims

1 Introduction

The court has wide powers to step in and upset a person's succession arrangements for the protection of his family and other dependants. In relation to lifetime transfers, the Matrimonial Causes Act 1973, s 37 empowers the court to set aside dispositions aimed at defeating a claim for financial relief in matrimonial proceedings.[1] For property passing on death, protection for the family lies under the family provision legislation, currently the Inheritance (Provision for Family and Dependants) Act 1975, which enables a qualifying member of the family and certain other dependants to apply to the court for provision from the estate, whether the deceased died testate or intestate.

The 1975 Act resulted from the recommendations of the Law Commission as contained in two reports on family property.[2] In their first report, the Law Commission considered the merits of a system of fixed rights of inheritance (particularly in relation to the surviving spouse)[3] as compared with improvement of the existing discretionary system of family provision[4] operating through application to the court.[5] Their second report contained detailed recommendations for the reform of the existing system, and these were embodied in the 1975 Act which repealed and replaced the existing system for those dying after March 1976.

Law Commission: First Report on Family Property[6]

Family provision and legal rights of inheritance

42 The advantage claimed for legal rights of inheritance is that they would operate automatically without the need to go to the courts. There are, of course, technical

---

1. For detailed consideration of this section see Bromley *Family Law* (6th edn 1981) pp 568–569.
2. 'First Report on Family Property: A New Approach' (1973) Law Com 52; 'Second Report on Family Property: Family Provision on Death' (1974) Law Com 61.
3. As in France, Scotland, USSR, Spain, Switzerland, Brazil, Jersey (CI), and most states of the USA (see Uniform Probate Code ss 2-201–2-207, ss 2-401–2-404). In Scotland, for example, the surviving spouse is entitled as of right to one third of the deceased's net moveable property or one half if there are no issue, the issue are entitled to one third and only the remainder ('the dead's part') can be disposed of by will. These fixed legal rights are subject to the statutory prior rights of the spouse on an intestacy (see p 130 n 14) and the widow and issue can still claim maintenance from the estate.
4. As contained in Inheritance (Family Provision) Act 1938 as amended by the Intestates' Estates Act 1952 and the Family Provision Act 1966.
5. As in New Zealand, Australia and all Canadian states except Quebec.
6. 'A New Approach' (1973) Law Com 52.

arguments to be adduced against a system of legal rights; its introduction would involve a new and possibly complex set of rules. But the essential issue is whether a fairer result would be achieved if a spouse who has been disinherited were entitled to a fixed share of the estate in addition to the right to claim family provision. Most cases of disinheritance involve some degree of marital breakdown whether open or below the surface. The circumstances of each case can vary enormously: one spouse may have had greater assets than the other; one spouse may be solely responsible for the breakdown; one spouse may have family obligations not shared by the other. Whatever the situation, the survivor would be entitled to a fixed proportion of the estate of the first to die. In some cases legal rights of inheritance would seem fair, in others they would not. In some cases the survivor may need to be provided for, in others he or she may be better off than the deceased. Legal rights could not be varied to suit the individual circumstances of each case. The fixed proportion would apply in every case; even the spouse who had lived separately for many years without ever being dependent on the deceased would be entitled to a fixed proportion. A high proportion might increase the number of cases where the survivor's claim to legal rights seemed unfair in all the circumstances. A low proportion might be unfair to the survivor. . . .

44 Another consideration is that unlike the principle of co-ownership of the home legal rights would not affect the spouses' interests in property during marriage but would apply at the end of marriage. As we have indicated, our view is that the surviving partner of a marriage should have a claim upon the family assets at least equivalent to that of a divorced spouse. The principle of co-ownership of the home,[7] if introduced, would close part of the gap left by the present law: it would operate during the marriage and its effects would survive the termination of the marriage, whether by divorce or death. For the rest, we believe that a strengthened family provision law, with its greater flexibility, is a better means of securing the survivor's interests than a system of legal rights. This view was supported by the majority of those consulted. The addition of a system of fixed legal rights of inheritance to the system of family provision law would, in our view, lead to uncertainty and confusion. Any advantage derived from the automatic operation of legal rights of inheritance would be offset by the disadvantage of rigidity and possible incompatibility with the new standards we propose for family provision law, and might even prejudice the survivor's interest in the estate.[8]

2 Who can claim?[9]

Inheritance (Provision for Family and Dependants) Act 1975

1. Application for financial provision from deceased's estate
(1) Where after the commencement of this Act a person dies domiciled in England and Wales and is survived by any of the following persons—
  (a) the wife or husband of the deceased;
  (b) a former wife or former husband of the deceased who has not remarried;
  (c) a child of the deceased;
  (d) any person (not being a child of the deceased) who, in the case of any marriage to which the deceased was at any time a party, was treated by the deceased as a child of the family in relation to that marriage;
  (e) any person (not being a person included in the foregoing paragraphs of this

---

7. Recommended in principle at para 30 and in detail in the Law Commission's Third Report on Family Property, (1978) Law Com 86 but not yet enacted.
8. See further for comparison between the two systems, Guest 'Family Provision and the Legitima Portico' (1957) 73 LQR 74.
9. Under the previous legislation the only permissible claimants were the deceased's spouse, former spouse, and, subject to various restrictions, his children.

subsection) who immediately before the death of the deceased was being
maintained, either wholly or partly, by the deceased;
that person[9a] may apply to the court[10] for an order under section 2 of this Act on the
ground that the disposition of the deceased's estate effected by his will or the law relating
to intestacy, or the combination of his will and that law is not such as to make reasonable
financial provision for the applicant.

(3) For the purposes of subsection (1)(e) above, a person shall be treated as being
maintained by the deceased, either wholly or partly, as the case may be, if the deceased,
otherwise than for full valuable consideration, was making a substantial contribution in
money or money's worth towards the reasonable needs of that person.[11]

(a) The spouse

This includes the judicially separated spouse[12] and a party to a void or voidable
marriage that was not annulled during the deceased's lifetime.[13]

Inheritance (Provision for Family and Dependants) Act 1975

25. Interpretation:—
(4) For the purposes of this Act any reference to a wife or husband shall be treated as
including a reference to a person who in good faith entered into a void marriage with the
deceased unless either—

   (a) the marriage of the deceased and that person was dissolved or annulled during the
        lifetime of the deceased and the dissolution or annulment is recognised by the law
        of England and Wales, or
   (b) that person has during the lifetime of the deceased entered into a later marriage.

(b) The former spouse who has not remarried

Remarriage will deny a former spouse the right to claim[14] as will an order made
in the matrimonial proceedings in question. Even when no such order is
imposed, it seems that the courts will generally take the view that the parties'
financial claims on one another were settled for all time in the course of those
proceedings, so that a subsequent claim against the estate is unlikely to succeed.

Inheritance (Provision for Family and Dependants) Act 1975

25. Interpretation
(1) In this Act—
'former wife' or 'former husband' means a person whose marriage with the deceased

---

9a. The claim is personal to the applicant: if the applicant dies before the hearing it cannot be
continued by his personal representative; *Whyte v Ticehurst* [1986] 2 All ER 158, [1986]
2 WLR 700.
10. The High Court unless the value of the net estate does not exceed £30,000 in which event
application may be made to the County Court: 1(PFD)A 1975, s 25(1), County Courts Act 1959,
s 52A, County Courts Jurisdiction (Inheritance—Provision for Family and Dependants) Order
1981, SI 1981/1636.
11. In their 22nd Report 'The Making and Revocation of Wills' (1980) Cmnd 7902 para 3.25, the
Law Reform Committee recommended the addition of a further class of applicant, see p 168 n 4
ante.
12. Unless an order under s 15 has been made, see p 244 post.
13. It also includes the concurrent spouses of a polygamous marriage: *Re Sehota* [1978] 3 All ER
385, [1978] 1 WLR 1506.
14. See Law Com 61 para 57.

was during the deceased's lifetime dissolved or annulled by a decree of divorce or of nullity of marriage made under the Matrimonial Causes Act 1973;

(5) Any reference in this Act to remarriage or to a person who has remarried includes a reference to a marriage which is by law void or voidable or to a person who has entered into such a marriage, as the case may be, and a marriage shall be treated for the purposes of this Act as a remarriage, in relation to any party thereto, notwithstanding that the previous marriage of that party was void or voidable.

15.   Restriction imposed in divorce proceedings, etc on application under this Act[15]

(1) On the grant of a decree of divorce, a decree of nullity of marriage or a decree of judicial separation[16] or at any time thereafter the court, if it considers it just to do so, may on the application of either party to the marriage, order that the other party to the marriage shall not on the death of the applicant be entitled to apply for an order under section 2 of this Act.

In this subsection 'the court' means the High Court or, where a county court has jurisdiction by virtue of Part V of the Matrimonial and Family Proceedings Act 1984, a county court.

(2) In the case of a decree of divorce or nullity of marriage an order may be made under subsection (1) above before or after the decree is made absolute, but if it is made before the decree is made absolute it shall not take effect unless the decree is made absolute.

(3) Where an order made under subsection (1) above on the grant of a decree of divorce or nullity of marriage has come into force with respect to a party to a marriage, then, on the death of the other party to that marriage, the court shall not entertain any application for an order under section 2 of this Act made by the first-mentioned party.

(4) Where an order made under subsection (1) above on the grant of a decree of judicial separation has come into force with respect to any party to a marriage, then, if the other party to that marriage dies while the decree is in force and the separation is continuing, the court shall not entertain any application for an order under section 2 of this Act made by the first-mentioned party.

Re Fullard [1981] 2 All ER 796, [1981] 3 WLR 743, CA; Ormrod LJ and Purchas J

The applicant married the deceased in 1938 and divorced him in 1976. They had both worked throughout the marriage and had accumulated savings of about the same amount. They settled their financial affairs after the divorce by agreement; she used her savings to buy out his share in the former matrimonial home and each party acknowledged that neither party would make a claim for periodical payments against the other.[17] Shortly afterwards he died, leaving his small estate of £7,100 elsewhere. The applicant's claim for reasonable provision under s 1(1)(b) was dismissed; the applicant appealed.

Held: Appeal dismissed.

Ormrod LJ: With the coming into effect of the Matrimonial Proceedings and Property Act 1970 with the new powers to make property adjustments orders and very much freer power to order lump sums, the court now has power to make appropriate capital adjustments as between spouses after divorce and those powers, although they are not necessarily comprehensive (and that is plain from s 15 of the 1975 Act which clearly contemplates that proceedings may be taken under the 1975 Act after divorce) nonetheless the number of cases in which it would be possible for an applicant to bring

---

15. As amended by Matrimonial and Family Proceedings Act 1984, s 8(1).
16. See p 243 ante.
17. No application was made to the court under s 15 ante.

himself (or herself) within the terms of s 2 of the 1975 Act, in my judgment, would be comparatively small. Where the estate, like this one, is small, in my view the onus on an applicant of satisfying the conditions in s 2 is very heavy indeed and these applications ought not to be launched unless there is (or there appears to be) a real chance of success, because the result of these proceedings simply diminishes the estate and is a great hardship on the beneficiaries if they are ultimately successful in litigation.

The question is, and it is a simple question to my mind: is it unreasonable, or was it unreasonable, that this man made no financial provision by his will for his former wife? He thought he and his wife had sorted out their financial claims as between each other when they reached the agreement about the house. It is right to say that if the wife had been dissatisfied with that arrangement, she had her remedy. She could have applied to the court for an order and she might have succeeded in getting the whole of the house transferred to her without having to pay anything, or perhaps on payment of very much less.

The final irony of this case is to be seen in looking at the estate of the deceased which amounted to £7,100 the greater part of which consisted of the £4,500 which his former wife had paid for his share of the house. So, if she is right on this application, what she is in fact doing is asking for her money back. It is as simple as that. It does not get any less simple and any less stark by going through all the steps that s 3(1) of the 1975 Act directs the court to do.[18] We come back to the same position which is: is it reasonable to expect a husband with assets of this kind who has made arrangements with his former wife which settled their financial affairs or is it reasonable for the court in his place to make provision for the wife out of his estate? To my mind the answer is plain and obvious. It is obviously No.

As I mentioned at the beginning of this judgment, it seems to me that the number of cases which, since the court acquired its wide powers under the 1970 Act to make property adjustments, can now get in within the umbrella of the 1975 Act post-divorce must be comparatively few. In the course of argument I suggested one case where a periodical payments order has been going on for a long time and the husband is found to have a reasonable amount of capital in his estate. That is one. Counsel for the applicant suggested that there was another possible situation, where a substantial capital fund was unlocked by the death of the deceased, such as insurance or pension policies. Those are cases which could come within the 1975 Act. Apart from those it seems there cannot be many cases which qualify.

(c) A child of the deceased[19]

Under the previous legislation only unmarried daughters, sons under 21, and children (without age limit) who were incapable of maintaining themselves by reason of mental or physical disability were permitted to claim provision from their parents' estate. On the recommendation of the Law Commission, these restrictions were abolished.

Law Commission: Second Report on Family Property[20]

Position of adult and unmarried children—age limits
74.   The argument against removing the age limit altogether is that it might encourage able-bodied sons capable of supporting themselves to apply for provision from the estate, thereby possibly incurring costs to be paid from the estate and reducing the share of the

---

18. See p 254 post.
19. 'Child' includes an illegitimate child and a child en ventre sa mère: 1(PFD)A 1975, s 25(1). An adopted child is brought within s 1(1)(c) by the Children Act 1975 s 8(9) Sch 1 Part II.
20. 'Family Provision on Death' (1974) Law Com 61.

surviving spouse or other beneficiaries. However an application by a son (or, indeed, by a daughter in the same position) could not succeed unless the court found that the deceased had failed to make reasonable provision for that child's maintenance.

75.   One solution would be to limit the right to apply to those children, of any age, who were actually dependent on the deceased at the time of his death but this would rule out a claim against the estate of a parent who had unreasonably refused to support an adult child during his lifetime where it could have been morally appropriate to provide such support. Moreover, an adult child, who is fully self-supporting at the time of the parent's death, may quite suddenly thereafter cease to be so. . . .

78.   There remains the question whether there is any merit in the provision that a daughter may claim only if she has not married. Although in principle the responsibility for maintaining her passes on marriage to her husband, in our view the restriction is capable of causing hardship, for example, where the daughter is a widow with young children who has not been provided for by her husband. To avoid possible hardship, we proposed [1] that the condition that a daughter can apply only if unmarried be removed. We thought the proposal unlikely to lead to any substantial increase in the number of cases, since a married daughter whose husband is supporting her would not be likely to make or succeed in an application against the estate of her deceased parent. The proposal was widely supported.

79.   *We accordingly recommend,* reaffirming the views expressed in the working paper, that any child or child of the family of the deceased, whether over or under 21 and whether married or unmarried, should be entitled to apply for family provision.

In **Re Coventry** [1979] 2 All ER 408, [1979] 2 WLR 853,[2] an application was made by the deceased's 46 year old son who was in good health and full time employment. In dismissing the application on the facts of the case, Oliver J warned at p 410:

Applications under the 1975 Act for maintenance by able-bodied and comparatively young men in employment and able to maintain themselves must be relatively rare and need, I should have thought, to be approached with a degree of circumspection.[3]

(d) A child of the family

This was a new class of applicant introduced on the recommendation of the Law Commission,[4] to remove the anomaly that a child treated as part of the family although not a child of the marriage in question, would fare better from the divorce[5] than the death of the non-parent.

Re Callaghan [1984] 3 All ER 790, [1984] 3 WLR 1076, Fam D; Booth J

When his mother married the deceased, the plaintiff was 35 years old with a family and home of his own, but he maintained a close relationship with his

---

1. Working Paper no 42, (1971) para 3.42.
2. Affirmed [1980] Ch 461, [1979] 3 All ER 815.
3. See also *Re Dennis* [1981] 2 All ER 140 at 145, *Re Rowlands* [1984] FLR 813 at 819.
4. 'Second Report on Family Property: Family Provision on Death' (1974) Law Com 61 paras 67–69.
5. By the Matrimonial Causes Act 1973, s 23 the court has power in granting a decree of divorce, nullity or judicial separation to order either spouse to make financial provision for a child treated by the parties as a child of their family albeit not a child of the marriage in question. Until the 1(PFD)A 1975 the court had no such power on the death of a spouse.

stepfather who had lived with his mother for many years before their marriage. The plaintiff's children treated the deceased as their grandfather, and after his mother's death, the plaintiff and his wife looked after the deceased, who was seriously ill, for some months before he died.

Held: The deceased had treated the plaintiff as a child of the family; the plaintiff was entitled to claim provision from the deceased's estate under s 1(1)(d).

Booth J: Undoubtedly, prior to the marriage and during the latter part of his minority, the plaintiff had lived with Mary and the deceased and was treated as a child of the family. From that time onwards and until his death, the deceased continued to treat the plaintiff as his son, and the plaintiff fully lived up to that role, but it is argued on behalf of the defendants that that does not entitle the plaintiff to apply; what the Act requires, it is said, is that the plaintiff should have been treated by the deceased within the family and after the marriage as a child in that he was maintained, nurtured, disciplined, educated and advised. That argument is founded, at any rate in part on s 3(3) of the Act,[6] which requires the court in considering an application made by virtue of s 1(1)(d) to have regard not only to the general matters set out in s 1(1)(d) of the Act, but also to have regard to the manner in which the applicant had been, or in which he might expect to be, educated or trained and the extent to which the deceased had assumed and discharged responsibility for his maintenance. So, it is argued, the words in s 1(1)(d), 'treated by the deceased as a child of the family', must be construed as treatment as a minor or a dependent child of the family and that it must be directly referable to the marriage, which means that it must have occurred after the marriage had taken place. I do not agree that the words in s 1(1)(d) require such a narrow construction. 'Child', for the purposes of s 1, clearly includes an adult child. One of the persons who may apply by virtue of s 1(1)(c) is 'a child of the deceased', and it cannot be suggested that in that context 'child' must be limited to a minor or dependent child. In s 1(1)(c) 'child' relates to the relationship between the deceased and the applicant. In my judgment this is precisely the same in s 1(1)(d) of the Act, and no different meaning should be given to the word 'child' in the context of the words 'treated by the deceased as a child of the family'. It is again a matter concerning the nature of the relationship between the deceased and the applicant, and it does not follow that treatment necessarily refers to the treatment of the applicant by the deceased as a minor or dependent child. In this case the acknowledgment by the deceased of his own role of grandfather to the plaintiff's children, the confidences as to his property and financial affairs which he placed in the plaintiff and his dependence on the plaintiff to care for him in his last illness are examples of the deceased's treatment of the plaintiff as a child, albeit an adult child, of the family. All these things are part of the privileges and duties of two persons who, in regard to each other, stand in the relationship of parent and child; it is the existence of that relationship that enables the plaintiff to apply under s 1(1)(d) of the Act.

In **Re Leach** [1985] 2 All ER 754, [1985] 3 WLR 413, the deceased's 53 year old stepdaughter applied for provision from the estate as a 'child of the family' notwithstanding the fact that the deceased's relationship with her had only become quasi-parental after the death of her father. The Court of Appeal held that she was nevertheless entitled to apply under s 1(1)(d), Slade LJ saying at p 760:

The phrase used is not 'during the subsistence of that marriage'; it is the wider phrase 'in relation to that marriage'. It seems to me that the treatment of an applicant by a surviving spouse after the death of the other spouse may be a relevant factor in deciding whether the applicant qualifies under s 1(1)(d), provided that such treatment is referable to or, as the deputy judge puts it, 'stems from' the marriage.

---

6. P 256 post.

(e) Any other person being maintained by the deceased

This was the other novel class of applicant and more controversial than the preceding class for it let in for the first time the possibility of claims by paramours.[7]

Law Commission: Second Report on Family Property[8]

Should the class of applicants be further extended?
90.   It is arguable that persons who have no rights enforceable against the deceased during his lifetime ought not to be entitled to claim family provision from the estate. However, where a deceased person was contributing to someone's maintenance before his death his failure to make provision for that person may have been accidental or unintentional; he may have made no will; his will may be stale; or his will may have operated in a way he did not anticipate (for example, the specific legacies may exhaust the estate and leave no residue). In these cases an order for family provision would be doing for the deceased what he might reasonably be assumed to have wished to do himself. This argument carries particular weight where the 'dependant' is a person with whom the deceased has been cohabiting. If the deceased dies intestate the person with whom he has been living has no claim; whereas any illegitimate children have rights under the rules of intestate succession as well as a claim to family provision.

91.   Another argument against any extension of the class of applicants is that the deceased may have been prepared to contribute to someone's support during his lifetime while he had a reasonable income, but he might be unwilling that the burden should be imposed on his estate to the possible detriment of his wife and children. However, though we accept that this position may arise in some cases, we think the objection fails to take account of two matters. The first is that, in any event, the court may always take into consideration the interests of other applicants and beneficiaries. The second is that it could (and should) be made clear that, if those who were dependent on the deceased at the time of his death are to be entitled to apply for family provision, the court should give special consideration to the basis upon which the deceased undertook responsibility for that person's maintenance.[9]

Jelley v Iliffe [1981] Fam 128, [1981] 2 All ER 29, CA; Stephenson, Cumming-Bruce and Griffiths LJJ

The applicant, a widower, and the deceased, a widow, lived together in the deceased's house for eight years until the deceased's death, pooling their resources, including their pensions, to meet their common living expenses. He provided some furniture, looked after the garden and did household jobs; she provided the rent-free accommodation and cooked and washed for him. He applied for reasonable provision from her estate under s 1(1)(e) of the Inheritance (Provision for Family and Dependants) Act 1975 as she had made no provision for him in her will. The registrar struck out his application on the ground that the evidence in support of it disclosed no reasonable cause of action and Bush J upheld the registrar's decision. The applicant appealed.
Held: Appeal allowed. There was an arguable case that he was being

---

7. 'The mistresses' charter . . . a blow to family life and to the Institution of Marriage' HC Deb, Vol 898, Col 172.
8. 'Family Provision on Death' (1974) Law Com 61.
9. See 1 (PFD)A 1975, s 3(4) p 256 post.

maintained by the deceased and the matter should be allowed to proceed to trial.

Stephenson LJ: In answering the question whether the statute gives the appellant the right which the registrar and judge have denied him we, like the statute, are concerned with dependency for support of that kind well known to family law as maintenance. What may be called matrimonial maintenance is mainly, if not exclusively, of two kinds, financial provision or the provision of accommodation in a house. A man maintains his wife and children by providing them with somewhere to live or by paying contributions of money or by both, and if he does that he maintains them, he assumes the responsibility of maintaining them and he discharges that responsibility as long as he continues to do so. That it seems to me is the background against which we have to consider the relevant provisions of the Act extending the right to apply for financial provision to those who have been maintained by a deceased person during his lifetime and immediately before his death, and to consider counsel's submissions on those provisions and their true interpretation.

I respectfully agree with Sir Robert Megarry V-C for the reasons that he gives in his exposition of the statute in *Re Beaumont* [1980] 1 All ER 266 at 270–276, [1980] Ch 444 at 450–458, on all points but one. (1) The deeming provision in s 1(3) exhaustively or exclusively defines what s 1(1)(e) means by 'being maintained', and does not include in those words a state of affairs which is not within s 1(1)(e) and would extend its ambit. To qualify within s 1(1)(e) a claimant must satisfy s 1(3) as if before the words 'if the deceased' the draftsman of s 1(3) had inserted the world 'only'. (2) In considering whether a person is being maintained 'immediately before the death of the deceased' it is the settled basis or general arrangement between the parties as regards maintenance during the lifetime of the deceased which has to be looked at, not the actual, perhaps fluctuating variation of it which exists immediately before his or her death. It is, I think, not disputed that a relationship of dependence which has persisted for years will not be defeated by its termination during a few weeks of mortal sickness. (3) Like Sir Robert Megarry V-C I reject the contention that the parenthetical words in s 1(3), 'otherwise than for full valuable consideration', apply only to full valuable consideration under a contract and agree with him and with Arnold J[10] that they apply whenever full valuable consideration is given, whether under contract or otherwise. . . .

Where, however, I feel bound to part company from Sir Robert Megarry V-C is in his interpretation of assumption of responsibility for the maintenance of the supported person. I do not question his opinion that the requirement of s 3(4) that the court should 'have regard to the extent to which and the basis upon which the deceased assumed responsibility for the maintenance of the applicant, and to the length of time for which the deceased discharged that responsibility' implies or 'assumes' (in another sense) that at the first stage, when the court is considering the applicant's right to apply under s 1(1)(e), he must prove that the deceased did 'assume responsibility' for his maintenance. But I cannot, with respect, agree with him, in spite of counsel's submission for the respondents that I should, that the bare fact of maintenance raises no presumption that responsibility for it has been assumed. I am of opinion that it generally does. I would not disagree with Sir Robert Megarry V-C when he says ([1980] 1 All ER 266 at 276, [1980] Ch 444 at 458):

'The word assumes . . . seems to me to indicate that there must be some act or acts which demonstrate an undertaking of responsibility or the taking of the responsibility on oneself.'

And the Act, here and elsewhere, has drawn a distinction between assuming and discharging responsibility. But how better or more clearly can one take on or discharge responsibility for maintenance than by actually maintaining? A man may say he is going to support another and not do it, promise to pay school fees but not pay; but if he does pay them, has he not both assumed and discharged responsibility for them whether or not he covenants to pay them? Surely A shoulders the burden of supporting B by

---

10. *Re Wilkinson* [1978] Fam 22, [1978] 1 All ER 221.

supporting him. If B is A's mistress and he maintains her by providing her with accommodation or money or both, has he not assumed or taken on responsibility for her maintenance? If it be said, as counsel for the respondents submitted, that he has a moral obligation which makes the assumption of responsibility easier to presume, is the presumption nevertheless not to be made where provision of a share in a home and/or financial support is made out of the donor's generosity of heart to a poor relation or friend? . . . I do not read the Act as expressing so limited a legislative intention. Its object is surely to remedy, wherever reasonably possible, the injustice of one, who has been put by a deceased person in a position of dependency on him, being deprived of any financial support, either by accident or by design of the deceased, after his death. To leave a dependant, to whom no legal or moral obligation is owed, unprovided for after death may not entitle the dependant to much or indeed any financial provision in all the circumstances, but he is not disentitled from applying for such provision if he can prove that the deceased by his conduct made him dependent on the deceased for maintenance, whether intentionally or not.

Accordingly, I am of opinion that the court has to consider whether the deceased, otherwise than for valuable consideration (and irrespective of the existence of any contract), was in fact making a substantial contribution in money or money's worth towards the reasonable needs of the appellant, on a settled basis or arrangement which either was still in force immediately before the deceased's death or would have lasted until her death but for the approach of death and the consequent inability of either party to continue to carry out the arrangement. To discover whether the deceased was making such a contribution the court has to balance what she was contributing against what he was contributing, and if there is any doubt about the balance tipping in favour of hers being the greater contribution, the matter must, in my opinion, go to trial. If, however, the balance is bound to come down in favour of his being the greater contribution, or if the contributions are clearly equal, there is no dependency of him on her, either because she depended on him or there was mutual dependency between them, and his application should be struck out now as bound to fail. Where what B does gives full valuable consideration for the substantial contribution A makes, there is no dependency and B's claim under the Act should be struck out. . . .

Can this difficult operation be carried out at this stage . . .? I have no doubt that the provision of free accommodation in these times is a substantial contribution to the needs of the accommodated and was a substantial contribution to the appellant's reasonable needs. If in describing the deceased as one who 'happens to own the house in which they live' the judge intended to treat that as an accidental and therefore insignificant circumstance, I cannot agree with him. It might qualify the appellant to pursue his claim because the pooling of their incomes and the remaining contributions of aid and comfort which each gave to the other cancelled out. In my judgment the statute, whether literally or purposively construed, requires the court to take a broad commonsense view of the question whether the applicant for the statutory relief was a dependant of the deceased before death and the ordinary man's answer to what, on this approach, is the right question, 'Was this man dependent on this woman during her lifetime for maintenance or did he give as good as he got?' might be (without regard to nice differences between the facts in this and other cases) that each was partly dependent on the other and he gave her, in companionship (whether or not it amounted to consortium) and help in money and in furnishing her house and caring for her and her house and garden, as much as she gave him in companionship and rent-free accommodation and money and looking after him by cooking and cleaning.

3   Standard of provision

Under the earlier law, the court's powers were restricted to making reasonable provision for the maintenance of applicants.[11] On the recommendation of the

---

11. Inheritance (Family Provision) Act 1938, s 1(1).

Law Commission, the 1975 Act removed the limitation to maintenance for spouse applicants only, although a saving provision was included for former or judicially separated spouses denied the opportunity of claiming a share of the family assets in matrimonial proceedings because of the supervening death of the other spouse.

Law Commission: Second Report on Family Property[12]

Should the aim of family provision be extended beyond maintenance?

14. . . . Recent decisions[13] have emphasised that maintenance is no longer the principal consideration in fixing the amount of financial provision on divorce and that the courts have the widest possible powers under Part II of the Matrimonial Causes Act 1973 to effect an equitable sharing of the family assets. We are of the opinion that the court's powers to order financial provision for a surviving spouse should be equally wide.

Inheritance (Provision for Family and Dependants) Act 1975

1. Application for financial provision from deceased's estate

(2) In this Act 'reasonable financial provision'—

  (a) in the case of an application made by virtue of subsection (1)(a) above by the husband or wife of the deceased (except where the marriage with the deceased was the subject of a decree of judicial separation and at the date of death the decree was in force and the separation was continuing), means such financial provision as it would be reasonable[14] in all the circumstances of the case for a husband or wife to receive, whether or not that provision is required for his or her maintenance;

  (b) in the case of any other application made by virtue of subsection (1) above, means such financial provision as it would be reasonable[14] in all the circumstances of the case for the applicant to receive for his maintenance.

14. Provision as to cases where no financial relief was granted in divorce proceedings etc

(1) Where within twelve months from the date on which a decree of divorce or nullity of marriage has been made absolute or a decree of judicial separation has been granted, a party to the marriage dies and—

  (a) an application for a financial provision order under section 23 of the Matrimonial Causes Act 1973 or a property adjustment order under section 24 of that Act has not been made by the other party to that marriage, or

  (b) such an application has been made but the proceedings thereon have not been determined at the time of the death of the deceased, then, if an application for an order under section 2 of this Act is made by that other party, the court shall, notwithstanding anything in section 1 or section 3 of this Act, have power, if it thinks it just to do so, to treat that party for the purposes of that application as if the decree of divorce or nullity of marriage had not been made absolute or the decree of judicial separation had not been granted, as the case may be.

(2) This section shall not apply in relation to a decree of judicial separation unless at the date of the death of the deceased the decree was in force and the separation was continuing.

---

12. 'Family Provision on Death' (1974) Law Com 61.
13. *Watchel v Watchel* [1973] Fam 72, [1973] 1 All ER 829, *Trippas v Trippas* [1973] Fam 134, [1973] 2 All ER 1, *Harnett v Harnett* [1974] 1 All ER 764, [1974] 1 WLR 219.
14. The test for reasonableness is objective not subjective, as recommended by the Law Commission: Law Com 61 para 101. See s 3(5) p 256 post and *Re Coventry* [1980] Ch 461 at 488, [1979] 3 All ER 815 at 822.

Re Besterman [1984] 2 All ER 656, [1984] 3 WLR 280, CA; Oliver, Fox and Goff LJJ

The plaintiff was the widow of the deceased who had left an estate of £1½ million; they had been married for 18 years during which she had enjoyed a very high standard of living. By his will he left her only his personal chattels and a life interest in a holding of War Loan which would produce an income of about £3,500 pa; the bulk of his estate was left to Oxford University. He had had no obligations to anyone other than his wife and she had no financial resources of her own other than her state pension. She applied for further provision from the estate; pending the hearing of the application, an interim order [15] of £75,000 was made to enable her to buy a smaller house and vacate the matrimonial home (worth £350,000). The trial judge awarded her further capital worth £125,000 and he also enlarged her interest in the War Loan to an absolute interest, worth £28,000, on the basis that these sums could then be used inter alia to purchase an annuity which would bring her total income up to £17,000 pa. She appealed on the grounds that the provision was too low as it was much less than she might have received had the marriage ended in divorce, and that the judge had misdirected himself in adopting as a criterion of reasonable financial provision the obligation of maintenance.
Held: Appeal allowed; the capital award would be increased from £125,000 to £275,000, so making an overall provision for her of £378,000.

Oliver LJ: The fundamental flaw in the judge's calculation appears from the following passage from the judgment which, I think, demonstrates his view that even in the case of the surviving spouse his or her needs for maintenance are the limiting factor or at least the paramount factor. He should I think have looked at the position as a whole for the purpose of assessing what a reasonable provision would be in all the circumstances for the widow of a millionaire with no obligations to anyone else, and, indeed, a millionaire who had expressed himself as desirous of making very ample provision for her. What he did in fact, as appears from the passage which I am about to quote, was to start from the position that particularly in the case of a large estate (and I am not quite clear why the size of the estate should be of particular relevance for this purpose) the court should start from the position that the provisions of the will must be upheld except to the extent that they are displaced by the obligation to maintain the widow during her lifetime. It was that which led him to adopt as the basis for his calculation the price of what he considered an adequate annuity and which led him to provide a figure which, for my part, I think was, in all the circumstances of this case, a good deal too low. What he said was this:

> 'I do not think that reasonable financial provision for [the plaintiff] within the 1975 Act requires the provision of so large a sum as [counsel for the plaintiff] suggested. The effect of that would be to make provision for [the plaintiff] and as well to enable her to benefit those who come after her. The 1975 Act requires no more than that provision be made for the applicant alone. In such a case as this, where a large estate is concerned and both sides desire a once and for all lump sum payment, the order made should ensure, if possible, that provision be made in a way that will interfere as little as possible with the deceased's testamentary dispositions. That means that in this case the applicant should be provided with a sum sufficient to enable her to purchase an appropriate annuity.'

In my judgment, therefore, the judge misdirected himself and this is, therefore, a case in which it is open to this court to review the exercise of his discretion and to form its own conclusion.

What then is to be done? In the first place, I think that we must give much greater weight than did the judge to the provision which the plaintiff might have expected to get

---

15. See 1(PFD)A 1975, s 5, p 260 n 4 post.

if the marriage had ended in divorce. What that is is a matter of speculation, but I would not seriously quarrel with the suggestion of counsel for the plaintiff that an overall sum of £350,000 could not be considered excessive. At the same time I do not think that I can accept that because the marriage did not terminate by divorce in fact, therefore and a fortiori, she must be entitled to more; counsel for the plaintiff puts it (perhaps rather arbitrarily) at £100,000 more. As I have pointed out, however odd the result may be, the two Acts are not necessarily directed to achieving the same result and under this Act the overall criterion is what is reasonable.

I also think that the absence, which is inherent in a lump sum order, of an opportunity to return to the court does mean that, in assessing the lump sum, the court must take rather greater account than might otherwise be the case of contingencies and inflation. I accept the submission of junior counsel for the plaintiff that reasonable provision, in the case of a very large estate such as this and a wholly blameless widow who is incapable of supporting herself, should be such as to relieve her of anxiety for the future. . . . I take the view that reasonable provision in this case would dictate that, in addition to the secure roof over her head, the widow should have available to her a capital sum of sufficient size not simply to enable her to purchase an adequate annuity according to present day needs, but to provide her with the income which she needs and a cushion in the form of available capital which will enable her to meet all reasonably foreseeable contingencies. What that sum is is a matter of judgment but I think that in assessing it we are entitled to take into account that, though the plaintiff is quite content with her present residence, it is in fact somewhat more modest than she might be thought to be entitled to expect to be provided for her by a husband in the financial position of the deceased. In confirming the title to the house and enlarging the life interest in the War Loan stock the judge was plainly right. It was also plainly right for the executors to forego any claim to recover the £31,000 expended between the death and the interim order, for this is, in effect, merely interim maintenance, although the judge should not, in my judgment, have brought this in to his calculation of the overall capital provision. In addition to that part of his order, however, which I would allow to stand, I would direct the payment of a capital sum which, on a broad calculation, will when invested produce a gross income broadly sufficient to meet the widow's likely needs, a sum which will leave it open to her, if she wishes to increase her income, to do so by an annuity purchase if she is so advised, but which will also enable her to have a substantial and safe fund of capital with which to supplement her income if need arises. One hopes that it will not be necessary for her to do so to any great extent, but she is not a young woman and one bears in mind that in case of prolonged illness or other emergency very substantial capital expenditure might well become necessary. I would accordingly increase the capital sum ordered by the judge from £125,000 to £275,000, thus making an overall provision for the plaintiff of £378,000 made up as follows: house, £75,000; War Loan £28,000; capital £275,000.

In **Re Coventry** [1980] Ch 461, [1979] 3 All ER 815, the applicant was the deceased's son whose claim under the Act was therefore limited to maintenance. The Court of Appeal considered the meaning of the word, Goff LJ saying at p 819:

There have been a number of cases under the Inheritance (Family Provision) Act 1938, previously in force, and also some cases from sister jurisdictions, which have dealt with the meaning of 'maintenance'. In particular, in this country there is *Re E* ([1966] 2 All ER 44, [1966] 1 WLR 709) in which Stamp J said that the purpose was not to keep a person above the breadline, but to provide reasonable maintenance in all the circumstances. If I may say so with respect, 'breadline' there would be more accurately described as 'subsistence level'. Then there was a case in this court, *Millward v Shenton*[16] ([1972] 2 All ER 1025, [1972] 1 WLR 711). I think I need only refer to one of the overseas reports, *Re Duranceau*, ([1952] 3 DLR 714 at p 720) where in somewhat poetic

---

16. See p 1028 where Lord Denning MR expressed the view that 'maintenance' might, depending on the circumstances, include the provision of a television set, a car, or even a better house.

language, the court said that the question is: 'Is the provision sufficient to enable the dependant to live neither luxuriously nor miserably, but decently and comfortably according to his or her station in life?'

What is proper maintenance must in all cases depend on all the facts and circumstances of the particular case being considered at the time, but I think it is clear on the one hand that one must not put too limited a meaning on it: it does not mean just enough to enable a person to get by, on the other hand it does not mean anything that may be regarded as reasonably desirable for his general benefit or welfare.

In **Re Dennis** [1981] 2 All ER 140, the applicant, described by Browne-Wilkinson J as a 'spendthrift drifter', had received substantial gifts from his wealthy father during his father's lifetime. In view of the extent of these gifts, his claim for provision from his father's estate was limited to the amount of the capital transfer tax,[17] some £50,000, which he was liable to pay in respect of them. He claimed that without such provision he would be made bankrupt by the Inland Revenue. Browne-Wilkinson J was unimpressed, however, saying at p 145:

The word 'maintenance' connotes only payments which, directly or indirectly, enable the applicant in the future to discharge the cost of his daily living at whatever standard of living is appropriate to him. The provision that is to be made is to meet recurring expenses, being expenses of living of an income nature. The provision can be by way of a lump sum, for example, to buy a house in which the applicant can be housed, thereby relieving him *pro tanto* of income expenditure. Nor am I suggesting that there may not be cases in which payment of existing debts may not be appropriate as a maintenance payment; for example, to pay the debts of the applicant in order to enable him to continue to carry on a profit-making business or profession may well be for his maintenance.

But no such case is made here. It is not suggested that the payment of capital transfer tax will do anything to help the applicant's future maintenance. It may save him from bankruptcy, but there is no evidence that being made bankrupt is going to prevent the applicant from earning his living in the kinds of ways he has sporadically chosen to do in the past. . . . Therefore in my judgment, he has not shown an arguable case that he is making a claim for maintenance which the court could allow, since the payment of the capital transfer tax would not in any way, direct or indirect, contribute to the cost of his future living.[18]

4   Matters to be taken into account

In deciding whether reasonable financial provision has been made for the applicant and if not, what, if any, provision the court should award, the court is specifically directed to take into account a number of matters, some of which apply to all applicants, some to particular classes of applicant.

Inheritance (Provision for Family and Dependants) Act 1975

3.   Matters to which court is to have regard in exercising powers under s 2

(1) Where an application is made for an order under section 2 of this Act, the court shall, in determining whether the disposition of the deceased's estate effected by his will or the

---

17. Now inheritance tax; see Ch 16 ante.
18. As the applicant had failed to make out an arguable case, Browne-Wilkinson J held that his application for leave to bring proceedings out of time should be dismissed.

law relating to intestacy, or the combination of his will and that law, is such as to make reasonable financial provision for the applicant and, if the court considers that reasonable financial provision has not been made, in determining whether and in what manner it shall exercise its powers under that section, have regard to the following matters, that is to say—

- (a) the financial resources[19] and financial needs which the applicant has or is likely to have in the foreseeable future;
- (b) the financial resources and financial needs which any other applicant for an order under section 2 of this Act has or is likely to have in the foreseeable future;
- (c) the financial resources and financial needs which any beneficiary of the estate of the deceased has or is likely to have in the foreseeable future.[20]
- (d) any obligations and responsibilities[1] which the deceased had towards any applicant for an order under the said section 2 or towards any beneficiary of the estate of the deceased;
- (e) the size and nature of the net estate of the deceased;[2]
- (f) any physical or mental disability[3] of any applicant for an order under the said section 2 or any beneficiary of the estate of the deceased;
- (g) any other matter, including the conduct[4] of the applicant or any other person, which in the circumstances of the case the court may consider relevant.[5]

(2) Without prejudice to the generality of paragraph (g) of subsection (1) above, where an application for an order under section 2 of this Act is made by virtue of section 1(1)(a) or 1(1)(b) of this Act, the court shall, in addition to the matters specifically mentioned in paragraphs (a) to (f) of that subsection, have regard to—

- (a) the age of the applicant and the duration of the marriage;[6]
- (b) the contribution made by the applicant to the welfare of the family of the deceased, including any contribution made by looking after the home or caring for the family;[7]

and, in the case of an application by the wife or husband of the deceased, the court shall also, unless at the date of death a decree of judicial separation was in force and the separation was continuing, have regard to the provision which the applicant might reasonably have expected to receive if on the day on which the deceased died the

---

19. This includes the availability of state aid including rent and rate rebates, see eg *Re E* [1966] 2 All ER 44, [1966] 1 WLR 709 where Stamp J said at p 48, that where the estate was a small one, the applicant was in receipt of social security benefits and the only result of provision from the estate would be to reduce those benefits, it would not be unreasonable to make no provision for the applicant; aliter if the estate were large.
20. See eg *Malone v Harrison* [1979] 1 WLR 1353.
1. See eg *Re Coventry* [1980] Ch 461 at 489 [1979] 3 All ER 815 at 823 where the lack of any moral obligation on the father to maintain his adult independent son was a decisive factor in the failure of the son's claim. See also *Re Besterman*, p 252 ante.
2. See p 258 post for the definition of 'net estate'. Judges have frequently expressed their reluctance to interfere with small estates where the costs of the litigation would often swallow up a substantial part of the estate, if not the whole of it, see eg *Re E* [1966] 2 All ER 44 at 48, [1966] 1 WLR 709 at 715. In *Re Fullard* [1981] 2 All ER 796 at 799, [1981] 3 WLR 743 at 745, Ormrod LJ pointedly suggested that judges should reconsider the practice of ordering the costs of both parties to be paid out of a small estate, particularly the costs of an unsuccessful applicant.
3. See eg *Millward v Shenton* [1972] 2 All ER 1025, [1972] 1 WLR 711.
4. See eg *Re Snoek* (1983) 13 Fam Law 18.
5. Eg the terms of any financial settlement reached on the divorce when the applicant is a former spouse, *Re Fullard* [1981] 2 All ER 796 at 799, [1981] 3 WLR 743 at 746, the source of the deceased's funds, *Sivyer v Sivyer* [1967] 3 All ER 429, [1967] 1 WLR 1482, where the whole of the estate was derived from the deceased's second wife but was to pass on his intestacy to his third wife. A daughter of the second wife was the claimant and was awarded £500 more than would otherwise have been the case but for this factor. See also *Re Wood* (1982) 79 LSG 774.
6. See eg *Re Fullard* p 244 ante.
7. See eg *Re Rowlands* [1984] FLR 813 where the marriage had lasted for 62 years but the deceased and his widow had lived apart for all but the first 19; the court took into account the contribution she had made to bringing up the family in those early years in awarding her a modest provision of £3,000 out of the £100,000 estate.

marriage, instead of being terminated by death, had been terminated by a decree of divorce.[8]

(3) Without prejudice to the generality of paragraph (g) of subsection (1) above, where an application for an order under section 2 of this Act is made by virtue of section 1(1)(c) or 1(1)(d) of this Act, the court shall, in addition to the matters specifically mentioned in paragraphs (a) to (f) of that subsection, have regard to the manner in which the applicant was being or in which he might expect to be educated or trained, and where the application is made by virtue of section 1(1)(d) the court shall also have regard—

  (a) to whether the deceased had assumed any responsibility for the applicant's maintenance and, if so, to the extent to which and the basis upon which the deceased assumed that responsibility and to the length of time for which the deceased discharged that responsibility;

  (b) to whether in assuming and discharging that responsibility the deceased did so knowing that the applicant was not his own child;

  (c) to the liability of any other person to maintain the applicant.

(4) Without prejudice to the generality of paragraph (g) of subsection (1) above, where an application for an order under section 2 of this Act is made by virtue of section 1(1)(e) of this Act, the court shall, in addition to the matters specifically mentioned in paragraphs (a) to (f) of that subsection, have regard to the extent to which and the basis upon which the deceased assumed responsibility for the maintenance of the applicant, and to the length of time for which the deceased discharged that responsibility.[9]

(5) In considering the matters to which the court is required to have regard under this section, the court shall take into account the facts as known to the court at the date of the hearing.[10]

(6) In considering the financial resources of any person for the purposes of this section the court shall take into account his earning capacity[11] and in considering the financial needs of any person for the purposes of this section the court shall take into account his financial obligations and responsibilities.

Re Crawford [1983] FLR 273, Fam D; Eastham J

The deceased had made no provision in his will for the plaintiff, his first wife, to whom he had been paying maintenance in his lifetime: she claimed provision from his estate under s 1(1)(b). The deceased's children and second wife were well provided for by the will, by benefits from his firm's pension scheme and by lifetime gifts from the deceased which included a lump sum payment he had received on retirement amounting to almost £70,000 and which he had paid into various joint accounts in the names of himself and his second wife.

Held: Having regard to the relevant s 3 factors, the plaintiff should receive a lump sum payment of £35,000, the deceased's half share in the joint accounts being treated as part of the net estate for this purpose.[12]

---

8. Reflecting the concern felt by the Law Commission to remove the discrepancy between the position of the widow or widower and that of the divorced spouse, see Law Com 52, para 41. See eg *Re Besterman*, p 252 ante, *Re Bunning* [1984] 3 All ER 1, [1984] 3 WLR 265.

9. Eg *Malone v Harrison* [1979] 1 WLR 1353, where a substantial factor in the court's award to the applicant, one of the deceased's mistresses, was the deceased's assumption of full responsibility for her maintenance for 12 years before his death. See *Jelley v Iliffe*, p 248 ante, for the qualifying effect of this subsection on s 1(1)(e).

10. As recommended by the Law Commission, Law Com 61 paras 102–104. The facts must be properly proved if they are to be 'known to the court', see *Re Coventry* [1980] Ch 461 at 491, [1979] 3 All ER 815 at 825.

11. See eg *Re Ducksbury* [1966] 2 All ER 374, [1966] 1 WLR 1226, where the applicant, although a trained secretary, chose to eke out a meagre living as an artist.

12. See s 9, p 260 post.

Eastham J: In order to determine whether the disposition of the deceased's estate effected by his will is such as to make or not to make reasonable financial provision for the plaintiff, the court has to have regard to the seven matters set out in s 3(1)(a) to (g), both inclusive, and, as this plaintiff is a s 1(1)(b) claimant, to the two further matters set out in s 3(2)(a) and (b). It is clear beyond doubt from a cursory glance at those nine considerations that the will of the deceased did not make reasonable financial provision for the plaintiff. Indeed the first defendant in her affidavit of 16 January 1981, sworn in her capacity as a beneficiary, stated that she conceded '. . . that it would be proper for the court to make some financial provision for the plaintiff out of my husband's estate'. She goes on to submit that it should be a very modest provision. . . .

Considering those matters, first of all s 3(1)(a), the plaintiff's financial resources are extremely slim. She has her house; she has £1,500 worth of capital; she has her supplementary benefit which I have described, which is likely to terminate once I make an order, and next year she will receive the old age pension. According to her affidavit her expenses only total £2,267 per annum; but these have been her expenses for the last 2 years when she was receiving nothing from the estate and using her small amount of capital in order to exist; and it was conceded in argument that those expenses are in fact subsistence-level expenses only. She plainly needs reasonable maintenance for the rest of her life.

Paragraph (b) is not applicable on the facts of this case. Paragraph (c), the resources and needs of the beneficiaries, the widow, the first defendant, and the children, the fourth and fifth defendants, are well placed. She has a half share in her house and a life interest in the other half; she has free capital, on any showing, of £100,000 and a pension which is now over £10,000 per annum. The children have pensions which are more than sufficient to cover their full-time education in the private sector; and so their position is in striking contrast to the position of the plaintiff.

Under (d), each of the two marriages was a long marriage, and the deceased, in my judgment, owed responsibilities towards the plaintiff and to the first defendant and to the two children of that marriage.

Under (e), the size and nature of the net estate of the deceased, that is either £30, 890 excluding s 9 or £65,774 if I exercise my discretion and bring in the whole of the deceased's half share in the lump sum.

Paragraph (f) is not applicable and (g), conduct, does not arise in this case, but I bear in mind the amounts that the deceased paid during the last year of his life by way of periodic payments to the plaintiff.

That concludes all the matters set out in s 3(1)(a) to (g), both inclusive, I now turn to s 3(2)(a) and (b), as the plaintiff is a claimant under s 1(1)(b), and I have to consider the age of the applicant and the duration of the marriage under para (a). She is 59 years of age; the marriage lasted for 24 years, and her life expectancy is 21.97 years on the actuarial table. Under para (b) I have to look to the contribution made by her to the welfare of the family of the deceased, including any contribution made by looking after the home or caring for the family. Under that head it is quite clear that for 24 years she looked after the deceased's home and brought up their only child, Alistair.

Finally, under s 3(6), in considering the financial resources of any person for the purpose of the section the court has to take into account his or her earning capacity. In my judgment, on the facts of this case, the fact that this plaintiff only worked during the war for a couple of years as a shorthand-typist, in my judgment her earning capacity is nil at the age of 59. She was never expected to work by the deceased and I see no reason why at her age she should go out and seek paid employment.

Those are the considerations that I have to bear in mind, and having regard to all the matters set out in s 3, bearing in mind further that she will have expenses in maintaining her property which is not in a very good condition at the moment, and replacing in due course her P registration Hillman Imp car which has done some 59,000-odd miles, I have come to the conclusion that a sum of approximately £4,000 per annum, on the basis of an escalation of 5% interest per annum compound, amounts to reasonable financial provision, and this involves the purchase of an annuity costing £35,000. Mr Marten accepted that any lump sum might properly come out of the deceased's half-share of the moneys in the joint account which would largely leave unaffected the provisions of the deceased's will so far as beneficiaries are concerned, and I therefore order, pursuant to the discretion vested in me under s 9, that the sum of £35,000 being a large part of the deceased's half share, be treated under s 9 as part of his net estate, and I order reasonable financial provision in favour of the plaintiff amounting, under s 2, to the lump sum of £35,000.

5   The net estate

In deciding whether reasonable financial provision has been made for the applicant and if not, as to the nature and amount of provision that should be made, close regard must be paid to the 'net estate' of the deceased out of which any provision will have to come.

(a) Definition

Inheritance (Provision for Family and Dependants) Act 1975

25.   Interpretation
(1) In this Act—... 'net estate,' in relation to a deceased person, means—
  (a) all property of which the deceased had power to dispose by his will (otherwise than by virtue of a special power of appointment) less the amount of his funeral, testamentary and administration expenses, debts and liabilities including any inheritance tax payable out of his estate on his death;
  (b) any property in respect of which the deceased held a general power of appointment (not being a power exercisable by will) which has not been exercised; [13]
  (c) any sum of money or other property which is treated for the purposes of this Act as part of the net estate of the deceased by virtue of section 8(1) [14] or (2) [15] of this Act;
  (d) any property which is treated for the purposes of this Act as part of the net estate of the deceased by virtue of an order made under section 9 of the Act; [16]
  (e) any sum of money or other property which is, by reason of a disposition or contract made by the deceased, ordered under section 10 or 11 of this Act to be provided for the purpose of the making of financial provision under this Act; [17]

(b) Nominated property

Inheritance (Provision for Family and Dependants) Act 1975

8.   Property treated as part of 'net estate'
(1) Where a deceased person has in accordance with the provisions of any enactment nominated any person to receive any sum of money or other property on his death and that nomination is in force at the time of his death, that sum of money, after deducting therefrom any inheritance tax payable in respect thereof, or that other property, to the extent of the value thereof at the date of the death of the deceased after deducting

---

13. Property over which the deceased had a special power of appointment was also considered by the Law Commission but rejected: Law Com 61, paras 129–133.
14. See post.
15. See p 259 post.
16. See p 260 post.
17. See p 265 post.

therefrom any inheritance tax so payable, shall be treated for the purposes of this Act as part of the net estate of the deceased; but this subsection shall not render any person liable for having paid that sum or transferred that other property to the person named in the nomination in accordance with the directions given in the nomination.

In **Re Cairnes** [1983] FLR 225, an attempt was made to argue that a non statutory nomination fell within the terms of the subsection. The deceased, an employee of TWA and a member of his company's pension scheme, had nominated in favour of his wife the benefits due on his death under the scheme. She subsequently divorced him but they remained on friendly terms and he never attempted to cancel the nomination. When he died, his mistress applied for provision from his estate, the value of which was small apart from the death benefit provided by the pension scheme. Holding that this could not be construed as part of the 'net estate' under s 8(1)[18] Anthony Lincoln J said at p 231:

> The conditions are wholly satisfied in this case save as to the words 'in accordance with the provisions of any enactment'. This nomination was not made in accordance with the provisions of any statute, any Act of Parliament. Mr Teverson (counsel for the applicant) argues that the word 'enactment' should be construed liberally to include the life assurance scheme rules drafted in accordance with the trust's scheme arranged by TWA. It is true that the word 'enactment' has in the decided cases been applied on occasions to regulations made in pursuance of an enactment and I can see that if the rules had been made in accordance with some statute, though themselves not a statute, then of course the condition of s 8(1) would be satisfied, but I cannot see anything in the authorities that have been presented to me which suggests that those authorities have widened the meaning of the word 'enactment' to embrace a scheme and a set of rules of this kind . . . the words of s 8(1) are very plain and Parliament seems to have stopped short of extending its protection to such schemes; it seems to me that the death benefit in this case does not fall into the residue of the net estate for the purposes of the 1975 Act.[19]

(c) Donationes mortis causa

Inheritance (Provision for Family and Dependants) Act 1975

8. Property treated as part of 'net estate'

(2) Where any sum of money or other property is received by a person as a donatio mortis causa[20] made by a deceased person, that sum of money, after deducting therefrom any inheritance tax payable thereon, or that other property, to the extent of the value thereof at the date of the death of the deceased after deducting therefrom any inheritance tax so payable, shall be treated for the purposes of this Act as part of the net estate of the deceased; but this subsection shall not render any person liable for having paid that sum or transferred that other property in order to give effect to that donatio mortis causa.

---

18. It was also argued that the death benefit fell within the definition by virtue of s 25(1)(a), p 258 ante, but the argument was rejected because of the scheme's restriction on the powers of members to dispose of death benefits, see [1983] FLR 225 at 230.
19. The application of the Act to death benefits payable under occupational pension schemes was specifically considered by the Law Commission but rejected as imposing too great a burden on the trustees of the scheme, 'who can confidently be expected to act conscientiously': Law Com 61 para 213. Cf Succession Law Reform Act 1977 (Ontario), s 79(1)(g) which brings such benefit within the net estate for the purpose of family provision claims.
20. A gift in contemplation of death: see Pettit pp 100–105.

(d) Joint tenancies[1]

Inheritance (Provision for Family and Dependants) Act 1975

9. Property held on a joint tenancy

(1) Where a deceased person was immediately before his death beneficially entitled to a joint tenancy of any property, then, if, before the end of the period of six months from the date on which representation with respect to the estate of the deceased was first taken out, an application is made for an order under section 2 of this Act, the court for the purpose of facilitating the making of financial provision for the applicant under this Act may[2] order that the deceased's severable share of that property, at the value thereof immediately before his death, shall, to such extent as appears to the court to be just in all the circumstances of the case, be treated for the purposes of this Act as part of the net estate of the deceased.[3]

(2) In determining the extent to which any severable share is to be treated as part of the net estate of the deceased by virtue of an order under subsection (1) above, the court shall have regard to any inheritance tax payable in respect of that severable share.

(3) Where an order is made under subsection (1) above, the provisions of this section shall not render any person liable for anything done by him before the order was made.

(4) For the avoidance of doubt it is hereby declared that for the purposes of this section there may be a joint tenancy of a chose in action.

6   The court's order

Having decided that it is going to make an order for financial provision for the applicant,[4] the court then has to decide what form its order shall take. Under the previous legislation the court could only award a lump sum or periodical payments: the additional powers introduced in the 1975 Act reflect the Law Commission's desire to equate the court's powers in family provision proceedings as far as possible with its powers in matrimonial proceedings.[5]

Inheritance (Provision for Family and Dependants) Act 1975

2. Powers of court to make orders

(1) Subject to the provisions of this Act, where an application is made for an order under this section, the court may, if it is satisfied that the disposition of the deceased's estate effected by his will or the law relating to intestacy, or the combination of his will and that law, is not such as to make reasonable provision for the applicant, make any one or more of the following orders—

    (a) an order for the making to the applicant out of the net estate of the deceased of such periodical payments and for such term as may be specified in the order;

---

1. Any interest held by the deceased as a tenant in common would be within s 25(1)(a), p 258 ante.
2. Cf the mandatory 'shall' in s 8(1)(2), p 259 ante; see *Kourkgy v Lusher* post.
3. As in *Re Crawford*, p 256 ante. See also *Kourkgy v Lusher* [1983] FLR 65 where on the facts of that case Wood J refused to order the deceased's severable share of the matrimonial home to be brought into the net estate on an application by his mistress.
4. Even before the merits of the application have been determined, the court has power to make an interim award to the applicant in immediate need of financial assistance: 1(PFD)A 1975, s 5, see eg *Re Besterman,* p 252 ante.
5. Law Com 61 paras 110–126.

  (b) an order for the payment to the applicant out of that estate of a lump sum[6] of such
       amount as may be so specified;[7]

  (c) an order for the transfer to the applicant of such property comprised in that estate
       as may be so specified;

  (d) an order for the settlement for the benefit of the applicant of such property
       comprised in that estate as may be so specified;[8]

  (e) an order for the acquisition out of property comprised in that estate of such
       property as may be so specified and for the transfer of the property so acquired to
       the applicant or for the settlement thereof for his benefit;[9]

  (f) an order varying any ante-nuptial or post-nuptial settlement (including such a
       settlement made by will) made on the parties to a marriage to which the deceased
       was one of the parties, the variation being for the benefit of the surviving party to
       that marriage, or any child of that marriage, or any person who was treated by
       the deceased as a child of the family in relation to that marriage.[10]

(2) An order under subsection (1)(a) above providing for the making out of the net estate
of the deceased of periodical payments may provide for—

  (a) payments of such amount as may be specified in the order,

  (b) payments equal to the whole of the income of the net estate or of such portion
       thereof as may be so specified,

  (c) payments equal to the whole of the income of such part of the net estate as the
       court may direct to be set aside or appropriated for the making out of the income
       thereof of payments under this section,

or may provide for the amount of the payments or any of them to be determined in any
other way the court thinks fit.

(3) Where an order under subsection (1)(a) above provides for the making of payments
of an amount specified in the order, the order may direct that such part of the net estate
as may be so specified shall be set aside or appropriated for the making out of the income
thereof of those payments; but no larger part of the net estate shall be so set aside or
appropriated than is sufficient, at the date of the order, to produce by the income thereof
the amount required for the making of those payments.[11]

(4) An order under this section may contain such consequential and supplemental
provisions as the court thinks necessary or expedient for the purpose of giving effect to
the order or for the purpose of securing that the order operates fairly as between one
beneficiary of the estate of the deceased and another[12] and may, in particular, but
without prejudice to the generality of this subsection—

  (a) order any person who holds any property which forms part of the net estate[13] of
       the deceased to make such payment or transfer such property as may be specified
       in the order;

---

6. 1(PFD)A 1975, s 7(1) enables the court to order payment of a lump sum by instalments.

7. In *Stead v Stead* (1985) 15 Fam Law 154 the Court of Appeal indicated that for elderly applicants periodical payments might well be more appropriate than a large lump sum award, particularly if a substantial part of the capital of the estate was left undistributed so as to be available for a s 6 application (see n 11 post) should any unforeseen circumstances arise.

8. See eg *Harrington v Gill* [1983] FLR 265 where the Court of Appeal ordered that the deceased's house in which the applicant (his mistress) had been living be vested in trustees on trust for sale for her for life and then for the defendant, his daughter, who was the sole beneficiary on his intestacy.

9. See eg *Re Haig* (1979) 76 LSG 476 where the court directed a sale of the house in which the deceased and his mistress had been living and the purchase of another by the personal representatives in which she should have the right to live during her life or until remarriage.

10. The Law Commission did consider recommending a general power to reopen settlements which had the effect of reducing the assets available to meet family provision claims, but decided that this was wider than was justified and that s 10 p 266 post would be sufficient to catch other settlements intended to defeat claims under the Act: Law Com 61 para 216.

11. S 6 gives the court power to vary a periodical payments order, for example on a change in the applicant's circumstances but only so as to affect property the income from which is already being used to meet periodical payments.

12. See eg *Malone v Harrison* [1979] 1 WLR 1353.

13. See p 258 ante.

(b) vary the disposition of the deceased's estate effected by the will or the law relating to intestacy, or by both the will and the law relating to intestacy, in such manner as the court thinks fair and reasonable having regard to the provisions of the order and all the circumstances of the case;

(c) confer on the trustees of any property which is the subject of an order under this section such powers as appear to the court to be necessary or expedient.

19. Effect, duration and form of orders

(1) Where an order is made under section 2 of this Act then for all purposes, including the purposes of the enactments relating to inheritance tax, the will or the law relating to intestacy, or both the will and the law relating to intestacy, as the case may be, shall have effect and be deemed to have had effect as from the deceased's death subject to the provisions of the order.[14]

(2) Any order made under section 2 or 5[15] of this Act in favour of—

(a) an applicant who was the former husband or former wife of the deceased, or

(b) an applicant who was the husband or wife of the deceased in a case where the marriage with the deceased was the subject of a decree of judicial separation and at the date of death the decree was in force and the separation was continuing,

shall, in so far as it provides for the making of periodical payments, cease to have effect on the remarriage of the applicant, except in relation to any arrears due under the order on the date of the remarriage.[16]

(3) A copy of every order made under this Act other than an order made under section 15(1) of this Act[17] shall be sent to the principal registry of the Family Division for entry and filing, and a memorandum of the order shall be endorsed on, or permanently annexed to, the probate or letters of administration under which the estate is being administered.

7 The time limit

The Act provides a time limit for applications to enable personal representatives to distribute an estate within a reasonable time without fear of personal liability to tardy applicants; the court does have a discretion to permit late applications, however.

Inheritance (Provision for Family and Dependants) Act 1975

4. Time limit for applications

An application for an order under section 2 of this Act shall not, except with the permission of the court, be made after the end of the period of six months[18] from the date on which representation[19] with respect to the estate of the deceased is first taken out.

---

14. See also Inheritance Tax Act 1984, s 146.

15. See p 260 n 4 ante.

16. See Law Com 61 paras 56–58.

17. See p 244 ante.

18. Cf New Zealand where the normal period for applications is twelve months, but applications in respect of minors or persons under any other incapacity can be made at any time within two years. Yet in the Committee stage of the House of Commons (HC Deb 1973, Col 173) the six month rule contained in the Inheritance (Provision for Family and Dependants) Bill was described as 'pernicious' because of the hardship it could cause to the deceased's widow and children waiting for the executors to distribute the estate. See further, Prime: 'Time Limits on Dependants' Applications for Family Provision' (1982) 31 ICLQ 862.

19. In *Re Freeman* [1984] 3 All ER 906 Thomas J held that this meant 'valid representation'; as the first grant had been revoked on proof that the will had not been duly executed, time would start to run from the date of the subsequent grant.

20. Provisions as to personal representatives
(1) The provisions of this Act shall not render the personal representative of a deceased person liable for having distributed any part of the estate of the deceased, after the end of the period of six months from the date on which representation with respect to the estate of the deceased is first taken out, on the ground that he ought to have taken into account the possibility—
- (a) that the court might permit the making of an application for an order under section 2 of this Act after the end of that period, or
- (b) that, where an order has been made under the said section 2, the court might exercise in relation thereto the powers conferred on it by section 6[20] of this Act,

but this subsection shall not prejudice any power to recover, by reason of the making of an order under this Act, any part of the estate so distributed.

Re Salmon [1981] Ch 167, [1980] 3 All ER 532, ChD; Megarry V-C

Application was made for leave under section 4 some five and a half months after the time limit had expired. The fault for the delay lay entirely with the applicant and her solicitors; there had been no warning to the bank-executor of the possibility of a late application until four and a half months after the expiration of the time limit, by which time most of the estate had been distributed.

Held: Permission to apply out of time was refused.

Megarry V-C: I am anxious not to go further than is proper in attempting to discover guidelines in exercising the court's discretion under s 4. I bear in mind what Ungoed-Thomas J said on this; and in saying what I do, I disclaim any intention to lay down principles, though I am not sure that it makes it much better to use the term 'guidelines' in place of 'principles'. However, after 14 years[1] I think that some progress can be made towards identifying some guidelines. A number of points seem reasonably plain. The first two are sufficiently supported by *Re Ruttie* ([1969] 3 All ER 1633 at 1636, [1970] 1 WLR 89 at 93). First, the discretion is unfettered. No restrictions or requirements of any kind are laid down in the Act. The discretion is thus plainly one that is to be exercised judicially, and in accordance with what is just and proper. Second, I think that the onus lies on the plaintiff to establish sufficient grounds for taking the case out of the general rule, and depriving those who are protected by it of its benefits. Further, the time limit is a substantive provision laid down in the Act itself, and is not a mere procedural time limit imposed by rules of court which will be treated with the indulgence appropriate to procedural rules. The burden on the applicant is thus, I think, no triviality: the applicant must make out a substantial case for it being just and proper for the court to exercise its statutory discretion to extend the time.

In addition to the two points which emerge from *Re Ruttie*, there are others which I think can properly be considered in deciding whether or not to extend time. In my view, a third point is that it must be material to consider how promptly and in what circumstances the applicant has sought the permission of the court after the time limit has expired. This is not, of course, a crude matter of simply looking at the length of time that has been allowed to elapse: it is not a mere matter of comparing, for instance, the six weeks of *Re Ruttie* with the $2\frac{1}{2}$ years of *Re Gonin* ([1979] Ch 16, [1977] 2 All ER 720). The whole of the circumstances must be looked at, and not least the reasons for delay, and also the promptitude with which, by letter before action or otherwise, the claimant gave warning to the defendants of the proposed application. Thus if the warning was given within time, but for some good reason the proceedings were not commenced until a short while after time had run, I would expect the applicant's task to be relatively simple.

---

20. The section enabling the court to make a variation order; see p 261 n 11 ante.
1. The court's discretionary power to permit late applications was introduced by the Family Provision Act 1966.

Where there has been some error or oversight, an obvious question is whether the applicant has done all that was reasonably possible to put matters right promptly, and keep the defendants informed. As I have said more than once, it is not only Heaven that helps those who help themselves.

This leads to a fourth point. For the reasons that I have already given, I think that it is obviously material whether or not negotiations have been commenced within the time limit; for if they have, and time has run out while they are proceeding, this is likely to encourage the court to extend the time. Negotiations commenced after the time limit might also aid the applicant, at any rate if the defendants have not taken the point that time has expired.

Fifth, I think that it is also relevant to consider whether or not the estate has been distributed before a claim under the Act has been made or modified. Section 20(1) provides that the Act is not to make a personal representative liable for distributing the estate after the six months has ended on the ground that he ought to have taken account of the possibility that the court might permit an application to be made after the six months; but this provision does not prejudice any power to recover, by reason of the making of an order under the Act, any part of the estate so distributed. The end of the six months thus marks a change from a period when any distribution by the personal representatives is made at their own risk (see *Re Simson* [1949] 2 All ER 826, [1950] Ch 38) to a period where there is some statutory protection for a distribution.

So far as the beneficiaries are concerned, there will usually be a real psychological change when the estate is distributed. Before the distribution, they would have only the expectation of payment; and if they are entitled to a share of residue, they will often have a considerable degree of uncertainty as to the amount. After the distribution, they have the money itself, and know the exact amount. If an order is made under the Act the difference will be the difference between the prospect of receiving in due course less than they had hoped, and on the other hand having something that they had already received and regarded as their own taken away from them. For most people, there is a real difference between the bird in the hand and the bird in the bush. In addition, of course, the beneficiaries are more likely to have changed their position in reliance on the benefaction if they have actually received it than if it lies merely in prospect. . . .

Sixth, I think that it is relevant to consider whether a refusal to extend the time would leave the claimant without redress against anybody. In *Re Gonin* ([1977] 2 All ER 720 at 736) Walton J considered the possibility that the plaintiff might sue her solicitors in negligence if in fact it was due to their faulty advice that her claim was not made in time. Although the subject matter is different, there seems to me to be considerable force in the approach to be found in the line of cases associated with the name of *Allen v Sir Alfred McAlpine & Sons Ltd* ([1968] 2 QB 229 at 256–257). There may appear to be some logical difficulty in making the decision whether the defendants should escape liability under the 1975 Act depend in any degree on whether the responsibility for the delay was that of the plaintiff personally or was that of the plaintiff's solicitors: the liability of the defendants, it may be said, ought not to depend on the distribution of fault between the plaintiff and his or her solicitors. Nevertheless, however logic may affect the defendants' position, there is a real and plain difference to a plaintiff between having a claim against his or her solicitors instead of against the defendants, and having no claim against anybody.

I am far from saying that the six considerations that I have stated are exhaustive: plainly they are not. I think, however, that they suffice for the present case. Here, the delay is substantial. It was some $4\frac{1}{2}$ months before the bank was even warned of the proposed proceedings, and a further unexplained month before proceedings were actually commenced. The fault for the delay is wholly on the widow's side: none of the delay can be laid to the charge of the defendants or of extraneous factors over which the widow had no control. Such explanations of the delay as have been given are inadequate and insubstantial. Even when the widow's solicitors realised that they would have to seek an extension of time, they did nothing prompt either to seek the extension or to warn the bank that they intended to do so. There were, of course, no negotiations either within time or out of time. Further, while the solicitors were delaying, nearly all the estate was being distributed to the beneficiaries without, of course, any warning that a claim had been made that might result in the beneficiaries having to give back some of the money that they were receiving.

In those circumstances, can the widow be said to have made out a sufficient case for extending a substantive statutory time limit, and not one that is merely procedural, when there lies to hand, if no extension is granted, possible, and indeed probable, proceedings for negligence against the solicitors who were responsibile for the delay and have put forward such unsatisfactory explanations? Would it be just to extend the time so that the beneficiaries must pay (if the claim succeeds) and the solicitors will escape? It seems to me that the answer must be No.[2]

8 Anti-avoidance provisions

There were no such provisions in the earlier legislation which was easily evaded;[3] a prime object of the Law Commission was to devise means of preventing the deceased from rendering ineffective the measures it was recommending.

(a) Lifetime gifts

The simplest method of avoiding family provision claims was for the deceased to make gifts in his lifetime, so reducing the net estate available to meet claims on his death.

Law Commission: Second Report on Family Property[4]
The case in principle for interfering with dispositions
190. . . . In general, people do not try to evade their obligations to their family, but there will always be some who will seek to put their property beyond the reach of certain members of their family who may have a just claim for family provision.

191. It may be argued that any provision designed to call in question dispositions made with this intention would involve too great an interference with the freedom of an individual to dispose of his property as he pleases, that uncertainty would be introduced into inter vivos transactions and that it would be difficult in the case of a deceased person to produce evidence of an intention to defeat the claim of family members. In our view, however, it is a matter of overriding importance to ensure that family provision laws are effective. The introduction of measures to prevent a person from defeating family provision by dispositions in his lifetime would not only give the court power to protect the dependants but would also discourage a testator from acting to their prejudice.

Avoidance of transactions in matrimonial proceedings
192. The case for such a provision is strengthened by the fact that the court has power under the Matrimonial Causes Act 1973, section 37, to avoid transactions made with the

---

2. In *Re Dennis*, p 254 ante, Browne-Wilkinson J added a seventh guideline: the need for the applicant to establish that he has an arguable case. The applicant before him had failed to satisfy this requirement (see p 254 ante), his delay was also lengthy (19 months) and in part inexcusable so Browne-Wilkinson J refused him leave to bring proceedings out of time.
3. In addition to the methods mentioned post, nominations, donationes mortis causa and property subject to a beneficial joint tenancy all escaped family provision claims; with the exception of non statutory nominations they have all now been brought within the definition of the net estate, see p 258 ante.
4. 'Family Provision on Death' (1974) Law Com 61.

intention of defeating a claim for financial provision in matrimonial proceedings.[5] It is difficult to see why a person should be allowed to defeat a claim for family provision on his death but not a claim for financial provision on the breakdown of his marriage. It may be that he is more likely to want to defeat the latter but that is hardly an adequate justification for the distinction.

Our conclusion

197. A provision for 'setting aside' dispositions will raise difficult problems of third or fourth parties into whose hands the property has come before the deceased's death. What we envisage is a different and simpler type of provision, the object of which is to require a person, who in certain circumstances has received property from the deceased during his lifetime, to make a payment to provide the funds from which a claim for family provision could be satisfied.

Inheritance (Provision for Family and Dependants Act) 1975

10. Dispositions intended to defeat applications for financial provision

(1) Where an application is made to the court for an order under section 2 of this Act, the applicant may in the proceedings on that application, apply to the court for an order under subsection (2) below.

(2) Where on an application under subsection (1) above the court is satisfied—

(a) that, less than six years[6] before the date of death of the deceased, the deceased with the intention of defeating an application for financial provision under this Act[7] made a disposition,[8] and

(b) that full valuable consideration[9] for that disposition was not given by the person to whom or for the benefit of whom the disposition was made (in this section referred to as 'the donee') or by any other person, and

(c) that the exercise of the powers conferred by this section would facilitate the making of financial provision for the applicant under this Act;

then, subject to the provisions of this section and of sections 12 and 13 of this Act, the court may order the donee (whether or not at the date of the order he holds any interest in the property disposed of to him or for his benefit by the deceased) to provide, for the purpose of the making of that financial provision, such sum of money or other property as may be specified in the order.

(3) Where an order is made under subsection (2) above as respects any disposition made by the deceased which consisted of the payment of money to or for the benefit of the donee, the amount of any sum of money or the value of any property ordered to be provided under that subsection shall not exceed the amount of the payment made by the deceased after deducting therefrom any inheritance tax borne by the donee in respect of that payment.

(4) Where an order is made under subsection (2) above as respects any disposition made by the deceased which consisted of the transfer of property (other than a sum of money) to or for the benefit of the donee, the amount of any sum of money or the value of any property ordered to be provided under that subsection shall not exceed the value at the date of the death of the deceased of the property disposed of by him to or for the benefit of

---

5. This enables the court to set aside a transaction in matrimonial proceedings if satisfied that the transaction was made with the intention of defeating a claim for financial relief; this intention is presumed if the transaction took place within three years of the application and has had the effect of preventing the grant of financial relief to the applicant or reducing its amount.

6. The Law Commission considered the case for no cut-off period but decided that in the interests of certainty and in view of the difficulty of investigating a person's intentions at too remote a time, the court's power to reopen inter vivos dispositions should be so limited: Law Com 61, para 211.

7. See further s 12(1).

8. Defined in s 10(7) post.

9. 'Valuable consideration' for this purpose does not include marriage or a promise of marriage: s 25(1).

the donee (or if that property has been disposed of by the person to whom it was transferred by the deceased, the value at the date of that disposal thereof) after deducting therefrom any inheritance tax borne by the donee in respect of the transfer of that property by the deceased.[10]

(5) Where an application (in this subsection referred to as 'the original application') is made for an order under subsection (2) above in relation to any disposition, then, if on an application under this subsection by the donee or by any applicant for an order under section 2 of this Act the court is satisfied—

    (a) that, less than six years before the date of the death of the deceased, the deceased with the intention of defeating an application for financial provision under the Act made a disposition other than the disposition which is the subject of the original application, and

    (b) that full valuable consideration for that other disposition was not given by the person to whom or for the benefit of whom that other disposition was made or by any other person,

the court may exercise in relation to the person to whom or for the benefit of whom that other disposition was made the powers which the court would have had under subsection (2) above if the original application had been made in respect of that other disposition and the court had been satisfied as to the matters set out in paragraphs (a), (b) and (c) of that subsection; and where any application is made under this subsection, any reference in this section (except in subsection (2)(b)) to the donee shall include a reference to the person to whom or for the benefit of whom that other disposition was made.

(6) In determining whether and in what manner to exercise its powers under this section, the court shall have regard to the circumstances in which any disposition was made and any valuable consideration which was given therefor, the relationship, if any, of the donee to the deceased, the conduct and financial resources of the donee and all the other circumstances of the case.

(7) In this section 'disposition' does not include—

    (a) any provision in a will, any such nomination as is mentioned in section 8(1) of this Act or any donatio mortis causa, or

    (b) any appointment of property made, otherwise than by will, in the exercise of a special power of appointment,

but, subject to these exceptions, includes any payment of money (including the payment of a premium under a policy of assurance)[11] and any conveyance, assurance, appointment or gift of property of any description, whether made by an instrument or otherwise.

(8) The provisions of this section do not apply to any disposition made before the commencement of this Act.[12]

12. Provisions supplementary to ss 10 and 11[13]

(1) Where the exercise of any of the powers conferred by section 10 or 11 of this Act is conditional on the court being satisfied that a disposition or contract was made by a deceased person with the intention of defeating an application for financial provision under this Act, that condition shall be fulfilled if the court is of the opinion that, on a balance of probabilities, the intention of the deceased (though not necessarily his sole intention) in making the disposition or contract was to prevent an order for financial

---

10. Thus instead of giving the donee an asset which is likely to appreciate in value, the donee would be better served by a cash gift which would enable him to buy the asset; his potential liability will be limited thereby to the amount of money handed over.

11. Thus if the deceased took out an insurance policy for the benefit of another with a view to defeating family provision claims on his death, the liability of the beneficial owner of the policy will be limited to the amount of the premiums paid within six years of death, rather than a proportionate part of the policy proceeds: see Law Com 61 para 205.

12. 1 April 1976: s 27(3).

13. See p 269 post.

provision being made under this Act or to reduce the amount of the provision which might otherwise be granted by an order thereunder.[14]

(3) Where the court makes an order under section 10 or 11 of this Act it may give such consequential directions as it thinks fit (including directions requiring the making of any payment or the transfer of any property) for giving effect to the order or for securing a fair adjustment of the rights of the persons affected thereby.

(4) Any power conferred on the court by the said section 10 or 11 to order the donee, in relation to any disposition or contract, to provide any sum of money or other property shall be exercisable in like manner in relation to the personal representative of the donee, and—

 (a) any reference in section 10(4) to the disposal of property by the donee shall include a reference to disposal by the personal representative of the donee, and

 (b) any reference in section 10(5) to an application by the donee under that subsection shall include a reference to an application by the personal representative of the donee;

but the court shall not have power under the said section 10 or 11 to make an order in respect of any property forming part of the estate of the donee which has been distributed by the personal representative; and the personal representative shall not be liable for having distributed any such property before he has notice of the making of an application under the said section 10 or 11 on the ground that he ought to have taken into account the possibility that such an application would be made.[15]

In **Re Kennedy** (1980) CLY, 2820, (Shoreditch County Court) the deceased had voluntarily transferred his leasehold house into the joint names of himself and his mistress as beneficial joint tenants, a few months before he died. There was no evidence that he had ever directed his mind at the time of the transfer to what would otherwise happen on his death. His widow applied for an order under s 10 that the mistress' estate[16] provide out of the proceeds of sale of the house a sum of money for the purpose of her claim for financial provision under the Act. Willis J dismissed the application, holding that whilst it was not necessary for a s 10 applicant to show that the deceased had the Act in mind when the transaction in question was made, there still had to be evidence that he intended to defeat a claim made after his death against his estate; there was no such evidence on the facts before him.

(b) Contracts

Less common than the inter vivos gift but just as feasible as a method of avoiding the family provision legislation was the contract[17] to create liabilities to be discharged out of the net estate. Such a contract generally took one of two forms: the contract to leave property to X by will[18] and the contract simply creating a liability which would have to be met out of the net estate if unsatisfied

---

14. It will be noted that on s 10 applications there is no presumption of an intent to defeat a claim; cf the position in relation to contracts, post and transactions intended to defeat claims for financial provision in matrimonial proceedings, p 266 n 5 ante.

15. See Law Com 61 para 243. S 13 contains similar provisions to limit the liability of the donee-trustee.

16. The mistress had died shortly after the deceased.

17. Under seal or supported by consideration.

18. See eg *Schaefer v Schuhmann* [1972] AC 572, [1972] 1 All ER 621 where the testator had bound himself by an enforceable contract to leave his house by will to his housekeeper and the Privy Council, on appeal from the Supreme Court of New South Wales, held that as a result it had no power to place any part of the burden of his daughters' family provision claim on that part of his property.

by the time of the deceased's death.[19] The Law Commission considered whether to recommend that all contracts be reviewable whether made with intent to defeat a family provision claim or not, but finally decided that such a measure would be too extreme.

Law Commission: Second Report on Family Property[20]

Our conclusion
226. We think that a distinction should be drawn between a contract to leave property by will where the intention of the promisor is to defeat a claim for family provision and a contract to leave property by will where there is no such intention. In the former case, we think that the court should have power to order family provision out of the net benefit accruing to the promisee after taking account of any valuable consideration which has been given for the contract (marriage or a promise to marry not being regarded as valuable consideration for this purpose). In the latter case, where the necessary intention is not established, we can see no ground for giving the court power to interfere.

Time limit
237. We have considered whether the power of the court to review contracts to leave property by will, or to pay money or to transfer other property out of the deceased's estate, should be limited to contracts made within a specified period before death. We have given reasons for recommending that dispositions inter vivos made more than six years before death should not be liable to be called in question.[1] We do not think, however, that contracts of the kind with which we are now concerned are comparable with dispositions inter vivos. In the case of a disposition inter vivos, the donor is immediately divesting himself of property and this must in most cases have a restraining effect upon him. In the case of contracts of the kind with which we are concerned there is no similar disincentive, because the deceased remains in full enjoyment of his property during his lifetime. We think that any rule rendering such contracts immune from challenge if made more than a specified period before death might be a positive encouragement to make them. Accordingly, we do not recommend any such rule.

Inheritance (Provision for Family and Dependants) Act 1975

11. Contracts to leave property by will
(1) Where an application is made to a court for an order under section 2 of this Act, the applicant may, in the proceedings on that application, apply to the court for an order under this section.
(2) Where on an application under subsection (1) above the court is satisfied—
  (a) that the deceased made a contract by which he agreed to leave by his will a sum of money or other property to any person or by which he agreed that a sum of money or other property would be paid or transferred to any person out of his estate,[2] and

---

19. Eg a covenant by A to pay £30,000 to B. If left unsatisfied at A's death, the debt would be a liability payable out of A's estate so reducing the amount available to meet family provision claims. If A's estate was only £30,000 or less the whole of it would be used up in satisfying the debt, so thwarting any family provision claims completely.
20. 'Family Provision on Death' (1974) Law Com 61.
1. At para 211, where the Law Commission stated that they were 'disturbed by the prospect of litigation in which it is necessary to investigate a man's intentions at remote periods of time.'
2. The section on its terms therefore applies only to contracts relating to the passing of property on death; if A covenants to transfer property in his lifetime to B and that contract is unfulfilled at A's death, it seems that such a contract will escape s 11; A's personal representatives will stand in A's shoes to carry out the contract.

(b) that the deceased made that contract with the intention of defeating an application for financial provision under this Act,[3] and

(c) that when the contract was made full valuable consideration[4] for that contract was not given or promised by the person with whom or for the benefit of whom the contract was made (in this section referred to as 'the donee') or by any other person, and

(d) that the exercise of the powers conferred by this section would facilitate the making of financial provision for the applicant under this Act,

then, subject to the provisions of this section and of sections 12[5] and 13[6] of this Act, the court may make any one or more of the following orders, that is to say—

(i) if any money has been paid or any other property has been transferred to or for the benefit of the donee in accordance with the contract, an order directing the donee to provide, for the purpose of the making of that financial provision, such sum of money or other property as may be specified in the order;

(ii) if the money or all the money has not been paid or the property or all the property has not been transferred in accordance with the contract, an order directing the personal representatives not to make any payment or transfer any property, or not to make any further payment or transfer any further property, as the case may be, in accordance therewith or directing the personal representatives only to make such payment or transfer such property as may be specified in the order.

(3) Notwithstanding anything in subsection (2) above, the court may exercise its powers thereunder in relation to any contract made by the deceased only to the extent that the court considers that the amount of any sum of money paid or to be paid or the value of any property transferred or to be transferred in accordance with the contract exceeds the value of any valuable consideration given or to be given for that contract, and for this purpose the court shall have regard to the value of property at the date of the hearing.

(4) In determining whether and in what manner to exercise its powers under this section, the court shall have regard to the circumstances in which the contract was made, the relationship, if any, of the donee to the deceased, the conduct and financial resources of the donee and all the other circumstances of the case.

(5) Where an order has been made under subsection (2) above in relation to any contract, the rights of any person to enforce that contract or to recover damages or to obtain other relief for the breach thereof shall be subject to any adjustment made by the court under section 12(3)[7] of this Act and shall survive to such extent only as is consistent with giving effect to the terms of that order.

(6) The provisions of this section do not apply to a contract made before the commencement of this Act.[8]

12.   Provisions supplementary to s . . . 11

(2) Where an application is made under section 11 of this Act with respect to any contract made by the deceased and no valuable consideration was given or promised by any person for that contract then, notwithstanding anything in subsection (1) above, it shall be presumed, unless the contrary is shown, that the deceased made that contract with the intention of defeating an application for financial provision under this Act.[9]

20.   Provisions as to personal representatives[10]

(3) Where a deceased person entered into a contract by which he agreed to leave by his will any sum of money or other property to any person or by which he agreed that a sum

---

3. As to the burden of proof, see s 12(2) post.

4. See p 266 n 9 ante.

5. P 267 ante.

6. S 13 contains provisions limiting the liability of a trustee to whom payment is made or property transferred by a contract caught by the provisions of s 11.

7. P 268 ante.

8. 1 April 1976: s 27(3).

9. Cf s 10 dispositions where no such presumption lies.

10. See also s 12(4), p 268 ante.

of money or other property would be paid or transferred to any person out of his estate, then, if the personal representative of the deceased has reason to believe that the deceased entered into the contract with the intention of defeating an application for financial provision under this Act, he may, notwithstanding anything in that contract, postpone the payment of that sum of money or the transfer of that property until the expiration of the period of six months from the date on which representation with respect to the estate of the deceased is first taken out or, if during that period an application is made for an order under section 2 of this Act, until the determination of the proceedings on that application.

QUESTIONS

1. What would be the advantages and disadvantages of a system of fixed rights of inheritance as opposed to the present discretionary system of family provision?

2. Tom has just died leaving his estate, worth £200,000, to his favourite charity. He is survived by the following:

(a) His former wife Wanda, from whom he was divorced six years ago;

(b) His former mistress Flo; the relationship ended in 1984 but he continued to pay her £50 per week 'for old time's sake';

(c) Delilah, who was living with him in a house provided by Tom who paid all the outgoings although she had her own sources of income;

(d) Ian (aged two) his child by Delilah.

Which of these persons would be entitled to claim from Tom's estate? What further information would you need to assess their prospects of success? What orders might the court make?

3. In 1978 Tony gave £10,000 to his girlfriend Lucy. In 1984 he bought a flat worth £30,000 in the joint names of himself and another girlfriend, Gail. In 1985 he died leaving his estate worth £60,000 (excluding the above items) to his mistress Mandy, who took out a grant of probate in September of that year. In September 1986 his wife Polly, who had left him some years ago, learns of his death and wishes to claim provision from his estate.

Advise her.

4. Before the 1975 Act, it was simplicity itself, given a wily lawyer, to thwart the hopes of potential applicants for provision from the estate.

To what extent is this still true? (Read Mellows, pp 203–12, Sherrin 'Defeating the Dependant' [1978] Conv 13, Cadwallader 'Inheritance Act Applications by Financial Dependants: a Loophole?' (1981) 125 Sol J 175.

PART THREE
Winding up the estate

CHAPTER 18

Getting in and managing the assets

1 Introduction

The first concern of the personal representatives in winding up the deceased's estate will be to assume control over his assets. This chapter is concerned with the 'getting in' of the assets, the steps the personal representatives should take to preserve them during the administration, their powers to deal with those assets and their position in relation to the carrying on of any business owned by the deceased. The other aspects of administration are considered in the following chapters.

Administration of Estates Act 1925

25. Duty of personal representative[1]

The personal representative of a deceased person shall be under a duty to—
    (a) collect and get in the real and personal estate of the deceased and administer it according to law;
    (b) when required to do so by the court, exhibit on oath in the court a full inventory of the estate and when so required render an account of the administration of the estate to the court;
    (c) when required to do so by the High Court, deliver up the grant of probate or administration to that court.

2 Vesting of the property in the personal representative

Pure personalty has always vested in the personal representative at common law including rights of action in contract, but not rights of action in tort until the passing of the Law Reform (Miscellaneous Provisions) Act 1934. Realty, including leaseholds, now vests in the personal representative by virtue of the Administration of Estates Act 1925.[2] In either case, if the personal

---

1. This section was substituted by the Administration of Estates Act 1971, s 9. Section 25 as originally drawn dealt only with the duties as to supplying an inventory and account; the amendment was made on the recommendation of the Law Commission: 'Administration Bonds, Personal Representatives' Rights of Retainer and Preference and related matters' Law Com 31 (1970), paras 10, 11.
2. Realty originally vested in the heir or, if there was a will, in the devisee, immediately on death. The position was altered by the Land Transfer Act 1897, s 1, now replaced by AEA 1925, s 1 post.

representative is an executor, since his authority derives from the will the deceased's property vests in him automatically on the deceased's death. If he is an administrator, the property vests in the President of the Family Division until the would-be administrator gets his grant, at which point the deceased's property vests in him; the vesting is also treated as relating back to the date of death in so far as this validates an act done for the benefit of the estate.

Law Reform (Miscellaneous Provisions) Act 1934

1. Effect of death on certain causes of action

(1) Subject to the provisions of this section, on the death of any person after the commencement of this Act all causes of action subsisting against or vested in him shall survive against, or, as the case may be, for the benefit of, his estate. Provided that this subsection shall not apply to causes of action for defamation.

(2) Where a cause of action survives as aforesaid for the benefit of the estate of a deceased person, the damages recoverable for the benefit of the estate of that person—

    (a) shall not include any exemplary damages . . . ;

    (c) where the death of that person has been caused by the act or omission which gives rise to the cause of action, shall be calculated without reference to any loss or gain to his estate consequent on his death,[3] except that a sum in respect of funeral expenses may be included.

(5) The rights conferred by this Act for the benefit of the estate of deceased persons shall be in addition to and not in derogation of any rights conferred on the dependants of deceased persons by the Fatal Accidents Act, 1976 or the Carriage by Air Act, 1961.

In **Warren-Gash v Lane** (1984) 14 Fam Law 184, a consent order had been made in divorce proceedings by which in return for a lump sum payment from the husband, the wife agreed to transfer her interest in the former matrimonial home to him. The husband paid the money before his death but no steps had been taken to complete the transfer of the wife's interest when he died, and after his death she took up residence in the property. Sheldon J held that the consent order remained enforceable against her for the benefit of the husband's estate saying at p 185, that:

The fundamental question was whether a claim made by or against the husband's estate arose out of a cause of action which was vested in or subsisted against the deceased at the time of death. If so, by s 1(1) of the Law Reform (Miscellaneous Provisions) Act 1934 it survived for the benefit of or against his estate. (In his Lordship's judgment) there was no doubt in the instant case that the deceased prior to his death could have applied to the court for an order compelling the respondent to comply with the terms of the order of 1977. That being so, it was vested in him at the date of his death and was a cause of action within the meaning of s 1(1) of the 1934 Act.

Administration of Estates Act 1925

1. Devolution of real estate on personal representative

(1) Real estate to which a deceased person was entitled for an interest not ceasing on his

---

3. In *Gammell v Wilson* [1982] AC 27, [1981] 1 All ER 578, the House of Lords held that this applied only to a loss or gain directly consequent on the death (eg insurance monies falling due on death), not to a loss or gain resulting from a right to recover damages which had vested in the deceased before his death. The result of this interpretation was that the estate was not precluded by s 2(1) from recovering substantial damages under the 1934 Act for the deceased's loss of future earnings during the years of life lost to him because of the defendant's negligence.

death[4] shall on his death, and notwithstanding any testamentary disposition thereof, devolve from time to time[5] on the personal representative of the deceased, in like manner as before the commencement of this Act chattels real devolved on the personal representative from time to time of a deceased person.

3. Interpretation of Part I
(1) In this Part of this Act 'real estate' includes—
    (i) Chattels real,[6] and land in possession, remainder or reversion, and every interest in land to which a deceased person was entitled at the time of his death; and
    (ii) Real estate held on trust (including settled land) or by way of mortgage or security,[7] but not money to arise under a trust for sale of land,[8] nor money secured or charged on land.

(2) A testator shall be deemed to have been entitled at his death to any interest in real estate passing under any gift contained in his will which operates as an appointment under a general power to appoint by will,[9] or operates under the testamentary power conferred by statute to dispose of an entailed interest.[10]

(3) An entailed interest of a deceased person shall (unless disposed of under the testamentary power conferred by statute)[11] be deemed an interest ceasing on his death, but any further or other interest of the deceased in the same property in remainder or reversion which is capable of being disposed of by his will shall not be deemed to be an interest so ceasing.

(4) The interest of a deceased person under a joint tenancy where another tenant survives the deceased is an interest ceasing on his death.

9. Vesting of estate of intestate between death and grant of administration
Where a person dies intestate, his real and personal estate, until administration is granted in respect thereof, shall vest in the Probate Judge[12] in the same manner and to the same extent as formerly in the case of personal estate it vested in the ordinary.

In **Mills v Anderson** [1984] QB 704, [1984] 2 All ER 538, Benet Hytner QC, sitting as a deputy judge of the High Court, had to consider the doctrine of 'relation back' in the context of a plaintiff administrator who sought to escape an agreement he had made on behalf of the estate before he received his grant. The plaintiff was the father of the deceased who had died in a road accident allegedly due to the defendant's negligence. Before letters of administration had been granted the plaintiff, through his solicitor, had accepted an offer of £375 damages and funeral expenses from the defendant's insurers in respect of the

---

4. So eg, a life interest ceasing on the death of the deceased will not pass to his personal representative, nor will the interest of a beneficial joint tenant (see s 3(4) post).

5. Ie the real estate will pass automatically from personal representative to personal representative if changes occur eg because the personal representative dies before having completed the winding-up of the estate and a *de bonis non* grant has to issue to an administrator (see p 292 post).

6. Ie leaseholds.

7. Eg if the deceased had lent money to A on the security of a mortgage of Blackacre, the benefit of that mortgage would pass to the deceased's personal representative.

8. Beneficial interests held under a trust for sale of land are therefore classified as personalty for this purpose.

9. Oddly there is no similar provision either by statute or by common law applying to personalty which passes under a general power of appointment, so that if T has a general power of appointment over pure personalty and he exercises that power by will the appointed interest does not vest in his personal representative but passes straightaway to the appointee.

10. LPA 1925, s 176. Oddly, there is no similar provision in respect of an entailed interest in personalty which has been effectively barred by the will.

11. LPA 1925, s 176.

12. Defined to mean the President of the Family Division of the High Court: AEA 1925, s 55(1)(xv) as substituted by AJA 1970, s 1(6) Sch 2, para 5.

estate's claim under the Law Reform (Miscellaneous Provisions) Act 1934.[13] When the insurer's cheque arrived, however, the plaintiff's solicitor rejected it, having learned in the meantime of the House of Lords decision in *Gammell v Wilson* which would enable the plaintiff to increase the estate's claim substantially by virtue of their Lordships' interpretation of s 2(1)(c) of the 1934 Act.[14] The defendant argued that when the plaintiff subsequently obtained his grant, that grant related back to the date of death and the plaintiff was therefore bound by the agreement he had entered into. Benet Hytner QC held that this would only be so where the agreement was for the benefit of the estate which this agreement, as it transpired, was not. He added at p 543:

I have, however, to consider whether an act done for the benefit of the estate means an act which looking back objectively is of benefit to the estate or whether it may include acts which are done subjectively for the benefit of the estate even though looking back they have not benefited the estate at all. It is perfectly clear that, in arriving at his decision to conclude an agreement with Mr Dodgson, Mr Peacock (the plaintiff's solicitor) believed that he was acting for the benefit of the estate. Indeed, had the House of Lords in *Gammell v Wilson* decided that damages for loss of expectation of life should be a token figure never intended to rise with inflation at all and consequently should have reverted to £250, the agreement would have been of considerable benefit to the estate.

I am satisfied, looking at all the cases as a whole,[15] that relation back only occurs when it would be beneficial to the estate for the general doctrine not to operate. The exception applies to prevent injury to the estate, and, in my judgment, the approach should be a purely objective one.

3   Getting in and preserving the assets

The personal representatives are under a duty to take reasonable care in preserving the deceased's estate and will be liable for any loss caused by their failure to do so.[16] They should therefore make sure at an early stage in their administration that all title deeds, share certificates, building society pass-books and other papers relating to the estate are securely under their control. Oddly, there is no specific duty on personal representatives to insure buildings and any other insurable property against loss or damage,[17] only a statutory power to do so, the limitations of which were recently considered by the Law Reform Committee.

Trustee Act 1925

19. Power to insure
(1) A trustee may insure against loss or damage by fire any building or other insurable property to any amount, including the amount of any insurance already on foot, not exceeding three fourths parts of the full value of the building or property and pay the premiums for such insurance out of the income thereof or out of the income of any other property subject to the same trusts without obtaining the consent of any person who may be entitled wholly or partly to such income.

---

13. See p 276 ante.
14. See p 276 n 3 ante.
15. *Morgan v Thomas* (1853) 8 Ex Ch 302, *Bodger v Arch* (1854) 10 Ex Ch 333, *Waring v Dewberry* (1718) 1 Stra 97.
16. See p 411 post.
17. See eg *Re McEacharn* (1911) 103 LT 900.

(2) This section does not apply to any building or property which a trustee is bound forthwith to convey absolutely to any beneficiary upon being requested to do so.

69. Application of Act

(1) This Act, except where otherwise expressly provided, applies to trusts including, so far as this Act applies thereto, executorships and administratorships constituted or created either before or after the commencement of the Act.

(2) The powers conferred by this Act on trustees are in addition to the powers conferred by the instrument, if any, creating the trust, but those powers, unless otherwise stated, apply if and so far only as a customary intention is not expressed in the instrument, if any, creating the trust, and have effect subject to the terms of that instrument.

Law Reform Committee: Twenty-Third Report[18]

(1) Power to Insure the Full Value of the Property

4.31 We find it difficult to reconcile section 19(1) with the general scheme of the (Trustee) Act, which places such an emphasis on the standards expected of an ordinary prudent man of business. We agree, therefore, that the sensible approach is that trustees[19] should have the power to insure the trust property up to its full replacement value in all cases in which it would be sensible to do that, and in other cases up to its market value. The standard of the ordinary prudent man should be used in this context, as it is used in the rest of the Act, in deciding whether it is necessary to insure up to market value or up to full replacement value.[20]

(2) Insurance against Damage by Fire

4.33 We agree . . . that no absolute duty should be imposed on trustees to insure against damage caused by fire since there are so many different sorts of circumstances which would have to be taken into account. We recommend that the trustees should be under a duty to insure against any risk in all the circumstances in which an ordinary prudent man of business would insure, which would necessarily include fire. The trustees will have the power to insure up to the full replacement value of the property in certain circumstances, as we have discussed above. We have taken this rather broader approach to the limited question of the extent to which a trustee should insure against the risk of damage by fire because we think that this question is part of the more fundamental question of what risks in general a trustee should be expected to insure against. We also agree with the view expressed by some of the witnesses, that it would be impracticable to lay down a fixed list of risks which should be insured against and that this should be a matter for the discretion of the trustees.[1]

---

18. 'The Powers and Duties of Trustees' (1982) Cmnd 8733.
19. The Law Reform Committee state at p 53: 'the conclusions we have reached apply equally to the positions of both trustees and personal representatives'.
20. In the United States, the Uniform Probate Code contains a similar provision at s 3–715: 'Except as restricted or otherwise provided by the will or by an order in a formal proceeding . . . a personal representative, acting reasonably for the benefit of the interested persons, may properly . . . (15) insure the assets of the estate against damage, loss and liability on himself against liability as to third persons.'
1. The Law Reform Committee further recommended: at para 4.34, that the new duty to insure (ante) should not apply to existing trusts (or estates presumably); at para 4.35 that TA 1925, s 19(2) be extended so as to enable trustees holding on bare trusts to insure the trust property in certain circumstances (presumably this would apply to a personal representative holding for a beneficiary property not required for the purposes of the administration); at para 4.36 that trustees (and personal representatives) should have power to pay insurance premiums out of capital as well as income.

4   Powers of management

Personal representatives have wide powers of management granted by statute including the power to sell any of the deceased's assets if the proceeds are required for the purpose of administration. A sole personal representative can act without having to appoint another personal representative to give a good receipt on a sale of realty; where there are two or more personal representatives, their powers must be exercised jointly over realty[2] whereas their authority over the deceased's pure personalty is several, enabling one personal representative to pass a good title without the other(s) joining in.[3] There is statutory protection for a purchaser in the event of the administration of the estate having been completed at the time of the sale.

Administration of Estates Act 1925

2. Application to real estate of law affecting chattels real
(2) Where as respects real estate there are two or more personal representatives, a conveyance of real estate devolving under this Part of the Act shall not, save as otherwise provided as respects trust estates including settled land, be made without the concurrence therein of all such representatives or an order of the court,[4] but where probate is granted to one or some of two or more persons named as executors, whether or not power is reserved to the other or others to prove, any conveyance of the real estate may be made by the proving executor or executors for the time being, without an order of the court, and shall be as effectual as if all the persons named as executors had concurred therein.

39. Powers of management
(1) In dealing with the real and personal estate of the deceased his personal representatives shall, for purposes of administration, or during a minority of any beneficiary or the subsistence of any life interest, or until the period of distribution arrives, have—
    (i) the same powers and discretions, including power to raise money by mortgage or charge (whether or not by deposit of documents), as a personal representative had before the commencement of this Act, with respect to personal estate vested in him, and such power of raising money by mortgage may in the case of land be exercised by way of legal mortgage; and
   (ii) all the powers, discretions and duties conferred or imposed by law on trustees holding land upon an effectual trust for sale[5] (including power to overreach equitable interests and powers as if the same affected the proceeds of sale); and
  (iii) all the powers conferred by statute on trustees for sale, and so that every contract entered into by a personal representative shall be binding on and be enforceable against and by the personal representative for the time being of the deceased, and may be carried into effect, or be rescinded by him, and, in the case of a contract entered into by a predecessor, as if it had been entered into by himself.

36. Effect of conveyance by personal representative
(8) A conveyance of a legal estate by a personal representative to a purchaser shall not

---

2. Including leaseholds, see AEA 1925, s 3(1) (p 277 ante), s 55(xix).
3. Cf the authority of trustees over personalty which is always joint. See p 281 post, for the Law Reform Committee's criticism of this distinction.
4. Cf a contract for the sale of realty: in *Fountain Forestry v Edwards* [1975] Ch 1, [1974] 2 All ER 280, Brightman J was prepared to assume that one of two or more personal representatives could enter into such a contract which would bind the estate although he could not implement it without the concurrence of the other personal representative(s) or a court order.
5. See LPA 1925, s 28.

be invalidated by reason only that the purchaser may have notice that all the debts, liabilities, funeral, and testamentary or administration expenses, duties and legacies of the deceased have been discharged or provided for.

Law Reform Committee: Twenty-Third Report[6]

7.12 Disposal of Property by Personal Representative

One of our witnesses has criticised the rule which allows one of two or more personal representatives to dispose of property from the deceased's estate without the concurrence of the others. It is suggested that, like trustees, personal representatives should be required to act with each other's agreement. We think that the position must be that even where one personal representative has acted without the authority of the others in selling the deceased's goods, the law should always protect the purchaser, but leaving this aside, we do agree that the distinction between trustees and personal representatives is difficult to justify. A further absurdity of the present position is that the consequences of the sale will depend upon whether or not the administration of the estate has been completed. If it has, then the personal representatives will have become trustees, and will be subject to a different rule. One possibility which has been put forward as a remedy is to provide that where title to property has to be passed by deed, then all the personal representatives must agree to the transfer, but leaving the position with respect to the transfer of chattels unchanged. We think it would be illogical to distinguish between chattels and other kinds of property and we therefore reject this suggestion. Our conclusion is that the position for personal representatives should be exactly the same as it is for trustees. This should not cause any practical difficulties, as in many cases an implied authority to take a particular course of action can be imputed to one particular personal representative. We accordingly recommend that personal representatives should be placed under a duty to act unanimously (subject to any contrary provision in the will, where this is relevant) when disposing of property from the deceased's estate.

5 Carrying on the deceased's business

(a) The power to carry on the business

Where the deceased's assets include a business, the personal representatives have power to carry on the business but only for a reasonable time with a view to selling it as a going concern. However the testator may have authorised them to carry on the business indefinitely; even if he has not done so expressly, so long as the will gives the personal representatives power to postpone sale of the business, by implication they have power to carry on the business in the meantime.[7]

Re Crowther [1895] 2 Ch 56, Ch D; Chitty J

The testator left the whole of his estate (including his businesses of a rope and twine manufacturer and shopkeeper) to his personal representatives as trustees

---

6. 'The Powers and Duties of Trustees' (1982) Cmnd 8733.
7. In the United States, the Uniform Probate Code s 3–715 (24) also empowers a personal representative (save in so far as the will provides otherwise) to continue the deceased's business after his death but only for a period not exceeding 4 months from the date of his appointment unless the court authorises a longer period or unless the personal representative incorporates the business with the consent of the beneficiaries in which case he can continue it throughout the administration of the estate so long as the beneficiaries have no objection.

on trust for sale, the proceeds to be held on trust for his wife for life and then for his children. The will contained an express power to postpone the sale, directing that the income until sale should be paid to the same persons as if the sale had actually taken place. For 22 years the trustees carried on the testator's businesses not with a view to a sale but for the benefit of the widow to whom the profit was paid as income.

Held: The power to postpone sale inevitably involved a power to carry on the businesses in the meantime so that the widow, as life tenant, was entitled to the whole of the income until a sale.

Chitty J: It is said by the plaintiff that the trustees have committed a breach of trust in carrying on these businesses under this power, though it is not suggested that any loss to the estate has been thereby occasioned; and it has been argued that this power to postpone conversion does not mean, as the testator says, that these trustees may postpone 'for such period as to them shall seem expedient', but that some limitation must be imposed on this period—a limitation arising out of some artificial rule, said to have been laid down by the Court of Chancery, which, according to the plaintiff's argument, is that the trustees may postpone for such period as they deem expedient, 'provided such postponement is only made with a view to a subsequent sale', or something to that effect. It seems extraordinary that there should be any such arbitrary rule inserting additional words in a power so expressed in its terms as this one, and restraining the testator's own words; and I have been searching in vain to see if any such limitation can be extracted from the authorities, and have failed to find it. If a testator says, 'I empower my trustees to postpone the conversion of my estate for as long as they shall deem it expedient to do so,' why is the Court to say that such a clause only authorises a short postponement, and then only with a view to a sale at the end of some two or three years?

Executors have in all cases a year in which to realise their estate,[8] and can always, even without any special power, postpone its conversion for a comparatively short time beyond this year, with a view to a more advantageous sale; and yet this is practically the result of this special power according to the plaintiff. When the estate becomes divisible, the power to postpone ceases, and comes to an end of itself; but when the power is existing, why such a power is not to be read so as to justify trustees in carrying on the testator's business, if they think right so to do, I am at a loss to understand.

I take it that a power to postpone the sale of a business involves a power of continuing the business in the meantime. That was Fry LJ's opinion in *Re Chancellor* ((1884) 26 Ch D 42); and Cotton LJ in his judgment (at p 46) says: 'Without impugning any of the authorities that have been referred to, there is in this will an implied authority to the trustee to carry on the business, and the testator has said how the profits of the business pending a sale are to be paid and applied.' That applies to the present case. So long as the trustees carry on the business under this implied power, the language of the will is unmistakable, the income or yearly profit derived from the businesses is income for all the purposes of the will, and passes under the words of the will to the tenant for life. To hold that the discretion of the trustees is limited in the way suggested by the plaintiff would be tantamount to inserting in this will words which are not there, and to say that the trustees were not justified under this power in carrying on these businesses would be to invent a trap to catch unwary trustees.[9]

---

8. See p 389 post.
9. Cf *Re Smith* [1896] 1 Ch 71 where the testator's residuary estate was subject to a trust for sale but the trustees were specifically directed 'with all convenient speed after my decease' to sell the deceased's pawnbroking business. In the light of this direction North J held that the trustees could not carry on the business indefinitely but a delay of 2 years from the testator's death would not be unreasonable unless a favourable opportunity to sell arose in the meantime.

(b) The personal liability of the personal representatives

The personal representatives will be personally liable to the business creditors in relation to debts incurred in carrying on the business after the deceased's death, but in so far as the personal representatives have power to carry on the business they are entitled, as against the beneficiaries of the estate, to be indemnified against the claims of the business creditors out of the assets they were authorised to use to carry on the business. When the right of indemnity exists, the business creditors can therefore enforce their claims direct against those assets by subrogation.[10] The personal representatives' right to an indemnity is subject to any claims the estate may have against them and the business creditors' right of subrogation is similarly limited.

In **Re Garland** (1804) 10 Ves Jun 110, Eldon LC, commenting on the personal liability of a personal representative carrying on the deceased's business, said at p 119:

> The case of the executor is very hard. He becomes liable, as personally responsible, to the extent of all his own property; also, in his person; and as he may be proceeded against, as a bankrupt; though he is but a trustee. But he places himself in that situation by his own choice; judging for himself, whether it is fit and safe to enter into that situation and contract that sort of responsibility.[11]

In **M'Neillie v Acton** (1853) 4 De GM & G 744, 43 ER 699, Knight-Bruce LJ considered the extent of the personal representative's right of indemnity against the estate for the claims of the business creditors. The will authorised the executor-trustees to carry on the deceased's colliery business. To raise money for this purpose, the executor-trustees mortgaged some of the testator's real estate that was not employed in the trade when the testator died. Holding that the mortgage was invalid as against the beneficiary of the property concerned, Turner LJ said at p 702:

> There appears, therefore, to be no case which has gone to the extent of saying, that a mere direction to continue the trade is to operate as a charge of the trade debts contracted in continuing the trade on all the estate of the testator; and the question is whether, upon any fair construction, it can be so considered? The consequence of it would be, that all the other directions which are contained in the will must be suspended during the period for which the trade is to be continued. If the debt contracted in the course of the trade or the right of the executors to be indemnified in respect of the expense incurred in carrying on the trade, is to be a charge on the whole of the estate of the testator, the necessary consequence would be that no part of the estate could in the meantime be applied in payment of any of the legacies given by the will, and that all administration of the testator's estate must stop until the period when the trade is wound up. That is a construction so unreasonable that, unless there are words sufficient for the purpose, it is one, in my opinion, to which the Court would not resort.
>
> Looking at the language of this will, containing as it does merely a direction to continue the trade, without any specific directions as to the assets which are to be employed in it, I am satisfied that it was not the meaning of this testator that any portion of his assets, beyond that which was employed in the trade at the time of his death, should be considered as the fund for carrying it on after his death. Suppose a grocer in London to say by his will, 'I direct my grocery business to be continued'; and suppose him to have

---

10. Standing in the shoes of the personal representative to enforce his right against the assets; this is particularly useful when the personal representative has gone bankrupt.
11. See also *Owen v Delamere* (1872) LR 15 Eq 134 at 139, per Bacon V-C: 'An executor authorised to carry on business, carries it on; he is liable for every shilling on every contract he enters into.'

had real estate in Northumberland, would it be a probable intention to ascribe to him that his estate in Northumberland was to be sold in order to supply assets to continue the trade carried on in London?

It is, however, said that the executors may not have the means of carrying on the trade, if they are confined to assets which were engaged in it at the time of the testator's death. The answer to that argument is plain. The executors, if they find that they have not the means of carrying on the trade according to the directions contained in the will, should come to this Court for directions to know what they are to do in the administration of the estate. It is no greater difficulty than occurs in other cases where the assets of a testator are insufficient for the purposes to which the testator has devoted them.

In **Re Johnson** (1880) 15 Ch D 548, the nature of the business creditor's right of indemnity by subrogation was considered by Jessel MR. The executor had been authorised by the will to carry on the deceased's business but in doing so he had received substantially more profit than he had accounted for to the trust estate. Certain business creditors claimed the right to have their debts met out of that part of the testator's estate which the executor had been authorised to use in carrying on the business but Jessel MR dismissed their claims saying at p 555:

What is the nature of the right of the creditors against the assets specifically appropriated by the testator for the purpose of carrying on the trade? . . . If the right of the creditors is, as is stated by Lord Justice Turner, [12] the right to put themselves, so to speak, in the place of a trustee, who is entitled to an indemnity, of course, if the trustee is not entitled, except on terms to make good a loss to the trust estate, the creditors cannot have a better right. They do get some additional benefit so as to avoid a supposed injustice; but the injustice to be avoided is the injustice of the cestui que trust walking off with the assets which have been earned by the use of the property of the creditor: but where the cestui que trust does not get that benefit, there is no injustice as between him and the creditors, and there is no reason for the Court interfering at the instance of the creditors to give them a larger right than that they bargained for, namely, their personal right against the trustee. It appears to me, therefore, that if the trustee has no such right in such a case, they have none here.

(c) The position of the estate creditors

The personal representatives' right of indemnity is also subject to the prior claims of the estate creditors[13] against the assets in question save (i) where the business debts were incurred with a view to selling the business as a going concern and (ii) where the estate creditors have assented to the carrying on of the business; in either case the personal representatives, and hence the business creditors by subrogation, have priority over the estate creditors against the assets in question.

Dowse v Gorton [1891] AC 190, HL; Lords Herschell, MacNaghten and Hannen

The testator gave his executors an unlimited discretion to carry on his two businesses for as long as they thought fit. They did so for 3 years with the consent of the testator's creditors (the estate creditors) in the course of which

---

12. In *Re Edmonds* (1862) 4 De GF & J 488.
13. Ie creditors of the estate at the time the deceased died, as opposed to business creditors to whom the personal representatives become indebted in the course of carrying on the deceased's business after his death.

they were able to pay off all the estate creditors except the appellants, but in the course of so doing they incurred other debts to business creditors. The appellants claimed payment of their debts out of the business assets in priority to any claim for an indemnity by the executors or by the business creditors (by subrogation).

Held: The executors were entitled to be indemnified for the business debts they had incurred in priority to the claims of the appellants.

Lord Herschell: I think it is clear that where a business has been carried on under such an authority as was conferred upon the executors by the will of this testator, they would be entitled to a general indemnity out of the estate as against all persons claiming under the will. But I take it to be equally clear that they could not, by reason only of such authority, maintain this right against the creditors of the testator. The executors would, no doubt, be entitled to carry on a business of the testator for such reasonable time as was necessary to enable them to sell his business property as a going concern, and would even, as against his creditors, be entitled to an indemnity in respect of the liabilities properly incurred in so doing. But, in the present case, the businesses were carried on for a period of three years; and it is obvious that this was not done merely for the purpose of effecting a sale.

I agree with the contention of the learned counsel for the appellants, that the mere fact that a creditor stood by under such circumstances, and did not immediately take steps to enforce his debt, would not of itself entitle the executors, as against him, to be indemnified out of the estate. But when all the circumstances of the case are considered, I do not think this is the true view of them. . . .

Under the circumstances I think the proper inference is that the businesses were not merely continued for the benefit of those interested under the will, but that they were also carried on with the assent of the (appellants), for the purpose of securing the payment of the debt due to them.

If this be the true view it can hardly be contested, that the executors of (the testator) are, as against the appellants, entitled to be indemnified out of their testator's estate, against the liabilities which they have properly incurred.

In **Re Oxley** [1914] 1 Ch 604, the will did not empower the executors to continue the deceased's business of a boilermaker but the executors nevertheless carried on the business for another four years. The estate creditors knew that the business was being carried on but made no attempt to interfere. Business creditors (in respect of debts subsequently incurred by the executors) applied for a declaration that the executors were entitled to an indemnity out of the assets for their debts in priority to the estate creditors so that the business creditors would have the benefit of that indemnity by subrogation. Joyce J refused the application and the decision was affirmed by the Court of Appeal. Holding that the estate creditors had never lost their prior claim to the business assets, Buckley LJ said at p 616:

In order to introduce the principle of *Dowse v Gorton* ([1891] AC 190) it must I think be established that the old creditor has so acted, either by claiming (as he did in that case) the assets of the continued business or by affirmative acts by which he so adopts the action of the executors in carrying on the business, as to show that he has abandoned that which is prima facie his right, that which has been asserted by the plaintiffs in this case, to have the assets of their debtor administered in due course for payment of their debts, and that he has assented to another course, namely, that the fund to which he is entitled to look shall be risked in trade with the result that there may be loss or there may be further additions for his benefit. It is necessary I think to show an active affirmative assent. Mere standing by with knowledge and doing nothing is not sufficient.[14]

---

14. Cf *Re Brooke* [1894] 2 Ch 600 where Kekewich J said that knowledge that the business was being carried on coupled with a failure to interfere would amount to an assent by the estate creditor; this dictum was disapproved of by the Court of Appeal in *Re Oxley*, at p 612.

QUESTIONS

1. The common law and civil law systems for winding up a deceased's estate have the same objects in view but very different methods of achieving them. This is primarily because in the civil law system the general rule is that the deceased's estate vests automatically and directly in the beneficiaries; it is only in exceptional circumstances that a personal representative is appointed, and even then his function is to supervise rather than to administer.

Read Neville Brown 'Winding up Decendents' Estates in French and English Law' (1959) 33 Tul LR 631 for an interesting comparison between the two approaches.

2. T was carrying on business as a grocer when he died, leaving a will appointing A as his executor and placing all his property on trust for sale (with power to postpone sale), the net proceeds of sale and income until sale to be held on various trusts for his family. At the time of T's death, £5,000 was owed to X for the installation of a new shop front.

A has carried on the business for 3 years in the hope that market conditions for a sale will improve. In the meantime he has incurred debts totalling £2,000 to a supplier Y who knows of the outstanding debt to X and is becoming increasingly nervous about his own position. Advise Y.

CHAPTER 19

Executors and administrators

The deceased person's estate will be administered by his personal representative(s); his function is to obtain control of the deceased's assets, discharge his debts, funeral expenses and any Inheritance Tax liability and distribute the balance in accordance with the deceased's will or under the intestacy rules.[1] The personal representative will be an executor if the deceased left a will appointing him as such, otherwise he will be an administrator; the executor will apply for a grant of probate, the administrator for letters of administration.[2]

1 Appointment of executors

(a) Capacity to act

Anyone can be appointed an executor, but probate will not be granted to an infant nor to a person suffering from an incapacitating mental or physical disability whilst the disability continues. A corporation sole can be an executor;[3] so can a corporation aggregate if it is a trust corporation, otherwise it can only take out a grant through its nominee[4] and even then only if the corporation has power in its memorandum of association to act as personal representative. A testator often wants to appoint a partnership, eg a firm of solicitors, as his executor but a partnership has no legal persona in English law; such an appointment is construed as an appointment of all the partners at the date of execution of the will,[5] unless the testator has shown a contrary intention.

(i) *Infants*

Supreme Court Act 1981

118. Effect of appointment of minor[6] as executor
Where a testator by his will appoints a minor to be an executor, the appointment shall

---

1. See p 123 ante.
2. See Ch 20 post. In 1984 there were 269,171 non-contentious grants of which 176,195 were probate grants, 83,492 were grants of letters of administration and 9,484 were grants of letters of administration with the will annexed (see p 289 post): Judicial Statistics, Annual Report 1984, Cmnd 9599.
3. See eg *Re Haynes* (1842) 3 Curt 75 (appointment of the 'Archbishop of Tuam').
4. Eg a director or a general manager, see eg *In the Goods of Hunt* [1896] P 288.
5. *In the Goods of Fernie* (1849) 6 Notes of Cas 657.
6. Ie a person under the age of 18, see Family Law Reform Act 1969, s 1(3) and Sch 1. See also the report of the Committee on the Age of Majority (1967) Cmnd 3342, paras 419–423.

not operate to vest in the minor the estate, or any part of the estate, of the testator, or to constitute him a personal representative for any purpose, unless and until probate is granted to him in accordance with probate rules.

Non-Contentious Probate Rules 1954[7]

31.   Grants on behalf of infants[8]

(1) Where the person to whom a grant[9] would otherwise be made is an infant, administration for his use and benefit until he attains the age of eighteen years shall, subject to paragraphs (3) and (5) of this Rule, be granted—

  (a) to both parents of the infant jointly or to the statutory or testamentary guardian of the infant or to any guardian appointed by a court of competent jurisdiction, or
  (b) if there is no such guardian able and willing to act and the infant has attained the age of sixteen years, to any next of kin nominated by the infant or, where the infant is a married woman, to any such next of kin or to her husband if nominated by her.

(2) Any person nominated under sub-paragraph (b) of the last foregoing paragraph may represent any other infant whose next of kin he is, being an infant below the age of sixteen years entitled in the same degree as the infant who made the nomination.[10]

(3) Notwithstanding anything in this rule, administration for the use and benefit of the infant until he attains the age of eighteen years may be granted to any person assigned as guardian by order of a registrar in default of, or jointly with, or to the exclusion of, any such person as is mentioned in paragraph (1) of this rule; and such an order may be made on application by the intended guardian, who shall file an affidavit of fitness sworn by a responsible person.

(4) Where a grant is required to be made to not less than two administrators and there is only one person competent and willing to take a grant under the foregoing provisions of this rule, administration may, unless a registrar otherwise directs, be granted to such person jointly with any other person nominated by him as a fit and proper person to take the grant.

(5) Where an infant who is sole executor has no interest in the residuary estate of the deceased, administration for the use and benefit of the infant until he attains the age of eighteen years shall, unless a registrar otherwise directs, be granted to the person entitled to the residuary estate.

(6) An infant's right to administration may be renounced only by a person assigned as guardian under paragraph (3) of this rule and authorised to renounce by a registrar.

32.   Grants where infant co-executor[11]

(1) Where one of two or more executors is an infant, probate may be granted to the other executor or executors not under disability, with power reserved of making the like grant to the infant on his attaining the age of eighteen years, and administration for the use and benefit of the infant until he attains the age of eighteen years may be granted under rule 31 if and only if the executors who are not under disability renounce or, on being cited to accept or refuse a grant, fail to make an effective application therefor.

(2) An infant executor's right to probate on attaining the age of eighteen years may not be renounced by any person on his behalf.

---

7. SCA 1981, s 127 authorises the making of rules of Court by statutory instrument for 'regulating and prescribing the practice and procedure of the High Court with reference to non-contentious or common form probate business.' The current rules are the Non-Contentious Probate Rules 1954, SI 1954/796 as amended.
8. As amended by SI 1967/748, SI 1982/446. These grants are sometimes referred to as grants of administration *durante minoris aetate*.
9. Probate or letters of administration; cf rule 32 post.
10. See eg *Re Cope* (1880) 16 ChD 49.
11. As amended by Family Law Reform Act 1969, s 1(3) and Sch 1, Pt II.

(ii) *Physical or mental incapacity*

Non-Contentious Probate Rules 1954[12]

33. Grants in case of mental or physical incapacity[13]

(1) Where a registrar is satisfied[14] that a person entitled to a grant[15] is by reason of mental or physical incapacity incapable of managing his affairs, administration for his use and benefit, limited during his incapacity or in such other way as the registrar may direct, may be granted—
  (a) in the case of mental incapacity, to the person authorised by the Court of Protection to apply for the grant, or
  (b) where there is no person so authorised, or in the case of physical incapacity—
      (i) if the person incapable is entitled as executor and has no interest in the residuary estate of the deceased, to the person entitled to such estate;
      (ii) if the person incapable is entitled otherwise than as executor or is an executor having an interest in the residuary estate of the deceased, to the person who would be entitled to a grant in respect of his estate if he had died intestate;
  or to such other person as a registrar may by order direct.[16]
(2) Unless a registrar otherwise directs, no grant of administration shall be made under this rule unless all persons entitled in the same degree as the person incapable have been cleared off.

(iii) *Corporations*

Supreme Court Act 1981

115. Grants to trust corporations

(1) The High Court may—
  (a) where a trust corporation is named in a will as executor, grant probate to the corporation either solely or jointly with any other person named in the will as executor, as the case may require; or
  (b) grant administration to a trust corporation, either solely or jointly with another person;
and the corporation may act accordingly as executor or administrator, as the case may be.
(2) Probate or administration shall not be granted to any person as nominee of a trust corporation.

128. Interpretation of Part V and other probate provisions

In this Part and in the other provisions of this Act relating to probate causes and matters, unless the context otherwise requires—'trust corporation' means the Public Trustee or a corporation either appointed by the court in any particular case to be a trustee or

---

12. See n 7 ante.
13. Amended by SI 1967/748.
14. Where the applicant has been authorised by the Court of Protection to apply for the grant this authority will satisfy the registrar of the patient's incapacity. Otherwise, if the patient is resident in an institution the registrar will normally accept a certificate of incapacity from the medical officer responsible; if not so resident, then from the patient's doctor: see *Practice Direction* [1969] 1 All ER 494, [1969] 1 WLR 301.
15. Probate or letters of administration.
16. Such as the attorney of the incapable person, if he holds an enduring power of attorney registered under the Enduring Powers of Attorney Act 1986: see *Practice Direction* [1986] 2 All ER 41.

authorised by rules made under section 4(3) of the Public Trustee Act 1906 to act as a custodian trustee.[17]

Non-Contentious Probate Rules 1954[12]

34.   Grants to . . . other corporate bodies[18]

(3) Where a corporation (not being a trust corporation) would, if an individual, be entitled to a grant, administration for its use and benefit, limited until further representation is granted, may be granted to its nominee or, if the corporation has its principal place of business outside England, its nominee or lawfully constituted attorney, and a copy of the resolution appointing the nominee or, as the case may be, the power of attorney, sealed by the corporation or otherwise authenticated to the registrar's satisfaction, shall be lodged with the application for the grant, and the oath shall state that the corporation is not a trust corporation.[19]

(iv)   *A partnership*

Re Horgan [1971] P 50, [1969] 3 All ER 1570, PDA; Latey J

The testator left a will containing the following clause: 'I appoint the firm of Rodgers, Horsley & Burton . . . who may act through any partner or partners of that firm or their successors in business at the date of my death not exceeding two in number to be the executors and trustees of this my will . . . .' The applicant, sole surviving partner in that firm, sought probate of the will. It was argued by the Attorney-General[20] that the clause was void for uncertainty. **Held:** Probate should issue to the applicant.

Latey J: The law does not permit the appointment as executor of a partnership firm as such. Where a clause in a will is so phrased as to purport to do this, the court construes it as appointing the individual partners as executors: see *In the Goods of Fernie*[1] ((1849) 6 Notes of Cases 657). That case was decided 120 years ago, there is no other reported decision on the point and it has never been questioned. Where the testator appointed 'any two of my sons' as executors the appointment failed as void for uncertainty: see *In the*

---

17. See Public Trustee Rules 1912, SR & O 348, as amended by SI 1971/1894 and SI 1975/1189. These rules bring within the definition of trust corporation the Treasury Solicitor and also any corporation (i) constituted under the law of the UK or any other EEC Member State (see eg *Re Bigger* [1977] Fam 203, [1977] 2 All ER 644 (Bank of Ireland)), (ii) empowered by its constitution to take on the business of acting as a trustee or personal representative, (iii) with a place of business in the UK, (iv) incorporated by special Act of Parliament or Royal Charter or registered in the UK or other EEC Member State (having a share capital of at least £250,000 of which no less than £100,000 is paid up). The most widely appointed trust corporations are the trust companies created by the clearing banks, eg Barclays Bank Trust Company Ltd, Midland Bank Executor and Trustee Company Ltd.
18. As amended by SI 1971/1977, SI 1982/446 and SI 1985/1232.
19. Practice Direction [1956] 1 All ER 305, [1956] 1 WLR 127 also requires a corporation seeking a grant under rule 34(3) to produce a copy of its constitution to establish its power to take a grant through a nominee.
20. Invited to assist the court as *amicus curiae*, as was the Law Society, in the light of the considerable number of enquiries directed by solicitors to the Probate Registry and to the Law Society on this point. In 1967 the Law Society's Gazette had published an article by Oerton on the subject which is referred to by Latey J in his judgment.
1. Whilst a valid authority for the proposition stated, it should be noted that the appointment in that case was simply one of the partnership concerned; it was therefore construed as an appointment of the partners at the date of the will, despite the fact that the partnership had subsequently dissolved. It was to overcome problems of this nature that clauses of the kind adopted by the testator in *Re Horgan* became increasingly popular.

Goods of Baylis ((1862) 2 Sw & Tr 613). In *In the Goods of Blackwell* ((1877) 2 PD 72) a testator who had three sisters appointed 'one of my sisters my sole executrix' without stating which. When the testator died only one of his sisters was surviving, but this appointment, too, was held to be void for uncertainty.

Counsel for the Attorney-General said rightly that the phraseology of the clause as a whole is unhappily chosen and is far from clear. But, he argued, the main defect is that on its proper construction, what is done is to appoint as executors any two of however many partners as may be surviving at the time of the testator's death without identifying them; and therefore, the appointment is indistinguishable from those in *In the Goods of Baylis* ((1862) 2 Sw & Tr 613) and *In the Goods of Blackwell* ((1877) 2 PD 72). If the construction for which he contends is the proper one the conclusion of failure for uncertainty is, in my judgment, inescapable and no one has argued to the contrary . . . .

For the applicant and for The Law Society it is argued that while there are defects they are not fatal. It is stressed that however many people a testator appoints as executors, no more than four can obtain a grant (s 160(1) of Supreme Court of Judicature (Consolidation) Act 1925)[2] and that power will be reserved to the others; and that, apart altogether from the statutory restriction for a variety of reasons it is not uncommon for, say, one executor to take a grant with power reserved to others.

Counsel for the Law Society argued that prima facie it is wholly inappropriate to say 'I appoint X, Y and Z and they can act through A, B and C.' But, he says, meaning can be given to it if one were to treat the firm as though it were a company and say 'I want the partners at the date of my death to act.' One gets out of the difficulty of the use of the word 'any' by the fact that the first line of the clause appoints all the partners. What the clause means is that the testator appointed 'the firm in the person of the partner or partners at the date of my death.' The words 'not exceeding two in number to be the executors' would result in the failure for uncertainty if what they meant was any two of however many partners at the time of the death. But these words have to be read conjunctively with the first line which appoints as executors all the partners. So, he argues, the natural construction of the clause as a whole is that the testator was contemplating and intending the appointment of all, a grant to two and power reserved to the others. Those, then, are the two constructions suggested. I have found it far from easy to decide which is to be preferred. On balance, in my judgment, the construction urged by counsel for the Law Society makes more sense of the clause as a whole and I construe the clause accordingly. It follows that the appointment is not void for uncertainty.

On behalf of The Law Society I was informed that there are probably thousands of wills in existence with appointments of this kind. Although it is an agreeable circumstance that if I am right then these appointments will not fail, I repeat that I have reached the decision with a good deal less than entire confidence in its correctness. This clause may come before the court again and a decision the other way may result.

Counsel wisely did not attempt to draft a formula which would cater for all contingencies such as dissolution (with one partner taking one part of the practice and another the other), amalgamation and purchase. But they were all agreed that the formula suggested by Mr Oerton in his article[3] was probably the best which could be devised and was greatly to be preferred to the one which has been under consideration. Although, of course, I cannot adjudicate in advance I agree with counsel. Mr Oerton's suggested clause is this:

> 'I appoint the partners at the date of my death in the firm of . . . . of . . . . or the firm which at that date has succeeded to and carries on its practice to be the executors and trustees of this my will (and I express the wish that two and only two of them shall prove my will and act initially in its trusts).'

the words in brackets being precatory only.[4]

---

2. Now SCA 1981, s 114(1).

3. Oerton 'Solicitors as Executors' (1967) 64 LSG 244–45, 343–46.

4. In *Re Yearwood* (1982) 30 SASR 169 (South Australia Supreme Court) the testatrix had adopted this clause but the appointment nevertheless failed; before her death the partnership of the firm in question had dissolved and the partners had formed three new firms, none of which could be regarded as succeeding to or carrying on the business of the original firm.

(b) Who appoints an executor?

Normally the testator will appoint his own executor(s), but there are some exceptions to this rule.

(i) *The chain of representation*

If B, the last proving executor of A, dies without having completed the winding up of A's estate, but himself leaves a will appointing C as his executor, C, on proving B's will automatically becomes executor of A's will as well and will have to complete the winding up of A's estate as well as wind up the estate of B.

Administration of Estates Act 1925

7. Executor of executor represents original testator
(1) An executor of a sole or last surviving executor of a testator is the executor of that testator.[5]

This provision shall not apply to an executor who does not prove the will of his testator, and, in the case of an executor who on his death leaves surviving him some other executor of his testator who afterwards[6] proves the will of that testator, it shall cease to apply on such probate being granted.[7]

(2) So long as the chain of such representation is unbroken, the last executor in the chain is the executor of every preceding testator.

(3) The chain of such representation is broken by—
   (a) an intestacy; or
   (b) the failure of a testator to appoint an executor; or
   (c) the failure to obtain probate of a will;[8]

but is not broken by a temporary grant of administration if probate is subsequently granted.

(4) Every person in the chain of representation to a testator—
   (a) has the same rights in respect of the real and personal estate of that testator as the original executor would have had if living; and
   (b) is, to the extent to which the estate whether real or personal of that testator has come to his hands, answerable as if he were an original executor.

Law Reform Committee: Twenty-Third Report[9]

7.4. . . . The evidence we have received indicates that the results of the operation of the chain of representation are often unsatisfactory. An executor can find himself responsible for the administration of estates with which he has no real connection; he will not, however, be able to renounce the executorship of any of them while retaining that of the one for which he was originally appointed.[10]

---

5. See eg *In the Goods of Beer* (1851) 2 Rob 349.
6. Power having been originally reserved to him to come in to prove at a later stage.
7. Eg A dies leaving a will appointing P and Q as his executors; P proves the will with power reserved to Q to prove; P then dies leaving a will appointing R his executor. R proves P's will and so becomes executor of P and of A (by chain of representation). If Q then applies for probate of A's will he will oust R from his position as executor of A. If Q subsequently dies without having completed the winding up of A's estate, the chain can only continue through him as he will have been the last surviving proving executor of A, so that if he dies eg intestate, the chain is broken.
8. Once the chain is broken, a grant of letters of administration *de bonis non administratis* will have to be taken out to complete the winding up of the original estate.
9. 'The Powers and Duties of Trustees' (1982) Cmnd 8733.
10. See eg *Brooke v Haymes* (1868) LR 6 Eq 25.

7.5. We agree that this is an unsatisfactory state of affairs and that since we have already decided that personal representatives generally should be able to retire with the leave of the court for good cause,[11] we see no reason why executors who have become responsible for more than one estate through a chain should not be able to renounce in respect of those estates. We recommend that a person who finds himself the executor of more than one estate through a chain of representation should be able to renounce in part provided that he has not inter-meddled in the affairs of those estates he wants nothing to do with. He should be able to do this at whatever stage it comes to his notice that he has become the executor of another estate through a chain of representation.[12]

(ii) *Appointment by the court*

The court has no general power to appoint an executor; if the deceased has left a will but no proving executor or the court exercises its power to pass over the person entitled to a grant of probate,[13] the appropriate step is for letters of administration with the will annexed to issue.[14] However, the court does have power to appoint an additional executor where there is a minority or life interest involved;[15] it also has power to make a substitutional appointment when it is removing a personal representative from office.[16]

Supreme Court Act 1981

114. Number of personal representatives
(4) If at any time during the minority of a beneficiary or the subsistence of a life interest under a will or intestacy there is only one personal representative (not being a trust corporation), the High Court may, on the application of any person interested or the guardian or receiver of any such person, and in accordance with probate rules,[17] appoint one or more additional personal representatives to act while the minority or life interest subsists and until the estate is fully administered.
(5) An appointment of an additional personal representative under subsection (4) to act with an executor shall not have the effect of including him in any chain of representation.

(iii) *An executor de son tort*

A person who is not an executor or administrator of the deceased's estate but who intermeddles in some way with the deceased's assets as if he was a personal representative can thereby constitute himself an executor *de son tort*;[18] this does not entitle him to any grant of representation, it merely fixes him with liability for his actions towards the creditors and beneficiaries of the deceased as if he were the lawful representative.

---

11. See p 302 post.
12. See also Barker: 'Executors: the Case Against the Chain of Representation' (1980) 77 LSG 265.
13. See p 303 post.
14. See p 299 post.
15. The court also has power to appoint an additional executor where a settled land grant is necessary: AEA 1925, s 23(2), see p 316 post.
16. See p 305 post.
17. See NCPR 1954, r 24 as amended by SI 1967/748, SI 1982/446.
18. This expression is used even if the deceased left no will.

Administration of Estates Act 1925

28. Liability for fraud

If any person, to the defrauding of creditors or without full valuable consideration, obtains receives or holds any real or personal estate of a deceased person or effects the release of any debt or liability due to the estate of the deceased, he shall be charged as executor in his own wrong to the extent of the real and personal estate received or coming to his hands, or the debt or liability released, after deducting—

   (a) any debt for valuable consideration and without fraud due to him from the deceased person at the time of his death; and

   (b) any payment made by him which might properly be made by a personal representative.

Inland Revenue Commissioners v Stype Investments (Jersey) Ltd [1982] Ch 456, [1982] 3 All ER 419, CA; Templeman, Watkins and Fox LJJ

The defendant was a company resident in Jersey (Channel Islands); it held a large estate in Hertfordshire as the nominee of Sir Charles Clore. At Sir Charles' request, the defendant company entered into a contract to sell the estate to the Prudential Assurance Co Ltd but between contract and completion, Sir Charles died. The sale was duly completed a few weeks after his death; on the instructions of the defendant company the Prudential paid the £20m proceeds of sale direct to the company's account in Jersey. No grant of representation in relation to Sir Charles' English estate had been taken out at that stage. The Inland Revenue claimed capital transfer tax[18a] of £15m on Sir Charles' beneficial interest in the Hertfordshire estate at his death. Sir Charles' remaining assets in the United Kingdom were worth only £4m so the Inland Revenue claimed that the defendant company had intermeddled with Sir Charles' English estate in removing the £20m to Jersey, an act which could have been lawfully done only by personal representatives duly constituted in England after payment of all English liabilities, including capital transfer tax. The company was therefore an executor *de son tort*, it was claimed, and as such liable to pay the £15m capital transfer tax due on this property. The Inland Revenue obtained leave under RSC Ord 11 r 1(1) to issue and serve a summons outside the jurisdiction against the defendant company claiming an account of this property for capital transfer tax purposes and an injunction freezing the company's United Kingdom assets (worth £28m) until the account had been delivered and the tax paid. The company successfully applied to Goulding J to have the order set aside;[19] the Revenue appealed. **Held:** Appeal allowed; Goulding J's order discharged.

Templeman LJ: After the death of Sir Charles, Stype Investments (the defendant company) was entitled and bound to complete the contract with the Prudential and to receive the purchase price of £20m. But the right in equity to the purchase price was property situate in England at the death of Sir Charles and the £20m therefore belonged to the personal representatives of Sir Charles when constituted in England and to nobody else for the purpose of carrying out and completing administration of the English estate. By procuring payment of the £20m in Jersey, Stype Investments transferred the right to the £20m from the personal representatives constituted in England to the personal representatives constituted in Jersey. If this were not the case, Stype

---

18a. Now inheritance tax. See Ch 16 ante.
19. See [1981] Ch 367, [1981] 2 All ER 394.

Investments would have no difficulty now in transferring the £20m from Jersey to England where it belongs. The act of transferring title from English personal representatives to Jersey personal representatives constituted an intermeddling with the English estate and constituted Stype Investments executor *de son tort.*

In *New York Breweries Co v A–G* ([1899] AC 62) an English company transferred shares in the company from the name of a deceased domiciled American into the names of his executors, who had proved his will in New York but, to the knowledge of the company, had not obtained, and did not intend to obtain, probate in England. The company also paid dividends and interest to the executors. It was held that the company had 'taken possession of and administered' part of the testator's estate, that the company was executor *de son tort* and that the company was personally liable to deliver an account and pay such duty as would have been payable if probate had been obtained in England.

Goulding J said that payment of the £20m in Jersey did not affect any such change of title as founded the decision in the New York Breweries case. But just as the intermeddling in the New York Breweries case transferred title from the English representatives when constituted to the American representatives already constituted, so in the present case Stype Investments transferred title from the English representatives when constituted to the Jersey representatives when constituted ... In our judgment Stype Investments is liable for intermeddling with the English estate. At the very least the Inland Revenue establish a strong arguable case.

(c) Manner of appointment

When the appointment is made by the testator, as is usual, he will normally appoint the executors expressly.[20] Sometimes, particularly in home-made wills, the testator, without expressly designating X as his executor has shown that he intends him to be an executor by virtue of the executor-like duties he has expressly conferred on him. In such a case the executor is said to be appointed 'according to the tenor' of the will, in other words, by implication.

In **Re Fawcett** [1941] P 85, [1941] 2 All ER 341, the testatrix had directed that her residuary estate be sold and the proceeds after repayment of debts should go to A. 'Barclays Bank will do this' she added. Langton J held, inter alia, that this was enough to show that she intended the bank to act as her executor, saying at p 345:

I think that the reference to them by the testatrix in this unprofessional language— namely, 'Barclays Bank will do this'—meant that she thought that they would act as her executors, as indeed, she had named them as joint-executors in her earlier will. Therefore, in so far as it is necessary to decide that point I decide also that Barclays Bank are executors according to the tenor of the will.[1]

In **Re Adamson** (1875) LR 3 P & D 253, the testator left all his estate to A, B and C as trustees on trust for sale and out of the proceeds of sale to pay his debts and funeral expenses and to pay the balance to X, Y and Z as his trustees on certain trusts, Hannen J had no difficulty in holding that A, B and C were executors according to the tenor of the will, saying, at p 254:

The essential duties of an executor are to collect the assets of the deceased, to pay his funeral expenses and debts, and to discharge the legacies. Of these three duties two are expressly assigned by the testator to (A, B and C), for he directs them to pay his debts and funeral expenses, and to pay the balance to the Scotch trustees; and I think the reasonable construction of the language used by the testator is that the three persons

---

20. See eg specimen will, p 62 ante.
1. See also *Re Cook* [1902] P 114.

named should also collect his assets in England. If the language of the will stood alone, I should deem it highly improbable that the testator intended that some person as administrator should collect the assets and hand them over to the three persons named, but there is a passage in the will which makes it clear that the testator intended to appoint and thought that he had appointed executors, for he says, 'each executor only accountable for his own intromissions.'[2] A meaning can only be given to this passage by holding that the three persons named are executors according to the tenor.[3]

In **Re Punchard** (1872) L R 2 P & D 369, by contrast, the testator appointed X 'as trustee to this estate' but he was given no executor-like duties to perform and Lord Penzance rejected his application for probate saying, at p 371:

In this case nothing was bequeathed to the person called a trustee; there is nothing for him to do as such, no duty to perform. The whole matter resolves itself into this: he is said to be a trustee. That is not enough.[4]

(d) Number of executors

A testator can appoint only one executor if he so wishes, although if the will involves a minority or life interest the court has power to appoint an additional executor.[5] There is no upper limit in so far as the testator can appoint as many as he likes, but the grant of probate will only issue to a maximum of four: if more than four are appointed and wish to take out the grant, the first four to apply will be given the grant, power being reserved to the others to prove on a vacancy occurring.

Supreme Court Act 1981

114. Number of personal representatives
(1) Probate or administration shall not be granted by the High Court to more than four persons in respect of the same part of the estate of a deceased person.[6]

(e) Must an executor take on the job?

An executor is not obliged to accept the position: he can renounce his entitlement to apply for the grant so long as he has not accepted the office by implication by intermeddling with the estate in some way. If he does not wish to act at the moment but wants to keep his position open for the future, he can reserve the right to prove later so long as more than one executor has been appointed and the other one is willing to take out a grant. If a sole executor is delaying his decision whether to accept or renounce,[7] he can be forced to make

---

2. An 'intromission' is a dealing or acts of intermeddling in Scots law; the testator in question was a Scot although he died domiciled in England.
3. See also *Re Baylis* (1865) LR 1 P & D 21, *Re Way* [1901] P 345, *Re Wilkinson* [1892] P 227.
4. See also *Re Mackenzie* [1909] P 305.
5. See SCA, 1981 s 114(4) p 293 ante.
6. So a testator could appoint eg four persons as executors of his literary works and four other persons as his executors of the rest of his estate and the grant would issue accordingly.
7. As a sole executor he will not be in a position to ask for power to be reserved for him to prove later on.

up his mind by a citation (a formal demand usually made by the person who would be entitled to an administration grant); if the executor does not appear to the citation his rights as executor wholly cease.

Long & Feaver v Symes & Hannam (1832) 3 Hagg Ecc 771, 162 ER 1339, Prerog Ct; Nicholl J

The executors, A and B, had inserted advertisements in the local newspaper requesting creditors of the testator's estate to put in their accounts without delay to themselves, A and B, 'his executors in trust'. After $2\frac{1}{2}$ years A and B had still not applied for probate and two legatees brought proceedings to compel them to do so.

Held: Having intermeddled in the estate the executors were not in a position to renounce and must take out a probate grant.

Nicholl J: The question then is whether there has been such an intermeddling as to render the executors compellable to take probate? There is no doubt on the law that if a person named executor intermeddles, he cannot afterwards refuse to take probate; and if not named executor, he becomes so *de son tort*. There are certain acts of necessity, such as feeding the deceased's cattle and the like, which do not bind a party; and if a party even has shewn himself willing to take upon himself the execution of a will, he may, in aid of justice, be dismissed by the Court, in order to become a witness;[8] but otherwise slight circumstances are obligatory and sufficient to compel a person to take probate if really executor, or to render him executor *de son tort* if not really executor. Swinburne in several passages lays down the obligation, and says (part 6, s 22) 'he must beware not to administer the effects as executor.' He is compellable 'when he does those acts which are proper to an executor.' 'The most safe course is not to meddle at all, but utterly to abstain:' 'the refusal cannot be by word only, it must be entered and recorded in Court' . . . .

What then are the facts? Have the executors done anything that shewed an intention on their part to take upon them the executorship? It is unnecessary to go one step further than the advertisements: nothing can be a more strong intermeddling than the insertion of such an advertisement, and expressly in the character of executors. It does not merely 'shew an intention to take upon them the executorship,' but it is an absolute acceptance of the executorship. Nor was this done by (A) alone, for (B) admits that it was done with his concurrence; that it was their joint act: and after this concurrence the acts of (A) in a great degree bind (B).

They subsequently make inquiries, and they find that the executorship may turn out a troublesome business, and then they give notice to the family that they will not act; the matter lies dormant till the following year, when in answer to an application by letter, they decline to undertake the office. That was too late in time and insufficient in form—'the refusal must be recorded in Court:' till that was done no person could take administration. They should have decided at once; they might have delivered up or brought in the will and given a proxy of renunciation. As the authorities point out, they should 'beware' how they do slight acts. I think they have not been cautious; they should not have first acted and given notice to the debtors to the estate, and afterwards leave the substituted residuary legatees without that protection for their legacies which the testator intended. For two years and a half they have left this estate, though small, without a representative or any person even to collect the debts.

---

8. The case was decided in 1832; before WA 1837, s 17 (p 99 ante) an executor of a will was not competent to be a witness as to the due execution of a will.

I am of opinion that the executors have so far intermeddled as to be compellable to take probate.[9]

Administration of Estates Act 1925

5.   Cesser of right of executor to prove

Where a person appointed executor by a will—

(i) survives the testator but dies without having taken out probate of the will; or
(ii) is cited to take out probate of the will and does not appear to the citation; or
(iii) renounces probate of the will;

his rights in respect of the executorship shall wholly cease, and the representation to the testator and the administration of his real and personal estate shall devolve and be committed in like manner as if that person had not been appointed executor.

6.   Withdrawal of renunciation

(1) Where an executor who has renounced probate has been permitted, whether before or after the commencement of this Act, to withdraw the renunciation and prove the will, the probate shall take effect and be deemed always to have taken effect without prejudice to the previous acts and dealings of and notices to any other personal representative who has previously proved the will or taken out letters of administration, and a memorandum of the subsequent probate shall be endorsed on the original probate or letters of administration.[10]

In **In the Goods of Stiles** [1898] P 12, A and B were appointed executors. A took out the grant of probate, B having renounced, but A subsequently absconded. Jeune P held that in these circumstances, B should be permitted to retract his renunciation saying at p 13:

I see no reason in the nature of things why, in a proper case, where circumstances have altered, one of several executors should not be allowed to retract his renunciation and carry on the executorship.[11]

Non-Contentious Probate Rules 1954[12]

46.   Citation to accept or refuse to take a grant[13]

(1) A citation to accept or refuse a grant may be issued at the instance of any person who would himself be entitled to a grant in the event of the person cited renouncing his right thereto.

(2) Where power to make a grant to an executor has been reserved, a citation calling on him to accept or refuse a grant may be issued at the instance of the executors who have proved the will or of the executors of the last survivor of deceased executors who have proved.

(3) A citation calling on an executor who has intermeddled in the estate of the deceased to show cause why he should not be ordered to take a grant may be issued at the instance

---

9. Cf *Holder v Holder* [1968] Ch 353, [1968] 1 All ER 665, where the Court of Appeal expressed the opinion (obiter) that the acts of an executor who simply co-operated with the other executors in (1) opening an executors' bank account and signing cheques on it, (2) allowing the endorsement of insurance policies in the names of all the executors, (3) joining with the other executors in instructing solicitors to wind up the estate, were so technical and trivial that they should not have prevented him from renouncing probate. See also *Re Stevens* [1897] 1 Ch 422, *Mordaunt v Clarke* (1868) LR 1 P & D 592.
10. See further NCPR 1954, s 35 as amended by SI 1967/748.
11. See also *In the Goods of Thacker* [1900] P 15.
12. See p 288 n 7 ante.
13. As amended by SI 1967/748.

of any person interested in the estate at any time after the expiration of six months from the death of the deceased:

Provided that no citation to take a grant shall issue while proceedings as to the validity of the will are pending.

(4) A person cited who is willing to accept or take a grant may apply *ex parte* to a registrar for an order for a grant on filing an affidavit showing that he has entered an appearance and that he has not been served by the citor with notice of any application for a grant to himself.

(5) If the time limited for appearance has expired and the person cited has not entered an appearance, the citor may—

    (a) in the case of a citation under paragraph (1) of this rule apply to a registrar for an order for a grant to himself;

    (b) in the case of a citation under paragraph (2) of this rule, apply to a registrar for an order that a note be made on the grant that the executor in respect of whom power was reserved has been duly cited and has not appeared and that all his rights in respect of the executorship have wholly ceased;

    (c) in the case of a citation under paragraph (3) of this rule, apply to a registrar by summons (which shall be served on the person cited) for an order requiring such person to take a grant within a specified time or for a grant to himself or some other person specified in the summons.

2 Appointment of administrators

(a) Letters of administration with the will annexed

If the deceased dies leaving a valid will but no executor able and willing to act, the grant of representation will be one of letters of administration with the will annexed.

Supreme Court Act 1981

119. Administration with will annexed

(1) Administration with the will annexed shall be granted, subject to and in accordance with probate rules, in every class of case in which the High Court had power to make such a grant immediately before the commencement of this Act.

(2) Where administration with the will annexed is granted, the will of the deceased shall be performed and observed in the same manner as if probate of it had been granted to an executor.

Non-Contentious Probate Rules 1954[14]

19. Order of priority for grant where deceased left a will[15]

Where the deceased died on or after January 1, 1926, the person or persons entitled to a grant of probate or administration with the will annexed shall be determined in accordance with the following order of priority,[16] namely—

    (i) The executor;

    (ii) Any residuary legatee or devisee holding in trust for any other person;

---

14. See p 288 n 7 ante.
15. As amended by SI 1974/597.
16. Subject to SCA 1981, s 116 (p 303 post), a grant can only issue to someone lower in the priority order when those higher in the order have either renounced their prior right or have been cited to accept or refuse administration under NCPR 1954, r 46 (p 298 ante).

(iii) Any residuary legatee or devisee for life;

(iv) The ultimate residuary legatee or devisee, including one entitled on the happening of any contingency, or, where the residue is not wholly disposed of by the will, any person entitled to share in the residue not so disposed of (including the Treasury Solicitor when claiming *bona vacantia* on behalf of the Crown), or, subject to paragraph (3) of rule 25[17] the personal representative of any such person:

Provided that: (a) unless a registrar otherwise directs a residuary legatee or devisee whose legacy or devise is vested in interest shall be preferred to one entitled on the happening of a contingency; and (b) where the residue is not in terms wholly disposed of, the registrar may, if he is satisfied that the testator has nevertheless disposed of the whole or substantially the whole of the estate as ascertained at the time of the application for the grant, allow a grant to be made (subject however to rule 37)[18] to any legatee or devisee entitled to, or to a share in, the estate so disposed of without regard to the persons entitled to share in any residue not disposed of by the will;

(v) Any specific legatee or devisee or any creditor or, subject to paragraph (3) of rule 25[17] the personal representative of any such person or, where the estate is not wholly disposed of by will, any person who, notwithstanding that the amount of the estate is such that he has no immediate beneficial interest therein, may have a beneficial interest in the event of an accretion thereto;

(vi) Any specific legatee or devisee entitled on the happening of any contingency, or any person having no interest under the will of the deceased who would have been entitled to a grant if the deceased had died wholly intestate.

(b) Letters of administration

If the deceased dies without leaving a will, the grant of representation will simply be one of letters of administration.

Non-Contentious Probate Rules 1954[19]

21.   Order of priority for grant in case of intestacy[20]

(1) Where the deceased died on or after January 1, 1926, wholly intestate, the persons having a beneficial interest in the estate shall be entitled to a grant of administration in the following order of priority, namely—

(i) The surviving spouse;

(ii) The children of the deceased, or the issue of any such child who has died during the lifetime of the deceased;

(iii) The father or mother of the deceased;

(iv) Brothers and sisters of the whole blood, or the issue of any deceased brother or sister of the whole blood who has died.

(2) If no person in any of the classes mentioned in sub-paragraphs (ii) to (iv) of the last foregoing paragraph has survived the deceased, then, in the case of—

(a) a person who died before January 1, 1953, wholly intestate, or

(b) a person dying on or after January 1, 1953, wholly intestate without leaving a surviving spouse,

---

17. See p 301 post.
18. R 37 requires notice of intended application for a grant to be given by the applicant to the Treasury Solicitor in any case in which it appears that the Crown is or may be beneficially interested in the estate of a deceased person.
19. See p 287 n 7 ante.
20. As amended by SI 1969/1689, SI 1971/1977, SI 1976/1362.

the persons hereinafter described shall, if they have a beneficial interest in the estate, be entitled to a grant in the following order of priority namely—

(i) Brothers and sisters of the half blood, or the issue of any deceased brother or sister of the half blood who has died;

(ii) Grandparents;

(iii) Uncles and aunts of the whole blood, or the issue of any deceased uncle or aunt of the whole blood who has died;

(iv) Uncles and aunts of the half blood, or the issue of any deceased uncle or aunt of the half blood who has died.

(3) In default of any person having a beneficial interest in the estate, the Treasury Solicitor shall be entitled to a grant if he claims *bona vacantia* on behalf of the Crown.

(4) If all persons entitled to a grant under the foregoing provisions of this rule have been cleared off, a grant may be made to a creditor of the deceased or to any person who, notwithstanding that he has no immediate beneficial interest in the estate, may have a beneficial interest in the event of an accretion thereto.[1]

(5) Subject to paragraph (3) of rule 25,[2] the personal representative of a person in any of the classes mentioned in paragraphs (1) and (2) of this rule or the personal representative of a creditor shall have the same right to a grant as the person whom he represents:

Provided that the persons mentioned in sub-paragraphs (ii) to (iv) of paragraph (1) and in paragraph (2) of this rule shall be preferred to the personal representative of a spouse who has died without taking a beneficial interest in the whole estate of the deceased as ascertained at the time of the application for the grant.

(6) In this rule references to children of the deceased include references to his illegitimate children, and 'father or mother of the deceased' shall be construed accordingly.

(c) Persons entitled in same degree

Non-Contentious Probate Rules 1954[3]

25. Grants where two or more persons entitled in same degree[4]

(1) A grant may be made to any person entitled thereto without notice to other persons entitled in the same degree.

(2) A dispute between persons entitled to a grant in the same degree shall be brought by summons before a registrar.

(3) Unless a registrar otherwise directs,[5] administration shall be granted to a living person in preference to the personal representative of a deceased person who would, if living, be entitled in the same degree and to a person not under disability in preference to an infant entitled in the same degree.

In **Budd v Silver** (1813) 2 Phill Ecc 115, 161 ER 1094, the parties were both

---

1. Eg if the intestate dies leaving a net residuary estate of £80,000 and survived by a spouse but not issue, the spouse would be entitled to the whole of the estate (see p 123 ante) but if further assets materialised, other relatives might come into benefit, such as the intestate's parents (see p 124 ante); this possibility would enable the parents to apply for a grant now under this sub-rule, having cleared off the spouse's prior entitlement (see p 299 n 16 ante).

2. See post.

3. See p 288 n 7 ante.

4. As amended by SI 1967/748, SI 1985/1232.

5. See eg *In the Goods of Mary Carr* LR (1867) 1 P & D 291 where the personal representative of the intestate's brother was granted letters of administration in preference to the intestate's sister because the only asset of the estate was the damages that might be recovered from X, a debtor of the intestate, and the intestate's sister was living with X and was thought to be adverse to the proceedings.

cousins of the intestate and equally entitled to the grant of letters of administration. Neither wished to act with the other. Ordering the grant to be made to Budd, Nicholl J said at p 1094:

There is no objection to Budd's character or his competency; the only point argued is that his competitor is a person of superior situation in life, being an alderman of the city of Winchester; whereas Budd is only a small shopkeeper in that city but, independently of the majority of interests being in Budd's favour, there is another reason why he should be preferred; for it seems a considerable question is likely to arise between the estate of the deceased and a son of Mr Silver, respecting the validity of a gift. The parties interested in the property might entertain a great deal of jealousy that the claims of the estate might not be so strongly asserted by the father against his son; the more so, as he has produced affidavits to shew that in his opinion it was a valid gift.

The Court grants to the person who has the majority of interests, unless there be some ground for setting him aside: here there is no ground.[6]

(d) Number of administrators

As with a grant of probate, letters of administration with or without the will annexed, will not issue to more than four.[7] Should a minority or life interest arise, the administration grant must be made to at least two individuals or a trust corporation (unless the court rules otherwise) whilst if the number in such circumstances ever drops to one individual, the court has power to appoint another administrator to act whilst the minority or life interest subsists.[8]

Supreme Court Act 1981

114. Number of personal representatives
(2) Where under a will or intestacy any beneficiary is a minor or a life interest arises, any grant of administration[9] by the High Court shall be made either to a trust corporation (with or without an individual) or to not less than two individuals, unless it appears to the court to be expedient in all the circumstances to appoint an individual as sole administrator.
(3) For the purpose of determining whether a minority or life interest arises in any particular case, the court may act on such evidence as may be prescribed.

3   Removal and retirement of personal representatives

The court has power to pass over a personal representative's entitlement to a grant and to make a grant of letters of administration instead to someone else where there are special circumstances to justify this. Otherwise, until recently, the court had no power to remove an unsatisfactory personal representative,[10]

---

6. Cf *In the Goods of Stainton* (1871) LR 2 P & D 212. See also *Bell v Timiswood* (1812) 2 Phill Ecc 22.
7. SCA 1981, s 114(1) p 296 ante.
8. SCA 1981, s 114(4) p 293 ante.
9. SCA 1981, s 128 interprets 'administration' as including 'all letters of administration of the effects of deceased persons, whether with or without a will annexed, and whether granted for general, special or limited purposes.'
10. Save by an application for the appointment of a judicial trustee in his place.

nor could a personal representative who had accepted office subsequently retire.

The Law Reform Committee was concerned about the hardship this might cause to a personal representative and their recommendation that he be permitted to retire for good cause appears to have been provided for in the Administration of Justice Act 1985 which permits the removal and substitution of personal representatives in the absolute discretion of the court.

Supreme Court Act 1981

116. Power of court to pass over prior claims to grant[11]
(1) If by reason of any special circumstances it appears to the High Court to be necessary or expedient to appoint as administrator some person other than the person who, but for this section, would in accordance with probate rules have been entitled to the grant,[12] the court may in its discretion appoint as administrator such a person as it thinks expedient.
(2) Any grant of administration under this section may be limited in any way the court thinks fit.[13]

In **Re Mathew** [1984] 2 All ER 396, [1984] 1 WLR 1011, the court considered the extent of its discretion under SCA 1981 s 116(2), Lincoln J saying at p 398:

> By s 116(2) the court is equipped with a power, in exercising this discretion, which is without fetter; it may define the grant in any way it thinks fit, ordering an unlimited or limited grant.

He upheld the registrar's decision to exercise the power by passing over the two executors named in the will, one of whom was currently the subject of bankruptcy proceedings whilst the other was outside the jurisdiction of the court, in order to make a grant of letters of administration with the will annexed to three grantees, as agreed by all parties involved, but with power reserved to the two executors to come in to prove subsequently should they wish to do so.

Re Clore [1982] Ch 456, [1982] 3 All ER 419, CA; Templeman, Watkins and Fox LJJ

The executors of Sir Charles Clore were both Jersey residents and both directors of Stype Investments (Jersey) Ltd, the company that had been closely involved with the transfer of £20m from Sir Charles' English estate to Jersey and hence out of the jurisdiction of the court without accounting for the £15m capital transfer tax due on it.[14] On the application of the Inland Revenue the senior registrar of the Probate Registry had acted under the Supreme Court of Judicature (Consolidation) Act 1925 s 162[15] to pass over the executors' entitlement to a grant and had instead made a grant to the Official Solicitor of

---

11. This power was previously contained in Supreme Court of Judicature (Consolidation) Act 1925, s 162(1).
12. Defined in s 128 as 'a grant of probate or administration'.
13. See further NCPR 1954, r 51 as amended by SI 1967/748, SI 1982/446.
14. See *IRC v Stype Investments (Jersey) Ltd* p 294 ante.
15. Now SCA 1981, s 116 ante.

letters of administration *ad colligenda bona*.[16] The senior registrar's decision was upheld by Ewbank J;[17] the executors appealed.
Held: Appeal dismissed.

Templeman LJ: The executors contend that the administration of the estate will be cheaper and more expeditious if they are given a grant. They do not intend to make provision or offer security for the payment of any capital transfer tax which may be found to be due and payable by the executors. Nor do they intend to pay or offer security for the capital transfer tax which may be found to be due and payable by them as trustees of the personal settlement of Sir Charles.

The executors as directors of Stype Investments share responsibility for the fact that £20m of the English assets are now locked up in Jersey. The executors as directors of Stype Investments share responsibility for opposing strenuously the efforts of the Inland Revenue to obtain payment by Stype Investments at least to the extent of its assets now in England of any capital transfer tax which may be found to be payable in respect of the English estate of Sir Charles. The executors, for reasons which are paltry and disingenuous, have opposed a grant to the Official Solicitor and have thus delayed investigation into the affairs of the estate of Sir Charles.

The appointment of the Official Solicitor will render academic the dispute as to whether Stype Investments constituted itself executor *de son tort*. If the £20 million now in Jersey represents property of Sir Charles situated in the United Kingdom at his death, the Official Solicitor, as personal representative of Sir Charles constituted in this country, will be able to sue Stype Investments in this country for failing to collect the debt owed by the Prudential in this country and for failing to retain the £20 million in this country available to be paid over to the Official Solicitor as personal representative of Sir Charles constituted in England. At the request of the Inland Revenue the English court would grant an injunction restraining Stype Investments from transferring any of its assets out of the jurisdiction until the Official Solicitor has taken a grant, instituted proceedings against Stype Investments and obtained an interlocutory injunction in those proceedings.

In the circumstances, the appointment of the executors as personal representatives duly constituted in this country would be bizarre. The appeal of the executors against the decision of Ewbank J is a sinister and time-wasting exercise and must be dismissed.[18]

Law Reform Committee: Twenty-Third Report[19]

7.2.   The retirement of personal representatives
In most cases, the administration of a deceased person's estate will cause no unforeseen problems. However it may well turn out to be a complicated and onerous task, and the personal representative, whether executor or administrator, will have taken the job on without appreciating the time and trouble to which he will be put. Once the personal representative has accepted the office, or done anything which indicates his acceptance, he will not (except in exceptional circumstances) be able to retire. Of course, an executor may renounce before he has accepted the office and a potential administrator may decide not to apply for a grant of letters of administration, but this does not assist the

---

16. A special grant limited to getting in and preserving the assets of the estate until a general grant is made.
17. [1982] 1 Fam 113, [1982] 2 WLR 314.
18. For further examples of the court exercising its power under s 116, see *Re S* [1968] P 302, [1967] 2 All ER 150 (executor convicted of manslaughter of testator and sentenced to life imprisonment, letters of administration with the will annexed granted to the testator's daughters); *In the Goods of Chapman* [1903] P 192 (the intestate's father had disappeared 20 years previously and was believed to be dead; the grant was issued instead to the intestate's brother. See also *Re Biggs* [1966] P 118, [1966] 1 All ER 358, where the court passed over an executor even though he had intermeddled in the estate.
19. 'The Powers and Duties of Trustees' (1982) Cmnd 8733.

personal representative who decides he does not want to carry on with the administration when the onerous nature of the task becomes apparent. Exceptionally, an executor may apply to the court under the provisions of section 1 of the Judicial Trustees Act 1896 for the appointment of a judicial trustee in his place.[20] However, the courts are generally reluctant to relieve personal representatives of their duties, although an application for replacement on the grounds of ill health would probably succeed. The evidence which we have received shows that the law is lacking in not allowing personal representatives to retire, especially since many personal representatives accept the office with no real understanding of what it entails.

7.3. Although we would not wish to encourage personal representatives to retire without good cause, as this would invariably cause upset and postpone the completion of the administration, we do think that both executors and administrators should be allowed to retire for good cause. Our view is that where the demands of the office are such as to impose unreasonable and unforeseen burdens upon a personal representative, he should be allowed to retire with the leave of the court.[1] Serious supervening ill health should be a separate ground for allowing the retirement of a personal representative, and both this and the previous suggested ground should be specified in any legislation which results from the recommendations of this Report.

Administration of Justice Act 1985

50. Power of High Court to appoint substitute for, or to remove personal representative

(1) Where an application relating to the estate of a deceased person is made to the High Court under this subsection by or on behalf of a personal representative of the deceased or a beneficiary of the estate, the court may in its discretion—
  (a) appoint a person (in this section called a substituted personal representative) to act as personal representative of the deceased in place of the existing personal representative or representatives of the deceased or any of them; or
  (b) if there are two or more existing personal representatives of the deceased, terminate the appointment of one or more, but not all, of those persons.

(2) Where the court appoints a person to act as a substituted personal representative of a deceased person, then—
  (a) if that person is appointed to act with an executor or executors the appointment shall (except for the purpose of including him in any chain of representation)[2] constitute him executor of the deceased as from the date of the appointment; and
  (b) in any other case the appointment shall constitute that person administrator of the deceased's estate as from the date of the appointment.

(3) The court may authorise a person appointed as a substituted personal representative to charge remuneration for his services as such, on such terms (whether or not involving the submission of bills of charges for taxation by the court) as the court may think fit.

(4) Where an application relating to the estate of a deceased person is made to the court under subsection(1), the court may, if it thinks fit, proceed as if the application were, or included an application for the appointment under the Judicial Trustees Act 1896 of a judicial trustee in relation to that estate.[3]

(5) In this section 'beneficiary', in relation to the estate of a deceased person, means a

---

20. See p 420 post.
1. The United States Uniform Probate Code s 3–610 permits a personal representative to resign his position by simply filing a written statement of resignation with the Registrar after 15 days written notice to the beneficiaries. So long as someone applies for the appointment of a successor representative within the time indicated in the notice, the resignation is effective.
2. See p 292 ante.
3. See p 420 post.

person who under the will of the deceased or under the law relating to intestacy is beneficially interested in the estate.

QUESTIONS

1. A dies intestate leaving a net estate of £60,000, a surviving spouse and one child. Who will take out what grant? Would it affect your answer if the child was under 18?

2. B dies leaving a will appointing C as his executor and leaving his net estate of £50,000 to his widow for life and then for his son absolutely. C has advertised for creditors but then decides not to take out probate after all. Who will take out what grant? Would it affect your answer if the son was under 18?

3. D dies leaving a will appointing 'my solicitors, Sharp & Fiddle', as her executors and leaving all her estate to her husband. When D executed her will there were four partners in Sharp & Fiddle: E, F, G and H. By the time D died, E had retired, F had died and G and H had dissolved the partnership and formed separate firms of their own. Who will take out what grant?

4. J dies leaving a will appointing K, L and M as his executors. K renounces probate and L takes out a probate grant with power reserved to M. L dies before completing the winding up of J's estate, leaving a will appointing N as his executor. Who will complete the winding up of J's estate? Would it affect your answer if L had died intestate?

5. Consider the advantages and disadvantages of permitting personal representatives to retire from office.

CHAPTER 20

Obtaining and revoking the grant

A grant of representation is not always necessary to deal with the deceased's property. Under the Administration of Estates (Small Payments) Act 1965 various authorities, notably the National Savings Bank and Friendly Societies, are able to hand over assets up to a certain amount which cannot exceed £5,000[1] to the beneficiaries without production of a grant. Otherwise, the personal representative must make a formal application for his grant of probate or letters of administration.

1 Applying for the grant

(a) Place

Supreme Court Act 1981

105. Applications
Applications for grants of probate or administration and for the revocation of grants may be made to—
   (a) the Principal Registry of the Family Division[2] (in this Part referred to as 'the Principal Registry'); or
   (b) a district probate registry.[3]

---

1. Administration of Estates (Small Payments) (Increase of Limit) Order 1984 (1984 SI/539). The 1984 Order also increases to £5,000 the limit of £1,500 specified in the Trustee Savings Bank Act 1981, s 27(4) in relation to Trustee Savings Bank balances.
2. The Family Division through the Principal and District Registries has jurisdiction in non-contentious matters; where the application is contentious, eg as to the validity of a will, the Chancery Division of the High Court has jurisdiction, also County Courts where the value of the deceased's estate after allowing for funeral expenses, debts and encumbrances does not exceed £30,000.
3. SCA 1981, s 104 empowers the Lord Chancellor to direct by statutory instrument that there be district probate registries at such places and for such districts as he shall specify. There are currently 13 district probate registries, namely Birmingham, Brighton, Bristol, Ipswich, Leeds, Liverpool, Llandaff, Manchester, Newcastle upon Tyne, Nottingham, Oxford, Sheffield and Winchester (see SI 1981/726 amending SI 1968/1676). These district registries between them control 17 sub-registries.

(b) Time

Non-Contentious Probate Rules 1954[4]

5.   Duty of registrar on receiving application for grant[5]
(3) Except with the leave of two registrars no grant of probate or of administration with the will annexed shall issue within seven days of the death of the deceased and no grant of administration shall issue within fourteen days thereof.

(c) Documents in support of application

Certain documents must be lodged at the Principal Registry or at one of the district or sub-registries as the case may be. The applicant may apply in person[6] or through a solicitor.[7] Of these documents, an Oath must always be lodged whether the application is for probate or letters of administration; the Will (if any) duly marked as an exhibit to the Oath must always be lodged; an Inland Revenue Account must be lodged and the inheritance tax on the personalty duly paid[8] unless the gross value of the estate does not exceed £40,000 and certain other conditions are met;[9] when the application is for letters of administration, sureties may be required to provide a guarantee[10]. Finally, the probate fees must be paid.[11]

(i) *Oath*

Non-Contentious Probate Rules 1954[12]

6.   Oath in support of grant[13]
(1) Every application for a grant shall be supported by an oath in the form applicable to the circumstances of the case, which shall be contained in an affidavit sworn by the applicant, and by such other papers as the registrar may require.
(2) On an application for a grant of administration the oath shall state whether, and if so, in what manner, all persons having a prior right to a grant have been cleared off, and whether any minority or life interest arises under the will or intestacy.
(3) Where the deceased died on or after January 1, 1926, the oath shall state whether, to the best of the applicant's knowledge, information and belief, there was land vested in the deceased which was settled previously to his death and not by his will and which remained settled land notwithstanding his death.

---

4. See p 288 n 7 ante.
5. As amended by SI 1971/1977.
6. See NCPR 1954 r 4 (as amended by SI 1968/1675, SI 1971/1977, SI 1982/446). A personal application is defined in NCPR 1954, r 2(1) as 'a person other than a trust corporation who seeks to obtain a grant without employing a solicitor'. A trust corporation must act through a solicitor when applying for a grant: see the Lord Chancellor's letter to the Law Society reprinted in (1982) 79 LSG 1597.
7. See NCPR 1954, r 3 (as amended by SI 1968/1675, SI 1969/1689, SI 1982/446).
8. See p 218 ante.
9. See p 309 n 16 post.
10. This requirement only applies exceptionally nowadays, see p 309 post.
11. Nil where the net value of the estate does not exceed £10,000, £40 where the net value is between £10,000–£25,000; £80 where the net value is between £25,000 and £40,000; £2.50 per £1,000 where the net value is between £40,000 and £100,000; £250 where the net value exceeds £100,000 and for every additional £100,000 or part thereof a further fee of £50 (Non-Contentious Probate Fees Order 1981, SI 1981/861, as amended by SI 1983/1180).
12. See p 288 n 7 ante.
13. As amended by SI 1971/1977. See specimen executor's oath at p 323 post.

(4) Unless otherwise directed by a registrar, the oath shall state where the deceased died domiciled.

(ii) *Will*

Non-Contentious Probate Rules 1954[12]

8. Marking of wills
Every will in respect of which an application for a grant is made shall be marked by the signatures of the applicant and the person before whom the oath is sworn, and shall be exhibited to any affidavit which may be required under these Rules as to the validity, terms, condition or date of execution of the will:

Provided that where the registrar is satisfied that compliance with this rule might result in the loss of the will, he may allow a photographic copy thereof to be marked or exhibited in lieu of the original document.

(iii) *Inland Revenue Account*[14]

Supreme Court Act 1981

109. Refusal of grant where inheritance tax unpaid
(1) Subject to subsections (2) and (3), no grant shall be made, and no grant made outside the United Kingdom shall be resealed, except on the production of an account prepared in pursuance of [the Inheritance Tax Act 1984][15] showing by means of such receipt or certification as may be prescribed by the Commissioners of Inland Revenue (in this and the following section referred to as 'the Commissioners') either—
  (a) that the inheritance tax payable on the delivery of the account has been paid; or
  (b) that no such tax is so payable.
(3) Nothing in subsection (1) applies in relation to a case where the delivery of the account required by that Part of that Act has for the time being been dispensed with by any regulations under section [246(1)(a) of the Inheritance Tax Act 1984].[16]

(iv) *Sureties' guarantee*[17]

Supreme Court Act 1981

120. Power to require administrators to produce sureties
(1) As a condition of granting administration to any person the High Court may, subject to the following provisions of this section and subject to and in accordance with probate rules, require one or more sureties to guarantee that they will make good, within any

---

14. See specimen Account at pp 324–7 post.

15. Words substituted by IHTA 1984 s 276, Sch 8 para 20 as amended by Finance Bill 1986 s 79(1).

16. Ibid. See now the Inheritance Tax (Delivery of Accounts) Regulations 1981 SI 1981/880 as amended by SI 1983/1039 dispensing with completion of an Inland Revenue Account where the total gross value of the estate does not exceed £40,000 provided that (a) the estate comprises only property which passed under the deceased's will or intestacy or by nomination or beneficially by survivorship; (b) no more than the higher of 10% of the total gross value or £2,000 consists of property situated outside the UK and (c) the deceased died domiciled in the UK and had made no lifetime gifts chargeable to IHT.

17. Until 1972 an administrator was always required to supply a bond for the due administration of the estate; unless the administrator was a trust corporation, sureties were also required. In 1970 the Law Commission (Law Com No 31) recommended the abolition of the bond on the basis that the only useful purpose it served was to provide a remedy against the sureties, which was seldom appropriate in practice. As a result, AEA 1971, s 8 abolished the requirement for a bond and substituted a new s 167 to the Judicature Act 1925 providing new guarantee requirements for grants made after 1971 and these new requirements are re-enacted by SCA 1981, s 120.

limit imposed by the court on the total liability of the surety or sureties, any loss which any person interested in the administration of the estate of the deceased may suffer in consequence of a breach by the administrator of his duties as such.

(2) A guarantee given in pursuance of any such requirement shall enure for the benefit of every person interested in the administration of the estate of the deceased as if contained in a contract under seal made by the surety or sureties with every such person and, where there are two or more sureties, as if they had bound themselves jointly and severally.

(3) No action shall be brought on any such guarantee without the leave of the High Court.

(4) Stamp duty shall not be chargeable on any such guarantee.

(5) This section does not apply where administration is granted to the Treasury Solicitor, the Official Solicitor, the Public Trustee, the Solicitor for the affairs of the Duchy of Lancaster or the Duchy of Cornwall or the Crown Solicitor for Northern Ireland, or to the consular officer of a foreign state to which section 1 of the Consular Conventions Act 1949 applies or in such other cases as may be prescribed.

Non-Contentious Probate Rules 1954[18]

38. Guarantee[19]

(1) The registrar shall not require a guarantee under section 120 of the Act as a condition of granting administration except where it is proposed to grant it—

    (a) by virtue of rule 19 (v)[20] or rule 21 (4)[1] to a creditor or the personal representative of a creditor or to a person who has no immediate beneficial interest in the estate of the deceased but may have such an interest in the event of an accretion to the estate;

    (b) under rule 27 to a person or some of the persons who would, if the person beneficially entitled to the whole of the estate died intestate, be entitled to his estate;

    (c) under rule 30 to the attorney of a person entitled to a grant;

    (d) under rule 31 for the use and benefit of a minor;[2]

    (e) under rule 33 for the use and benefit of a person who is by reason of mental or physical incapacity incapable of managing his affairs;[3]

    (f) to an applicant who appears to the registrar to be resident elsewhere than in the United Kingdom;

or except where the registrar considers that there are special circumstances making it desirable to require a guarantee.[4]

(2) Notwithstanding that it is proposed to grant administration as aforesaid, a guarantee shall not be required, except in special circumstances, on an application for administration where the applicant or one of the applicants is—

    (a) a trust corporation;[5]

    (b) a solicitor holding a current practising certificate under the Solicitors Act 1974;

    (c) a servant of the Crown acting in his official capacity;

    (d) a nominee of a public department or of a local authority within the meaning of the Local Government Act 1972.

(5) Unless the registrar otherwise directs—. . .

    (d) the limit of the liability of the surety or sureties under a guarantee given for the

---

18. See p 288 n 7 ante.

19. As amended by SI 1971/1977, SI 1982/446 and by SI 1985/1232.

20. See p 300 ante.

1. See p 301 ante.

2. See p 288 ante.

3. See p 289 ante.

4. NCPR 1954, r 5(4) further states that where the registrar intends requiring a guarantee as a condition of granting administration he must first give the applicant or his solicitor an opportunity of being heard with regard to the application.

5. See p 289 ante.

purposes of section 120 of the Act shall be the gross amount of the estate[6] as sworn on the application for the grant;

(d) Further evidence that may be required

Non-Contentious Probate Rules 1954[7]

5.   Duty of registrar on receiving application for grant[8]
(1) A registrar shall not allow any grant to issue until all inquiries which he may see fit to make have been answered to his satisfaction.

(2) The registrar may require proof of the identity of the deceased or of the applicant for the grant beyond that contained in the oath.

10.   Evidence as to due execution of will[9]
(1) Where a will contains no attestation clause or the attestation clause is insufficient or where it appears to the registrar that there is some doubt about the due execution of the will, he shall, before admitting it to proof, require an affidavit as to due execution from one or more of the attesting witnesses or, if no attesting witness is conveniently available, from any other person who was present at the time the will was executed.

(2) If no affidavit can be obtained in accordance with the last foregoing paragraph, the registrar may, if he thinks fit having regard to the desirability of protecting the interests of any person who may be prejudiced by the will, accept evidence on affidavit from any person he may think fit to show that the signature on the will is in the handwriting of the deceased, or of any other matter which may raise a presumption in favour of the due execution of the will.

(3) If the registrar after considering the evidence—
   (a) is satisfied that the will was not duly executed, he shall refuse probate and shall mark the will accordingly;
   (b) is doubtful whether the will was duly executed, he may refer the matter to the court on motion.

11.   Execution of will of blind or illiterate testator[10]
Before admitting to proof a will which appears to have been signed by a blind or illiterate testator or by another person by direction of the testator, or which for any other reason gives rise to doubt as to the testator having had knowledge of the contents of the will at the time of its execution, the registrar shall satisfy himself that the testator had such knowledge.

12.   Evidence as to terms, condition and date of execution of will
(1) Where there appears in a will any obliteration, interlineation, or other alteration which is not authenticated in the manner prescribed by section 21 of the Wills Act 1837,[11] or by the re-execution of the will or by the execution of a codicil, the registrar shall require evidence to show whether the alteration was present at the time the will was executed and shall give directions as to the form in which the will is to be proved:

---

6. Until 1972 sureties were required to enter into a guarantee for twice the value of the gross estate. The Law Commission (Law Com No 31) found this to be unnecessary 'since it can only be in the rarest of cases that the loss can exceed the value of the gross estate' (para 13) and recommended this alteration effected by SI 1971/1977.

7. See p 288 n 7 ante.

8. As amended by SI 1971/1977.

9. As amended by SI 1967/748. See further p 189 ante.

10. See p 80 ante.

11. See p 182 ante.

Provided that this paragraph shall not apply to any alteration which appears to the registrar to be of no practical importance.

(2) If from any mark on the will it appears to the registrar that some other document has been attached to the will, or if a will contains any reference to another document in such terms as to suggest that it ought to be incorporated in the will, the registrar may require the document to be produced and may call for such evidence in regard to the attaching or incorporation of the document as he may think fit.

(3) Where there is doubt as to the date on which a will was executed, the registrar may require such evidence as he thinks necessary to establish the date.

13.   Attempted revocation of will

Any appearance of attempted revocation of a will by burning, tearing or otherwise, and every other circumstance leading to a presumption of revocation[12] by the testator, shall be accounted for to the registrar's satisfaction.

16.   Wills of persons on military service and seamen

If it appears to the registrar that there is *prima facie* evidence that a will is one to which section 11 of the Wills Act 1837,[13] as amended by any subsequent enactment, applies, the will may be admitted to proof if the registrar is satisfied that it was signed by the testator or, if unsigned, that it is in the testator's handwriting.

52.   Applications for leave to swear death[14]

An application for leave to swear to the death of a person in whose estate a grant is sought may be made to a registrar and shall be supported by an affidavit setting out the grounds of the application and containing particulars of any policies of insurance effected on the life of the presumed deceased.

53.   Grants in respect of nuncupative wills and of copies of wills[15]

(1) An application for an order admitting to proof a nuncupative will,[16] or a will contained in a copy, a completed draft, a reconstruction or other evidence of its contents where the original will is not available,[17] may be made to a registrar:

Provided that where a will is not available owing to its being retained in the custody of a foreign court or official, a duly authenticated copy of the will may be admitted to proof without any such order as aforesaid.

(2) The application shall be supported by an affidavit setting out the grounds of the application and by such evidence on affidavit as the applicant can adduce as to—

  (a) the due execution of the will,
  (b) its existence after the death of the testator, and
  (c) the accuracy of the copy or other evidence of the contents of the will, together with any consents in writing to the application given by any persons not under disability who would be prejudiced by the grant.

Supreme Court Act 1981

107.   No grant where conflicting applications

Subject to probate rules, no grant in respect of the estate, or part of the estate, of a deceased person shall be made out of the Principal Registry or any district probate registry on any application if, at any time before the making of a grant, it appears to the

---

12. See p 181 ante.
13. See privileged wills, Ch 9 ante. As to privileged wills in verbal form see r 53 post.
14. As amended by SI 1967/748.
15. As amended by SI 1967/748.
16. Ie a verbal privileged will: as to privileged wills in written form see rule 16 ante.
17. See p 190 ante.

registrar concerned that some other application has been made in respect of that estate or, as the case may be, that part of it and has not been either refused or withdrawn.

122. Examination of person with knowledge of testamentary document
(1) Where it appears that there are reasonable grounds for believing that any person has knowledge of any document which is or purports to be a testamentary document, the High Court may, whether or not any legal proceedings are pending, order him to attend for the purpose of being examined in open court.
(2) The court may—
   (a) require any person who is before it in compliance with an order under subsection (1) to answer any question relating to the document concerned; and
   (b) if appropriate, order him to bring in the document in such a manner as the court may direct.
(3) Any person who, having been required by the court to do so under this section, fails to attend for examination, answer any question or bring in any document shall be guilty of contempt of court.[18]

123. Subpoena to bring in testamentary document
Where it appears that any person has in his possession, custody or power any document which is or purports to be a testamentary document, the High Court may, whether or not any legal proceedings are pending, issue a subpoena requiring him to bring in the document in such manner as the court may in the subpoena direct.[19]

(e) Caveats and citations

Before a grant can issue, the registrar will check the index of caveats at the registry in case a caveat has been entered, for example by someone who wants to contest the will, in which event no grant will be sealed until the caveator has been warned off.[20] It may also be necessary for a citation to issue from the registry in order to clear the way for the applicant, for example where the applicant is not first in priority of entitlement for the grant.[20a]

Supreme Court Act 1981

108. Caveats
(1) A caveat against a grant of probate or administration may be entered in the Principal Registry or in any district probate registry.
(2) On a caveat being entered in a district probate registry, the district probate registrar shall immediately send a copy of it to the Principal Registry to be entered among the caveats in that Registry.

In **Moran v Place** [1896] P 214, Lindley LJ described a caveat at p 216 as follows:

A caveat is not a notice to any opponent in particular. It is a notice to the registrar or officer of the court not to let anything be done by anybody in the matter of the will, or the

---

18. See further NCPR 1954, r 49(1) as amended by SI 1971/1977, SI 1982/446, SI 1985/1232.
19. See further NCPR 1954, r 49(2) as amended by SI 1971/1977, SI 1982/446.
20. The caveator has eight days in which to enter an appearance to a warning; if he fails to do so, the caveat will cease to have effect. See further NCPR 1954, r 44 as amended by SI 1967/748, SI 1971/1977, SI 1976/1362, SI 1982/446, SI 1985/1232.
20a. See p 298 ante. See also NCPR 1954, r 45 as amended by SI 1985/1232 and r 47 as amended by SI 1971/1977, SI 1974/597.

goods of the deceased, without notice to the person who lodges the caveat. It is impossible to look at it as commencing any litigation—it merely requests the registrar to tell the caveator if anybody stirs in the matter.

(f) Issuing the grant

The grant will be sent by post to the applicant or his solicitors.[1]

Supreme Court Act 1981

111.   Records of grants
(1) There shall continue to be kept records of all grants which are made in the Principal Registry or in any district probate registry.[2]
(2) Those records shall be in such form, and shall contain such particulars, as the President of the Family Division may direct.

124.   Place for deposit of original wills and other documents
All original wills and other documents which are under the control of the High Court in the Principal Registry or in any district probate registry shall be deposited and preserved in such places as the Lord Chancellor may direct; and any wills or other documents so deposited shall, subject to the control of the High Court and to probate rules, be open to inspection.[3]

2   Settled land grants

The three grants so far considered,[4] probate, letters of administration with the will annexed and letters of administration are the most common grants in practice but there are other grants that can issue,[5] one of which is the settled land grant.

If the deceased was a life tenant under a settlement governed by the Settled Land Act 1925 and that settlement continues after his death, special personal representatives will have to take out a grant limited to the settled land in order to vest the legal estate in the next person entitled as tenant for life under the settlement.[6] If the deceased life tenant died testate, priority for this special grant goes to the trustees of the settlement at the date of death; if there are no such trustees or if the life tenant dies intestate, priority is governed by the Non-Contentious Probate Rules 1954, r 28(3), failing which the court has power to appoint a special representative to deal with the settled land.

---

1. See specimen grant at p 328 post.
2. By NCPR 1954, r 57 (as substituted by SI 1982/446) each district probate registrar is required to make a weekly return of grants issued by his registry with a copy in each case for filing in the Principal Registry.
3. Official copies of all grants and original wills can be obtained on payment of the prescribed fee: see SCA 1981, s 125 and NCPR 1954, r 58 as amended by SI 1982/446.
4. See Ch 19 ante.
5. Eg letters of administration de bonis non administratis (see p 292 n 8 ante), the grant of administration durante minoris aetate (p 288 ante) and the grant of administration during a mental or physical incapacity (p 289 ante).
6. SLA 1925, s 7(1). The vesting instrument will be a vesting assent: SLA 1925, s 8. The settled land grant will not identify the land to which it relates; for criticism of this see Withers, (1946) 62 LQR 167.

Administration of Estates Act 1925

22. Special executors as respects settled land

(1) A testator may appoint, and in default of such express appointment shall be deemed to have appointed, as his special executors in regard to settled land, the persons, if any, who are at his death the trustees of the settlement thereof,[7] and probate may be granted to such trustees specially limited to the settled land.

In this subsection 'settled land' means land vested in the testator which was settled previously to his death and not by his will.

(2) A testator may appoint other persons either with or without such trustees as aforesaid or any of them to be his general executors in regard to his other property and assets.

Re Bridgett and Hayes' Contract [1928] Ch 163, Ch D; Romer J

Land was vested in the testatrix as tenant for life under a settlement governed by the Settled Land Act 1925. Under the terms of the settlement, on the death of the testatrix the land became subject to a trust for sale and so ceased to be settled land at that point. A general grant of probate was made to the sole executor of the testatrix, the grant in question issuing in respect of the whole of the testatrix's estate including the hitherto settled land. Was this general grant one on which a prospective purchaser of the previously settled land could rely or should the purchaser insist on the trustees of the settlement taking out a special grant of probate under the Administration of Estates Act 1925, s 22(1) in order to pass a good title?

Held: The general personal representative could pass a good title to the land; s 22(1) only applied where the land remained settled after the death of the tenant for life.

Romer J: (Having read s 22(1), he continued:) So far down to the words 'previously to his death' the section applies to the present case, because here land was vested in the testatrix and it had been settled previously to her death. Then the sub-section says she shall be deemed to have appointed as her special executors the persons, if any, who are at her death the trustees of the settlement. Now before any one can go to the Court of Probate and get probate specially limited to the settled land granted to him, he must be in a position to say to the Court that he is to be deemed to have been appointed special executor of this land, because at the death of the testator he was trustee of the settlement thereof. But in my opinion he is not in a position to make that statement if the settlement comes to an end the moment the testator dies. It is to be observed that the sub-section does not refer to the persons who immediately before the death of the testator were the trustees of the settlement, but to the persons who at his death are the trustees of the settlement.

The words 'persons who are at his death the trustees of the settlement' connote to my mind persons who are trustees notwithstanding his death, especially when it is realised that the section is dealing with the testator's will, which comes into operation only when he is dead.

For these reasons I think this sub-section does not apply in a case like the present, where, upon the death of the testatrix in question the settlement existing up to that date comes to an end.[8]

---

7. SLA 1925, s 30(1) identifies the trustees of the settlement, failing which recourse can be had to s 30(3) if the settlement was created by will or intestacy; in such a case the personal representatives of the deceased settlor will be the trustees of the settlement and the persons with entitlement to a grant of probate limited to the settled land under AEA 1925, s 22(1): see *Re Gibbings* [1928] P 28.

8. Cf *In the Estate of Taylor* [1929] P 260 where *Re Bridgett and Hayes' Contract* was successfully distinguished as on the terms of the settlement in the former case, the settlement had not come to an end on the death of the life tenant so a special grant of probate limited to the settled land would lie.

Non-Contentious Probate Rules 1954[9]

28.   Grants in respect of settled land[10]

(1) In this rule 'settled land' means land vested in the deceased which was settled previously to his death and not by his will and which remained settled land notwithstanding his death.[11]

(2) The special executors in regard to settled land constituted by section 22 of the Administration of Estates Act 1925 shall have a prior right to a grant of probate limited to the settled land.

(3) The person or persons entitled to a grant of administration limited to settled land shall be determined in accordance with the following order of priority, namely—

    (i)   The trustees of the settlement[12] at the time of the application for the grant;

    (ii)   The personal representative of the deceased.

(4) Where the persons entitled to a grant in respect of the free estate are also entitled to a grant of the same nature in respect of settled land, a grant expressly including the settled land may issue to them.

(5) Where there is settled land and a grant is made in respect of the free estate only, the grant shall expressly exclude the settled land.

Administration of Estates Act 1925

23.   Where representation is not granted to trustees of settlement

(1) Where settled land becomes vested in a personal representative, not being a trustee of the settlement,[13] upon trust to convey the land to or assent to the vesting thereof in the tenant for life or statutory owner in order to give effect to a settlement created before the death of the deceased and not by his will, or would, on the grant of representation to him, have become so vested, such representative may—

    (a)   before representation has been granted, renounce his office in regard only to such settled land without renouncing it in regard to other property;

    (b)   after representation has been granted, apply to the court for revocation of the grant in regard to the settled land without applying in regard to other property.

(2) Whether such renunciation or revocation is made or not, the trustees of the settlement, or any person beneficially interested thereunder, may apply to the High Court for an order appointing a special or additional personal representative in respect of the settled land, and a special or additional personal representative, if and when appointed under the order, shall be in the same position as if representation had originally been granted to him alone in place of the original personal representative, if any, or to him jointly with the original personal representative, as the case may be, limited to the settled land but without prejudice to the previous acts and dealings, if any, of the personal representative originally constituted or the effect of notices given to such personal representative.[14]

24.   Power for special personal representatives to dispose of settled land

(1) The special personal representatives may dispose of the settled land without the

---

9. See n 7 ante.

10. As amended by SI 1967/748.

11. See eg *In the Estate of Bordass* [1929] P 107.

12. See n 7 ante. It will be noted that whilst AEA 1925, s 22(1) applies only to the trustees of the settlement at the date of death of the tenant for life, NCPR 1954, r 28(3) allows trustees of the settlement appointed after the date of death to take out or join in taking out the grant of letters of administration limited to the settled land.

13. Ie when NCPR 1954, r 28(2) and (3)(i) do not apply.

14. So as a last resort if there are no trustees of the settlement or none of them is willing to act and there are no general personal representatives of the tenant for life or they have renounced their entitlement to the settled land grant, the court has power to appoint a special personal representative to deal with the settled land.

concurrence of the general personal representatives, who may likewise dispose of the other property and assets of the deceased without the concurrence of the special personal representatives.

(2) In this section the expression 'special personal representatives' means the representatives appointed to act for the purposes of settled land and includes any original personal representative who is to act with an additional personal representative for those purposes.

3 Foreign grants

The grant of representation enables the deceased's personal representatives to deal with his property in England and Wales; if he has assets in another country, the probate requirements of that other country will have to be met, normally by taking out a fresh grant in that other country. Similarly, if the testator's will has already been proved in some other country but he has assets in England and Wales, it will usually not be sufficient for the personal representative merely to produce the foreign grant; normally the will will have to be proved again and a fresh grant issued to the person entitled to deal with the testator's estate.[15] In two instances, however, this rule is relaxed.

(a) Resealing Commonwealth and colonial grants

The grants of any country to which the Colonial Probates Act 1892[16] has been applied are simply resealed by the Family Division and then have the same effect as if originally granted here.

Colonial Probates Act 1892

1. Application of Act by Order in Council
Her Majesty the Queen may, on being satisfied that the legislature of any British possession has made adequate provision for the recognition in that possession of probates and letters of administration granted by the courts of the United Kingdom, direct by Order in Council that this Act shall, subject to any exceptions and modifications specified in the Order, apply to that possession and thereupon, while the Order is in force, this Act shall apply accordingly.[17]

2. Sealing in United Kingdom of colonial probates and letters of administration
(1) Where a court of probate in a British possession to which this Act applies has granted

---

15. The Convention concerning the International Administration of the Estates of Deceased Persons (1972) is designed to obviate this duplication by the introduction of an international certificate designating the person entitled to administer the deceased's estate, which would be recognised by all Contracting States. The UK has signed but not yet ratified this Convention.
16. As extended to certain Protected States and Mandated Territories by the Colonial Probates (Protected States and Mandated Territories) Act 1927.
17. See the Colonial Probates Act Application Order 1965, SI 1965/1530. The 1892 Act as extended by the 1927 Act currently applies to all the Australian States, most of the Canadian States, New Zealand, Bahamas, Barbados, Bermuda, Botswana, Falkland Islands, Fiji, Ghana, Gibraltar, Hong Kong, Jamaica, Kenya, Malawi, Malaysia, Nigeria, Singapore, Zimbabwe, (see PD [1980] 2 All ER 324, [1980] 1 WLR 553), Sri Lanka, Swaziland, Tanzania, Uganda and Zambia among others.

probate or letters of administration in respect of the estate of a deceased person, the probate or letters so granted may, on being produced to, and a copy thereof deposited with, a court of probate in the United Kingdom, be sealed with the seal of that court,[18] and, thereupon, shall be of the like force and effect, and have the same operation in the United Kingdom, as if granted by that court.

(2) Provided that the court shall, before sealing a probate or letters of administration under this section, be satisfied—

    (a) that probate duty[19] has been paid in respect of so much (if any) of the estate as is liable to probate duty in the United Kingdom.[20]

(b) Recognition of Scottish confirmations[1] and Northern Irish grants

Originally these had to be resealed but the Administration of Estates Act 1971 rendered this unnecessary so long as the deceased died domiciled in Scotland or Northern Ireland; in either case the Scottish or Northern Irish grant will now be accepted in England and Wales without the need for any further formality.

Administration of Estates Act 1971

1. Reciprocal recognition of grants

(1) Where a person dies domiciled in Scotland—

    (a) a confirmation granted in respect of all or part of his estate and noting his Scottish domicile, and

    (b) a certificate of confirmation noting his Scottish domicile and relating to one or more items of his estate,

shall, without being resealed, be treated for the purposes of the law of England and Wales as a grant of representation (in accordance with subsection (2) below) to the executors named in the confirmation or certificate in respect of the property of the deceased of which according to the terms of the confirmation they are executors or, as the case may be, in respect of the item or items of property specified in the certificate of confirmation.

(2) Where by virtue of subsection (1) above a confirmation or certificate of confirmation is treated for the purposes of the law of England and Wales as a grant of representation to the executors named therein then, subject to subsections (3) and (5) below, the grant shall be treated—

    (a) as a grant of probate where it appears from the confirmation or certificate that the executors so named are executors nominate,[2] and

    (b) in any other case, as a grant of letters of administration.

(3) Section 7 of the Administration of Estates Act 1925[3] (executor of executor represents original testator) shall not, by virtue of subsection (2)(a) above, apply on the death of an executor named in a confirmation or certificate of confirmation.

(4) Subject to subsection (5) below, where a person dies domiciled in Northern Ireland a

---

18. See NCPR 1954, r 41 for the procedure. 638 grants were resealed in 1984: Judicial Statistics, Annual Report 1984, Cmnd 9599.
19. 'Probate duty' is defined by s 6 of the Act as including 'any duty payable on the value of the estate and effects for which probate or letters of administration is or are granted': it would thus include inheritance tax.
20. See further AEA 1971, s 11.
1. Equivalent to an English grant of probate or letters of administration.
2. Equivalent to an English executor.
3. See p 292 ante. It should be noted that AEA 1971, s 1(3) only applies to Scottish grants not to Northern Irish grants to which the chain of representation will therefore apply.

grant of probate of his will or letters of administration in respect of his estate (or any part of it) made by the High Court in Northern Ireland and noting his domicile there shall, without being resealed, be treated for the purposes of the law of England and Wales as if it has been originally made by the High Court in England and Wales.

(5) Notwithstanding anything in the preceding provisions of this section, a person who is a personal representative according to the law of England and Wales by virtue only of those provisions may not be required, under section 25[4] of the Administration of Estates Act 1925, to deliver up his grant to the High Court.[5]

4 Revoking the grant

(a) In general

A grant is conclusive evidence that the grantee is the personal representative of the deceased so long as it is in force. However the court[6] has power to revoke it whenever it appears to the court that the grant should not have been made or contains an error.[7]

Supreme Court Act 1981

21. Revocation of grants and cancellation of resealing at instance of court
(1) Where it appears to the High Court that a grant either ought not to have been made or contains an error, the court may call in the grant and, if satisfied that it would be revoked at the instance of a party interested, may revoke it.

(2) A grant may be revoked under subsection (1) without being called in, if it cannot be called in.

(3) Where it appears to the High Court that a grant resealed under the Colonial Probates Act 1892 and 1927 ought not to have been resealed, the court may call in the relevant document and, if satisfied that the resealing would be cancelled at the instance of a party interested, may cancel the resealing.

In **In the Goods of Loveday** [1900] P 154, the deceased died intestate leaving a widow, and six children by a former marriage. The widow obtained letters of administration but subsequently disappeared before completing the winding up of the estate. Granting the children's application to revoke her grant and make a grant of letters of administration *de bonis non*[8] to one of their number, Jeune P said at p 156:

The real object which the Court must always keep in view is the due and proper administration of the estate and the interests of the parties beneficially entitled thereto; and I can see no good reason why the Court should not take fresh action in regard to an

---

4. See p 275 ante.
5. Ss 2 and 3 make similar provision for the recognition of English grants in Northern Ireland and Scotland if the deceased died domiciled in England.
6. If the application is non-contentious, the revocation will normally be dealt with by the Family Division of the High Court and is a relatively simple procedural matter (see NCPR 1954, r 42 as amended by SI 1967/748). If it is contentious, a revocation action is normally necessary; this will usually be assigned to the Chancery Division of the High Court, although the County Court also has jurisdiction if the value of the deceased's estate after debts and funeral expenses does not exceed £30,000 (County Courts Jurisdiction Order 1981, SI 1981/1123).
7. 319 grants were revoked in 1984: Judicial Statistics, Annual Report 1984, Cmnd 9599.
8. See p 292 n 8 ante.

estate where it is made clear that its previous grant has turned out abortive or inefficient. If the Court has in certain circumstances made a grant in the belief and hope that the person appointed will properly and fully administer the estate, and if it turns out that the person so appointed will not or cannot administer, I do not see why the Court should not revoke an inoperative grant and make a fresh grant.[9]

In **In the Estate of Cope** [1954] 1 All ER 698, [1954] 1 WLR 608, however, Collingwood J distinguished *In the Goods of Loveday* on its facts. Letters of administration had been granted to A and B. An application had since been made for the revocation of their grant on the grounds that A and B had not made a full disclosure of the deceased's assets in the Inland Revenue Account and had shown as a liability against the estate a debt allegedly due to A which the applicant disputed. The applicant argued that, as in *In the Goods of Loveday*[10] and in *In the Goods of Galbraith*,[11] the special circumstances of the case would justify the revocation of the grant and the substitution of a new grant. Collingwood J held that there were no such circumstances on the facts before him, saying at p 700:

In my opinion, none of those cases covers the present one. There is no suggestion in the present case that there is any defect in the title of the grantees of the letters of administration, or any supervening incapacity. There may be, on the evidence that has been put forward, a prima facie case for an inventory and an account under s 25 of the Administration of Estates Act, 1925, but, in my opinion, it is not a case in which the court can order revocation of the grant.[12]

(b) The effect of revocation

The former personal representative is well protected by statute for acts carried out under the authority of the grant, as are debtors of the estate and purchasers whose transactions with him took place before his grant was revoked. A former beneficiary to whom distributions were made under the authority of the revoked grant has no protection in so far as his entitlement does not survive the revocation; he is both personally liable to the true beneficiaries to reimburse them[13] and in so far as he still holds the property concerned, a tracing action will lie.[14]

Administration of Estates Act 1925

27.   Protection of persons acting on probate or administration
(1) Every person making or permitting to be made any payment or distribution in good faith under a representation shall be indemnified and protected in so doing,

---

9. See also *In the Goods of Galbraith* [1951] P 422, [1951] 2 All ER 470n where the two surviving executors had become incapable of completing the winding up of the estate by reason of their mental and physical infirmity; their grant of probate was revoked and letters of administration *de bonis non* were issued to someone else.
10. Ante.
11. N 9 ante.
12. See also *Re Heslop* (1846) 1 Rob Ecc 457 where the administratrix wished her grant to be revoked as a matter of convenience, the administration having proved to be more onerous than she had anticipated; her application was refused.
13. See eg *Ministry of Health v Simpson* [1951] AC 251, [1950] 2 All ER 1137 p 421 post.
14. See eg *Re Diplock* [1948] Ch 465, [1948] 2 All ER 318, p 420 post.

notwithstanding any defect or circumstance whatsoever affecting the validity of the representation.[15]

(2) Where a representation is revoked, all payments and dispositions made in good faith to a personal representative under the representation before the revocation thereof are a valid discharge to the person making the same; and the personal representative who acted under the revoked representation may retain and reimburse himself in respect of any payments or dispositions made by him which the person to whom representation is afterwards granted might have properly made.

37. Validity of conveyance not affected by revocation of representation

(1) All conveyances of any interest in real or personal estate made to a purchaser either before or after the commencement of this Act by a person to whom probate or letters of administration have been granted are valid, notwithstanding any subsequent revocation or variation, either before or after the commencement of this Act, of the probate or administration.

55. Definitions

(1) . . . (xviii) 'Purchaser' means a lessee, mortgagee or other person who in good faith acquires an interest in property for valuable consideration, also an intending purchaser and 'valuable consideration' includes marriage but does not include a nominal consideration in money.

Law of Property Act 1925

204. Orders of court conclusive

(1) An order of the court under any statutory or other jurisdiction shall not, as against a purchaser, be invalidated on the ground of want of jurisdiction, or of want of any concurrence, consent, notice, or service, whether the purchaser has notice of any such want or not.

(2) This section has effect with respect to any lease, sale, or other act under the authority of the court, and purporting to be in pursuance of any statutory power notwithstanding any exception in such statute.

205. General definitions

(1) In this Act unless the context otherwise requires, the following expressions have the meanings hereby assigned to them respectively, that is to say:—. . . (xxi) 'Purchaser' means a purchaser in good faith for valuable consideration and includes a lessee, mortgagee or other person who for valuable consideration acquires an interest in property . . .; and in reference to a legal estate includes a chargee by way of legal mortgage; and where the context so requires 'purchaser' includes an intending purchaser; 'purchase' has a meaning corresponding with that of 'purchaser'; and 'valuable consideration' includes marriage but does not include a nominal consideration in money.

In **Re Bridgett and Hayes' Contract** [1928] 1 Ch 163,[16] Romer J first considered whether the sale of the formerly settled land by the deceased's general executor (Thomas William Bridgett) could stand even if a grant of probate limited to the settled land should have been issued to the trustees of the

---

15. See eg *In the Estate of Bloch* (1959) The Times July 2nd: a grant of letters of administration had been made to A and B but had to be revoked when the deceased person turned up alive. It was held that A was entitled to an indemnity for payments made under AEA 1925, s 27(1) but not B for B had withheld material evidence when an application was made for leave to swear death prior to the grant and so had not acted in good faith.

16. See p 315 ante.

settlement under the Administration of Estates Act 1925, s 22. He found that it could, saying at p 168:

On January 17, 1926, (the deceased life tenant) died, and on April 7, 1926, a general grant of probate of her will was made to Thomas William Bridgett, a person whom she had thereby appointed as executor. As from that date, at any rate, wherever the legal estate in this property may have been as between the date of her death and this act of probate, the legal estate in this land vested in Thomas William Bridgett, and, while that act of probate remains unrevoked, he can in my opinion properly convey the legal estate to the purchaser. Sect 204 of the Law of Property Act, 1925, sub-s 1, says this: . . . (Having recited the terms of the section he continued:) Sect 22, sub-s 1 (if the purchaser is right as to its application at all to this case), provided that probate might have been granted to this sole surviving trustee. In point of fact the Court of Probate did not grant probate to him, but granted probate to Thomas William Bridgett. That being so, it appears to me that s 204 of the Law of Property Act applies to the case with regard to the taking of a conveyance from the legal personal representative. Further, the purchaser would be protected in the event of any subsequent revocation of that grant of probate by s 37, sub-s 1, of the Administration of Estates Act, 1925. It can hardly be doubted that in this case, if the purchaser does take a conveyance from the person to whom the grant of probate was granted, he would be acting in good faith, within the meaning of s 55 sub-s 1 (xviii), of the Act.[17]

---

17. He went on to find that in fact the grant was correctly made to the deceased's general executor, see p 315. Unfortunately LPA 1925, s 204 and AEA 1925, s 37 will not always protect the purchaser, eg if unbeknown to him the grant has already been revoked at the time of his purchase, see Phillips 'The Revocation Trap: an Additional Conveyancing Search?' (1982) 126 Sol J 107.

Specimen Oath for executors[18]

Oath for Executors

IN THE HIGH COURT OF JUSTICE

Family Division

Extracting Solicitor .... Messrs Tup & Griffiths

Address .... 6 Lampire Lane Llandaff, South Glamorgan

The District Probate Registry at   Llandaff

IN the Estate of*   DAI TUP

                                       deceased.

(¹) We, CYRIL OWEN TUP of 19 Rhubarb Row, Radyr, South Glamorgan, Retired Miner and GWYN TUP of 6 Lampire Lane Llandaff, South Glamorgan, Solicitor

make Oath and say, (²)   that
(¹) we believe the paper writing   now produced to and marked by (³) us
to contain the true and original last Will and Testament (⁴)   with one codicil
of*   Dai Tup
of   21 Sunny Street, Splott in the County of South Glamorgan
~~formerly of~~

                                        deceased,
who died on the   15th   day of   May   19 86 ,
aged   50   years (⁵) domiciled in (⁶) England and Wales
and that to the best of   our   knowledge, information and belief there was (⁷) [no]
land vested in the said deceased which was settled previously to his   death (and
not by his   Will (⁴) with one codicil   )
and which remained settled land notwithstanding h is   death (⁸)

Power reserved to

                the other
Executor.

And (¹) we further make Oath and say (²)
       that (⁹) (¹⁰)   we are the

                                    Executors

named in the said   will

and that (¹)   we   will (i) collect, get in and administer according to the law
the real and personal estate (¹¹)
of the said deceased; (ii) when required to do so by the Court, exhibit on oath in
the Court a full inventory of the said estate (¹¹)
and when so required render an account of the administration of the said estate to
the Court; and (iii) when required to do so by the High Court, deliver up the grant
of probate to that Court; and that to the best of   our   knowledge, information
and belief

~~(¹²) [the gross estate passing under the grant does not exceed (¹³)£~~   ,
~~and the net estate does not exceed (¹⁴) £----------, and that this is not a~~
~~case in which an Inland Revenue Account is required to be delivered]~~

(¹⁵) [the gross estate passing under the grant amounts to £ 42,562. 75
and the net estate amounts to £ 42,045.00   ].
      *

SWORN by   the above-named
Deponents
at   10 Lampire Lane Llandaff
this 10th day of July 1986

Before me,

A ~~Commissioner for Oaths~~/Solicitor.

Glyn Roberts

Cyril Tup

Gwyn Tup

Marginal notes

*If necessary to include alias of deceased in grant, add "otherwise (alias name)" and state below which is true name and reason for requiring alias.

(1) "I" or "We", insert the full name, place of residence and occupation or if none, description of the deponent(s) adding "Mrs", "Miss", as appropriate for a female deponent.

(2) Or "do solemnly and sincerely affirm".

(3) Each testamentary paper must be marked by each deponent and by the person administering the oath.

(4) "with one, two (or more) Codicils", as the case may be.

(5) If exact age is unknown, give best estimate.

(6) Where there are separate legal divisions in one country, the state, province, etc , should be specified.

(7) Delete "no" if there was land vested in deceased which remained settled land notwithstanding his death.

(8) Settled land may be included in the scope of the grant provided the executors are also the special executors as to the settled land; in that case the settlement must be identified.

(9) "I am" or "we are". Insert relationship of the executors to the deceased only if necessary to establish title or identification.

(10) "the sole", or "one of the", or "are the ", or "two of the", (If power is to be reserved the marginal note to that effect should be completed by giving the name of the non-acting Executor).

(11) If there was settled land and the grant is to include it, insert "including settled land" but if the grant is to exclude the settled land insert "save and except settled land".

(12) Complete this paragraph only if the deceased died on or after 1 April 1981 and an Inland Revenue Account is not required; the next paragraph should be deleted.

(13) Insert currently "25,000".

(14) Insert currently "10,000" or "25,000" as appropriate.

(15) Complete this paragraph only if an Inland Revenue Account is required and delete the previous paragraph.

---

18. See p 62 ante for the will referred to in the Oath.

Specimen Inland Revenue Account[19]

Inland Revenue
Capital Transfer Tax

Inland Revenue Account

For use for an original full grant where

* the deceased died on or after 27 March 1981 domiciled in the United Kingdom;
* the estate comprises only property which has passed under the deceased's Will or Intestacy or by nomination or beneficially by survivorship, and all that property was situate in the United Kingdom; and
* the total net value of the estate, after deducting any Exemptions and Reliefs claimed, does not exceed the threshhold above which Capital Transfer Tax is payable at the date of death.

In all other cases form 200 or 201 as appropriate must be used, unless the estate is an excepted estate under the CTT (Delivery Of Accounts) Regulations. For an excepted estate no account need be completed, although exceptionally one may be required later.

For Official Use

A

Date of Grant		
Index	Reader	Stats

Name and address of person to whom any communication should be sent   Messrs. Tup & Griffiths, 6 Lampire Lane

Reference GT/T.550

Telephone No. 0222 6150

Post town Llandaff   Postcode LL41 5AG

(a) Insert "Principal or "District" as required, and in the latter case add the name of the district.

In the High Court of Justice Family Division (Probate)
The (a) Llandaff District   Registry
In the estate of (please use CAPITAL letters)

Surname	TUP
Title and Forenames (*In full*)	DAI (Mr)

Date of Birth	4	2	3 6		Date of Death	1 5	5	8 6	

Last usual address	21 Sunny Street, Splott, South Glamorgan.	**Marital Status**	*tick "✓" as appropriate* married ☐ single ☑	divorced ☐ widowed ☐
		Surviving Relatives	*tick "✓" as appropriate* Husband ☐ Wife ☐	Child(ren) ☐ Parent(s) ☐
	Postcode	Occupation	Electrician	

Country of Domicile (*tick "✓" as appropriate*) England and Wales ☑   Scotland ☐   N. Ireland ☐

Names and addresses of executors or intending administrators:

CYRIL OWEN TUP 19 Rhubarb Row, Radyr, South Glamorgan **Postcode** LL40 5AM	GWYN TUP 6 Lampire Lane, Llandaff, South Glamorgan **Postcode** LL41 5AG
Postcode	**Postcode**

Cap Form 202

---

19. An Inland Revenue Press Release issued after the Budget Speech on 18 March 1986 stated that Accounts in this form should be continued to be used for the time being; until new forms are produced, references in the existing forms to capital transfer tax should be read as if they were references to inheritance tax: see (1986) STI 192.

Declaration

(b) Insert kind of grant

1. I/We desire to obtain a grant of (b)   probate

2. To the best of my/our knowledge and belief all the statements and particulars furnished in this account and its accompanying schedules are true and complete.

No alteration is permitted to paragraphs 2, 3, 4, 5, 6 and 7

3. The deceased made no transfers of value chargeable with Capital Transfer Tax (ie no transfers of value that were not covered by the CTT exemptions) after 26 March 1974 and within 10 years of the death.

4. Account "A" is a complete and true account of all the property comprised in the estate at the death in respect of which the grant is to be made and of its value at that time.

5. Account "B" is a complete and true account of any nominated property, and of any property held jointly with any other person(s) the beneficial interest in which passed by survivorship, and of its value at the date of death.

6. No property situate outside the United Kingdom was comprised in the estate at the death.

7. The deceased did not have an interest in settled property at his death nor had he after 26 March 1974 and within 10 years of his death an interest in settled property or settled any property.

Signed by the above-named   *Cyril Tup*

date 10.7.1986

Signed by the above-named   *Gwyn Tup*

date 10.7.1986

Signed by the above-named

date

Signed by the above-named

date

Warning: An executor or intending administrator who fails to make full enquiries and personally verify that the statements in this account are true may make himself liable to prosecution or penalties.

Account A — property of the deceased in respect of which the grant is to be made

Property without instalment option	Gross Value at date of death (before deduction of exemption(s) or relief(s))
	£
1. British Savings Bonds and other Government Securities, Savings Certificates and Premium Bonds. (Give description and state amount of each security held, attaching a schedule if necessary.) In the case of Savings Certificates please attach a letter from the Savings Certificates Division or a list giving details of purchase and value of each certificate at date of death.	
2. Other Stocks, Shares or Investments including Unit Trusts. (Give details on Form 40 or similar schedule attached and state in adjoining column total value of all investments.)	
3. Cash and Cash at Bank, Savings Banks or in Building, Co-operative or Friendly Societies, including interest to date of death (state each separately and attach a schedule if necessary). Barclays Bank Current Account	225.50
4. Policies of Insurance Principality Building Society Share Account	6,435.50
a. on the life of the deceased, including any bonuses thereon (state each item separately, giving names of companies) Pearl Assurance Company	10,000.00
b. on th life of any other person (enter surrender value and attach letter from the Company).	
5. Household and Personal Goods (furniture, jewellery, clothes, car, etc).	300.00
6. Other Assets not included above or as instalment option property opposite. (If space is insufficient please give details on schedule attached and state in adjoining column total value of these assets.)	
Joe Bloggs Ltd: Salary to date of death	451.50
Inland Revenue: Income tax repayment	150.25
Total 1	17,562.75

2

Debts due from the deceased	Amount
	£

1. Debts (other than mortgage and business debts)

Name and address of creditor	Description of debt	
Wales Gas, Ferry Road, Grangetown, Cardiff.	Gas Account	49.50
British Telecom, 38 Newport Road, Cardiff.	Telephone Account	53.25

(If there is insufficient space to list all debts a schedule should be attached)

2. Funeral expenses (cost of tombstone must not be included).   415.00

Total 2	517.75

Instalment option property	Gross value at date of death (before deduction of exemption(s) or relief(s))
	£

1. Freehold and leasehold property (Form 37B should also be completed) situated at
    21 Sunny Street, Splott, South Glamorgan   25,000.00

2. Business interests (state nature of business ....)

    a. Net value of deceased's interest in business, as statement or balance sheet annexed.

    b. Net value of deceased's interest as a partner in the firm of

    as statement annexed.

Total 3	25,000.00

Debts due in respect of instalment option property	Amount

1. Mortgages on freehold and leasehold property (amount outstanding at date of death)

Date of mortgage

Property on which mortgage charged

To whom owed

2. Other debts (If space is insufficient please attach a schedule)

Name and address of creditor	Description of debt	

Total 4	n.L

3

Joint Property

Was the deceased joint owner of any property of any description or did he hold any money on a joint account (apart from property or money of which he was merely a trustee)?

Tick "√" as appropriate

Yes [ ]   No [√]

If so, please give full particulars including

    a. the date when the joint ownership began (or the date of opening the joint account)

    b. the name(s) of the other owner(s)

    c. by whom and from what source the joint property was provided and, if it or its purchase price was contributed by one or more of the joint owners, the extent of the contribution made by each

    d. how the income (if any) was dealt with and enjoyed

    e. what is considered to be the extent of the deceased's share or interest.

Account B — Nominated and joint property

Gross value at date of death (before deduction of exemption(s) and relief(s))

£

Full description of property, real and personal, being nominated property and property held jointly with any other person(s) the beneficial interest in which passed by survivorship. (Show gross value at date of death of the proportion chargeable to tax. If space is insufficient, please attach a schedule.)   **Total 5**

Less appropriate share of debts or incumbrances thereon. (Give details. If space is insufficient, please attach a schedule.)   **Total 6**

£

Value for probate purposes

Gross estate	per total 1	17,562.75		
	per total 2	25,000.00	**Total 7**	42,562.75
Less debts	per total 2	517.75		517.75
	per total 4			

Net estate for probate purposes Total 8   42,045.00

£

Value of estate for tax purposes

Nominated and joint property (net)   as total 6

Net estate for Probate purposes   as total 8   42,045.00

Deduct Exemptions and Reliefs claimed   Total 9   42,045.00

1. Agricultural relief: Schedule annexed

2. Business relief   : Schedule annexed

3. Spouse exemption: Schedule annexed

4. Other (please specify)

Net estate for tax purposes   42,045.00

4

Specimen grant of probate

COPIES OF THIS GRANT ARE NOT VALID UNLESS
THEY BEAR THE IMPRESSED SEAL OF THE COURT

In the High Court of Justice

The District Probate Registry at   LLANDAFF

BE IT KNOWN that   DAI TUP

died on   the   15th   day of   May   19 86

domiciled in   England and Wales

AND BE IT FURTHER KNOWN that at the date hereunder written the last Will and Testament

with one Codicil

(a copy whereof is hereunto annexed) of the said deceased was proved and registered in the said Registry of the High Court of Justice

and Administration of all the estate which by law devolves to and vests in the personal representative of the said deceased was granted by the aforesaid Court to

CYRIL OWEN TUP of 19 Rhubarb Row Radyr South Glamorgan and GWYN TUP of

6 Lampire Lane Llandaff South Glamorgan the Executors named in the said

Will

It is hereby certified that it appears from information supplied on the application for this grant that the gross value of the said estate in the United Kingdom
~~does not exceed~~/amounts to £   42,562.75   and that the net value of such estate
~~does not exceed~~/amounts to £   42,045.00

Dated the   28th day of   July 1986

A.J. Davies

District Registrar.

Probate

11.9

Extracted by   Tup & Griffiths,
6 Lampire Lane, Llandaff,
South Glamorgan.

Printed in the UK for HMSO D64?0211 3R62/5854L

DR2

KW

QUESTIONS

1. Common law legal systems generally require there to be some public grant of authority to a personal representative to administer and distribute the deceased's estate before the deceased's property can be dealt with. Under civil law systems, however, the usual rule is that the deceased's estate automatically and directly vests in his heirs or universal legatee. For an interesting comparison of the two approaches, see Neville Brown 'Winding up Decedent's Estates in French and English Law' (1959) 33 Tul LR 631. See also the Convention concerning the International Administration of the Estates of Deceased Persons 1972, signed by the UK but not yet ratified, designed to bridge the difference between the two approaches.

2. D died intestate leaving an estate of £60,000; he is survived by his wife W and his parents X and Y. W takes out a grant of letters of administration but dies before she has completed the winding up of D's estate. She leaves a will appointing X as her executor. Who will complete the winding up of D's estate?

3. T has died leaving a will appointing E as his executor. T was also a life tenant of Blackacre which was devised by his late father's will to T for life, then to S for life, then to R in fee simple. Who will take out what grant? Would your answer be different if (i) T had died intestate or (ii) S had died before T?

4. When A died no will could be found, so letters of administration were granted to B. Six months after A's death, B sold A's farm Greenacre to C. Three months later A's will was found, by which he appointed D his executor. Advise D. Would it make any difference to your answer if C had known at the time of the conveyance of the existence of the will?

CHAPTER 21

Payment of the debts

1 In general

(a) What assets are available?

The whole of the deceased's realty and personalty can be utilised if necessary for the payment of his debts.

Administration of Estates Act 1925

32. Real and personal estate are assets for payment of debts
(1) The real and personal estate, whether legal or equitable, of a deceased person, to the extent of his beneficial interest therein, and the real and personal estate of which a deceased person in pursuance of any general power (including the statutory power to dispose of entailed interests[1]) disposes by his will,[2] are assets for payment of his debts (whether by specialty or simple contract) and liabilities, and any disposition by will inconsistent with this enactment is void as against the creditors, and the court shall, if necessary, administer the property for the purpose of the payment of the debts and liabilities.

This subsection takes effect without prejudice to the rights of incumbrancers.
(2) If any person to whom any such beneficial interest devolves or is given, or in whom any such interest vests, disposes thereof in good faith before an action is brought or process is sued out against him, he shall be personally liable for the value of the interest so disposed of by him, but that interest shall not be liable to be taken in execution in the action or under the process.[3]

(b) What debts are payable?

All causes of action subsisting against the deceased survive against the estate;[4] the personal representatives stand in the deceased's shoes to perform his

---

1. See LPA 1925, s 176.
2. Pure personalty disposed of by will under a general power of appointment vests in the appointee, not in the personal representatives (see p 277 n 9 ante), but the personal representatives can give a valid receipt for it and use it for the payment of debts under s 32: *O'Grady v Wilmot* [1916] 2 AC 231. Otherwise the creditors can take an administration action against the beneficiary to whom the property has devolved.
3. The subsection thus protects the property from the deceased's creditors once it reaches the hands of a person deriving title from a beneficiary; on its terms it would also protect an assignee from the personal representative but this can hardly have been intended: see AEA 1925, s 38 p 420 post.
4. See Law Reform (Miscellaneous Provisions) Act 1934 s 1, p 276 ante.

contracts, other than those for personal services, and to discharge his debts and liabilities. They must plead all proper defences to any claim, however, with one exception: they are not obliged to plead the Limitation Act and so may pay a debt that is statute-barred.

In **Farrow v Wilson** (1869) LR 4 CP 744, the deceased had hired the plaintiff as a farm bailiff at a weekly wage on the basis that the plaintiff would remain in his service until the arrangement was determined by six months notice by either party, or six months pay in lieu of notice if determined by the deceased. When the deceased died, his personal representative dismissed the bailiff without notice or pay in lieu and her action was upheld by Willes J who said at p 746:

> Generally speaking, contracts bind the executor or administrator, though not named. Where, however, personal considerations are of the foundation of the contract, as in the cases of principal and agent and master and servant, the death of either party puts an end to the relation; and, in respect of service after the death, the contract is dissolved, unless there be a stipulation express or implied to the contrary. It is obvious that, in this case, if the servant had died, his master could not have compelled his representatives to perform the service in his stead, or pay damages, and equally by the death of the master the servant is discharged of his service, not in breach of the contract, but by implied condition.

In **Stahlschmidt v Lett** (1853) 1 Sm & Giff 415, 65 ER 182, the deceased owed his son (who was also his executor) £1,071 at the time of his death. It was argued that as the debt was statute-barred the son had no right to claim it but Stuart V-C disagreed, saying at p 184:

> It is clear that there was a debt. It is equally clear that, at the time of the testator's death, there had been no payment or acknowledgement, or entry amounting to an acknowledgement in respect of it, for the period of six years and eleven days. It is clear also that, at the time of the testator's death, it was a debt as to which, in an action, the testator might, if he were alive, have pleaded the Statute of Limitations. But it is equally clear that the testator was not bound to plead the statute if it had been a debt to a stranger; and that the debt remained, although the defence afforded by the statute, the testator, if he had lived, would have had the right to use. He died, however, without asserting any such right; and I am of opinion that, if this had been a debt due to a stranger, arising from a loan to the testator under the same circumstances, and that stranger, after the testator's death, had applied to the son for payment of the debt, the son as executor would have had a right to refuse payment, on the ground that it was barred by the statute. But I am of opinion also that the son might, if he pleased, say that, being satisfied there was a debt due by his father, he would be doing an unrighteous and improper thing—a thing the testator would not himself have done, if he attempted to avoid the payment of a just debt, and which he knew to be a just debt, by setting up the defence of a statute. I, therefore, think it is clear in this case that the son, the executor, if it had been the case of a stranger, might properly have paid the debt after the death of the testator, and after it was barred by the statute, and that such payment would have been allowed him.
>
> If then the son, the executor, might have done this where the debt was due to a stranger, the Court can hardly say that with reference to his own debt he had not the same right.[5]

---

5. Aliter where the debt has been judicially declared to be statute-barred, in which event the personal representatives must not pay it: *Midgley v Midgley* [1893] 3 Ch 282.

(c) Time for payment

Personal representatives are required to pay the deceased's debts with all due diligence, but not necessarily by the end of the 'executor's year'.[6]

Re Tankard [1942] 1 Ch 69, [1941] 3 All ER 458, Ch D; Uthwatt J

By his will the testator left his residuary estate on trust for sale, his debts to be paid out of the proceeds and the balance to be held on certain trusts for the beneficiaries. He also authorised his executors to retain any part of the estate in its unconverted form for so long as they thought fit. Requiring money to pay the debts, the executors sold the testator's shares in a particular company over an eighteen month period after his death, the bulk of them after the first anniversary of his death, by which time the value of the shares had more than halved. The beneficiaries claimed that the executors were guilty of a devastavit[7] in that they should have sold sufficient assets to meet the debts at the time most favourable to the estate within a year of the death.
Held: The executors had acted in accordance with the directions in the will and were not liable to the beneficiaries for the loss.

Uthwatt J: With respect to the period within which debts should be paid, there is, in my opinion, no rule of law that it is the duty of executors to pay such debts within a year from the testator's death. The duty is to pay with due diligence. Due diligence may, indeed, require that payment should be made before the expiration of the year, and the circumstances affecting the estate and the assets comprised in it may justify non-payment outside the year, but if debts are not paid within the year, the onus is thrown upon the executors to justify the delay. . . .

That, in my view, is the position, apart from any provision contained in the will of the testator. As against creditors, the provisions of the testator's will which relate to the realisation of his assets, or which otherwise bear upon the payment of debts, are irrelevant. As against beneficiaries, the position is different. Beneficiaries take their interest under the will only upon the terms of the will. As respects them, full effect has to be given to any provisions which, either in express terms or by implication, modify the executor's duty of paying debts with due diligence.

In the present case the provision relied on is the power to retain assets. Upon the construction of the will, I am of opinion that the power of retention was exercisable notwithstanding the facts that debts of the testator were outstanding and that there was not sufficient cash in hand to meet the debts. The primary trust for conversion applies to the whole residue of the testator's estate other than money, and the proceeds resulting from the execution of that trust are treated by the testator as the fund from which debts are to be paid. The power of retention is in terms applicable to all the assets comprised in the estate. Assets as respects which the power is for the time being duly exercised are excluded from the assets which, under the testator's scheme, need—so far as beneficiaries are concerned—be applied in payment of debts. Beneficiaries cannot complain if the directions given by testators are adhered to.

(d) Solvent or insolvent estate?

A crucial matter for the personal representatives to consider at an early stage is the solvency or otherwise of the estate, as if the estate is insolvent, they are obliged to follow the bankruptcy order for the payment of debts and will be

---

6. See AEA 1925, s 44 p 389 post.
7. See p 411 post.

personally liable if they deviate therefrom. A personal representative used to have the right to retain any debt due from the deceased to himself in priority to other creditors in the same class and to prefer one creditor in the same class[8] to another, rights that were particularly useful when the deceased died insolvent. These rights were abolished by the Administration of Justice Act 1971 which gave personal representatives instead a limited protection when paying debts in an insolvent estate in the belief that it was solvent.

Law Commission: Administration Bonds, Personal Representatives' Rights of Retainer and Preference and Related Matters[9]

8.   As we see it, there is only one respect in which the right of preference may be said to perform a useful function. It protects a personal representative who, reasonably enough, has paid the tradesmen's bills without waiting until all claims are received in response to the statutory notice for creditors. Should the estate ultimately prove to be insolvent the personal representative will not be liable at the suit of creditors of the same class as those paid. Real hardship might be caused to small tradesmen (and indeed to the widow and children of the deceased who may be dependent on their goodwill) if debts of this sort could not be paid promptly. We suggest, however, that this would best be dealt with by an express provision to the effect that where a personal representative reasonably and in good faith pays a creditor at a time when he has no reason to believe that the estate will be insolvent he shall not be liable to account to any creditor of the same class if the estate subsequently proves to be insolvent. We see no reason why this provision should not be capable of applying to one who has obtained a grant as a creditor, although it is unlikely that it would operate in such a case since the estate will usually be known to be insolvent. If, however, a creditor has obtained letters of administration to an estate which appears to be solvent we see no reason why he, to the same extent as any other personal representative, should not be allowed to pay the tradesmen immediately. What is objectionable is that he should prefer himself to the other creditors (ie exercise a right of retainer) and this the recommended provision does not permit. There is no need to provide any special protection to the creditors who have been paid: as they are not volunteers, the payment cannot be followed into their hands and recovered from them (*Thorndike v Hunt* (1857) 3 De G & J 563).

9.   Subject to the provision suggested in the preceding paragraph we recommend that the rights of retainer and preference be abolished and that this should apply to executors as well as administrators.

Administration of Estates Act 1971

10.   Retainer, preference and the payment of debts by personal representatives
(1) The right of retainer of a personal representative and his right to prefer creditors are hereby abolished.
(2) Nevertheless a personal representative—
  (a) other than one mentioned in paragraph (b) below, who, in good faith and at a time when he has no reason to believe that the deceased's estate is insolvent, pays the debt of any person (including himself) who is a creditor of the estate; or
  (b) to whom letters of administration had been granted solely by reason of his being a creditor and who, in good faith and at such time pays the debt of another person who is a creditor of the estate;

---

8. See p 335 post for the various classes of priority in an insolvent estate.
9. Law Com No 31 (1970).

shall not, if it subsequently appears that the estate is insolvent, be liable to account to a creditor of the same degree as the paid creditor for the sum so paid.[10]

2   Insolvent estates

If the assets of the estate are insufficient to pay all the debts and liabilities (including the funeral, testamentary and administration expenses) the estate is insolvent.[11] The debts must then be paid in the order set out in the Insolvency Act 1985[12] which gives priority to the funeral, testamentary and administration expenses and thereafter requires the normal bankruptcy order to be followed.[13] If a personal representative fails to observe the statutory order and pays creditors in a lower class when he has notice of a debt in a higher class, he commits a devastavit[14] for which he is personally liable; similarly where he neglects to pay debts in the same class pari passu, save in so far as the Administration of Estates Act 1971 s 10 protects him.

(a) The funeral, testamentary and administration expenses

In **Goldstein v Salvation Army Assurance Society** [1917] 2 KB 291, the plaintiff had taken out an insurance policy for the express purpose of providing for his mother's funeral expenses. Holding that 'funeral expenses' within the meaning of the Assurance Companies Act 1905 could include the cost of a tombstone, Rowlatt J said at p 295:

Undoubtedly it could not be said as a matter of law that the erecting of a memorial in the shape of a church or chapel, or the founding of a bed in a hospital, or even wearing mourning, was part of the funeral expenses; but the memorial upon a grave may be the completion and identification of the grave itself, and while I do not say that in every case a tombstone must be part of the funeral expenses, I do not say as a matter of law that it is not. We have no jurisdiction to review the findings in this case upon the facts, and I think in every case the learned judge must consider whether a tombstone is reasonable under all the circumstances or not. Speaking for myself, I should say that prima facie £50 is a very large sum to spend on a funeral; but the learned judge has said that among Jews a very large measure is to be allowed.[15]

In **Sharp v Lush** (1879) 10 Ch D 468, Jessel MR had to consider the ambit of

---

10. For a critical examination of these provisions, see Sunnucks: 'Debts—Preference and Retainer' (1972) 122 NLJ 26.
11. Insolvency Act 1985, s 228.
12. The provisions of the Insolvency Act 1985 referred to in this chapter have not yet been brought into force. The present provisions which they are to replace are contained primarily in AEA 1925, s 34(1), Sch I, pt I and in the Bankruptcy Act 1914 and are similar save where indicated.
13. Only the areas of bankruptcy law of particular relevance to the winding up of an estate are considered here.
14. See p 411 post.
15. McCardie J added at p 297; 'He [the judge] must remember the station in life, the occupation, and the creed of the dead person, and the general circumstances of the case, and he ought not to allow as a funeral expense anything beyond these reasonable and proper limits'. See also *Hart v Griffith-Jones* [1948] 2 All ER 729 (costs of embalming body of young child allowed in a claim for funeral expenses in assessing damages due under the Law Reform (Miscellaneous Provisions) Act 1934, s 1(2)(c) but not the cost of an expensive monument over the grave). See also *Stanton v Ewart F Youldon* [1960] 1 All ER 429, [1960] 1 WLR 543.

the expression 'executorship expenses' when it occurred in the will he was construing and he said at p 470:

I cannot distinguish between 'executorship expenses' and 'testamentary expenses'. As I understand the words 'executorship expenses', they are expenses incident to the proper performance of the duty of the executor in the same way as testamentary expenses are, neither more nor less.

Now what is the proper performance of the duty of an executor? It is ascertaining the debts and liabilities due from the testator's estate, the payment of such debts and liabilities, and the legal and proper distribution of the estate among the persons entitled. . . .

That being so, when a testator directs 'executorship expenses' to be paid out of a given fund he does, in my opinion, include the expenses incurred in relation to the administration of his estate whether incurred in an administration suit, or whether incurred simply by taking the advice of a solicitor and counsel outside the administration suit as to the distribution of the estate. It very often is cheaper to take the opinion of the Court than even the opinion of counsel. I cannot see any solid distinction; and I think, therefore, whatever this testator may have intended, he has used words which clearly cover the whole costs of the administration.

(b) The bankruptcy order for payment of unsecured[16] debts

The Cork Committee, reporting in 1982, recommended a substantial reduction in the categories of preferential debts on an insolvency and this was subsequently achieved by the Insolvency Act 1985. Once the preferential debts have been paid in full (without interest), the balance is available for the ordinary creditors whose claims will abate proportionally in so far as there is insufficient for all to be paid in full. If there happens to be any surplus remaining, interest will then be paid to the preferential and ordinary creditors and any balance will then pass to the deferred creditors.

Report of the Cork Committee[17]

1396. It is a fundamental objective of the law of insolvency to achieve a rateable, that is to say *pari passu*, distribution of the uncharged assets of the insolvent among the unsecured creditors. In practice, however, this objective is seldom, if ever, attained. In the overwhelming majority of cases it is substantially frustrated by the existence of preferential debts. These are unsecured debts which by force of statute, fall to be paid in bankruptcy or winding up in priority to all other unsecured debts.

Insolvency Act 1985[12]

166. Priority of debts
(1) In the distribution of the bankrupt's estate, the preferential debts listed in part I of

---

16. Secured creditors are permitted to rely on their security and need only prove in the bankruptcy for any balance due to them: see Bankruptcy Act 1914, ss 32, 167, 2nd Sch. These provisions have not been extracted as they are about to be replaced by rules, not yet published, made under the Insolvency Act 1985, s 163.
17. 'Insolvency Law and Practice' (1982) Cmnd 8558.

Schedule 4 to this Act shall be paid in priority to other debts; and Part II of that Schedule shall have effect for the interpretation of the said Part I.

(2) Preferential debts shall rank equally between themselves after the expenses of the bankruptcy and shall be paid in full unless the bankrupt's estate is insufficient for meeting them, in which case they shall abate in equal proportions between themselves.

(3) Debts[18] which are neither preferential debts nor debts falling within subsection (6) below shall also rank equally between themselves and, after the preferential debts, shall be paid in full unless the bankrupt's estate is insufficient for meeting them, in which case they shall abate in equal proportions between themselves.

(4) Any surplus remaining after the payment of the debts that are preferential or rank equally under subsection (3) above shall be applied in paying interest on those debts in respect of the periods during which they have been outstanding since the commencement of the bankruptcy; and interest on preferential debts shall rank equally with interest on debts other than preferential debts.

(5) The rate of the interest payable under subsection (4) above in respect of any debt shall be whichever is the greater of—

(a) the rate specified in section 17 of the Judgments Act 1838[19] at the commencement of the bankruptcy; and

(b) the rate applicable to that debt apart from the bankruptcy.

(6) Bankruptcy debts owed in respect of credit provided by a person who (whether or not the bankrupt's spouse at the time the credit was provided) was the bankrupt's spouse at the commencement of the bankruptcy shall—

(a) rank in priority after the debts and interest required to be paid in pursuance of subsections (3) and (4) above;[20] and

(b) be payable with interest at the rate specified in sub-section (5) above in respect of the period during which they have been outstanding since the commencement of the bankruptcy;

and the interest payable under paragraph (b) above shall have the same priority as the debts on which it is payable.

(7) This section is without prejudice to any provision of this Act or of any other Act under which the payment of any debt or the making of any other payment is, in the event of bankruptcy, to have a particular priority[1] or to be postponed.[2]

SCHEDULE 4—PREFERENTIAL DEBTS

PART I—LIST OF PREFERENTIAL DEBTS[3]

Debts due to Inland Revenue

1.—(1) Sums due at the relevant date from the debtor on account of deductions of income tax from emoluments paid during the period of twelve months next before that date, being deductions which the debtor was liable to make under section 204 of the Income and Corporation Taxes Act 1970 (pay as you earn) less the amount of the repayments of income tax which the debtor was liable to make during that period.

(2) Sums due at the relevant date from the debtor in respect of such deductions as are

---

18. Ie ordinary debts.

19. Currently 15%: Judgment Debts (Rate of Interest) Order 1985, SI 1985/437.

20. Ie as a deferred debt. This subsection has replaced Bankruptcy Act 1914, s 36 which reduced a loan between spouses to deferred status only where the loan was made in connection with the borrower's trade or business.

1. Eg the funeral, testamentary and administration expenses, p 334 ante. See also Friendly Societies Act 1974, s 59 and Regimental Debts Act 1893, s 2.

2. In addition to loans between spouses (ante, ss (6)), a loan to a trader where the lender is to receive a rate of interest varying with the profits or a share of the profits, is a deferred debt: Partnership Act 1890, ss 2, 3.

3. Until the Insolvency Act 1985 this list included one year's general rates and one year's taxes; the Cork Committee on 'Insolvency Law and Practice' Cmnd 8558, recommended the abolition of their priority as unfair to other creditors and out of date but advised that priority should continue for PAYE, National Insurance Contributions, VAT and car tax, where the debtor could be regarded as a tax collector rather than a tax payer (para 1418).

required to be made by the debtor for that period under section 69 of the Finance (No 2) Act 1975 (sub-contractors in the construction industry).

Debts due to Customs and Excise
2.—(1) Any value added tax which is referable to the period of six months next before the relevant date.
(2) The amount of any car tax which is due at the relevant date from the debtor and which became due within a period of twelve months next before that date.
(3) Any amount which is due—
  (a) by way of general betting duty or bingo duty; or
  (b) under section 12(1) of the Betting and Gaming Duties Act 1981 (general betting duty and pool betting duty recoverable from agent collecting stakes); or
  (c) under section 14 of, or Schedule 2 to, that Act (gaming licence duty),
from the debtor at the relevant date and which became due within the period of twelve months next before that date.

Social security contributions
3.—(1) All sums which on the relevant date are due from the debtor on account of Class 1 or Class 2 contributions under the Social Security Act 1975 or the Social Security (Northern Ireland) Act 1975 and which became due from the debtor in the twelve months next before the relevant date.
(2) All sums which on the relevant date have been assessed on and are due from the debtor on account of Class 4 contributions under either of the said Acts of 1975, being sums which—
  (a) are due to the Commissioners of Inland Revenue (rather than to the Secretary of State or a Northern Ireland department); and
  (b) are assessed on the debtor up to 5th April next before the relevant date,
but not exceeding, in the whole, any one year's assessment.

Contributions to occupational pension schemes etc
4. Any sum which is owed by the debtor and is a sum to which Schedule 3 to the Social Security Pensions Act 1975 (contributions to occupational pension scheme and state scheme premiums) applies.

Remuneration of employees etc
5.—(1) So much of any amount which—
  (a) is owed by the debtor to a person who is or has been an employee of the debtor; and
  (b) is payable by way of remuneration in respect of the whole or any part of the period of four months next before the relevant date,
as does not exceed such amount as may be prescribed by order made by the Secretary of State.[3a]
(2) An amount owed by way of accrued holiday remuneration, in respect of any period of employment before the relevant date, to a person whose employment by the debtor has been terminated, whether before, on or after that date.
(3) So much of any sum owed in respect of money advanced for the purpose as has been applied for the payment of a debt which, if it had not been paid, would have been a debt falling within sub-paragraph (1) or (2) above

3 Solvent estates

When an estate is solvent, the personal representatives' problem is not in deciding which debts should be satisfied but rather the order in which the deceased's assets should be used to satisfy the creditors, a matter of vital interest to the beneficiaries. A set order for the application of the assets for payment of

---

3a. The limit currently in force under a similar provision in the Bankruptcy Act 1914 s 33(1)(b)(c) and (5) as amended by Insolvency Act 1976 s 1(1) and Sch 1 Pt 1 is £800.

the debts in a solvent estate is contained in the Administration of Estates Act 1925 and in the absence of a contrary intention shown by the deceased, this order must be followed.

(a) Secured creditors

Any debts secured on the deceased's property when he died must first be identified as these must be met primarily out of the property so charged, unless the deceased has shown a contrary intention.

Administration of Estates Act 1925

35.   Charges on property of deceased to be paid primarily out of the property charged
(1) Where a person dies possessed of, or entitled to, or, under a general power of appointment (including the statutory power to dispose of entailed interests)[4] by his will disposes of, an interest in property, whether by way of legal mortgage, equitable charge or otherwise (including a lien for unpaid purchase money)[5] and the deceased has not by will deed or other document signified a contrary or other intention, the interest so charged shall, as between the different persons claiming through the deceased, be primarily liable for the payment of the charge; and every part of the said interest, according to its value, shall bear a proportionate part of the charge on the whole thereof.
(2) Such contrary or other intention shall not be deemed to be signified—
  (a) by a general direction for the payment of debts or of all the debts of the testator out of his personal estate,[6] or his residuary real and personal estate, or his residuary estate; or
  (b) by a charge of debts upon any such estate;
unless any such intention is further signified by words expressly or by necessary implication referring to all or some part of the charge.
(3) Nothing in this section affects the right of a person entitled to the charge to obtain payment or satisfaction thereof either out of the other assets of the deceased or otherwise.

Re Wakefield [1943] 2 All ER 29, CA; Lord Greene MR, Luxmoore and Goddard LJJ

The testator contracted to buy a farm and paid the usual 10% deposit with the contract. He then instructed stockbrokers to sell some stock and send him two cheques, one for the exact amount he needed to complete his purchase and the other in his favour for the balance. This was duly done and he then sent the first cheque on to his solicitors endorsed over to them, with a letter in which, after referring to the property he said 'Cheque enclosed for the balance of the purchase-money.' He died before the sale could be completed, leaving a will in which he devised all his real estate to X. X wished to take the farm free of the vendor's lien for the 90% unpaid purchase money with which it was charged when the testator died, and so argued that the testator's letter to his solicitor showed that the testator intended that the balance of the purchase money

---

4. See LPA 1925, s 176.
5. See eg *Re Wakefield* [1943] 2 All ER 29 post, *Re Birmingham* [1959] Ch 523, [1958] 2 All ER 397. As to the point at which the vendor's lien arises, see *Lysaght v Edwards* (1876) 2 Ch D 499 at 506, *Re Coxen* [1948] Ch 747, [1948] 2 All ER 492.
6. See eg *Re Neeld* [1962] Ch 643, [1962] 2 All ER 335.

should come from another source, namely the cheque. As a contrary intention had therefore been shown, X argued, s 35 should not apply.

Held: The letter did not indicate a contrary intention, so X took the property subject to the vendor's lien for the unpaid purchase money.

Lord Greene MR: The whole question, in my opinion, is whether the letter enclosed with the cheque can be said to indicate a contrary or other intention within the meaning of s 35. The first thing to notice about that letter is that there is no reference in it as to what is to happen after the death of the testator. It is a mandate given to the solicitors, which is not merely revocable in the testator's lifetime, but which necessarily comes to an end on his death. It is not a direction which is to operate after his death, but it is merely a direction of the character which I have described. The proceeds of that cheque, which the solicitors paid into their clients' account, became part of the testator's estate on his death and passed to his executors. There was no trust attached to the cheque and no enforceable mandate because the mandate to the solicitors had come to an end. It follows, therefore, that the intention disclosed by the testator in that letter could have no effect upon anything which was to happen after his death. It had reference to what was to take place in his lifetime and had no reference to what would happen after his death. That, in my opinion, is sufficient to dispose of the appeal because, if that is right, no such contrary or other intention as the section requires is to be found. That view was taken by Farwell J,[7] and in my opinion, he was perfectly correct. He found support for it in *Re Nicholson, Nicholson v Boulton* ((1923) WN 251). That was a case in which the testatrix, subsequently to the date of her will, had mortgaged her freehold property and had served notice upon the mortgagee that she intended to pay off the mortgage, but she died before that could be done. It was contended that the letter giving notice of intention to pay off the mortgage should be treated as being an indication of a contrary or other intention. It was said by Russell J at p 251:

'Now it is said that the letter written by the lady's solicitor to the mortgagee, giving notice of an intention on the part of the lady herself to pay off the mortgage in 6 months' time, is an 'other document' within the meaning of the section by which she has shown a contrary or other intention within the meaning of the Act. In my opinion that view is quite unsound. The letter shows no intention of any sort or kind that, as between the specific legatee and the residuary legatee, the debt should be borne by the latter. It merely shows an intention by the testatrix to pay off the mortgage herself in her own lifetime, and, above all, the letter shows no intention at all in relation to a mortgage which would be in existence at the date of the death of the testatrix.'

Those observations appear to me to apply with equal force to the present case. The only difference is that in the present case a cheque was sent to the solicitors for the purpose of paying the purchase money. That seems to me to make no difference. It merely shows an intention on the part of the testator to pay the unpaid balance of the purchase money in his lifetime and it had no reference as to what the position would be after his death as regards the administration and distribution of his estate. In my opinion, the judgment of Farwell J was right and this appeal must be dismissed with costs.[8]

In **Re Valpy** [1906] 1 Ch 531, the testator was more successful in establishing a contrary intention for the purpose of s 35. His will included a direction that all his debts 'except mortgage debts, if any, in (Blackacre)' be paid out of residue. Swinfen Eady J said at p 533:

A general direction that the testator's debts shall be paid out of his personal estate shall not be deemed to be a declaration of an intention contrary to the rule established by the Real Estate Charges Act 1854[9] unless such contrary intention shall be further declared

---

7. At first instance.
8. See also *Re Birmingham* [1959] Ch 523, [1958] 2 All ER 397.
9. A fore-runner of AEA 1925, s 35.

by words 'expressly or by necessary implication' referring to 'all or some' of the testator's debts or debt charged by way of mortgage 'on any part' of his real estate. Now, this will refers to the mortgage debts, if any, on Blackacre, and directs all other debts to be paid out of the mixed residuary fund. That is a clear implication that the mortgage debts other than those, if any, on Blackacre are included in the general direction to pay the debts. There is therefore a contrary intention within the Real Estate Charges Act 1867,[9] and the mortgage on Whiteacre must be born rateably by the mixed residuary fund.

In **Re Fegan** [1928] Ch 45, the testator left his four daughters legacies of £1,000 each to be paid out of the proceeds of certain life policies which were worth about £5,600 on his death but had been mortgaged by the testator to secure debts of about £2,000. He left another fund[10] to be used to pay all his debts but that other fund proved to be insufficient. It was argued that in so far as the mortgage debts had not been met by the other fund, the balance of the debts should be met in accordance with the statutory order in the Administration of Estates Act 1925, s 34(3)[11] but Tomlin J did not agree, saying at p 52:

The testator has indicated that a particular fund should be used for paying debts. That seems to me to be a direction that the mortgage debt is to be paid out of that fund so far as it is available, but not a direction that the property charged is to be exonerated beyond that so as to throw the burden of the balance of the sum charged on the general personal estate. . . .

Therefore I will declare that in so far as the special fund is insufficient for payment of debts the money charged will remain payable primarily out of the fund charged.[12]

(b) Unsecured creditors

Having allowed for the secured debts to which s 35 applies, the personal representatives should then apply the statutory order for the application of assets in payment of the debts in a solvent estate as contained in the first Schedule of the Administration of Estates Act 1925 unless the statutory order has been varied by a contrary intention shown in the will.

Administration of Estates Act 1925

34.   Administration of assets
(3) Where the estate of a deceased person is solvent his real and personal estate shall, subject to rules of court and the provisions hereinafter contained as to charges on property of the deceased, and to the provisions, if any, contained in his will, be applicable towards the discharge of the funeral, testamentary and administration expenses,[13] debts and liabilities payable thereout in the order mentioned in Part II of the First Schedule to this Act.

55.   Definitions
(1) In this Act, unless the context otherwise requires, the following expressions have the meanings hereby assigned to them respectively, that is to say—
(xvii) 'Property' includes a thing in action and any interest in real or personal property.

---

10. Non-residuary, see AEA 1925 s 35(2), p 338 ante.
11. Post.
12. See also *Re Birch* [1909] 1 Ch 787.
13. Including any inheritance tax payable on the deceased's estate, whether realty or personalty: IHTA 1984, s 211. Cf IHT payable on property of which the deceased was a beneficial joint tenant; such property does not vest in the personal representative (see p 277) and any inheritance tax payable on it will be borne by the surviving joint tenant.

FIRST SCHEDULE

PART II—ORDER OF APPLICATION OF ASSETS WHERE THE ESTATE IS SOLVENT

1.   Property of the deceased undisposed of by will,[14] subject to the retention thereof of a fund to meet any pecuniary legacies.[15]
2.   Property of the deceased not specifically devised or bequeathed but included (either by a specific or general description) in a residuary gift,[16] subject to the retention out of such property of a fund sufficient to meet any pecuniary legacies,[15] so far as not provided for aforesaid.
3.   Property of the deceased specifically appropriated or devised or bequeathed (either by a specific or general description) for the payment of debts.
4.   Property of the deceased charged with, or devised or bequeathed (either by a specific or general description) subject to a charge for the payment of debts.
5.   The fund, if any, retained to meet pecuniary legacies.[15]
6.   Property specifically devised or bequeathed,[17] rateably according to value.
7.   Property appointed by will under a general power, including the statutory power to dispose of entailed interests,[18] rateably according to value.
8.   The following provisions[19] shall also apply—
  (a) The order of application may be varied by the will of the deceased.

In **Re John** [1933] Ch 370, the testator left Blackacre (subject to a mortgage he had created) to X and Whiteacre (subject to certain legacies he gave by his will) to Y. It being necessary to resort to paragraph 6 property for the payment of the debts, Farwell J held that 'value' meant the value of the property to the testator, saying at p 372:

The testator had, in fact, in respect of (Blackacre), only an equity of redemption, and that is the value which, in my judgment, must be taken for this purpose. The 'value' cannot mean the actual price which the property would fetch in the open market free from incumbrances: it must mean the value to the testator, and since all he had was the equity of redemption, that is the value which must be taken.

Also, it seems to me that it is quite impossible to read the word 'value' in para 6 as meaning the interest the beneficiary takes. It must mean the value of the property to the testator. Where the testator imposes on a legatee an obligation to make certain payments thereout as legacies, I cannot read 'value' as meaning what the beneficiary is ultimately going to receive from the property. There will, therefore, be a declaration that there be deducted from the probate values the amount of the mortgage on (Blackacre) so charged, and that there be no deduction from the value of (Whiteacre) devised to the defendant, (Y), in respect of the several legacies which under the will he is bound to pay.

In **Re Eve** [1956] Ch 479, [1956] 2 All ER 321, Roxburgh J decided that there was one further category of asset available for the payment of debts when the assets contained in the statutory order had been exhausted, namely, the benefit of an option given by will, saying at p 322:

The question is where the benefit of the option stands in the hierarchy of assets for the payment of debts in a solvent estate. The option is a right to purchase one thousand shares at par value, ie, at a price below their true value. Once exercised, it involves a contract between the trustees as vendors to sell and the purchaser to buy the shares at the

---

14. Including a lapsed share of residue: *Re Lamb* [1929] 1 Ch 722.
15. See p 373 post as to the incidence of legacies.
16. See *Re Wilson*, p 61 ante.
17. A demonstrative legacy is treated as specific in so far as the designated fund is available, otherwise it is treated as general: *Tempest v Tempest* (1857) 7 DeG M & G 470.
18. See LPA 1925, s 176.
19. Provision (b) was repealed by Finance (No 2) Act 1983.

stated price, free from incumbrances, and this is so notwithstanding that there is a strong element of bounty in the transaction. The shares are not bequeathed subject to a charge or condition. An option to purchase cannot be a specific bequest of shares. If there is a specific bequest at all, it must be of the difference between the price stated in the will and the market value of the shares.

Such a benefit has never yet been held to be a specific bequest: nor does it fit in with any reported definition of a specific bequest . . . . In my judgment that beneficial interest is not a specific bequest.

It is said that if that is so, it has no place in Part 2 of Sch 1 to the Administration of Estates Act 1925, and that that is surprising. I do not find it surprising if, as I think, the property subject to an option is the last to be available for the payment of debts. For, indeed, in so far as the property subject to the option is required for the payment of debts, the option over that property cannot be exercised at all and the benefit of it is totally destroyed by operation of law. So long as the purchase price stated in the will is, with the other available assets, sufficient for the payment of debts, it, and not the shares, constitutes the fund available for that purpose.

Re Kempthorne [1930] 1 Ch 268, Ch D, Maugham J, CA; Lord Hanworth MR, Lawrence and Russell LJJ

The testator left his residuary personalty 'subject to and after payment of my funeral and testamentary expenses and debts' in shares to various beneficiaries, two of whom predeceased him so that their shares lapsed. Out of what property were the debts payable?

Held: (Maugham J) The undisposed of shares would be primarily liable for the payment of the debts under paragraph 1 of the statutory order, the only effect of the words quoted being to place the remainder of the deceased's personalty into paragraph 4.

(On appeal) Appeal allowed. The testator had shown an intention that the statutory order should not apply and that the debts should be paid out of the residuary personalty as a whole before division into shares.

Maugham J: Now in both of those cases (paragraphs 3 and 4 of the statutory order) it is to be noticed that the Legislature is assuming that the testator by his will has specifically appropriated in one case, or devised or bequeathed in the other, property for the payment of debts; or that he charged with payment of debts specific property, or some property, under a general description, or devised or bequeathed property subject to a charge for payment of debts, and I cannot help concluding that those two paragraphs mean that the fact that the testator has done one of those things is not per se to constitute, to use the words of s 34, subs 3, a provision in the will which operates to alter the order of application which is specified in Part II of the Schedule.

Russell LJ: The first thing to do, is to ascertain whether the testator's will contains any and what provisions relating to the discharge of his funeral, testamentary and administration expenses, debts and liabilities. If such provisions exist in the will, they will control the operation of s 34, sub-s 3 of the Administration of Estates Act, 1925.

The testator in the present case has made, as it seems to me, a particularly clear provision by his will. As to all his personal estate he directs that, subject to and after payment of his funeral and testamentary expenses and debts and legacies it is to be divided into seven equal parts, which he bequeaths to five named persons in unequal shares. There is no gift to any of those persons except of a share of the balance of the general personal estate remaining after the expenses and debts and legacies have been borne and paid out of the entirety thereof. If the words used in the will left any doubt on this score (which they do not) the doubt would be removed by the codicil, which recites that by his will the testator had bequeathed to his sister Elizabeth 'one seventh part of my . . . personal estate and effects after certain payments had been made thereout.'

In the circumstances of the present case I fail to see how Part II of Sch I can come into play as regards the real and personal estate of this testator. The statutory order of application of assets is overridden by the testator's own provisions, the effect of which is (to put the result in another way) that the only personal estate as to which he has died intestate is a share of what personal estate remains after the expenses and debts have in fact been paid thereout.'

As I read the judgment of Maugham J its foundation is this: that although s 34, sub-s 3 of the Administration of Estates Act 1925, is stated to be subject to the provisions, if any, contained in the will of the deceased person, yet the provisions contained in this particular will are not strong enough to negative the operation of the sub-section. He argues thus, that a consideration of paras 3 and 4 of Part II of Sch I indicates that even if a testator has made a disposition of property, as described in paras 3 or 4, nevertheless the property described in para 1 must first be applied; this shows that a disposition of property as described in para 4 will not be a provision contained in the will strong enough to negative the operation of the sub-section. He then states that the provision contained in this will is a disposition of property as described in para 4 and that, accordingly, he is driven to hold that it is ineffective to override the subsection. That is the reasoning of the judgment as I read it.

In my opinion however, the learned judge erred in treating the provision made by this testator as being a disposition of property as described in para 4 of Part II of Sch 1. Neither para 3 nor para 4 can apply or be intended to apply to a disposition of a general or residuary nature: because the operation of the Schedule is such that resort is not to be had to the items covered by paras 3 and 4 until all property of the deceased comprised in a residuary gift has been exhausted. Thus the reason which compelled Maugham J to decide as he did had, as I construe the Schedule, no foundation in fact. For these reasons I would allow the appeal.[20]

Re James [1947] Ch 256, [1947] 1 All ER 402, Ch D; Roxburgh J

The testator gave specific property to his bank-executor to hold on trust for sale 'and after payment of my just debts, funeral and testamentary expenses, to invest the proceeds' and hold the same on certain trusts. He gave the residue of his estate to his wife absolutely. On the face of it the primary fund for the payment of the debts etc was the residuary gift (paragraph 2 property) rather than the property specifically given for the payment of debts (paragraph 3). **Held:** The testator had shown an intention to vary the statutory order. In making the specific gift for the payment of debts when the only other gift in the will was residuary and therefore preceded the specific gift in the statutory order, he must have intended to exonerate the residuary gift and make the specific gift the primary fund.

Roxburgh J: In my opinion the testator, when he directed the bank to sell and after payment of just debts to invest, was directing the bank to pay the debts. They could not carry out his direction to invest after payment without paying them. Therefore, I should hold that the testator had specifically appropriated or devised or bequeathed property for the payment of debts, within the meaning of the Administration of Estates Act, 1925, Sched 1, pt II, para 3. Secondly, I should hold that the direction to pay debts out of a particular fund necessarily involved an intention to exonerate some other fund which

---

20. See also *Re Harland-Peck* [1941] Ch 182, [1940] 4 All ER 347; *Re Berrey's Will Trusts* [1959] 1 All ER 15, [1959] 1 WLR 30; *Re Feis* [1964] 1 Ch 106, [1963] 3 All ER 303. In each case there was a similarly worded residuary gift: 'subject to the payment of my debts and funeral expenses etc. I give my residuary estate to A and B in equal shares;' one of the residuary beneficiaries died before the testator but the residue (para 2) was held to be the primary fund for the payment of the debts, notwithstanding the existence of undisposed of (para 1) property.

the testator disposed of in some other part of the will—in other words, necessarily involved an intention to exonerate the residue of his estate which he devised and bequeathed to his wife absolutely.

Am I right in reaching those conclusions? This depends on a difficult line of authorities. In *Re Kempthorne* Maugham J (as he then was) made these observations in reference to Sched 1, pt II, paras 3 and 4 ([1930] 1 Ch 269 at 278): (Having read out that part of Maugham J's judgment extracted on p 342 ante, he continued:)

Counsel for the nephew has referred to that paragraph, which, as I shall show in a moment, has since been applied in another case[1] and he has submitted that those words apply to the present case, but, in my judgment, they do not, because in that passage the words 'per se' are of vital importance, and in this case there is to be found, not only a devise or bequest of particular property for the payment of debts, but also an intention to exonerate another category of property disposed of by this will, namely residue, and I think that a review of subsequent cases will show that this ground of distinction is valid. . . .

In *Re Littlewood* ([1931] Ch 443) Maugham J had to deal with a will in which Hannah Littlewood . . . gave and bequeathed 'all my farm stock, implements and tenant right, but charged with the payment of all my just debts and funeral and testamentary expenses and also with the payment thereout of the legacies mentioned in the will of my late husband William Littlewood, and an additional legacy of £50 which I bequeath to my stepdaughter Eleanor Booth, unto and equally between my stepson George Littlewood and my son Frederick Littlewood' and the will contained also a gift of the testatrix's residuary estate to Frederick Littlewood absolutely. Maugham J said ([1930] 1 Ch 443 at pp 445, 446):

'But if the testator chooses to charge debts by his will on certain specific items of personal estate, and then gives his residue to some person other than the legatee of the specific property, there can be no doubt, on the construction of his will, that he intends the specific property to be primarily applied in payment of the debts, to the exoneration of the person to whom the residue is given: *Re Smith* ([1913] 2 Ch 216). Accordingly, in my view, the testatrix in this case intended to give George Littlewood and Frederick Littlewood her farm stock, implements, and tenant right, after the payment thereout of all just debts and funeral and testamentary expenses and the legacies therein mentioned and therein bequeathed: and to the residuary legatee Frederick Littlewood she intended to give the whole of the rest of the real estate, discharged from the payment of debts and legacies, provided that the specific gift of farm stock, implements, and tenant right was of sufficient value to discharge the liabilities.'

It appears to me that the language there used by Maugham J is extremely appropriate to the present case. It is interesting to note that he considered the words 'after payment' as equivalent to a direction to pay. Maugham J continued (ibid at p 466):

'I have now to consider the effect of the Administration of Estates Act 1925, Sched I, pt II, having regard to the authorities and also to the provisions of s 34(3) of the Act, and Sched I, pt II para 8, which provides that 'the order of application may be varied by the will of the deceased'. In *Re Kempthorne* ([1930] 1 Ch 268) I endeavoured to explain the difficulty which I felt in giving effect to some of the provisions of that part of that schedule. . . .'

I have no doubt that those words are a reference to the passage which I read earlier in my judgment.[2] Maugham J continued:

' . . . and I understand that the Court of Appeal, who differed from me on one point in that case, also felt some difficulty in explaining the precise effect of those provisions. I think however, that I am justified in taking the view that, prima facie, the paragraphs of the schedule are to have effect subject to the provisions of the will

---

1. *Re Gordon* [1940] Ch 769, [1940] 3 All ER 205.
2. Extracted on p 342 ante.

of the deceased, in cases where there is a reasonably clear indication of the intention of the deceased; and a fortiori, I think, is that the case where the will was executed before the coming into force of the Administration of Estates Act, 1925.'

In my opinion, that passage shows two things. It shows that the proposition which Maugham J is there enunciating is not limited to wills which were executed before the coming into force of the Administration of Estates Act 1925. It also shows that the passage which I have read from a judgment of his own occasioned him no difficulty when he came to decide *Re Littlewood* ([1931] 1 Ch 443) and I feel little doubt that that was because the words 'per se' are emphatic. In *Re Littlewood* ([1931] 1 Ch 443) the judge found (and, if I may say so, very naturally found) that there was not only a direction to pay debts out of the particular fund, but a clear intention to exonerate another fund which was disposed of by the testatrix.

This analysis of that passage, in my judgment, supplies the clue to *Re Gordon* ([1940] Ch 769, [1940] 3 All ER 205), which is a decision of Bennett J. In that case ([1940] Ch 769):

'A testatrix by her will gave certain specific legacies and a legacy of £50 in trust thereout to pay debts, funeral and testamentary expenses, and to pay any balance remaining to a society. There was no residuary gift: Held, that there was an intestacy as to the residue and there being no direction in the will to vary the statutory order of application of assets, the debts, funeral and testamentary expenses of the testatrix were primarily payable out of property undisposed of. Ruling of Maugham J in *Re Kempthorne* ([1930] 1 Ch 47) applied.'

In my judgment, the underlying ground of the decision in *Re Gordon* ([1940] Ch 769) was that there was no residuary gift. If a testator directs a particular fund to bear debts and makes no other disposition, it is, of course, impossible to hold that he intends to exonerate some other fund. That, I think, is why Bennett J said at an early point in his judgment ([1940] Ch 769, at pp 772, 773):

'It is said, and I think truly, that there has been no case which decides what the interpretation of the statutory provisions is, and what their effect is where a testator has made such a will as has to be considered in the present case.'

The real distinction between *Re Littlewood* ([1931] 1 Ch 443) which was cited to the judge but was not referred to by him in his judgment) and *Re Gordon* ([1940] Ch 769, [1940] 3 All ER 205) is that in *Re Littlewood* there was a residuary gift and in *Re Gordon* there was not. Moreover, at the end of his judgment Bennett J said (ibid at pp 775, 766):

'In the present case it is clear that the testatrix has either bequeathed property for the payment of her debts or has bequeathed the property charged with the payment of her debts. She has made no other disposition of her property. The facts of the case plainly fall within the reasoning of Maugham J, with which, if I may respectfully say so, I entirely agree. Where a solvent testator has made by his will a disposition of property which falls either within para 3 of the schedule or within para 4 and has made no other disposition of his property and has not otherwise indicated his intentions there seem to me to be no grounds for a conclusion that such a testator has intended to vary or interfere with or alter the order in which the statute has said that assets are to be applied for the payment of debts and funeral and testamentary expenses.'

Of those three conditions precedent enumerated by the judge, only the first applies in the present case, and, accordingly, it is, in my judgment, clear that the decision in *Re Gordon* ([1940] Ch 769, [1940] 3 All ER 205) is not applicable to the present case. On the contrary, *Re Littlewood* ([1931] 1 Ch 443) is, in my judgment, directly applicable and would, I think, have compelled me to reach the conclusion which I should have wished to reach independently of all authorities.[3]

---

3. See also *Re Meldrum* [1952] 1 Ch 208, [1952] 1 All ER 274, where there was a gift of a bank deposit account to A 'after all legacies, debts, funeral and other expenses have been liquidated' (para 4) followed by a residuary gift to B and C (para 2) but the court held that the testator had shown an intention to exonerate the residue and charge the debts primarily on the deposit account and the Schedule had therefore been effectively varied.

(c) Marshalling

Unlike the beneficiaries, the creditors of a solvent estate are in no way bound by
these statutory rules and may obtain payment out of any of the assets; it is then
for the personal representatives to adjust matters between the beneficiaries (the
doctrine of marshalling) to ensure that as between the beneficiaries the rules are
observed.

Re Broadwood [1911] 1 Ch 277, Ch D; Neville J

The testator left a specific gift of shares to trustees to transfer to his son on
attaining 21. The executors used a part of the shareholding (para 6 property) to
pay a debt although it subsequently transpired that the residuary estate (para
2) was sufficient to pay the debt in full. When the son became 21, he claimed
compensation from the residuary estate, namely the value of the shares at the
date of their transfer to the creditor (the shares having since fallen in value).
Held: He was entitled to compensation but the measure of his loss was the value
of the shares at the date he became entitled to their transfer, that is on the date
he became 21.

Neville J: On the general principle that has to be applied to this case I think there is no
doubt that where the creditors have resorted, for the satisfaction of their debts, to a fund
which is not primarily liable to satisfy them the owner of that fund, is entitled to stand in
the shoes of the creditors for the purpose of compensation, and, of course, where you are
dealing with a pecuniary legacy, the compensation cannot vary from the amount of the
fund exhausted by the creditors. Where you have to deal with a specific legacy, a
different question arises, but you still undoubtedly have the right, where your specific
legacy has been resorted to for the payment of debts, to be put in the same position as
though the creditor had satisfied his debt out of the fund primarily liable. The only
question is, to what extent does that compensation go? Are you entitled under any
circumstances to be put into a better position than you would have been in if the creditor
had never resorted to your legacy at all? I do not think that you are. I think that in that
case you have to consider what it is that the legatee was disappointed of. In the present
case, if the son had attained the age of twenty-one years before the testator's death, he
would have been disappointed of the transfer of these shares upon his attaining twenty-
one, and, therefore, so far as the shares could not be transferred to him on his attaining
twenty-one, he would require compensation out of the general estate, and that
compensation would be measured by the loss to him at the date when he is entitled to the
transfer; that is the value of the shares which have been sold for the purpose of the
payment of debts, at the date of his attaining his right to the enjoyment.
    Now comes this question: Does it make any difference that here the fund was directed
by the will to be transferred to a trustee, the beneficial interest being still contingent
upon the son attaining the age of twenty-one? Upon consideration I do not think it does,
and for this reason, that I am dealing solely with an equity, and I think what I have to
consider is the loss sustained by the beneficiary, and not the loss, if there could be such a
thing, which the trustee could assert in equity. The trustee is merely the hand to hold the
legacy until the happening of the contingency in question, and what I have to look at is
how far the beneficial legatee was disappointed, and I think he was only disappointed to
the extent to which the shares could not be transferred to him.[4]

---

4. He did, however, allow the son any dividends paid on the shares as from the testator's death
(p 282).

QUESTIONS

1. Tom dies leaving a will appointing Edward as his executor; Tom's assets are worth £20,000. Edward obtains probate and pays the undertaker's account of £500; he also pays himself £2,000 in repayment of a loan he had made to Tom. Edward subsequently discovers that Tom also owed £14,000 to the Inland Revenue for arrears of income tax, £3,000 to Wendy (his wife), £2,000 to his bank, £600 to his home help in respect of arrears of wages (payable at £25 per week), £250 to the local authority for general rates and £100 by way of unpaid car tax.
Advise Edward.

2. Tilly makes a will leaving her house Blackacre to Brenda, her jewellery to Janet and her residuary estate to Dick and Harry in equal shares. When Tilly dies, Blackacre is worth £20,000 and is subject to a mortgage debt of £10,000, the jewellery is worth £10,000 and the remainder of Tilly's assets amount to £15,000. Tilly's debts, including the mortgage debt, amount to £40,000. Dick died a few weeks before Tilly. Advise the executors as to the distribution of Tilly's estate.

3. The statutory order for the application of assets of a deceased testator in payment of his debts will not necessarily be varied by a direction in the will for payment of the debts out of a specified part of the estate.
Consider this statement and then decide in which of the following wills the statutory order has been effectively varied:

   (a) 'Subject to the payment of my debts, I give all my residuary estate to A and B in equal shares.' A dies before the testator.

   (b) 'I give my house, subject to the payment of my debts, to Y and the residue of my estate to Z'.

   (c) 'I give all my stocks and shares, subject to the payment of my debts, to P.' The will contains no gift of residue (see *Re Gordon*, p 345 ante).

CHAPTER 22

Failure of gifts by will

1 Effect of failure

If a gift fails, in so far as it is non-residuary, it will simply fall into residue; if residuary, it will devolve under the intestacy rules. If successive interests are created and one of the prior interests fails, then the remainder interests following the failed interest are accelerated, unless the testator has shown a contrary intention.

In **Leake v Robinson** (1871) 2 Mer 363, 35 ER 979, Sir Wm Grant said at p 990:

A question has been made, whether the particular bequests thus declared void do or do not fall into the residue. I have always understood that, with regard to personal estate, everything which is ill given by the will does fall into the residue; and it must be a very peculiar case indeed, in which there can at once be a residuary clause and a partial intestacy, unless some part of the residue itself be ill given. It is immaterial how it happens that any part of the property is undisposed of, whether by the death of a legatee, or by the remoteness, and consequent illegality, of the bequest. Either way it is residue,— ie something upon which no other disposition of the will effectually operates. It may in words have been before given; but if not effectually given, it is, legally speaking, undisposed of, and consequently included in the denomination of residue.

Wills Act 1837

25. Residuary devises shall include estates comprised in lapsed and void devises Unless a contrary intention shall appear by the will, such real estate or interest therein as shall be comprised or intended to be comprised in any devise in such will contained, which shall fail or be void by reason of the death of the devisee in the lifetime of the testator or by reason of such devise being contrary to law, or otherwise incapable of taking effect, shall be included in the residuary devise (if any) contained in such will.

In **Re Flower's Settlement Trusts** [1957] 1 All ER 462, [1957] 1 WLR 401, Jenkins LJ considered the doctrine of acceleration, saying at p 465:

The principle, I think, is well settled, at all events in relation to wills, that where there is a gift to some person for life, and a vested gift in remainder expressed to take effect on the death of the first taker, the gift in remainder is construed as a gift taking effect on the death of the first taker or on any earlier failure or determination of his interest, with the result that if the gift to the first taker fails—as, for example, because he witnessed the will—or if the gift to the first taker does not take effect because it is disclaimed, then the person entitled in remainder will take immediately upon the failure or determination of the prior interest, and will not be kept waiting until the death of the first taker. It has long been settled that this principle applies not only to realty (in respect of which I think it was first introduced) but equally in respect of personalty; and although all the authorities to which we have been referred have been concerned with wills, counsel for the trustees submits . . . that there is no reason for applying any different rule to a settlement inter vivos. As to that I would say that I am disposed to agree that the principle must be broadly the same; but I cannot help feeling that it may well be more difficult, in the case of a settlement, to collect the intention necessary to bring the doctrine of acceleration into play.[1]

In **Re Townsend's Estate** (1887) 34 Ch D 357, the remainder interest following the failed interest was contingent. The testatrix had left the income from her residuary estate to A for life, then to B for life and then as to capital and income for the children of B in equal shares but if B died without leaving issue, for the children of C instead. The will had been attested by the wife of B so that the life interest to B was void,[2] but B had no children and Chitty J held that until he had a child the gifts on the determination of his estate could not be accelerated and that during his life, so long as he had no children, the income of the trust fund was undisposed of. As Upjohn J subsequently said when examining this case in *Re Taylor* [1957] 3 All ER 56 at 58, 1957] 1 WLR 1043 at 104:

It is, I think, made quite clear by the observations of Chitty J in *Re Townsend's Estate* that if at the time of the determination of the prior estate, whether it be by disclaimer or because the person to whom the will purported to give it witnessed the will, or for other reason, the gifts following on that estate are still contingent, there can be no acceleration because the gifts being still contingent, it cannot be seen whether they will take effect.[3]

2 Ademption

(a) In general

A specific gift, devise or bequest, is always at risk of ademption.[4] A gift is said to be adeemed if the gifted property has ceased to be part of the testator's estate by the date of his death so that there is nothing for it to operate on, for example because it has been destroyed, given away or sold.

Harrison v Jackson (1877) 7 Ch D 339, Ch D; Jessel MR

The testator's will included a legacy of '£1,000 D Stock in the London and North Western Railway Company now standing in the names of the trustees of my marriage settlement and bequeathed to me by my late wife (and which stock it is my intention to have transferred into my name).' The stock never was transferred into the testator's name but was paid off by the company and at the

---

1. As a matter of construction of the inter vivos deed before him, he held that the settlor had shown that he did not intend acceleration to apply.
2. WA 1837, s 15, p 359 post.
3. See also *Re Scott* [1975] 2 All ER 1033, [1975] 1 WLR 1260.
4. The only exception to this is a specific gift of a generic kind eg 'all my shares in ABC Ltd' instead of 'my 1000 shares in ABC Ltd' see p 57.

testator's request the proceeds were reinvested in the names of the marriage settlement trustees in other securities.

Held: The legacy was adeemed; the replacement securities would fall into the residuary estate.

Jessel MR: If I were allowed to guess what was the intention of the testator in this case and in other cases where specific bequests have been held to be adeemed, I should say that the doctrine of ademption very often defeats that intention.

But the law is that a specific legacy is adeemed when the subject-matter of it has been aliened by the testator in his lifetime. I cannot read the gift in this will as the gift of a particular fund coming from the testator's wife. All he gives is the '£1,000 D Stock of the *London and North Western Railway Company*,' which he describes as 'standing in the names of the trustees of my marriage settlement, and which have been bequeathed to me by my late wife;' one part of the description is not more essential than another, and it is to be observed that the reference to the wife's bequest comes after the names of the trustees. There is also on the face of the will a clear intention on the part of the testator not to allow the fund to remain in their names. This sum of D Stock was paid off in the lifetime of the testator, and the money arising therefrom was reinvested in other securities, which were transferred almost immediately before the testator's death into the names of the trustees of the settlement. The testator then has, as it were, sold the D Stock, and bought something else with the money. To my mind there is no difference whether that money was applied to buy shares or horses or anything else. He has applied his own money to buy something which is not the specific article bequeathed by him.[5]

In **Re Carrington** [1932] 1 Ch 1, the testator had included in his will a specific gift of 420 preference shares in a particular company to various legatees. Subsequently, by an agreement in writing, he gave X an option, to be exercised within one month of the testator's death, to purchase all his shares in that company. Within one month of the testator's death X gave notice of his intention to exercise the option. The Court of Appeal held that the specific gift of the shares was adeemed by the exercise of the option and the proceeds of the sale would pass to the residuary beneficiaries, Romer LJ saying at p 16:

As the cases stand,[6] where an option has been given by a testator over part of his real estate then, whether given before or after the date of the will, that real estate is to be treated for the purposes of devolution on death as devolving from the date of the exercise of the option as proceeds of sale and not as real estate. I do not myself understand apart from the authorities why this should be so. Conversion obviously takes effect from the exercise of the option only, and in the hands of the devisee of real estate the property as from the exercise of the option would be personal and not real estate. That is to say upon his death it would pass as part of his personal estate. But why the exercise of the option should have the effect of taking away the real estate from the person to whom it has been devised and giving it to the person who has the personal estate is what I have never been able to understand. But there it is, and applying that rule to the present case, from the moment of the exercise of the option the shares ceased to belong to the legatees and the proceeds of sale of the shares passed to the residuary legatees. It is impossible for us to escape from the effect of those decisions, and therefore the appeal must be dismissed.

(b) Effect of a nominal change

If the gift is divisible and only part of it is disposed of, only that part is adeemed; the remainder will still pass under the gift. The whole of the gift will be saved

---

5. See also *Manton v Tabois* (1885) 30 Ch D 92, *Stanley v Potter* (1789) 2 Cox 180.
6. *Lawes v Bennett* (1785) 1 Cox 167, *Weeding v Weeding* (1860) 1 J & H 424.

from ademption, however, if at the date of his death, the testator still has substantially what was given by the will, so long as the change in the property is only nominal.

Re Slater [1907] 1 Ch 665, CA; Cozens-Hardy MR, Gorell Barnes P, Kennedy LJ

The testator made a gift by will of 'the interest arising from money invested in (inter alia) the Lambeth Waterworks Company', a small waterworks company that was subsequently acquired by the giant Metropolitan Water Board under the provisions of the Metropolis Water Act 1902. The shareholders in the old company, including the testator, were compensated by way of stock in the Metropolitan Water Board.

Held: The Metropolitan Water Board Stock would not pass under the gift, which therefore failed.

Cozens-Hardy MR: Has not this gift, so far as the Lambeth Waterworks Company's stock is concerned, been adeemed by the subsequent transaction? Speaking for myself, although it may not be absolutely necessary for the decision of this case, I think it has been. There was a time when the Courts held that ademption was dependent on the testator's intention, on a presumed intention on his part; and it was therefore held in old days that when a change was effected by public authority, or without the will of the testator, ademption did not follow. But for many years that has ceased to be law, and I think it is now the law that where a change has occurred in the nature of the property, even though effected by virtue of an Act of Parliament, ademption will follow unless the case can be brought within what I may call the principle of *Oakes v Oakes* ((1852) 9 Hare 666), in which Turner V-C held that a bequest of shares in a railway company was not revoked by the subsequent change of those shares into stock by reason of a vote of the company under the powers of their special Act. At the end of his judgment the Vice-Chancellor says this (ibid p 672): 'The testator had this property at the time he made his will, and it has since been changed in name or form only. The question is, whether a testator has at the time of his death the same thing existing, it may be in a different shape,—yet substantially the same thing.' Remembering the extraordinary accuracy of the language used by Turner V-C, I think there is great force in those words which he used 'changed in name or form only, . . . yet substantially the same thing.' Applying that to the present case, in the first place the Lambeth Waterworks undertaking was sold, and sold for cash—sold, that is, for cash in this sense, that the price was ascertained in cash and could only be paid otherwise than in cash if both the vendors and the purchasers agreed to a scheme providing for satisfying the purchase money otherwise. That agreement was obtained in the present case. A scheme was prepared, and the Water Board B stock was allotted to the testator in respect of his shares in the old company. But can it possibly be said that that is the same thing? Instead of having shares in a company dependent for its profits upon water rates which they, and they alone, were able to demand from the limited area within the ambit of their Act of Parliament, the Water Board B stock is a stock which is payable out of water rates levied not merely upon the Lambeth Waterworks area, but upon the whole metropolitan area, and, I think, also on some districts even outside the metropolitan area. But, more than that, in the event of the water rates being insufficient to provide for the interest the present stock has a claim upon the rateable property in London, and any deficiency has to be made good out of the general rates. I cannot bring myself to say that that is the same thing.

In **Re Leeming** [1912] 1 Ch 828, by comparison, the company concerned went into voluntary liquidation in order to alter its share structure. A new company of the same name was formed and the business of the old company was sold to the new company in consideration of the issue of shares in the new company to the various shareholders including the testator. The result was that instead of owning 10 £4 shares in the old company when he died, the testator held 20 £5 ordinary and 20 £5 preference shares in the new company. The testator's gift was of 'my ten shares in the Kirkstall Brewery Company Ltd.' (the old company) but Neville J held that the new shares would pass to the legatee, saying at p 830:

I think that the shares in the new company are really in substance the same as the shares in the old company and represent the specific bequest. The subject matter of the bequest remains though changed in number and form. They are substantially the same shares. The testator gave 'my ten shares in the Kirkstall Brewery Company Limited' to a legatee. There has been a dissolution of that company and a new company has taken its place, but in substance it is the same company. It seems to me that the amount of the testator's interest in the old company remains and is represented by the shares in the new company and is practically the same, and is changed in name and form only. I think, therefore, that there has been no ademption, and that the legatee is entitled to the shares in the new company.

(c) Effect of a codicil

Once a gift has been adeemed, a confirming codicil will not save it unless the testator shows a clear intention in the codicil that the property in its changed form is still to pass to the specific beneficiary, or unless the words used in the testator's will as republished[7] at the date of the codicil are sufficiently apt to describe the property subsequently acquired.[8]

Re Galway's Will Trusts [1950] Ch 1, [1949] 2 All ER 419, Ch D; Harman J

The testator owned certain mines and minerals. He made a will in 1922 specifically giving them to X, but by the Coal Act 1938 they were compulsorily acquired by the Coal Commission, so that when he died in 1943, his only interest was in the compensation money which was still to be assessed. However he had made a confirming codicil in 1941 and it was argued that the effect of this was to enable the compensation money to pass to X.
Held: The gift was adeemed.

Harman J: It is . . . suggested on behalf of the testator's widow and daughters that by republishing his will by a codicil dated after the valuation the testator must be held to have intended that the compensation money should pass under the devise of mines and minerals and to have sufficiently expressed that intention. I cannot accept this contention. It is old law, at least as old as the days of Lord Hardwicke LC, that a republication cannot operate to make good a legacy once adeemed: see the judgment in *Drinkwater v Falconer* ((1755) 2 Ves Sen 636) and also the decision of Lord Cottenham LC in *Powys v Mansfield* ((1837) 3 Myl & Cr 359). The cases, indeed, show that even a contract to sell will work an ademption: see the decision of Sir Charles Hall V-C in *Watts v Watts* ((1873) LR 17 Eq 217). Much more so, therefore, will a contract which has been brought to completion as this one was in the testator's lifetime. It is said, however, that

---

7. See p 54 ante.
8. As in *Re Reeves* [1928] Ch 351 (gift of 'all my interest in my present lease of No 1 Chesterfield Street.' The lease the testator held at the date of the will subsequently expired and was renewed for a 12 year term. He thereafter made a codicil which enabled Russell J to save the 12 year lease for the beneficiary).

there is a modern line of authority which prevents me coming to this conclusion, and my attention was drawn to a number of cases connected with the subject of the conversion into personal property by the Law of Property Act, 1925, of an undivided share in real estate. The earlier cases, and in particular the decision of Clauson J in *Re Price* ([1928] Ch 579) seem to have accepted the conversion worked by the Act of 1925 at its full value, but it seems to me that this was seen to defeat the intention of testators and the more recent cases, in particular *Re Warren* ([1932] 1 Ch 42 and *Re Harvey* ([1947] 1 Ch 285), have emphasised the fact that the owner of an undivided share in real estate still has an interest in the real estate under the statutory trusts for sale, which are after all only a conveyancing device for avoiding the complication of partition actions, and it has, therefore, been held that a confirmatory codicil after 1926 may save from ademption by the legislation of 1925 an undivided share in real property. Those cases seem to me to have very little to do with the present. Here there was no conveyancing device leaving a man substantially in the same position as before, but a real statutory disappropriation of the proprietor in favour of the State, subject to the payment of statutory compensation. I ought, perhaps, to add that a question akin to this appears to have been decided by Evershed J in *Re Hatfield* ((1944) 198 LT Jo 55). In the upshot, I hold that, on the true construction of the testator's will and codicil, the compensation to which the testator was entitled at his death under the Coal Act passed under the gift of the testator's residuary personal estate.

3 Lapse

(a) In general

A will only comes into operation on the testator's death. If by that time the beneficiary has died, or being a company has been dissolved, the gift fails: it is said to lapse. In so far as it is uncertain whether or not the beneficiary did die before the testator there is a rebuttable presumption provided by the Law of Property Act 1925 to the effect that the younger person is deemed to have survived the elder.[9]

Law of Property Act 1925

184. Presumption of survivorship in regard to claims to property[10]
In all cases where, after the commencement of this Act, two or more persons have died in circumstances rendering it uncertain which of them survived the other or others, such deaths shall (subject to any order of the court), for all purposes affecting the title to property, be presumed to have occurred in order of seniority, and accordingly the younger shall be deemed to have survived the elder.[11]

In **Re Lindop** [1942] Ch 377, [1942] 2 All ER 46, it was suggested that the words 'subject to any order of the court' meant that the court had a discretion not to allow the presumption to apply if it concluded that that would produce

---

9. The presumption does not apply between spouses in so far as the older spouse died intestate, see p 126 ante.
10. Previously, at common law, if a claim to property depended on A surviving B, it had to be positively proved that A had survived B: *Wing v Angrave* (1860) 8 HLC 183.
11. Cf the United States Uniform Probate Code which provides at s 2-601 that a beneficiary who fails to survive the testator by 120 hours is treated as if he predeceased the testator, unless the will provides otherwise.

an unfair result. A husband and wife had been killed when a bomb hit their house in an air raid; he had left his residuary estate to her by will, she had left him a legacy of £200 in her will. Holding that s 184 would apply so that the older husband's residuary estate would pass into his wife's estate and thence by the provisions of her will to her relatives, Bennett J said at p 48:

The meaning I put upon the language of the section is this. Once it has been proved (as it has been in the present case) that two or more persons have died in circumstances rendering it uncertain which of them survived the other or others, a presumption of fact arises, the presumption being that the deaths occurred in the order of seniority. The section, however, gives rise to nothing more than a presumption, that is to say, the law will act upon the footing that death has occurred in the order of seniority unless and until evidence to the contrary is forthcoming. The presumption is one capable of being rebutted and, in my judgment, the words 'subject to any order of the court' find a place in the section to make it clear that the statutory presumption is a rebuttable presumption. The effect of the words is to enable the court, although the circumstances in which the persons have died are such as to make it uncertain which survived, to receive evidence upon the question, and if the evidence is such as to displace the statutory presumption, to act upon that evidence. I do not think these words give, as counsel for the next of kin suggested they did, a discretion to the court to disregard the statutory presumption, if the court came to the conclusion that it would be unfair or unjust to act upon it.

Hickman v Peacey [1945] AC 304, [1945] 2 All ER 215, HL; Viscount Simon LC, Lords Macmillan, Wright, Porter and Simonds

An entire household died when the house was bombed in an air raid in 1940. Two members had left wills leaving legacies to each other and to other members of the household so it was necessary to decide their order of deaths. It was argued that the Law of Property Act 1925, s 184 did not apply, because there was no uncertainty; they had all died at exactly the same time and no-one had survived any one else.

Held: (Viscount Simon and Lord Wright dissenting). The Law of Property Act 1925, s 184 would apply to determine the order of deaths whenever it could not be affirmatively proved that A survived B.

Lord Macmillan: Two views have been advanced as to (the section's) meaning and effect. According to one view, which is the view of Lord Greene MR and Goddard LJ[12] ... the statutory presumption is strictly limited in its application to cases in which:

'the court is satisfied as to two things—one that the proper inference from the circumstances is that the deaths took place consecutively, the other, that the circumstances leave the court in uncertainty as to which death took place first'.[13]

that is to say, all that the statute does is to fix artificially the order of sequence among consecutive deaths, where that order cannot in fact be ascertained. If the circumstances are such as to justify an inference that all the parties concerned died simultaneously then the circumstances are not such as to render it uncertain which of them survived the other or others, for it is certain that none survived the other or others. This, according to Goddard LJ, is the literal construction of the plain words of the enactment.

The other view is that when the circumstances are such that it cannot be ascertained that one of the deceased survived the other then the uncertainty which the section

---

12. As expressed in the Court of Appeal hearing of the case where it was held (Luxmoore LJ dissenting) that the deaths were simultaneous and that as there was therefore no uncertainty, s 184 would not operate ([1944] Ch 138, [1944] 1 All ER 81).
13. Ibid per Lord Greene MR, [1944] Ch at 146.

postulates exists and the statutory presumption applies. One reason why it cannot be ascertained that one survived the other may well be that the deaths occurred so closely in time that they were practically simultaneous. I say 'practically' for reasons which will appear later.

Having carefully weighed the arguments in support of each of these rival constructions I pronounce unhesitatingly in favour of the latter. It would be indeed unfortunate if the former were to prevail. For one thing it would mean that the legislature had signally failed to provide any remedy for an admitted defect in the law in a large and unhappily increasing number of cases in which evidence that the victims died consecutively is not available. Having set out, as I think may be reasonably assumed, to remedy the law as to *commorientes*, or persons dying together, the legislature is ironically found not to have made any provision for the case of *commorientes* who die together but to have dealt only with persons proved to have died consecutively. In the next place I would observe that where two persons perish in a common calamity and there is no evidence as to which died first it is necessarily left uncertain whether they died consecutively or simultaneously, although the circumstances may point with high probability to their not having both died at the same moment. The operation of the statutory presumption is, in the view of Lord Greene MR, made dependent on the ascertainment of a fact, namely, that the deaths were consecutive, which is itself necessarily conjectural in the absence of any positive evidence. The only case in which it can be demonstrated that the deaths were consecutive is where one of the persons concerned is proved to have been alive after the other is proved to have died: but in such a case there is no need for any presumption of survivorship. Nevertheless it is said that unless the court is satisfied that one of two victims of a common calamity survived the other the circumstances are not such as to render it uncertain which victim survived the other. I prefer to read the enactment as meaning that where the circumstances are such that it is not possible to say with certainty that one of the victims survived the other there is then uncertainty as to which survived the other. . . .

Without resorting to fantastic or far-fetched conjectures it is perfectly possible that the blast of the explosion did not annihilate the whole of these five victims at the same instant. Thus, one of them may quite well have been out of the shelter in another part of the house at the moment of the impact of the bomb and the blast though by an infinitesimal interval may have struck him sooner or later than the others. I simply do not know. Nobody can know. Where everything depends, as Lord Cranworth LC said on 'survivorship for a second'[14] I cannot accept the view that in the circumstances of this case there was no element of uncertainty, legal or other, on the cardinal issue.

Viscount Simon LC: I cannot agree with the submission of counsel for the appellants that the form of the section shows that Parliament recognised the proposition that proof of simultaneous deaths is impossible. This would be to attribute to the legislature conclusions as to a problem of considerable refinement in the realms of physics and philosophy which I hardly think the two Houses can be expected to have studied and inferentially pronounced upon. The circumstances that Parliament provides for what is to happen if one condition is fulfilled is no reason at all for saying that Parliament has impliedly expressed the view that another and different condition can never arise. A rule of racing which provided that, where the judge was uncertain which of two horses passed the winning post first, the younger horse should take the prize, would not prevent the sharing of the prize in a dead-heat. . . .

There thus remain three questions which must be answered in determining this appeal. If any one of them should be answered in the negative, the appeal must succeed. These three questions are (i) Can two or more persons die at the same time? (ii) Can it be proved in a court of law that two or more persons died at the same time? (iii) In the present case, is the proper conclusion on the evidence that the two testators and their beneficiaries in the shelter died at the same time? (Answering all three questions in the affirmative and dissenting from the majority, he said that in his judgment the appeal should be dismissed.)

---

14. *Wing v Angrave* (1860) 8 HL Cas 183 at 207.

(b) Exceptions

In a well-drawn will the testator will avoid the doctrine of lapse by including substitutional provisions.[15] A gift to a charity which ceases to exist before the testator's death will in any case be saved from lapse if the testator has shown a general charitable intention; it will be applied cy-près to another charity.[16] Other exceptions are illustrated below.

In **Re Leach** [1948] Ch 232, [1948] 1 All ER 383, a codicil contained a recital that when the testatrix's son died he was indebted to P in the sum of £1,000. The testatrix then went on to direct her executors to pay 'the said sum of £1,000' to P. P predeceased the testatrix but Vaisey J held that the legacy should be paid into his estate, saying at p 385:

The question which I have to consider is whether that legacy lapses or whether it comes within the principle of *Stevens v King*, ([1904] 2 Ch 30), where it was held that:

'Where on the true construction of a will the court finds that the testator's intention in giving a legacy was not merely bounty to the legatee, but to discharge a moral obligation recognised by the testator, whether legally enforceable or not, the legacy will not lapse by the legatee's death in the testator's lifetime.'

The facts of that case were much stronger than the facts of this case,[17] but, looking at this codicil and trying to consider whether I can or ought to find in it an expression of some moral duty resting on the testatrix in pursuance of which she made this gift, I think on the whole that that is the proper way of reading it. This is not an ordinary legacy of a sum of money. It is a direction to the executors to pay the actual sum which (P) had lent to the son of the testatrix and in respect of which the testatrix's son was indebted to (P) at the date of the codicil. I think that this case does come within the principle of *Stevens v King* and I will so decide.

Real Property Commissioners: Fourth Report[18]

The rule, that gifts lapse if the person to whom they are made dies in the lifetime of the Testator, sometimes operates with great hardship, and defeats in many cases the intention of the Testator. When an estate is devised to a person in tail with remainder to another, it is manifestly the intention of the Testator that the tenant in tail and his issue should take, and the person to whom the remainder is given should not take until all the issue of the intended tenant in tail have failed; and yet if such intended tenant in tail die in the Testator's lifetime, leaving issue, and the Testator is not aware of his death, or neglects to alter his will, the issue are wholly excluded in consequence of the gift to the parent having lapsed, and the remainderman obtains the Testator's estates. The hardship is very apparent in the usual case of a devise to the eldest, and every other son successively according to seniority in tail, if an elder son dies in the Testator's lifetime leaving issue, such issue are excluded, and the estate goes to the younger branch of the family. In another usual case, where a Testator gives his property among his children, and a daughter or other child dies before him leaving a family, such family are disappointed. In all these cases, if the issue or family were to become entitled to the property given to their parent, the person to whom the remainder or residue is given would still be entitled to the property intended for him by the Testator, and would have no reason to complain. It is true that the event of death might always be provided for, but it is found in practice that such provision is very rarely made. A Testator does not

---

15. See eg specimen will, p 62 ante. See also *Re Smith* [1916] 2 Ch 368.
16. See Pettit, pp 262–273; Picarda, 'The Law and Practice relating to Charities', (1977) Part III.
17. The obligation on the facts of that case was more in the way of a legal obligation as the testator was repaying overpaid trust moneys to his trustee.
18. 1833, p 73.

contemplate that the immediate objects of his bounty, and especially his children, will die before him; he does not like to encumber his Will with provisions which appear to be unnecessary, and he imagines that if the event should happen, he shall be able to alter his Will. . . . We propose that devises of estates tail to persons who die in the lifetime of the Testator, leaving issue, and devises and bequests to children and grandchildren of the Testator, who die in his lifetime, leaving issue at the time of his death, shall not lapse, but shall take effect as if the death of the Testator had happened before the deaths of such tenants in tail or children or grandchildren, that is, in the case of an estate tail the issue shall take, and in the case of a devise of real, or a bequest of personal property, the property devised or bequeathed shall pass to the real or personal representatives as part of the estate of the deceased Devisee or Legatee.[19]

Wills Act 1837

32. Devises of estates tail shall not lapse where inheritable issue survive
Where any person to whom any real estate[20] shall be devised for an estate tail . . . shall die in the lifetime of the testator leaving issue who would be heritable under such entail, and any such issue shall be living at the time of death of the testator, such devise shall not lapse, but shall take effect as if the death of such person had happened immediately after the death of the testator, unless a contrary intention shall appear by the will.

33. Gifts to children or other issue who leave issue at the testator's death shall not lapse[1]
(1) Where—
  (a) a will contains a devise or bequest to a child or remoter descendant of the testator; and
  (b) the intended beneficiary dies before the testator, leaving issue, and
  (c) issue of the intended beneficiary are living at the testator's death, then, unless a contrary intention appears by the will, the devise or bequest shall take effect as a devise or bequest to the issue living at the testator's death.[2]
(3) Issue shall take under this section through all degrees, according to their stock, in equal shares if more than one, any gift or share which their parent would have taken and so that no issue shall take whose parent is living at the testator's death and so capable of taking.
(4) For the purposes of this section—
  (a) the illegitimacy of any person is to be disregarded; and
  (b) a person conceived before the testator's death and born living thereafter is to be taken to have been living at the testator's death.

In **Re Meredith** [1924] 2 Ch 552, the operation of s 33 gave way to a contrary intention. The testator had left a share of furniture and a legacy of £100 to his son, and his residuary estate in equal shares to his five children by name, including this son. The son died in the testator's lifetime survived by children of his own. The testator made a codicil to his will in the following terms: 'Whereas since the date of my said will my son has died and the legacy and share of residue given to him by my said will have lapsed. Now with a view of making some provision for the two children of my said son I give to each of them a legacy of

---

19. See n 2 post.
20. By LPA 1925, s 130(1) the section was made applicable to personalty too.
1. As amended by AJA 1982, s 19 for testators dying after 1982.
2. S 33 as originally drawn embodied the Real Property Commissioners' recommendation (ante), in providing that the property saved from lapse should pass into the deceased beneficiary's estate as if that beneficiary had died immediately after the testator. This provision caused a number of difficulties, see eg *Re Pearson* [1920] 1 Ch 247, where the property so saved from lapse went straight to the deceased beneficiary's trustee in bankruptcy; see also *Re Hensler* (1881) 19 ChD 612, hence the introduction of this amended version which brings the statutory position into line with the usual form of express substitutional gift.

£100.' Holding that the son's legacy of £100 and his share of residue would lapse, the testator having shown a contrary intention within the meaning of the Wills Act 1837, Romer J said at p 556:

> Now approaching this codicil to see whether it shows such an intention, it appears to me that it does. For although the testator recites that the legacy and share had lapsed, no lapse at that moment had taken place because the testator was still living and he could still make such testamentary disposition as he thought fit to meet the case that had arisen. When therefore he recites that the legacy and share had lapsed what he means is: 'Whereas since the date of my will my son James Meredith has died, and having regard to the dispositions made by my will the legacy and share of residue given to him by my will will lapse, if I do not make some other disposition of them.' Now he could, had he so wished, have provided that notwithstanding the death of James Meredith in his lifetime the legacy and share of residue should be paid to James Meredith's executors as part of James Meredith's estate, or he could have given the legacy and share direct to the children of James Meredith, or he could have said that 'as James Meredith has died I will not make any provision as to his legacy and share of residue, but I will let them lapse.' It seems that by not disposing of the share and legacy and by bequeathing the £200 to his children he has in effect said: 'I do not desire that the said legacy and share shall be paid to my son's executors as part of his estate, but that subject to paying his children £100 each the legacy and share of residue shall lapse.' For these reasons I come to the conclusion that the codicil shows a contrary intention within the meaning of s 33.[3]

(c) Class gifts

The doctrine of lapse has never applied to a class gift[4] because, as a matter of construction, a person who is within the class description but predeceases the testator never qualifies as a member of the class. Where the class gift is in favour of the testator's issue, however, the Administration of Justice Act 1982 has written a new provision into the Wills Act 1837 so as to save the share of a potential member of the class for his issue where that potential member predeceases the testator.

In **Re Harvey** [1893] 1 Ch 567, Chitty J explained the pre-1983 position[5] in the following terms, saying at p 570:

> The difference between a gift to named individuals, and a gift to a class, in reference to lapse is firmly established. A gift by will to a class is taken, in Law and in Equity, to be a gift, where it is immediate, to those only who survive the testator; and, where it is not immediate but postponed, to be a gift to those only who survive the testator, or come into being before the period of distribution. Take gifts to children: when the gift is to a child named, and he dies in the testator's lifetime, it fails to take effect, apart from the 33rd section. The reason of its thus lapsing is found in the ambulatory nature of a will, which does not come into operation until the testator's death; a deceased person cannot take under a will, just as a deceased person cannot take under a deed, which has an immediate operation. But where the gift is to children as a class, to take as tenants in common, a child dying in the testator's lifetime, was excluded by the law as it stood before the passing of the Wills Act; and, according to the decisions already cited, the 33rd section does not apply, although the child leaves issue that survives the testator. The principle acted upon was, that the section leaves the construction of these class gifts

---

3. As there was no mention of the furniture in the codicil he went on to hold, at p 558, that s 33 would save this gift in the will.
4. A gift to persons falling within a general description, eg 'the children of A' as opposed to gifts to persons identified as individuals, eg 'X, Y and Z, the children of A'.
5. This will still represent the position post 1982 for class gifts other than those in favour of the testator's issue.

unaltered; and that these gifts are still to be read as gifts to those only who survive, and not as gifts to the possible members of the class who die in the testator's lifetime; and that the gift, in regard to those children who so die, is not to be treated as a gift to individuals.

In this case the testator had left a share of his residuary estate to his daughter's 'children'; she only had one child who predeceased the testator, leaving a child of her own who survived the testator, but Chitty J held that s 33 would not apply and the gift would lapse.[6]

Wills Act 1837

33. Gifts to children or other issue living at the testator's death shall not lapse[7]
(2) Where—
  (a) a will contains a devise or bequest to a class of persons consisting of children or remoter descendants of the testator; and
  (b) a member[8] of the class dies before the testator, leaving issue; and
  (c) issue of that member are living at the testator's death,
then, unless a contrary intention appears by the will, the devise or bequest shall take effect as if the class included the issue or its deceased member living at the testator's death.
((3) and (4), see p 357 ante.)

4   The witness beneficiary

(a) In general

By Wills Act 1837 s 15, if a beneficiary witnesses a will, that person is a competent witness, but the gift to the beneficiary is void.

Wills Act 1837

15. Gifts to an attesting witness to be void
If any person shall attest the execution of any will to whom or to whose wife or husband any beneficial devise, legacy, estate, interest, gift or appointment, of or affecting any real or personal estate (other than and except charges and directions for the payment of any debt or debts), shall be thereby given or made, such devise, legacy, estate, interest, gift, or appointment shall, so far only as concerns such person attesting the execution of such will, or the wife or husband of such person, or any person claiming under such person or wife or husband, be utterly null and void, and such person so attesting shall be admitted as a witness to prove the execution of such will, or to prove the validity or invalidity thereof, notwithstanding such devise, legacy, estate, interest, gift, or appointment mentioned in such will.

---

6. Aliter had the testator died after 1982 when WA 1837, s 33(2) post would have applied to save the gift for the grandchild who survived the testator.
7. The subsection was inserted by AJA 1982, s 19 for testators dying after 1982. It should be noted that the subsection only applies to a class gift to the testator's children or remoter descendants; it would not apply for example to a class gift to the testator's 'nephews and nieces'.
8. A 'potential' or 'presumptive' member would have been a more accurate description as under the normal rules of class gifts no one becomes a member of a class unless he is living at the testator's death or is born afterwards (in the case of a class gift postponed by a prior interest).

In **Re Pooley** (1889) 40 Ch D 1, the testatrix had appointed A, a solicitor, as one of her executors and trustees, and the will contained the usual charging clause:[9] 'I declare that any trustee of this my will who may be a solicitor shall be entitled to charge my estate for all business done by him in relation to my estate in the same manner as if he had been engaged to do such business by my executors as their solicitor.' A was one of the attesting witnesses to the will. As a result, the Court of Appeal held that he could not charge profit costs for any professional work he did for the estate, Cotton LJ saying at p 4:

We have only to consider whether this direction (the charging clause) is not in substance a gift to him of so much of the estate as is required to pay the profit costs, and therefore void. It is urged that it is not a gift, for that he has to work for what he receives. That is true, but the clause gives him a right which he would not otherwise have to charge for the work if he does it, and that, in my opinion, is a beneficial gift within the meaning of the section.

In **Re Bunting** [1974] 2 NZLR 219 (New Zealand), the will appointed a solicitor as a trustee and was witnessed by a partner of that solicitor, but White J held that the solicitor-trustee could still enjoy the benefit of the charging clause it contained, saying at p 219:

A solicitor who is a witness to a will appointing a partner of the solicitor witness a trustee is not a person claiming an interest within the terms of s 15 of the Wills Act. In my view, s 15 is specific and personal in its prohibitions and I do not consider that it extends to a partner of a solicitor-trustee appointed by the will.[10]

(b) Exceptions to the rule

There are a number of possible escape routes for a beneficiary who appears to be caught by s 15.

Re Royce's Will Trusts [1959] Ch 626, [1959] 3 All ER 278, CA; Lord Evershed MR, Hodson and Romer LJJ

The testator's will had been witnessed by a solicitor. It contained a charging clause empowering a professional trustee to charge for his services, but the solicitor was not named as an executor or trustee, nor were any of his partners. After the testator's death, one of the trustees named in the will died and the surviving trustee appointed the solicitor to be a trustee in his place. It was argued that as he had witnessed the will, the charging clause was void so far as his services were concerned.

Held: As he had no beneficial interest under the will at the date of its execution, s 15 would not apply.

Lord Evershed MR: It is, I think, clear that the effect of s 5 of the Statute of Frauds was this, that, unless the devise or bequest was attested by three 'credible' (ie not

---

9. A person in a fiduciary position such as an executor or trustee, may not profit from the relationship without authority: *Bray v Ford* [1896] AC 44. A solicitor or other professional person who is to be appointed as an executor or trustee will therefore wish to see a charging clause in the will or trust instrument authorising him to charge for any professional services carried out by him or his firm.
10. See also the Australian case of *Re Oberg* [1952] QLR 45 where the will was witnessed by a clerk in the solicitor's firm but the charging clause was upheld. Cf the Scottish case *Gorrie's Trustee v Stiven's Executrix* [1952] SC 1.

disqualified) witnesses, the whole instrument, or at the very least the whole devise or bequest, was entirely void; and a witness was held to be incompetent if he, under the will, took any interest whatever in the subject matter of the devise or bequest. The result was that if a non-competent person did attest a will, and there were not three other competent ones who did, the whole instrument, or (as I have said) at least a very material part of it, was avoided altogether.

The Wills Act, 1752, was clearly intended somewhat to mitigate that effect. The Wills Act, 1752, was (so far as is relevant for present purposes) exactly in the terms of s 15 of the Act of 1837, save that in the latter there is a reference to the wife or husband of an attesting witness. . . . But it was admitted by counsel for the second defendant (and, if I may say so, rightly so) that the object of these enactments was to protect a testator who was in extremis, or otherwise weak and not capable of exercising judgment, from being imposed on by someone who came and presented him with a will for execution under which the person in question was himself substantially interested; and if that is indeed the real object (as I think it is) of these enactments, then, to my mind, the object is not achieved if this section is construed so as to disqualify someone who, at the time he attested the execution of a will had no interest whatever under the will as it stood and only became interested under it by some later event or act—what I have called a *novus actus interveniens*: eg, if he should be the object of some appointment made by some person named in the will having a power to appoint; or (as in the present case) if he happened to be a person who was later appointed a trustee of the will by the then existing trustees.[11]

In **Re Ray's Will Trusts** [1936] Ch 520, [1936] 2 All ER 93, the testatrix was a nun in a convent. By her will she gave all her property to the person who at the time of her death should be abbess of the convent. The will was witnessed by two nuns at the convent, one of whom was subsequently elected abbess, and held that office when the testatrix died. Holding in favour of the gift, Clauson J said at p 99:

The will is attested by the lady who happens to be the lady who will be the hand to receive this gift. If she receives it as a trustee only, and I think she does receive it as a trustee only, the fact that she was an attesting witness to the will, can, on well settled authority be no objection to the validity of the gift. But the two ladies who were the attesting witnesses were at the time of the execution of the will and both are now, members of the convent, and the argument is that, in so far as they form part of the community, the gift, according to my construction of it, will enure in some sense to their benefit. But does that circumstance afford any objection to the validity of the gift? If it does, it must be because the circumstances come within the terms of the Wills Act 1837, s 15. (Having recited the terms of s 15 he continued:) I do not see my way to hold that the attesting witness here obtained under the will, as I construe it, any such beneficial legacy or interest as to bring her within the terms of that section. The truth is that the gift is a gift to swell the community funds, to be administered for the benefit of the community. I do not think it is a fair construction of the section to treat the fact that an attesting witness may, as a member of a community, get some benefit in some shape or form out of the administration of the fund, as amounting to a legacy or gift by the will to such individual member of the community. Accordingly, in my view, the point taken under s 15 of the Wills Act is a false one.

Re Trotter [1899] 1 Ch 764, Ch D; Byrne J

A beneficiary witnessed the will under which he benefited. The testator subsequently made a first codicil to it which that beneficiary did not witness; it approved and confirmed the will save in so far as it specifically altered it. It was followed by a second codicil which the same beneficiary witnessed; the codicil

---

11. See also *Thorpe v Bestwick* (1881) 6 QB 311 where the witness married the beneficiary after the will was executed; the beneficiary was allowed to retain her beneficial interest.

approved and confirmed the will and first codicil save in so far as it specifically altered them.

Held: The beneficiary could claim his benefit through the first codicil, the instrument he did not witness.

Byrne J: I think that these points in respect of wills made since the Wills Act have been thus established. (1) That a will invalid in itself may operate as a valid instrument when referred to and incorporated in or with a subsequent and validly-executed codicil. (2) That a valid gift by will to a legatee is not rendered invalid by reason of his subsequently attesting a codicil, although the codicil has the effect of republishing and incorporating the will.[12] (3) That, although a gift by a valid will to an attesting witness is utterly null and void, such gift may be rendered effectual if the will is republished by a codicil referring to the will but not attested by the legatee.[13] (4) That the legatee must be able to point to an instrument giving him his legacy not attested by himself before he can establish his right to his legacy. Bearing in mind these principles, the question appears to be whether or not John Trotter can point to an instrument not attested by himself and giving him the benefit he claims. It cannot be to the will alone, for though a valid instrument it is utterly null and void so far as the disposition in his favour is concerned. But, just as had the original will been altogether void he would have been able to point to a codicil republishing and incorporating the whole of it, and as validating the whole of the dispositions intended to be made by the will, so in like manner I think he can point to the first codicil republishing and incorporating an instrument valid as to some of its dispositions, but invalid as to the dispositions in his favour, as being the instrument under which he claims. I think that the true view is that, where the original gift is by the operation of s 15 of the Wills Act utterly null and void, the will is pro tanto null and void, as it would have been, if unattested, null and void altogether; and that, just as in the latter case the whole will would, if referred to in a duly-executed and duly-attested codicil, operate in its entirety as from the date of the codicil, so where void in part as to its dispositions by reason of improper attestation, it will, so far as void, operate for the first time by the incorporation and republication effected by the due execution of the codicil. I think that John Trotter is entitled here to point to the first codicil as the instrument conferring upon him the benefit in question, inasmuch as that codicil incorporates the whole will, including the originally void disposition, and that this being so, upon the authority of *Gurney v Gurney* ((1855) 3 Drew 208) and *Re Marcus* ((1887) 57 LT 399),[14] he has not lost this benefit by reason of his having subsequently attested the second codicil.

In **Re Bravda** [1968] 2 All ER 217, [1968] 1 WLR 479, the failure of the gift to the beneficiary-witness led directly to remedial legislation. The testator's will had been witnessed by two non-beneficiaries. Then the testator asked his two daughters, the sole beneficiaries under the will, to sign as well 'to make it stronger'. They signed in the place left above the signature of the two independent witnesses and below the words 'witnessed 14.12.65'. It was argued that they did not intend to sign as attesting witnesses, but merely to please their father who thought that in some way the addition of their signatures would improve the will, but the Court of Appeal held that their beneficial interests failed, Salmon LJ saying at p 224:

The law is quite plain. The presumption is that any signature appearing on a will after that of the testator is presumed to be the signature of a witness to the will. The strength of this presumption depends to some extent on where the signature on the will is found. Sometimes there are just two signatures on the back of a will and nothing on the document which expressly states the capacity in which the signatories are signing. There

---

12. As in *Gurney v Gurney* (1855) 3 Drew 208.
13. As in *Anderson v Anderson* (1872) LR 13 Eq 381.
14. One beneficiary in this case had witnessed both the will and the two codicils; another beneficiary had not witnessed the will by which the benefit was given, but had witnessed the codicils. North J held that the latter beneficiary could benefit, but not the former.

is still a presumption that they sign as witnesses. In this case, however, as my lords have pointed out, the signatures of the plaintiffs appear immediately under the words 'witnessed 14.12.65'. It really is not a question here even of presumption. The document which they signed states on its face that they signed as witnesses.

In spite of that, I can imagine evidence which might justify us in holding that when they signed they had no intention of signing as witnesses, that they were signing merely to verify the contents of the will or for some other purposes which had nothing to do with attestation. There have been many cases in which beneficiaries who have signed a will have, on the evidence before the court, been able to persuade the court that they were not signing as witnesses; but in all those cases there has been the most clear and unequivocal express evidence that the beneficiaries signed in some other capacity (see, for example, *In b Sharman* ((1869) LR 1 P & D 661) and *In b Smith* ((1889) 15 PD 2).[15]

Wills Act 1968

1. Restriction of operation of Wills Act 1837 s 15

(1) For the purposes of section 15 of the Wills Act 1837 (avoidance of gifts to attesting witnesses and their spouses) the attestation of a will by a person to whom or to whose spouse there is given or made any such disposition as is described in that section shall be disregarded if the will is duly executed without his attestation and without that of any other such person.

(2) This section applies to the will of any person dying after the passing of this Act, whether executed before or after the passing of this Act.[16]

(c) Reform

The application of s 15 usually flies in the face of the testator's intention and the section has been much criticised as a result. Statutory reform has been frequently considered over the years[17] but none has transpired.[18]

Justice Committee: Report on Home-Made Wills[19]

13. We are all agreed that the rule that automatically invalidates gifts to a witness is unreasonable and requires alteration, but we think that it does give a limited degree of

---

15. All three members of the court expressed their dissatisfaction with the outcome of the case, Russell LJ, at p 224, urging amending legislation to enable a beneficiary who had signed as a witness to retain his benefit where there were still two independent (ie non-beneficiary) witnesses to the will.

16. It was thus too late to help the Bravda beneficiaries. It should also be noted that the Act is only of assistance where, without the beneficiary witness, there are two independent witnesses. If there was only one such witness and two beneficiary witnesses, the cases decided before the Act would still be relevant in attempting to show that one of the beneficiary witnesses did not sign as a witness. Care would have to be taken to see that this argument did not succeed in relation to both beneficiary witnesses otherwise the will would be invalid for want of compliance with the witnessing requirements of WA 1837, s 9 anyway.

17. For a general review of the history of the section and the various suggestions for reform, see Yale: 'Witnessing Wills and Losing Legacies', (1984) 100 LQR 453.

18. The disappointed beneficiary may have a remedy in negligence against the testator's solicitors, however, see *Ross v Caunters* [1980] Ch 297, [1979] 3 All ER 580.

19. Published 1971. The recommendation was not adopted. See, however, the Australian Administration and Probate Act 1958 (Victoria) which provides at s 101(1) that where the court is satisfied that the entitlement of the applicant under the will was known to and approved by the testator, and was not included in the will as the result of any undue influence it may allow the gift to stand notwithstanding the Wills Act 1958, s 13(3)(c) (the Victoria equivalent of WA 1837, s 15); see eg *Re Emanuel* [1981] VR 113.

protection against undue influence and probably should not be abolished altogether. We think that the best solution would be to impose a rebuttable presumption of undue influence in the case of gifts to witnesses (with certain exceptions, such as, for example, gifts of not more than £100 or not exceeding a specified percentage of the net estate).

Law Reform Committee: Twenty-Second Report[20]

The rule prohibiting witnesses from taking any benefit under the will
2.15   In our consultative document we asked for views on the value of this rule, which has come under a certain amount of criticism. Its clear purpose is to discourage misconduct on the part of witnesses who, if they were in a position to benefit under the will, might exert undue pressure on the testator. On the other hand it is argued that it is those who help the testator to prepare his will who are really in a position to influence its content and yet there is no rule which prevents them from benefiting under it. We see the force of this argument and in particular think it unfortunate that a beneficiary should be deprived of the testator's bounty through nothing but good intentions on all sides. Nonetheless we think it right in principle that a witness should be independent, objective and have no 'axe to grind'. Further the rule is an obvious safeguard against abuse and on balance we think that it should be retained.

2.16   We also considered two possible modifications of the rule. First, it was suggested to us that the rule could safely be abolished in its application to the spouses of attesting witnesses, on the basis that it is anomalous to single out the spouse when abuse can come from others such as partners or close friends. Secondly, we considered whether a partial exception could be made for small gifts. However our general view about these suggestions is that the first would open greatly the possibilities for abuse and the second would be of limited value. There would be formidable practical difficulties in defining a small gift and any figure would quickly become out of date. In any event we believe that small legacies are likely to be honoured by the other beneficiaries where possible.[1]

5   Contrary to public policy

As Cozens-Hardy MR said in *Re Hall* [1914] P 1, at p 5: 'You do not look for public policy in the sense in which that expression is used, in an Act of Parliament. It is something which is really part of the common law of the land and does not depend on statute.' Gifts by will which offend public policy are at risk of being declared void.[2] One particular rule of public policy that has been developed by the courts is that no one guilty of unlawfully killing another

---

20. 'The Making and Revocation of Wills' (1980) Cmnd 7902.
1. No recommendation for change was therefore made by the Committee and none accordingly followed in the Administration of Justice Act 1982 which embodied most of the Committee's recommendations. Cf the United States Uniform Probate Code which provides, at section 2-505, that no will or provision thereof shall be invalid because the will is signed by an interested witness. The official commentary points out that a substantial gift to a witness would still be regarded as suspicious and could be attacked on other grounds, such as fraud or undue influence; the provision is intended to protect in particular the innocent use of a member of the testator's family in a home-made will.
2. Eg *Thrupp v Collett* (1858) 26 Beav 125 where the testator had left £5,000 to his executors for obtaining the discharge of convicted poachers imprisoned for non-payment of fines. Romilly MR declared the gift contrary to public policy and void; it was calculated to encourage offences prohibited by the Legislature. See also *Re Millar* [1938] 1 DLR 65 (the 'Baby Derby' case).

should be allowed to take any benefits from that person's estate[3] whether by will or under the intestacy rules.[4] Forfeiture of benefit was automatic in such circumstances, applying equally to those guilty of manslaughter[5] as to those guilty of murder. This inflexibility became a source of judicial and academic disquiet[6] with the result that the Forfeiture Act was passed in 1982, giving the court a very wide discretion to modify the rule, save in relation to convicted murderers.

In **Re Giles** [1972] Ch 544, [1971] 3 All ER 1141, the testator made a will leaving his estate to his second wife, who subsequently killed him by a single blow from a 'domestic chamber pot'; she was found guilty of manslaughter through diminished responsibility. Pennycuick V-C was urged not to apply the public policy rule where there was no moral culpability involved, but he refused to relax the rule, saying at p 1146:

> Counsel for the widow pointed out, and I am entirely in agreement with him on this, that the principles of public policy on which the courts act change over the generations and the centuries, but I am not persuaded that there is any sufficient ground for qualifying the established rule in the manner that counsel seeks to qualify it, and further I am quite satisfied that if the rule is to be qualified in any way that is something that can only be done by a higher tribunal. I hope that I will not be thought to be unsympathetic to the widow. Obviously, this is a tragic case, as are many of the cases in which a person kills a near relation, sometimes out of love for that person. On the other hand, it is very easy to imagine cases of diminished responsibility of an entirely different kind where relaxation of the established rule could be harmful and dangerous.

He held that the widow was disqualified from taking any benefit either under the deceased's will or intestacy; the entire estate would pass under the intestacy rules to the deceased's only child, a son of his first marriage.

Forfeiture Act 1982

1. The 'forfeiture rule'
(1) In this Act, the 'forfeiture rule' means the rule of public policy which in certain circumstances precludes a person who has unlawfully killed another from acquiring a benefit in consequence of the killing.
(2) References in this Act to a person who has unlawfully killed another include a reference to a person who has unlawfully aided, abetted, counselled or procured the death of that other and references in this Act to unlawful killing shall be interpreted accordingly.

2. Power to modify the rule
(1) Where a court determines that the forfeiture rule has precluded a person (in this section referred to as 'the offendor') who has unlawfully killed another from acquiring

---

3. 'A man shall not slay his benefactor and thereby take his bounty' per Hamilton LJ In *Re Hall* [1914] P 1 at p 7. See also *Cleaver v Mutual Reserve Association* [1892] 1 QB 147, *Re Crippen* [1911] P 108.
4. Where the victim dies intestate, the slayer is simply passed over in the application of the order of entitlement to an intestate's estate, as in *Re Callaway* [1956] Ch 559, [1956] 2 All ER 451.
5. So long as the person seeking to benefit deliberately and intentionally inflicted the unlawful violence on his victim, even if he did not thereby intend the victim's death: *R v National Insurance Commissioner ex p Connor* [1981] 1 All ER 769.
6. See Tarnow 'Unworthy Heirs: The Application of the Public Policy Rule in the Administration of Estates' (1980) 58 Can Bar Rev 582; Youdan 'Acquisition of Property by Killing' (1973) 89 LQR 235.

any interest in property mentioned in subsection (4) below, the court may make an order under this section modifying the effect of that rule.

(2) The court shall not make an order under this section modifying the effect of the forfeiture rule in any case unless it is satisfied that, having regard to the conduct of the offender and of the deceased and to such other circumstances as appear to the court to be material, the justice of the case requires the effect of the rule to be so modified in that case.

(3) In any case where a person stands convicted of an offence of which unlawful killing is an element, the court shall not make an order under this section modifying the effect of the forfeiture rule in that case unless proceedings for the purpose are brought before the expiry of the period of three months beginning with his conviction.[7]

(4) The interests in property referred to in subsection (1) above are—

    (a) any beneficial interest in property which (apart from the forfeiture rule) the offender would have acquired—

        (i) under the deceased's will (including as respects Scotland, any writing having testamentary effect) or the law relating to intestacy or by way of ius relicti, ius relictae or legitim;[8]

        (ii) on the nomination of the deceased in accordance with the provisions of any enactment;

        (iii) as a donatio mortis causa made by the deceased; or

        (iv) under a special destination[9] (whether relating to heritable or moveable property); or

    (b) any beneficial interest in property which (apart from the forfeiture rule) the offender would have acquired in consequence of the death of the deceased, being property which, before the death, was held on trust for any person.[10]

(5) An order under this section may modify the effect of the forfeiture rule in respect of any interest in property to which the determination referred to in subsection (1) above relates and may do so in either or both of the following ways, that is—

    (a) where there is more than one such interest, by excluding the application of the rule in respect of any (but not all) of those interests; and

    (b) in the case of any such interest in property, by excluding the application of the rule in respect of part of the property.

(6) On the making of an order under this section, the forfeiture rule shall have effect for all purposes (including purposes relating to anything done before the order is made) subject to the modifications made by the order.

(7) The court shall not make an order under this section modifying the effect of the forfeiture rule in respect of any interest in property which, in consequence of the rule, has been acquired before the coming into force of this section[11] by a person other than the offender or person claiming through him.

(8) In this section—

'property' includes any chose in action or incorporeal moveable property and 'will' includes codicil.

3. Application for financial provision not affected by the rule

(1) The forfeiture rule shall not be taken to preclude any person from making any application under a provision mentioned in subsection (2) below or the making of any order on the application.

(2) The provisions referred to in subsection (1) above are—

---

7. The Act was thus too late to assist the offender in *Re Giles*, p 365 ante.
8. 'Ius relicti' and 'ius relictae' are the respective rights of inheritance of surviving husbands and surviving wives in Scotland; 'legitim' is the right of inheritance of children in Scotland.
9. A form of inheritance operating outside a will in Scotland.
10. Eg the property that would have accrued to a joint tenant by the right of survivorship, see eg *Re K*, post.
11. 13th October 1982. As to the application of this subsection, see *Re K* post.

(a) any provision of the Inheritance (Provision for Family and Dependants) Act 1975[12]. . . .

5. Exclusion of murderers

Nothing in this Act or in any order made under section 2 or referred to in section 3(1) of this Act shall affect the application of the forfeiture rule in the case of a person who stands convicted of murder.[13]

Re K [1985] Ch 85, [1985] 1 All ER 403, Ch D; Vinelott J[14]

After enduring a number of violent assaults by her husband over the years, on 30th September 1982[15] the deceased's wife picked up his loaded shotgun to defend herself; she released the safety catch and the gun went off, killing him. Her plea of manslaughter was accepted and she was put on two years' probation. The deceased had left her substantial benefits by will in his £400,000 estate; they were also beneficial joint tenants of the matrimonial home, worth £80,000.

Held: Having regard to all the circumstances, the forfeiture rule would be modified to permit her to take all the benefits which the deceased had conferred on her by will and which accrued to her by survivorship.

Vinelott J: (Having first decided that on the facts of the case the forfeiture rule would apply, continued:)

It (the Forfeiture Act 1982) is very wide in its scope. I think the word 'acquired' in s 2(7) is used in a quite intelligible sense to denote property which has actually been transferred to a person entitled thereto by virtue of the operation of the rule or who has thereby acquired an indefeasible right to have it transferred to him or to her. Whether it extends to a present or future interest in property settled by a will which on completion of administration has vested either in the executors or others as trustees is a question which does not arise and on which I express no opinion. In my judgment it clearly does not extend to property which, when the section came into force, was held by personal representatives who had not completed the administration of the estate.

Before turning to the substantial question whether the court should make an order relieving the widow in whole or in part from the operation of the rule, there are two other matters which I should mention.

(He read out s 2(5) (p 366 ante) and continued:)

Literally construed para (a) gives the court power to modify the effect of the forfeiture rule where more than one interest in property is affected by it in respect of some but not all of those interests, and under para (b) in relation to any given interest in property the court can modify the rule in respect of part of it. So it is said that the court cannot relieve the applicant from the consequences of the rule altogether. . . . I cannot believe that the framers of the 1982 Act intended a result as bizarre as that. The answer to this submission

---

12. See ante Ch 17. In *Re Royse* [1984] 3 All ER 339, [1984] 3 WLR 784, the Court of Appeal nevertheless held that a person for whom reasonable provision was made by the deceased's will but who forfeited that provision by virtue of the forfeiture rule, could not make a claim under the 1975 Act because that person could not satisfy the precondition in the 1975 Act, s 2(1), the absence of reasonable financial provision being attributed not to the deceased's will or intestacy but to the application of the forfeiture rule. Such a person could therefore only claim, if at all, under Forfeiture Act 1982, s 2 but the offender in question was well outside the time limit in s 2(3) of that Act.
13. In the absence of a murder conviction, the Act would thus still apply, eg in circumstances such as those in *Re Callaway*, n 4 ante, where the murderer committed suicide before criminal proceedings could be taken.
14. Affirmed on appeal, see n 17 post.
15. The Forfeiture Act came into force on 13th October 1982 but has retrospective effect subject to the restrictions imposed by s 2(3) and (7) ante.

in my judgment is that sub-s (5) is intended to enlarge the power conferred by sub-s (1) by making it clear that the court is not bound either to relieve against the operation of the forfeiture rule altogether or not to relieve against the operation of the rule at all. The draftsman assumed that sub-s (1) alone conferred power to relieve an applicant from the operation of the rule in respect of the entirety of all interests affected by the rule. Subsection (5) then in effect enlarges the court's powers.

As I have mentioned, the matrimonial home (which is registered land) was vested in the deceased and the widow as joint tenants at law and in equity. Counsel for the widow accepts that the forfeiture rule, unless modified under the 1982 Act, applies in effect to sever the joint tenancy in the proceeds of sale and in the rents and profits until sale. I think that concession is rightly made. . . .

I turn therefore to the substantial question. Section 2(2) requires that before making any order under that section modifying the effect of the forfeiture rule the court must be satisfied that, having regard to the conduct of the offender and of the deceased and to such other circumstances as appear to the court to be material, the justice of the case requires the effect of the rule to be so modified in that case. (He examined the parties' respective financial position and continued:)

In a case where reasonable provision is made by the will, the first question is whether, having regard to the conduct of the deceased and of the claimant in particular in relation to the unlawful killing, justice required that the claimant should be relieved against forfeiture in respect of all or any interest accruing on the death. The 1982 Act was clearly passed with the decision of Pennycuick V-C and earlier decisions in mind. In *Re Giles* ([1971] 3 All ER 1141, [1972] Ch 544)[16] Pennycuick V-C declined to enter into any investigation of the degree of moral culpability attending the killing. The purpose of the 1982 Act as I see it is to entitle and indeed require the court to form a view on that very matter.

I have reached the conclusion after anxious consideration that in the very unusual circumstances of this case it would be unjust that the widow should be deprived of any of the benefits which the deceased chose to confer on her by his will or which accrued to her by survivorship. As Lord Salmon observed in *DPP v Newbury, DPP v Jones* ([1976] 2 All ER 365 at 367, [1977] AC 500 at 507), it being unnecessary in cases of manslaughter to prove that the accused knew that the act causing death was unlawful or dangerous, cases of manslaughter necessarily vary infinitely in their gravity. Despite the revulsion which any person must feel at conduct which leads to the death of another human being it is impossible in the tragic circumstances of this case not to feel sympathy for the widow. If cases vary infinitely in their gravity, this is, I think, one of the cases which weighs least heavily. The widow, as I have said, was a loyal wife who suffered grave violence at the hands of the deceased. When she took hold of the gun and released the safety catch she was in a state of great distress and feared further violence. She must accept the blame for what happened but she should not, in my judgment, suffer the further punishment of being deprived of the provision which her husband made for her which was, it seems to me, wholly appropriate having regard to the fact that the widow gave up a worthwhile and satisfying career when she married him, to her conduct towards him to the very end of his life and to the fact that there were no other persons for whom he was under any moral duty to provide.[17]

---

16. See p 365 ante.
17. On all points this decision was affirmed by the Court of Appeal: *Re K* [1985] ... .ll ER 833, [1985] 3 WLR 234. The court also rejected a submission that a judge who exercised the discretion under the Forfeiture Act 1982 should not permit a spouse-offender to inherit more than she would have obtained on a divorce from the deceased or under the Inheritance (Provision for Family and Dependants) Act 1975. 'The short answer to that submission', said Ackner LJ at p 842 'is that, if that was what Parliament intended to be the limit of the discretion, it would have been very easy to say so.'

6 Disclaimer

No one is obliged to accept a gift by will or under the intestacy rules.[18] A beneficiary may disclaim the gift at any time before acceptance and the disclaimer may be by word, deed or by conduct.[19]

Re Hodge [1940] Ch 260, Ch D; Farwell J

The testatrix appointed her husband as her executor and residuary beneficiary and also left him certain freehold properties 'in consideration of him paying my sister (C) the sum of £2 per week during her life and I further direct that in the event of my said husband disposing of the whole of the property the annuity of £2 a week shall cease and in lieu thereof he shall invest the sum of £2,000' for the benefit of C for life and then for her children. If the husband had disclaimed the gift, the properties would have fallen into residue and would have passed to him as residuary beneficiary. He never did so, however, but proved the will and for five years paid C the £2 a week, making up any deficiency out of his own pocket when the rental income was insufficient. When the properties were then sold, he sought to disclaim to avoid the provision of the £2,000 for C and her children.

Held: He had accepted the gift by his conduct, it was too late for him to disclaim.

Farwell J: The question, therefore, in my view on this part of the case is whether the evidence is such that the Court must come to the conclusion that the plaintiff has accepted the gift, taken the devise as beneficial owner, and therefore taken the burden upon himself, or whether it is still open to him to disclaim. It is to be noted that the testatrix died so long ago as 1934. No doubt in 1939 when selling a portion of the property to the London County Council, the plaintiff sold as legal personal representative, but apart from that there is nothing to show that he ever took any steps to disclaim this devise during the years since the lady's death. He collected the rents, he paid the outgoings, and he has made payments to this lady out of his own pocket. He says that he did that because he thought he was a trustee for her of this property, not because he thought he was under any personal obligation and that there is nothing which he has done which now precludes him from saying: 'I am not and I never have been beneficial owner of the property and I now disclaim that position altogether, and so escape from this obligation.' In my judgment I am bound to come to the conclusion that, taking the evidence as a whole, the plaintiff has made it now impossible for him to disclaim. There is sufficient evidence, in my judgment, to show quite plainly that he did accept this devise and has in fact treated himself as the owner in equity of the property, as distinguished from ownership as legal personal representative. I have come to the conclusion though with considerable regret, that the plaintiff is under an obligation from which he cannot escape to provide this £2,000 for the benefit of Mrs Griffiths (C) and her children. I say I have come to that conclusion with regret, because if the plaintiff had fully appreciated his legal position he could have disclaimed the property and avoided the burden which I

---

18. As to intestacy, see *Re Scott* [1975] 2 All ER 1033, [1975] 1 WLR 1260, but see also Goodhart: 'Disclaimer of Interests on Intestacy' (1976) 40 Conv 292 where he argues that unlike a gift by will, an interest in intestacy vests automatically on death and cannot be disclaimed.

19. Cf the much more tightly drawn provisions of the United States Uniform Probate Code which require a written instrument describing the property or interest disclaimed, signed by the disclaimant and filed in the probate registry no later than 9 months after the deceased's death: s 2-801.

now hold rests upon him, but unfortunately for him he did not appreciate the position or take the necessary steps which would have enabled him to disclaim the property and thereby put an end to any question as to the liability under this will.

In **Guthrie v Walrond** (1883) 22 Ch D 573, the testator had left to his son 'all my estate and effects in the island of Mauritius absolutely.' His property in Mauritius included an onerous lease; the son wished to disclaim the lease and accept the rest of the gift. Holding that he must either take the whole of the estate and effects in Mauritius or disclaim the gift altogether, Fry J said at p 577:

It appears to me plain that when two distinct legacies or gifts are made by a will to one person he is, as a general rule, entitled to take one and disclaim the other, but that his right to do so may be rebutted if there is anything in the will to show that it was the testator's intention that that option should not exist. For there are cases in which the Court has held that a legatee has no right to take one gift and leave another, because it has discovered an intention on the part of the testator to couple the two gifts together. But in the present case the question arises upon a single and undivided gift, and it appears to me that such a gift is prima facie evidence that it was the testator's intention that the gift shall be one, and that the legatee shall either take it all or take none of it. It may be that even in such a case the Court would sometimes be able to discover some subtle indication of an intention that the legatee should be at liberty to take part of the gift and leave the rest, but I think that prima facie the fact that there is only one gift is an indication of an intention that the legatee shall take either the whole or none at all.

In **Re Cranstoun** [1949] Ch 523, [1949] 1 All ER 871, the testatrix left her residuary estate to the Home of Rest for Horses on such terms as led the Committee of the Home to assume that the gift was subject to onerous liabilities and was of little value. They signed a written renunciation of all claims to the estate but when it was finally wound up almost 20 years after the testatrix's death, there was some £4,000 left for distribution. Romer J permitted the Home to retract its disclaimer, saying at p 873:

From the scanty material available on this principle of renunciation, it seems that it was introduced for the benefit of beneficiaries, so that a beneficiary should not be obliged to take what might be an onerous burden, but a natural corollary of the principle is that, if anyone acted on the faith of his renunciation and altered his position to his detriment in consequence thereof, the beneficiary would not be allowed to retract his renunciation. Where, as here, no one has altered his position, I cannot see why the claim to retract should not prevail.[20]

QUESTIONS

1. Anthea and her two children, Bill and Coral, all die in a plane crash; it is known that Bill died first but the order of death of Anthea and Coral is unknown. Two days after the tragedy, Bill's widow, Daisy, gives birth to a child, Eve. By her will Anthea has left the whole of her estate 'to my children'. Advise Anthea's executors as to whom the estate should be distributed.

2. Consider the various reforms that have been suggested to Wills Act 1837, s 15. What measure of reform, if any, would you support and why?

3. The Forfeiture Act 1982 is an undoubtedly well-intentioned measure but it

---

20. See also *Re Young* [1913] 1 Ch 272. Cf *Re Paradise Motor Co* [1968] 2 All ER 625, at 632, [1968] 1 WLR 1125 at 1143 in relation to disclaimer of inter vivos gifts.

is very limited and is arguably an unnecessarily complicating factor in relation to forfeiture of inheritance,
(Mithani and Wilton 'The Forfeiture Act 1982', (1983) 80 LSG 910).
Do you agree?

4. Tom died recently. By his will made in 1981 he left 'my share in the proceeds of sale of Yellowacre to Brenda.' At the date of the will, the fee simple in Yellowacre was held on trust for sale for Tom and Joe in equal shares. In 1983 Tom bought out Joe's half share and the trustees conveyed the legal fee simple in the property to him. Consider the validity of the gift to Brenda. Would it make a difference to your answer if Tom had made a codicil in 1985 for the sole object of appointing an executor? (See *Re Warren* [1932] Ch 42; cf *Re Newman* [1930] 2 Ch 409.)

CHAPTER 23

Payment of pecuniary (general) legacies

1 In general

Having paid the debts and funeral expenses, the next concern of the personal representatives will be to discharge the pecuniary (or general) legacies because, subject to any contrary intention shown by the testator, and to the problems of incidence discussed below, these are payable out of the residuary estate. If the residuary estate is insufficient for this purpose, the pecuniary legacies abate, that is, they are reduced proportionately; specific legatees and devisees are not required to contribute to any deficiency. As Lord Blackburn said in *Robertson v Broadbent* (1883) 8 AC 812 at p 819:

Let us suppose that a testator leaves his library, such as it should be at the time of his death, to A, £10,000 to B, and the residue of his personal estate to C, very probably believing, perhaps even indicating on the face of his will, that he thought his library would be worth £10,000 and the whole of his personal estate, including the library, worth £50,000; and owing either to miscalculation on his part, or to unforeseen disasters, his personal estate, including his library, turns out, after all debts and charges are paid, to be £19,000 only. No one can doubt that the testator, if alive, would remodel his will and give something to C, perhaps burthening the library with a payment to C, and reducing the legacy to B, so as to get the means of giving something to C. But he is dead and the Court cannot make a will for him. C, hard as it may seem, can get nothing under the bequest of the residue, for there is no residue; and it is settled by decisions, and, I think, if it was res integra I should hold that, as the intention on the face of the will is that A should have the library as a specific thing such as it should be at the testator's death, he must have it, whether it is of more or less value than the testator supposed, and that B can only get the £9,000.

Administration of Estates Act 1925

55. Definitions
In this Act, unless the context otherwise requires, the following expressions have the meanings hereby assigned to them respectively, that is to say—
(1) (ix) 'Pecuniary legacy' includes an annuity, a general legacy, a demonstrative legacy so far as it is not discharged out of the designated property, and any other general direction by a testator for the payment of money, including all death duties free from which any devise, bequest, or payment is made to take effect.

2 Incidence of pecuniary legacies

The general rule before 1926 was that in the absence of a contrary intention shown in the will, pecuniary legacies were payable only out of residuary personalty. If that was not sufficient, the legacies abated; no recourse could be had to realty at all. In identifying the residuary personalty for this purpose, failure of any part of the residuary gift was ignored.[1] It was always possible for a testator to show a contrary intention in his will and in this connection two well-known rules of construction existed: the rule in *Greville v Browne*[2] which applied when there was a gift of residuary realty and residuary personalty together ('all my real and personal property to X' 'all the residue of my estate to X on trust for Y') in which case the testator was presumed to have intended that the residuary realty could be taken after the personalty was exhausted,[3] and the rule in *Roberts v Walker*[4] where there was a gift of residuary realty and personalty together, but this time the testator expressly directed that the legacies were to be paid from the mixed fund ('I give all the residue of my estate to X subject to the payment of the legacies bequeathed herein') in which case the realty and personalty were proportionately liable to satisfy the legacies. To what extent has this pre-1926 position been altered by the Administration of Estates Act 1925?

(a) The effect of section 33

It has been generally accepted that post 1925, when there is undisposed of residue which is subjected to the statutory trust for sale of the Administration of Estates Act 1925, s 33(1), the old law has been altered; pecuniary legacies must then be paid out of the proceeds of the sale regardless of whether the undisposed of property originally consisted of realty, personalty or both.

Administration of Estates Act 1925

33. Trust for sale
(1) See p 122 ante.

In **Re Worthington** [1933] Ch 771, after leaving certain pecuniary legacies, the testatrix gave all her residuary estate, both real and personal, to X and Y in equal shares. X predeceased the testatrix and so his share lapsed and went as on the testatrix's intestacy. There was no express trust for sale in the will. Bennett J at first instance held that although the debts and funeral expenses were payable primarily out of the lapsed share on the application of the Administration of Estates Act 1925, s 34(3) and Part II of the First Schedule,[5] the rule in *Greville v*

---

1. So eg, if T's residuary personalty amounted to £15,000, he left it to A & B in equal shares and he also left, inter alia, pecuniary legacies totalling £10,000, on A's death before T the £10,000 legacies would be taken out of the residuary personalty before division into shares so that £5,000 would be left, of which £2,500 would go to B and £2,500 to those entitled on T's intestacy. Had the legacies amounted to £20,000, neither B nor those entitled on T's intestacy would have received anything, the residuary personalty being swallowed up completely by the legacies which would abate proportionately, for no recourse could be had to any realty or specific legacies.
2. (1859) 7 HLC 689.
3. See eg *Re Bawden* [1894] 1 Ch 693.
4. (1830) 1 Russ & M 752.
5. See p 340 ante.

Browne[6] would apply to the pecuniary legacies which would be payable in the first instance out of the residuary personalty (disregarding the fact that part of the gift had lapsed). The Court of Appeal disagreed. Having recited the provisions of the Administration of Estates Act 1925, ss 33(2), 34(3) and para 1 of Part II of the First Schedule ('Property of the deceased undisposed of by will, subject to the retention thereout of a fund sufficient to meet any pecuniary legacies'), Lord Hanworth MR continued at p 775:

Having regard to those sections and the paragraph of Part II of the First Schedule which I have read, is there any reason for the distinction made by Bennett J between debts and funeral expenses on the one hand and pecuniary legacies on the other? The learned judge seems to have read the will as providing for the payment of the legacies first and to have thought that the residue was not to be ascertained until after they had been paid. But the provisions of the statute[7] indicate that unless there is some provision in the will which negatives the prescribed order of administration, that order of administration must apply both to legacies and to debts. The learned judge seems to have thought that because of the specific reference to legacies in the will there was an indication of an intention that the statutory order of administration should not apply to them. But, after all, if legacies are given by a will, there must be a specific reference to them, and I do not see how that can be sufficient to alter the statutory order of administration.

Similarly in **Re Berrey's Will Trust** [1959] 1 All ER 15, [1959] 1 WLR 30, where the testatrix gave certain pecuniary legacies and then left her residuary estate equally between four persons, one of whom died before her so that that share lapsed. Before 1926 the pecuniary legacies would have been paid out of the residuary estate before dividing it into shares, but Danckwerts J held otherwise, saying at p 22:

There is no trust for sale contained in the will and, therefore, it seems to me that, following the decision of the Court of Appeal in *Re Worthington*, ([1933] 1 Ch 771) I must infer that with regard to the undisposed-of one-fourth share, in the same way as regards the undisposed-of one-half share in *Re Worthington*, ([1933] 1 Ch 771) that the trusts which create a trust for sale with a disposition of the resulting fund according to section 33 of the Administration of Estates Act, 1925, must be applied in the present case.

(b) The effect of section 34(3)

Where there is no undisposed of property or there is, but the residuary estate has been subjected to an express trust for sale by the will,[8] s 33 is of no assistance, and the unresolved question is then whether the pre-1926 law should continue to be applied or whether it has been effectively altered by the Administration of Estates Act 1925, s 34(3). Although this subsection expressly incorporates the statutory order of application of assets only for the payment of debts[9] as set out in Part II of the First Schedule to the Act, many judges and some academic commentators argue that by implication it also alters the old law governing the incidence of pecuniary legacies. Until the House of Lords rules on the point or Parliament legislates, following the precedent, perhaps, of the Queensland Succession Act 1981, the uncertainty will, it seems, remain.

6. (1859) 7 HLC 689.
7. It will be noted that Lord Hanworth MR was apparently utilising s 34(3) post as well as s 33(2) in reaching his decision, so also Romer LJ at p 777.
8. See *Re Mckee*, p 142 ante. The only circumstance where the statutory trust for sale would still apply would be if the express trust for sale failed owing to a complete failure of its objects.
9. See p 340 ante.

Administration of Estates Act 1925

34. Administration of assets
(3) and First Schedule Part II: see pp 340–341 ante.

Re Thompson [1936] 1 Ch 676, [1936] All ER 141, Ch D; Clauson J

The testator left certain pecuniary legacies and then all his residuary realty and personalty to certain charities. It was necessary to know for estate duty[10] purposes out of which property the pecuniary legacies were payable.

Held: The pre-1926 law has not been altered by the Administration of Estates Act 1925, s 34(3); under the rule in *Greville v Browne*[11] the residuary personalty would be primarily liable with recourse to the realty only when the personalty was exhausted.

Clauson J: The law which operates in these circumstances is well settled, and I will take the statement of it from the headnote in *Re Boards, Knight v Knight* ([1895] 1 Ch 499): 'When a testator bequeaths legacies and then bequeaths the residue of his real and personal estate, the legacies are charged upon the real estate or its proceeds, but they are payable primarily out of the personalty,[12] unless the testator directs that they are to be paid out of the mixed fund, in which case they are paid rateably out of realty and personalty.'[13] So it follows that the strict way to administer these assets is to apply the personal estate in paying legacies so far as it will go, and in so far as there is left something payable in respect of the legacies, that will be charged on realty. . . .

It is suggested that, having regard to certain provisions, to which I will draw attention in a moment, of the Administration of Estates Act, 1925, the rule stated in *Re Boards* ([1895] 1 Ch 499) is no longer law. It is suggested that by that Act a vast alteration has been made, which results in the law now being, so it is suggested, that, if a testator bequeaths legacies and then bequeaths the residue of his real and personal estate, the legacies are charged on the real estate or its proceeds and are not payable primarily out of the personalty but are payable out of personalty and realty pro rata, according to the proportions of personalty and realty. The suggestion that that is now the law is founded on this:

(He recited the terms of the Administration of Estates Act 1925, s 34(3) and the second paragraph of Part II of the First Schedule and continued:)

It is suggested that the effect of that provision is to alter the law and to provide that the fund which is to be retained out of the residuary realty and personalty in order to meet pecuniary legacies is to be retained in this way, that a proportionate part is to be retained out of realty and personalty pro rata the amount of the realty and personalty respectively. The provision does not say that. And the provision is not concerned with any such matter. The provision is concerned with the way in which funeral, testamentary and administration expenses, debts and liabilities are to be met. There is no indication there that there is any intention to alter the law in regard to the rights of legatees as against those interested in the residuary real estate, and I can see no foundation for the suggestion that that provision has in any way altered the law as laid down in *Re Boards* ([1895] 1 Ch 499).[14]

Re Midgley [1955] Ch 576, [1955] 2 All ER 625, Ch D; Harman J

The testatrix left certain pecuniary legacies and then her residuary estate on an express trust for sale for the benefit of six people equally. She subsequently made

---

10. A fore-runner of inheritance tax.
11. P 373 ante.
12. Under the rule in *Greville v Browne*, p 373 ante.
13. Under the rule in *Roberts v Walker*, p 373 ante.
14. See also *Re Anstead* [1943] Ch 161, [1943] 1 All ER 522.

a codicil revoking the gift to one of the six without making any substitutional provision, so that one-sixth of the residue was undisposed of. It was argued that the pre-1926 law would apply so that the pecuniary legacies would be payable out of the proceeds of sale before division into shares.

Held: Applying the Administration of Estates Act 1925, s 34(3) the pecuniary legacies were payable primarily out of the lapsed share by virtue of paragraph 1 of Part II of the First Schedule.

Harman J: The question now arises: Out of what sum are legacies to be paid? Having regard to the form of the will, it is clear that the debts, funeral and testamentary expenses are to be paid out of the whole fund before the division of the shares, and that is conceded, but the trust for sale created by the will says nothing about legacies and they are not charged by the will on any specific portion of the estate.

I am to look, as it seems to me, to s 34 of the Administration of Estates Act, 1925. Section 34(3) deals with the method of administering the estate of a deceased person who is solvent. The section only purports to apply to the method of the discharge of the funeral, testamentary and administration expenses, debts and liabilities and there is nothing in the section about legacies. So far apparently the law about payment of legacies has not been altered, but in Part 2 of Sch I, referred to in s 34(3) as controlling the order of administration, I find: 'Order of application of assets where the estate is solvent. 1. Property of the deceased undisposed of by will, subject to the retention thereout of a fund sufficient to meet any pecuniary legacies.' Therefore, one has first to retain out of the property undisposed of a fund sufficient to meet any pecuniary legacies, and one has to pay the debts, testamentary expenses and so forth out of the rest of the undisposed of property. What is one to do then with the fund that has been retained thereout? The answer, it seems to me, is that one must pay the pecuniary legacies because it has been retained to meet them. It is if I may say so a tortuous way of legislating, but that is what I should have thought it inevitably meant and so, indeed, Danckwerts J concluded recently in *Re Martin* ([1955] Ch 698, [1955] 1 All ER 865). It is quite true that in that case there was undisposed of real estate and no trust for sale which applied to it.[15] Any trust for sale would have failed because of the failure of the gift. Danckwerts J said ([1955] 1 All ER at p 868): 'It seems to me that here I am dealing simply with one asset, the undisposed of real estate, and out of that undisposed of real estate a fund is to be raised to provide for the pecuniary legacies, and if the fund is not to be raised for the payment of the pecuniary legacies, it is difficult to see what reason there is for setting aside the fund. Therefore, I am necessarily driven to the conclusion that according to the provisions contained in para 1 of Part 2 of Sch 1 to the Act the proper fund to meet the legacies in the present case is the undisposed of property.' That seems to me, if I may say so, to be right.

I am told, however, that that does not apply in a case where there is a trust for sale and I was referred to a former decision of the same judge, *Re Beaumont's Will Trusts* ((1950) Ch 462, [1950] 1 All ER 802). The end of the headnote reads as follows ([1950] Ch 463): 'Held, that, in effect, no provision at all was made by s 34(3), with regard to such things as legacies, so that the law in force before 1926 applied to the legacies in question, and the pecuniary and specific legacies and the duty on them were all payable out of the whole estate before the division of the residuary estate into four equal parts . . . .' The learned judge purports to follow *Re Thompson* ([1936] Ch 676, [1936] 2 All ER 141). The argument that prevailed in *Beaumont's* case ([1950] Ch 462, [1950] All ER 802) was apparently that a trust for sale imposed by the will excluded the Act altogether, because it excluded s 33 of the Act. I confess that I do not follow that argument. The decision of Roxburgh J in *Re Gillett's Will Trusts*, ([1950] Ch 102, [1949] 2 All ER 893) was not apparently cited to the learned judge. In the latter case, Roxburgh J (it is true on some concessions from counsel), held that para 1 of Part 2 of Sch 1 made the legacies payable out of the undisposed of property. That rule may not

---

15. Ie Danckwerts J could have reached the same decision by the application of AEA 1925, s 33(2) anyway as in *Re Worthington, Re Berrey*, p 373 ante.

apply when there is no intestacy apparent at the death of the testator. I am not suggesting that anything I say covers that case, but where, as here, it is apparent that the testator is to some extent intestate at his death and where no contrary intention appears from the will, then, as it seems to me, the effect of para 1 of Part 2 of Sch 1 applies to make the pecuniary legacies payable out of the undisposed of property, and I so hold.

Re Taylor's Estate [1969] 2 Ch 245, [1969] 1 All ER 113, Durham Chancery Court; Salt QC, Chancellor

The testatrix left various pecuniary legacies and then gave the residue of her real and personal estate to her personal representatives on an express trust for sale and division among certain persons, one of whom died before her so that there was an undisposed of share of residue. Should the burden of the pecuniary legacies fall on the total converted proceeds of sale as a whole before division, as under the pre-1926 law, or out of the lapsed share in accordance with the Administration of Estates Act 1925, paragraph 1, Part 2, Sch 1?
Held: The pecuniary legacies would be payable out of the converted proceeds of sale before division into shares, in accordance with the pre-1926 law.

Salt QC, Chancellor: Section 33 and s 34(3) and Sch 1, Pt 2, of the Administration of Estates Act 1925, read with the definition section, s 55, and against the background of pre-1926 law, are notoriously obscure. No one can say that they are old Wolstenholme (Wolstenholme and Cherry's Conveyancing Statutes) writ large. They have given rise to numerous judicial decisions, some of which are not readily reconcilable. . . .

Section 33(2) requires the personal representatives out of that ultimate balance of undisposed of property to set aside a fund sufficient (although it may have become insufficient by exhaustion) to provide for any pecuniary legacies bequeathed by any will of the deceased. None of the counsel contended that s 33 could have any application to this present case. They all shared my difficulty in appreciating how anything in Sch 1, Pt 2, dependent on a different section, viz, s 34, became relevant in *Re Martin (decd), Midland Bank Executor & Trustee Co Ltd v Marfleet* ([1955] Ch 698, [1955] 1 All ER 856), in so far as it was concerned with the incidence of pecuniary legacies. For in that case there was immediately undisposed of realty not subjected to any express trust for sale by the will and s 33(2) applied apparently, without looking beyond it, to throw on to that realty the burden of the pecuniary legacies. I say 'apparently' because the section is mandatory only in positively and unequivocally directing a fund to be set aside, after payment of funeral, testamentary and administration expenses, debts and other liabilities sufficient to provide for any pecuniary legacies: and in order to render that balance liable to meet payment of them it requires the further but modest implication that it is mandatory that they should be so paid. . . .

Now it seems to me that in interpreting and applying what Harman J has described in *Re Midgley* ([1955] Ch 576, [1955] 2 All ER 625) as this tortuous legislation, the court is faced with a dilemma—always assuming that the pre-1926 law does not directly apply in this particular regard irrespective of the Act, instead of as a result of lacunae in the Act. Either (a) the next-of-kin in order to succeed here require the importation into Sch 1, Pt 2, para 1 of some such words, following the phrase 'subject to retention', as 'if appropriate' or 'at the discretion of the personal representatives' so as to render 'subject to the retention' not mandatory, much less paramount, in point of payment of pecuniary legacies out of undisposed of property; or (b) the residuary legatees in order to succeed require the importation into s 34(3) itself, following the phrase 'discharge of the funeral, testamentary and administration expenses, debts and liabilities' of the words 'and pecuniary legacies': in as much or in so far as they cannot get what they want out of the wording of Sch 1, Pt 2 as it stands linked with s 34(3) or alonê. . . .

In my judgment it is not permissible to read 'and pecuniary legacies' into s 34(3). It is in terms confined to dealing with the 'discharge of the funeral, testamentary and administration expenses, debts and liabilities' payable out of a solvent estate and the order of resort therefore is prescribed by Sch 1, Pt 2. To read 'and pecuniary legacies' into it would be to do strong violence to the Act. On the other hand, I am of the opinion that it is possible, and permissible as a matter of construction, to import into Sch 1, Pt 2, para 1 the words 'where appropriate' or 'at the discretion of the personal representatives' in the context 'subject to the retention thereout of a fund sufficient to meet any pecuniary legacies'. Indeed I regard this as a reasonable construction of Sch 1, Pt 2, read as a whole and of the Act read as a whole, and for these reasons: First, whereas where s 33 applies sub-s (2) thereof expressly makes mandatory provision for setting aside a fund for pecuniary legacies out of the *balance* of the fund arising by statutory conversion of undisposed of real and personal estate *after* requiring primary provision out of *that* fund for 'funeral, testamentary and administration expenses, debts and other liabilities . . .' s 34(3) and Sch 1, Pt 2, would reverse that order if the words 'subject to setting aside . . .' were read as mandatory in para 1 thereof; and a curious inconsistency would emerge between s 33 on the one hand and s 34(3) and Sch 1, Pt 2, on the other hand. Secondly, when one turns to para 5 of Pt 2 of Sch 1 one finds the words 'The fund, *if any*, retained to meet *pecuniary legacies*'. This contemplates that the will has or may have bequeathed pecuniary legacies but that no fund has been retained under para 1 to meet them, and that para 1 is not mandatory, much less paramount, in this respect. The words are not 'The fund retained to meet *pecuniary legacies if any*'. Thirdly, the words in para 1 'subject to the retention . . .' are a curious formula if the legislature had intended to impose (as in s 33(2)) a clear obligation on the personal representatives to retain a fund to meet pecuniary legacies. Fourthly, s 34(3) and Sch 1, Pt 2, linked with it would (if the words 'subject to the retention . . .' were read in a mandatory sense, which I do not think they will bear in the total context thereof, and in the absence in s 34 of such imperative direction to retain as is contained in s 33) operate to substitute for the established pre-1926 law a new conception of provision for pecuniary legacies: and one which would favour them above funeral, testamentary and administration expenses debts and liabilities so far as concerns undisposed of property. And, finally, s 33(2) (as contrasted with s 34(3)) can only by a great stretch of canons of construction be read in any relation whatever to Sch 1, Pt 2, since they are mutually inconsistent in the order of resort which they may be thought to prescribe for provision or payment of pecuniary legacies.[16] Nor is this obstacle surmounted by the words in s 33(2) 'properly payable thereout having regard to the rules of administration contained in this Part of this Act'. Those words only underline any inconsistency.

I conclude that the pre-1926 law continues to apply, notwithstanding anything contained in the Administration of Estates Act 1925 in regard to pecuniary legacies, to the situation disclosed at (the testatrix's) death: and I accept that the argument for the next-of-kin of (the testatrix) must prevail. It does less violence to the statute than any other construction. Accordingly I answer question 3 of the summons by declaring in accordance with para (a) thereof that her pecuniary legacies totalling (effectively) £400 must be paid out of her converted residuary estate as a whole.

Ryder, 'The incidence of general pecuniary legacies'[17]

(Having reviewed the above authorities, other than *Re Taylor's Estate* which had not then been decided, he concludes at p 100:)

It is to be hoped that the House of Lords may some day have an opportunity of considering the problems discussed above. Meanwhile, in the present state of the authorities the draftsman has a plain duty whenever he draws a will even of the simplest kind, if it contains a pecuniary bequest, to consider the question of incidence of legacies

---

16. AEA 1925, s 33(2) directs debts to be paid first out of undisposed of property, then legacies, whilst Sch 1, Pt 2, para 1 seems to expect that legacies will be paid first out of undisposed of property, then debts.

17. [1956] CLJ 80. Salt QC, Ch, in *Re Taylor's Estate* ante, expressed his indebtedness to Professor Ryder for this article. Professor Ryder decides firmly in favour of the old rules, save in so far as AEA 1925, s 33(2) applies; cf Albery, (1969) 85 LQR 464, writing after *Re Taylor's Estate* was decided.

and, if necessary, to insert express provisions which will prevent any of the difficulties discussed above from arising.[18]

Succession Act 1981 (Queensland, Australia)

59.   Payment of debts in the case of solvent estates

(1)   Where the estate of a deceased person is solvent the estate shall, subject to this Act, be applicable towards the discharge of the debts payable thereout in the following order, namely—

Class 1—Property[19] specifically appropriated devised or bequeathed (either by a specific or general description) for the payment of debts; and property charged with, or devised or bequeathed (either by a specific or general description) subject to a charge for the payment of debts;

Class 2—Property comprising the residuary estate[20] of the deceased including property in respect of which any residuary disposition operates as the execution of a general power of appointment;

Class 3—Property specifically devised or bequeathed including property specifically appointed under a general power of appointment and any legacy charged on property so devised bequeathed or appointed;

Class 4—Donationes mortis causa.

(2)   Property within each class as aforesaid shall be applied in the discharge of the debts and, where applicable, the payment of pecuniary legacies rateably according to value; and where a legacy is charged on a specific property the legacy and the property shall be applied rateably.

(3)   The order in which the estate is applicable towards the discharge of debts and the incidence of rateability as between different properties within each class may be varied by a contrary or other intention signified by the will, but a contrary or other intention is not signified by a general direction, charge or trust for the payment of debts or of all the debts of the testator out of his estate or out of his residuary estate or by a gift of any such estate after or subject to the payment of debts.

60.   Payment of pecuniary legacies

Subject to a contrary or other intention signified by the will;

(a)   pecuniary legacies shall be paid out of the property comprised in Class 2 referred to in section 59 after the discharge of the debts or such part thereof as are payable out of that property; and

(b)   to the extent to which the property comprised in Class 2 referred to in section 59 is insufficient the pecuniary legacies shall abate proportionately.

3   Annuities

Included within the statutory definition of a pecuniary legacy[1] the annuity by will has been described by Cross J in *Re Berkeley*[2] as 'a series of legacies payable at intervals', usually yearly and for the duration of the annuitant's life or such other period as the will specifies. The rules as to the incidence of pecuniary

---

18.   See eg residuary gift in the specimen will at p 62 ante.

19.   Defined in s 5(1) as including real and personal property.

20.   Defined in s 55 as meaning (a) property of the deceased that is not effectively disposed of by his will; and (b) property of the deceased not specifically devised or bequeathed but included (either by a specific or general description) in a residuary disposition. There is no provision equivalent to AEA 1925, s 33(1) & (2) in the Act.

1.   See p 372 ante. See also *Gaskin v Rogers* (1866) LR 2 Eq 284, at 291.

2.   [1968] 1 Ch 154, 165, [1967] 3 All ER 170, 176.

legacies[3] apply to identify the property out of which the annuity is payable, from which it follows that it will usually be payable out of the residuary estate, unless charged on some other fund. Unless the executors are authorised by the will or by the court[4] to set aside a particular part of the residue to meet the annuity to the exoneration of the rest of the residuary estate, the annuitant is entitled to be paid in full out of the residuary income with resort to capital if necessary, before the residuary beneficiary receives anything, so that executors making a distribution to the residuary beneficiary during the annuitant's lifetime will do so at their peril.[5] In the following circumstances the annuitant has the right to demand a capital sum in lieu of his annuity.

(a) Direction to purchase an annuity

Where the will directs the executors to purchase an annuity for the beneficiary, the beneficiary may demand the cash equivalent of the purchase price instead.

In **Stokes v Cheek** (1860) 28 Beav 620, 54 ER 504, the testatrix left annuities to various beneficiaries, including annuities of £30 each to X & Y; she directed her executors to sell her assets and use the proceeds to buy 'Government annuities' for the respective annuitants, none of whom, she declared, was to be entitled to claim the value of the annuity in lieu thereof. Despite the declaration, Romilly MR held that the annuitants were entitled to such sums as would be required to purchase their annuities, saying at p 505:

It would be an idle form to direct an annuity to be purchased, which the annuitants might sell immediately afterwards.[6]

(b) Commercial risk of insufficiency

Where the will includes other pecuniary legacies[7] and there is a real commercial risk of insufficient capital to provide for all the pecuniary legacies, including the annuity, in full, the annuitant may call for the actuarial value of his annuity, abated if necessary along with the other pecuniary legacies.

Re Cottrell [1910] 1 Ch 402, Ch D; Warrington J

By her will the testatrix gave certain pecuniary legacies and then left her husband an annuity of £1 per week for life, directing her trustees to set aside and invest such sum as would produce by its income an annual sum equal to the amount of the annuity and to apply the income and if necessary the capital of

---

3. P 373 ante.
4. As in *Harbin v Masterman* [1896] 1 Ch 351.
5. The risk may only be a technical one, depending on the size of the residuary estate and the amount of the annuity: eg if the annuity was for £100 a year and the executors were to set aside say £1,500 from the residuary estate to meet it, and distribute the remainder to the residuary beneficiary, it would be most unlikely that the income of the £1,500 with resort to capital if necessary, would be insufficient to meet the annuity in full.
6. See also *Re Robbins* [1907] 2 Ch 8 where there was a direction to purchase an annuity but the annuitant died 16 days after the testator. The Court of Appeal held that the annuity and the right to take its value in cash had vested in her on the testator's death so that the cash sum could be claimed by her personal representatives for her estate.
7. Or annuities, see p 372 ante.

the fund so appropriated, in payment of the annuity; on the death of the annuitant, the fund would fall into residue. The estate was insufficient to pay the pecuniary legacies in full and to set aside the sum in question, but it was sufficient to pay the pecuniary legacies and the actuarial value of the annuity at the date of the testatrix's death.

Held: The annuitant was entitled to call for the actuarial value of the annuity.

Warrington J: Now the amount of the estate of the testatrix is sufficient to pay in full the pecuniary legacies and the value as at the date of the testatrix's death of the annuity of £52. It is not sufficient to pay the pecuniary legacies in full and to set apart in full a fund sufficient by the income thereof to pay the annuity. If, therefore, the directions of the testatrix are to be carried into effect in the form in which they are expressed in the will the pecuniary legacies and the amount to be set aside to answer the annuity will have to abate.[8] It is true that if the annuity did not in the result exhaust the abated fund set aside the pecuniary legatees might in the end get paid in full—they might or they might not. Under those circumstances what is the course which the Court ought to pursue? In the ordinary case where there is a gift of an annuity to an annuitant with a direction to set aside a fund to answer the annuity, and the annuity is payable out of capital as well as income and there is a gift over of the residue, it was decided in *Wright v Callender* ((1852) 2 De G M & G 652), and I think it is the law, that the right of the annuitant is to have the directions of the testator carried into effect, and that if the estate is not sufficient to pay the annuity in full he is entitled to have the deficiency made up out of capital, but he must take the estate as it stands and is not entitled to have the value of the annuity paid over to him. That is the law where the question is one simply as between an annuitant and residuary legatees. But where the question is one as between an annuitant and pecuniary legatees, and the estate is insufficient for the payment of the annuity and the pecuniary legacies, then, where there is a direction in the will to set apart and invest a sufficient sum to answer the annuity, the course adopted by the Court has been to value the annuity as at the date of the testator's death, to treat the amount of the valuation as a legacy, and to make it abate in its due proportion, and then to pay the abated amount to the annuitant. In each of those two cases respectively those are the proper courses to pursue, as is shewn by *Wright v Callender* ((1852) 2 De G M & G 642). But the case with which I have to deal is the intermediate case. It is this: If the course is to be pursued in the present case which is pursued in the case where the estate is insufficient to pay both the pecuniary legatees and an annuitant in full, the pecuniary legacies will be paid in full and the annuitant will receive the full value of his annuity at once. If, however, I take the amount directed to be set aside to answer the annuity and treat it as a legacy and make it abate with the other pecuniary legacies, then three courses are possible; either (1) the annuitant is to receive his annuity in full out of the abated fund, or (2) he is to receive his annuity in full out of both income and capital, or (3) by some intricate calculation he is to receive out of income supplemented by capital a yearly sum abated in proportion to the actual abatement of the pecuniary legacies. Whichever of those three courses be adopted, an injustice will be done to the pecuniary legatees, which would be avoided by adopting the course which is contended for on behalf of the pecuniary legatees. The right of the pecuniary legatees is to be paid at the expiration of one year from the testator's death, that is, in the present case, at once, the amounts of their legacies. If I adopt the course pressed upon me by counsel for the residuary legatee I do not pay the pecuniary legatees the amounts of their legacies in full. The annuitant may get paid in full, the pecuniary legatees may or may not be paid in full, at some time hereafter, when it is known how long the annuitant has lived, and possibly if both the annuitant and the pecuniary legatees are paid in full there may be something left for the residuary legatee. But that course is wholly speculative. By adopting the other course I can do justice at once without any speculating to both the pecuniary legatees and the residuary legatee. The pecuniary legatees are entitled to be paid in full at once; so also is the annuitant. It is

---

8. Ie reduce proportionately, see eg *Miller v Huddlestone* (1851) 3 Mac & G 513.

true that here the testatrix has provided a means by which the annuity can be secured, but to follow that course would be to do injustice to the pecuniary legatees. In my judgment justice can be done to all the three classes of beneficiaries by adopting the course suggested by counsel on behalf of the pecuniary legatees, namely, by valuing the annuity as at the date of the death of the testatrix according to the Government tables or according to ordinary actuarial principles and treating the amount of the valuation as a pecuniary legacy, and paying the pecuniary legatees in full and the annuitant the amount of the valuation of his annuity, if he is willing to accept it, or investing it in the purchase of a Government annuity of £52. There will thus remain a residue to which the residuary legatee will be entitled.

In **Re Hill** [1944] 1 Ch 270, [1944] 1 All ER 502, this ruling was qualified by the Court of Appeal. The testator's will included a number of pecuniary legacies and annuities. At the outset there was insufficient capital for all the pecuniary legacies to be paid in full and for sums to be set aside to meet the annuities from the income therefrom although in view of the age of the annuitants there was no commercial risk that the annuities would not be paid in full.[9] As soon as even the smallest of the annuities ceased, the income of the residue would be sufficient to meet all the annuities and in the meantime the executors could have recourse to capital to the small degree necessary. The annuitants claimed that under the rule in *Re Cottrell* they nevertheless had the right to call for the capital value of their respective annuities. The Court of Appeal held that as there was no commercial risk of insufficiency they had no such right; the annuities should be paid out of the income of the residuary estate with recourse to capital if necessary. Lord Greene MR said at p 505:

The reason for the application of the rule in *Re Cottrell* ([1910] 1 Ch 402) is we think, correctly stated by Simonds J in *Re Cox* ([1938] Ch 556, 563, [1938] 1 All ER at p 666). 'The reason is clear from a hypothetical example. Suppose an annuity of £100 is bequeathed to one annuitant, A, who is ninety years of age, and a similar annuity to another, B, who is nineteen years of age, and suppose that the whole estate available for satisfaction of the annuities is only £1,000. If both the income and the capital of that sum are applied year by year until it is exhausted in payment of the two annuities, A will probably get his annuity paid in full for the whole of his life, but B will not do so. There is thus an inequality in that treatment which the testator is presumed not to have intended. The only fair way of dealing with annuities as between annuitants of different ages is to make an actuarial valuation of the annuities, and to pay the value of each so ascertained to the annuitants . . . .'

The reason so stated has obviously no application to a case like the present where it is plain that the available estate is more than sufficient to provide for the payment in full of the annuities out of income and capital as directed by the testator unless a series of events should transpire entirely outside the scope of human expectation, namely, the joint survival of all the annuitants for a period of time of impossible length having regard to their respective ages at the time when the matter is to be considered.

Although Uthwatt J[10] obviously felt the hardship on the residuary legatees that would be caused by so doing, he applied the rule because he thought it was one of universal application and that to refuse to do so would create confusion in the administration of other estates. But the rule is not a rule of law. It is one of convenience . . . . No confusion can be caused if the court refuses to apply the rule where

---

9. The annuitants' ages were between 59 and 64; the court calculated that to outlive the funds available in the residuary estate (after payment of the pecuniary legacies in full) all four annuitants would have to live to at least the age of 103.
10. At first instance.

it is clear on the evidence that all the annuities can properly be satisfied in full out of the estate and there is no commercial risk of any insufficiency.[11]

4 Payment of income or interest[12]

(a) The general rule

Specific legacies and devises have always included the right to the income earned by the property concerned from the testator's death[13] (subject to any contrary intention shown by the testator), as have gifts of residuary realty or personalty. The Law of Property Act 1925, s 175 confirmed that this position also applies to contingent specific and residuary gifts[14] but there is no mention in that section of general or pecuniary legacies. The common law rule therefore remains, that unless a contrary intention has been shown, the general legacy bears simple interest at 5%[15] but only from the time when payment is due.[16]

Law of Property Act 1925

175. Contingent and future testamentary gifts to carry the intermediate income
(1) A contingent or future specific devise or bequest of property, whether real or personal, and a contingent residuary devise of freehold land, and a specific or residuary devise of freehold land to trustees upon trust for persons whose interests are contingent or executory shall, subject to the statutory provisions relating to accumulations, carry the intermediate income of that property from the death of the testator, except so far as such income, or any part thereof, may be otherwise expressly disposed of.

In **Re Raine** [1929] 1 Ch 716, Eve J had to decide whether the income of two pecuniary legacies bequeathed contingently upon the legatees attaining twenty-one was applicable for their maintenance. Holding that it was not, as the gifts did not carry the right to the intermediate income, he said at p 719:

On behalf of the legatees s 175 of the Law of Property Act 1925[17] is first relied upon. There is nothing in the will by which the income of these legacies or any part thereof is expressly disposed of; if not applicable for maintenance it falls into residue. But does a

---

11. See also *Re Bradberry* [1943] 1 Ch 35, [1942] 2 All ER 629; two of the three annuitants had died after the testator's death as a result of which there was sufficient in the estate to pay the pecuniary legacies in full and to set aside a fund sufficient to meet the surviving annuitant's entitlement. The court took this into account in refusing to award capital sums to the surviving and deceased annuitants.
12. See generally Ker: 'Trustees' Powers of Maintenance', (1953) 17 Conv 273.
13. Save in so far as the income relates to the period before the date of death, when an apportionment must be made under the Apportionment Act 1870 so that such part as relates to the pre-death period falls into the residuary estate, see eg Meads 'Treatment of Income in Probate' (1978) 122 Sol J 689.
14. Oddly the section makes no mention of contingent gifts of residuary personalty but their entitlement to the intermediate income had already been established, see eg *Re Adams* (1893) 1 Ch 329.
15. Originally 4% but increased to 5% by SI 1972/1898. The rate still seems very low: c/f for example the 8% allowed by the Succession Act 1981 (Queensland) s 52(1)(e).
16. One year after the testator's death in the case of an immediate legacy; the date of satisfaction of the contingency where the legacy is contingent.
17. Ante.

pecuniary legacy come within the words 'A contingent or future specific devise or bequest of property, whether real or personal'? In my opinion it does not. I think the adjectives 'contingent future and specific' apply both to the devise and the bequest, and that a pecuniary legacy cannot be said to be a specific bequest of personal property. Had it been intended to include pecuniary legacies I think more appropriate language would have been employed. That being so, one is relegated to the law prior to the passing of the Act, and I think that is fully and accurately stated by Younger J in *Re Boulter* ([1918] 2 Ch 40) where at p 44 he says: 'The rule of the Court on this subject is, I think, quite settled. It depends, first, to some extent, upon the question whether the testator was the father or stood *in loco parentis* to the infant.[18] In such a case, even if the legacy be not by the testator directed to be set apart for the benefit of the legatee, the legacy will bear interest for maintenance for so long as no maintenance is expressly provided for the infant by the testator.' In support of that he cites *Re Bowlby* ([1904] 2 Ch 685, 706): 'On the other hand, a contingent legacy in favour of an infant of whom the testator is not the father, or towards whom he does not stand in loco parentis, and which is not directed to be set apart for the benefit of the infant, bears no interest either for maintenance or otherwise until it vests.'[19]

(b) The exceptions

To this general rule there are three important exceptions that favour the legatee:[20]

(i) *Where the testator is the parent of or in loco parentis to the legatee*

Whether the legacy is immediate or contingent it will bear 5% interest from the date of death, provided in the case of a contingent legacy that the contingency is only the attaining of majority by that child or marrying under that age.

In **Re Abrahams** [1911] 1 Ch 108, the testator left a legacy to each son of his who should attain 25 and a further legacy to each son to attain 30. He left two sons, one aged 25 when the testator died, the other aged 13. Holding that the exception would not apply in the case of either legatee, Eve J said at p 115:

This much I think is clear from the historical examination of the cases through which (Counsel) has taken us, that the exception had its origin in the desire of the Court to give effect to what the Court presumed must have been the intention of the testator, that is to say, to provide for the maintenance of the infant, an intention which might well be presumed in cases where the suspensory period was limited to the years when the infant would in the ordinary course require to be maintained, but which could not be presumed as readily, if indeed at all, where the legacy was made contingent upon events having no reference to the infancy of the legatee, and in this connection it certainly is remarkable that in all the cases to which my attention has been directed the contingencies have been the attainment by the child of full age or marriage under that age. There is no case in which I can see that the exception has been held to apply when the contingency is anything but the attainment of full age or marriage under that age. In that state of things and bearing in mind that I am dealing with an exception engrafted on a general rule, ought I to be the first judge to hold that the exception extends so as to include

---

18. In the case before him the testator was not the parent nor *in loco parentis* to the children, see the exception (i) to the general rule, post.
19. See also *Re Hall* [1951] 1 All ER 1073.
20. There are two other exceptions but these seldom arise in practice, namely where the legacy is immediate and payable to a creditor in satisfaction of a debt (*Re Rattenbury* [1906] 1 Ch 667; where the legacy is immediate and charged on realty (*Pearson v Pearson* (1802) 1 Sch & Lef 10). If either of these exceptions does apply, 5% interest will run from the date of death unless a contrary intention has been shown.

contingencies of every description and having no relation to the attainment of full age? I do not think I ought to be.[1]

(ii) *Where the testator directs the legacy to be set apart from the rest of the estate*

The legacy will carry 5% interest even if contingent, but only from the end of the executor's year.

Re Medlock (1886) 55 LJ Ch 738, 54 LT 828, Ch D; Kay J

The testator appointed certain persons to be the 'executors and trustees' of his will and then left £750 to his 'trustees' on trust to pay and divide it among certain children contingent on them attaining the age of 21 or (in the case of females) marrying under that age. If no one attained a vested interest then 'the said sum of £750 and the investments representing the same' should fall into his residuary estate.

Held: The contingent legatees were entitled to the intermediate income from the £750 and that income could therefore be applied for their maintenance during their infancy.

Kay J: It is said first, that this will contains no direction to sever; and secondly, that even if there be such a direction, that is not sufficient to entitle the infants to the intermediate income. First of all, let us consider the question apart from authority. Suppose a testator were to say, 'I direct £1,000 to be set apart and invested for the benefit of such children of A as shall attain twenty-one years.' How is it possible to say that the fund is not to go to them with all the accretions it may acquire? I should be extremely reluctant to hold that that is not the result of a direction of that kind. The thing given to the children of A is the segregated fund, and why that fund should not carry interest I cannot conceive. Again, suppose a policy of assurance on the life of A is given and the policy acquires a bonus, it could not be said that a contingent legatee to whom the policy was given was not entitled to the bonus. It seems to be therefore clear that, where a testator has so set apart a fund for the benefit of certain objects when the contingency happens, that fund, with its accretions, belongs to the legatee. Is there here a segregation directed? I have tried to express in *Re Judkin's Trusts* (50 LT Rep N S 200; 25 Ch Div 743), and in *Re Dickson, Hill v Grant* (51 L T Rep N S 891; 1b 707; 28 Ch Div 291; 29 ibid 331), that where there is no direction to set apart the legacies, and the setting apart is only because there is a wish to divide the residue, then the fund set apart remains as part of the residue until the contingency happens, and the income belongs to the residuary legatee. In this particular case the testator appoints three persons executors and trustees. He shows that he thoroughly understands the difference between the duties of executors and trustees, because he says, 'I bequeath to my said trustees the sum of £750 upon trust to pay and divide the same unto and equally between such of my three grandchildren,' and so on, 'and in default of any such person attaining a vested interest the sum of £750 and the investments representing the same shall fall into my residuary estate.' I pause there a moment to ask this question: Suppose the executors were different persons from the trustees, is there any reason to doubt that the trustees could have required the executors to hand over the £750 to them? It seems to me impossible to doubt that they could have done so. It is clear, therefore that the legacies were to be set apart and invested in the names of the trustees to answer the contingent legacies. The will then continues as follows: [His Lordship read the residuary gift, and continued:] The testator's widow, therefore, is entitled to the residue after providing for the legacies. I have, therefore, no

---

1. Nor does the exception apply where the legacy is expressed to be payable not to the child but to someone else, such as trustees, on behalf of the child, see *Re Pollock* [1943] Ch 338, [1943] 2 All ER 443; nor where the testator has provided some other fund for the child's maintenance: *Re George* (1876) 5 Ch D 837, 843.

doubt but that the legacies are to be first set apart, and the residue, after setting aside the legacies, is to be invested and the income thereof is to be paid to the widow. Turning to the authorities, is there any authority against this construction? Quite the contrary. With the exception of the Irish case of *Johnston v O'Neill* (3 L Rep Ir 476) there does not seem to be a case very much in point. But in *Festing v Allen* (5 Hare 573) there was a will framed like this one. Wigram V-C in that case does not say that the direction to sever a legacy from the bulk of an estate is absolutely conclusive; but it is a weighty argument in favour of a claim of interest on a deferred legacy. I hold, therefore, that in this case the purport and effect of the will is that the infant legatees are entitled to the income; and that the intermediate income may therefore be applied for their maintenance.

(iii) *Where the testator has otherwise shown a contrary intention*

In **Re Riddell** (1936) 155 LT 247, the legacy was in the following terms: 'I bequeath to (X) free of death duties the sum of £100,000. I direct that such legacy shall be paid immediately after my death, and that the same shall be paid in priority to all other legacies and annuities bequeathed by my will and treated as a first charge on my estate.' Farwell J said at p 247:

Generally speaking a legacy carries interest from one year after the death, but there are exceptions, as in the case where the testator was the father of, or stood in loco parentis to, the legatee. In this case there is an express direction that the legacy shall be paid immediately after the death. It is plain, in my judgment, that these words do entitle the widow to immediate payment and, that being so, she is entitled to interest as from the date of the death.[2]

In **Re Churchill** [1909] 2 Ch 431, the testatrix had given a legacy of £200 to her grandnephew contingent on his attaining twenty-one. Elsewhere in her will she empowered her trustees at their discretion 'to apply the whole or any part of the share to which any beneficiary hereunder may be contingently entitled in or towards the advancement in life or otherwise for the benefit of such beneficiary whether male or female and whether under the age of twenty-one years or not.' Warrington J said at p 433:

There is a further exception where the testator has shewn an intention that the legatee should be maintained as part of the testator's bounty; in such a case the legacy will bear interest from the testator's death until the legacy becomes payable. It is said that the present case comes within that exception. That the exception exists is shewn by *Leslie v Leslie* ((1835) Ll & Gt Sug 1). There the testator had shewn twice over his intention that the £2,000 given by his will should be 'for the use and support of the younger children.' He said so in the recital, and he used those words again in the actual gift. So that case is, I think, an illustration of the exception to the general rule. In the present case what I have to determine is whether in the will before me there is sufficient to bring the matter within that exception. Has the testatrix expressed an intention that the infant legatee shall be maintained out of her bounty? In support of the contention that she has done so counsel for the infant legatee relies on the direction in the will (He recited the power in the will and continued): If the direction had been 'towards the advancement in life' of the legatee only, that would clearly not have been sufficient; but the testatrix goes on to say 'or otherwise for the benefit of such beneficiary whether male or female and whether under the age of twenty-one years or not'—that is, for maintenance as distinguished from advancement. Here, therefore, the legacy is payable at twenty-one, but power is given to the trustees to apply the legacy for maintenance of the infant. Is that sufficient to

---

2. See also *Re Pollock* [1943] Ch 338, [1943] 2 All ER 443.

justify the Court in holding that the legacy bears interest from the death of the testatrix until the date at which it becomes payable? (He held that it was).[3]

(c) Annuity arrears

There is one further exception to the rule, this time against the interest of the legatee, namely that an annuitant is not entitled to interest on the arrears of his annuity. Established since at least 1723[4] this exception was confirmed by the House of Lords in *Torre v Browne* (1854) 24 LJ Ch 757, where Lord Cranworth LC said at p 761:

> The general rule of the Court was, that arrears of an annuity did not carry interest, and the only cases in which of late years the Court had held interest on the arrears of an annuity to be payable, were those in which the annuitant held some enforceable security, or where the accumulation of arrears had been expressly occasioned by the misconduct of the party who was bound to pay.

On the facts before him, no security was held by the annuitants and it was difficult to say whose fault it was that the annuity had fallen into arrears; mere delay alone did not entitle the annuitants to interest, so no interest would be payable.

In **Re Hiscoe** (1902) 71 LJ Ch 347, the unfairness of the exception was pointed out by Kekewich J who could find no justification for it but felt himself bound to apply the House of Lords ruling, saying at p 349:

> Now, on principle I have been unable to see why interest should not be payable. An annuity is, after all, nothing but a legacy payable by instalments, and as it is our ordinary practice to calculate interest on legacies, as a general rule from twelve months after the testator's death, it is extremely difficult to my mind to see why the arrears of an annuity should not carry interest in the same way. To take the simplest, because the commonest possible, case. On the death of a testator, who has bequeathed both legacies and annuities—possibly a legacy to one child, and an annuity to another—the question arises, whether his estate is solvent or not; and that depends, we will say, on one of two questions of this character—either whether a certain asset can be realised so as to bring in enough to pay everything, or whether a certain claim against the estate can be established. It may take a very long time to settle either of those practical questions. The claim may be carried through the Courts to the Court of Appeal and to the House of Lords. The asset may be doubtful, and may not be realised for a very long time. Then the child who has the legacy will, in the ordinary course, be paid that legacy (I am assuming that the estate after all turns out to be solvent), with interest from twelve months after the testator's death. The child who has an annuity surely ought also to have interest on the annuity on the instalments of the legacy which that child has not received. That seems to me perfectly plain on principle. But, this notwithstanding, it seems to me equally plain that there is a distinction in practice, and that the interest cannot be allowed.[5]

---

3. See also *Re Selby-Walker* [1949] 2 All ER 178 where the trustees were empowered to use any part of the legacy (before the legatee satisfied the contingency) for the education of the legatee; Roxburgh J followed *Re Churchill* on the basis that "'education' and 'maintenance' are so closely akin that the same principle ought to apply,' at p 179). Aliter where the testator has made some other provision in his will for the maintenance of the beneficiary: *Re West* [1913] 2 Ch 345.
4. *Batten v Earnley* (1723) 2 P Wms 163.
5. See also *Re Berkeley* [1968] Ch 154, [1967] 3 All ER 170, affd on this point [1968] Ch 744, [1968] 3 All ER 364.

Law Commission: Fifth Annual Report 1969–1970[6]

63.   Interest on arrears of annuities

Our study of the suggested abrogation of the rule that arrears of an annuity given by will do not carry interest is complete. Consultations have revealed a strong body of informed opinion against the abolition of this rule. The view is taken that there is a valid distinction between legacies and annuities and that, moreover, the abolition of the rule, even if justified as a matter of principle, would create a disproportionate amount of work and expense. It is in any event probable that, if the rule were altered so that arrears of a testamentary annuity carried interest, most professionally drawn wills would provide to the contrary.[7]

QUESTIONS

1. 'The effect of the Administration of Estates Act 1925 has been to produce lasting uncertainty as to the rules governing the incidence of general legacies'.
Read Ryder, 1956 CLJ 80, Albery (1969) 85 LQR 464 and then discuss. In what way does the Queensland Succession Act 1981 seek to resolve that uncertainty?
2. Terence dies leaving a will by which he gives £10,000 to Albert, and 'the residue of my real and personal estate to Brenda and Carole in equal shares.' Carole died before Terence. Terence's realty is worth £30,000 and his personalty is worth £10,000 but he also leaves debts totalling £20,000. Out of which property will the debts and legacy be payable? Would it make any difference to your answer if the residuary estate had been left 'on trust for sale for Brenda and Carole in equal shares'?
3. Tim dies recently; by his will he left his widow an annuity of £1,000, legacies of £500 each to his two sons and the rest of his estate to his daughter. His executors estimate that the residuary estate will not be sufficient to pay the annuity out of income. Advise them as to the distribution of the estate.
4. Which of the following gifts in M's will will earn interest for the beneficiary and from what point in time?
  (a) 'I give £1,000 to A if he attains 18.'
  (b) 'I give £1,000 to B.' B is M's son.
  (c) 'I give £1,000 to C if she attains 21.' C is M's daughter.
  (d) 'I give £5,000 to such of my grandchildren as attain 18 in equal shares.'
  (e) 'I give £500 to my niece N if she attains 18; my executors may at their discretion pay or apply any part of this gift for her maintenance in the meantime.'

---

6. Law Com No 36.
7. On 7th July 1970 the Lord Chancellor was informed that the Law Commission advised that no action shoud be taken on the proposal.

CHAPTER 24

Distribution of the estate

1 The time for distribution

Personal representatives have at least a year from the date of death[1] before the beneficiaries can call on them to distribute the estate;[2] often the administration of the estate may justify them in taking much longer than this[3] whilst many estates are wound up and distributed well within the year.[4]

Administration of Estates Act 1925

44. Power to postpone distribution
. . . . a personal representative is not bound to distribute the estate of the deceased before the expiration of one year from the death.

2 Rights of the beneficiaries during administration

Whilst the estate is still being administered, the entire ownership in the deceased's unadministered property is in the personal representative for the purposes of administration and no beneficiary, whether under the deceased's will or intestacy, has any proprietary interest in any particular asset comprised in the deceased's unadministered estate. The beneficiary's entitlement during this period is to a chose in action, namely, the right to require the deceased's estate to be duly administered.

Commissioners of Stamp Duties (Queensland) v Livingston [1965] AC 694, [1964] 3 All ER 692, PC; Visct Radcliffe, Lords Reid, Evershed, Pearce and Upjohn

Mrs Coulson's husband had predeceased her, leaving her a one-third interest in his residuary estate, which included real property in Queensland. She died whilst his estate was being administered and it was necessary to know for the

---

1. The so-called 'executor's year' applies equally to administrators.
2. Cf creditors, see p 332 ante.
3. See eg *Re Neeld* [1962] Ch 643, 688, [1962] 2 All ER 335, 359.
4. See eg *Re Palmer* [1916] 2 Ch 391 ('the executor is not bound to wait twelve months before he hands over or pays a legacy', per Pickford LJ at p 401).

purpose of liability to succession duty in Queensland, whether, at the time of her death, she owned a beneficial interest in that Queensland realty.

Held: The testator's property, real and personal, was still vested in his executors when she died and no beneficial interest in any part of that property belonged to her at the date of her death; no succession duty was therefore payable.

Lord Radcliffe: When Mrs Coulson died she had the interest of a residuary legatee in the testator's unadministered estate. The nature of that interest has been conclusively defined by decisions of long established authority, and its definition no doubt depends upon the peculiar status which the law accorded to an executor for the purposes of carrying out his duties of administration. There were special rules which long prevailed about the devolution of freehold land and its liability for the debts of a deceased, but subject to the working of these rules whatever property came to the executor *virtute officii* came to him in full ownership, without distinction between legal and equitable interests. The whole property was his. He held it for the purpose of carrying out the functions and duties of administration, not for his own benefit; and these duties would be enforced upon him by the Court of Chancery, if application had to be made for that purpose by a creditor or beneficiary interested in the estate. Certainly, therefore, he was in a fiduciary position with regard to the assets that came to him in the right of his office, and for certain purposes and in some aspects he was treated by the court as a trustee. Kay J in *Re Marsden* ((1884) 26 Ch D 783, at p 789) said:

> 'An executor is personally liable in equity for all breaches of the ordinary trusts which in courts of equity are considered to arise from his office.' He is a trustee 'in this sense'.

It may not be possible to state exhaustively what those trusts are at any one moment. Essentially, they are trusts to preserve the assets, to deal properly with them, and to apply them in a due course of administration for the benefit of those interested according to that course, creditors, the death duty authorities, legatees of various sorts, and the residuary beneficiaries. They might just as well have been termed 'duties in respect of the assets' as trusts. What equity did not do was to recognise or create for residuary legatees a beneficial interest in the assets in the executor's hands during the course of administration. Conceivably, this could have been done, in the sense that the assets, whatever they might be from time to time, could have been treated as a present, though fluctuating, trust fund held for the benefit of all those interested in the estate according to the measure of their respective interests; but it never was done. It would have been a clumsy and unsatisfactory device, from a practical point of view; and, indeed, it would have been in plain conflict with the basic conception of equity that to impose the fetters of a trust on property, with the resulting creation of equitable interests in that property, there had to be specific subjects identifiable as the trust fund. An unadministered estate was incapable of satisfying this requirement. The assets as a whole were in the hands of the executor, his property; and, until administration was complete, no one was in a position to say what items of property would need to be realised for the purposes of that administration or of what the residue, when ascertained, would consist or what its value would be. . . .

Where, it is asked, is the beneficial interest in those assets during the period of administration? It is not, ex hypothesi, in the executor: where else can it be but in the residuary legatee? This dilemma is founded on a fallacy, for it assumes mistakenly that for all purposes and at every moment of time the law required the separate existence of two different kinds of estate or interest in property, the legal and the equitable.

There is no need to make this assumption. When the whole right of property is in a person, as it is in an executor, there is no need to distinguish between the legal and equitable interest in that property any more than there is for the property of a full beneficial owner. What matters is that the court will control the executor in the use of his rights over assets that come to him in that capacity; but it will do it by the enforcement of remedies which do not involve the admission or recognition of equitable rights of property in those assets. . . . Their Lordships regard it as clearly established that Mrs Coulson was not entitled to any beneficial interest in any property in Queensland at the date of her death. What she was entitled to in respect of her rights under her deceased husband's will was a chose in action, capable of being invoked for any purpose connected with the proper administration of his estate.[5]

3 Power to appropriate

A personal representative has a statutory power[6] to appropriate any part of the deceased's property in or towards satisfaction of a legacy or any other interest (eg a share of residue) in the deceased's estate.

Administration of Estates Act 1925

41. Powers of personal representative as to appropriation

(1) The personal representative may appropriate any part of the real or personal estate, including things in action, of the deceased in the actual condition or state of investment thereof at the time of appropriation in or towards satisfaction of any legacy bequeathed by the deceased, or of any interest or share in his property, whether settled or not, as to the personal representative may seem just and reasonable, according to the respective rights of the persons interested in the property of the deceased:
   Provided that—
   (i) an appropriation shall not be made under this section so as to affect prejudicially any specific devise or bequest;[7]
   (ii) an appropriation of property, whether or not being an investment authorised by law or by the will, if any, of the deceased for the investment of money subject to the trust, shall not (save as hereinafter mentioned) be made under this section except with the following consents—
      (a) when made for the benefit of a person absolutely and beneficially entitled in possession, the consent of that person;
      (b) when made in respect of any settled legacy share or interest, the consent of either the trustee thereof, if any (not being also the personal representative), or the person who may for the time being be entitled to the income: If the person whose consent is so required as aforesaid is an infant or is incapable, by reason of mental disorder within the meaning of (the Mental Health Act 1983)[8] of managing and administering his property and affairs, the consent shall be given on his behalf by his parents or parent, testamentary or other guardian, or receiver, or if, in the case of an infant, there is no such parent or guardian, by the court on the application of his next friend;
   (iii) no consent (save of such trustees as aforesaid) shall be required on behalf of a person who may come into existence after the time of appropriation, or who cannot be found or ascertained at that time;
   (iv) if no receiver is acting for a person suffering from mental disorder, then, if the appropriation is of an investment authorised by law or by the will, if any, of the

---

5. The beneficiary's chose in action is transmissible inter vivos or on death: *Re Leigh's WT* [1970] Ch 277, [1969] 3 All ER 432.
6. Save in relation to an appropriation of the matrimonial home on an intestacy where the surviving spouse of the intestate is entitled to demand that the personal representative exercises the power: see p 130 ante.
7. Eg the personal representatives cannot appropriate Blackacre to a pecuniary legatee if Blackacre has been specifically devised to someone else.
8. Substituted by Mental Health Act 1983, s 148, Sch 4 para 7.

deceased for the investment of money subject to the trust, no consent shall be required on behalf of the said person;

(v) if, independently of the personal representative, there is no trustee of a settled legacy share or interest, and no person of full age and capacity entitled to the income thereof, no consent shall be required to an appropriation in respect of such legacy share or interest, provided that the appropriation is of an investment authorised as aforesaid.

(2) Any property duly appropriated under the powers conferred by this section shall thereafter be treated as an authorised investment, and may be retained or dealt with accordingly.

(3) For the purposes of such appropriation, the personal representative may ascertain and fix the value of the respective parts of the real and personal estate and the liabilities of the deceased as he may think fit, and shall for that purpose employ a duly qualified valuer in any case where such employment may be necessary; and may make any conveyance (including an assent) which may be requisite for giving effect to the appropriation.

(4) An appropriation made pursuant to this section shall bind all persons interested in the property of the deceased whose consent is not hereby made requisite.

(5) The personal representative shall, in making the appropriation, have regard to the rights of any person who may thereafter come into existence, or who cannot be found or ascertained at the time of appropriation, and of any other person whose consent is not required by this section.

(6) This section does not prejudice any other power of appropriation conferred by law or by the will (if any) of the deceased, and takes effect with any extended powers conferred by the will (if any) of the deceased,[9] and where an appropriation is made under this section, in respect of a settled legacy, share or interest, the property appropriated shall remain subject to all trusts for sale and powers of leasing, disposition, and management or varying investments which would have been applicable thereto or to the legacy, share or interest in respect of which the appropriation is made, if no such appropriation had been made.

(7) If after any real estate[10] has been appropriated in purported exercise of the powers conferred by this section, the person to whom it was conveyed disposes of it or any interest therein, then, in favour of a purchaser, the appropriation shall be deemed to have been made in accordance with the requirements of this section and after all requisite consents, if any, had been given.

(8) In this section, a settled legacy, share or interest includes any legacy, share or interest to which a person is not absolutely entitled in possession at the date of the appropriation, also an annuity, and 'purchaser' means a purchaser for money or money's worth.

(9) This section applies whether the deceased died intestate or not, and whether before or after the commencement of this Act, and extends to property over which a testator exercises a general power of appointment, including the statutory power to dispose of entailed interests,[11] and authorises the setting apart of a fund to answer an annuity by means of the income of that fund or otherwise.

Re Collins [1975] 1 All ER 321, [1975] 1 WLR 309, Ch D; Pennycuick V-C

The intestate's spouse was exercising her right under the Intestates' Estates Act 1952, s 5, Sch 2 to demand the appropriation of the matrimonial home in part

---

9. A will often includes an express power of appropriation incorporating the statutory power but making it exerciseable without any consents, thereby avoiding the payment of ad valorem stamp duty on the value of the appropriated property: see *Jopling v IRC* [1940] 2 KB 282, [1940] 3 All ER 279 and FA 1985, s 84(4)(5).
10. Defined in AEA 1925, s 55(1)(xix) as including chattels real, ie leaseholds.
11. See LPA 1925, s 176.

satisfaction of her statutory legacy.[12] The question before the court was whether the house should be valued for that purpose at the date of death or the date when the personal representatives made the appropriation.

Held: The house should be valued at the date of the appropriation.

Pennycuick V-C: Leaving aside the statutory provisions as to the matrimonial home[13] there can be no doubt that where a personal representative exercises the statutory power of appropriation under section 41 of the Act of 1925 he must do so at the value of the property appropriated as at the date of appropriation: see as to this the note in Wolstenholme and Cherry (Conveyancing Statutes, 13th ed (1972), vol 5, p 74): 'The value of appropriated securities should be taken as at the date of appropriation.' And the case there cited, *Re Charteris* ([1917] 2 Ch 379), contained this statement by Swinfen Eady LJ, at p 386:

> 'Upon that proposition being communicated to the solicitors for the plaintiff they objected to the appropriation. They pointed out that their client, Colonel Richard Charteris, was entitled to have £230,000 in cash, or the value thereof, as at the date of the appropriation; that almost all the securities comprised in the list had dropped in value since February 21, 1915, the date of the death, and some of them considerably, and that if their client liked to invest in any of these securities he should do so on the basis that the value of the securities appropriated should be the value as at the date of appropriation, and not as at the date of the testatrix's death. In my opinion that contention was well founded; and upon that point being raised by the plaintiff's advisers the executors took the opinion of counsel with regard to the appropriation, and, having taken it, they sent a copy of it to the plaintiff's advisers. . . .'

The point is sometimes put by treating the appropriation as a notional sale of the appropriated assets to the beneficiary, the legacy to the beneficiary being applied in discharge of the purchase price on the sale. This is a rule of administration too well established to require further discussion.

In **Ballard v Marsden** [1880] 14 Ch D 374, Fry J considered the position of the beneficiary (a life tenant of a legacy of £1,000) once property had been appropriated to meet the legacy saying, at p 376:

A sum of East Indian Railway stock has been set apart by the executors of (the testator's) will to meet this legacy, and it is material to observe that before such setting apart Miss Harvey (the life tenant) could not have recovered her legacy without administration of the estate of the testator, but since such setting apart she could have gone against the Indian Railway stock as a trust fund without interfering with the general estate. Similarly, had the investment in the Indian Railway stock turned out badly, she could not after such appropriation have gone against the general estate to make good her loss, while, had the stock improved, she and not the estate would have had the benefit of the rise. The stock was a trust fund held by the two executors for the purpose of meeting Miss Harvey's legacy.[14]

---

12. See p 130 ante.
13. Ie those contained in Intestates' Estates Act 1952, s 5, Sch 2, see p 130 ante.
14. Similarly in the case of partial appropriation where the appropriated property only partially satisfies the beneficiary's entitlement; he only has to bring into the final reckoning the cash value of the appropriated property at the date of the appropriation, without giving credit for any subsequent appreciation in the appropriated property (or receiving any allowance for subsequent depreciation)—see *Re Marquess of Abergavenny's Estate Act Trusts* [1981] 2 All ER 643, [1981] 1 WLR 843: 'some such possibility of good or ill fortune is inherent in the very nature of payments made under a duty or power on successive occasions up to an aggregate limit; per Goulding J at p 646.

4   Method of distribution

The personal representative can transfer assets to the beneficiaries by any means available for the transfer of property inter vivos.[15] Alternatively he can use an assent, described by Pennycuick J in *Re King's Will Trusts*[16] as 'the instrument or act whereby a personal representative effectuates a testamentary disposition by transferring the subject matter of the disposition to the persons entitled to it.'

(a) Assent of pure personalty

This is provided for at common law. No writing is required; all that is necessary is an indication by the executor either expressly or by implication that he does not need the property concerned for administration purposes and that the property may pass under the will. It activates the gift of the property to the beneficiary even if further documentation is necessary to transfer the actual title to the property concerned.[17]

In **Barnard v Pumfrett** (1841) 5 My & Cr 63, the executor wrote to one of the legatees, referring to the testator's death and saying:

> 'By his last will and testament I perceive you are entitled to a legacy of £500, to be paid to you on your attaining the age of twenty-five years; the same legacy of £500 to each of your brothers on attaining the same age, and a similar sum to your sister on her arriving at twenty-one. The above legacies I assure you, my dear Philip, shall be most cheerfully paid to you all, in just compliance with your late dear uncle's bequests. . . .
>
> I shall, as soon as the legal time arrives for payment, give you a line, so that you may please yourself in what way you would like best to receive it.'

The executor subsequently refused to pay the legacies on the grounds of insufficiency of assets, but Lord Cottenham LC held that the words in the letter amounted to an assent, an admission that the assets were sufficient for the legacies to be paid and the executor would be personally liable to pay them.[18]

In **Wise v Whitburn** [1924] 1 Ch 460, the question arose as to whether the executors had assented in their own favour as trustees of a leasehold house left to them on trust to permit the widow to occupy it for her life and after her death to hold it on other trusts.[19] Finding on the evidence that they had, Eve J said at p 467:

The question of assent is one, no doubt, mainly of fact. It is not suggested that in order to prove assent it is necessary, to show affirmatively that the executors, either verbally or in writing, formally expressed assent; it is conceded that assent may be implied from conduct on their part, and the plaintiffs rely upon conduct which they say is unequivocal

---

15. See Ch 2 ante.

16. [1964] Ch 542 at 547, [1964] 1 All ER 833 at 835. See p 396 post.

17. Eg signing the appropriate stock transfer forms, see Companies Act 1985, ss 182–183, p 20 ante.

18. See also *Camden v Turner* (1719) (cited in *Hawkes v Saunders* (1782) 1 Cowp 289, 293) where King CJ gave as an example of an assent an executor telling the legatee that the legacy was ready for him 'whenever he would call for it'.

19. A strict settlement, but as it was created before 1926(i) the legal estate could nevertheless be held by the trustees (albeit they would have to give effect to the tenant for life's wish to exercise his powers under the Settled Land Act 1882), (ii) a written form of assent was not necessary; cf now AEA 1925, s 36(4) p 396 post.

and unambiguous as establishing the assent. The conduct is of this character. The testator left a large estate, and appointed as his executors his son and daughter; the son, as was to be supposed, took the active share in the administration, and has told us that his one desire was to get the estate clear and settled up as quickly as he could. Having regard to the magnitude of the estate no time was lost in obtaining probate. The death was in November (1911) and probate was granted in January. No unnecessary time was expended in payment of the debts, which were very small, or in paying or providing for the pecuniary and other legacies, some of them of large amount. Everything was done with as much expedition as circumstances and the magnitude of the estate, which consisted both of realty and personalty, permitted, and the residuary account was passed in June, 1913. Nor was this all. Before the residuary account was finally passed and the duty paid it became necessary to provide for the duty on the specific bequest to which this action relates, and in August, 1912, less than a year after the testator's death, accounts were delivered and the duty paid in respect of the widow's succession and the settlement created by the bequest. All these are acts indicative of the promptness with which this administration was conducted and ultimately concluded, so far as the executors were concerned. Nor do matters rest there. The widow was left in occupation of the house. As was said in the course of the argument, no one would have expected to see her turned out for a reasonable time after the testator's death, but she was left in possession for the whole of the remainder of her life, a period of a little over ten years, and her possession was throughout upon the terms imposed upon her as tenant for life by the bequest. She paid the ground rent, rates and outgoings, and observed the covenants of the lease—covenants involving in that period of ten years the expenditure on her part of considerable sums of money. Upon the facts I have already stated I think the conclusion is almost irresistible that the executors had assented to the bequest.'

(b) Assent of land

An assent of realty (including leasehold land) made after 1925 has to comply with the statutory formalities contained in the Administration of Estates Act 1925 if a legal estate is to pass, even where the legal estate is already vested in the assentee in some other capacity, eg because the beneficiary or trustee concerned is also the personal representative.

Administration of Estates Act 1925

36. Effect of assent or conveyance by personal representative

(1) A personal representative may assent to the vesting, in any person who (whether by devise, bequest, devolution, appropriation or otherwise) may be entitled thereto, either beneficially or as a trustee or personal representative, of any estate or interest in real estate[20] to which the testator or intestate was entitled or over which he exercised a general power of appointment by his will, including the statutory power to dispose of entailed interests,[1] and which devolved[2] upon the personal representative.

(2) The assent shall operate to vest in that person the estate or interest to which the assent relates, and, unless a contrary intention appears, the assent shall relate back to the death of the deceased.

---

20. AEA 1925, s 55(1)(xix) defines real estate as 'including chattels real (ie leaseholds) which by virtue of Part I of this Act devolves on the personal representatives of a deceased person.'
1. See LPA 1925, s 176.
2. See *Re Stirrup's Contract* [1961] 1 All ER 805, [1961] 1 WLR 449 where the land had not devolved on the personal representative at the deceased's death because the deceased had not completed his contract to buy it. Fortunately for the personal representative the 'assent' he subsequently signed was under seal which enabled Wilberforce J to treat it as an effective conveyance under LPA 1925, s 52(1).

(3) The statutory covenants[3] implied by a person being expressed to convey as personal representative, may be implied in an assent in like manner as in a conveyance by deed.
(4) An assent to the vesting of a legal estate shall be in writing, signed by the personal representative, and shall name the person in whose favour it is given and shall operate to vest in that person the legal estate to which it relates; and an assent not in writing or not in favour of a named person shall not be effectual to pass a legal estate.

Law of Property Act 1925

206. Forms of instruments and examples of abstracts

Instruments in the form of and using the expressions in the forms given in the Fifth Schedule to this Act or in the like form or using expressions to the like effect, shall in regard to form and expression be sufficient.

SCHEDULE 5

Form No 8

ASSENT[4] BY PERSONAL REPRESENTATIVE IN FAVOUR OF A PERSON ABSOLUTELY ENTITLED FREE FROM INCUMBRANCES

> I, AB, of [etc] as the personal representative of XY, late of [etc] deceased, do this   day of   19   hereby As Personal Representative, assent to the vesting in CD of [etc] of [All that farm etc] or [All that property described in the Schedule hereto] for all the estate or interest of the said XY at the time of his death [or for an estate in fee simple][5]
> As witness etc.[6]

Re King's Will Trusts [1964] Ch 542, [1964] 1 All ER 833, Ch D; Pennycuick J

By her will the testatrix (T) appointed A and B to be her executors and specifically devised certain realty to them to be held on certain trusts. After they had obtained probate, A died. B appointed C as a trustee of the will jointly with himself and B then died. B's executor, X, became an executor by chain of representation[7] of T's estate. C appointed D to be a trustee of T's will jointly with himself and C then died. No written assent was ever made by A, B or X to the vesting of the legal estate in the realty in the trustees.
Held: The legal estate remained in T's estate, vested in X as executor by representation of T.

Pennycuick J: (Having read the Administration of Estates Act 1925, s 36) Subsection (4) presents no difficulty where the person entitled to the estate or interest is someone other than the personal representative himself. It has been suggested that where the

---

3. See LPA 1925, ss 76–77.
4. Unregistered title. For registered title see LRA 1925, s 41, Land Registration Rules 1925, SR & O 1925 No 1093, r 170 and the Schedule, Form 56.
5. An acknowledgement for production is usually added in view of AEA 1925, s 36(5) and (6) p 397 post.
6. An assent is usually under hand, not under seal; a 50p deed stamp is thereby avoided.
7. See p 292 ante.

personal representative is also entitled in some other capacity, for example as trustee of the will, as beneficiary or otherwise, to the estate or interest he may come to hold the estate or interest in that other capacity without any written assent.

Counsel who appeared for the plaintiff, has mentioned but not stressed this contention, and, in my judgment, the contention is not well-founded. It is well recognised by judicial decision that a personal representative may make a written assent in favour of himself in some other capacity; see *Re Yerburgh* ([1928] WN 208) where Romer J said: 'At the moment when that event happened they ought to make a vesting assent under s 36, vesting the property in themselves as trustees.' Such cases are of every day occurrence in conveyancing practice. The first sentence of subs (4) accordingly contemplates that for this purpose a person may by assent vest in himself in another capacity, and such vesting, of course, necessarily implies that he is divesting himself of the estate in his original capacity. It seems to me impossible to regard the same operation as lying outside the negative provision contained in the second sentence of the subsection. To do so involves making a distinction between the operation of divesting and vesting the legal estate and that of passing the legal estate. I do not think that this highly artificial distinction is legitimate. On the contrary, the second sentence appears to me to be intended as an exact counterpart to the first.[8]

In **Re Edwards Will Trusts** [1982] Ch 30, [1981] 2 All ER 941, the problem exposed by *Re King's Will Trusts*, ante, was avoided by resorting to an assent of the equitable estate in the realty by conduct. Buckley LJ said at p 949:

The argument presented by counsel for the defendant has been that, since Mr Edwards (the husband) as administrator of his wife's estate never made any written assent in respect of the property or any part of it in his own favour as the sole beneficiary entitled to it, the legal estate was at his death vested in him as such administrator and so did not pass to his executors but remains an unadministered asset of Mrs Edwards' estate. He relied on *Re King's Will Trusts* [1964] 1 All ER 833, [1964] Ch 542. I proceed on the basis that this is correct. It does not follow that the equitable beneficial interest in the property did not vest in Mr Edwards in his lifetime so as to form part of his estate at his death: see *Re Hodge* [1940] Ch 260 at 264. Mr Edwards enjoyed the beneficial occupation of the property for nearly twenty years after Mrs Edwards' death. Nothing in the evidence suggests that during the greater part of that period any liabilities of Mrs Edwards's estate remained outstanding. . . . An assent to the vesting of an equitable interest need not be in writing. It may be inferred from conduct. In my judgment there are ample grounds for inferring that Mr Edwards assented in his lifetime to the vesting in himself of the full beneficial interest in the property. If so, that beneficial interest passed to his executors on his death and became subject to the trusts of his will. For these reasons I am of the opinion that the property is subject to the trusts of Mr Edwards' will.

(c) Protection of a purchaser

Administration of Estates Act 1925

36. Effect of assent or conveyance by personal representative

(5) Any person in whose favour an assent or conveyance of a legal estate is made by a personal representative may require that notice of the assent or conveyance be written or endorsed on or permanently annexed to the probate or letters of administration, at the

---

8. A much criticised decision, not least for its practical inconvenience for although on the facts of the case there was an executor by chain of representation to complete the winding up of the estate and make an effective assent or exercise his executor's power of sale, had this not been the case (eg because the last proving executor had died intestate,) a *de bonis non* grant would have been necessary. See Ryder 'Re King's Will Trusts: A Reassessment' (1976) 29 CLP 60; Walker (1964) 80 LQR 328; Garner 'Assents today' (1964) 28 Conv 298.

cost of the estate of the deceased, and that the probate or letters of administration be produced, at the like cost, to prove that the notice has been placed thereon or annexed thereto.

(6) A statement in writing by a personal representative that he has not given or made an assent or conveyance in respect of a legal estate, shall, in favour of a purchaser, but without prejudice to any previous disposition made in favour of another purchaser deriving title mediately or immediately under the personal representative, be sufficient evidence that an assent or conveyance has not been given or made in respect of the legal estate to which the statement relates, unless notice of a previous assent or conveyance affecting that estate has been placed on or annexed to the probate or administration.[9]

A conveyance by a personal representative of a legal estate to a purchaser accepted on the faith of such a statement shall (without prejudice as aforesaid and unless notice of a previous assent or conveyance affecting that estate has been placed on or annexed to the probate or administration) operate to transfer or create the legal estate expressed to be conveyed in like manner as if no previous assent or conveyance had been made by the personal representative.

A personal representative making a false statement, in regard to any such matter, shall be liable in like manner as if the statement had been contained in a statutory declaration.

(7) An assent or conveyance by a personal representative in respect of a legal estate shall, in favour of a purchaser, unless notice of a previous assent or conveyance affecting that legal estate has been placed on or annexed to the probate or administration, be taken as sufficient evidence that the person in whose favour the assent or conveyance is given or made is the person entitled to have the legal estate conveyed to him, and upon the proper trusts, if any, but shall not otherwise prejudicially affect the claim of any person rightfully entitled to the estate vested or conveyed or any charge thereon.

(9) An assent or conveyance given or made by a personal representative shall not, except in favour of a purchaser of a legal estate, prejudice the right of the personal representative or any other person to recover the estate or interest to which the assent or conveyance relates, or to be indemnified out of such estate or interest against any duties, debt, or liability to which such estate or interest would have been subject if there had not been any assent or conveyance.

(10) A personal representative may,[10] as a condition of giving an assent or making a conveyance, require security for the discharge of any such duties, debt, or liability, but shall not be entitled to postpone the giving of an assent merely by reason of the subsistence of any such duties, debt or liability if reasonable arrangements have been made for discharging the same; and an assent may be given subject to any legal estate or charge by way of legal mortgage.

(11) This section shall not operate to impose any stamp duty in respect of an assent,[11] and in this section 'purchaser' means a purchaser for money or money's worth.

Re Duce and Boots Cash Chemists (Southern) Ltd's Contract [1937] Ch 642, [1937] 3 All ER 788, Ch D; Bennett J

The testator had left his realty to his son as his executor and trustee, on trusts which created a settlement governed by the Settled Land Act 1925 of which his daughter would be the tenant for life. The son should therefore have signed a

---

9. Note the subsection therefore only protects a purchaser from a previous assent, not from a previous sale of the same property, nor does it protect an assentee from a previous assent should the personal representative by accident or design attempt to transfer the same property again.

10. The word 'may' should be noted; a personal representative cannot be compelled to make such an assent, if he needs to sell the property for the purpose of administration: *Williams v Holland* [1965] 2 All ER 157, [1965] 1 WLR 739.

11. See *Kemp v IRC* [1905] 1 KB 581; cf *GHR Company Ltd v IRC* [1943] KB 303, [1943] 1 All ER 424.

vesting assent in her favour[12] but he in fact assented in his own favour and subsequently contracted to sell the property as beneficial owner. When contracts had been exchanged the purchaser's solicitor received the abstract of title. Normally this would not have revealed the true situation, a purchaser not being entitled to call for a copy of a will, only for an abstract of the assent, but the assent as abstracted by the son's solicitors quite unnecessarily recited details from the will which made it apparent that the son was not the beneficial owner of the property. The purchaser claimed the title was defective. The son argued that the purchaser was protected by the Administration of Estates Act 1925, s 36(7) (ante).

Held: A proper investigation of title having revealed the defect, s 36(7) did not protect the purchaser who was entitled to reject the title offered.

Bennett J: The fact is that the proper interpretation of the words depends upon the context in which they are placed, and I think one must find some context of a compelling kind before one can decide that the word 'sufficient' has the same meaning as 'conclusive'. Now I can find no context in the Administration of Estates Act, 1925, which affords a foundation for a decision that there ought to be placed upon the word 'sufficient' in sect 36(7) a meaning which it does not usually bear, still less for a decision that it has the same meaning as 'conclusive'.

In my judgment, the meaning and effect of sect 36(7) are that a purchaser, when investigating title, may safely accept a vesting assent as evidence that the person in whose favour it has been made was the person entitled to have the legal estate conveyed to him, unless and until, upon a proper investigation by a purchaser of his vendor's title, facts come to the purchaser's knowledge which indicate the contrary. When that happens, in my judgment, the vesting assent cannot be and ought not to be accepted as sufficient evidence of something which the purchaser has reason to believe is contrary to the fact, still less so when, as in the present case, he knows it to be contrary to the fact.[13]

5 Expenses

Unless provided otherwise by the testator, any expense incurred in the upkeep and preservation of any property specifically devised or bequeathed must be borne by the beneficiary concerned. The personal representative's expenses incurred in relation to other assets, however, are regarded as part of the administration expenses and paid out of the estate in accordance with the statutory order contained in the Administration of Estates Act 1925, s 34(3) First Schedule Part II.[14]

In **Re Pearce** [1909] 1 Ch 819, the testator had specifically bequeathed all his furniture and effects, horses, carriages, cars, yachts and jewellery to his wife absolutely (the residuary estate being left elsewhere). His personal representative spent a considerable amount of money in paying staff to look after these items. Holding that this expenditure should fall on the specific legatee, Eve J said at p 821:

The question which I have to decide is whether the moneys which have been expended ought to come out of the general estate or ought to be borne by the specific legatee. Now

---

12. SLA 1925, ss 6, 8.
13. The draftsman of an assent should therefore take care to avoid unnecessary recitals; had the son's solicitor followed the usual form of assent (see p 396 ante) the purchaser would have been protected by s 36(7).
14. See p 340 ante.

it seems to be settled law that when an executor gives his assent to a specific legacy the assent relates back to the death of the testator, and the specific legatee is entitled to the profits accrued due from the time of the testator's death. That being so, it seems to me to be right and fair that the specific legatee should be charged with the costs of the upkeep, care, and preservation of the specific legacy from the time of the death until the executor's assent, and I shall make a declaration to that effect, and direct an inquiry into what expenses were properly incurred in and for such upkeep, care, and preservation.[15]

6   Passing the residuary accounts

The final act in the administration of the estate is usually the preparation of the estate accounts showing how the estate has been administered and the balance due to the residuary beneficiaries.[16] As Rowlatt J said in *Re Claremont* [1923] 2 KB 718 at p 721: 'When an executor carries in the residuary account, it seems to me, looking at the form of it and at its purpose, that prima facie he must be taken to be declaring that he has brought the administration to an end.'

This somewhat unstructured end to the winding up of an estate can be compared with the relatively tightly drawn provisions of the United States Uniform Probate Code.

Uniform Probate Code (USA)

3-1003.   Closing Estates; By Sworn Statement of Personal Representative
(a) Unless prohibited by order of the Court and except for estates being administered in supervised administration proceedings, a personal representative may close an estate by filing with the court no earlier than 6 months after the date of original appointment of a general personal representative for the estate, a verified statement stating that he, or a prior personal representative whom he has succeeded, has or have:
    (1) published notice to creditors as provided by Section 3-801 and that the first publication occurred more than 6 months prior to the date of the statement;
    (2) fully administered the estate of the decedent by making payment, settlement or other disposition of all claims which were presented, expenses of administration and estate, inheritance and other death taxes, except as specified in the statement, and that the assets of the estate have been distributed to the persons entitled. If any claims remain undischarged the statement shall state whether the personal representative has distributed the estate subject to possible liability with the agreement of the distributees or it shall state in detail other arrangements which have been made to accommodate outstanding liabilities; and
    (3) sent a copy thereof to all distributees of the estate and to all creditors or other claimants of whom he is aware whose claims are neither paid nor barred and has furnished a full account in writing of his administration to the distributees whose interests are affected thereby.
(b) If no proceedings involving the personal representative are pending in the Court one year after the closing statement is filed, the appointment of the personal representative terminates.

---

15. See also *Re Rooke* [1933] Ch 970, *Re Scott* [1915] 1 Ch 592; cf *Re Collins ST* [1971] 1 All ER 283, [1971] 1 WLR 37 where the testator gave X 'such articles of furniture and personal effects as X shall select.' Brightman J held that the title of the beneficiary in such a case would stem from his selection; any profit earned by the assets concerned before he made his choice would belong to the residue, as therefore would any pre-selection expenses for storing the assets etc.
16. For an example of an estate account, see p 407 post.

7 Personal representative or trustee?

The will may contain trusts which survive the completion of the administration[17] and it is common in such a case for the testator to appoint his personal representatives to be the trustees as well.[18] It can be very important to know when such a personal representative-trustee is acting in his capacity as trustee as opposed to personal representative, eg because their duties are different;[19] different limitation periods apply;[20] their authority over pure personalty differs.[1] If the personal representative has expressly assented in his own favour as trustee, the transition has clearly occurred,[2] indeed in so far as the property is land it would seem that an express assent complying with AEA 1925, s 36(4) is essential if the legal estate is to be held in the new capacity.[3] Otherwise it is a matter of examining all the evidence to decide whether an assent can be inferred from the conduct of the personal representatives and all the circumstances of the case.[4]

Attenborough v Solomon [1913] AC 76, HL; Viscount Haldane LC, Lords Atkinson and Shaw of Dunfermline

The testator appointed A and B to be his executors and trustees, and after certain pecuniary legacies, left his residuary estate (including some silver plate) to them to be held on certain trusts. Within a year of the death, A and B had paid all the debts and legacies and prepared the estate accounts showing the balance that was left to be held on the residuary trusts. Fourteen years after the testator's death A, without B's knowledge, fraudulently pawned the silver plate and misappropriated the proceeds. If A and B were still holding the silver plate in their capacity as executors when A pawned it, the pawnbroker would have a good title because A as a personal representative, would have the authority to make a valid pledge of pure personalty in the estate.[5] If A and B were holding the plate in their capacity as trustees, the pawnbroker would have no title to the silver plate, A having no authority to make the pledge without his co-trustee joining in.

Held: By the date of the pledge the executors held the plate as trustees; A accordingly had no power to pledge the plate on his own and the existing trustees were entitled to recover it.

Haldane LC: The position of an executor is a peculiar one. He is appointed by the will, but then, by virtue of his office, by the operation of law and not under the bequest in the will, he takes a title to the personal property of the testator, which vests him with the *plenum dominium* over the testator's chattels. He takes that, I say, by virtue of his office. The will becomes operative so far as its dispositions of personalty are concerned only if and when the executor assents to those dispositions. It is true that by virtue of his office he

---

17. Such trusts may also arise under the intestacy rules, eg where the spouse has a life interest in half the residuary estate; see eg *Re Yerburgh* p 62 post.
18. See eg specimen will at p 62 ante.
19. See *Re Hayes' WT* [1971] 2 All ER 341, [1971] 1 WLR 758.
20. See p 413 post. See eg *Phillipo v Munnings* (1837) 2 My & Cr 309.
1. See p 281 ante.
2. See eg *Clegg v Rowland* (1866) LR 3 Eq 368, 373.
3. *Re King's Will Trust*, p 396 ante.
4. Per Kekewich J in *Re Timmis* [1902] 1 Ch 176, 182: 'It is extremely difficult to draw the line, even when the facts are fully ascertained.'
5. See p 281 ante.

has a general power to sell or pledge for the estate. He is executor and he remains executor for an indefinite time. Authorities were cited to us by (Counsel) to the effect that an executor can sell at a period long after the death of the testator, and that where it is a question of conveyancing, as for instance in the case of the sale of leaseholds by the executor, the purchaser is not entitled to make requisitions as to whether debts remain unpaid, because the executor's office remains intact and he may exercise his functions at any time. That is true as a general principle, and I have no comment to make upon it except that it is qualified by another principle, which is this: The office of executor remains, with its powers attached, but the property which he had originally in the chattels that devolved upon him, and over which these powers extended, does not necessarily remain. So soon as he has assented, and this he may do informally and the assent may be inferred from his conduct, the dispositions of the will become operative, and then the beneficiaries have vested in them the property in those chattels. The transfer is made not by the mere force of the assent of the executor, but by virtue of the dispositions of the will which have become operative because of this assent.

Now, my Lords, in view of the residuary account passed as it was and in the form it was, in view of the evidence of (B), and in view of the fourteen years which had passed since the testator died before the time when (A) made the pledge to the appellants in 1892, I am of opinion that the true inference to be drawn from the facts is that the executors considered that they had done all that was due from them as executors by 1879, and were content when the residuary account was passed that the dispositions of the will should take effect. That is the inference I draw from the form of the residuary account; and the inference is strengthened when I consider the lapse of time since then, and that in the interval nothing was done by them purporting to be an exercise of power as executors. My Lords, if this be so, this appeal must be disposed of on the footing that in point of fact the executors assented at a very early date to the dispositions of the will taking effect. It follows that under these dispositions the residuary estate, including the chattels in question, became vested in the trustees as trustees. That they were the same persons as the executors does not affect the point, or in my opinion present the least obstacle to the inference. But if that was so, then the title to the silver plate of (A) as executor had ceased to exist before he made the pledge of 1892.[6]

In **Re Cockburn's Will Trusts** [1957] Ch 438, [1957] 2 All ER 522, it was suggested by Danckwerts J that the transition from personal representative to trustee would occur automatically once the administration was complete, without the need for an assent.[7] He said at p 524:

The questions which I am asked to decide are whether the administrators of the estate, having cleared the estate and completed the administration in the ordinary way, are in a position, the testator having been dead for about ten years, to appoint new trustees of the will, and whether those new trustees, when so appointed by the administrators, will be able to exercise the powers which are conferred by the will on the trustees for the time being of the will. I feel no doubt about the matter at all. Whether persons are executors or administrators, once they have completed the administration in due course, they become trustees holding for the beneficiaries, either on an intestacy or under the terms of the will, and are bound to carry out the duties of trustees, although in the case of administrators they cannot be compelled to go on indefinitely acting as trustees and are entitled to appoint new trustees in their place and thus clear themselves from duties which were not expressly conferred on them under the terms of the testator's will and which they were not bound to accept.

It seems to me that, if the administrators do not appoint the new trustees to proceed to execute the trusts of the will they will become trustees in the full sense. Further, it seems to me that they have the power, conferred by s 36 of the Trustee Act, 1925, to appoint

---

6. See also *Re Timmis* [1902] 1 Ch 176.
7. On this argument see in particular Ryder 'Re King's Will Trusts: A Reassessment' (1976) 29 CLP 60.

new trustees of the will to act in their place. That seems to me to have been clearly established by the decision of Sargant J in *Re Ponder*.[8]

In **Re Ponder** [1921] 2 Ch 59, the deceased, who died intestate in 1919, left a widow and two infant children. The widow obtained letters of administration, realised the assets, paid all the liabilities and invested each child's share of the personalty in her name. Sargant J held that she no longer held these assets as administratrix but as trustee which gave him jurisdiction to appoint the Public Trustee as a trustee jointly with her, saying at p 61:

That the Court may appoint a new trustee to act with an executor where all the debts and the expenses of the estate have been paid, and the estate has been cleared, and the executor is left merely a trustee for the residuary legatees, seems quite clear. That is so, because when the estate has been wound up and the residue ascertained, the executor has ceased to be an executor and has become a trustee for the persons entitled to the residue. And I cannot see why the same reasoning should not apply to the case of the administratrix before me.[9]

In **Re Yerburgh** (1928) WN 208, by contrast, the deceased died intestate in 1926, leaving a widow and two infant children. His administrators cleared the estate of liabilities and applied to the court for directions as to whether they should now appoint themselves as trustees of the residuary estate, and as to how the land comprised in the residuary estate should be held by them. Romer J said at p 208, that his view:

was that s 33 of the Administration of Estates Act had imposed certain duties on legal personal representatives under which they became trustees when the estate had been fully administered. They ceased to be legal personal representatives and became trustees at a particular date. Sect 33 did not draw a distinction between trusts arising before and trusts arising after the commencement of the Act. In those circumstances the old law applied and determined the time when the applicants ceased to be legal personal representatives and became trustees for sale. At the moment when that event happened they ought to make a vesting assent under s 36 vesting the property in themselves as trustees.[10]

8 Infant beneficiaries

The existence of infant beneficiaries may prolong the administration of the estate as unless the will expressly authorises payment to an infant beneficiary[11] or directs that the receipt of his parent or guardian shall be a good discharge,

---

8. Post. See also *Eaton v Daines* [1894] WN 32, *Re Pitt* (1928) 44 TLR 371.
9. This decision has been criticised, see eg *Harvell v Foster* [1954] 2 QB 367, 379, 382, [1954] 2 All ER 736, 743, 745 and p 404 post and as Ryder points out in (1976) 29 CLP 60 at p 64, strictly speaking pre-1926 the intestacy rules applicable to personalty did not actually declare any trusts for the next of kin in any case. Cf the statutory trusts under AEA 1925, s 33 which arose in *Re Yerburgh* post.
10. Ryder argues in (1976) 29 CLP 60 at p 67 that this last sentence must be read in the light of the one immediately preceding it, that the reference to the 'old law' must mean the law as laid down in *Re Ponder* ante and therefore that Romer J was not suggesting that a written assent was essential under s 36 to effect the transition of the legal estate, merely evidentially desirable. In the light of the inconclusive nature of the authorities, personal representative-trustees would be well advised always to make a written assent in their own favour (as trustees) and relating to all the trust property as soon as the winding up of the estate is complete.
11. See eg *Re Somech* [1957] Ch 165, [1956] 3 All ER 523 at 524.

the personal representatives cannot obtain a binding receipt either from the infant himself or from his parent or guardian on his behalf.[12] There is a statutory power for personal representatives to appoint trustees to hold the property concerned on trust for the infant, and thereby obtain their own discharge, but this is only available where the infant is absolutely entitled to the property in question.

Administration of Estates Act 1925

42.   Power to appoint trustees of infants' property

(1) Where an infant is absolutely entitled under the will or on the intestacy of a person dying before or after the commencement of this Act (in this subsection called 'the deceased') to a devise or legacy, or to the residue of the estate of the deceased, or any share therein, and such devise, legacy, residue or share is not under the will, if any, of the deceased, devised or bequeathed to trustees for the infant, the personal representatives of the deceased may appoint a trust corporation of two or more individuals not exceeding four (whether or not including the personal representatives) or one or more of the personal representatives), to be the trustee or trustees of such devise, legacy, residue or share for the infant, and to be trustees of any land devised or any land being or forming part of such residue or share for the purposes of the Settled Land Act 1925 and of the statutory provisions relating to the management of land during a minority, and may execute or do any assurance or thing requisite for vesting such devise, legacy, residue or share in the trustee or trustees so appointed.

On such appointment the personal representatives, as such, shall be discharged from all further liability in respect of such devise, legacy, residue, or share, and the same may be retained in its existing condition or state of investment, or may be converted into money, and such money may be invested in any authorised investment.

Harvell v Foster [1954] 2 QB 367, [1954] 2 All ER 736, CA; Evershed MR, Jenkins and Hodson LJJ

The testator left all his estate to his daughter whom he appointed as his sole executrix. She was under age when he died so administration with the will annexed was granted to her husband for her minority.[13] He and two solicitors gave an administration bond[14] that the husband would 'well and truly administer the estate' and deliver proper accounts of his administration. The solicitors acting for the husband got in the assets, paid all the debts and liabilities and handed over the residue to the husband who subsequently absconded with most of it. When the daughter came of age, she claimed the balance from the solicitors as sureties under the bond. They argued that once the residue was in the husband's hands, his character changed from administrator to trustee and the sureties' obligation under the bond ended.

Held: The administrator not having availed himself of the Administration of Estates Act 1925, s 42, he continued to hold the residue as personal representative and the sureties were therefore liable under their bond.

---

12. See eg *Cooper v Thornton* (1790) 3 Bro CC 96. Cf the United States Uniform Probate Code whereby payment can be made to the infant himself, if married, otherwise to the infant's parent or guardian or to a federally insured financial institution savings account in the infant's name and with notice to the infant of the deposit (s 5–103).
13. An example of a grant *durante minore aetate*, see p 288 ante.
14. See p 309 n 17 ante.

Evershed MR: The novel point raised in *Re Ponder*[15] ([1921] 2 Ch 59) and decided by Sargant J was that one appointed administrator of an intestate's estate could in due course of time assume the character and functions of a trustee in the same way as one appointed by will executor and trustee (as was the case in *Eaton v Daines* ([1894] WN 32) so as to be able to invoke the statutory powers of appointing new or additional trustees. *Re Ponder* seems to have been since followed on one occasion—in *Re Pitt* ((1928) 44 TLR 371). Whether or not it was rightly decided on its own facts it is unnecessary for us to determine. But we are unable to accept the view, which Sargant J's language read without qualification would seem to support, that because a personal representative who has cleared the estate becomes a trustee of the net residue for the persons beneficially interested, the clearing of the estate necessarily and automatically discharges him from his obligations as personal representative and in particular from the obligation of any bond he may have entered into for the due administration of the estate. We would add that, in our view, the duty of an administrator as such must at least extend to paying the funeral and testamentary expenses and debts and legacies (if any) and where, as here, immediate distribution is impossible owing to the infancy of the person beneficially entitled, retaining the net residue in trust for the infant. At least until the administrator can show that he has done this, it cannot, in our judgment, be said of him that he has duly administered the estate according to law. The husband in the present case did not retain the net residue in trust for the infant plaintiff, but on the contrary, converted the greater part of it (ie, all except the £300) to his own use, and moreover, sought in his letter of Dec 30, 1949, to justify his conduct by claims of right which, as he has not condescended to come forward and prove them, cannot now be regarded, but which were wholly inconsistent with any recognition or acknowledgment on his part that the assets in his hands represented a clear residue held by him in trust for the plaintiff. In any event, as counsel for the plaintiff contended, the Administration of Estates Act, 1925, s 42, to which we have already referred, now makes provision for the case of an infant, who is absolutely entitled to a legacy or residue or some share therein under a will or intestacy, there being (in the case of a will) no appointment of trustees on the infant's behalf; and enables the personal representative to appoint a trust corporation or two or more individuals as trustees for such infant and, on such appointment and vesting of the property in the trustees so appointed, to be discharged from further liability in respect thereof. That provision (which incidentally meets the difficulty pointed out by Lord Goddard CJ[16] as to the protracted liability of bondsmen in the case of a very young infant beneficiary) seems to us to carry a necessary implication to the effect that, until a personal representative having in his hands assets to which an infant is absolutely entitled either avails himself of the prescribed method of obtaining his discharge from further liability (scilicet, as personal representative) in respect of those assets, or accounts for and pays them over to the infant on his or her attaining the age of twenty-one years, he remains liable for them in his capacity as personal representative. This, in our judgment, makes it still more difficult and, indeed, impossible, for the defendants to assert that the husband's obligations as administrator, and consequently their own liability under the bond, ceased automatically on his receiving the net residue, although the procedure laid down by s 42 for relieving the husband from further liability as administrator was not complied with.

QUESTIONS

1. X has been left a legacy of £10,000 under the will of T. He asks T's executors to transfer to him T's shares in ABC Ltd to the value of £10,000 in satisfaction of his legacy. What factors should the executors bear in mind in considering his

---

15. See p 403 ante.
16. The first instance judge: [1954] 1 QB 591, [1954] 1 All ER 851.

request? Would it make any difference if (i) the value of the shares had depreciated since T's death or (ii) the legacy had been left to X for life and then to Y absolutely?

2. D died leaving a will appointing his wife W as his executrix and leaving all his property to her. His estate included a freehold house, Greenacre, in which she continued to live for 15 years after his death. No assent was ever made in relation to this house and W has now died intestate. Advise P who wishes to buy the house. Would it make any difference if W had died testate?

3. 'In this connection (the transition from personal representative to trustee), two questions arise: (a) do the authorities, apart from *Re King's Will Trusts*, indicate that a change of capacity may occur without an assent or conveyance and (b) is *Re King's Will Trusts* really an authority for the proposition that such a change is impossible?' Read Ryder 'Re King's Will Trusts: A Reassessment' (1976) 29 CLP 60 (from which the quotation is taken, at p 63) for his answer to both questions.

4. In the United States, the Uniform Probate Code requires a personal representative within 30 days of obtaining his grant to notify beneficiaries of his appointment and of the recipient's interest in the estate (s 3-705). See also other references to the Uniform Probate Code in this chapter. Would it be desirable to have similar legislation in this country?

Specimen estate account[17]

Executors of Dai Tup deceased

Estate Account

Receipts	£	Payments	£	£
		Funeral expenses: Messrs Morbid & Moribund		415.00
Assets in the estate at probate value		Creditors:		
Personal chattels	300.00	Wales Gas—gas account	49.50	
Freehold property: 21 Sunny St, Splott	25,000.00	British Telecom—telephone account	53.25	102.75
Principality Building Society Share Account	6,435.50	Administration expenses:		
Pearl Assurance Co: Proceeds life policy	10,000.00	Messrs. Tup & Griffiths, costs and		
Barclays Bank Splott: Current account	225.50	disbursements as statement		790.00
Joe Bloggs Ltd: Salary to date of death	451.50	To Miss S Siren:		
Inland Revenue: Income tax repayment	150.25	Personal chattels as valued for probate	300.00	
Death Grant—DHSS	30.00	21 Sunny St, Splott as valued for probate	25,000.00	
Income of administration period		Income of administration period	370.25	25,670.25
Principality Building Society interest to		To Mr G Tup, legacy (cost of 'Real Property')		20.00
closure of account	370.25	To Mrs M Tup, legacy		250.00
		To Mr G O Tup, legacy		100.00
		Balance, being net residue of estate to be held by		
		the trustees on the trusts of the Will of the		
		deceased		15,615.00
	42,963.00			42,963.00

17. The account relates to the hypothetical estate of Dai Tup deceased whose will and codicil are to be found at pp 62–64 ante, Oath, Inland Revenue Account and grant at pp 323–328 ante.

CHAPTER 25

Remedies

There are various proceedings that dissatisfied creditors and beneficiaries can bring against the personal representative, but there are also numerous defences available to him. If the personal representative manages to escape liability or is insolvent, the creditors and beneficiaries can proceed against the wrongful recipient of the assets, as illustrated in the last part of this chapter.

1   Liability for the acts of the deceased

All causes of action subsisting against a deceased person survive against his estate, so that the deceased's personal representative stands in the deceased's shoes to be sued in his capacity as personal representative on the deceased's contracts[1] and torts. All the defences available to the deceased can be used by the personal representative who is, in general, only liable to the extent of the deceased's assets. If he has fully administered the estate at the time of the action and pleads the defence of *plene administravit,* the creditor can only get judgment against any future assets that come into the personal representative's hands.[2] The personal representative must plead this defence if applicable because his failure to do so will amount to an admission of sufficient assets to satisfy the claim so that if such assets are not available there will be a presumption of a devastavit[3] by the personal representative for which he will be personally liable unless he can rebut the presumption.[4]

Law Reform (Miscellaneous Provisions) Act 1934

1. Effect of death on certain causes of action[5]
(1) . . . on the death of any person after the commencement of this Act all causes of action

---

1. Other than contracts that are personal to the deceased, such as contracts of service and of agency; see further Williams, Mortimer and Sunnucks, p 491.
2. Alternatively he may plead *plene administravit praeter,* viz, that he has administered all the assets that have come into his hands except assets of a stated amount which are still in his hands in which event the creditor can proceed only against those assets; as to the balance of his claim he has to look to any future assets.
3. See p 411 post.
4. See eg *Marsden v Regan* [1954] 1 All ER 475, [1954] 1 WLR 423, *IRC v Stannard* [1984] 2 All ER 105, 107.
5. See further RSC 1965 Ord 15, r 7.

subsisting against or vested in him shall survive against, or, as the case may be, for the benefit of,[6] his estate. . . .

In **Midland Bank Trust Co Ltd and another v Green and others (No 2)** [1979] 1 All ER 726, [1979] 1 WLR 460, a father gave his son an option to purchase a farm, to be exercisable within ten years. The son failed to register the option as an estate contract so that when six years later the father sold the farm to his wife for £500 (at a time when the market value of the farm was £50,000) the option was defeated.[7] The son brought an action claiming, inter alia, damages for the tort of conspiracy against his father. The father died and his executrix, Mrs Kemp, took his place as defendant to the action. The father's estate had been sworn for probate at only £9,000 but she inadvertently failed to plead *plene administravit praeter.*[8] The son's claim succeeded on the conspiracy allegation and judgment was entered against Mrs Kemp for damages and costs estimated at £100,000. She applied for leave to serve the defence of *plene administravit praeter*, but Oliver J held that judgment having been entered against her, he had no jurisdiction to permit this. He added at p 729:

The principles are not in doubt. I take the principle from Williams and Mortimer on Executors, Administrators and Probate (1970 p 1008)[9] where it is said that:

'If a personal representative has not assets to satisfy the debt, upon which an action is brought against him, he must take care to plead *plene administravit* or *plene administravit praeter*, etc. For it seems that, even under the present system of pleading, if a personal representative fails to plead that he has fully administered the assets, or that with the exception of certain assets he has fully administered, and judgment, whether by default or otherwise, is given for the plaintiff, this amounts to a conclusive admission that he has assets to satisfy such judgment.'

I think therefore that although I have very great sympathy with Mrs Kemp in the position in which she finds herself and although, as her counsel has pointed out, it was said as long ago as the 18th century that the rule relating to *plene administravit* (or rather the failure to plead it) bore very hardly on personal representatives and although it might I think be looked at by those interested in law reform, I do not think that I can assist in this case by giving her the relief which she seeks in the action.

2 Administration proceedings

A creditor or beneficiary may bring administration proceedings.[10] These may take the form of asking the court to make a general administration order[11] so that the personal representatives thenceforth have to act under the direct supervision of the court. Alternatively (and more commonly) it will take the form of asking for specific relief on a particular point of concern, often asking for

---

6. See p 276 ante.
7. Land Charges Act 1925, s 13(2), now Land Charges Act 1972, s 4(6).
8. See n 2 ante.
9. See now 16th edn (1982) 803–804.
10. Administration proceedings are not always contentious; they are often brought by the personal representatives themselves, particularly when seeking the court's guidance on questions referred to in Ord 85, r 2 post.
11. Described by the Law Reform Committee in their 23rd Report 'The Powers and Duties of Trustees' (1982) Cmnd 8733 as 'an extremely clumsy, costly and time-consuming procedure; in practice it is only in wholly exceptional cases that its use can be recommended' (para 7.13, p 419 post).

an order requiring the personal representatives to account. When called upon to account, the personal representative is usually required to bring into the account only the assets he has actually received (and payments made) unless there has been some wilful default on his part (a devastavit[12] or breach of trust) in which event he will be ordered by the court to account also for assets that he would have received but for that wilful default.

Rules of the Supreme Court, Order 85

1. Interpretation
In this Order 'administration action' means an action for the administration under the direction of the Court[13] of the estate of a deceased person or for the execution under the direction of the Court of a trust.

2. Determination of questions etc without administration
(1) An action may be brought for the determination of any question or for any relief which could be determined or granted, as the case may be, in an administration action and a claim need not be made in the action for the administration or execution under the direction of the Court of the estate or trust in connection with which the question arises or the relief is sought.

(2) Without prejudice to the generality of paragraph (1), an action may be brought for the determination of any of the following questions—
   (a) any question arising in the administration of the estate of a deceased person or in the execution of a trust;
   (b) any question as to the composition of any class of persons having a claim against the estate of a deceased person or a beneficial interest in the estate of such a person or in any property subject to a trust;
   (c) any question as to the rights or interests of a person claiming to be a creditor of the estate of a deceased person or to be entitled under a will or on the intestacy of a deceased person or to be beneficially entitled under a trust.

(3) Without prejudice to the generality of paragraph (1), an action may be brought for any of the following reliefs—
   (a) an order requiring an executor, administrator or trustee to furnish and, if necessary, verify accounts;
   (b) an order requiring the payment into court of money held by a person in his capacity as executor, administrator or trustee;
   (c) an order directing a person to do or abstain from doing a particular act in his capacity as executor, administrator or trustee;
   (d) an order approving any sale, purchase, compromise or other transaction by a person in his capacity as executor, administrator or trustee;
   (e) an order directing any act to be done in the administration of the estate of a deceased person or in the execution of a trust which the Court could order to be done if the estate or trust were being administered or executed, as the case may be, under the direction of the Court.

Re Tebbs [1976] 2 All ER 858, [1976] 1 WLR 924, Ch D; Slade J

By his will the testator gave a family company an option to buy some eight acres of land ('the Wash Land') at the current market value at the date of exercise of the option. The executors sold the Wash Land to the company some four years after the testator's death, but at the probate value of £5,642 (itself a figure

---

12. See p 411 post.
13. The High Court (Chancery Division) unless the net estate is no more than £30,000 in which event the County Court has jurisdiction: County Courts Jurisdiction Order 1981, SI 1981/1123.

estimated by the executors without a professional valuation) and not at the market value at the date of sale which the plaintiff contended was very much higher. The plaintiff, who was one of the beneficiaries, had repeatedly warned the executors through her solicitors that they would be in breach of their duties if they sold for less than market value at the date the option was exercised. She issued a summons for relief[14] including an order for an account of the whole of the testator's estate to be taken on the footing of a wilful default. The executors conceded that she was entitled to such an account in relation to the Wash Land but one of them (the first defendant) disputed her entitlement to such an account in relation to the rest of the estate.

Held: An account should be taken of the Wash Land on the footing of wilful default and of the rest of the estate in common form with liberty to apply in the event of evidence of further wilful default arising.

Slade J: Counsel have not been able to refer me to any reported case in which the court has discussed the principles which should be applied in exercising its discretion whether or not a general account on the footing of wilful default should be ordered in a case where one or more past breaches of trust have been proved or admitted. In the absence of such authority it seems to me that the test should be this: is the past conduct of the trustees such as to give rise to a reasonable prima facie inference that other breaches of trust not yet known to the plaintiff or the court have occurred? . . . .

Bearing in mind that the honesty of the executors is not in question and that the enquiries already made have revealed nothing beyond the Wash Land transaction, I do not think I am justified in assuming the probability that other improper transactions may have occurred. In all the circumstances I do not think it would be right at this stage to take the somewhat drastic step of ordering an account of the whole of the estate on the footing of wilful default. I therefore propose to order that an account be taken of the rest of the testator's real and personal estate in common form. But I should emphasise in conclusion that I am not finally dismissing the plaintiff's claim for an account on the footing of wilful default in respect of the estate. At any subsequent stage of the proceedings it will be open to the court, on evidence of further wilful default being produced to it, to direct further accounts and enquiries on that footing. If the plaintiff wishes to have express liberty to apply for further accounts and enquiries on producing such evidence, I shall give her such liberty.[15]

3 Devastavit

Any breach of his duty as personal representative which results in a loss to the estate is a devastavit[16] for which the personal representative will be personally liable.[17]

---

14. She originally asked for the appointment of a judicial trustee and for a general administration order (see at p 859) but in the event, as is often the case, the proceedings became simply for an order for an account.

15. Slade J also took into account (at p 863) the executors' frank admission of wilful default in relation to the Wash Land. 'If in contrast (the court) has before it a case where a trustee has persisted in denying the relevant facts or persisted in wrongful assertions as to the legal position, even after it has become plain, the court may be more inclined to consider that this is a case where the wider form of account should be taken, because the wrongful or misguided persistence of the trustee itself supports the inference that the trustee may have been guilty of other wrongful or misguided acts in the administration of the trust.'

16. Ie a wasting of the assets.

17. A personal representative's duties are often referred to as 'trusts' and any failure to perform them as a 'breach of trust'. Strictly this is incorrect unless the will or the intestacy rules impose on the personal representative the office of a trustee, either in relation to particular tasks or generally. Usually the loose way in which the term is used will not matter as the provisions of the Trustee Act 1925 apply to personal representatives where the context so admits: see TA 1925, s 69, p 279 ante.

In **Job v Job** (1877) 6 Ch 562, it was suggested that once the assets had come into his hands a personal representative would always be liable for any loss suffered thereto. The testator in that case was a watchmaker and when he died his executor entrusted part of the testator's stock-in-trade to the executor's son who was himself a watchmaker, for the son to sell in the course of his business. The son went bankrupt before doing so and his trustee in bankruptcy took possession of all his stock-in-trade, including the testator's goods, and sold them. Jessel MR held that the executor was not liable to make good the loss, saying at p 564:

It should seem, at least in a Court of Equity, that an executor or administrator stands in the condition of a gratuitous bailee; with respect to whom the law is that he is not to be charged, without some default in him.

In **Marsden v Regan** [1954] 1 All ER 475, [1954] 1 WLR 423, the executrix spent money from the estate in cleaning certain of the deceased's personal effects, only to give them all away subsequently at a total loss to the estate of £22. The Court of Appeal held that she was liable for the devastavit, Evershed MR saying at p 481:

It is clear that the defendant proceeded to give away furniture which was comprehended in the miscellaneous items valued for probate, and, further, that before she gave it away she improved or embellished some bedding by spending £2 of the estate money on it for that purpose. So far as the value is concerned, there is no evidence except that the defendant herself stated the sum of £20 for the purpose of obtaining probate, and since there can be no possible defence against a charge of devastavit by an executor who admits having given the furniture away, I do not think she can be heard to say that it was of less value than that which she herself swore it had for the purpose of probate. The result is that as to £22, the plaintiff must be entitled to recover.

In **Re Kay** [1897] 2 Ch 518, the executor paid the testator's widow her legacy of £300 out of apparent assets of £22,000, before advertising for creditors.[18] It subsequently transpired that the estate was insolvent and he was held liable for devastavit, but the court relieved him from liability by the application of the Judicial Trustees Act 1896 s 3,[19] Romer J saying at p 521:

S 3 clearly applies to the case of an executor who has been guilty of devastavit. What the executor in this case has done is to pay his legatees when the assets, in the result, proved to be insufficient to pay the debts. In my opinion it is clear that this executor has acted honestly. The question I have to consider is whether he has acted 'reasonably, and ought'—in the words of s 3—'fairly to be excused for the breach of trust and for omitting to obtain the directions of the Court in the matter in which he committed such breach.' The circumstances under which this breach of trust was committed are as follows: The testator was in good reputation at the time of his death, and died leaving assets amounting to £22,000; no suspicion existed that he had left anything but small debts, and certainly there was no ground for supposing that he had been guilty of any dishonesty. Substantially there were no debts except that due to the plaintiffs, which I will refer to later on. What was the executor to do under these circumstances? The estate was apparently solvent with substantial assets; the will bequeathed to the widow an immediate legacy of £300 for pressing expenses, and there was the widow, the children, and the household to be maintained; it was clear that money must be found for what I may call household expenses, unless the executor had reason to suspect that the assets would be insufficient; and this, as I have already said, was not the case. It would be

---

18. See p 415 post.
19. See now Trustee Act 1925, s 61 p 415 post.

monstrous to suppose that it is the duty of an executor preremptorily to stop all supplies, and allow the family to go to the workhouse when he has every reason to believe that the testator has left ample means for their support. The executor here pays the £300 legacy, and I note that this sum was not large in proportion to the testator's available assets as they then appeared; and he also pays sums on account of income to the widow for the support of the household. It is clear that some payments were bound to be made at once; and, under the peculiar circumstances of this case, I think the defendant acted reasonably in paying the £300 legacy and such further sums on account of income as were reasonably necessary until the testator's debts, if any, could be fully ascertained.

4 Defences

The defences available to a personal representative when sued in respect of his own acts and omissions (as opposed to the acts and omissions of the deceased) are generally the same as those available to trustees[20] save in so far as the limitation periods differ.

(a) Limitation of actions

Claims against trustees for breach of trust are statute-barred after six years.[1] Whilst this is usually the same for creditors' claims against personal representatives, beneficiaries' claims against personal representatives are not statute-barred until 12 years from the date the cause of action arose.[2]

(i) *Claims by creditors*

Limitation Act 1980

2. Time limit for actions founded on tort[3]
An action founded on tort shall not be brought after the expiration of six years from the date on which the cause of action accrued.

5. Time limit for actions founded on simple contract
An action founded on simple contract shall not be brought after the expiration of six years from the date on which the cause of action accrued.

8. Time limit for actions on a specialty[4]
(1) An action upon a specialty shall not be brought after the expiration of twelve years from the date on which the cause of action accrued.

---

20. For more detailed consideration see, therefore, Pettit, pp 434–445, Maudsley and Burn, pp 772–784.
1. Limitation Act 1980, s 21(3).
2. All these periods are subject to extension in the case of disability such as infancy, unsoundness of mind, see Limitation Act 1980, s 28, or where the right of action was deliberately concealed by the defendant, ibid s 32. See further Maudsley and Burn 778–779. If the executor acknowledges the claim or makes any payment in respect of it before the right of action is statute-barred, time will start to run only as from the date of the acknowledgment or payment and not before: Limitation Act 1980, ss 29–31.
3. This would include a creditor's action for devastavit.
4. Ie a contract under seal.

(ii) *Claims by beneficiaries*

Limitation Act 1980

15.   Time limit for actions to recover land

(1) No action shall be brought by any person to recover any land after the expiration of twelve years from the date on which the right of action accrued to him or, if it first accrued to some person through whom he claims, to that person.

(2) Subject to the following provisions of this section, where:

  (a) the estate or interest claimed was an estate or interest in reversion or remainder or any other future estate or interest and the right of action to recover the land accrued on the date on which the estate or interest fell into possession by the determination of the preceding estate or interest; and

  (b) the person entitled to the preceding estate or interest (not being a term of years absolute) was not in possession of the land on that date;

no action shall be brought by the person entitled to the succeeding estate or interest after the expiration of twelve years from the date on which the right of action accrued to the person entitled to the preceding estate or interest or six years from the date on which the right of action accrued to the person entitled to the succeeding estate or interest, whichever period last expires.

21.   Time limit for actions in respect of trust[5] property

(1) No period of limitation prescribed by this Act shall apply to an action by a beneficiary under a trust, being an action—

  (a) in respect of any fraud or fraudulent breach of trust to which the trustee was a party or privy; or

  (b) to recover from the trustee trust property or the proceeds of trust property in the possession of the trustee, or previously received by the trustee and converted to his use.

(2) Where a trustee who is also a beneficiary under the trust receives or retains trust property or its proceeds as his share on a distribution of trust property under the trust, his liability in any action brought by virtue of sub-section (1)(b) above to recover that property or its proceeds after the expiration of the period of limitation prescribed by this Act for bringing an action to recover trust property shall be limited to the excess over his proper share.

   This sub-section only applies if the trustee acted honestly and reasonably in making the distribution.

22.   Time limit for actions claiming personal estate of a deceased person

Subject to section 21(1) and (2) of this Act—

  (a) no action in respect of any claim to the personal estate of a deceased person or to any share or interest in any such estate (whether under a will or on intestacy) shall be brought after the expiration of twelve years from the date on which the right to receive the share or interest accrued; and

  (b) no action to recover arrears of interest in respect of any legacy, or damages in respect of such arrears, shall be brought after the expiration of six years from the date on which the interest became due.

(iii) *In general*

Limitation Act 1980

23.   Time limit in respect of actions for an account

An action for an account shall not be brought after the expiration of any time limit under this Act which is applicable to the claim which is the basis of the duty to account.

---

5. By LA 1980, s 38(1) the expressions 'trust' and 'trustee' have the same meanings as those ascribed to them in the Trustee Act 1925, ie 'trust' includes the duties incident to the office of a personal representative and 'trustee', where the context so admits, includes a personal representative: TA 1925, s 68(17).

(b) Relief by the court

Trustee Act 1925

61. Power to relieve trustee[6] from personal liability
If it appears to the court that a trustee, whether appointed by the court or otherwise, is or may be personally liable for any breach of trust, whether the transaction alleged to be a breach of trust occurred before or after the commencement of this Act, but has acted honestly and reasonably, and ought fairly to be excused for the breach of trust and for omitting to obtain the directions of the court in the matter in which he committed such breach, then the court may relieve him either wholly or partly from personal liability for the same.[7]

(c) Consent

The consent of the creditor or beneficiary to the wrongful act of the personal representative or trustee is a complete defence to any proceedings by the consenting party so long as the consent was made with full knowledge of all the relevant facts.[8] Furthermore the court has power to impound a consenting beneficiary's beneficial interest in certain circumstances.

Trustee Act 1925

62. Power to make beneficiary indemnify for breach of trust
(1) Where a trustee[6] commits a breach of trust at the instigation or request or with the consent in writing of a beneficiary, the court may, if it thinks fit . . . make such order as to the court seems just, for impounding all or any part of the interest of the beneficiary in the trust estate by way of indemnity to the trustee or persons claiming through him.

(d) Advertising for claimants

As a general rule the personal representative is liable for all the deceased's debts, even those of which he has no notice at the time of distribution of the assets,[9] but he can protect himself from liability for late claims completely by following the procedure for 'statutory advertisements':

Trustee Act 1925

27. Protection by means of advertisements
(1) With a view to the conveyance to or distribution among the persons entitled to any real or personal property, the trustees of a settlement or of a disposition on trust for sale or personal representatives, may give notice by advertisement in the Gazette,[10] and in a newspaper circulating in the district in which the land is situated, and such other like notices, including notices elsewhere than in England and Wales, as would, in any special case have been directed by a court of competent jurisdiction in an action for

---

6. The expression includes a personal representative, see TA 1925, s 68(17), s 69(1), p 279 ante.
7. See eg *Marsden v Regan* [1954] 1 All ER 475, [1954] 1 WLR 423; *Re Kay* [1897] 2 Ch 518, p 412 ante.
8. See eg *Re Somerset* [1894] 1 Ch 231, *Re Pauling* [1964] Ch 303, [1963] 3 All ER 1.
9. See eg *Knatchbull v Fearnhead* (1837) 3 My & Cr 122.
10. Ie the London Gazette: TA 1925, s 68(1), (4).

administration, of their intention to make such conveyance or distribution as aforesaid, and requiring any person interested to send to the trustees or personal representatives within the time, not being less than two months, fixed in the notice or, where more than one notice is given, in the last of the notices, particulars of his claim in respect of the property or any part thereof to which the notice relates.

(2) At the expiration of the time fixed by the notice the trustees or personal representatives may convey or distribute the property or any part thereof to which the notice relates, to or among the persons entitled thereto, having regard only to the claims, whether formal or not, of which the trustees or personal representatives then had notice[11] and shall not, as respects the property so conveyed or distributed, be liable to any person of whose claim the trustees or personal representatives have not had notice at the time of conveyance or distribution; but nothing in this section—

(a) prejudices the right of any person to follow the property, or any property representing the same, into the hands of any person, other than a purchaser, who may have received it;[12] or

(b) frees the trustees or personal representatives from any obligation to make searches or obtain official certificates of search similar to those which an intending purchaser would be advised to make or obtain.

(3) This section applies notwithstanding anything to the contrary in the will or other instrument, if any, creating the trust.

In **Re Aldhous** [1955] All ER 80, [1955] 1 WLR 459, the statutory advertisements protected the personal representatives from the claims of unknown beneficiaries. The testatrix had died partially intestate; her executor had made the statutory advertisements under Trustee Act 1925, s 27. No one put in any claim as the testatrix's next-of-kin and the executor knew of none, so he paid the undisposed of property to the Treasury Solicitor on behalf of the Crown, as bona vacantia. In fact there was a niece but as Danckwerts J said at p 82:

'It is perfectly plain that that section (s 27) applies equally to the claims of beneficial owners as to the claims of creditors in respect of any estate or trust fund'

and he held that the statutory advertisements were a complete defence for the executor in respect of the wrongful payment.[13]

(e) Future liabilities under a lease

Future liabilities, particularly those of a contingent nature, can prolong the administration of an estate for many years unless the personal representatives can obtain an order from the court authorising them to distribute without making provision for the liability. In relation to one potential source of liability, however, statutory protection is provided, viz the personal representative's continuing liability where the deceased was an original lessee.[14]

---

11. Either as a result of the advertisement or in any other way, including constructive notice: *Re Land Credit Company of Ireland,* (1872) 21 WR 135.

12. See p 420 post.

13. In fact the Treasury Solicitor, whilst not admitting liability, consented to an order to account to whoever should be shown to be the next-of-kin following an enquiry to that end.

14. A liability that enures in contract no matter how often the lease is assigned and whether before or after the death of the deceased: see Cheshire and Burn, pp 437–438.

Trustee Act 1925

26. Protection against liability in respect of rents and covenants

(1) Where a personal representative or trustee liable as such for—
   (a) any rent, covenant, or agreement reserved by or contained in any lease; or
   (b) any rent, covenant or agreement payable under or contained in any grant made in consideration of a rentcharge; or
   (c) any indemnity given in respect of any rent, covenant or agreement referred to in either of the foregoing paragraphs;
satisfies all liabilities under the lease or grant which may have accrued, or been claimed, up to the date of the conveyance hereinafter mentioned, and, where necessary, sets apart a sufficient fund to answer any future claim that may be made in respect of any fixed and ascertained sum which the lessee or grantee agreed to lay out on the property demised or granted, although the period for laying out the same may not have arrived, then and in any such case the personal representative or trustee may convey the property demised or granted to a purchaser, legatee, devisee, or other person entitled to call for a conveyance thereof and thereafter—
   (i) he may distribute the residuary real and personal estate of the deceased testator or intestate, or, as the case may be, the trust estate (other than the fund, if any, set apart as aforesaid) to or amongst the persons entitled thereto, without appropriating any part, or any further part, as the case may be, of the estate of the deceased or of the trust estate to meet any future liability under the said lease or grant;
   (ii) notwithstanding such distribution, he shall not be personally liable in respect of any subsequent claim under the said lease or grant.

(2) This section operates without prejudice to the right of the lessor or grantor, or the persons deriving title under the lessor or grantor, to follow the assets of the deceased or the trust property into the hands of the persons amongst whom the same may have been respectively distributed,[15] and applies notwithstanding anything to the contrary in the will or other instrument, if any, creating the trust.

(f) Acting under the court's directions

It is always open to a personal representative to seek the court's directions if any problem arises as to the distribution of the estate; so long as the personal representative complies with the order, that will give him complete protection without taking away the right of a creditor or beneficiary who thereby loses out, from pursuing his remedies against the recipient of the assets.[16]

In **Re Benjamin** [1902] 1 Ch 723, the testator left his son a share of residue but the son had disappeared some nine months before the testator's death. The executors made enquiries but no information was forthcoming, so they applied to court and Joyce J made the following order:

In the absence of any evidence that the said PD Benjamin survived the testator, let the trustees of the testator's will be at liberty to divide the share of the testator's estate devised and bequeathed in favour of the said PD Benjamin, his wife and children, upon the footing that PD Benjamin was unmarried and did not survive the testator.[17]

In **Re Gess** [1942] Ch 37, (1942) 111 LJ Ch 117, the testator was of Polish nationality but domiciled in England where he died intestate in 1939. His

---

15. See p 420 post.
16. Ibid.
17. An order in such terms is now known as a 'Benjamin Order', see eg *Re Taylor's Estate* [1969] 2 Ch 245, [1969] 1 All ER 113, *Re Green's WT* [1985] 3 All ER 455.

administrators made the usual statutory advertisements[18] in this country but were unable to advertise in Poland for creditors' claims owing to the outbreak of war. Holding that the administrators could wind up the estate on the basis that all debts and liabilities had been ascertained, Morton J said at p 38:

> There appears to be no reported precedent for the relief asked, but, in the analogous case where leave is sought to distribute among beneficiaries notwithstanding that a particular beneficiary, or his issue, cannot be traced, leave is frequently given to distribute on the footing that the beneficiary in question has predeceased the testator or intestate or has so predeceased without leaving issue who survived the testator or intestate. This is in accordance with a practice which has been in operation since the decision of Joyce J in *Re Benjamin* ([1902] 1 Ch 723) and it would only be following the principle of that decision if its application were extended to debts. Such orders are made, not as of course, but only on satisfactory prima facie evidence of practical impossibility of proof of the fact or event sought to be established. Moreover, if leave to distribute is given, it only operates to protect the personal representative. It does not prevent the missing beneficiary or the absent creditor (if any) from following the assets.[19]

(g) Payment into court

If none of the above measures solves the problem of the missing beneficiary, personal representatives, like trustees, have the right to pay money into court; alternatively, and in practice much more usually, the personal representatives will insure against the risk of the missing beneficiary turning up and then distribute in full to those otherwise entitled.

Trustee Act 1925

63.   Payment into court by trustees[20]
(1) Trustees, or the majority of trustees, having in their hands or under their control money or securities belonging to a trust, may pay the same into court; and the same shall, subject to rules of court, be dealt with according to the orders of the court.
(2) The receipt or certificate of the proper officer shall be a sufficient discharge to trustees for the money or securities so paid into court.
(3) Where money or securities are vested in any persons as trustees, and the majority are desirous of paying the same into court, but the concurrence of the other or others cannot be obtained, the court may order the payment into court to be made by the majority without the concurrence of the other or others.

5   The dilatory personal representative

One particular problem that was drawn to the attention of the Law Reform Committee in 1982 was the difficulty experienced by beneficiaries where the personal representative was not actually in breach of his duties but took a very long time to carry them out. The Committee made no recommendation for reform, preferring instead to draw attention to existing methods of alleviating the situation.

---

18. See p 415 ante.
19. See further p 420 post.
20. Including personal representatives, see TA 1925, s 68(17), s 69(1), p 279 ante.

Law Reform Committee: Twenty-Third Report[1]

The problem of the dilatory personal representative

7.13. . . . A common complaint by beneficiaries is that it takes a very long time to wind up an estate and that little, if any, information is provided on the progress of the administration. It seems that solicitors are the most frequent target for complaint though it is possible that other personal representatives, whether lay or professional, might well be open to the same criticism. No doubt there are many instances when what seems to be inexcusable delay on the part of the personal representative is necessitated by matters outside his control, but there are also occasions when he is at fault and it is, in any case frustrating for the beneficiary to be left in the dark. We have considered what, if anything, ought to be done, by way of law reform to meet this problem.

7.14. Before considering changes in the law we think it would be helpful to set out in outline the remedies which are available at the moment to a beneficiary who is dissatisfied with the actions of the personal representative. The time honoured remedy of an administration action[2] in which the Court, in effect, takes over the whole administration of the estate is still available; it is, however, an extremely clumsy, costly and time-consuming procedure and in practice it is only in wholly exceptional cases that its use can be recommended. In practical terms, in the kind of case we are considering, the beneficiary's main remedy is to apply to the court for the appointment of a judicial trustee under section 1(2) of the Judicial Trustees Act 1896.[3] The object of this statute is to provide a middle course in cases where the administration of the estate by the ordinary trustees has broken down and it is not desired to put the estate to the expense of a full administration. We are not aware of any case where this remedy has been adopted and found unsatisfactory.

7.15 In any event, a personal representative is under a duty to keep clear and accurate accounts of the estate and, at the request of a beneficiary, to give him full and accurate information as to its state. As a further alternative course of action, machinery does exist whereby complaints can be made against solicitors to the Law Society, which is able to exercise quite considerable control over their actions in matters concerned with the administration of estates. We also understand that equivalent machinery exists in the case of the professional accountancy bodies.

7.16 We have considered whether matters might be improved by giving the beneficiary additional rights by statute, such as the right to have the personal representative provide him, on request, with certain information about the administration of the estate. This would encourage the personal representative to expedite matters and would also give the beneficiary a route to the courts if the personal representative did not comply with the request. However, we think that there would be considerable difficulties in formulating such a right, that the provision to all beneficiaries (who might be numerous) of regular information would in some cases add significantly to the expense of administering estates and, most important, that it might be open to abuse in that beneficiaries might make frequent and vexatious requests for information in situations where the personal representative was in fact doing everything required of him. In any event, such a right is only needed where the personal representative is not a solicitor and has not taken legal advice since, as we have pointed out above, the Law Society can control the actions of solicitors in this area.

7.17 We appreciate the worries of the beneficiary who is not told what is happening to the estate but we do not believe that additional remedies should be provided. We doubt whether the introduction of a statutory right to information would remedy matters to any great extent. Moreover, it may well be that greater use of the existing procedures, in

---

1. 'The Powers and Duties of Trustees' (1982) Cmnd 8733.
2. See p 409 ante.
3. See p 420 post. See also AJA 1985, s 50, p 305 ante, which is more likely to be used in future for the removal or replacement of personal representatives.

particular the appointment of a judicial trustee and the right to call for accounts, would solve many of the problems that are encountered at the moment and we hope that by referring to them in this Report we have drawn attention to the fact that they are available.

Judicial Trustees Act 1896

1. Power of court on application to appoint judicial trustee[4]
(1) Where application is made to the court by or on behalf of the person creating or intending to create a trust, or by or on behalf of a trustee or beneficiary, the court may, in its discretion, appoint a person (in this Act called a judicial trustee) to be a trustee of that trust, either jointly with any other person or as sole trustee, and, if sufficient cause is shown, in place of all or any existing trustees.
(2) The administration of the property of a deceased person, whether a testator or intestate, shall be a trust, and the executor or administrator a trustee, within the meaning of this Act.
(3) Any fit and proper person nominated for the purpose in the application may be appointed a judicial trustee, and, in the absence of such nomination, or if the court is not satisfied of the fitness of a person so nominated, an official of the court may be appointed, and in any case a judicial trustee shall be subject to the control and supervision of the court as an officer thereof.
(7) Where an application relating to the estate of a deceased person is made to the court under this section, the court may, if it thinks fit, proceed as if the application were, or included, an application under section 50 of the Administration of Justice Act 1985 (power of High Court to appoint substitute for, or to remove, personal representative).[5]

6   Liability of the wrongful recipient

(a) In rem

This is the right to trace or follow the assets of the estate or their products into the hands of anyone holding them; insofar as the assets have been mixed with other property, the tracing action will lie in equity (as opposed to common law) and will be of no avail against a bona fide purchaser of a legal estate for value without notice.[6] An assent or conveyance by the personal representative (other than to such a purchaser) does not prejudice the right in any way.

Administration of Estates Act 1925

38. Right to follow property and powers of the court in relation thereto
(1) An assent or conveyance by a personal representative to a person other than a purchaser[7] does not prejudice the rights of any person to follow the property

---

4. See further the Judicial Trustee Rules 1972, SI 1972/1096.
5. The sub-section was added by AJA 1985, s 50(6). See p 305 ante.
6. For further discussion of the tracing action see Pettit, pp 446–456, Maudsley and Burn, 784–812, Goff and Jones 'The Law of Restitution' (2nd edn 1978) 46–63, and in particular that classic illustration of a tracing action, *Re Diplock* [1948] Ch 465, [1948] 2 All ER 318.
7. 'Purchaser' is defined in AEA 1925, s 55(1)(xviii) as 'a lessee, mortgagee or other person who in good faith acquires an interest in property for valuable consideration, also an intending purchaser and 'valuable consideration' includes marriage but does not include a nominal consideration in money.' The exception in favour of a purchaser in s 38(1) is therefore not on its terms restricted to a purchaser of a legal estate; cf s 36(9), p 398 ante.

representing the same, into the hands of the person in whom it is vested by the assent or conveyance, or of any other person (not being a purchaser) who may have received the same or in whom it may be vested.

(2) Notwithstanding any such assent or conveyance the court may, on the application of any creditor or other person interested—

    (a) order a sale, exchange, mortgage, charge, lease, payment, transfer or other transaction to be carried out which the court considers requisite for the purpose of giving effect to the rights of the person interested;

    (b) declare that the person, not being a purchaser, in whom the property is vested is a trustee for those purposes;

    (c) give directions respecting the preparation and execution of any conveyance or other instrument or as to any other matter required for giving effect to the order;

    (d) make any vesting order, or appoint a person to convey in accordance with the provisions of the Trustee Act 1925.

(3) This section does not prejudice the rights of a purchaser or a person deriving title under him, but applies whether the testator or intestate died before or after the commencement of this Act.

(b) In personam

An unpaid or underpaid creditor or beneficiary has an equitable right to claim a refund from a wrongful recipient from a personal representative. The existence of this equitable right in personam had been recognised as long ago as 1682 but for very many years it had been suggested that it would only lie if the estate was being administered by the court, if the wrongful payment was a mistake of fact as opposed to a mistake of law, and if the defendant was an overpaid beneficiary as opposed to a stranger to the estate, someone with no title to the assets at all. In 1951 these apparent restrictions on the action were swept away by the House of Lords.

Ministry of Health v Simpson [1951] AC 251, [1950] 2 All ER 1137, HL; Lords Simonds, Normand, Oaksey, Morton of Henryton and Macdermott

Acting under a mistake of law, the personal representatives of Caleb Diplock, whose residuary gift was found to be invalid,[8] had distributed his residuary estate, worth approximately £250,000, on the basis that it was valid, to some 139 charitable institutions who had received the payments in good faith. Having exhausted their personal remedy against the personal representatives,[9] the testator's next-of-kin brought various actions against the charities to recover the balance, including an equitable action in personam which succeeded in the Court of Appeal.[10] The Ministry of Health on behalf of one of the hospital charities appealed, arguing that the action in personam could not succeed, because the estate was not being administered by the court, it was a mistake of law not fact, and the charities were strangers to the estate.

Held: None of these limitations was valid. So long as the next-of-kin had exhausted their remedy against the personal representatives, the equitable action in personam would lie.

---

8. *Chichester Diocesan Fund v Simpson* [1944] AC 341, [1944] 2 All ER 60.

9. This action (unreported) was compromised in the sum of £15,000, the court approving the settlement terms.

10. *Re Diplock* [1948] Ch 465, [1948] 2 All ER 318.

Lord Simonds: I will first refer to a statement made by Lord Davey early in this century, which, as I think, illuminates the position. In *Harrison v Kirk* ([1904] AC 1) Lord Davey says this ([1904] AC 7): 'But the Court of Chancery, in order to do justice and to avoid the evil of allowing one man to retain what is really and legally applicable to the payment of another man, devised a remedy by which, where the estate had been distributed either out of court or in court without regard to the rights of a creditor, it has allowed the creditor to recover back what has been paid to the beneficiaries or the next-of-kin who derive title from the deceased testator or intestate.'

The importance of this statement is manifold. It explains the basis of the jurisdiction, the evil to be avoided and its remedy. Its clear implication is that no such remedy existed at common law. It does not suggest that it is relevant whether the wrong payment was made under error of law or of fact. It is immaterial whether those who have been wrongly paid are beneficiaries under the will or next-of-kin. It is sufficient that they derive title from the deceased. It is true that Lord Davey expressly dealt with the case of a claimant creditor, not a beneficiary or next-of-kin. I shall show your Lordships that what he said of the one might equally be said of the other. It would be strange if a court of equity, whose self-sought duty it was to see that the assets of a deceased person were duly administered and came into the right hands and not into the wrong hands, devised a remedy for the protection of the unpaid creditor, but left the unpaid legatee or next-of-kin unprotected. . . .

I pass over numerous cases in which the equitable remedy was refined and elaborated. Their effect is stated in the judgment of the Court of Appeal and summarised in the passage from Roper on Legacies (4th ed) which is cited in that judgment ([1948] 2 All ER 327), but I should in passing mention *Orr v Kaines* ((1750) 2 Ves Sen 194) in which it was clearly established that the right of an underpaid legatee to claim directly against the overpaid legatee is subject to this qualification, that he must first exhaust his remedy against the executor who has made the wrongful payment. It was for this reason that I mentioned at an earlier stage of this opinion that the next-of-kin must be deemed to have recovered from the executors all that they could recover. They had then no other way to recover the balance that was due to them than by proceeding directly against the appellant and other institutions amongst which the executors had distributed the estate. It must at this point be said that a distinction on which Wynn-Parry J relied[11] has no validity. Not having had his attention called to the earlier authorities, the learned judge was disposed to think that the equitable remedy, even where it existed, was only available to an unpaid creditor or legatee if the estate had been administered by the court. There is no ground for this broad distinction, though it may well be that a distinction exists, viz: that, where the executor has distributed the estate under an order of the court, the unpaid creditor would not be required to bring a further action against him before proceeding against persons wrongfully paid. . . .

It remains to deal with two other arguments. It was said that the equity was not applicable against a 'stranger' and that the appellant (or the hospital[12] through whom it claimed) having been paid money to which it was not lawfully entitled, since the disposition under which it took was invalid, was to be regarded as a stranger. This argument is wholly without substance. The hospital[12] received £4,000 for no other reason than that the executors thought that it was a proper object for the testator's bounty. It was treated as a beneficiary under the testator's will and, to use Lord Davey's words, derived title under it. It does not appear to me that a person so receiving money from the estate of a testator is in a different position from any other person to whom money is paid on the footing that under the testator's will money can be lawfully paid to him though, in fact, the payment is wrongful.

I come, finally, to the argument on which counsel for the appellant laid the greatest stress, relying not only on the judgment of Wynn-Parry J, but on the other cases which have yet to be examined. It was that the equitable remedy was subject at least to this

---

11. *Re Diplock* [1947] Ch 716 at 731, [1947] 1 All ER 522 at 529.
12. Westminster hospital, one of the 139 charitable institutions to which the executors had wrongfully paid a part of the residuary estate.

qualification—that it was not applicable where the wrongful payment was made in error of law. It was said that in every case where it had been applied the wrongful payment had been made under a mistake of fact, and that, wherever the principle had been stated without any such qualification, it must be read, nevertheless, as subject to it. I think, my Lords, that this argument which found favour with the learned judge is misconceived. In the first place, though in almost all the reported cases the probability is that the wrongful payment was made under a mistake of fact, that is not true of all of them and in many of them, while the probability is in one direction, there can be no certainty without further information which is not now available. This leads directly to the second reason. In not one of the many cases where the equity was applied was any suggestion made in argument or judgment that the issue depended on the nature of the mistake under which the wrongful payment had been made. It is not credible that, if the distinction between mistake of fact and law was relevant, it would never have been mentioned, particularly at a time when in the courts of common law it was being established. In the third place, the most satisfactory reason for the distinction rests in the maxim, itself probably taken from the criminal law, *ignorantia juris neminem excusat*: see *Baylis v Bishop of London* ([1913] 1 Ch 127). The man who makes a wrong payment because he has mistaken the law may not plead his own ignorance of the law and so cannot recover what he has wrongfully paid. It is difficult to see what relevance this distinction can have, where a legatee does not plead his own mistake or his own ignorance but, having exhausted his remedy against the executor who has made the wrongful payment, seeks to recover money from him who has been wrongfully paid. To such a suit the executor was not a necessary party and there was no means by which the plaintiff could find out whether his mistake was one of law or of fact or even whether his wrongful act was mistaken or deliberate. He could guess and ask the court to guess, but he could prove nothing. I reject, therefore, the suggestion that the equitable remedy in such circumstances was thus restricted, and repeat that it would be a strange thing if the Court of Chancery, having taken on itself to see that the assets of a deceased person were duly administered, was deterred from doing justice to creditor, legatee or next-of-kin because the executor had done him wrong under a mistake of law. If, in truth, this were so, I think that the Father of Equity would not recognise his child. . . .

Finally, my Lords, I must say some words on an argument of a more general character put forward on behalf of the appellant. The Court of Chancery, it was said, acted on the conscience, and, unless the defendant had behaved in an unconscientious manner, would make no decree against him. The appellant, or those through whom he claimed, having received a legacy in good faith and having spent it without knowledge of any flaw in their title, ought not in conscience to be ordered to refund. My Lords, I find little help in such generalities. Upon the propriety of a legatee refusing to repay to the true owner the money that he has wrongly received I do not think it necessary to express any judgment. It is a matter on which opinions may well differ. The broad fact remains that the Court of Chancery, in order to mitigate the rigour of the common law or to supply its deficiencies, established the rule of equity which I have described, and this rule did not excuse the wrongly paid legatee from repayment because he had spent what he had been wrongly paid. No doubt the plaintiff might by his conduct, and, particularly, by laches, have raised some equity against himself; but, if he had not done so, he was entitled to be repaid. In the present case the respondents have done nothing to bar them in equity from asserting their rights. They can only be defeated if they are barred at law by some statute of limitations.[13]

---

13. Holding that this was a claim to the personal estate of the testator (see now Limitation Act 1980, s 22, p 414 ante) and had been brought within 12 years of the expiration of the executor's year, the claim was not statute barred (see pp 1147–8). Cf the United States Uniform Probate Code where in general claims by creditors or beneficiaries against wrongful distributions are 'forever barred at the later of (1) three years after the decedent's death; or (2) one year after the time of distribution thereof': s 3–1006. The section does not bar an action to recover property or value received as the result of fraud however.

QUESTIONS

1. In 1982 Trevor died. By his will he left his estate 'to my children, Alfred, Brenda and Clarence, in equal shares'. Alfred had disappeared on a visit to South America in 1980 and Trevor's executors were unable to trace him, so in 1984 they divided Trevor's estate equally between Brenda and Clarence. In 1986 Alfred returns to England and demands his share of his father's estate. Discuss.

2. Compare the personal representative's position in regard to the Limitation Act 1980 with the corresponding provision in the United States Uniform Probate Code:

3-1005.   Limitation on proceedings against personal representative
Unless previously barred by adjudication and except as provided in the closing statement, the rights of successors (beneficiaries) and of creditors whose claims have not otherwise been barred against the personal representative for breach of fiduciary duty are barred unless a proceeding to assert the same is commenced within 6 months after the filing of the closing statement (see p 400 ante.) The rights thus barred do not include rights to recover from a personal representative for fraud, misrepresentation, or inadequate disclosure related to the settlement of the decedent's estate.

3. In the light of the suggestions supplied by the Law Reform Committee in their 23rd Report (see p 419 ante) what advice would you give to someone complaining about the length of time it is taking his solicitor to wind up an estate?

4. Read Goff and Jones 'The Law of Restitution' (2nd edn 1978) pp 46–63, 450–453 on the actions in rem and in personam against wrongful distributees and note in particular their criticism of the ruling that claims against the personal representatives must first be exhausted before the wrongful recipient can be proceeded against.

Index